1 MONTH OF
FREE
READING

at

www.ForgottenBooks.com

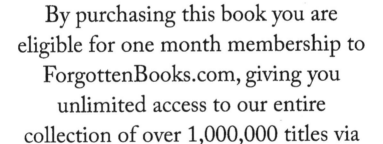

By purchasing this book you are eligible for one month membership to ForgottenBooks.com, giving you unlimited access to our entire collection of over 1,000,000 titles via our web site and mobile apps.

To claim your free month visit:

www.forgottenbooks.com/free267498

ISBN 978-0-265-61902-5
PIBN 10267498

This book is a reproduction of an important historical work. Forgotten Books uses
state-of-the-art technology to digitally reconstruct the work, preserving the original format
whilst repairing imperfections present in the aged copy. In rare cases, an imperfection in
the original, such as a blemish or missing page, may be replicated in our edition. We do,
however, repair the vast majority of imperfections successfully; any imperfections that
remain are intentionally left to preserve the state of such historical works.

For support please visit www.forgottenbooks.com

1861.

THE

COMMERCIAL ADVERTISER

DIRECTORY

FOR THE

CITY OF BUFFALO,

TO WHICH IS ADDED A

BUSINESS DIRECTORY,

AND

Advertisements of Merchants and Manufacturers

OF THE CITY OF BUFFALO.

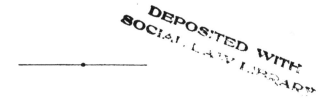
BUFFALO:

PUBLISHED BY R. WHEELER & CO.

161 Main St., Commercial Advertiser Buildings.

1861.

Dir 431

GENERAL INDEX.

INDEX TO BUSINESS DIRECTORY.

'INDEX TO BUFFALO ADVERTISEMENTS.

BUFFALO

Commercial Advertiser Directory,

FOR 1861.

CITY GOVERNMENT.—1861.

Mayor.—F. A. Alberger.

Aldermen — First Ward — John Hanovan, Patrick Walsh. 2d Ward—Nath. Jones, Joel Wheeler. 3d Ward—Z. G. Allen, Alexander Brush. 4th Ward—Everard Palmer, Edward Storck. 5th Ward—Chas. Beckwith, Andrew Grass. 6th Ward — Paul Goembel, Jacob Scheu. 7th Ward—J. F. Schwartz, F. M. Pratt. 8th Ward—Robert Mills, Chas. E. Felton. 9th Ward—Jas. Adams, E. P. Dorr. 10th Ward—Geo. R. Yaw, A. S. Bemis. 11th Ward—Jacob Crowder, A. A. Howard. 12th Ward—Washington Russell, S. W Howell. 13th Ward—Thos. Savage, Thomas Rutter.

President of the Common Council—Asaph S. Bemis.

Standing Committees. — *Finance*—Howard, Pratt, Yaw, Palmer, Beckwith.

Schools—Wheeler, Howell, Howard, Pratt, Dorr, Storck, Beckwith.

Streets—Palmer, Yaw, Howell, Mills, Brush, Wheeler, Walsh.

Sewers — Brush, Palmer, Schwartz, Mills, Hanovan.

Side and Cross Walks—Schwartz, Adams, Allen, Storck, Grass.

Fire—Yaw, Adams, Palmer, Allen, Jones.

Water — Pratt, Jones, Crowder, Brush Walsh.

Claims—Howell, Howard, Beckwith, Yaw, Wheeler.

Police—Mills, Storck, Pratt, Allen, Felton.

Markets—Storck, Dorr, Schwartz, Yaw, Hanovan.

Wharves, Harbors and Ferries—Allen, Dorr, Mills, Yaw, Scheu.

Public Grounds—Dorr, Russell, Brush, Wheeler, Walsh.

Public Lamps—Adams, Yaw, Mills, Savage, Goembel.

License—Russell, Jones, Savage, Crowder, Rutter.

Sanitary Measures—Savage, Adams, Crowder, Jones, Goembel.

New Territory—Crowder, Howell, Howard, Russell, Rutter.

CITY OFFICERS.

Comptroller.—Alonzo Tanner.

City Attorney.—Geo. Wadsworth.

Street Commissioner.—Levi J. Waters.

City Treasurer.—J. S. Trobridge.

Receiver of Taxes.—Michael Weidrich.

Auditor.—Wm. Fleming.

Superintendent of Schools.—Sanford B. Hunt,

Police Justice.—Daniel D. Bidwell.

Chief of Police.—Geo. Drulard.

Overseer of the Poor.—Chas. B. Morse.

Assessors.—Job Gorton, Lorenz Gillig, Francis G. Pattison.

City Clerk.—Otis F. Presbrey,

Supervisors.—1st Ward—John O. Donnelly. 2d Ward—J. K. Tayler. 3d Ward—Joshua Barnes. 4th Ward—L. K. Haddock. 5th Ward

—Orrin Lockwood. 6th Ward—John Davis. 7th Ward—Geo. Ricketts. 8th Ward—James Ryan. 9th Ward—Albert Sawin. 10th Ward—Joseph Candee. 11th Ward—Thos. R. Stocking. 12th Ward—Jacob Richert. 13th Ward—Aaron Martin. Amherst—C. C. Grove. Alden—A. P. Vandervoort. Aurora—Seth Fenner. Boston—George Brindley. Brant—Thos. Judson. Checktowaga—Eldridge Farwell. Clarence—David Woodward. Collins—Elisha Henry. Concord—S. W. Godard.—Colden — Nathan Francis. Elma — Z. Hemstreet. East Hamburg—H. Dowel. Eden—Lyman Pratt. Evans—James Ayer. Grand Island—O. Bedell. Holland—Nathan Morey. Hamburg—Hoel White. Lancaster—Wm. W. Bruce. Marilla—H. T. Foster. Newstead—E. P. Goslin. North Collins—Wilson Rogers. Sardinia—Jas. Rider. Tonawanda—E. Hensler. West Seneca—John G. Langler. Wales—John Macbeth.

Health Commissioners.—Jason Sexton, President; Thos. R. Stocking, Jacob Gittere, Otis F. Presbrey, Clerk.

Health Inspectors.—John Elliot, George J. Rheinhardt.

Health Physician.—J. Whitaker.

Constables.—1st Ward—Mort. O'Brian. 2d Ward—Daniel B. Williams. 3d Ward—Louis Otto. 4th Ward—Carl Anderson. 5th Ward—B. Kreig. 6th Ward—Michael Kester. 7th Ward—Theodore Seele. 8th Ward—Peter Dietrich. 9th Ward—Henry McLane. 10th Ward Samuel W. Bagnall. 11th Ward—L. D. Jerome. 12th Ward—Wm. Hastings. 13th Ward—Anthony Brosso.

Street Inspectors.—John Drexler, F. Schmelzer, Jacob Sohm, Patrick Scanion, Chas. Broshart

Inspectors of Election.—1st Ward—Hermon Ohlmer, Lorenzo Kent. 2d Ward—1st District — James Boyd, Chandler J. Wells; 2d District—Lyman B. Knapp, William H. Moore. Cyrenius C. Bristol. 3d Ward—Rodolph W. Ransom, Robt. W. Voas, Christian Smith. 4th Ward—1st District—Arthur McArthur, Christian Bonner, Jr., William H. Smith; 2d District—William Dana Forbes, Louis Hackmeir, Frank Fisher. 5th Ward—1st District—Frank Smith, Carper Retel; 2d District—John Benzinger, John A. Weimer. 6th Ward—1st District—John Stengel, Michael Beck, John R. Walter; 2d District—Jacob Heimenz,Wendell Stern, Frederick Jacobs. 7th Ward—1st District—Frederick Schmelzer, Seymour Bennett, Geo. F. Pfeiffer; 2d District—Edward Hazard, George Reinheimer, Morris Hazard, Jr. 8th Ward—Hamilton Courter, Dennis M. Enright, M. P. Wellman, Jr. 9th Ward—1st District—David Kissock, James Adams, Amasa Graham; 2d District—James Turner, James D. G. Stevenson, John D. Smith. 10th Ward—Wm. Fleming, P. Augustus Hodge, David F. Day. 11th Ward—John Elliott, A. Hull Thompson, Casper Hoffmeyer. 12th Ward—

1st District—Albert H. Blossom, John Drewer, Wm. Post. 13th Ward—Jacob Faber, Horace Buffum, Jas. M. Galloway.

General Clerk of Markets—Cornelius Boorom.

Sealers of Weights and Measures.—Conrad Seiber, Thos. Smith.

City Sexton.—Philip Nothnagel.

Harbor Masters. — Levi Villers, Joseph Whittel.

Captains of Police.—Morris Helms, Elijah K. Richardson, Jerome B. Shumway, William Messing.

Watch House Justice.—Warren Lampman.

Justices.—C. A. Waldron, Charles Gardner, Charles T. Shattuck, Geo. Talbot, Martin H. Woodward, Warren Lampman, H. B. Burt, Moses Bestol.

Police Constables. — Jacob Emerick, Benj. Toles, David S. Reynolds, Jacob Bloom, Geo. B. Mitchell, Jno. F. E. Plogsted, Stephen Thornton, John O. Hopkins, Adam Jones, Eli Fountain, Jas. Van Valkenburgh.

Police and Justices' Court.—Police Justice.—D. D. Bidwell.

City Scavenger.—Peter Hurbert.

Salaries of City Officers.—Mayor, $1,600; all Aldermen, $100 per year; Comptroller, $1,500; City Attorney, $1,200; Receiver of Taxes, $1,100; Street Commissioner, $1,200; Superintendent of Schools, $1,200; City Surveyor, $900; Treasurer, $1,100; Assessors, $1,150 each; Chief of Police, $1,000; Overseer of the Poor, $800; City Clerk, $900; City Clerk, as Clerk of the Board of Health, $100; Deputy City Clerk, $800; General Clerk of Markets, $750; Health Physician, $500; Harbor Masters, each, $500; Deputy Comptroller, $800; First Clerk to Receiver of Taxes, $800; First Clerk to Street Commissioner, $700; Second Clerk to Street Commissioner, $600; Clerk to City Surveyor, $700; Clerks to Overseer of the Poor, $400; Clerk to Chief of Police, $500; Street Inspectors, while in actual employ, per day, $1.25; Messenger to Common Council, per year, $100; Watch House Justices, per year, $150; Police Justice, $2,000.

BUFFALO FIRE DEPARTMENT.

OFFICERS FOR 1861.

Fire Commissioners.—Geo. Jones, President; Francis H. Root, Sam'l Smith, Oliver G. Steele, Jarvis Davis. R. L. Burrows, Clerk.

Fire Marshal.—David Kissock.

Chief Engineer.—Wm. Taylor.

1st Assistant Engineer.—John T. Spaulding.

2d Assistant do ———

3d Assistant do Lewis P. Maurer.

LOCALITIES OF ENGINES.

Steam Fire Engine Chan. J. Wells.—House on South Division, between Washington and Ellicott streets.

Steam Engine Niagara.—House on Niagara street, between Mohawk and Georgia streets.

Steam Engine City of Buffalo.—House on Huron street, between Washington and Ellicott streets.

Live Oak Engine Co. No. 2.—South side of Elk street, 200 feet east of Louisiana street.

Fillmore Engine Co. No. 3—South side of Genesee street, 20 feet west of Spruce street.

Niagara Engine Co. No. 7.—East side of Pine street, 65 feet south of William street.

Hydraulic Engine Co. No. 9.—South side of Seneca street, 150 feet east of Red Jacket street.

Defiance Engine Co. No. 10.—East side of Terrace, 125 feet south of Court street.

Jefferson Engine Co. No. 12—North side of Batavia street, 150 feet east of Michigan street.

Pioneer Hook and Ladder Co. No. 1.—South side South Division street, 75 feet west of Ellicott street.

Rescue Hook and Ladder Co. No. 2.—South side Huron street, 100 feet west of Ellicott street.

Taylor Hose Co. No. 1.—No. 106 Pearl street.

Eagle Hose Co. No. 2.—No. 316 Washington street.

Seneca Hose Co. No. 3.—Corner of Seneca and Chicago streets.

Excelsior Hose Co. No. 4.—In alley on South Division street, between Main and Washington streets.

Neptune Hose Co. No. 5.—North side of Perry street, 80 feet west of Washington street.

Store House.—Junction Mohawk, Pearl, and Genesee.

FIRE DISTRICTS.

No. 1. Embraces all that portion of the city lying south of Court street and west of Main street.

No. 2. All south of Clinton street and east of Main street.

No. 3. All north of Court street and west of Main street.

No. 4. All north of Clinton street and east of Main street.

CANAL OFFICERS.

Collector.—Wm. Foot.

Clerks.—Seymour Bennett, R. S. Foote, J. T. Spaulding, Louis Pfeifer, Wm. Foote, Jr.

Superintendent.—Chester S. Shelly, Lockport.

ERIE CANAL ENLARGEMENT.

Resident Engineer's Office.—Prosser's Block, corner Pearl and W. Seneca streets.

Resident Engineer.—W J. Keeler.

Assistant Engineer.—S. D. Charles.

Draftsman.—T. F. Bohn.

GOVERNMENT BUILDING.

Custom House and Post Office.—Corner of Washington and Seneca streets.

Collector.—Christian Metz.

Deputy.—Wm. Flemming.

Clerks.—Oscar F. Crary, Hiram P. Thayer.

Inspectors.—Sam'l Strong, Sanford Halbert, Wm. H. Bostwick. Geo. Weohnert, E. A. Maynard.

COUNTY OFFICERS.

County Judge.—James Sheldon.

District Attorney.—F. J. Fithian.

Assistant District Attorney.—Ed. P. Chapin.

Surrogate.—C. C. Severance.

County Clerk.—O. J. Green.

Deputy Clerk.—S. Carey Adams.

Special Deputy Clerk.—J. L. Fairchild.

Superintendents of Poor.—John J. Weber, Buffalo; Joseph Bennett, Evans; Silas Taber, Lancaster.

County Treasurer and County Tax Receiver.—Norman B. McNeal, Spaulding's Exchange.

Coroners.—Nelson Randall, Buffalo; S. V. R. Graves, East Hamburg.

Sheriff.—G. A. Scroggs.

Under Sheriff.—Nelson Hopkins.

Office Deputy.—Noah P. Sprague.

Deputies.—Adam Renewaldt, Amherst; Geo. Mayo, Concord; D. C. Welch, Eden; Albert W. Marshall, Alden; Stafford Pike, Wales; Charles P. Persons, Aurora; Benj. Toles, James Kester, Jacob Emerick, Joseph K. Tyler, Tucker T. Bloomer, Jacob F. Kuhn, Samuel Fursman, Peter Corbin, Linus Reynolds, Jas. Waller, Geo. Orr, Buffalo.

Jailor and Deputy Sheriff.—Giles P. Glass.

Turnkey.—Zealous Sperry.

Commissioners of Deeds—From Jan. 1, 1861, for two years.—Wm. C. Bryant, Josiah A.

Mills, Chas. W. Hamlin, Wm. Hodge, Cuyler Garrett, John Rudy, Mark B. Moore, Lyman D. Hodge, Leonard Wilson, John Stellwagon, Lyman P. Perkins, DeForest Crandall, Cyrus P. Lee, Chas. Shiels, Augustus S. Brooks, Jno. S. Seibold, Thomas Parsons, Lorenzo K. Haddock, Thos. Bath, Daniel Kelley, Jacob Krettner, Wm. W. Mann, H. J. Marshall, Joel L. Walker, Edmund S. Ralph, Jas. Sheldon, Elnathan G. Luce, Millard P. Fillmore, J. D. Hoyt Chamberlain, Alfred B. Bidwell, John Dodge, Stephen M. Evry, Wm. H. Gurney, Geo. P. Barker, Grover Cleveland, Geo. Hinson, Thos. Edmonds. Thos. B. Shepard, Benj. H. Williams, Perry M. Sayles, Lyman K. Bass, Hiram Chambers, Jos. A. Rathbun, Seth Newman, Christopher Schmidt, Jno. G. Johnson, Albert S. Merrill, Geo. Zillig, James E. Ford, Sylvanus O. Gould, Oscar Folsom, Jas. Mooney, Peter M. Vosburgh. Myron Stillwell, Jacob Domedian, Jas. M. Baker, Louis D. Voltz, David N. Marvin, Geo. S. Wardwell, Geo. A. Stinger, Frederick Keppel, Samuel O. Bigelow, Wm. Philips, Jas. W. Booth, DeWitt Clinton, Chas. McCarthey, Jos. S. A. Judson, Jos. Timmerman, Wm. H. Albro, Jas. S. Lyon, L. F. Bissell, Edwin S. Husted, Lucien Hawley, Orlando McCumber, Henry F. Allen, Abbott C. Calkins, Geo. Zeiler, Geo. Mugridge, Ira Barnard, Jr., Wallace W. French, Talmadge Ewers, Geo. M. Noyes, Christopher M. Baldy, Geo. J. Bryan, Harry H. Clapp, Jos. Warren, Cyrenius C. Bristol, Michael Hagan, Julius Vortriede, Frederick Held, Edward M. Jewett, Geo. W. Allen, John G. Schuhler, Christopher Rodenbach, Harry Thompson, Jr., Gilbert Hyatt, Darius F. Gates, Jas. S. Gibbs, Geo. F. Haywood, Amos B. Tanner, Adam Metz, Thos. R. Clinton, Samuel S. Kellogg, Edward Stevens, Jas. C. Brown, John F. Gardner, Bela H. Colegrove, Nelson Janes, John E. McMahon, Edward L. Ferris, John W. A. Meyer, Henry A. Swartz, Stephen B. Porter, Christian Lapp, Patrick Goodwin, Derrick L. Pomeroy, Theodore Hamilton, Marshall N. Jones, Henry Zink, Jacob Gall, Edward H. Myers, Thos. S. Cutting. John Otto, Andrew J. Buckland, Jos. P. Dudley, Louis Kuempel, Jonathan Austin, Mathew A. Whitney, Louis Goembel, Fayette Rumsey, Philander A. Hodge, Edward W. Palmer, Harmon H. Griffin, David F. Day, Amos A. Blanchard, Ephraim S. Havens, Albert G. Stevens, Roswell L. Burrows, Edward Fuchs, David Tucker, Samuel Sizer, Stephen B. Charles, Edward Bennett, William H. Hoyt, Truman Ohlmer, Nelson Hopkins, John W. Stewart, Roswell Chapin, Carl Hutter, Samuel Lake, Lorenz Gillig, James C. Strong, Oliver C. Houghton, John Hellriegel, Jas. Inglis, Harry H. Matteson, Gordon Bailey, Jas. Miller, Wm. B. Hoyt, Charles J. Thomas, Conrad Baer, Donald McDonald.

Commissioners of Deeds for other States.— L. P. Perkins, for every State in the Union; James S. Gibbs, for New York, Alabama, Arkansas, California, Connecticut, Florida, Georgia, Illinois, Indiana, Iowa, Kentucky, Louisiana, Maine, Massachusetts, Michigan, Minnesota, Missouri, New Hampshire, New Jersey, Ohio, Pennsylvania, Rhode Island, South Carolina, Tennessee, Texas, Vermont, Virginia and Wisconsin. Frederick P. Stevens, for New Hampshire, Pennsylvania, Ohio, Indiana, Michigan and Wisconsin. W. W. Mann, for Massachusetts. Le Grand Marvin, for Connecticut, Ohio, Indiana and Pennsylvania. G. L. Marvin, for Ohio, Michigan and Wisconsin. L. K. Haddock, for Maine. Nelson K. Hopkins, for Massachusetts, Ohio, Michigan and Wisconsin. Joseph L. Fairchild, for Wisconsin. B. H. Colegrove, for Connecticut and Pennsylvania. Henry C. Tillinghast, for Michigan. Lucien Hawley, for Iowa. A. A. Blanchard, for Massachusetts and New Hampshire. Geo. Wadsworth, for California, Pennsylvania, Virginia, Indiana, Connecticut, Vermont, Wisconsin, Maine. North Carolina, South Carolina, Georgia and Tennessee. P. J. Douw, for Wisconsin. J. Stellwagen, for every State in the Union.

Loan Commissioners.—Thos. J. Sizer, Buffalo. Samuel S. Read, East Hamburgh.

Notaries Public.—Albert K. Allen, Edgar P. Perkins, Geo. A. Stringer, Abbott C. Calkins, E. St. John Bemis, S. Carey Adams, Elisha T. Smith, E. Dexter Belden, James H. Fisher, Jacob Gall, Edgar P. Pickering, Christopher Rodenbach, John Stellwagen, John Whytock, Otis F. Presbrey, Frederick L. Danforth, John C. Clifford, Lorenz Gillig, Abram L. Griffin, Jas. C. Strong, Julius Vordtriede, Andrew William Gleason. Watson A. Fox, E. B. Forbush, Chas. M. Hopkins, Samuel M Brunck, Sylvanus O. Cobb, George W. Allen, Robert P. Hayes, H. W. Burt, Richard J. Sibley, Joseph M. Gaylord, Hosea S. Heath, Chas. L. Mayer, Jacob Krettner, Joseph E. Baldwin, Wm. A. Best, John Brown, Harry H. Clapp, Henry P. Clinton, Hermann Doerffel, Henry W. Faxon, Edward Fuchs, Sylvanus O. Gould. Reuben Justin, Lyman P. Perkins, Jos. Salter, Wm. H. Slade, Joseph Whittel, Clifford A. Baker, J. John Chard, Michael Danner. Christian Eggert, David F. Day, Samuel B. Hard, Wm. C. Russell, Eben P. Dorr, Phocian Hoffman. Samuel Hurr, Geo. L. Marvin, Nicholas Ottenot, Michael Pinner, John W. Wilkeson, George H. Ganson, Lorenzo K. Haddock, Chas. Huetter, Jas. H. Fisher, John R. Lee, Wm. A. Chard, Henry Starkweather, Jos. L. Fairchild, Chas. W. Kraetzer, Henry J. Shuttleworth, Augustus Paul. Alden Barker, Hiram H. Blodgett, Seymour Bennett, Octavius O. Cottle, Cyrus P. Lee, Jas. H. Madison, Henry H. Martin, Edward Pierson, Geo. Wadsworth, Christian Lapp, John H. Parsons, Charles Townsend, Buffalo.

Seth Newman, White's Corners. Chas. W. Morse, Louis E. Filbert, Eden. John A. Case, Holland. Johnson Parsons, Lancaster. Gottleb J. Wolfle, North Buffalo. Stephen Sisson, Samuel Healey, Gowanda. Anson G. Conger, Noah H. Bartlett, Collins.

District Clerk, new appointment.—Geo. Gorham, vice Aurelian Conkling, deceased.

COURTS.

EIGHTH JUDICIAL DISTRICT.

County Court and Court of Sessions.—James Sheldon, Buffalo, County Judge. James Morrison, of Clarence, and S. G. Johnson, of Tonawanda, Justices of Sessions. Obadiah J. Green, Clerk. F. J. Fithian, District Attorney.

General Terms.—1861.—In Erie County, 2d Monday in February; 2d Monday in May; 1st Monday in September; 2d Monday in November.

Erie County Special Terms.— 1861.— 2d Tuesday in January, by Justice Grover; 4th Tuesday in March, by Justice Davis; 3d Tuesday in June, by Justice Marvin; 4th Tuesday in August, by Justice Grover; 1st Tuesday in Movember, by Justice Marvin.

Erie County Circuit Courts and Courts of Oyer and Terminer.—1861.—2d Monday in March, by Justice Marvin; 1st Monday in June, by Justice Davis; 1st Monday in October, by Justice Grover; 3d Monday in December, by Justice Davis.

Circuit Courts, Courts of Oyer and Terminer, and Special Terms of the Supreme Court.—Allegany County.—1861.—2d Monday in March, by Justice Davis; 1st Monday in July, by Justice Marvin; 4th Monday in October, by Justice Grover. Cattaraugus County.—1861.— 3d Monday in January, by Justice Grover; 4th Monday in June, by Justice Davis; 3d Monday in October, by Justice Marvin. Chautauqua County.—1861.—4th Monday in January, by Justice Grover; 1st Monday in June, by Justice Marvin; 1st Monday in October, by Justice Davis. Genesee County.—1861.—4th Monday in March, by Justice Grover; 4th Monday in June, by Justice Marvin; 4th Monday in October, by Justice Davis. Niagara County.—1861.—4th Monday in January, by Justice Davis; 4th Monday in May, by Justice Grover; 4th Monday in September, by Justice Marvin. Orleans County.—1861.—3d Monday in January, by Justice Davis; 3d Monday in May, by Justice Grover; 3d Monday in September, by Justice Marvin. Wyoming County.—1861.—4th Monday in April, by Justice Grover; 4th Monday in August, by Justice Davis; 4th Monday in December, by Justice Marvin.

SUPERIOR COURT OF BUFFALO.

George W. Clinton, Isaac A. Verplanck, Joseph G. Masten, Judges; D. Tillinghast, Clerk; S. U. Brunck, Deputy Clerk; C. Lake, Crier.

Special Civil Terms.—1st Monday in January; 1st Monday in March; 1st Monday in May; 1st Monday in July; 1st Monday in September; 1st Monday in November.

Special Criminal Terms.—4th Monday in January; 4th Monday in April; 4th Monday in June; 4th Monday in September; 4th Monday in November.

General Terms.—3d Monday in March; 2d Monday in June; 2d Monday in October; 2d Monday in December.

Special Terms for all Civil Business, except Trial of Calendar Causes.—1st Monday in February; 1st Monday in April; 1st Monday in June; 1st Monday in October; 1st Monday in December.

Erie County Courts, 1861.—4th Monday in March; 2d Monday in May; 4th Monday in September; 4th Monday in December.

Court of Sessions, 1861.—3d Monday in February; 4th Monday in May; 2d Monday in November.

County Courts for all motion purposes are held with Courts of Sessions.

Court of Appeals.—At Albany, 1st Tuesday in January; 4th Tuesday in March; 3d Tuesday in June; 5th Tuesday in September.

UNITED STATES COURTS.

District Court United States.—3d Tuesday in January, at Albany; 3d Tuesday in May, at Rochester; 2d Tuesday in July, at Utica; 3d Tuesday in August, at Auburn; 2d Tuesday in November, at Buffalo; and one Term, by appointment, in one of the Counties of St. Lawrence, Franklin or Clinton.

Circuit Court United States.—3d Tuesday in May, at Albany (not held); Tuesday after 3d Monday in June, at Canandaigua; 3d Tuesday in October, at Albany.

U. S. District Judge, N. District New York.—N. K. Hall. Office and Court Room over Post Office, U. S. buildings, corner Washington and Seneca streets, Buffalo.

Justice of the Supreme Court of the Eighth Judicial District.—James G. Hoyt.

Clerk District Court.—Aurelian Conkling. Office corner Washington and Seneca streets.

U. S. Attorney, Potsdam, St. Lawrence Co., N. Y.—Wm. A. Dart.

U. S. Marshal, Lockport, Niagara Co., N. Y.—Edward I. Chase.

Deputy U. S. Marshal.—Albert G. Stevens.

U. S. Commissioners.—Dennis Bowen, Aurelian Conkling, A. P. Nichols, Perry G. Parker and George Gorham.

BUFFALO POST OFFICE.—1861.

Government Building, corner of Washington and Seneca streets.

Postmaster.—Almon M. Clapp.

Assistant Postmaster.—Thos. Blossom.

Clerks.—James H. Lee, Henry White, John Powers, Geo. Walker, Willis Dodge, Henry Smith, Louis Weber, Dennis Collins, Jr., Mi-

2

chael Wolf, C. Bronner, Jr., J. C. West, Louis Filner, John Zoll, H. Krausskopf, Chas. E. Johnson, T. C. O'Grady, Alexander McKay, Wm. C. Armes, Edward Morris, John W. Stewart, John G. Weimar, Geo. Niess, Isaac Sanford, John Hellriegel, Lucian Sierret and Francis Stevens.

BANKS.

White's Bank of Buffalo.—Capital $200,000. Geo. C. Whie, President; Wm. Williams, Vice President; F. Gridley, Cashier; J. H. Madison, Assistant Cashier; Wm. H. Hutchinson, Teller; G. A. Schafer, Assistant Book-keeper. Office, 146 Main street.

Bank of Attica.—Capital, $250,000. A. J. Rich, President; C. Townsend, Cashier; Wm. K. Allen, Teller; C. Dygert, Clerk; Geo. H. Gridley, Book-keeper. Office, No. 1 Spaulding's Exchange.

New York and Erie.—Capital, $300,000. John S. Ganson, President; James Sweeney, Cashier; J. M. Gwinn, Teller; John B. Seymour, Book-keeper; Geo. H. Dunbar, Assistant Teller; F. A. Rathbun, Clerk. Office, Iron Building, Seneca street, between Main and Pearl.

Marine.—Capital, $200,000. Geo. Palmer, President; H. E. Howard, Cashier; Henry E. Howard, Assistant Cashier and Notary Public; Samuel A. Provost, Jr., Book-keeper; Ed. Fiske, Clerk. Office, 90 Main street.

Buffalo City.—Capital, $140,000. John L. Kimberly, President; A. P. Thompson, Cashier; H. B. Starkweather, Teller and Notary Public; J. L. Kimberly, Jr., Book-keeper; Chas. Pickering, Jr., Discount Clerk. Office, 177 Main street.

Farmers and Mechanics.—Capital, $150,000. E. G. Spaulding, President; Edward Pierson, Cashier; E. D. Belden, Teller; E. D. Lacy, Book-keeper; H. H. Mills, Clerk. Office, No. 3, Spaulding's Exchange.

International.—Capital $400,000. M. S. Hawley, President; E. S. Prosser, Vice President; Chas. T. Coit, Cashier; B. B. Hamilton, Teller; E. W. Seymour, Book-keeper. Office, Iron Building, Seneca street, between Main and Pearl.

The Manufacturers' and Traders' Bank.— Capital, $500,000. Henry Martin, President; Pascal P. Pratt, Vice President; Henry H. Martin, Cashier; Jared P. Fairman, Teller; Salem G. Kennedy, Book-keeper; Charles E. Sprague, Book-keeper and Discount Clerk. Office, 219 Main street.

Clinton Bank.—Capital, $250,000. Gibson T. Williams, President; J. M. Hutchinson, Vice President; James M. Smith, Cashier; E. T. Smith, Teller; A. L. Bennett, Book-keeper; C. H. Langdon, Clerk. Office, corner Pearl and West Seneca streets.

Buffalo Savings.—Chartered May 8th, 1846. This institution has been in operation nearly fifteen years. Whole number of depositors, 21,000. Office, 330 Main street. Hours of Business from 9 A. M. to 3 P. M. E. D. Efner, President; E. L. Stevenson, Pice President; Henry Howard, Secretary; Charles Shields, Book-keeper; John U. Wayland, Assistant Book-keeper; Peter Young, Clerk; O. H. Marshall, Attorney.

Trustees—E. D. Efner, E. L. Stevenson, Francis J. Handel, N. H. Gardner, R. H. Heywood, E. G. Grey, Wm. Tweedy. N. K. Hall. Geo. R. Babcock, Hiram Barton, Albert H. Tracy, J. Beyer, John L. Kimberly, F. C. Brunck, Geo. Coit, Warren Bryant, Dr. Hauenstein, Samuel F. Pratt.

Buffalo Trust Company.—Organized under a charter passed April 16th, 1852. Office. 223 Main street, corner of Main and Swan. Open from 9 A. M. to 3 P. M. Peter Curtiss, President; G. R. Wilson, Vice President; Dennis Bowen, Attorney.

Trustees—George Coit, Henry W. Rogers, Guilford R. Wilson, Orlando Allen, John Stellwagen, Alanson Robinson, Stephen Bettinger, S. S. Jewett, Samuel F. Pratt, Orsamus H. Marshall, Edw'd Bennett, Peter Curtiss, Chandler J. Wells.

This Company has deposited with the Bank Department $100,000 in stocks and bonds and mortgages, which, together with the personal liability of the Trustees, is held as security for all classes of depositors.

Erie County Savings.—Incorporated April 10th, 1854. Opened September 1st, 1854. Office, 244 Main street. Office hours from 9 A. M. to 3 P. M. Wm, A. Bird, President; S. V. R. Watson, 1st Vice President; Jas. C. Harrison, 2d Vice President; Cyrus P. Lee, Secretary and Treasurer; E. C. Sprague, Attorney; H. H. Stanley and Jacob L. Gall, Clerks.

Trustees—Wm. A. Bird, S. V. R. Watson, Henry Roop, Richard Bullymore, Jacob Krettner, Michael Danner, Wm. C. Sherwood, Wm Wilkeson, F. Augustus Georger, N. H. Gardner, Wm. Fiske, Noah P. Sprague, C. J. Wells, Chas. D. Norton, J. C. Harrison, Jno. R. Evans, Oliver G. Steele, L. K. Plimpton.

Western Savings Bank.—Main street, corner Mohawk, 1861. Geo. Palmer President; Ph. Beyer, 1st Vice President; George Urban, 2d Vice President; Chas. Schmidt, Secretary; N. K. Hopkins, Attorney.

Trustees—Henry Martin, Jas. Hollister, C. A. Van Slyke, A. L. Schryver, Wm. O. Brown, L. L. Hodges, E. S. Warren, A. Schmidt, P. Houck, John R. Lee, Nic. Ottenot, George C. White, Jacob Scheu, Elijah Ford, Charles Chretien, A. Weppner.

Emigrant Savings.—Main street, corner LaStephen Bettinger, President; Edwin Thomas, Vice President; P. T. Beirne, Secretary; E. C. Chase, Treasurer; Tillinghast & McMahon, Attorneys.

BUFFALO COMMERCIAL COLLEGE.

Entrance on Main street, directly opposite the Metropolitan Theater, No, 194, and over Cone's Emporium.

D. Clinton Hicks, President; Horatio Seymour Counsellor.

Directors—Rev. J. C. Lord, George Palmer, Chas. G. Playter, Wm. Luther, Rev. Otto Berger, Rev. Frederick Schelle, T. T. Lockwood, M. D., Lucius H. Pratt, Geo. C. White, Rev. G. S. Voght, J. S. Semon, Elijah Hadley, Rev. Dr. Burtis, Rev. Christian Volz, H. Parmelee, Jacob Beyer.

Faculty — D. Clinton Hicks, Lecturer on the Collective, Collateral, and Demonstrative Branches of the Science of Accounts, Penmanship and Commercial Problems.

BUFFALO MERCANTILE COLLEGE.

Brown's Buildings, corner Main and Seneca streets.

Founded October 10th, 1854. H. B. Bryant, H. D. Stratton and J. C. Bryant, Principals.

Faculty—H. B. Bryant, H. D. Stratton, J. C. Bryant, W. P. Spencer, Professors of the Science of Accounts and Lecturers on Business Customs. P. R. Spencer, W. P. Spencer, R. W. Hoadley, Instructors in Business and Ornamental Penmanship, and Lecturers on Mercantile Correspondence. Hons. Horace Mann, Geo. W. Clinton, Elihu Burritt, Special Lecturers. Hon. Judge Masten, W. P. Spencer and others, Lecturers on Commercial Law. John R. Lee and others, Lecturers on Banking, Finance, &c. Revs. J. Hyatt Smith and M. R. Atkins, Lecturers on Political Economy. Revs. M. L. R. P. Thompson, G. W. Hosmer, G. W. Heacock, C. W. Dennison, A. T. Chester, Lecturers on Mercantile Ethics. Oliver Arey, M. J. Oatman, E. C. Pomeroy, Lecturers on Commercial Computations.

Directors—Hons. E. G. Spaulding, Geo. W. Clinton, I. V. Verplanck, Victor M. Rice, N. K. Hall, Wm. A. Mosely, Washington Hunt, S. G. Haven, Eli Cook, O. G. Steele, Esq., J. L. Kimberly, Wm. A. Bird, John R. Lee, Peter A. Porter, C. M. Reed, P. R. Spencer, A. H. Tracy.

BUFFALO FEMALE ACADEMY.

This Institution is situated in the most eligible and delightful part of the city, and commands a beautiful view of the city, the river and the lake. The grounds consisting of a whole block, fronting on Delaware avenue, and extending to a charming private park in the rear, are tastefully laid out and ornamented with trees and shrubbery.

The buildings, "The Cottage" and "Goodell Hall" combine all that is desirable in arrangement and convenience. The former is built of stone, and is exclusively occupied by the family of the Principal. the young ladies entrusted to his care as boarders, and the teachers of the Institution boarding with the Principal. The latter, "Goodell Hall," has been expressly erected for academic instruction, and for spaciousness and convenience, may well challenge comparison with any similar establishment in the country. It has abundant accommodations for four hundred pupils.

Board of Trustees—Hon. N. K. Hall, President; Rev. A. T. Chester, D. D., Secretary and Treasurer. Samuel F. Pratt, Dennis Bowen, Noah H. Gardner, Henry W. Rogers, Bronson C. Rumsey, Joseph Dart, Sherman S. Jewett, John R. Lee, Thomas Farnham, Jas. M. S'n'th, Geo. N. Burwell, Myron P. Bush, Chas. E. Clark, Andrew J. Rich.

RAILROAD COMPANIES.

New York Central.—Capital, $23,000,000. Erastus Corning, President; Dean Richmond, Vice President; C. Vibbard, General Superintendent; J. Collamer, Superintendent of Western Division; J. V. L. Pruyn, Counsel; G. L. Wilson, Secretary and Treasurer.

Directors — Erastus Corning, Dean Richmond, John H. Chedell, Hamilton White, Livingston Spraker, Alonzo C. Paige. Cornelius L. Tracy, Jacob Gould, R. M. Bealchford, Nathaniel Thayer, John V. L. Pruyn, Henry H. Martin, Chas. Russel.

Great Western, Canada. — From Niagara Falls to Windsor, C. W., 229 miles; Branches, Hamilton to Toronto, 38 miles; Harrisburg to Guelph, 27 miles; Komoka to Sarina, 51 miles; Total, 345 miles. Office—Hamilton, Canada West. Capital paid in, $15,024,987.65; funded debt, 6,442,006.69; total cost of Road, $22,583,202.30. Time of election—2d Tuesday in November. Gauge of Road, 5 feet 6 inches. Robert Gill, Surrey, Eng., President.

American Officers—J. Young, Vice President; C. J. Brydges, Managing Director; T. Reynolds, Financial Director: W. C. Stephens, Secretary; E. G. S. Colpoys, Supt. East Div.; J. Peacock, Supt. West Div.; G. L. Reid, Chief Engineer; Julius Movius, Gen. Agent; Thos. Bell, Gen. Ft. Agent; Richard Eaton, Locomotive Supt.; S. Sharp, Car Supt.

Canadian Board of Directors—John Young, Chas. John Brydges, Thos. Reynolds, Henry C. R. Becher, F. W. Gates, Geo. H. Mills.

English Board—Robert Gill, Alex. Hoys, Thos. Cullen, F. S. Head, M. Faulconer.

General Agency, No. 175 Washington Street, Buffalo.

Detroit and Milwaukee.—From Detroit to Grand Haven, 188 miles. Office, Detroit, Mich. Gauge of Road, 4 feet 8½ inches. Charles John Brydges, President; Thomas Reynolds, Vice President; C. C. Trowbridge, Secretary; W. K. Muir, Gen. Supt.; Jas. H. Muir, Auditor; J. A. Armstrong, General Freight Agent; Benj. Briscoe, Mast. of Mach.; John Kitching, Road Master; G. L. Reid, Chief Engineer.

Directors—C. J. Brydges, Thos. Reynolds, C. C. Trowbridge, H. N. Walker, W. K. Muir,

E. A. Brush, Robt. Gill, Thomas Cullen, Henry C. R. Becher. Julius Movius, General Agent, 175 Washington street, Buffalo.

Buffalo, New York and Erie.—A. D. Patchin, President; C. G. Miller, vice President; Gilbert Cameron, Treasurer; William F. Miller, Secretary; L. M. Schermerhorn, General Ft. Agent.

Directors—Geo. W. Tifft, Aaron D. Patchin, Chas. G. Miller, Henry Martin, Guilford R. Wilson, John G. Deshler; Daniel W. Tomlinson, Batavia; Thos. Brown, Caledonia; A. O. Comstock, Le Roy; John Arnot, Elmira; Geo. Briggs, James G. King, R. S. Carter, Brantford, C. W.

Executive Committee—A. D. Patchin, Geo. W. Tifft, Henry Martin, Chas. G. Miller, Thos. Brown.

New York and Erie.—Directors — Samuel Marsh, President; Daniel Drew, Dudley S. Gregory, John Arnot of Elmira, William B. Skidmore, Hermann Gelpcke, Ralph Mead, D. A. Cushman, Ambrose S. Murray, of Goshen; William Evans, of England; George T. Cobb, Robert H. Berdell, William F. Splatt, of England. Nathaniel Marsh, J. C. B. Davis, Henry L. Pierson, Cornelius Vanderbilt.

Buffalo and Lake Huron.—R. S. Carter, Managing Director, Brantford, C. W.; William McLean, Secretary, Brantford, C. W.; A. Fell, Road and Tariff Superintendent. Office, Erie Street Depot, Buffalo.

Buffalo and State Line.—Geo Palmer, President; Dean Richmond, Vice President; R. N. Brown, Supt.

Directors—George Palmer, James S. Wadsworth, Joseph Field, Daniel Drew, Dean Richmond, John Wilkinson, Charles H. Lee, Henry L. Lansing, Hamilton White, Alanson Robinson, George W. Patterson, Nathaniel Marsh, Wm. Keep.

ROAD COMPANIES.

Buffalo and Hamburg Turnpike.—Capital, $21,500. Henry W. Rogers, President; Geo. Palmer, Secretary; Joseph Foster, Treasurer.

Buffalo and Williamsville McAdam.—T. A. Hopkins, President; John R. Lee, Secretary and Treasurer.

Directors—Warren Granger, Samuel F. Pratt, H. Seymour, Jr., William Hodge, William F. Miller. L. K. Plimpton, T. A. Hopkins. Capital, $60,000. Annual dividends, five per cent.

White's Corners and Buffalo Plank.—Geo. A. Moore, President; Wm. H. Glenny, Secretary and Treasurer.

Directors —Wm. H. Glenny, Allen Potter, Geo. A. Moore, A. A. Howard, Isaac Long.

Aurora and Buffalo Plank.—Capital Stock, $60,000. L. M. Bullis, President; W. S. Rogers, Secretary, Treasurer and Superintendent.

Directors—R. H. Maynard, Robert Persons,

Chas. D. Mayer, W. S. Rogers, L. M. Bullis, Nelson Janes, Horace Parmalee.

Buffalo and Batavia Plank.—F. P. Adams, President; Eli H. Bowman, Secretary and Treasurer.

Directors—Levi Otis, Theodore Eldred, Henry Darrow. L. G. Wilsey, George Smiley, E. P. Adams, John Wood, Eli H. Bowman, B. C. Curtland.

Batavia Street Plank Road.—Apollos Hitchcock, President; George L. Marvin, Secretary and Treasurer.

Directors—S. V. R. Watson, Joseph F. Hill, Milo W. Hill, Eurotas Marvin, Alex. Hitchcock, Apollos Hitchcock, Amos Ray, Jesse Vaughn, James Demarest, Geo. L. Marvin.

TELEGRAPH COMPANIES.

Western Union Telegraph.—Office, No. 5 Spaulding's Exchange. Hiram Sibley, President; I. R. Elwood, Secretary, Rochester; J. H. Wade, General Agent; A. Stager, General Superintendent, Cleveland; Emery Cobb, Chicago, and C. Davenport, Cincinnati, Division Superintendents; N. Hucker, Manager; C. E. Williams, Assistant Book-keeper; R. Newell, Chief Operator; P. Kelley and G. B. Haynes, Assistant Operators.

Montreal Telegraph.—Office, No. 5 Spaulding's Exchange. Hugh Allen, President; Jas. Dakers, Secretary; O. S. Wood, General Superintendent, Montreal; H. P. Dwight, Assistant Superintendent, Toronto; N. Hucker, Manager; C. Robinson, Operator.

New York, Albany and Buffalo Electro-Magnetic Telegraph.—Office, No. 5 Spaulding's Exchange. Thos. R. Walker, President; E. Chapman, Treasurer; Jas. D. Reid, General Superintendent, Utica; N. Hucker, Manager; C. E. Williams, Assistant Book-keeper; J. C. Bowles, Chief Operator; J. A. Osburn, and Wm. Wallace, Jr., Operators.

Buffalo, New York and Erie Railroad Telegraph.—Office, corner Washington and Exchange streets. L. E. Babb, Superintendent; C. N. Sawin, Operator.

PUBLIC SCHOOLS.

Superintendent—Sanford B. Hunt.

Central School.—Situated on Court, Franklin and Genesee streets. Oliver Arey, Principal.

School District No. 1, Seventh near Hudson —Principal, A. Z. Barrows.

School District No. 2, Terrace near Genesee —Principal, N. G. Benedict, Jr.

School District No. 3, Perry east of Burwell Place—Principal, James E. Gilbert.

School District No. 4, Elk near Louisiana— Principal, John B. Sackett.

School District No. 5, E. Seneca near Pollard—Principal, E. T. Benedict.

School District No. 6, South Division near Chestnut—Principal, E. F. Cook.

School District No. 7, South Division below Ellicott—Principal, N. B. Barker.

School District No. 8, Church above Delaware—Principal, Samuel Slade.

School District No. 9, Vine near Elm—Principal, Chas. C. Johnson.

School District No. 10, Delaware street—Principal, Geo. W. Stowitt.

School District No. 11, Elm near Clinton—Principal. C. W. Colyer.

School District No. 12, Spruce above Batavia—Principal, E. C. Pomeroy.

School District No. 13, Oak near Sycamore—Principal. W. W. Newman.

School District No. 14, Franklin between Edward and Tupper—Principal, John S. Fosdick

School District No. 15, Oak corner Burton alley—Principal, James H. French.

School District No. 16, Delaware above Bryant—Principal, P. E. Dye.

School District No. 17, Main near toll gate—Principal. Harriet Patterson.

School District No. 18, Tenth near School—Principal, E. L. Chamberlayne.

School District No. 19, North Washington near Eighteenth—Principal, Wm. L. French.

School District No. 20, Amherst corner East—Princpal, A. B. Elsworth.

School District No. 21, Emslie near Peckham—Principal, E. A. Austin.

School District No 22, Main near Burt Scott's—Principal, ——

School District No. 23, Delevan Avenue beyond Adams—Principal, Esther E. Carr.

School District No. 24, Best near Walden—Principal, Wm. S. Rice.

School District No. 25, Batavia beyond toll gate—Principal. Miss Alida M. Hakstein.

School District No. 26, Seneca near Whitmore's Tavern—Principal, Rascelia Vasseler.

School District No 27, near Seneca beyond Hydraulics—Principal, Charles Fosdick.

School District No. 28, White's Corners Plank Road—Principal, — Kennedy.

School District No. 30, Ohio near toll Gate—Principal, Jane N. Dunn.

School District No. 31, Emslie and Krettner near William—Principal, P. E. Brown.

School District No. 32, Cedar near Clinton—Principal, J. W. Barker.

School District No. 33, Elk near Smith—Principal, H. J. French.

Of these Schools, Nos. 1, 3, 4, 5, 6, 7, 10, 12, 13, 14, 15, 16, 20 and 32, in all fourteen schools, are organized with three departments.

Nos. 2, 8, 9, 11, 18, 19, 24 and 31, in all eight schools, have two departments.

Nos. 17, 21, 22, 23, 25, 26, 27, 28, 29, 30 and 33, in all eleven schools, have one department.

ASSOCIATIONS AND SOCIETIES.

Medical College of Buffalo.—The University of Buffalo was chartered during the legislative session of 1846, and endowed with all the powers and privileges which belong to any College or University in the State. The Medical Department was established and organized in August of the same year. The lectures commence on the first Wednesday in November, and continue sixteen weeks. A preliminary term commences four weeks before the regular term, which is devoted to dissection, clinical instruction, and lectures on special subjects. The preliminary term is voluntary and gratuitous.

Hon. Millard Fillmore, Chancellor.

Council—Orsamus H. Marshall, President; Joseph G. Masten, Vice President; Geo. Hadley, Secretary; James Hollister, Treasurer; Henry W. Rogers, James P. White, Orsamus H. Marshall, Geo. Hadley, Elbridge G. Spaulding, John D. Shepard, John R. Wilkeson, Millard Fillmore, Orson Phelps, Orlando Allen, Sanford B. Hunt, Geo. R. Babcock, Jas. Hollister, Albert H. Tracy, Thos. F. Rochester, Member elect from the Medical Faculty. Mayor of the City of Buffalo, Recorder of the City of Buffalo, *ex officio.*

Faculty—Sandford Eastman, M. D., Dean; Geo. Hadley, Registrar and Treasurer; C. B. Coventry, M. D., Emeritus Professor of Physiology and Medical Jurisprudence; Charles Alfred Lee, M. D., Professor of Pathology and Materia Medica; Sandford Eastman, M. D., Professor of Anatomy; Jas. P. White, M. D., Professor of Obstetrics and Diseases of Women and Children; E. M. Moore, M. D., Professor of Principles and Practice of Surgery and Clinical Surgery; Thos. F Rochester, M. D., Professor of Principles and Practice of Medicine, and Clinical Medicine; Geo. Hadley, M. D., Professor of Chemistry and Pharmacy; A. J. Steel, M. D., Demonstrator of Anatomy; J. R. Lothrop, M. D., Professor of Materia Medica; Wm. Mason, M. D., Professor of Physiology and Microscopy.

Buffalo Medical Association.— Organized July 16, 1845; incorporated April 1, 1856. This Association meets regularly on the first Tuesday evening of each month, at its rooms, No. 7 South Division street. The objects of the Association are strictly of a scientific character. The membership is confined to those who are in regular membership with the Medical Society of the County of Erie. Initiation fee, $2. Annual dues, $3.

Officers—Drs. C. C. F Gay, President; Jas. P. White, Vice President; J. B. Samo, Treasurer; J. F. Miner, Secretary; Wm. Ring, Librarian.

Trustees—Drs. C. C. F. Gay, Jas. P. White, J. B. Samo, J. F. Miner. Wm. Ring.

Members—Drs. W. W. Mason, George N. Burwell. John Boardman, Charles L. Dayton, Daniel Devening. Sanford Eastman, C. C. F. Gay, William Gould, Geo. Hadley. C. W. Harvy, S. B. Hunt, C. B. Hutchins, J. E. King,

T. T. Lockwood, S. F. Mixer, J. F. Miner, Henry Nichell, Wm. Ring, Thomas F. Rochester, J. B. Sarno, Edward Storck, P. H. Strong, Wm. Treat, James P. White, I. C. Whitehead, Jr., B. L. Whitney, C. H. Wilcox, C. C. Wyckoff, H. M. Conger, A. Jansen, J. I. Richards, John Croyn.

Medical Society of the County of Erie.—Officers—Drs. Sandford Eastman, President; J. B. Sarno, Vice President; Samuel D. Flagg, Jr., Secretary; C. C. F. Gay, Treasurer; C. C. Wyckoff, Librarian.

Primary Board—Drs. E. Storck, J. F. Miner and J. Hauenstein.

Censors—Dr. John Boardman, Examiner in Anatomy and Physiology; Dr.W. Gould, Examiner in Practical Medicine and Obstetrics; Dr. J. R. Lathrop, Examiner in Chemistry and Pharmacy; Dr. W. Ring, Examiner in Materia Medica and Botany; Dr. H. M. Congar, Examiner in Medical Jurisprudence and Pathology.

Buffalo City Dispensary.—Organized, March, 1847; Incorporated, February, 1859, for the purpose of relieving such poor, sick and indigent persons as are unable to procure medical aid.

Officers—R. H. Heywood, President; Jason Sexton, Vice President; Isaac D. White, Secretary; S. N. Callender, Treasurer.

Managers—Russell H. Haywood, Samuel N. Callender, Chas. H. Coleman, Peter Curtiss, George A. Moore, Isaac D. White, Myron P. Bush, Jason Sexton, Jacob H. Koons, George Jones, Samuel Cary, M. D., Francis P. Wood, C. W. Harvy, M. D.

Physicians—1st Ward—H. D. Gravin; 2d Ward—P. H. Strong; 3d Ward—Julius F. Miner; 4th Ward—J. R. Lathrop; 5th Ward—J. A. Felgemacher; 6th Ward—James B. Samo; 7th Ward—William Treat; 8th Ward—Sandford Eastman; 9th Ward—C. C. Wyckoff; 10th Ward—C. C. F. Gay; 11th Ward—L. P. Dayton; 12th Ward—Henry Nichell; 13th Ward—Benj. H. Lemon.

Consulting Physicians—Thos. F. Rochester and Geo. N. Burwell. Consulting Surgeons—C. H. Wilcox and James P. White. Apothecary—Wm. H. Peabody, cor. Main and South Division streets.

Buffalo General Hospital.—Chas. E. Clarke, President; Andrew J. Rich, Vice President; Wm. T. Wardwell, Secretary and Treasurer.

Trustees—Geo. S. Hazard, Chas. E. Clarke, Andrew J. Rich, Bronson C. Rumsey, Roswell S. Burrows, Wm. T. Wardwell, Isaac Holloway, George Howard, Henry Martin.

Attending Physicians—Thos. F. Rochester, C. C. F. Gay, C. C. Wyckoff. Consulting Physicians—G. F. Pratt, Geo. N. Burwell, Phineas H. Strong. Attending Surgeons—Charles H. Wilcox, Sandford Eastman, Julius F. Miner. Consulting Surgeons—J. P. White, H. N. Loomis, J. Hauenstein. Resident Physician—N. L. Bates. Warden—J. M. Crozier.

Young Men's Association. — The Young Men's Association is an institution of a literary and scientific character, and was established by the Young men of this city in the winter of 1835 and '36, and subsequently incorporated by an act of the Legislature, passed March, 1843.

The library numbers about ten thousand volumes, comprising many rare and valuable works, and is gradually increasing.

The Reading Room is supplied with all the daily city newspapers, and many from the principal cities of the Union, together with the ablest American and Foreign quarterlies and monthly periodicals. It is open every week-day from 8, A. M. to 9, P. M., to members and strangers introduced by members, the latter being entitled to its free use for one month from their introduction. The Rooms are in the American Hotel Block.

Lectures, literary and scientific, are maintained during the winter months.

Officers for 1861—Joseph Warren, President; Rufus L. Howard, 1st Vice President; Edward Stevens, 2d Vice President; Wm. C. Sweet, 3d Vice President; Charles H. Morse, Corresponding Secretary; Geo. T. Bentley, Recording Secretary; Edward S. Rich, Treasurer.

Managers—Frank A. Sears, Alfred D. Daw, James H. Penfield, Junius S. Smith, Everard Palmer, Charles E. Young, Wm. H. Peabody, Talmadge Ewers, Benj. H. Austin, Jr., Geo. S. Wardwell.

Standing Committees—Ways and Means—Howard, Palmer and Rich. Library—Palmer, Young and Rich. Lectures—Stevens, Morse, Daw, Sears, Bentley, Wardwell and Ewers. Newspapers and Periodicals—Sears, Austin and Penfield. Natural Sciences—Wardwell, Palmer and Stevens. Local History—Sweet, Austin and Penfield. Donations and Subscriptions—Peabody, Howard and Rich. Rooms and Fixtures—Young, Sears and Daw. Law—Ewers, Stevens and Austin. Printing—Penfield, Bentley and Young. By-Laws—Austin, Sweet and Wardwell. Auditing—Bentley, Smith and Peabody. Collecting—Morse, Howard, Sweet, Peabody, Sears and Smith. Membership—Smith, Ewers and Peabody. Library Fund—Daw, Howard and Young. Fine Arts—Rich, Howard, Ewers, Morse and Palmer.

Librarian—Wm. Ives.

Assistant Librarian—Wm. W. Stewart.

German Young Men's Association.—Instituted 1841—incorporated 1846. The object of this Association is for the purpose of establishing and maintaining a library and reading rooms, lectures and other means of promoting moral and intellectual improvement, and has about 200 members. The library consists of about 2000 volumes. The rooms are located in Hauenstein's Block, corner Main and Mohawk streets, and is open every Wednesday and Saturday nights from 7 to 9 o'clock.

Officers—Carl Frieschmann, President; F. Georger, Vice President; John B. Schlund, Recording Secretary; Otto Besser, Corresponding Secretary; Augustus Paul, Treasurer; Fr. Frankenstein, Librarian.

Managers—H. F. Juengling, F. C. Brunck,

J. Schuntz, F. A. Georger, F. Lautenbacher, Fr. Held, C. Loeberick. J. Hauenstein, A. Luesenhop and Geo. Seebach.

Young Men's Christian Union —This Society has for its primary object the moral and intellectual improvement of young men. It was organized in May, 1852, incorporated in March. 1853, and now contains about 850 members. Its Library and Reading Rooms are in Arcade Building, opposite American Hotel. Initiation fee, $1. Semi-annual dues, $1.

Officers—John D. Hill, M. D., President; W. C. Bryant, 1st Vice President; Samuel D. Sikes, 2d Vice President; A. H. Bryant, 3d Vice President; C. B. Armstrong, Corresponding Secretary; L. R. Casey, Recording Secretary. Thos. G. Parsons, Treasurer.

Managers—Wm. F. Miller, M. L. Comstock, Robt. Keating, Jas. B. Parke, Fred. W. Taylor, Joseph B. Sweet, Wm. R. Bradford, P. B. Peterson.

Buffalo Orphan Asylum.—Organized in 1835. Incorporated April 24th, 1837, and an amendment of the Charter in 1839. Located on Virginia street, near Delaware. Russell H. Heywood, President; J. G. Deshler, Vice President; Geo. Wadsworth, Secretary; Peter Curtiss, Treasurer.

Trustees—S. N. Callender, Jason Sexton, George Howard, H. Daw, Francis H. Root, Amasa R. Ransom, F. P. Wood, J. D. Hill, Joseph Dart, Jr., R. L. Burrows, George S. Hazard.

Buffalo Industrial School Association.—President, Mrs. L. S. Athearn; Vice President, Mrs. S. S. Guthrie, Treasurer; Mrs. H. R. Seymour; Secretary, Miss E. S. Athearn.

Managers—Mrs. Clapp, Mrs. R. Williams, Mrs. H. H. Hale, Mrs. Chas. Coleman, Mrs. H. Shumway, Mrs. O. E. Sibley, Miss E. Athearn, Mrs. H. R. Seymour, Mrs. Stanbery, Mrs. S. S. Guthrie, Mrs. L. S. Athearn, Mrs. E. Thayer.

Association for the Relief of the Poor.—Jason Sexton. President; R. H. Heywood, G. B. Rich. A. C. Moore, Samuel Carey, E. G. Grey, Vice Presidents; S. N. Callendar, Treasurer; F. P. Wood, Secretary.

Managers—Geo. Howard, I. D White, Wm. Ashman, Joshua Barnes, C. H. Coleman.

Friendly Sons of St. Patrick.—James Whealan, President; Nicholas Higgins, 1st Vice President; V. P. P. Gorman, 2d Vice President; P. Scanlon, Secretary; John Rose, Treasurer; Edward Hanley, Banner Bearer; Richard Duggan, Messenger.

Committee—William Flanagan, Wm. Riggs, Owen Connell, Patrick Woods, Jeremiah Kavanagh. John Butler, Patrick O'Day, Jeremiah Keleber, Thos. Hennessy.

Mutual Benefit Catholic Temperance Society.—President, Michael Hagan; Vice President, Daniel Vaughan; Treasurer, Jas. McCool; Secretary, Michael Nellany; Financial Secretary, John E. Walsh; Marshal, Edward Hardy.

Executive Committee—Alexander Forthing-

ham, Timothy Corcorane, John C. McManus, James Kavanagh and Maurice Vaughan.

Buffalo Building Society —Edwin Thomas, President; James B. Dubois, Vice President; Seth Austin, Secretary and Treasurer.

Trustees—Cooley S. Chapin, Fernando C. Candee, James McCredie, Philo Dubois, Walter Porter, John H. Coleman, Peter Gowans.

City Building and Loan Association.—President, A. S. Merrill; Secretary, Seth Austin; Treasurer, C. P. Lee.

Buffalo Horticultural Society.—President, Jason Sexton; Vice Presidents, Noah H. Gardner, Thos. Stephenson; Treasurer. Edward S. Rich; Recording Secretary, Henry Waters; Corresponding Secretary, Wm. Coleman.

Managers—Horace Williams. Dennis Bowen, James W. Brown, Wm. R. Coppock, Otis F. Presbrey, Benjamin Hodge, Warren Granger, Jno. B. Eaton, Amos I. Mathews.

Trustees—John Hellreigel, C. Longstreet, Wm. A. Hart, O. H. P. Champlin, E. A. Swan, F. J. Handel, John W. Schwinn.

St. Vincent Female Orphan Asylum, Catholic. —Corner Batavia and Ellicott streets. Under the care of the Sisters of Charity. Rev. Martin Kavanagh, Chairman; Sister Neri Mathews, Superior and Treasurer.

Martha Industrial School. — Incorporated March 18, 1857.

Trustees—Mary Vaughan, Julia M. Beers, Mary Chase, Francis O'Farrell, Margaret Estop, M. A. Jackson, Anne Hardy.

Buffalo Hospital of the Sisters of Charity.— Corner of Franklin and Virginia streets. Rev. F. O'Farrell, President; Martin Kavanagh, Secretary; Sister Camilla, Superior and Treasurer; Edwin Thomas and Sister Appollonia, Trustees.

Young Men's Catholic Association.—James Mooney, President; Wm. Clinglen, Vice President; Chas. W. McCarthy, Secretary; James Ryan, Treasurer.

Conference of St. Vincent de Paul.—Founded in 1837. James McCool, President; Daniel Vaughan, Vice President; John Walsh, Secretary; Timothy Cochrane, Treasurer.

Firemen's Benevolent Association.—President, Wm. A. Robinson, exempt; 1st Vice President, L. P. Marer, engineer; 2d Vice President, M. Gardiner, Hose 1; Secretary, Harry H. Clapp, Eagle Hose 2; Treasurer, Geo. W. Hayward, Neptune Hose 5; Collector, Peter Ripon, exempt.

Benevolent Society of the Evangelical Lutheran St. John's Church.—President, Andrew Grass; Vice President, John Laux; Recording Secretary, Henry Sheppard; Corresponding Secretary, Louis Rodenbach; Treasurer, Geo. Jager.

Western Loan Company.—Edwin Thomas, President; Guy H. Salisbury, Vice President;

John Brown, Secretary and Treasurer; J. J. Cottle, Attorney.

Trustees—Lewis T. White, Wm. Lovering, Jr., Chas. E. Clarke, C. C. Wells, James Duthie, O. T. Flint, C. M. Woodward, Anton Bussman, W. G. Thomas.

Turnverein.—C. P. Wertsch, Speaker. Meets Turner's Hall, Ellicott street, near Genesee.

Deutsche Leidertafel.—Dr. Ed. Storck, President; Andrew Brunn, Vice President; Gustave Wemicke, Secretary; Chas. Adam, Leader. Meets Market corner Genesee and Ellicott.

Deutscher Sængerbund.—W. Braun, President. Meets corner Genesee and Oak.

Buffalo Water Works.—Henry W. Rogers, President; Geo. Coit, Vice President; A. R. Ketcham, Secretary and Treasurer.

Directors—H. W. Rogers, Geo. Coit, O. G. Steele, H. L. Lansing, Jos. Dart, Jr., A. H. Tracy, George R. Babcock, Robert Campbell, (New York,) and Henry Cartwright, (Philadelphia.) Office Erie near Pearl.

Buffalo Gas Light Company. — Organized February, 1848. Capital $400,000.

Officers—Samuel F. Pratt, President and Treasurer; Oliver G. Steele, Secretary and Superintendent.

Directors—S. F. Pratt, O. G. Steele, S. G. Austin, E. G. Spaulding, W. K. Scott, George Coit, Wm. Bucknell.

The Company was organized under the General Gas Light Law of 1848, and the works were completed and gas supplied to the city in November of the same year.

The works are situated on the block bounded by Genesee, Jackson and Fourth streets and the Wilkeson Slip, and comprise about five acres in all occupied by the company.

The whole construction is of the most substantial character, embracing all modern improvements, and with the extensions and additional machinery added the past season, makes it one of the most complete works in the United States.

The quantity of street mains now laid and in use, is about fifty-seven miles, with gasometer room and retort-house facilities for the manufacture and supply of a daily consumption of 500,000 cubic feet.

FREE MASONS.

There are eight Lodges in this city, two Chapters of Royal Arch Masons, two Councils, and two Commandaries.

"*Hiram*"—James Barton, Master; mets Friday evenings, corner Swan and Main.

"*Concordia*"—Joseph L. Haberstro, Master; meets every alternate Tuesday evenings, corner Washington and Exchange.

"*Erie*"—Wm. Gould, Master; meets Thursday evenings, corner Swan and Main.

"*Washington*"—M. Pinner, Master; meets Thursday evenings, 326 Main.

"*Modestia*"—B. H. King, Master; meets every other Tuesday, 326 Main.

"*Queen City*"—C. G. Fox, Master; meets first and third Mondays in each month, corner Court and Main.

"*The Ancient Landmarks*"—Wm. Hersee, master; meets first Wednesday in each month, 326 Main street.

"*Parish*"—(Black Rock), H. P. Clinton, Master; meets Thursday evenings.

"*De Molay*"—J. T. Wilbnr, Master; meets every Tuesday, corner Swan and Main. .

Buffalo Chapter—Royal Arch—James McCredie, H. P.; meets first and third Wednesdays, corner Swan and Main.

Keystone Chapter—Royal Arch—M. Pinner, H. P.; meets second and fourth Wednesdays, 326 Main.

Lake Erie Commandery of Knights Templar. —James McCredie, E. C.; meet first and third Mondays of each month, corner Swan and Main.

Hugh de Payen Commandery—R. N. Brown, E. C.; meets first and third Tuesdays of each month, Free Mason's Hall, corner Main and Court.

STAGE LINES.

Routes—All stages start from the Franklin House, corner Seneca and Ellicott streets, or Brown's Hotel, corner Seneca and Michigan streets.

Williamsville and Clarence Express, leaves every day at half past 2, P. M.

Buffalo and Springville Express, leaves daily at half past 2, P. M., via East Hamburgh, Haines' Corners, West Falls, Colden, Glenwood and Springville.

Buffalo and Springville Express, leaves daily at half past 2, P. M., through White's Corners, North Boston, Boston Center, Boston Corners, to Springville; connecting at White's Corners with stages through Water Valley, Eden Valley, Eden Corners and North Collins.

Buffalo and Arcade Mail Stage, leaves Tuesdays, Thursdays and Saturdays, at 9, A. M., through Aurora, South Wales, Holland, Protection, Sardinia, Yorkshire, to Arcade; connecting at Yorkshire with stages for Lime Lake, Machias, Franklinville, Farmersville, to Hinsdale.

Buffalo and Aurora Express, leaves daily at 3 o'clock, P. M.

Buffalo and Marilla Express, leaves Mondays, Wednesdays and Saturdays.

INDEPENDENT ORDER OF ODD FELLOWS.

There are five Lodges of this Order in the city, and one Degree Lodge, under charters granted by the Grand Lodge of the I. O. O. F. of Northern New York.

The oldest is Niagara Lodge, No. 25, instituted Nov. 6, 1839. Regular meetings, Monday evening of each week, over old Post Office.

The next is Buffalo Lodge No. 37, instituted May, 1840. Regular meetings, Tuesday evening of each week.

The third is Tehoseroron, No. 48, instituted Dec. 28, 1840. Regular meetings, Thursday evening of each week.

The fourth is Walhalla (German) Lodge, No. 260, instituted Nov. 7, 1846. Regular meetings, Thursday evening of each week.

The fifth is Odin (German) Lodge, No. 178, instituted Feb. 19, 1849. Regular meetings. Monday evening of each week.

Erie Degree Lodge, No. 3. Regular meetings, second and fourth Wednesday evenings of each month.

Mount Vernon Encampment, No. 8, I. O. of O. F., instituted August 1, 1841. Regular meetings, first and third Wednesday evenings in each month. D. S. Rice, D. D. G. P., District of Erie.

The Niagara, Buffalo, Tehoseroron and Erie Degree Lodges meet in the hall over the old Post Office.

The Walhalla and Odin Lodges meet in the new room on Court near Pearl.

A. C. of G. F., Copernicus Lodge, No. 45, Buffalo Encampment, No. 1. Richard Flach, D. D. G. M. No. 8 Court street.

NEW YORK STATE MILITIA—EIGHTH DIVISION.

Major General, 8th Division—Nelson Randall.
Judge Advocate—Col. Jesse C. Dann.
Quartermaster—Lieut. Colonel Andrew J. Rich.
Inspector—Colonel Henry L. Lansing.
Paymaster —— ——
Surgeon—Colonel Walter Cary.
Engineer—Colonel Bronson C. Rumsey.
Aids—Maj. R. L. Howard and Maj. Alexander W. Harvey.
Col. 65th Regiment—Jacob Krettner, Buffalo.
Lieut. Colonel —— Buffalo.
Major—L. Gillig.
Adjutant—Acting Adj. Louis Krettner.
Quartermaster—Louis Krettner.
Paymaster—Anthony Diebold, Buffalo.
Surgeon—Chas. P. Fanner, Buffalo.
Chaplain—Rev. Otto Burger.
Engineer—Wm. Scheu.
Ass't Surgeon —— ——
Light Artillery—Michael Weidrich, Captain; Philip Howck, 1st Lieutenant; M. Schenkel-

berger, 2d Lieutenant; W. C. Zimmerman, 3d Lieutenant.
Cavalry Company—John Ordner, Captain; —— —— 1st Lieutenant; John Kamman, 2d Lieutenant; Daniel Schwartz, Cornet.
Company A—J. Weter, Captain; George Buckheit, 1st Lieutenant; Louis Fritz, 2d Lieutenant.
Company D. Krettner Guard—Gregory Ritt, Captain; Paul Dehlinger, 1st Lieut.; Michael Kimmerle, 2d Lieut.
Company E—J. Wolf, Captain; Peter Weigel, 1st Lieutenant; Martin Herbold, 2d Lieut.
Company F—Martin Roth, Captain; J. A. Lipp, 1st Lieutenant; H. Hitchler, 2d Lieut.
Company G—H. Erb, Captain; C. Betel, 1st Lieutenant; —— —— 2d Lieutenant.
Rifle Company—Chris. Schaeffer, Captain; Joseph Beck, 1st Lieutenant; Henry Schirmer, 2d Lieutenant.

Headquarters 65th Regiment, State Arsenal, Batavia street, Buffalo.

Field and Staff Officers of the 74th Regiment:
Colonel—Watson A. Fox.
Lieut. Colonel—Wm. P. Carlin.
Major—Freman J. Fithean.
Chaplain—Grosvenor W. Heacock, D. D.
Engineer—Frank Williams.
Surgeon—Ira D. Whitehead.
Surgeon's Mate—Chas. K. Winne.
Quartermaster—Frank Ritter.
Paymaster—Chas. J. Wing.
Sergeant Major—M. V. B. Buell.
Drum Major—Thos. D. Dodds.
Leader of the Band—Peter Cramer, Jr.

Line Officers of the 74th Regiment:
Company A—A. R. Root, Captain; C. W. Sternberg, 1st Lieutenant; P. C. Doyl, 2d Lieutenant.
Company B—H. M. Gaylord, Captain; A. M. Wheeler, 1st Lieutenant; J. McLish, 2d Lieutenant.
Company C—W. F. Rogers, Captain; A. M. Adams, 1st Lieutenant; J. P. Washburn, 2d Lieutenant.
Company D—D. D. Bidwell, Captain; W. C. Alberger, 1st Lieutenant; G. M. Baker, 2d Lieutenant.
Company E—J. McMannus, Captain; M. Bailey, 1st Lieutenant; Wm. Brown, 2d Lieut.
Company F—Geo. D. W. Clinton, Captain; J. H. Giffin, 1st Lieutenant; T. B. Wright, 2d Lieutenant.
Company G—J. H. Canfield, Captain; R. F. Atkins, 1st Lieutenant; A. Sinclair, 2d Lieut.
Company H—J. T. Wilbur, Captain; E. R. P. Shurley, 1st Lieutenant; J. V. Germain, 2d Lieutenant.
Company R—A. Sloan, Captain; J. Peterson, 1st Lieutenant; Hugh Sloan, 2d Lieutenant; A. F. Holt, 3d Lieutenant.

Headquarters 74th Regiment, State Arsenal, Buffalo.

NEWSPAPERS AND PERIODICALS.

Buffalo Commercial Advertiser.—The oldest Daily Paper in the city. Anson G. Chester, Editor. R. Wheeler & Co., Publishers. Issued daily and semi-weekly. Circulated in the city by W. G. Seely.

Patriot and Journal, Weekly.—R. Wheeler & Co., Publishers.

Buffalo Courier, Daily, Tri-Weekly and Weekly.—Joseph Warren & Co., Publishers. Joseph Warren and David Gray, Editors. Office, 178 Washington street.

Morning Express, Daily, Tri-Weekly and Weekly.—A. M. Clapp & Co., Publishers. Office, Exchange Buildings, 158 Main street.

Buffalo Republic, Daily, Tri-Weekly and Weekly.—Thomas Keene, Editor and Proprietor. Office, 186 Washington street.

Buffalo Christian Advocate, Weekly.—John E. Robie, Editor and Proprietor. Office, cor. Pearl and West Seneca, New Banking Buildings.

Der Democrat and Weltburger.—(German.) Published daily and weekly by Brunck, Held & Co. Office, 196 Washington street.

Buffalo Telegraph.—(German,) Published daily and weekly by P. H. Bender. Office, 358 Main street.

Evening Post, Daily.—George J. Brian, proprietor. Office 184 Washington street.

Ecclesiastical Informer.—(German.) Published semi-monthly, by J. A. A. Grabau, Genesee, near Oak street.

Buffalo Sentinel.—Published weekly, by Michael Hagan. Office, 111 Main street.

The Aurora.—(German.) Tri-weekly and weekly. Christian Wieckman, Publisher. Office, 67 Batavia street, between Elm and Michigan.

Buffalo Freie Presse.—(German.) Semiweekly. Frederick Reinecke & Co., Editors and Proprietors. Office, Genesee Block.

Historical Gazette.—(German.) Monthly. C. Baer, Editor and Proprietor. Office, 410 Main street.

CHURCHES AND PASTORS.

First Presbyterian.—On the triangle bounded by Church, Pearl and Niagara streets. Rev. Walter Clark, D. D., Pastor.
Trustees—George R. Babcock, J. D. Sawyer, T. Butler, George Coit, Jr., Wm. H. Glenny, Chas. Rosseel, A. R. Root, Chas. Hopkins, Wm. F. Miller.

Lafayette Street Presbyterian.—Between Main and Washington, north of the Park. G. W. Heacock, Pastor.
Trustees—George Howard, S. Sears, O. F. Presbrey, Seth Clark, L. White, Edward Brews-ter, G. L. Squares, Clifford Baker, Peter Gowans.

Central Presbyterian.—Corner Genesee and Pearl. John C. Lord, Pastor.
Trustees—L. K. Plimpton, Wm. Tweedy, Stephen Lockwood, Oscar Cobb, Patrick Smith, Robert Dunbar, Geo. L. Marvin, Wm. H. Abell, Horace Utley.

North Presbyterian.—Main street, between Huron and Chippewa.
Trustees—Jason Sexton, President of the Board; A. J. Rich, P. P. Pratt, A. A. Howard, G. L. Hubbard, O. P. Ramsdell, H. N. Loomis, F. P. Wood, J. V. W. Annin.

United Presbyterian.—Washington street, below Eagle. Clark Kendall, Pastor.
Trustees—Robert Latta, Alexander Sloan, D. McGilvray, Wm. Jamison, David Donaldson, Archibald Robinson.

Westminster.—Delaware street, above North. J. H. Towne, Pastor.
Trustees—Jesse Ketchum, Isaac F. Bryant, Horace Parmelee, Aaron Rumsey, Dexter P. Rumsey, Wm. Hodge, L. Enos, Dan B. Castle, N. A. Halbert.

East Presbyterian.—(Colored.) Elm street, between North and South Division streets.
Trustees—Geo. Weir, Jr., E. P. Williams, John Simpson, Henry Moxley, N. D. Thompson, A. Young, Wm. Cooper.

Church of the Puritans. — (Presbyterian.) Breckenridge street, near Niagara, Black Rock.
Trustees—Lewis F. Allen, Daniel Kelley.

Niagara Street Methodist Episcopal.—Niagara street, between Pearl and Franklin. Griffin Smith, Pastor.
Trustees—H. O. Cowing, Wm. Baker, P. M. Vosburg, Nelson Hopkins, Amos Williams, Robert Fero.

Asbury Methodist Episcopal.—Corner Pearl and Chippewa streets. W. H. DePuy, Pastor.
Trustees—Joel Wheeler, David Walls, John Benson, Abram Twichell, Isaac Holloway, Samuel Jocelyn, Salmon Shaw.

Grace Methodist Episcopal.—Michigan st., between North and South Division. A. D. Wilbur, Pastor.
Trustees—F. H. Root, A. Swan, W. Dodsworth, H. B. Burt, D. B. Hull, P. L. Sternberg, C. G. Playter, Jas. Howells.

German Methodist Episcopal.—Sycamore st., cor. Ash. Louis Wallon, Pastor.
Trustees—John Weber, D. Provoost, J. S. Lyon, Wm. Hibbert, John Spiess, H. H. Matteson, Joel Wheeler.

River Side Methodist.—Dearborn street.— Rev. R. C. Welsh, Pastor.
Trustees—Joseph Corns, William D. Davis, Capt. D. Gazely, E. Bandell, Orrin Stickney, Isaac Ashton, Sam'l Blossom, Wm. Hughes.

Fillmore.—Near Whitmore's Tavern. Rev. Mr. Green, Pastor.

St. Mark's Methodist Episcopal.—Elk street, near Alabama. S. Hunt, Pastor.
Trustees—James N. Scratchard, Leonard Crocker, J. Butler, S. Hume, S. Collinson, J. Coatsworth, R. Evans, C. Bartholemew, H. O. Perry.

Free Baptist.—Corner Pearl and Genesee streets.
Trustees—E. Farwell, Peter Corbin, Fred'k Hughsong, Matthew McComb, A. J. Davis.

Michigan Street Baptist.—(Colored.) Between Clinton and Batavia streets.
Trustees—James Thomas, C. Johnson, Chas. Smith, Robert Smith.

First German Baptist.—Spruce street, north of Batavia. Wm. Meyer, Pastor.

North Buffalo Baptist.—Dearborn street, —— Spoor, Pastor.

Vine Street Methodist Episcopal.—(Colored) J. M. Williams, Pastor.
Trustees—Joseph Peterson, John Farbush, Wm. Carter, Lewis Smith, Thos. Harmon.

Washington Street Baptist. — Washington street, north of Swan. D. Moore, Pastor.
Trustees—F. W. Breed, Daniel C. Beard, S. S. Jewett, Lyman Knapp, James H. Chase.

Niagara Square Baptist.—Northwest corner Niagara Square.
Trustees—P. A. Balcom, A. L. Baker, Velorus Hodge, M. H. Tryon, R. M. Eddy, E. B. Smith.

Cedar Street Baptist.—Cedar street, between North and South Division. B. D. Marshall, Pastor.
Trustees — W. W. Case, W. H. Bonnell, Joshua Burns, John Bush, E. H. Mellington, Hugh Webster.

St. Luke's Episcopal.—Maryland street, near Virginia. Wm. White Montgomery, Rector.
Wardens—Michael Willis, Charles Armstrong.
Vestrymen—E. P. Pierce. Wm. Hingston, Wm. H. Pease, Thos. I? Parker, Thos. Phillips, Robt. Newton, Edward Drew, John T. Douglas.

St. John's Episcopal.—Corner Washington and Swan streets. Orlando Witherspoon, Rector.
Wardens—Samuel Provoost, Julius Movius.
Vestrymen—Henry Dee, James N. Matthews, Jerome F. Fargo, Charles E. Noble, Thos. H. Mendsen, Chas. K. Loomis, Horace Williams, D. B. Waterman.

Trinity Episcopal.—Corner Washington and Mohawk streets. Edward Ingersoll, Rector.
Wardens—Henry Daw, H. W. Rogers.
Vestrymen—J. M. Smith, R. Hollister, A. A. Eustaphieve, S. V. R. Watson, H. Martin, S. K. Worthington, J. C. Harrison, R L. Howard.

St. Paul's Episcopal. — On the triangle bounded by Erie, Church and Pearl streets. Wm. Shelton, Rector.

Wardens — Russell H. Heywood, Lester Brace.
Vestrymen—Walter Joy, John S. Ganson, Erastus B. Seymour, Chas. W. Evans, E. M. Atwater, Carlos Cobb, A. P. Nichols, W. H. Walker.

Church of the Ascension, Episcopal.—North street, at the head of Franklin. O. F. Starkie, Rector.
Wardens—Wm. Dickson, Geo. C. Webster.
Vestrymen—Warren Granger, Dean S. Manley, Thaddeus C. Davis, Wm Monteith, Wm. Hersee, John Bosche, Jr., Wm. S. Scott, John T. Hingston.

St. James', Episcopal.—Corner Swan and Spring streets. L. S. Stevens, Rector.
Wardens—M. Wilder, Geo. Mills.
Vestrymen—J. B. Sloan, Geo. Beals, Wm. Powell, Chas. E. Williams, Arthur Christy, H. J. Shuttleworth, Jesse Peck, J. H. Montgomery.

Grace, Episcopal.—Niagara street, corner Bidwell, Black Rock. H. G. Wood, Rector.
Wardens—H. F. Penfield, Thos. Millard.
Vestrymen —A. Bull, W. A. Bird, H. P. Clinton, S. W. Howell, Geo. Pooley, W. G. Underhill, Thos. Thornton, Jas. Warr.

Union Bethel.—Perry street. P. Griffin, Pastor.

First Unitarian.—Corner Eagle and Franklin streets. Geo. W. Hosmer, Pastor.
Trustees—C. S. F. Thomas, Augustus F. Tripp, O. G. Steele, M. P. Fillmore, E. P. Dorr, Jas. Hollister.

First Universalist.—Washington street, near corner of South Division. J. Hazard Hartzell, Pastor.
Trustees—Geo. W. Scott, Seth Austin, Norman H. Barnes, B. H. Austin, Chas. H. Morse, Thos. B Shepard, Jas. Brayley, A. J. Decker, H. Guild.

First French Protestant.—Northeast corner of Ellicott and Tupper streets. Geo. S. Vogt, Pastor.
Trustees—Geo. S. Peugeot, Geo. F. Monnier, Geo. Tods, Chas. Monnin, Fred. Chamot, P. Peugeot, Jaques Marshand.

German, Evangelical.—Corner Spruce and Sycamore streets. Rev. Mr. Hurlong, Pastor.
Trustees—Geo. Schoot, John Bauer, George Hofhein.

Evangelical Lutheran. — Hickory street, between Batavia and William. Christian Volz, Pastor.
Trustees—Geo. Kney, Andrew Debus, Nicholas Hiller, Daniel Lang, Anton Hasselbach, Geo. Gager.

Evangelical Lutheran Trinity German.—Corner of Goodell and Maple streets. J. A. A. Grabau and C. W. Hochstetter, Pastors.
Trustees—J. H. Hilgeneck, M. Schaumloeffel, Fr. Bräunlich, Conrad Baer, Charles Korn, F. Landwehr.

German Evangelical.—North Buffalo, Amherststreet. Chas. Sieben Pfeiffer, Pastor.

German United St. Paul's Evangelical.—Washington street, between Genesee and Chippewa. Otto Burger, Pastor.
Trustees—Henry C. Persch, Philip Wagner, Jacob Bauer, Philip Beyer, Philip Houch, Valentine Schumacher.

Zion's German Reformed.—Lemon street. John Lichtenstein, Pastor.
Trustees—Adam Good, Christian Muenich, Frederick Brich, —— Heihopf.

Lutheran Trinity, German.—William street, Louis Dulitz, Pastor.
Trustees—Chas. Graeser, Fr. Zimmerman, F. Kamprath.

St. Peter's.—Genesee street, corner Hickory. G. S. Vogt, Pastor.
Trustees—John Scheifer, Geo. Gross, Wm. Schneider, Daniel Deitzer.

St. Joseph's Cathedral.— Franklin street, near Swan. John Timon, Bishop of Buffalo. F. O'Farrell, M. Kavanagh, Officiators.

St. Michael's, Catholic.—Washington street, between Chippewa and Tupper. Luke Caveng, J. Blettner, and G. Fortsch, Pastors.
Committee—S. Bettinger, Martin Zinns, John Swartz, F. Haefner.

St. Francis Xavier, Catholic.—East street, near Amherst. John Zawistoski, Pastor.

St. Patrick's, Catholic.—North Canal street, near Emslie. Rev. M. Sesto, Pastor.

Holy Angels, Catholic.—Prospect Hill. Rev. Edward Chevalier, Pastor; Joseph Guilard, Assistant.

Holy Cross.—Main street, near Poorhouse. Rev. S. F. Hynes, Pastor.

Hospital of the Sisters of Charity, and Chapel at the Asylum.—Rev. F. Gery, Pastor.

Immaculate Conception.—Edward st., near the Buffalo Orphan Asylum. Michael Purcell, Pastor.

St. Peter's, French Catholic.—Corner Clinton and Washington streets. F. N. Sester, Pastor.

St. Louis, German Catholic.—Main street, opposite Goodell. W. Dieters, Pastor.
Trustees—Chas. Chreiten, Martin Roth, Geo. Richert, Nicholas Harry, Mathias Hausle, Anthony Diebold.

St. Mary's, Catholic.—(Order of the Redemptorists) Cor. Batavia and Pine streets. Rev. Kleimeidom, Pastor.

St. Bonifacius.—Mulberry street. Henry Feldman, Pastor.

St. Bridget's.—Lousiana street, cor. Fulton. Rev. M. O'Connor, Pastor.

St. Anne's.—Emslie street, near Lovejoy.— B. Fritsch, Pastor.

North Street Methodist.—North street, near Twelfth.

Thirteenth Street Church.—Thirteenth street, near Jersey.

Calvary Church.—Delaware street, below Tupper.

Second German.—Hickory street, near Sycamore.

Mission Church. — Goodell street, corner Boston.

St. Stephen's.—Peckham street, cor. Adams.

St. Andrew's.—Peckham street, cor. Sherman.

Evangelical Association. — William street, corner Elmalie. Rev. Mr. Alles, Pastor.

Ebenezer Church.—Grape street, near Virginia.

Zion Church.—Williamsville Road, near Delavan Avenue.

Old Indian Church.—Indian Church street, near Whitmore's Tavern.

Jewish Synagogue.—Pearl street, near Eagle.

Free Methodist Church.—Pearl street, near Eagle.

House of Bethel.—Seneca street, near Jefferson.

BUFFALO BOARD OF TRADE.

President, Jason Parker; Vice President, A. W. Cutter; Secretary and Treasurer, Horace Wilcox.
Arbitration Committee—P. S. Marsh, S. H. Fish, G. S. Hazard.

LIST OF STREETS

REFERRED TO IN THIS WORK.

Abbott, from Elk to south line of city.
Adams, from Eagle to Genesee.
Alabama, from Seneca to Buffalo Creek.
Albany, from Hampshire to Niagara River
Allen, from Main to Wadsworth.
Amherst, from Main to Niagara River.
Arkansas, from Hampshire to North Washington.
Ash, from Genesee to Batavia.
Auburn, from De Wit to Niagara River.
Aurora, from Ohio to Buffalo Creek.
Austin, from Military Road to Niagara River.
Babcock, from Seneca to William.
Balcom, from Main to Linwood Avenue.
Barker, from Main to Delaware.
Barker's Alley, from Seneca to Swan.
Barton, from Albany to north line of Ferry lot.
Batavia, from Washington to east line of city.
Beak, from Exchange to Green.
Beaver from Perry to Scott.
Beech, from Virginia to Carlton.

Bennett, from William to Batavia.
Berlin, from High to Best.
Best, from Main to east line of city.
Bidwell, from Niagara to North Washington.
Bird, from Colvin to Niagara River.
Bird Ave., from Delaware to Niagara River.
Blossom, from Batavia to Huron.
Blossom, from Amherst to Military Road.
Bolton, from Tonawanda to Winans.
Bond, from North Canal to Howard.
Boston, from Tupper to Virginia.
Bouck Ave., from Main to Niagara.
Bowery, from Allen to North.
Brace, from Niagara to Erie Canal.
Brayton, from Vermont to Utica.
Breckenridge, from State Reservation Line to Niagara River.
Bremen, from Vermont to Rhode Island.
Bridge, from Niagara to Erie Mills.
Bristol, from Spring to Jefferson.
Bristol, from Emslie to East.
Brown, from Jefferson to Adams,
Bryant, from Main to Rogers.
Buffum, from Seneca to south line of lot 130¼.
Bull, from North Washington to De Witt.
Bundy's Alley, from Sycamore to North.
Burton, from Main to Maple.
Burwell Place, from Scott to Perry.
Bush, from Amherst to north line of lot No. 352.
Butler, from Delaware to Rogers.
California, from North Washington to North Jefferson.
Camp, from Sycamore to Genesee.
Canal, from Main to Erie.
Canal Alley, from Court to Jackson.
Carey, from Delaware to State Res. Line.
Carlton, from Main to Genesee.
Carolina, from Tupper to Lake Erie.
Carroll, from Washington to Indian Res. Line.
Cazenovia, from Seneca to Abbott.
Cedar, from Swan to Batavia.
Center, from Seneca to Swan.
Central Wharf, from foot of Main street to foot of Commercial.
Champlin, from Spring to Mortimer.
Chapin, from Main to Delaware.
Charles, from Terrace to Erie Canal.
Chenango, from Utica to Massachusetts.
Cherry, from Michigan to Virginia.
Chestnut, from Swan to North Division.
Chicago, from Swan to Buffalo Creek.
Chippewa, from Genesee to Georgia.
Church, from Main to Erie Canal.
Cincinnati, from Ohio to Buffalo Creek.
City Ship Canal, from Buffalo Creek, near the lighthouse, to south channel.
Clifton Place, from Cottage to Allen.
Clinton, from Main to east line of city.
Clinton Alley from Clinton to William.
Clinton Ave., from Delaware to Niagara River.
College, from Cottage to North.
College Place, from Johnson Place to Park Place.
Colton, from Erie Canal to Lake Erie.
Columbia, from Scott to Buffalo Creek.
Colvin, from Bird to Amherst.
Commercial, from Terrace to Buffalo Creek.

Connecticut, from Rogers to Niagara River.
Cornelia, from North Canal to Little Buffalo Creek.
Cottage, from Hudson to junction with Virginia.
Court, from Main to Erie Canal.
Cypress, from Michigan to Pine.
Dann, from Amherst to Hamilton.
Daugherty's Alley, from Seneca to Folsom.
Davis, from Genesee to Jefferson.
Dayton, from Main to Prime.
Dearborn, from Tonawanda to Bird.
Delavan Avenue, from Niagara to east line of city.
Delaware, from Terrace to north line of city.
Delaware Place, from Delaware to Virginia.
De Witt, from Breckenridge to Scajaquada Creek.
Dingens, from Williamsville Road to east line of city.
Doat, from Williamsville Road to east line of city.
Dock, from Water to Buffalo Creek.
Dodge, from Main to Michigan.
Dole, from Seneca to Elk.
Eagle, East, from Main to Indian Res. Line.
Eagle, West, from Main to Terrace.
East, from Clinton to Howard.
East, from South to Bird.
East Bennett, from Clinton to William.
East Market, from Main and Hamburgh Canal to Elk.
Edward, from Main to Virginia.
Efner, from Georgia to Virginia.
Eggert, from Sugar to north line of city.
Eleventh, from Carolina to Albany.
Eley Road, from Main, near Poor House, to north line of city.
Elizabeth, from North Canal to Little Buffalo Creek.
Elk, from Ohio, to junction with Seneca.
Ellicott, from Seneca to Northampton.
Ellicott Turnpike, from Walden to east line of city.
Elm, from Swan to High.
Elm, from North to Best.
Elmwood Avenue, from Ferry to Delavan ave.
Emily, from Delaware to Carolina.
Emslie, from Seneca to Batavia.
Erie, from Main to Erie Basin.
Erie Canal, from Main to north line of city.
Erie Slip, from Erie Canal to Erie Basin.
Essex, from Rhode Island to Massachusetts.
Evans, from Terrace to Water.
Evans Ship Canal, from Peacock Slip to Buffalo Creek.
Exchange, from Main to junction with Seneca.
Express, from Pearl to Franklin.
Farmer, from Tonawanda to Erie Canal.
Ferry, from Williamsville Road to Niagara River.
Fifteenth, from Vermont to Connecticut.
Fifth, from Court to Vermont.
Fitzgerald, from Elk to Indian Res. Line.
Fletcher, from Hamburgh Turnpike to Sophia.
Florida, from Main street, east.
Fly, from Maiden Lane to Evans.
Folsom, from Michigan to Jefferson.

Forest Avenue, from Delaware to Niagara River.

Forest Avenue, from Main to Ellicott Turnpike.

Fort, from Niagara to Erie Canal.

Fourteenth, from Pennsylvania to Hampshire.

Fourth, from Genesee to Vermont.

Fougeron, from Walden to Genesee, (extended).

Fox, from North to north line of Love's lot.

Franklin, from Terrace to North.

French, from Walden to east line of lot 7.

Fulton, from Michigan to Smith.

Garden, from Carolina to Virginia.

Gay, from Michigan to Potter.

Genesee, East, from Main to junct'n with Best.

Genesee, West, from Main to Erie Basin.

Genesee, from Williamsville Road to east line of city, (extended).

Georgia, from State Res. Line to Lake Erie.

German, from Genesee to Sycamore.

Germain, from Amherst to north line of lot 250.

Gibson, from Amherst to Military Road.

Goodell, from Main to Cherry.

Goodell Alley, from Tupper to Burton.

Goodrich, from Main to Michigan.

Gorton, from Amherst to Austin.

Granger, from Chicago to Ohio Slip.

Grape, from Cherry to North.

Green, from Washington to Michigan.

Grey, from Batavia to Genesee.

Grider, from Delavan Avenue to Ellicott Turnpike.

Griffin, from Porter to Carroll.

Grosvenor, from North Canal to Eagle.

Grove, from Race to north line of lot 86.

Gull, from Niagara to Erie Canal.

Hagerman, from Swan to South Canal.

Hamburgh, from Seneca to Buffalo Creek.

Hamburgh Turnpike, from Ohio street at Toll Bridge to south line of city.

Hamilton, from Spring to Jefferson.

Hamilton, from Emslie to East.

Hamilton, from Tonawanda to Niagara River.

Hampshire, from Sixth to Ferry.

Hanover, from Main to Prime.

Hayward, from Elk to Otto.

Heacock, from Seneca to Elk.

Henry, from Terrace to Erie Canal.

Herman, from Best to north line of Love's lot.

Hickory, from Swan to Cherry.

High, from Main to Johnson.

Hinckley, from Spring to Jefferson.

Hodge, from Vermont to Rhode Island.

Hoffman Alley, from Hamilton, south.

Hollister, from Spring to Mortimer.

Hopkins, from Abbott to south line of lot 45.

Hospital, from junction with Mohawk to Erie Basin.

Howard, from Jefferson to Williamsville Road.

Howell, from Amherst to north line of lot 251.

Hudson, from Wadsworth to Lake Erie.

Huron, from Oak to Niagara.

Hydraulic, from Seneca to Scott.

Hydraulic Canal, from junction with M. & H. St. Canal to east line of city.

Illinois, from Scott to Buffalo Creek.

Indiana, from Perry to Buffalo Creek.

Indian Church, from Seneca to County Fair Ground.

Jackson, from Church to Wilkeson Slip.

James, from Emslie to East.

James, from Military Road to Austin.

Jane, from Erie to Coit Slip.

Jefferson, from Mill to Ferry.

Jefferson Alley, from Jefferson street, east, between Genesee and Carlton street.

Jerry, from Raze to East.

Jersey, from Rogers to Lake Erie.

John, from Seneca street, south, between Main and Pearl.

Johnson, from Batavia to North.

Johnson Place, from Delaware to Carolina.

Joy, from Water to Erie Basin.

Kaene, from Genesee to Sycamore.

Katharine, from Elk to Indian Res. Line.

Kentucky, from Mackinaw to St. Clair.

Ketchum, from Carlton to High.

Kinney, from Seneca to Swan.

Koon's Alley, from Ellicott to Oak.

Krettner, from Batavia to Howard.

Lacy, from St. Clair to Buffalo Creek.

La Fayette, from Main to Washington.

Lake, from River to Erie Basin.

Landon, from Jefferson to Walden.

Lathrop, from Batavia to Genesee.

Laurel, from Linden to Jefferson.

Le Couteulx, from Canal to Water.

Lemon, from Cherry to North.

Le Roy Avenue, from Main to Ellicott Turnpike.

Lewis, from Military Road to Austin.

Liberty, from Main & H. St. Canal to Buffalo Creek.

Linden, from Riley street, north.

Linwood Avenue, from North to Delavan Avenue.

Lloyd, from Main to Buffalo Creek.

Lock, from Terrace to Erie.

Locust, from Cherry to North.

Long Wharf, from foot of Commercial street to Evans Ship Canal.

Lord, from Howard to Little Buffalo Creek.

Louisiana, from Seneca to Buffalo Creek.

Lovejoy, from Emslie to east line of city.

Lutheran, from William to Batavia.

Mackinaw, from Ohio to Indian Res. Line.

McPherson, from Bird to Amherst.

Madison, from Eagle to Brown.

Maiden Lane, from Erie Canal to Water.

Main, from Buffalo Creek to north line of city.

Main and Hamburg Street Canal, from Main to Hamburg.

Maple, from Cherry to North.

Mariner, from Virginia to North.

Mark, from William to Gay.

Marvin, from Elk to Perry.

Mary, from Mississippi to Indiana.

Maryland, from State Res. Line to Lake Erie.

Mason, from Breckenridge to Auburn Avenue.

Massachusetts, from Sixth to Ferry.

Mathews, from Mortimer to Jefferson.

Meach, from Virginia to Allen.

Mechanic, from Terrace to Erie Canal.

Miami, from Ohio to Hamburgh.

Michigan, from Buffalo Creek to junction with Main street.

Military Road, from Amherst to north line of city.

Mill, from Alabama to Indian Res. Line.

Miller's Alley, from Milnor street, east.

Milnor, from William to Batavia.

Mineral Spring, from Seneca to east line of city.

Mississippi, from M. & H. St. Canal to Buffalo Creek.

Mohawk, from Ellicott to junction with Hospital.

Monroe, from Eagle to Brown.

Montgomery, from Howard to Eagle.

Moore, from Elk to Ohio.

Morgan, from West Eagle to Chippewa.

Morgan, from Virginia to south line of lot 35.

Mortimer, from William to Genesee.

Mulberry, from Cherry to North.

Mulligan, from Pennsylvania to Hudson.

Niagara, from Main to north line of city.

Niagara Square, at junction of Court, Delaware, Genesee and Niagara.

Niagara Slip, from Erie Canal to Erie Basin.

Nichols Alley, from Seneca, below Center, half way to Swan.

Ninth, from Huron to junction with Niagara.

Norris Place, from Cottage to Wadsworth.

North, from York to Jefferson.

North, from Jefferson to Herman.

Northampton, from Main to Jefferson.

North Adams, from Albany to within 200 feet of Breckenridge.

North Canal, from junction with Swan to Indian Res. Line.

North Division, from Main to Indian Res. Line.

North Jefferson, from Albany to north line of Ferry lot.

North Ogden, from William to Batavia.

North Railroad Avenue, from Emslie to Howard.

North Washington, from Albany to Scajaquada Creek.

North William, from Virginia to North.

Norton, from Peacock to Water.

Oak, from Swan to High.

Oak, from North to Best.

Ohio, from Main to Buffalo Creek at the Toll Bridge.

Ohio Basin, between Mackinaw, Ohio, Louisiana and Wabash streets.

Ohio Slip, from M. & H. St. Canal to Ohio Basin.

O'Neil, from Niagara to State Res. Line.

Ontario, from Niagara to Military Road.

Ontario, from Seneca to South Canal.

Orange, from Cherry to North.

Otis, from Bouck Avenue to Delavan Avenue.

Otsego, from Main to Jefferson.

Ottawa, from Louisiana to Hamburgh.

Otto, from Hayward to Alabama.

Page, from Bird to Race.

Palmer, from Georgia to Hudson.

Parish, from Tonawanda to Niagara River.

Park, from Virginia to North.

Park Place, from Delaware to junction with Johnson Place.

Peach, from Cherry to North.

Peacock, from Evans to Erie.

Pearl, from Erie Canal to Tupper.

Pearl, from Virginia to North.

Peckham, from Jefferson to Smith.

Pennsylvania, from North to Lake Erie.

Perry, from Main to Dole.

Peter, from Amherst to north line of lot 250.

Peterson, from Walden street, east.

Peugeot, from White's Corners Plank Road to Buffalo & State Line Railroad.

Pine, from Swan to Sycamore.

Pink, from Lord to Montgomery.

Pooley Place, from De Witt to east line of lot 154.

Porter, from Heacock to Indian Res. Line.

Porter, from Ferry to Bouck ave.

Potter, from William to Batavia.

Potter's Corners Plank Road, from Abbott to east line of city.

Pratt, from Eagle to Genesee.

Preston, from Ferry to north line of Ferry lot.

Prime, from Main to Commercial.

Prospect, from North to junction with Main.

Puffer, from Main to Walden.

Quay, from Main to Washington.

Race, from Grove street, west.

Randall, from Hamilton to William.

Raze, from Howard to Eagle.

Red Jacket, from Seneca to Elk.

Reservation, from Amherst to north line of lot 252.

Rhode Island, from Rogers to Sixth.

Rich, from Batavia street north.

Riley, from Main to Jefferson.

River, from Erie to Genesee.

Rock, from Genesee to Hospital.

Rogers, from North to Ferry.

Roos, from William to Batavia.

Root, from Fifth to Erie Canal.

Rose, from Virginia to North.

Sandusky, from Louisiana to Smith.

Scajaquada, from Ferry to Scajaquada Creek.

School, from Niagara to Albany.

Scott, from Main to Chicago.

Scott, from Alabama to Indian Res. Line.

Seneca, East, from Main to east line of city.

Seneca, West, from Main to Terrace.

Seventh, from Court to junction with Sixth.

Sherman, from Howard to North.

Sherwood, from Hampshire to Arkansas.

Shumway, from William to Batavia.

Sidway, from Elk to Indian Res. Line.

Sixth, from Court to junction with Niagara.

Skillen, from O'Neil to south line of Allen farm.

Sloan, from Church to Erie Canal.

Sloan, from Niagara to Erie Canal.

Smith, from Batavia to Buffalo Creek.

Sophia, from Fletcher to south line of city.

South, from Hamburgh to Buffalo Creek.

South, from Tonawanda to Niagara River.

South Canal, from Hagerman to Indian Res. Line.

South Division, from Main to Little Buffalo Creek.

South Ogden, from Mineral Spring to William.

South Railroad Avenue, from Emslie to Howard.

Spring, from Seneca to Cherry.
Spruce, from Batavia to Cherry.
Staats, from Mohawk to Court.
Stauton, from William to Batavia.
State, from Canal to Water.
Steele, from Main to junction with Ellicott Turnpike.
Stevens, from Mechanic to Canal Slip.
St. Clair, from South to Ohio.
St. Paul, from Main to Oak.
Sugar, from Williamsville Road to east line of city.
Summer, from Delaware to Rogers.
Sutton Lane, from Main to south line of lot 66.
Swan, East, from Main to junction with Seneca.
Swan, West, from Main to Terrace.
Sycamore, from Oak to Adams.
Tecumseh, from Louisiana to Hamburgh.
Tennessee. from South to Mackinaw.
Tenth, from Carolina to junction with Niagara.
Terrace, from Main to Court street and State Res. Line.
Thirteenth, from Pennsylvania to Albany.
Thompson, from Parish to Austin.
Tifft, from Hamburgh Turnpike to White's Corners Plank Road.
Tonawanda, from junction with Niagara street, at Scajaquada Creek, to north line of city.
Tousey, from Batavia to Sycamore.
Town Line Road, from Eley Road to Delaware.
Townsend, from Erie Canal to Lake Erie.
Tracy, from Delaware to Carolina.
Triangle, from Abbott to White's Cor's Road.

Tupper, East, from Main to Michigan.
Tupper, West, from Main to Virginia.
Twelfth, from Viginia to Albany.
Union, from Eagle to William.
Utica, from Jefferson to Massachusetts.
Vandalia, from South to Mackinaw.
Van Rensselaer, from Seneca to Elk.
Vary, from Spring to Jefferson.
Vermont, from Rogers to Fourth.
Vincennes, from Mackinaw to South.
Vine, from Oak to Michigan.
Virginia, from Jefferson to Erie Canal.
Wabash, from Mackinaw to Ohio.
Wadsworth, from Allen to Pennsylvania.
Wadsworth Place, from College to Wadsworth.
Walden, from Batavia to Le Roy ave.
Walnut, from Eagle to Genesee.
Warren, from Chicago to Ohio slip.
Warren, from Smith to Indian Res. Line.
Washington, from High to Buffalo Creek.
Water, from Commercial to Erie.
Watson, from Eagle to Batavia.
Watts, from Tonawanda to Winans.
Weaver, from Goodell to Virginia.
Weiss, from Clinton to Dingens.
West Bennett, from Clinton to William.
West Market, from Elk to M. and H. St. Canal.
White's Corners Road, from Seneca street, at toll bridge, to south line of city.
William, from Michigan to east line of city.
Williamsville Road, from Seneca to North.
Winans, from Amherst to Bolton.
York, from Rogers to Niagara River.

BUFFALO ADVERTISEMENTS.

BUFFALO ADVERTISEMENTS

FOR 1861.

HENRY DAW & SON,

COMMISSION MERCHANTS

AND DEALERS IN

Timothy and Clover Seed, Flour, Wheat, Corn,
Rye, Oats and Barley.

HENRY DAW,
ALFRED D. DAW. }

No. 26 CENTRAL WHARF.

CASH ADVANCES ON CONSIGNMENTS.

A. W. HORTON,

Forwarding and Commission Merchant,

AGENT FOR THE CORN EXCHANGE LINE.

Particular attention given to Purchasing and Shipping Produce. Will receive consignments and make advances.

OFFICE 10 CENTRAL WHARF.

M. S. HAWLEY & CO.,

PRODUCE COMMISSION MERCHANTS

18 and 19 CENTRAL WHARF.

M. S. HAWLEY.   E. J. HAWLEY.   JAS. H. PENFIELD.

JOSEPH A. HEAD,
PRODUCE
COMMISSION MERCHANT,
DEALER IN
HAMBURGH CHEESE, BUTTER,
Beans, Timothy and Clover Seed, Green and Dried Fruit, and all kinds of Country Produce.
No. 60 MAIN STREET.

A. L. DODGE,
Wholesale and Retail Dealer in
GROCERIES, LIQUORS, CIGARS,
FOREIGN AND DOMESTIC FRUITS,
AND RECTIFIED WHISKY.
No. 17 MAIN STREET.

SAMUEL BOGARDUS,
DEALER IN
HAMBURGH AND ERIE CO. CHEESE
No. 29 MAIN STREET.

D. C. BEARD.   G. W. HAYWARD.
BEARD & HAYWARD,
DEALERS IN
HAMBURGH CHEESE,
DRIED FRUIT, GROCERIES, PRODUCE, BUTTER, &c.
CORNER WASHINGTON AND GREEN STREETS, HEAD OF QUAY STREET.

GOWANS & BEARD,
MANUFACTURERS OF SOAP AND CANDLES.
P. GOWANS.   D. C. BEARD.

ANDREW M. JOHNSON,
DEALER IN
GROCERIES, FLOUR, PORK,
BEEF, FISH, SALT, &c.
FLOUR BAGS IN EVERY VARIETY, PLAIN AND PRINTED TO ORDER.
NO. 52 MAIN STREET.

MATHEWS & TALMAN,

WHOLESALE AND RETAIL

AND

PROVISION DEALERS.

We have always on hand a large Stock of

FINE GROCERIES AND PROVISIONS,

—ALSO—

PURE WINES AND LIQUORS,

HAVANA AND MANILLA CIGARS.

The attention of Dealers and Consumers is respectfully invited.

334 MAIN STREET, COR. COURT.

LOUIS MATHEWS.   WM. S. TALMAN.

1861.   MORTON'S TRANSPORTATION LINE.   1861.

MORTON, FOOTE & CO.

Forwarding and Commission Merchants,

AND GENERAL FREIGHT AGENTS,

Nos. 7 CENTRAL WHARF, and 32 and 36 LLOYD ST.

Particular attention paid to the Purchase and Sale of Produce, and procuring down and up
Cargoes for Erie and Lateral Canals. Agents for Sale of Ohio and Lake Huron
Grindstones at manufacturers' prices.

JOHN F. MORTON.   WILLIAM FOOTE.   WILLIAM B. HOYT.

JOHN McNAUGHTON,

COMMISSION MERCHANT

FOR THE SALE OF

Wheat, Flour, Oat Meal, Pot Barley and Seed.

No. 58 MAIN STREET.

CANADA FLOUR AT ALL TIMES ON HAND AT WHOLESALE AND RETAIL.

EDWARD HARRIES,
(SUCCESSOR TO JOHN W. WILLIAMS,)
DEALER IN

CHOICE FAMILY GROCERIES

DRUGS, MEDICINES, DYE WOODS AND DYE STUFFS,

Satinet Warps, Reeds and Shuttles, Pickers, Picker String and Lacing Leather, Leicester Machine Cards, Paints, Oils, Window Glass, &c.,

NO. 180 MAIN STREET.

AGENT FOR PARSONS' IMPROVED SHEARING MACHINES.

ROBERT HOLLISTER.   WILLIAM LAVERACK.

HOLLISTER & LAVERACK,
WHOLESALE DEALERS IN

GROCERIES, WINES, LIQUORS

DRUGS, PAINTS, OILS, WINDOW GLASS, DYE WOODS, &c.

No. 202 Washington Street,

FIRST BUILDING BELOW SENECA STREET,   CHEQUERED BLOCK.

S. N. CALLENDER,
DEALER IN

CHOICE FAMILY GROCERIES

FOREIGN AND DOMESTIC FRUITS,

No. 229 Main Street,   Four Doors above Swan.

GEO. W. SCOTT,
Wholesale and Retail Dealer in

GROCERIES, PROVISIONS

FLOUR, SALT, GREEN AND DRIED FRUITS,

Stone Ware, Wooden Ware, Baskets, Mats, Brooms, Pails, Tubs; also, Clover, Timothy, Hemp and Canary Seed,

No. 9 East Seneca Street, opposite the Post Office.

☞ Cash paid for all kinds of Country Produce.

ELLIS WEBSTER,
GENERAL DEALER IN

GROCERIES AND PROVISIONS

FRUITS, SEEDS, &c.

No. 7 SENECA STEET.

☞ Produce sold on Commission. All orders promptly attended to.

WEBSTER & CO.

WHOLESALE AND RETAIL DEALERS IN

CHOICE FAMILY GROCERIES

CHEESE, PROVISIONS,

Dried and Green Fruit, Flour, Salt, Wooden Ware, &c., &c.

H. WEBSTER.   *No. 1 Seneca Street.*   D. J. WEBSTER.

A. S. WEBSTER,

DEALER IN

GROCERIES AND PROVISIONS,

Also, Vegetables, Flour. Salt, Fish, Pork. Butter, Cheese, Poultry, Green and Dried Fruit, Wood and Stone Ware, &c.

No. 33 EAST SENECA STREET.

N. B.—Cash Paid for all kinds of COUNTRY PRODUCE.

F. S. FITCH,

WHOLESALE AND RETAIL DEALER IN

GROCERIES, DRY GOODS,

BOOTS AND SHOES, &c.

3 Stores corner Michigan and Seneca Sts., opp. Brown's Hotel.

All kinds of Produce Bought and Sold.

A. L. SMITH, formerly of Evans, Superintendent of Grocery Department.

S. DOBBINS,

DEALER IN

GROCERIES, PROVISIONS

FOREIGN AND DOMESTIC FRUITS,

Corner of Swan and Michigan Streets.

CASH PAID for all kinds of COUNTRY PRODUCE.

SAMUEL PORTER,

DEALER IN

GROCERIES, PROVISIONS,

FRUITS AND VEGETABLES,

No. 360 MAIN STREET, OPP. THE OLD PHŒNIX HOTEL.

GEO. MUGRIDGE,

WHOLESALE DEALER IN

Soda Biscuit, Bread, Crackers

AND EVERY VARIETY CAKES AND CONFECTIONERY.

Com'l Hotel Block, Ohio St., near foot Main.

W. H. CLARK,

WHOLESALE DEALER IN

Soda Biscuit, Bread, Crackers

AND EVERY VARIETY CAKES AND CONFECTIONERY.

JUNCTION OF ELK AND OHIO STREETS.

FRANKLIN & RAND,

SAIL MAKERS,

AND DEALERS IN ALL KINDS OF

DUCK, CANVAS, BUNTING, AND RUSSIA BOLT ROPE.

Awnings, Tents, Marquees and Wagon Covers made to order,

ALSO, FLAGS MADE AND TRUNKS COVERED ON SHORT NOTICE.

MARINE BLOCK.

JOHN BENSON,

Manufacturer and Wholesale Dealer in all kinds of

CONFECTIONERY

NO. 131 MAIN STREET.

G. A. VAN SLYCK,

Manufacturer and Wholesale Dealer in all kinds of

CONFECTIONERY

ALSO, THE GENUINE ICELAND MOSS CANDY.

39 Seneca St., nearly opposite New Post Office.

ALCOHOL DISTILLERY.

HENRY T. GILLET,

Nos. 18, 20 and 22 LLOYD STREET,

Manufacturer and Wholesale Dealer in

85 and 95 Per Cent. Alcohol, Camphene,

BURNING FLUID, TRIPLE REFINED PURE SPIRITS,

COLOGNE SPIRITS,

BOURBON, OLD RYE AND RECTIFIED

ALSO, DOMESTIC BRANDIES & GIN.

A Superfine article of RECTIFYING COAL always on hand.

COAL AND PETROLEUM OILS

For Sale at the lowest Manufacturer's Prices, in Barrels and Half Barrels.

Address,   **HENRY T. GILLET,**
                                   Distiller, Buffalo, N. Y.

Purchasers may rely on having good Packages and correct Guages.

N. CASE,

Wholesale and Retail Dealer in

LEATHER, HIDES & OIL

CURRIERS' TOOLS, SHOE FINDINGS, &c.

No. 14 Exchange Street, nearly opposite the Mansion House.

BUSH & HOWARD,

DEALERS IN

LEATHER, HIDES AND OIL

NO. 91 MAIN STREET, ADJOINING THE CANAL BRIDGE.

Cash Paid for Hides.

MYRON P. BUSH.   GEORGE HOWARD.

AARON RUMSEY & CO.

DEALERS IN

LEATHER, HIDES, OIL

CURRIERS' TOOLS, SHOE FINDINGS, &c.

NO. 4 EXCHANGE STREET, OPPOSITE THE MANSION HOUSE.

AARON RUMSEY.   BRONSON C. RUMSEY.   DEXTER P. RUMSEY.

JAMES HARRADEN,

CONTRACTOR AND BUILDER

OFFICE, NO. 37 ELM STREET, NEAR EAGLE.

AUGUSTUS SCOFIELD,

MANUFACTURER OF

ROUND BANISTER FENCE

CAPSTAN BARS, PUMP SPEARS,

CURTAIN ROLLS AND SLATS.

ON MECHANIC STREET, AT JOHN R. EVANS & CO.'S PLANING MILL.

BANGASSER & BROTHER,

SIGN OF THE

CROSS KEYS.

LOCKSMITHS

BELL HANGERS,

SILVER PLATERS,

BRASS FOUNDERS AND FINISHERS,

No. 15 SENECA ST., Opposite the Post Office.

FIRE ENGINES AND HOSE CARRIAGES

Built to order at Prices to compete with Eastern Manufacturers.

Gong Bells and Lightning Rod Trimmings on Hand,

AUTHORIZED AGENTS FOR THE SALE OF

LYON'S CELEBRATED LIGHTNING CONDUCTORS in Erie Co.

Job Work done with dispatch.   Special attention given to orders for the protection of Buildings.

DOOR PLATES MADE TO ORDER.

Also, Builders of PORTABLE STEAM ENGINES of all sizes.

J. BANGASSER.   F. BANGASSER.

A. GOOD.

Lafayette Brass and Bell Foundry

No. 21 OHIO STREET,

MANUFACTURE

STATIONARY AND PORTABLE

STEAM ENGINES

AND BOILERS

OF EVERY VARIETY.

Double Acting Lift and Force and Fire Engine Pumps,

PLUMBERS' WORK, BRASS COCKS OF ALL KINDS,

Leather Rollers, Steam Whistles, Copper Rivets, Couplings, Steamboat and R. R. Castings, Machine Stretched Leather Belting and Hose.

MILL WORK AND SHAFTING.

Jobbing and Repairs done on short notice, and on Reasonable Terms.

QUEEN CITY IRON WORKS.

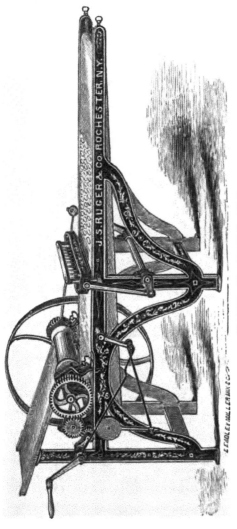

CRACKER AND BISCUIT MACHINE.

J. S. RUGER & CO.

PRACTICAL MACHINISTS,

Having taken the above Works, situated on Chicago Street, are prepared to furnish

Steam Engines, Boilers, Shafting, Pulleys, Mill Gearing, Models,

AND ALL KINDS OF MACHINERY TO ORDER.

F. C. HILL,

MANUFACTURER OF

Tin, Copper and Sheet Iron Ware

DEALER IN

Stoves, Hollow and Britannia Ware

CISTERN PUMPS, &c.

AGENT FOR

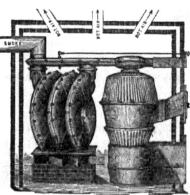

PORTABLE FURNACES,   **VENTILATORS,**

Hedenburgh Heaters,   **Cooking Ranges**

Furnace Registers,   &c., &c.

BARROW'S PATENT HOT AIR AND HOT WATER FURNACE.

Particu'ar attention paid to Warming and Ventilating Private and Public Buildings. Galvanized Gutters, Cornishes, and all kinds of Job Work made to order.

NO. 269 MAIN STREET, OPPOSITE THE CHURCHES.

GEORGE B. BULL & CO.

UNION STOVE WORKS.

Office and Warehouse Nos. 95 Main and 1 and 2 Quay Sts. Foundry corner Swan and Jefferson Streets.

Manufacturers, Wholesale and Retail Dealers in

STOVES OF EVERY CLASS

FOR PUBLIC OR PRIVATE USES.

THE CONQUEST COOKING STOVE,

An entire new style, combining all the recent improvements, and especially adapted for family use for economy in fuel, convenient Broiling arrangements and Hot Water Tank.

The Best assortment of Hotel Cook Stoves in the United States,

Refrigerators, all sizes, and at very low prices.

Water Coolers, from 1 to 10 gallons' capacity.

Dr. Thomson's Patent Filter, the best in Market.

HOUSE FURNISHING GOODS

COMPRISING COMPLETE OUTFITS IN

WOODEN, TIN, JAPANNED AND BRITANNIA WARE.

GRINDSTONES OF ALL WEIGHTS,

POTASH KETTLES,

CAULDRONS AND COOLERS.

With a variety of MISCELLANEOUS CASTINGS always on hand. Special inducements to Wholesale Buyers.

GEORGE B. BULL.   JOHN M. ROCKWELL.

MASON & BIDWELL.

SHIP BUILDING

AND

REPAIRING,

On Buffalo Creek (Opposite Foot of Chicago Street).

The undersigned would respectfully inform the public that they are prepared to contract for the Building of

STEAMERS, PROPELLERS

TUGS AND VESSELS,

Of every description, for the LAKES, SEABOARD and CANALS, on as reasonable terms as any other establishment.

Having two of the

BEST DRY DOCKS

In this section of the country, we are prepared to do all kinds of

REPAIRING

On the shortest possible notice, and in the most thorough manner.

ALSO, ALL KINDS OF

JOINER, BLACKSMITH AND SPAR WORK

DONE TO ORDER.

We have always on hand, and for sale, all kinds of

SHIP TIMBER, PLANK, KNEES, &c.

A. S. MASON.   C. S. BIDWELL.

CABINET WAREHOUSE

ON THE CASH SYSTEM.

The increasing demand for good FURNI-TURE at a low price, induced the undersigned to make this the largest Establishment in the State, embracing Nos. 197, 199, 201 and 203 Main Street, through to Nos. 210 and 212 Washington Street. Main entrance, 203 Main Main Street. Here may be found the

LARGEST, CHEAPEST AND BEST ASSORTMENT

OF PLAIN AND ELEGANT

New Style Cabinet Furniture

EVER BEFORE OFFERED.

Embracing almost every article that can be named; among which are Mahogany and Rose-wood Sofas, Tete-a-tetes, Divans, Ottomans and Lounges, covered in Brocatelle, Plush, Dam-ask and Hair Cloth, at prices ranging from $6 to $150 each. Patent Premium Sofa Beds, Pat-ent Self-rocking Cradles, Patent Spring Bed Bottoms, of all the latest improvements. Also, Patent Recumbent Extension Easy Chairs of all kinds. Rocking, Sewing, Easy and Common Chairs, over 110 different patterns, of Mahogany, Rosewood, Walnut, Oak, Maple, and Fancy Painted, at prices varying from 25 cents to $60 each. Also, a great variety of Book Cases, Bu-reaus, Commodes, Sideboards, Wardrobes, Bedsteads, Tables, Stands, Hat Racks, Piano Stools, Music Racks, Corner Stands, What-nots, &c., &c.

OFFICE FURNITURE, CHAIRS, DESKS, &c.

Painted Bedroom Sets, at prices varying from $30 to $150. Upholstery Goods, Curled Hair, Cotton, and Palm Leaf Mattresses, Bolsters, Pillows, and Cushions. Looking Glasses at Man-ufacturers' prices. Cane, Flag and Wood Seat Chairs.

Cabinet Hardware and Upholstery Materials for sale to the Trade.

Having largely increased manufacturing facilities, it is my purpose, by a large increase o business, to sell at a reduction on former Low Prices, while the quality of the work will be maintained, as heretofore, unrivaled. Every article sold will therefore be warranted to be properly made, and of good material.

FURNITURE MADE TO ORDER.

Repairing, Boxing and Packing done in the best manner and on the most reasonable terms.

Any one can understand that the CASH SYSTEM does not require large profits to make up losses by bad debts, and those who wish, by paying cash, to obtain a good article and save from 20 to 50 per cent., are respectfully invited to give me a call.

ISAAC D. WHITE,
203 Main Street.

5

A. & J. KEOGH,

Piano Forte Manufacturers

NOS. 257, 259 AND 281 WASHINGTON STREET,

Between North and South Division Streets.

The subscribers keep constantly on hand an extensive and choice assortment of Piano Fortes, in elegant Rosewood Cases, which we warrant to be equal in tone, touch and finish, to any manufactured in this country. As a proof of the superiority of our instruments, the subscribers would respectfully call the attention of the public to the subjoined testimonial from Professor Gottschalk (one of the most distinguished pianists in this country), being one of the many they are daily receiving from professors and others, assuring them of the merits of their Pianos. Persons desirous of obtaining a superior instrument are earnestly invited to give us a call. Dealers supplied on liberal terms.

A. & J. KEOGH.

TESTIMONIAL.

SARATOGA, 27th July, 1856.

I was excessively satisfied with the piano which Mr. Richard Owen, of Quebec, was kind enough to lend me for my concert here.

That instrument, of the manufacture of Messrs. A. & J. Keogh, of Buffalo, was one of the most powerful, if not the most powerful, two stringed square pianos I had ever met with. The tone was full and round, without harshness, and of a remarkable evenness in all its registers. As to its strength, I will merely state the fact that it stood at my concert during two hours, without intermission, under five or six heavy fantasias, and as many small pieces, in a moist and hot atmosphere, without one single string breaking, or the instrument getting out of tune ; which is more than I could say of many grand pianos, even of the most eminent makers.

The Messrs. Keogh are personally unknown to me, and this was the first instrument of theirs I had ever performed on ; my opinion, therefore, cannot be influenced by partiality. In recommending it, I simply respond to an artistic feeling, and a desire to do justice to manufacturers whose popularity is so well deserved.

(Signed)   L. GOTTSCHALK.

BUFFALO CITY STEAM TURNING WORKS.

JOSEPH SUOR,

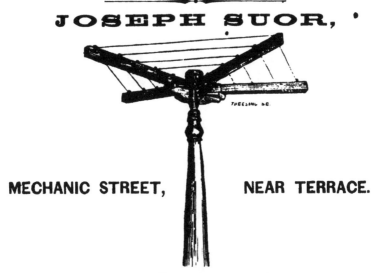

MECHANIC STREET,   NEAR TERRACE.

TURNER AND MANUFACTURER OF ALL KINDS OF

MAHOGANY, ROSEWOOD, WALNUT AND CHERRY

NEWEL POSTS

AND

REVOLVING CLOTHES DRYERS.

Would call the attention of the public to his REVOLVING CLOTHES DRYERS, which possess the following advantages over any other mode of drying clothes : Its rotary motion produces a circulation of air, causing the clothes to dry rapidly, and prevents the liability of their being torn. The labor and time in hanging up the articles to be dried and of taking them down are materially lessened.

It occupies but little space, and may be set up in any yard, however small, without inconvenience. The machine will be found to give entire satisfaction wherever it is used, and no family should be without one.

For particulars address, if by letter, POST OFFICE, BOX 4287.

Orders will be promptly executed, and the machine put up in any part of the city on short notice.

PARTICULAR ATTENTION PAID TO

TEN-PIN BALLS AND PINS.

Newel Posts, Banisters, &c., constantly on hand or made to order. Also, all kinds of heavy turning, Windlasses, &c., for boat work. All work done in the neatest manner, and warranted

HART, BALL & HART,

MANUFACTURERS AND DEALERS IN

PLUMBERS' GOODS,

HOT WATER AND HOT AIR FURNACES

GAS AND STEAM FITTINGS,

HART'S PATENT COMPRESSION FAUCETS,

METAL ROOFING, GUTTERS, CONDUCTORS, &c.

Manufactory and Ware-Rooms, - - No. 237 Main Street.

Agents for Boyington's celebrated

HOT AIR FURNACES AND REGISTERS

HARDIKER & TOYE,

PLUMBERS

GAS AND STEAM FITTERS.

FURNACES BUILT AND REPAIRED,

TIN, COPPER AND SHEET IRON WORK.

CORNER OF NIAGARA AND PEARL STREETS, UNDER KREMLIN HALL.

ALL WORK WARRANTED.

W. HARDIKER.   T. W. TOYE.

CHARLES THEOBALD,

MANUFACTURER OF

COPPER, TIN AND SHEET IRON WARE

HAT AND BONNET STANDS.

ALSO, DEALER IN

STOVES, HARDWARE AND CUTLERY,

No. 406 Main Street, below the North Church.

JOBBING AND REPAIRING DONE TO ORDER.

GEO. A. DEUTHER,

DEALER IN

ARTISTS' MATERIALS

And everything requisite for the Fine Arts.

Paints, Brushes, Crayons, Drawing Papers,

PASTEL AND MONOCHROMATIC BOARDS.

Also, in Fancy and Gold Papers for Box Makers and Book Binders, Lithographs, Engravings, Prints, and all kinds of Pictures.

PORTRAIT AND PICTURE FRAMES MADE TO ORDER,

Gilt, Mahogany, Black Walnut and Rosewood Mouldings at wholesale. Gilders supplied with Prepared Moulding, Gold and Silver Leaves, &c. Also,

Looking Glass Plates, by the box and single plate, constantly on hand.

NO. 12 EXCHANGE STREET.

CHAMBERLAIN & CO.

MANUFACTURERS OF

CARRIAGES, BUGGIES

WAGONS, SLEIGHS, &c.,

CORNER OF NIAGARA AND MOHAWK STREETS.

J. CHAMBERLAIN.   S. M. CHAMBERLAIN.

G. HOUSE,

ORGAN BUILDER

CLINTON STREET, OPPOSITE NEW COURT HOUSE,

Is prepared to build Church and Parlor Organs of almost every description, on reasonably short notice. Twenty years experience, and a personal application to the subject of

VOICING, TUNING AND MAKING REED PIPES

Together with good facilities and competent workmen, enable him to do his work in the most thorough and satisfactory manner.

Tuning and Repairing done on short notice, and warranted to please.

N. B.—Specifications of different class Organs, and their prices, will be sent to any one on application

BUFFALO STEAM COFFEE AND SPICE MILLS.

J. H. CHASE,

Wholesale Dealer in

Green, Roasted and Ground Coffees

PREPARED COCOA, CHOCOLATE,

SPICES OF ALL KINDS, MUSTARD AND PEPPERSAUCE.

271 Main Street, directly opposite the Churches.

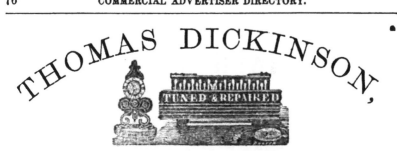

WATCH AND CLOCK MAKER

NO. 370 MAIN STREET.

T. D., having had thirteen years experience in a large manufacturing town in England, and twelve years in Buffalo, flatters himself he can give entire satisfaction to all who may favor him with their commands.

EVERY DESCRIPTION OF

MUSICAL, WEIGHT AND SPRING CLOCKS

CHRONOMETERS,

Repeating, Duplex, Horizontal and Common Watches,

CLEANED, ADJUSTED AND REPAIRED,

At unusually moderate terms. ☞ Charges always stated beforehand, if practicable.

JEWELRY CAREFULLY REPAIRED.

ACCORDEONS TUNED AND REPAIRED.

Fine Watches and Jewelry Constantly Kept for Sale.

OLD GOLD AND SILVER TAKEN IN EXCHANGE.

MODEL GEARING CUT ON THE SHORTEST NOTICE.

Country orders attended to at the

ILLUMINATED CLOCK, 370 MAIN STREET.

H. B. BURT,

JUSTICE OF THE PEACE.

OFFICE, NO. 147 MAIN STREET.

CHARLES T. SHATTUCK,

JUSTICE OF THE PEACE.

Office, 144 Main St., over White's Bank.

CHARLES GARDNER,

JUSTICE OF THE PEACE.

Office, over 150 Main Street, Williams' Hall.

WARREN LAMPMAN,

JUSTICE OF THE PEACE

OFFICE OVER NO. 142 MAIN STREET.

BENJAMIN TOLES,

DEPUTY SHERIFF

CIVIL AND CRIMINAL OFFICER.

OFFICE, 147 MAIN STREET, RESIDENCE, 167 FRANKLIN STREET.

☞ All business entrusted to me will be promptly and faithfully attended to.

LOUIS OTTO,

CONSTABLE AND COLLECTOR

Post Office Address, Box 1937; Residence, 107 Fulsom St.

All business entrusted to my care will be attended to with promptness and dispatch.

REFERENCES.—Hiram Adams & Co., Geo. A. Moore, Norman B. McNeal.

6

LYMAN B. SMITH,

ATTORNEY

AND

COUNSELOR,

OFFICE OVER THE OLD POST OFFICE.

ATTENDS TO

LAW BUSINESS IN ALL THE COURTS OF THIS STATE,

RENTING OF HOUSES

Paying of Taxes at Albany and Buffalo,

Purchase and Sale of Real Estate.

———

HIS LONG RESIDENCE IN BUFFALO, AND

PERSONAL KNOWLEDGE OF BUSINESS MEN

SITUATION AND VALUE OF REAL ESTATE,

Will, he hopes, commend him to those having business to be done in his line.

———

. He will give his Personal Attention to all Business entrusted to him.

LE GRAND & GEO. L. MARVIN,

ATTORNEYS, COUNSELORS, &C.

In the Several New York State and United States Courts,

NO. 156 MAIN STREET.

Notaries Public, Commissioners to take Acknowledgments and Depositions for Records and Courts in New York, Ohio, Michigan, Pennsylvania, Connecticut, Indiana, Wisconsin, &c. Their acquaintance (FROM 1830) with the laws and people in this, and Western, and other States, and in Canada (having statutes of most of the Northern States and Canada), enables them to give dispatch to business therein.
LE GRAND MARVIN, No. 461 Main St.   GEORGE L. MARVIN. No. 58 W. Mohawk St.

E. B. FORBUSH,

ATTORNEY AND COUNSELOR AT LAW

OFFICE CORNER MAIN AND SWAN STS.

Gives special attention as Attorney and Counselor in the LAW OF PATENTS in the United States Courts. Also, prepares specifications and acts as Solicitor of Patents in the United States and Foreign Countries. Inventors from abroad may have their business economically and safely attended to, by correspondence through the Post Office. Having had a large experience in PRACTICAL MECHANISM, as well as with the rules of the Patent Office, and the practice of the Courts in Patent cases, he feels authorized to say that all business which he undertakes in this behalf will be done promptly and correctly. Drawings of Machinery and Models neatly executed.

HOMER & CO.

(SUCCESSORS TO E. C. BROWN & CO.)

Importers and Dealers in Crockery

CHINA AND GLASS WARE.

NO. 175 MAIN STREET, NEXT TO HOLLISTER BUILDINGS.

WM. H. GLENNY,

IMPORTER AND DEALER IN

CHINA, GLASS, CROCKERY

GAS FIXTURES AND PLATED WARE.

162 Main and 17 Pearl Streets.

A. MAJOT,

LADIES' HAIR DRESSER, GENTLEMEN'S HAIR CUTTER

And Manufacturer of Wigs, Toupees, Scalps, Braids, Curls, &c.

Importer of French Perfumery and Fancy Articles.

273 MAIN STREET, CORNER NORTH DIVISION, UP STAIRS.

VENTILATED WIGS AND TOUPEES OF EVERY DESCRIPTION.

PIERCE & CO.,

LUMBER DEALERS

Office and Yard, Corner Michigan and Scott Streets.

We have constantly on hand a good assortment of

HEMLOCK JOIST, TIMBER, &c.

Of all lengths and sizes. Also,

PINE, WHITEWOOD, ASH, MAPLE, OAK AND CHERRY.

PINE AND HEMLOCK LATH.

Cedar, Oak, Beech and Chestnut Fence Posts.

SHINGLES.

We are manufacturing Cut, Sawed and Shaved Pine Shingles. Dealers supplied at the lowest market prices.

STAVES AND HEADING.

We are manufacturing, and have on hand, Oak and Elm Flour Barrel Staves and Sawed and Finished Heading. Also, manufacture Oak and Elm Flour Barrels.

Mill on Ohio Basin Slip, corner Perry Street.

SAW MILL.

We have just fitted up the Saw Mill corner of Alabama Street and Main and Hamburgh Street Canal, and are prepared to furnish bills of Pine and Oak of all sizes and lengths. Custom Sawing done.

CHARLES L. PIERCE.   JEROME PIERCE.

J. B. DUBOIS,

MERCHANT TAILOR

No. 149 MAIN STREET.

An elegant variety of Gentlemen's Furnishing Goods. Also, ready-made Clothing of first rate quality constantly on hand.

THOMAS KENNETT,

DRAPER AND TAILOR

NO. 183 MAIN STREET,

BROWN'S BUILDINGS.

W. S. COOLEY,

MERCHANT TAILOR

No. 7 Seneca Street, between Main and Washington.

A first class assortment of Cloths, Cassimeres and Vestings constantly on hand, which will be made to order in the most fashionable styles, at the lowest Cash Prices.

M. H. TRYON,

MERCHANT TAILOR

242 MAIN STREET,

NEXT TO ERIE COUNTY SAVINGS BANK.

CLARK & STORMS'

NEW CLOTHING EMPORIUM

No. 308 Main Street, - - - - - American Hotel.

Branch of CLARK'S Mammoth Clothing House, New York City. Principal Houses, 398 and 400 Bowery, New York City. Branch Houses, 83 Main Street, Rochester, and 308 Main Street, Buffalo, N. Y.

A Fashionable assortment of Men's, Boys' and Children's Clothing and Furnishing Goods constantly on hand at less than New York City Prices.

E. & B. HOLMES,

DEALERS IN ALL KINDS OF

LUMBER, TIMBER,

LATH. SHINGLES, FLOORING,

SIDING, CEILING, PANEL STUFF, BRACKETS AND MOULDINGS.

MACHINE FOR DRESSING RIVED STAVES.

SASH, DOORS AND BLINDS

PUMP TUBING,

PREMIUM ZINC WASHBOARDS.

PLANING MILL, LUMBER YARD AND STAVE MACHINE OFFICE,

Michigan Street, near New York Central R. R. Depot.

Patent Stave and Barrel Machinery

Patented, Manufactured and Sold by the Inventors,

E. & B. HOLMES,

MACHINE FOR JOINTING STAVES.

FOR MANUFACTURING

Oil, Pork, Liquor and Flour Barrels,

KEGS AND SHOOKS OF ALL SIZES.

CONSISTING OF

STAVE DRESSING MACHINES,

STAVE JOINTING MACHINES,

BARREL-HEAD ROUNDING MACHINES,

HOOP PUNCHING AND FLARING MACHINES,

Hoop Driving and Crosing Machines, Separate and Combined.

Apply to the Inventors,

E. & B. HOLMES, Buffalo.

☞ These Machines will work Sawed, Rived or Cut Staves and Headings.

COURTER HOUSE,

Corner of Terrace, Seneca and Erie Sts.

R. COURTER, ...MANAGER.

FRNAKLIN HOUSE,

Z. ELDRIDGE, --------------- ----------PROPRIETOR.

CORNER SENECA AND ELLICOTT STS.

BONNEY'S HOTEL,

BOARD $1.50 PER DAY...........................Z. BONNEY, Proprietor.

CORNER WASHINGTON AND CARROLL STS.

GLOBE HOTEL,

36 and 37 Exchange Street,

T. COTTER,...........Sole Owner and Proprietor.

WESTERN HOTEL.

(ON TEMPERANCE PRINCIPLES.)

CORNER PEARL AND TERRACE STREETS.

D. B. HULL,.....................Proprietor.

WASHINGTON HOTEL,

BY HENRY ITJEN,

15 Commercial St., near the Railroad, Packet Dock and Steamboat Landing.

BOARD ONE DOLLAR PER DAY.

Conveyances always in readiness to carry Passengers and Baggage to and from the House.

BROWN'S HOTEL,

CORNER SENECA AND MICHIGAN STREETS,

Near the Eastern and Western Railroad Depots.

Board One Dollar per Day. - - **CHARLES BROWN, Proprietor.**

EXTENSIVE STABLES AND YARDS ATTACHED.

SOUTHERN HOTEL,

Corner Seneca and Michigan Streets.

BOARD ONE DOLLAR PER DAY.

DICKEY & BOWEN, - - - Proprietors.

Drovers' and Stock Dealers' Headquarters. Extensive Yards, Livery and good Stabling for seventy-five horses.

NATIONAL HOTEL,

A. N. LARREAU, Proprietor.

No. 91 Exchange Street, Opposite Main Entrance New York Central and Lake Shore Railroad Depot.

The above House is new and entirely furnished with new furniture, and kept on the European and American plan.

REVERE HOUSE,

DOMENIC BOZZE,——————————PROPRIETOR.

Directly opposite the Depot of the Niagara Falls, Lockport, Buffalo and Lake Huron and Great Western Railroads.

F. MOUNT,

LIVERY STABLE KEEPER

On the Terrace, opposite the Western Hotel.

GOOD HORSES AND CARRIAGES AT ALL TIMES ON REASONABLE TERMS.

CHEESMAN & DODGE,

LIVERY STABLE

No. 116 PEARL STREET.

W. CHEESMAN. H. DODGE.

7

GREAT CENTRAL ROUTE TO THE WEST.

Leaving Detroit Daily, on arrival of all Trains from the East.

1861.   1861.

Michigan Central Rail Road

BETWEEN

DETROIT AND CHICAGO

ST. LOUIS, CAIRO,

BURLINGTON, PRAIRIE DU CHIEN,

GALENA, HANNIBAL, NEW ORLEANS, MILWAUKEE,

St. Paul, Rock Island, La Crosse, Quincy, St. Joseph, Memphis, and all points West and South-West.

PATENT SLEEPING CARS

Run on all Night Trains of this route, and on all its connections. Smoking Cars run on Day Trains. PATENT DUSTERS are applied to all Passenger Trains on this Road, and the ventilation is perfect, relieving passengers from all annoyance by reason of dust and foul air.

TIME THE SAME AND FARE AS CHEAP

AS BY ANY OTHER RAILROAD ROUTE.

☞ Baggage checked through to and from all important points in the West and South-West.

THROUGH TICKETS can be obtained at all principal Railroad and Steamboat Offices in the United States and Canadas, and at 17 Exchange Street, Buffalo, 21 State Street, Boston, 173 Broadway, New York.

CHARLES E. NOBLE,   **R. N. RICE,**

General Eastern Passenger Agt., 15 Exchange St., Buffalo.   General Supt., Detroit.

BUFFALO STEAM GAUGE COMPANY
CORNER WASHINGTON AND PERRY STREETS,
SOLE MANUFACTURERS OF

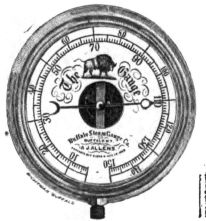 

A. J. ALLEN'S PATENT STEAM GAUGE.

We claim that this Gauge is superior to any other Gauge now in use, is not liable to get out of order, and is unlike most other Gauges ; is free from India Rubber or Steel that is brought in contact with water or steam. These Gauges are thoroughly constructed in all their parts, and warranted to perform all that is required of them. They are particularly adapted to Locomotives, as no jar will affect them.

TEST GAUGES, and FORCE PUMPS for adjusting Gauges, made to order. For further particulars, send for Circular. Address orders to BUFFALO STEAM GAUGE CO., Buffalo. N. Y.

BOOKS! BOOKS!

H. H. OTIS,

PUBLISHER
Wholesale and Retail Dealer in

BOOKS AND STATIONERY,
NO. 226 MAIN STREET.

Keeps constantly on hand a good stock of School and Miscellaneous Books, including all the standard and popular books of the day.

SUNDAY SCHOOL BOOK DEPOSITORY.

Fifteen thousand volumes of Sunday School Books on hand, adapted to Sunday Schools of all denominations. Also, a complete assortment of

BIBLES AND TESTAMENTS, HYMN AND TUNE BOOKS

Prize Books, Tickets, &c. All the Publications of the

METHODIST BOOK ROOM

Furnished at same prices as charged in New York. Also, the Depository of the AMERICAN BIBLE SOCIETY. Always on hand, a large and good variety of

STATIONERY OF EVERY KIND

CAP AND LETTER AND SERMON PAPERS

Of all sizes and qualities.

ENVELOPES OF ALL KINDS, GOLD PENS, &c.

Any Books will be sent by mail, postage paid, on receipt of price. Address H. H. OTIS, BUFFALO, N. Y

J. M. JOHNSON,

STEAM

BOOK MANUFACTORY

AND

BINDERS' FURNISHING HOUSE,

161 MAIN STREET,.............COMMERCIAL ADVERTISER BUILDINGS.

BOOK PRINTING AND BINDING

FOR PUBLISHERS AND AUTHORS.

FIRST CLASS BLANK BOOKS

ON HAND AT WHOLESALE AND RETAIL,

Or manufactured to order for the trade, of every desired pattern, style, or quality, at the lowest New York wholesale rates.

BANK, MERCANTILE, LAW, INSURANCE,

Railroad, Steamboat, and County Work, executed to order.

Bill Heads, Circulars, Blanks, and every variety of Ruling and Printing.

IMPORTER AND DEALER IN

BINDERS' STOCK, TOOLS AND MACHINERY.

Case Work, and every variety of Cloth and Leather Stamping for the trade.

Orders respectfully solicited and promptly attended to.

J. M. JOHNSON, Agent.

The Buffalo Courier.

JOSEPH WARREN & Co., - - - - Publishers and Proprietors.

178 Washington St., opposite Bonney's Hotel.

THE DAILY COURIER,

Six Dollars per annum, or One Shilling per week.

EVENING COURIER AND REPUBLIC,

A PENNY DAILY.

THE WEEKLY COURIER,

Published every Wednesday, $1.00 per annum, in advance.

THE COURIER JOB PRINTING HOUSE.

The Courier Job Printing Office is one of the most complete in Western New York, and is furnished with facilities for turning out every variety of Job Work in the most approved style. Commercial Printing, including Bills of Lading, Letter-Heads, Checks and Drafts, consecutively numbered, Business Cards, Circulars, &c. Railroad Printing, including Cards in Colors, Illuminated Show Bills, Blanks, Tickets, &c. Book and Pamphlet Work; we have the best facilities for printing Books, Pamphlets, Law Cases, &c. Ruling and Blank Work; connected with the Courier establishment is a well appointed Bindery and Blank Book Manufactory. Books Bound in all styles. Ruling done to order.

The Book and Job Office is provided with the latest styles of Types, Borders, Ornaments, &c., including all the latest improvements in Typography.

☞ Orders for any style of work executed in the very best manner.

JOSEPH WARREN.   **JOSEPH WARREN & CO.**   F. H. MARTEN.

1861.   NEW ARRANGEMENTS.   1861.

BUFFALO EVENING POST

STEAM PRINTING OFFICE.

Post Publishes List of Letters—has the Largest Circulation.

☞ GOES FOR THE UNION! ☜

THE BUFFALO EVENING POST,

An indomitable, outspoken, uncompromising independent

PENNY DAILY PAPER.

Is left at the residences of the Subscribers for Six Cents a week, or $3.00 per year, payable invariably in advance.

The Buffalo Evening Post is the Paper to advertise in; it is the organ of the honest masses instead of the selfish cliques. It always contains the general news of the day, Local Intelligence, Pointed and Indomitable Editorials, an entertaining Story, Anecdotes, the latest Telegraphic News, &c., &c., &c.

JOB PRINTING

Of all descriptions expeditiously and beautifully executed.

Office of the Post in Franklin Buildings, on Washington Street.

GEORGE J. BRYAN,

Editor and Proprietor of Post.

R. WHEELER & CO.

PUBLISHERS OF THE

Commercial Advertiser

THE OLDEST DAILY PAPER IN WESTERN NEW YORK.

DAILY, $6 PER ANNUM.

SEMI-WEEKLY COMMERCIAL,

$3.00 PER ANNUM.

PATRIOT AND JOURNAL,

WEEKLY, $1.00 PER ANNUM.

All subscriptions must be settled once in six months.   No subscriptions received for a less period than six months, *unless paid in advance.*

RATES OF ADVERTISING.

TERMS OF ADVERTISING BY THE SQUARE IN THE DAILY.

TWELVE LINES or less make a square.

For one square one insertion, 75 cents. For each subsequent insertion, up to one week, 25 cents.

1 Square, 2 weeks,	$3.00	1 Square, 3 months.	$10.00
1 Square, 3 weeks,	4.00	1 Square, 6 months,	16.00
1 Square, 4 weeks,	5.00	1 Square, 9 months,	18.00
1 Square, 2 months,	8.00	1 Square, 12 months,	20.00

YEARLY ADVERTISING, $40.00 per annum; the space occupied not to exceed two Squares at any one time. One square changeable quarterly if desired, $20.00. Two Squares, $35.00. Each additional Square, $10.00.

SPECIAL NOTICES, ten cents per line for each insertion; but no advertisement will be inserted among the Special Notices for less than ONE DOLLAR for a single insertion.

INSIDE ADVERTISEMENTS will be charged 50 per cent. in addition to our regular rates.

Advertisements for EXHIBITIONS, CONCERTS, or for any other purpose, which are required uniformly to be kept in any specified place, will be charged as *inside advertisements.*

All transient advertisements to be paid for in advance.

LIST OF NAMES.

OMISSIONS AND CORRECTIONS.

Albro, Jas. Courier office, h. cor. Huron and Delaware.

Ambs, Joseph, lab. h. 206 Genesee.

Baman, Frederick, clerk, 399 Main, b. Genesee House.

Barras, M. Charles, actor, 6th bet. Hospital and Georgia.

Berryman, John, capt. marine inspector, h. 205 Swan.

Bissell, E. L. M. D. office and residence cor. Main and Mohawk.

Bleuker, Henry, fireman, h. Cherry n. Jefferson.

Bowden, Richard, tinsmith, h. N. Div. n. Cedar.

Bristol & Bierne, auction and com. Arcade Buildings.

Burns, Geo. L. painter, 204 Washington.

Campbell, Jno. A. 258 Seneca.

Chrysler, George, broom and brush maker, 36 Green.

Cook & Crandall, attorneys, 136 Main.

Copenspiro, Jacob, waiter, Bonney's hotel.

Corning, Erastus & Co. Pearl cor. Seneca.

Dawzer, E. clerk, Wadsworth House.

Dellenbaugh, Chas. C. M. D. 358 Main, h. 133 Ellicott.

Dinwoodie & Shultz, grocers, S. Division cor. Mich.

Green & Stevens, attorneys, 3 N. Division.

Gorham, Geo. att'y, clerk, U. S. Dist. Court, 13 Gov't Buildings, b. 144 Franklin.

Graesser, C. G. shoemaker, h. 35 William.

Green & Stevens, attorneys, 3 N. Division.

Gregg, R. R. M. D. 237 Washington.

Hadley & Husted, hardware, 119 and 217 Main.

Hunn, Edmund, h. 139 S. Division.

Jenner, R. druggist, American Hotel Block.

Kenyon & Wright, M. D. 262 Washington.

Locke, Wm. C. auction and com. 3 Swan.

Mahbach, Valentine, painter, h. 3 Vine alley.

Moessner, L. fireman, h. 222 Clinton.

Quinn & Forrester, plain and ornamental plasterers, 365 Main.

Schaller, John, boarding house, Niagara cor School.

Seib, Mrs. midwife, h. 14th n. Vermont.

Seib, Philip, h. 14th n. Vermont.

Sloss, Maria, nurse, h. 222 Clinton.

Sweet, L. merchant tailor, 230 Main, h. Palmer n. Georgia.

Thornton, Wm. h. 159 Delaware.

Titus, O. B. dry goods, 385 Main, h. Franklin n. North.

Van Buren & Noble, for. and com. merch. 23 Central Wharf.

Weed, L. M. h. cor. Swan and Franklin.

Weller, J. J. with Hersee & Timmerman, h. cor. Elm and Tupper.

Whitaker, Jacob, M. D. 5 Kremlin Hall, h. American.

Commercial Advertiser Directory.

LIST OF NAMES.

ABBREVIATIONS.—In the pages following, h. stands for house ; b. for boards ; cor. for corner ; opp. for opposite ; lab. for laborer ; ab. for above ; bel. for below ; n. for near ; r. for rear ; carp. for carpenter ; N. S. E. W. for north, south, east and west ; N. Div. for North Division ; S. Div. for South Division ; Exch. for Exchange ; Wash. for Washington ; Com'l for Commercial ; and the abbreviations of the States for streets of similar names. The word *street* is implied.

* Compiler's Reference.

A.

Aardly, Bryan, lab. h. Exch. n. Heacock.

Aarons, Aaron, tailor, 23 Exchange, h. same.

Abb, Margaret, widow, h. Spruce n. Batavia.

Abbey. G. B. billiard, cor. Exchange and Mich. h. same.

Abbott, Geo. S. foreman, h. 21 6th.

Abbott, John H. melodeon maker, h. 10th n. Maryland.

Abbott, Walter S. boot and shoe store, 240 Main, h. Delaware cor. Virginia.

Abel, Chas. L. liquor store, Com. Hotel block, Ohio n. Main.

Abel, Adam, blacksmith, h. Maple n. Va.

Abel, John, farmer, Main n. poorhouse.

Abell, Louis, vinegar factory, h. 70 Del Place.

Abell, T. G. widow, h. 235 Franklin.

Abell, Wm. H. com. mer. 24 Central Wharf, h. 125 Chippewa.

Able, Adam, blacksmith, h. Mulberry n. Carlton.

Abernethy, Andrew, flour dealer, Elk n. La.

Abers, Wm. carpenter, h. Watson n. Clinton.

Abhau, Christian, tailor, h. Locust n. Cherry.

Abraham, Geo. carpenter, h. 301 Oak.

Abraham, Geo. carpenter, h. cor. Carolina and 6th.

Abraham, Solomon, clerk, b. 37 W. Seneca.

Abrahams, Abraham, clothing store, 98 Main, h. 90 E. Seneca.

Abwender, Joseph, shoemaker, h. 116 Cedar.

Ach & Stock. saddlers, 557 Seneca.

Ach, John. firm A. & Stock, h. 557 Seneca.

Achtziger, John, soap and candle maker, h. Clinton n. C. R. R.

Ackerman, Jacob. E. Swan cor. Wash. h. same.

Ackerman, John, cooper, Hofman alley n. Hamilton.

Acroyd, Hiram, watchman N. Y. C. R. R. h. 39 Church.

Acton, Henry, 31 Elk St. Market, h. 227 Seneca.

Ada, John, lab. h. Dearborn n. Austin.

Adam, Augustus, M. D. Russian steam bath, h. 29 Pearl.

Adam, Carl, music teacher, h. N. Pearl ab. Va.

Adam, Joseph, shoemaker, h. Johnson n. Gen.

Adams, A. M. firm James Adams & Co, b. Mansion House.

Adams, Albert H. clerk, b. 46 S. Division.

Adams, Ambrose, cooper, b. Walnut n. Wm.

Adams, Augustus E. b. 109 Seneca.

Adams, C. Charles, with Hiram Adams & Co. b. 23 Carroll.

Adams, Charles B. car builder, Folsom n. Jefferson.

Adams, Chas. W. at 23 Exch. b. 46 S. Div.

Adams, David L. clerk, h. Mackinaw n. Ala.

Adams, Fitch D. car builder, h. 220 Swan.

Adams, Hiram & Co. grocers, 37 E. Seneca.

Adams, Hiram, firm H. A. & Co. h. 23 Carroll.

ADAMS, JAMES & CO. tobacconists, 207 Wash.—*See adv. p. 74.*

Adams, Jas. firm J. A. & Co. h. 184 Pearl.

Adams, J. mason, h. Walnut n. William.

Adams, John, harness maker, h. Smith block, Carroll.

Adams, John, grocer, Exchange, h. 46 S. Div.

Adams, John H. clerk R. Dill, b. 30 7th.

Adams, J. T. grocer, on Aurora plank road, n. Whittmore's tavern.

Adams, Louise Ann, Miss, teacher children's Asylum, Erie Co. poorhouse.

Adams, Maria, wid. h. Amherst n. Dearborn.

Adams, Milan, h. 104 Fulton.

Adams, Philip, lab. h. Sycamore n. Jefferson.

Adams, S. Carey, clerk, h. N. Pearl n. Va.

Adams, Wm. blacksmith Buffalo Eagle Iron Works, h. Ky.

Adams, Wm. H. printer, Com. Adv. office, b. 252 Pearl.

Adams, Wm. H. engineer L. S. R. R. h. Seneca bel. R. R. crossing.

8

Ade. John M.* cooper, h. Genesee n. Sherman.
Addington, Samuel H. h. 19 Niagara.
Adler, August, butcher, h. 63 Genesee.
Adler, John, blacksmith, h. Maple ab. Goodell.
Adler, John, lab h. Johnson n. North.
Adler, John, lab. h. 104 Batavia.
Adler, Joseph, mason, h. Ash n. Batavia.
Adler, Max, tinsmith, Court n. 6th, h. same.
Adler, Michael, lab. h. Hickory n. Batavia.
Adoff, L. P. grocer. Genesee cor. Oak, h. same.
Adriance, Elizabeth, book sewer, b. Oak cor. Huron.
Adriance, J. V. S. with Beard & Hayward, h. cor. Oak and Huron.
Adriance, J. V. S. Jr. painter, with G. L. Burns, b. cor. Huron and Oak.
Adsit, John G. clerk, b. D. Brown, h. 1 Scott.
Agin, Jno. lab. h. Staats n. Genesee.
Agne, Charles, lab. h. Johnson n. Genesee.
Ahen, A. blacksmith, with Brayley & Pitts.
Ahern, Thomas, h. 46 Pine.
Abner, Frederick, cooper, h. W. Bennett n. William.
Ahr, Christian. blacksmith, h. 297 Oak.
Aigner, Geo. warehouseman, h. Maiden Lane.
Ailinger, Francis, grocer, Niagara n. Austin, h. same.
Ailinger, Gabriel, cooper, h. Dearborn n. Austin.
Ainler, Bulrick, lab. h. Amherst n. Thompson.
Ainsworth, Joshua, saloon, 74 Exchange, h. same.
Aiple, Daniel, grocer, 435 Seneca, h. same.
Akins, Dennis, cl'k Rowe & Co. h. 114 Folsom.
Albedeen, George, shoemaker, h. Hospital n. Niagara.
Alberger, F. A. Mayor, office cor. Church and Franklin, h. 3 Franklin.
Alberger, J. L. with Job A. h. Delaware n. Ferry.
ALBERGER, JOB, meat market, cor. Terrace and Franklin, h. Main n. Puffer, Cold Springs. —See adv. p. 42.
Alberger, Morris, Serg. N. Y. V. M.
Alberger, W. C. Capt. N. Y. V. M. h. 42 Morgan.
Albers, Albert, shoemaker, h. Best cor. Ellicott.
Albersdarfer, Susana, wid. h. Grape n. North.
Albert, Andrew, lab. h. Watson n. Batavia.
Albert, Charles, grocer, h. cor. Milnor and Wm.
Albert, Geo. lab. h. Lemon n. High.
Albert, John, potash maker, h. Adams n. Sycamore.
Albert, John, shoe dealer, 9 Commercial, h. Canal cor. Maiden Lane.
Albrecht, Fred. saloon, 150 Cherry, h. same.
Albrecht, Frederick,* brewery, Genesee cor. Jefferson, h. same.
Albrecht, Jacob, grocer, S. Div. cor. Pine, h. same.
Albrecht, Leonard, brewer, h. 219 Oak.
Albrecht, Michael, woodsawyer, h. 166 Clinton.
Albrecht. Wm. grocer, h. 12th n. Vermont.
Albright, Chris. in Frontier Mills, h. 11th n. Hampshire.
Albright, Michael, upholsterer, 203 Main, h. 166 Clinton.
Albro, Geo. A. b. 215 S. Division.

Albro, James, at Courier office, h. cor. Georgia and 7th.
Albro, Stephen, h. 215 S. Division.
Albro, Wm. H. firm Hannivan & A. b. 215 S. Division.
Alby, Lindley, with Bowen & Humason, h. Seneca n. old city line.
Aldred, John, tailor, b. cor. Niagara and Eagle.
Aldrich. S. Rev. h. 35 W. Tupper.
Alexander E. h. Md. n. 7th.
Alexander, Isaac, clothier, 138 Main, h. 32 Ex.
Alexander, Isaac, clothing store, 160 Main, h. 50 S. Division.
Alexander, John, with Murray, Cumming & Grant, h. 12 William.
Alexander, J. G. clerk at 273 Main, b. Johnson park n. Carolina.
Alexander, Mary, widow of John, h. S. Div. n. Emslie.
Alford, S. M. 349 Washington.
Allebrandt, Alois, cabinet maker, h. 206 Elm.
Allebrandt, Charles, engineer, h. Clinton n. Madison.
Allen, Albert J. machinist, b. Western.
Allen, Alex. hack driver, 303 Main, b. corner Pearl and Court.
Allen, Alexander, with Hamlin & Mendsen.
Allen, A. J. machinist, 137 E. Seneca.
Allen, Andrew J. awl maker, with Geo. Parr, h. 520 Michigan.
Allen, A. R. cl'k T. D. Dole, b. Main n. Barker.
Allen, Creighton O. h. 262 S. Division.
Allen, C. T. melodeon finisher, Prince & Co. h. 313 Franklin.
Allen, David, tollgate keeper, n. Red Jacket Hotel.
Allen, E. B. b. 61 E. Eagle.
Allen, Francis, boarding house, Miss. n. Ohio.
Allen, Geo. W. h. 61 E. Eagle.
Allen, Henry E. farmer, h. Main n. tollgate.
Allen, Henry F. clerk Hopkins & Halbert, b. 73 Swan.
Allen, Ira W. com. mer. foot Main, h. 27 Ellicott.
Allen, Jacob, b. 77 N. Division.
Allen, James, sailor, h. Perry, n. Illinois.
Allen, James, ship carp. b. Perry n. Hayward.
Allen, James, capt. h. 9th n. Hudson.
Allen, Jeremiah, h. 157 E. Seneca.
Allen, J. E. wood worker with Brayley & Pitts.
Allen, J. Gilbert, firm Harvey & A. b. cor. Mich. and N. Division.
Allen, John, Jr. prest West'n Transp. Co. h. American.
Allen, John P. grocer, Chicago n. Exchange.
Allen, John, painter, h. Carolina n. 7th.
Allen, J. P. b. 61 E. Eagle.
Allen, J. W. dept. sheriff, h. 127 Main.
Allen, Lewis F. h. Niagara n. Ferry.
Allen, Maria, widow, across creek.
Allen, Melissa K. widow, h. Morgan ab. Huron.
Allen, Montlebert, on L. H. R. R. b. Revere.
Allen, Orlando, h. 73 E. Swan.
Allen, Orlando, Jr. b. 73 E. Swan.
Allen, Otis, Mrs. b. Main n. Barker.
Allen, Philo, b. Delaware cor. Allen.
Allen, Wesley D. with E. P. Dorr, h. 69 E. Eagle.

Allen, Wm. master mech. B. S. Engine Works, h. 242 S. Div.
Allen, Wm. K. teller Bank Attica, h. 197 Pearl.
Allen, Wm. R. att'y, over 191 Main, h. 170 E. Swan.
Allen, W. J. clerk Sherman and Barnes, b. Jefferson n. William.
Allen, W. R. att'y, b. Bonney's Hotel.
ALLEN, Z. G. agent millwright, Miami bet.
· Moore and Chicago, h. Hidraulics.—*See adv.* p. 108 *and* 109.
Allenbrand. Geo. moulder. 5 State, h. Batavia bel. Walnut.
Alles, Peter, minister, h. Emslie n. William.
Allinger, John. laborer, h. Sherman n. Batavia.
Allis Allen, exch. office, h. 12 Goodell.
Allis, Geo. painter, h. Pratt n. Batavia.
Allison, Geo. M. joiner, 143 Pearl, h. College n. Allen.
Allman, Geo. F. clerk, h. 155 9th.
Allmendinger, Joseph, shoemaker, h. 89 Hospital.
Allmot, Jno. shoemaker, h. Wm. n. Madison.
Alman, Eugene, lab. h. Washington square.
Alperm. Nathan, peddler, h. William n. Vine.
Alphas, Jas. lab. b. Peckham n. Monroe.
Alphas, John, lab. h. Peckham n. Monroe.
Altemos, Nicholas, tailor, h. Locust ab. Cherry.
Altenburg, Augustus, sash and blind maker, h. Emslie n. William.
Altenburg, John E. sash and blind factory, Swan n. N. Y. C. R. R. h. Watson n. Clinton.
Altman & Co. wholesale clothiers, 40 Pearl.
Altman, A. & Co., clothing store, 140 Main.
Altman, A. firm A. & Co. h. Delaware n. Edw'd.
Altman, Frederick Wm. wagon maker, with W. Barker, h. Batavia n. Ash.
Altman, Isaac, b. 133 Pearl.
Altman, Jacob, firm A. & Co. 40 Pearl, h. 133 Pearl.
Altman, Jos. carriage trimmer, h. 251 Oak.
Altman, Wm. wagoner, h. 154 Batavia.
Altmeyer, F. A. tinsmith, 259 Main, b. 5 Church.
Alton, Mary, Mrs. dressmaker, over 12 Niagara.
Altschuck, Franz, lab. h. Goodell alley n. Tupper.
Altshafel, Joseph, at N. Y. & Erie R. R. Depot, h. Locust n. Virginia.
Alvord, Geo. engineer, b. Courter House.
Aman, Lorenz, lab. b. Washington n. Virginia.
Aman, Wm. tanner, Granger n. Chicago.
Amberg, John, shoemaker, h. Gray n. Genesee.
Ambrose, Altilia, widow, h. Delavan av. cor. Walden.
Ambrose, Augustus, painter, h. over 441 Mich.
Ambrose, Elijah, hackman, h. 162 Clinton.
Ambrose, Geo. drover, h. 128 Clinton.
Ambrose, Jno. builder, h. Main n. Steele.
Ambrose, Norman, carriage driver, h. 513 Washington.
Ambrose, Robert, grocer, h. Delavan av. cor. Walden.
Ambruster, Anton, cooper, h Syc. n. Michigan.
Ambs, Frank, carpenter, h. 206 Genesee.
Ambs, Gervas, hatter, 17 E. Genesee, h. same.
Ambs, Salome, widow, h. 335 Genesee.
Ambs, Hiram, carpenter, h. 206 Genesee.
American Express Co. 9 and 11 W. Seneca.

American Hall, 304 Main.
American Hotel, 314 Main.
Amer, Louisa, widow, h. r. 177 Genesee.
Amlah, John, with D. C. Beard, b. Franklin ab. Tupper.
Amos, John, lab. h. across creek.
Amos & Son, M. D. office 48 E. Genesee.
Amsden, Ira R. clerk, cor. 4th and Carolina, b. Georgia n. 6th.
Amstuts, Joseph. lab. h. Hickory n. Sycamore.
Amstuts, Catharine, midwife, h. Hickory n. Sycamore.
Andas, Pauline, Mrs. h. 174 Oak.
Anderle, Franz, painter, h. 578 Washington.
Anderson, Alex'r S. & Co. wholesale grocers and liquor dealers, 56 Main.
Anderson, Alex'r S. firm Alex'r S. A. & Co. h. 31 Niagara square.
Anderson, Andrew, capt. marine inspector, h. 9th cor. Pennsylvania.
Anderson, Carl, h. 1 Vine.
Anderson, Geo. cloth cleaner, h. 102 Oak.
Anderson, Jacob, waiter, h. Madison n. Batavia.
Anderson, James, plumber, h. 23 Illinois.
Anderson, James, engineer, h. 174 N. Div.
Anderson, James, capt. Exchange cor. Wash.
Anderson, John, whitewasher, h. 360 Michigan.
Anderson, John, farmer, h. r. White's Corners plank road and city line.
Anderson, John, colored, sailor, h. r. 20 Walnut.
Anderson, John, lab. h. 66 Cedar.
Anderson, Mary, widow, Clinton n. Walnut.
Anderson, Robert, cabinet maker, with Hersee & Timmerman, b. Michigan cor. High.
Anderson, Wm. A. firm D. C. Weed & Co. 222 Main, h. 6 S. Division.
Andoff. Mrs. Mary, upholsterer, h. 439 Main.
Andr, Edward, blacksmith, b. Clinton n. Spring.
Andre, C.· clerk, Brunck, Held & Co. h. Oak cor. Burton Alley.
Andre, Conrad, tailor, h. 76 Bennett.
Andre, Conrad, tailor, h. Oak cor. Burton alley.
Andre, Wm. clerk, b. Boston Hotel.
Andres, Chas. hostler, b. Geo. Andres.
Andres, Elizabeth, h. 249 Elm.
Andres, Frank, peddler, h. 231 Elm.
Andres, Geo. hostler, at Genesee House, h. Camp n. Genesee.
Andres, Geo. Jr. teamster, b. Geo. Andres.
Andrews, A. artist, over 216 Main.
Andrews, Ellen, widow, h. Georgia n. 4th.
Andrews, Robert E. firm Andrews & Son, h. 9th cor. York.
Andrews, Robert F. firm Andrews & Son, h. 9th cor. York.
ANDREWS & SON, opticians, &c. 221 Main cor. Swan.—*See adv. p.* 49.
Angel, John, mason, h. Cherry n. Jefferson.
ANGELS, SALLY, widow, milliner, 284 Main, h. 3 Edward.—*See adv. p.* 80.
Angle, Jno. wood sawyer, h. Spring n. William.
Anger, Chas. lab. h. Pratt n. Sycamore.
Angus, E. W. lab. h. Seneca n. tollgate.
Annin, J. W. prod. and com. merch. 9 Central Wharf, h. 227 Delaware.
Annis, Ezekiel, watchman, h. 171 Washington.
Annis, Wm. with C. W. Evans, b. 171 Wash.
Annon, Nicholas, lab. h. Pratt n. Clinton.

Annowsky, Henry, piano maker, h. 246 Ellicott.
Anont, Peter, milkman, Walden. n. Ferry.
Ansteth, Jacob, tailor, h. Genesee, cor. Elm.
Ansteth, Jacob, Jr. clerk, Howard, Whitcomb & Co. b. cor. Genesee and Oak.
Anthony, Jacob C. commission merchant, 2 Central Wharf, h. 68 S. Division.
Anthony, James, saloon, 3 Water, h. same.
Anton, Joseph, lab. h. Pine n. Cypress.
Antweiller, Jacob, carp. h. Grey n. Batavia.
Apel, Fred. printer, b. 516 Michigan.
Apel, Herman, carpenter, b. 516 Michigan.
Apel, Louis W. carpet weaver. h. 516 Michigan.
Apern, Nathan, peddler, h. William n. Pine.
Apfelbacher, Andrew, lab. h. Oak n. North.
Appenheimer, Philip, farmer, Walden n. Delavan avenue.
Apple, Jacob, shoemaker, h. Syc. cor. Ash.
Appleman, Jno. ship carpenter, h. Perry n. La.
Applement, Alice, widow, h. across creek.
Appleton, Jas. Jr. jeweller, 196 Main.
Arbor, Jacob, lab. h. Exch. n. Van Rensselaer.
Archer, Mary, seamstress, 112 Batavia.
Ardmen, Frank, lab, William n. Madison.
Arend, And. b. William Stanton.
Arend, Chas. clerk, h. William cor. Hickory.
Arent, Fred. shoemaker, 4 Commerc'l. b. same.
Arey, Chas. tailor, Abbott's Corners plank road n. Iron Bridge.
Arey, Oliver, teacher Central School, h. 47 7th.
Arft, John, baker, h. Pratt n. Batavia.
Argus, Adam, peddler, h. 64 William.
Argus, Antony,* cooper, h. Amherst n. Military Road.
Argus, Geo. grocer, cor. Niagara and Hamilton.
Argus, Geo. grocer, Amherst opp. Lewis.
Argus, Henry, shoemaker, 242 Main, h. 64 Wm. n. Pine.
Argus, James C. clerk National, b. same.
Ariell, Jno. sailor, 167 South Division.
Arkwright, E. hackdriver, h. 101 Ellicott.
Arllas, Wm. harness maker, William n. Adams.
Armbrast, John, tinsmith, 79 Genesee.
Armbraster, Joseph, grocer, Genesee cor. canal.
Armbruster, Geo. tailor, h. Oak cor. Goodell.
Armond. Ellen, saloon, n. 92 Main, h. same.
Arms, Wm. clerk, P. O. b. 109 Seneca.
Armstrong, Alonzo, carriage maker, 58 E. Sen.
Arm-trong. Andrew, engineer, W. E. Co. h. Eagle bel. Spring.
Armstrong, Charles, upholsterer. 3 Birckhead Buil., Com'l. h. Bowery bet. North and Va.
Armstrong, Chas. B. firm Fish & A. h. 28 Johnson Place.
Armstrong, Charles J. with C. Armstrong, b. Bowery.
Armstrong, C. J. grinder, h. Perry n. Hamburgh.
Armstrong, Galbraith, shoemaker, h. 65 Chippewa.
Armstrong, Geo. barber, 11 William.
Armstrong, H. with Brayley & Pitts.
Armstrong, John, boiler maker, h. 13 Miss.
Armstrong, John, h. Bidwell n. Niagara.
Armstrong, Susan, h. Bidwell n. Niagara.
Armstrong, Thos. carpenter, 276 Swan.
Armstrong, Thos. A. clerk, with Seymour & Wells, b. 276 E. Swan.

Armstrong, Wm. C., U. S. Express Co. h. Palmer n. Virginia.
Arnawine, Andrew, mason, h. Walnut n. Gen.
Arnawine, Ignatz, Sr. Hickory n. Batavia.
Arnett, Henry M. com. merchant, 7 C. Wharf, b. 408 Main.
Arnind, Nick, lab. h. Pratt n. William.
Arnold, John, saloon, Carroll n. Ala. h. same.
Arnold, Jos. lab. h. 59 Cedar.
Arnold, Peter. lab. h. Goodell alley bel. Goodell.
Arnold Philip, at cor. Washington and Swan, b. same.
Arnold, Theresia, widow, washer, h. Walnut n. Batavia.
Arnold, W. W. firm Little & A. h. Day's Park n. Cottage.
Arnwick, Jacob, heater, h. N. Washington n Forest avenue.
Arras, L. woodworker, Bradley & Pitt's.
Arres, Leonard, carp. h. Palmer ab. Md.
Arrus, Richard, Weyhman, b. Commercial.
Art, William, beer saloon, Main n. Tupper.
Arthur, Wm. H. capt. on lake, h. 288 Swan.
Ash, Jas. clerk in C. W. Evans' coal office, h. 44 Jackson.
Ash. Robert, h. cor. Bouck n. Washington.
Ashburn, John, lab. h. Thompson n. Austin.
Ashby, John, bookbinder, with J. V. W. Penfield.
Ashby, John, carp. h. Park ab. Virginia.
Ashley, Dorothy, widow, nurse, h. 75 Del. cor. Chippewa.
Ashley, Paul, mason, h. Oak n. High.
Ashman, Wm. h. 84 6th.
Ashton. Isaac, engineer in Buff. Iron and Nail Works, h. Niagara n. Bird avenue.
Ashton, Jas. b. I. Ashton.
Ashton, Jno. engineer, h. Hayward n. Perry.
Asmuss, John, manuf. wash blueing, h. 177 Genesee.
Ast, Frank, tanner, with Bush & Howard, h. N. Canal n. Emslie.
Ast, Nicholas, lab. with E. Palmer.
Atherton, Henry, benzoin distiller, h. Hospital n. 6th.
Atkins, Barton, blast furnace, h. Elk n. Hamburgh.
Atkins, Robt F. undertaker, 100 Pearl, h. same.
Atkinson, Edward J. soap and candle manufactory, h. Mich. bet. Seneca and Swan.
Atwater, Edward, firm A. & Hawes, h. 113 Niagara.
Atwater, F. J. h. 167 Delaware.
Atwater & Hawes, Niag. Oil Works, cor. Maryland and 3d.
Atwood, Luther, cooper, h. 79 Church.
Auchinleck, A. h. 140 Clinton.
Auchinvole, John, h. Niagara cor. Ferry.
Audenride, Jno. blacksmith, h. 528 Mich.
Auer, August, shoemaker, h. 40 William.
Auer, Fred. carpenter, h. 322 Elm.
Aueres, Barbara, b. Potter n. Batavia.
Auerhammer, H. M. glove maker, h. Alabama n. Fulton.
Augstell, Geo. locksmith, h. 107 Genesee.
Augstell, Peter, blacksmith. h. 62 Goodell.
Ault, Jas. clerk, 28 Main, h. 57 Oak.
Austin & Austin, attorneys, 289 Washington.
Austin, Anna, Mrs. nurse, h. Hamburgh n. Sen.

Austin, Benj. H. firm A. & A. h. 291 Wash.
Austin, Benj. H. Jr. firm A. & A. b. 21 Pearl.
Austin, D. S. firm C. & A. h. 101 E. Swan.
Austin, E. A. teacher, h. Parish n. East.
Austin, E. F. farmer, h. White's Cor. pl'k road.
Austin. Emmett, clerk, with D. S. Austin, b. 101 E. Swan.
Austin, Harriet E. T. Mrs. h. 183 Ellicott.
Austin. Jonathan, student at law, 289 Wash. b. 291 Washington.
Austin, Seth. sec. build. soc. h. 101 E. Swan.
Austin, Stephen G. attorney, 1 Granite Block, h. Niagara square.
Austin. Thomas J. carpenter, h. Niagara n. Austin.
Auth, Maria, widow, h. 137 Batavia.
Averell, Jas. M. mariner. h. 13 6th.
Avers, John, carpenter, Hickory n. Batavia.
Avers, Mary, widow, h. Hickory n. Batavia.
Avery, Geo. willow wagon maker, 384 Swan, h. same.
Avery. John T. sexton Unitarian Church, cor. Eagle and Franklin, h. same.
Avery, W. firm Judson & A. 24 Central Wharf, b. Main cor. Huron.
Axe. Geo. plane maker, 233 E. Seneca, Smith's block, h. same.
Axmacker. Gustavus, carpenter, h. 174 Oak.
Ayer, F. C. clerk, 180 Main, b. 118 6th.
Ayers J. on N. St. R. R.
Ayers, Wm. B. h. 24 Johnson Park.
Ayers, Wm. B. firm Knapp & A. h. 24 Johnson Place.
Ayers, Washington J. clerk, Knapp & A. b. 24 Johnson Place.
Ayers, W. J. distiller, 8 Hanover, h. 24 Johnson Park.

B.

Baader. Joseph, goldsmith, 403 Main, h. same.
Baar, Chas. lab. b. 43 Ash.
Baar, C. widow, h. 43 Ash.
Baas, Conrad, piano maker, with A. & J. Keogh, h. Spruce n. Batavia.
Babb, L. E. sup't telegraph B. N. Y. & E. R. R. b. Bloomer, room St. James.
Babbington, Hugh, joiner, h. Van Rensselaer n. Carroll.
Babbit, Jas. A. ship carp. h. 9th n. York.
Babcock, Benj. carpenter, h. 168 9th.
Babcock, Benj. engineer, h. 2 W. Bennett.
Babcock, Christopher, joiner, h. Palmer n. Va.
Babcock, Geo. R. firm B. & Moore, 330 Main, h. Niagara Square.
Babcock & Moore, attorneys, 330 Main.
Babcock, ——. b. Western.
Babcock, H. P. med. student, 9 Court, h. Niagara Square.
Babcock. S. piano maker, with A. & J. Keogh.
Babwish. John, whitewasher, h. 18 Walnut.
Bace, Curtis L. at J. R. Evans & Co. b. 48 Court.
Bach, Gabriel, carpenter, h. Maple bel. Va.
Bach, Gregor, cooper, h. 10 Bennett.
Bach, Philip, cook. h. 530 Michigan.
Bacheler, Henry, h. cor. Hospital and Court.
Bachmann, Jacob, cooper, h. Wash. n. Va.

Bachman, Anton, stone cutter, h. over 29 Huron.
Bachman, Fred. with Sherman & Barnes, h. Locust n. High.
Bachman, John, gardener, h. Locust n. High.
Bachman, Peter. cooper, h. Wash. n. Va.
Bachoff, Frederick, peddler, h. Hollister n Spring.
Bachover, John, upholsterer, h. Maple n. High.
Backofer, John, upholsterer, 34 Ellicott, b. Maple cor. High.
Backus, Peter. lab. h. Sycamore cor. Ash.
Bacon, Chas. E. book-keeper, h. Maryland n. 11th.
Bacon, Duncan, telegraph opp. b. 29 Swan.
Badder, John. mason, h. Clinton n. Madison.
Bader, John, lab. h. Mortimore n. Sycamore.
Baecke, Joseph, cigar maker, h. Mulberry n. Carlton.
Baecker, Charles, sawyer, b. Genesee cor. Davis.
Baecker, Daniel, lab. h. Genesee cor. Davis.
Baecker, Henry, with J. M. Johnston, b. D. Baecker.
Baecker, John, lab. h. 56 Bennett.
Baeitz, Dorotha, widow, Spruce n. Genesee.
Baer, Anton, varnisher, h. Elm n. Best.
Baer, Casper, lab. h. 215 Elm.
Baer, Conrad. bookseller and com. deeds, 410 Main, h. same.
Baer, Frank. lab. h. Mortimer cor. Hollister.
Baer, Frederick, lab. h. Grey n. Genesee.
Baer, George, tailor, 31½ Genesee, h. same.
Baer. George, cab. maker, b. 78 E. Genesee.
Baer. George. pail maker, h. Parish n. East.
Baer, Geo. Jr. pail maker, h. Parish n. East.
Baer, Jacob, lab. h. 451 Michigan.
Baer, Jacob, lab. Monroe n. Sycamore.
Baer, James, pail maker, h. Parish n. East.
Baer, John C. tailor, h. Peach n. High.
Baer, Martin, carpenter, h. Lemon n. Va.
Baer, Michael, lab. h. Mulberry n. Goodell.
Baer, Philip, mason h. Spring n. Genesee.
Baer, Sebastian, brewer, b. Max Roth.
Baer Ulrich, tailor, h. Lemon n. North.
Baesinger, Christian, lab. h. Steel n. Waldron.
Baetenger, Elizabeth, widow, butcher shop, 286 Genesee, h. same.
Baethig, Henry, h. 167 Oak.
Baeumler, Anton, lab. h. Elm n. Best.
Bagg, Charles, engineer, h. 261 N. Division.
Bagley, John, marnier, h. across creek.
Bagnall, Mrs. B. h. 210 Niagara.
Bagnall, S. W. constable, h. 62 Chippewa.
Bagnall, S. A. b. with S. W. Bagnall.
Bagon, John, lab. h. across creek.
Bahling, H. painter, over 113 Genesee.
Baider, John, jr. apprentice, h. Hickory n. Cherry.
Bailey, A. T. clerk, b. 256 Franklin.
Bailey, Charles. machinist, h. 24 Spruce.
Bailey, Chauncey C. organist, b. 256 Franklin.
Bailey, D. W. with Hamlin & Mendsen, h. 99 E. Seneca.
Bailey, E. W. firm Cutter & Bailey, h. 256 Franklin.
Bailey, Geo. machinery and printing, 9, 10, 11 & 12 Water, h. Edward bel. Delaware.

Bailey, Gordon, clerk, tax receiver's office, h. 43 S. Division.
Bailey, Jas. B. engineer, b. 132 Swan
Bailey, Jas. B. milk dairy, h. Batavia cor. Williamsville road.
Bailey, James, h. 117 Pearl.
Bailey, John, tanner. h. Cedar n. William.
Bailey, Wendling, mason, h. Walnut n. Wm.
Bailey, Wm. W. engineer, b. 132 Swan.
Bain, Donald, clerk, overseer poor. h. 298 Mich.
Bain, Lucy, over cor. 9th and Carolina.
Bain, James, b. 18 Johnson Place.
Bain, Malcolm, carp. h. 18 Johnson Place.
Baine, Sam'l S. joiner, h. Palmer n. Virginia.
Baine, Wm. mariner, h. 11th ab. Virginia.
Baird. John, tinsmith, b. 47 5th.
Baird, M. Mrs. widow, h. Wash. n. Burton alley.
Baker, A. D. with H. Hotchkiss, 210 Main.
Baker, A. L. attorney, 1 Brown's Building, h. Delaware cor. Huron.
Baker, A. L. Jr. b. cor. Delaware and Huron,
Baker, C. with Nelson & Co. h. cor. Washington and Exchange.
Baker, Chas. H. b. 7 Pearl.
Baker, Charles, with Nelson & Co. h. cor. Wash. and Exchange.
Baker, Clifford A. firm Lyon & Co. h. 252 Pearl.
Baker, Diana, Miss, matron children's asylum Erie Co. poorhouse.
Baker, E. L. prof. music and organist at St. Paul's church, b. 427 Main.
Baker, Geo. P. b. 154 Seneca.
Baker, Geo. W. h. 154 E. Seneca.
Baker, Geo. M. b. Moses Baker.
Baker, Henry, carp. h. Main n. Goodell.
Baker, Henry, sailor, h. Ohio cor. Mackinaw.
Baker, Henry, moulder, h. 14th n. Ct.
Baker, Howard, cor. Lloyd and Prime, b. 154 E. Seneca.
Baker, James, lab. h. Abbott road bel. Elk.
Baker, James M. com. of deeds, with A. L. Baker, b. cor. Delaware and Huron.
Baker, John, carp. h. 8 Mechanic.
Baker, John, carp. cor. Penn. and 7th.
Baker, John, machinist, h. 72 Bennett.
Baker, Jonathan, caulker, h. Fourth n. Ga.
Baker, Joseph, lab. h. Walnut n. William.
Baker, Joseph, Jr. mason, Jeff. n. Peckham.
Baker, J. shoemaker, h. Wm. n. Cedar.
Baker, Louis, grocer, Bat. n. Hickory, h. same.
Baker. Louis P. b. Batavia n. Hickory.
Baker, Mary, widow, h. Hospital n. Niagara.
Baker, Moses, agricultural works, Genesee cor. Washington, h. 427 Main.
Baker, O. P. painter, h. Exchange n. Van Rensselaer.
Baker, Peter, machinist, h. 21 14th.
Bakes, Peter, tailor, h. William n. Walnut.
Baker, Peter, moulder, h, 14th n. Ct.
Baker, Philip, harness maker, h. 22 Green.
Baker, Sarah, widow, h. Goodell cor. Oak.
Baker, Sam'l. ship carp. b Mechanic.
Baker, W. H. on N. St. R. R.
Baker, Wm, old Amer. hotel, 29 Commercial, h. same.
Baker, Wm. H. firm Rockwell & B. h. 103 E. Eagle.

Baker, Wm. lab. h. Ohio n. South.
Balcom, A. W. milk-dairy, Batavia n. tollgate.
Balcom, Jas. A. clerk, cor. Erie and Canal, h. 21 Union.
Balcom, Jno. A. machinist, b. Batavia n. Walden.
Balcom, Myron, peddler, h. A. W. Balcom.
Balcom. P. A. brickmaker, office and store Main cor. Ferry, h. same.
Balcom, P. A. Jr. book-keeper, b. with P. A. Balcom.
Baldarf, Aug. boiler maker. h. Pratt n. Eagle.
Baldauf, Geo. lab. h. Adams n. Batavia.
Baldauf, Henry, boiler maker, h. Pratt bet. E. Eagle and Clinton.
Baldolf, Peter, shoemaker, b. William bet. Bennett and Cedar.
Baldwin, Jane, book sewer, b. cor. Pine and Eagle.
Baldwin, Daniel, firm Hodge & B. cor. Niagara and Carolina, h. 121 Delaware.
Baldwin, Eliza, nurse, h. 436 Michigan.
Baldwin, Fred. L. clerk, b. Daniel Baldwin.
Baldwin, Henry D. agent Singer's sewing machine, b. 35 Swan.
Baldwin, Wm. carpenter, h. 158 E. Eagle.
Baldy, C. M. printer, Com. Adv. h. 15 Chestnut.
Balz, Peter, Jr, tinsmith, 31 Main, h. Cold Springs.
Ball, A. M. cor. Erie and River, h. 30 Park.
Ball, Chas. stone-cutter, h. 302 Oak.
Ball, C. W. book-keeper, Cobb & Co. 20 Prime, b. 36 Clinton.
Ball, Frank, carpenter, h. Adams n. Brown.
Ball, Franklin, carpenter, h. 70 Exchange.
Ball, Jacob, furnaceman, h. 237 Elm.
Ball, John M. firm Hart, B. & Hart, h. Georgia n. Niagara.
Ball, Joseph, h. 496 Washington.
Ball. Joseph, machinist, h. Wash. n. Tupper.
Ball, Jethro, lab. h. Pine n. William.
Ball, Jos. saloon, Main n. American Hotel.
Ballou, Charles, capt. h. 70 Oak.
Balmarian, Buskel, architect, h. 119 Batavia.
Baltz, Peter, Jr., b. Ferry n. Michigan.
Baltzer, Christopher, miller, h. Parish, cor. Thompson.
Baltzer, Frank, distiller, h. Niagara n. Austin.
Baltzer, Henry, cooper, h. Parish n. Thompson.
Balters, Geo. carpenter, h. Adams n. Peckham.
Baltzer, Wm. cooper, h. Parish n. Thompson.
Balz, Geo. shoemaker, h. 480 Michigan.
Balz, Mary, widow, h. 143 Batavia.
Balz, Peter, dairyman, h. Ferry n. Michigan.
Bamberg, John Adam, musician, h. Hickory n. Sycamore.
Bamberg, Martin, shoemaker, b. 128 Batavia.
Bamberger, Christ. blacksmith, Batavia, cor. Roos Alley, h. Watson cor. Batavia.
Bamberger, John, mason, h. S. Div. n. Jeff'n.
Bamberger, Henry, lab. b. 503 Michigan.
Bame, Sam'l S. manufac'r Monroe's pat. spring bedsteads, 45 Chippewa, h. same.
Bames, E. Butcher, 360 Swan.
Bamgonsger, David, lab. h. 92 Sycamore.
Bamler, Geo. J. family grocer, cor. Erie and Lock, h. same.
Bandell, E. foreman water w'ks, h. Lake n. 6th.

BANGASSER & BROTHERS, locksmiths and brass manufacturers, 15 E. Seneca.—*See adv.* p. 54.
Bangasser, Fred. firm B. & Bros. h. Elm n. High.
Bangasser, Geo. moulder, h. 100 Tupper.
Bangasser, Jacob, firm B. & Bros. h. Maryland n. Palmer.
Bangeder, John, stone cutter. h. 112 Cedar.
Bangratze, Joachim, glass blower, h. 530 Mich.
Banks, Levi A. grocer, 16 Niagara, h. 69 6th.
Banker, Wm.W. musician, h. Cedar cor. Clinton.
Bannister, John, carpenter, h. Ky. n. South.
Bannister, H. wagon maker, h. 5th above Pa.
Banta, Jacob W. h. Perry cor. Hayward.
Banta, Wm. S, finisher, h. Perry cor. Hayward.
Bancor, John, farmer, Martin's Corners.
Bapst, Casper, carpenter, h. Pratt n. Genesee.
Bapst, Louis, dining saloon, 198 Washington.
Barber, Daniel, grocer, h. 396 Seneca.
Barber, Ida, Miss, h. 40 Sycamore.
Barber, John, boatman. h. 35 Folsom.
Barber, Mary, Mrs. boarding house. 255 Wash.
Barber, Moses, baggage agent, L. S. R. R. h. 233 Swan.
Barber, Wm. B. printer Republic Office, b. National Hotel
Bardwell, C. firm Frink & Co. Central Wharf, h. 131 Niagara.
Barger, Fred. b. 126 Swan.
Bargin, Sophia, widow, h. 7th n. Hudson.
Barham, Wm. h. Oak, cor. Tupper.
Barker, A. land and insurance agt. 3 Brown's Buildings, h. 40 Niagara.
Barker, Dudson B. produce dealer, Elk St. Market, h. Perry n. Ohio basin slip.
Barker, Geo. P. att'y. 4 International Bank Building, b. cor. Swan and Pearl.
Barker, Geo. W. J. P. h. Martin's Corners.
Barker, Isaac, engineer, B. & E. R. R. h. Lee's Corners 13th Ward.
Barker, Jacob A. Mrs. widow, h. 72 Pearl.
Barker, James H. clerk Howard, Whitcomb & Co. b. 20 Carolina.
Barker, Jasper, deputy keeper poorhouse, Main n. city line.
Barker, Joseph B. carpenter, h. Hodge n. Vt.
Barker, J. W. teacher, h. 98 Clinton.
Barker. Nathan B. principal school 7, h. 20 Carolina.
Barker, Richard, with G. A. Prince & Co. h. 10th n. Carolina.
Barker, Stephen, h. Forest ave. n. Dewitt.
Barker, Wm. wagon manufacturer, 93 E. Seneca, h. 98 same.
Barleon, Charles, barber shop, 86 Batavia, h. Michigan n. Cypress.
Barlon, Ransom, h. 9 Terrace.
Barman, Jacob, clothier, 116 & 148 Main, h. 36 Exchange.
Barnaby, W. gardener. h. Summer n. Delaware.
Barnard, Abram, peddler, h. 102 E. Seneca.
Barnard, Albert, Mrs. h. 86 S. Division.
Barnard, Albert J. book-keeper, U. S. Express Company, h. 86 S. Division.
Barnard, Edward, blacksmith, h. 62 Eagle.
Barnard, Frederick, moulder, h. 103 Carroll.
Barnard, Geo. A. boarding house, 62 Eagle.

Barnard, Henry, lab. h. S. Exch. n. R. R. T.
Barnard, Ira, Jr. grocer, 182 Swan, h. same.
Barnard, Lewis J., U. S. Express Company, b. 86 S. Division.
Barnard, Margaret, widow, boarding house, 62 E. Eagle.
Barnard, Robert, firm Fero & B. h. 117 Eagle.
Barnd, Peter, furnaceman, h. 194 Elm.
Barnes, Alex. Sen. butcher, h. 191 E. Seneca.
Barnes, Bradford, builder, h. 88 Eagle.
Barnes, Ephraim, clerk at 3 E. Seneca, b. 360 Swan.
Barnes, Fred. lab. h. Walden n. Batavia.
Barnes, George N. clerk at 3 E. Seneca. b. 360 Swan.
Barnes, Henry, inspector of customs, h. 108 Chippewa.
Barnes, Jacob L. h. Niagara n. Hudson.
Barnes, John, lab. h. S. Exchange n. R. R. T.
Barnes, John, cooper, h. Porter n. Bouck.
Barnes. John L. meat market, 199 Seneca and 19 Main, h. 191 E. Seneca.
Barnes, Joseph, clerk. 1 Seneca, b. 360 Swan.
Barnes, J. C. firm Sherman & Co. h. 78 W. Chippewa.
Barnes J. & Son, meat store, 3 E. Seneca.
Barnes, Josiah, M. D. office 6 Exchange, h. 104 Swan.
Barnes. Joshua, firm J. B. & Son, h. 360 Swan n. Spring.
Barnes, Matilda, wid. h. Porter n. Auburn ave.
Barnes, Michael, drayman, b. 86 5th.
Barnes, Patrick, hostler, cor. Franklin and Va h. 4 Edward.
Barnes & Slocum, canal stables, Tow-path below Genesee.
Barnes, Smith, carp. h. 195 Eagle n. Cedar.
Barnes, Wm. lab. h. Scott cor. Market.
Barnes, Wm. H. joiner, h. 189 Eagle.
Barnes, William N. butcher, firm J. B. & Son, b. 360 Swan.
Barness, Wm. D. patentee, h. 30 E. Tupper.
Barnett, Albert, weighman, h. Eagle bel. Spring.
Barnett, James, tailor, h. Elm n. High.
Barnett, Jas. R. clerk, N. Y. & E. R. R. b. Elm n. High.
Barnett, Patrick, fisherman, h. across creek.
Barnett, Peter, Mrs. h. 18 Palmer.
Barnett, Wm. lab. h. cor. Dearborn and Austin.
Barnhard, Phillip, peddler, h. Gen. n. tollgate.
Barnhardt, H. D. joiner, h. 204 N. Division.
Barnhardt, H. H. shingle sawyer, h. N. Division n. Walnut.
Barnum, Geo. G. grocer, 74 Main, h. Chippewa cor. Morgan.
Barnum, S. O. variety store. 211 Main, h. Delaware bet. Allen and North.
Barnum, Theodore, clerk, S. O. Barnum, 211 Main, h. Delaware n. Allen.
Barr, A. lab. h. Main n. Ferry.
Barr, Charles W. student, b. Main opp. Cold Spring House.
Barr, Charles, h. Ferry n. Main.
Barr, F. H. teamster, h. 155 Elk.
Barr, Henry, with Wm. Barr, b. 29 E. Swan.
Barr, Michael, machinist, 16 Water, h. Mulberry n. Goodell.
Barr, Robert, lab. 64 Main, h. 63 Main.

Barr, Robert, liquor store, 212 Washington, h. 107 S. Division.
Barr, R. W. liquor dealer, h. 107 S. Division.
Barr, Wm. blacksmith, h. Monroe, bet. Batavia and Sycamore.
Barr, William, stock agent N. Y. C. R. R. h. 52 N. Division.
Barr, Wm. R. agt. L. S. and M. S. R. R. lines, 147 Main, b. American.
Barret, Thos. teacher, St. Nicholas Church.
Barrett, Bridget, widow, grocery, across creek.
Barrett, John, lab. h. Albany n. School.
Barrett, Stephen, sailor, h. across creek.
Barrett, Stephen, cabinet maker, John n. N. Y. & E. Bank, b. 6½ Swan.
Barrowman, Moses, blacksmith, h. 188 9th.
Barrows, Chester, b. 217 Delaware.
Barrows, E. G. & Co. liquor and cigar dealers, 213 and 215 Washington.
Barrows, E. G. firm E. G. B. & Co. h. 217 Del.
Barrows, G. S. firm E. G. B. & Co. b. 29 Swan.
Barry, D. L. cooper, b. National Hotel.
Barry, Jas. blacksmith, b. 27 Ohio.
Barry, Jerry, shoemaker, room Spaulding's Ex.
Barry, John, ship carp. h. Fulton n. Alabama.
Barry, John, Ontario n. Tonawanda.
Barry, Timothy, lab. h. across creek.
Barse, Samuel, mariner, Pennsyl'a n. Niagara.
Bartel, Fred. saloon. Ellicott n. Genesee.
Bartel. Jno. C. barber, Erie n. Canal, h. Mich. n. Batavia.
Bartel, Markus, collector, h. 22 Maple.
Bartell, Christian. barber, h. 409 Michigan.
Bartell, Fred. b. Niagara n. Austin.
Bartell, Frank, carpenter, h. 205 S. Division.
Bartell, Geo. mechanic, h. 205 S. Division.
Bartell, Jacob, joiner, h. 11th n. North.
Bartell, Joseph, Jr. N. Y. C. R. R. freight office, 229 S. Division.
Bartell, Jos. car builder, h. 229 S. Division.
Bartell. Victor, joiner, h. 231 Ellicott.
Barth, Christian, cigar maker, 6 Spruce n. Gen.
Barth, Fred. tailor, 64 S. Division, b. same.
Barth, Frederick, clerk, 92 E. Gen. h. 42 Ash.
Barth, Jacob, blacksmith, Batavia n. Pratt.
Barth, Jacob, lab. Roos alley n. William.
Barth, John, blacksmith, h. 126 Elm.
Barth, John. cigar maker. 6 Spruce n. Genesee.
Barth. Joseph, lab. h. 294 Elm.
Barth, Ludwig, lab. h. 197 Ellicott.
Barth, Matthias, boarding, h. Ex. n. Michigan.
Barth, Philip, bakery, 5 Canal.
Barth, Regina, widow of John P. h. Spruce n. Genesee.
Barthauer, Charles F. barber, American Hotel, h. 120 Clinton.
Barthauer, L. widow, Martin Luther College, Maple n. Virginia.
Barthauer, William, with C. F. Barthauer, b. 120 Clinton.
Barthing, Geo. teacher, b. William n. Milnor.
Barthol, William, carp. h. Watson n. Peckham.
Bartholomew, A. machinist, h. 241 7th n. Md.
Bartholomew, Chas. clerk, h. 187 9th.
Bartholomew, C. h. Elk n. Alabama.
Bartholomew, J. D. carriage mak'r, h. 5 Church.
Bartholomew, Peter, clerk, 229 Main, b. 9th n. Hudson.

Bartlett, F. W. M. D. 70 Pearl, h. same.
BARTLETT, GEO. upholsterer, cor. Clinton and Hickory, h. 178 Oak.—See adv. p. 45.
Bartlett. Joseph, marine block, b. 35 Swan.
Bartlett, Mary Ann, widow, h. 29 E. Eagle.
Bartlett, Thos. engineer, lead w'ks, h. 3 Palmer.
Bartmann, G. W. tailor, b. 3 Court.
Barton, Benj. book-keeper, h. 90 E. Swan.
Barton, Charles, tally clerk. b. 25 Commercial.
Barton. Chas. B. N. Y. & E. freight office, b. 167 E. Seneca.
Barton, Hiram, attorney, 6 Hollister block, h. 141 Franklin.
Barton, Jas. L. h. 122 Pearl.
Barton, J. H. b. 122 Pearl.
Barton, Joseph A. clerk of str. City of Buff. h. 3 Carolina.
Barton, L. H. h. 146 9th.
Barton, Pliny F. machinist at Vulcan foundry, h. 62 6th.
Barton, Theo. contractor, h. 532 Main.
Barton, Wm sailor, h. 1 Scott.
Bartow, Catharine, widow, h. 109 Franklin.
Baskett, G. W. London Hotel, Niagara n. Auburn.
Bass, C. piano maker, with A. & J. Keogh.
Bass, L. K. attorney, 18 Spaulding's Exchange, b. 83 S. Division.
Bass, Smith, barber, h. William cor. Union.
Bassett, G. hats and caps, 161 Main, h. 34 S. Division.
Bastion, Michael, teamster, b. J. F. Hoffiens.
Bastion, Wm. lab. h. Syc. cor. Bundy's alley.
Batch, Christian, lab. h. 151 Oak.
Batch, Joseph, lab. h. East n. Farmer.
Bates, — b. National Hotel.
Bates, C. Mrs. milliner, 275 Main, entrance N. Division.
Bates, George, brick maker, with P. A. Balcom, h. Ferry n. Jefferson.
Bates, George, lab. h. 12 Elm.
Bates, Henry, brick maker, h. Ferry n. Main.
Bates, James, brick maker, h. Ferry n. Mich.
Bates John, log sawyer, with Pierce & Co. h. Perry n. Alabama.
Bates. Samuel, brick maker, with P. A. Balcolm. h. Main n. Ferry.
Bates, W. J. cabinet maker, h. Morgan n. Court.
Bates, W. L. M. D. at Buff. Gen. Hospital.
Bates, Wm. C. tinsmith, 259 Main, b. 5 Church.
Bates, Wm. J. moulder, 124 Court n. 4th.
Bath, Thos. jr. at elevator cor. Water and Morton, h. 12th n. Hudson.
Bath, Thos. clerk with J. Ganson, b. 12th ab. Hudson.
Bathgate, Wm. L. machinist, b. 203 Wash.
Batles, Matthew, lab. h. Sycamore n. Ash.
Bats, Philip D. painter, h, Batavia n. Monroe.
Batsch, Jno. lab. h. Best n. Michigan.
Batsford, R. b. American.
Batt, Anton. millinery, 125 Genesee.
Batten, James, moulder, h. Alabama n. Elk.
Battle, Henry, lab. h. 12th n. Rhode Island.
Batty, Charles, clerk, Howard W. & Co. h. 240 S. Division.
Batty, Phebe H. widow, h. 240 S. Division.
Batuy, Geo. F. tinsmith, 240 S. Division.
Batzel, Peter, lab. h. Mortimer n. Sycamore.

COMMERCIAL ADVERTISER DIRECTORY.

Banch, John, lab. h. Grey bet. Genesee and Batavia.
Bauer, Adam, lab. h. Spring n. Sycamore.
Bauer, Bartholomy, tailor, h. Genesee n. Jeff.
Bauer, Chas. tinshop, b. William n. Bennett.
Bauer, Christian, tailor, h. Cherry n. Spruce.
Bauer, Conrad, shoemaker, h. Elm n. North.
Bauer, Geo. tinsmith, h. r. 233 Ellicott.
Bauer, Jacob, blacksmith, Goodell n. Elm, h. same.
Bauer, John, cooper, h Niagara n. South.
Bauer, John, butcher, h. 68 Tupper.
Bauer, John Ed. shoemaker, h. 26 Bennett.
Bauer, John, butcher, b. Genesee cor. Elm.
Bauer, John C. farmer, h. Hickory n Genesee.
Bauer, John, lab. h. Walnut n. Batavia.
Bauer, John, lab. h. Elm n. Best.
Bauer, Maria, widow, h. 103 Cedar.
Bauer, Matilda, widow, h. Lovejoy n. Krettner.
Bauer. Wolfgang, lab. h. Hickory n. Genesee.
Bauerfeind, Fred. cabinet maker, h. Genesee opp. Adams.
Bauerlein, Joseph, lab. h. Monroe n. Sycamore.
Bauers, Henry, lab. h. 124 Walnut.
Baum, Chas. F. organist, h. cor. Cherry and Michigan.
Baum, Herman, barber, cor. Pearl and Terrace, b. Washington Hotel.
Baum, Otto, finisher, h. 8 Walnut.
Baum, Peter, shoemaker, b. 583 Main.
Bauman, Mrs. widow, h Ash n. Batavia.
Banman, Regina, widow, gardener, h. Elm n. Carlton.
Baumann, Geo. lab. h. Walnut n. Batavia.
Baumann, George, tailor, h. Goodell alley bel. Goodell.
Baumann, John, lab. h. Hickory n. Clinton.
Baumeister, Jacob, cabinet maker, h. Boston alley n. Tupper.
Baumeister, Margaret, Miss, dress maker, b. Hickory n. Sycamore.
Baumister, Mary Ann, widow, b. Hickory bel. Sycamore.
Baumgaerten, Chr. lab. h. Shumway n. Lovejoy.
Baumgarten, Fred. joiner, h. Syc. n. Hickory.
Baumgarten, Jacob, firm Beck & B. h. Oak n. Tupper.
Baumgartner, John. lab. German alley n. Gen.
Baumler, Conrad, lab. Walnut n. Sycamore.
Baumler, John, tailor, h. cor. Cypress and Pine.
Baumler, Lorenz, mason. h. Walnut n. Batavia.
Baumstark, Ægidius, carp. h. Maple n. Goodell.
Baush, John, peddler, h. 304 Elm.
Baust, Adam, with Rumsey & Co. h. Monroe n. Peckham.
Baust, Henry, mason, h Adams n. Sycamore.
Baut, Jos. plasterer, h. Hickory n. Batavia.
Bautz, Jacob, tinsmith, h. Elk n. Chicago.
Baxter, Peter, printer, h. 269 N. Div.
Bayer, Jacob, b. River bel. Erie.
Baylis, Chas. green grocer, 5 Scott, h. Delaware n. Barker.
Bayne, S. Wm. carp. h. Rogers n. Summer.
Beadle, Irwin P. news dealer, 227 Main, h. 5 Franklin.
Beafer, Henry, stone mason, h. Spruce n. Syc.
Beal, John, with West. Trans. Co. h. 103 7th.
Beale, Edward C. clerk, 54 Main, b. 132 Elm.

Beals, E. P. firm Pratt & Co. h. 82 Del.
Beals, Geo. firm D. C. Weed & Co. 222 Main, h. 222 S. Division.
Beals, Sam. b. Bonney's Hotel.
Beam, John, moulder, h. 137 Oak.
Beaman, Wm. F. bellows maker, h. Wm. n. Jeff.
Beamer, Josiah, lab. h. Eagle n. Hickory.
Beamer, Mrs. dress maker, h. Eagle n. Hickory.
Beamer, S. fruit store, 94 E. Seneca.
Bean, Dixon, with Hamlin & Mendsen, b. 139 Eagle.
Bean, Geo. tinsmith, with Rand & Felthonsen, b. Tremont House.
Bean, J. & W. M. house & sign painters, 171 Main.
Bean, Wm. M., firm J. & W. M. B. h. 207 Oak.
Bean, Wm. painter. 171 Main, h. 207 Oak.
Beanan, Nicholas, lab. h. Spring n. Genesee.
Beard, D. C. firm B. & Hayward, h. Franklin n. Tupper.
Beard, D. C. firm Gowans & B. h. Franklin ab. Tupper.
Beard, Garret, lab. b. towpath n. Genesee
Beard, Geo. C. clerk, b. D. C. Beard.
BEARD & HAYWARD, grocers, 165 Washington.—See adv. p. 58.
Beardsley, Abraham, N. Y. C. R. R. agent, h. Folsom n. Chicago.
Beardsley, Geo. P. painter, b. 5 Franklin.
Beardsley, Josiah, land agent, 190½ Main, h. 5 Franklin.
Beatson, Boswell, painter, h. Clinton n. Spring.
Beattie, John, clerk, 305 Main, b. 13 Court.
Beattie, John, coal weigher, h. Canal alley n. Jackson.
Beaty, Geo. machinist, h. Miami n. Alabama.
Beauschamp, P. stone cutter, b. 101 Ellicott.
Beche, Andreas, lab. h. Maple cor. Virginia.
Bechemeyer, Anton, lab. 3 Sycamore.
Becherer, F. shoe shop, Seneca n. junct. Swan, h. same.
Bechtol, Michael, police, h. Ash n. Sycamore.
Bechtold, Geo. lab. h. Ash n. Genesee.
Bechtold, Peter, marble cutter, h. Spruce n. Sycamore.
Beck, Benj. cigar maker, b. Monroe n. Peckh'm
Beck & Baumgarten, brewers, 209 Oak.
Beck, Chas. cigar maker, Cherry n. Hickory.
Beck, Chas. gardener, h. Genesee n. Johnson.
Beck, Chas. blacksmith, h. Peckham n. Stanton.
Beck, C. C. boat house, foot Erie, h. Joy n. Lake.
Beck, Erhard, lab. h. Watson bet. Batavia and Peckham.
Beck, Fred.* baker, Pratt n. Sycamore, h. same.
Beck, Fred. lab. h. Grey n. Batavia.
Beck, H. J. lab. h. Utica n. Rogers.
Beck, John, tailor, h. Mulberry n. Carlton.
Beck, John, mason, h. Watson n. Batavia.
Beck, John, cooper, h. Adams n. Peckham.
Beck, Jos. melodeon maker. b. 99 Batavia.
Beck, Magnus, firm B. & Baumgarten, h. 209 Oak.
Beck, Mathias, lab. h. Grey n. Genesee.
Beck, Michael,* blacksmith, Elk n. Mich. h. Sycamore n. Pratt.
Becker, Anson U. h. Canal n. Emslie.
Becker, Anthony, lab. h. 10th n. Hampshire.

Becker, Christian. brewer, h. Walnut n. Wm.
Becker, Chas. shoemaker, 20 S. Division, h. 321 Ellicott.
Becker, Christian, b. 358 Michigan.
Becker, Christian,* blacksmith, Peckham n. Watson, h. same.
Becker Christophe, lab. h. Krettner n. Batavia.
Becker, & Co. grocers, 384 Main.
Becker, Eve, wid. h. 522 Michigan.
Becker, Ferdinand, shoemaker, Seneca n. junction Swan, h. same.
Becker, Frank, lab. h. Spring cor. Hollister.
Becker, Fred. moulder, h. 358 Mich.
Becker, Geo. shoemaker, h. Ash n. Batavia.
Becker, Geo. shoemaker, h. 212 Elm.
Becker, Geo. clerk, b. Frank Fisher.
Becker, Herman, fish peddler, b. 32 Genesee.
Becker, Hugo, rectifier, cor. Clinton and Elm.
Becker, Jacob, cooper, h. Parish n. Thompson.
Becker, John, grocer, Genesee n. Jeff. h. same.
Becker, John, cigar maker, h. Mulberry n. Va.
Becker, John, grocer, n. cor. Mich. h. same.
Becker, John C. liquor dealer, h. Oak n. High.
Becker, J. P. grocer, 356 Michigan, h. same.
Becker, Joseph, h. 66 E. Tupper.
Becker, Lorenz, grocer, h. 72 Bennett.
Becker, Mathias, lab. h. 29 Hickory.
Becker, Nich. with Jewett & Root, Spruce n. Batavia.
Becker, Peter, lab. h. Spruce n. Batavia.
Becker, Peter, policeman, h. Spruce n. Batavia.
Becker, Peter, cartman, h. Lutheran n. Batavia.
Becker, Philip, firm P. B. & Co. h. 384 Main.
Becker, Philip & Co. grocers, 384 Main.
Becker, Valentine, ship carp. Bennett n. Bat.
Becker, Wm. moulder, h. William n. Cedar.
Beckert, P. wood worker, with Brayley & Pitts.
Beckle, Michael, organ builder, h. Hickory cor. Genesee.
Beckler, John, lab. h. 28 Exchange.
Beckman, Peter. millinery. 386 Main, h. same.
Beckmann, Frederick, lab. h. Carlton n. Maple.
Beckstein, Henry, rag peddler, h. Sycamore n. Spring.
Beckstein, Lorenz, cigar maker, b. H. Beckstein.
Becktle, Louis, b. Western.
Beckwith. A. L. clerk, N. Y. C. R. R. Erie, b. 20 Goodell.
Beckwith, Bros. & Co. com. merchants, 1 Central Wharf.
Beckwith, Chas. attorney, 302 Main, h. Clinton n. Monroe.
Beckwith, E. M. firm B. Bros. & Co. h. 20 Goodell.
Beckwith, E. M. clerk, 171 Main, b. 20 Goodell.
Beckwith, J. L. capt. h. Fulton n. Hayward.
Beckwith, L. W. contractor, h. 20 Goodell.
Bedford, John M. clerk, B. N. Y. & Erie freight office, b. 202 Swan.
Bedford. Lyman. agent, h. 15 Court.
Beebe, Henry C. Sergeant U. S. Army.
Beecher, Hiram S. clerk N. Y. & E. R. R. h. 32 S. Division.
Beecher, Jas. C. law student, b. 32 S. Division.
Beecher, J. C. student at law, b. 32 S. Div.
Beecher, S. A. Mrs. at St. James Hotel.
Beedle, Chas. lab. h. Carroll n. Jefferson.

Beehan, Martin, lab. h. across creek.
Beeler, F. J. saloon, 157 Main, h. 178 Wash.
Beemer, August, shoemaker, b. 6 Water.
Beemer, Sylvanus, saloon, 3 Custom house block, grocery and h. 94 Seneca.
Beer. Anne, carpet weaver, h. 79 Sycamore.
Beer, Joseph, lab. h. Ellicott n. Burton alley.
Beers, Alfred, M. D. 6 S. Division.
Begg, Robert, at Harris' marble works, h. cor. Main and Virginia.
Beheimer, Fred. peddler, h. 61 Cedar.
Behle, Frederick, tanner, h. Ash n. Batavia.
Behm, Chr. lab. h. Johnson n. Genesee.
Behn, Fred. civil and mechanical eng'r, Prosser's building. Pearl cor. Seneca, h. 96 Oak.
Behre, Frederick, carp. h. Lemon n. North.
Behrens, Andrew, carriage manuf'r, Va. cor. Ellicott, h. same.
Behringer, Anton. painter, h. 16 Bennett.
Behringer, August, cigar maker, 111 Genesee.
Behringer, Henry, butcher, h. 294 Elm.
Behringer, Henry, lab. h. Adam n Goodell.
Behringer & Klaes, butchers, 14 Niagara.
Behringer, Maria, b. P. Behringer.
Behringer, Peter, firm B. & Klaes, 14 Niagara. h. 115 Batavia.
Behrmann, Casper, lab. h. Johnson n. Genesee.
Beichy, Wm. barber, with H. Pierson, b. same.
Beicke, Wm. lab. h. Madison n. Peckham.
Beier, Frederick. clerk. h. Tupper n. Elm.
Beier, Michael, tailor, h. 104 Hickory.
Beier, Wm. lab. h. 14 Maple.
Beier, Ignatz, lab. h. Steel n. Walden.
Beierl, Max, carpenter, h. Grey n. Batavia.
Beierle, Joseph, tailor, h. Boston n. Goodell.
Beierlein, Geo. lab. h. Boston alley n. Barton alley.
Beierlein, John S. butcher, Washington market, h. 271 Elm.
Beierlein, John, printer, h. 255 Oak.
Beierlein, John, mason, h. 97 Cedar.
Beierlein, Otto, lab. h. 14th n. Connecticut.
Beigler, Chas. lab. h. Pratt n. Clinton in r.
Beil, Jacob, lab. h. 202 Elm.
Beil, John, blacksmith, Amherst n. Lewis.
Beil, Mary, widow, h. Best n. Main.
Beileman, Jacob, painter, h. Mulberry n. Va.
Beilmaier, Frank,* shoemaker, cor. Niagara and Amherst.
Beilman, Elizabeth. h. Milnor opp. Arsenal.
Beilstein, Jacob, lab. h. Maple n. Carlton.
Beimler, John, bricklayer, h. 255 Elm.
Beimler, Joseph, silver plater, Carlton n. Orange.
Beimler. Theodore. farmer, h. Carlton n. Lemon.
Being, Henry. carpenter, h. 10 Bennett.
Beirne, Pat. T. h. 46 W. Tupper.
Beiser, L. Ph. A. boarding house, Washington cor. Huron.
Beisser, Frederica, Mrs. h. 274 Elm.
Beisser, Fred. teamster. h. 274 Elm.
Bekcken. F. tailor, h. Hickory n. William.
Beke. H.. N. Y. C. R. R. h. 120 William.
Beker. Henry, with George L. Fowler, h. 11 Sycamore.
Belden, C. b. Western.
Belden. E. D. teller Farmer and Mechanics Bank, b. D. Belden, Niagara square.

Belden, Dexter, h. Niagara square ab. Court.
Belden, H. clerk, People's line, b. cor. Oak and Swan.
Beler, Frank, musician, h. 30 Goodell.
Bell, Brampton, grocer, 22 E. Eagle, h. same.
BELL DAVID, steam eng. works, Norton n. Water, h. Swan cor. Mich.—*See adv. p. 55.*
Bell, Francis, pattern maker, 16 Water, h. Blossom n. Koon's alley.
Bell, John, blacksmith, h. 271 Exchange.
Bell, John, joiner, h. 13th n. Massachusetts.
Bell, John, cooper, h. Alabama n. Mackinaw.
Bell, Robert W. cabinet maker, 161 Washington, h. 24 Green.
Bell, Wm. cooper, h. Mackinaw n. Tenessee.
Bell, Wm. pattern maker, h. Blossom n. Koon's alley.
Bellein, Joseph, lab. h. Monroe n. Sycamore.
Beller, Peter, lab. h. Batavia cor. Williamsville road.
Belles, John, tailor, h. 143 Walnut.
Belliett, Henry, cigar maker, at 263 Main, b. 33 Genesee.
Bellinger, Franz, carpenter, h. Elm. cor. Va.
Bellinger, Henry, teamster, Niag. cor. Austin.
Bellows, Wm. E. blacksmith, b. Elk n. Chicago.
Belton, Henry, foreman in workhouse, h. York cor. 5th.
Belton, Wm. P. b. 104 Exchange.
Belvy, Wm. painter, b. cor. Market and Perry.
Belzer, Jacob, tailor, h. Cedar n. William.
Bem, John, lab. h. Walnut n. Batavia.
Bemer, Martin, on Main St. R. R. b. Mrs. J. S. Miller.
Bement, Annie M. teacher, b. Del. n. North.
Bement, Daniel H. boatman, h. East n. Ham'n.
Bement, R. widow, h. Delaware n. North.
Bement, W. H. liquors, &c., Merchant's Exch. h. cor. Delaware and Chippewa.
Bemis, Asaph S. Com'l. cor. Terrace, b. Mrs. Sidway.
Bemis, Aurelia, widow, h. 109 Franklin.
Bemis, E. St. John, office 6 and 7 Ohio cor. Miss. h. 271 Washington.
Bemis, Philo S. ship chandler, 6 and 7 Ohio, b. 271 Washington.
Bemisch, Antone, mason, h. Genesee n. Grey.
Bemish, Richard, ship carp. h. Miami n. La.
Bemler, F. lab. b. 123 William.
Bemler, J. baker, h. 123 William.
Bemler, W. carp. h. William n. Hickory.
Bemsley, Christian, lab. h. Ash n. Batavia.
Bender, Geo. Fred. printer, Buffalo Telegraph, h. Mulberry n. Virginia.
Bender, M. ship carp, h. Milnor opp. Arsenal.
Bender, Philip H. prop'r Buffalo Telegraph, 358 Main, h. 213 Oak.
Bendoerfer. Jno. lab. h. 265 Elm.
Benedict, Elenora, wid. washer, h. Elk n. Mich.
Benedict, Ezra T. teacher Public School No 5, h. 89 Niagara.
Benedict, John, worker in plaster paris, h. cor. Michigan and Perry.
Benedict, Nathan, principal Public School No. 2. b. 158 Seneca.
Benham, Thomas, cigar maker, b. J. Schaller.
Benjamin, Lysander, h. Spring bet. Seneca and Swan.

Beninger, Geo. lab. h. Chenango n. Ferry.
Benlinhof, Martin, tailor, h. Walnut n. Batavia.
Bennett, Alex. capt. h. 10th n. Virginia.
Bennett, A. L. book-keeper, Clinton Bank, b. Courter House.
Bennett, Alezo, cooper, b. Washington n. Ohio.
Bennett, David, coachman S. V. R. Watson.
Bennett, D. S. elevator, cor. dock and Water, b. American.
Bennett, Daniel C. engineer. h. Wm. n. Walnut.
Bennett, Edward, firm Miller, B. & Co. 14 Water, b. cor. Pine and Eagle.
Bennett, Edward, policeman, 7 5th.
Bennett, Elijah, cooper, Mortimer n. William, h. Adams n. William.
Bennett, Emeline, widow, b. 369 Washington.
Bennett, Edward, b. 44 Pearl.
Bennett, Frank, moulder, h. 94 Elm.
Bennett, James, ship carp. h. Perry cor. Mich.
Bennett, Jas. P. butcher, 17 Elk St. Market, h. Louisiana n. Carroll.
Bennett, Jas. S. with Hamlin & Mendsen, b. 5 Franklin.
Bennett, Lewis, lab. Clinton bel. R. R. crossing.
Bennett, L. S. with S. Bennett, 128 Main.
Bennett, Philander, cor. Pine and Eagle.
Bennett, S. clothing store, 126 and 128 Main and 1 and 2 Terrace, h. 16 Oak.
Bennett, Seymour, clerk canal collector's office, h. Ellicott cor. Virginia.
Bennett, Stephen, carp. h. 14th n. Vermont.
Benseler, Fred, upholsterer, b. 156 Batavia.
Benseler, Herman, cabinet maker, 156 Batavia, h. same.
Benson & Co. tea and coffee dealers, 313 Main.
Benson, Christian, shingle sawyer, Pierce & Co. h. 17 Ash.
Benson, D. D. clerk at 205 Main, h. Franklin n. North.
Benson. E. A. clerk 316 Main, b. Franklin n. North.
Benson, James, lab. b. 189 Exchange.
BENSON JOHN, confectioner, 131 Main, h. Franklin n. North.—*See adv. p. 47.*
Benson, Michael, sailor, h. Seneca n. Hamburgh.
Benson, Robt. P. b. 63 Delaware.
Benson, S. h. 63 Delaware.
Benstead, Edward, lab. h. Elk n. N. Y. & Erie R. R. track.
Benstead, John, farmer, h. n. Tifft's farm.
Benstead, Richard, blacksmith, h. Elk bet. Van Rensselaer and Smith.
Bentley, Geo. W. last maker, with H. Wing & Co. h. 98 Carroll.
Bentley, Geo. T. with J. R. Bentley & Co. h. 21 Ellicott.
Bentley, J. G. freight agent, b. Franklin House.
BENTLEY, J. R. & CO. com. mers. 17 Cent'l Wharf.—*See adv. p. 36.*
Bentley, J. R. firm J. R. B. & Co. h. 7 Beston block, Niagara.
Bentley, B. S. watchmaker, 189 Main, b. West'n.
Bentley, B. b. Western.
Benton, R. O. ambrotype goods and gilt frames, over 204 Main, b. 20 Ellicott.
Beny, David, watchman, h. 214 N. Division.
Bentz, Bernhard, cooper, h. Walnut n. Batavia.
Bentz, Henry, cooper, h. Spring n. Bristol.

Bentz, Henry, Jr. cooper, b. Spring n. Bristol.
Bentz, Nicholas, lab. h. Grey n. Genesee.
Bentz, Sam. shoemaker, h. 105 Genesee.
Benz, Geo. cook, h. 396 Michigan.
Benz, John, lab. h. Potter n. Gay.
Benz, John, Jr. painter, b. J. Benz, Sr.
Benz, Sophia, h. 249 Elm.
Benz, Xavier, tailor, h. Mulberry cor. Virginia.
Benzine, Margaret, widow, saloon, 335 N. Div
Benzing, Gott. N. grocer, Clinton cor. Madison.
Benzing, Jacob, carpenter, h. 22 Bennett.
Benzinger, Chris. grocer, h. Clinton cor. Jeff'n.
Benzinger, Conrad, lab. h. 528 Mich.
Benzinger, Jacob, mason, h. Jeff'n cor. Clinton.
Benzinger, John, milkman, h. Jeff'n n. Clinton.
Benzinger, Jos. Mrs. widow, saloon keeper, 219
  Washington.
Berch, Jno. musician, h. Bundy alley, n. Syc.
Berche, John, tailor, h. 158 Genesee.
Bercher, Geo. lab. h. Sherman N. of Genesee.
Bercht, Martin, machinist, h. 207 Elm.
Berck, Charles, cigar maker, b. junc. Genesee
  and Huron.
Berend, Mathias, shoemaker, h. Watson n. Ba-
  tavia.
Bergen, John, machinist, h. Howard n. Watson.
Berger, Christine, widow, h. Roos alley.
Berger, Gus. mason, h. Hinckley n. Mortimer.
Berger, Mathias, lab. h. Mulberry n. Va.
Berger, Moritz, musician, h. Genesee n. Spruce.
Berger, Philip, blacksmith, b. Hinkley n. Mort.
Berghauser, Adam, lab. h. Walden n. Steele.
Berghauser, Conrad, lab. ■ Steele n. Walden.
Berghauser, Peter, teamster, h. Steele n. Main.
Bergin, James, coachman, T. D. Barton, h. 253
  Franklin.
Bergin, Mathew, machinist, h Hayward n.
  Perry.
Bergholz, Charles, lab. h. 13 Cherry.
Bergholz, Fred. lab. h. Boston alley ab. Tupper.
Bergholz, Wm. lab. b. Boston alley ab. Tupper.
Bergman, Frank, cooper, h. Mortimer n. Wm.
Bergman, Henry, lab. h. William n. Cedar.
BERGMAN, S. & CO. clothing store, 142 & 198
  Main.—See adv. p. 87.
Bergman, S. firm S. B. & Co. h. 31 S. Div.
Bergmann, William, tailor, h. 215 Ellicott.
Bergtold, Catharine, wid. of John, h. 78 Wm.
Bergtold, Charles A. news depot, 147 Main, b.
  10 6th.
Bergtold, Daniel, carpenter. h. 230 Oak.
Bergtold, Jacob E. b. 10 6th.
Bergtold, Louis B. clerk, cor. Eagle and Frank-
  lin, b. 10 6th.
Berhorst, Wm. tailor, h. Wash. n. Chippewa.
Berkhause, Wm. tanner, h. 158 Clinton.
Berlin, Louis, grocer, 560 Seneca, h. same.
Bernard, Peter, lab. h. Carroll bel. Alabama.
Berndt, Mathias, coach painter, b. Ellicott n.
  Goodell.
Berner, John, mason, h. Monroe n. Batavia.
Bernerer, Gertrude, Mrs. h. Goodell alley ab.
  Tupper.
Bernhard, Chris. cooper, h. Thompson n. Ham-
  ilton.
Bernhardt, Christ. shoemaker, h. Ellicott cor.
  Burton alley.
Bernhardt, George, lab. h. 38 Cherry.

Bernheimer, J. E. store, 61 Ellicott, h. same.
Bernhoft, Geo. lab. h. Batavia cor. Pratt
Bernitzky, Charles, tailor, h. 225 Ellicott.
Berns, Fred. lab. h. Porter n. Van Rensselaer.
Bernstein, Sam'l. tailor, h. cor. Oak & Tupper.
Bernstone, Aaron, peddler, h. Folsom n. Jeff'n.
Berqul, T. painter, h. Clinton n. Walnut.
Berrick, Charles, mason, h. 288 S. Division.
Berry, Clinton R clerk, 14 Union.
Berry, Elizabeth W. M. D. h. 271 S. Division.
Berry, D. H. foreman Starkey & Co. n. Ohio
  basin, b. National Hotel.
Berry, James, lab. h. cor. Carolina & Tupper.
Berry, Joseph, painter, b. James Berry.
Berry, Mark, painter, b. James Berry.
Berry, Royal, N. Y. C. freight house, h. 60 Oak.
Berry, Philip, miller, h. Niagara n. Sloan.
Berry, Wm. painter, b. James Berry.
Berry, W. S. harness maker, b. 435 Main.
Berry, Wm. grocer. Forest ave. n. Washington.
Berry, W. W. conductor street cars, h. over
  435 Main.
Berryman, Charles, saloon, 16 Main, h. same.
Bersch, Joseph, tailor, h. 195 Ellicott.
Bersch, M. M. tailor, b. 195 Ellicott.
Bersch, Jno. moulder, h. Sycamore n. Ash.
Bersch, Johanna, midwife, h. 82 Sycamore.
Berst, Michael, on lake, h. 240 Elm.
Berst, F. J. machinist, h. 29 William.
Berst, Maria E. widow, b. 240 Elm.
Berstch, Christian, lab. h. Carlton n. Jefferson.
Berthing, John, Jr. book-keeper, b. Spring n.
  Cherry.
Bertling, Rhinhard, cooper, h. 139 Spring.
Bertram, Louis, carpenter, h. Maple n. Va.
Besancon, Felicien, saloon, cor. Oak and Syc.
Besancon, Frank, lab. h. Cherry n. Virginia.
Besnah, Philip, ship carp. h. Swan n. Jeff'n.
Bessart, Philip, bakery, 10th cor. Maryland.
Besse, Henry, lab. Batavia opposite tollgate.
Besser, Gottlob J. saloon, cor. Wm. and Pratt.
Besser, Gus. A. painter, b. Wm cor. Pratt.
Besser, Otto, clerk, h. William cor. Pratt.
Bessir, J. W. E. bookstore, 27 Genesee, b. Wm.
  cor. Pratt.
Bessmen, Jno. saloon, 309 Genesee. h. same.
Besstak, Jos. baker, h. Wm. cor. Mortimer.
Best, Chas. stove mounter, h. Oak n. Carlton.
Best, Chas. A. liquors and cigars, 180 Washing-
  ton. h. 231 Franklin.
Best, Frank Digley, teacher, h. 44 Blossom alley.
Best, Henry, iron works, h. N. Washington n.
  Clinton avenue.
Best, Joseph, sawyer, h. Alabama n. Fulton.
Best, Melchior, cooper, h. Mulberry n. Carlton.
Best, Robert H. agt. Am. Express Co. Mohawk.
Best, Peter, h. 106 Chippewa.
Best, Wm. F. dep. col. of customs, h. 36 Pine.
Besth, Mathias, lab. h. Sycamore n. Ash.
Betger, August, lab. h. Grey n. Genesee.
Bettinger & Co. dry goods. 399 Main.
Bettinger, Stephen, firm B. & Co. h. Franklin
  n. North.
Bettinger, Sebastian, cabinet maker, h. Pratt
  n. Clinton.
Betts, Hiram, foreman N. Y. C. R. R. b. Revere
  House.
Bettis, Henry A. 223 7th.

Bettis, Sallie, midwife, h. 48 Morgan.
Bettis, Sarah, Miss, teacher No. 8, b. 48 Morgan.
Betz, Ferdmand, produce dealer, Clinton Market, h. 111 Pine.
Betz, Henry, teamster, h. Ketchum n. Carlton.
Betz, Henry, Sr. potter, h. Genesee n. Sherman.
Betz, John, butcher, h. cor. Alabama & Perry.
Betz, Philip, Eagle Furnace, h. Hick'y n. Clin.
Betzendorfer, John, lab. h. Bat. n. Lutheran.
Betzer, Anton, shoemak'r, h. Emslie n. Lovejoy.
Betzhold, August, carp. h. bet. Jeff. and Walden.
Betzhold, Fred. shoemak'r, h. W'lden cor. Ferry.
Betzhold, John, lab. h. Maple n. Goodell.
Betzold, John, lab. h. Ketchum alley n. High.
Betzmeyer, Andrew, milk-dairy, h. Walden N. of Best.
Beuchat, Jos. furnaceman, h. Ellicott n. Burton alley.
Beuerleia, Jno. lab. h. Batavia n. Emslie.
Beuermann, August, lab. h. Pratt n. Genesee.
Beutler, Jacob, butcher, h. Pine n. Batavia.
Bever, Nich. shoemaker, Watson n. Peckham.
Beyer, Andreas, saloon, Cherry n. Maple.
Beyer, Andrew, lab. h. Adams n. Syracuse.
Beyer, Ernst, bakery, 238 Genesee, h. same.
Beyer, Frederick, lab. h. same.
Beyer, George, farmer, h. Main n. Eley Road
Beyer, Henry, carp. h. Monroe bet. Batavia and Sycamore.
Beyer, Jacob, mason, h. Walnut n. Genesee.
Beyer, Jacob, dry goods, h. 113 Genesee.
Beyer, Louis, * pump maker, Mich. cor. Cherry, h. same.
Beyer, Mart. daguerrean, h. 538 Michigan.
Beyer, Philip, dry goods and groceries, 430 Main. h. same.
Beyer, Phil. grocer, 482 Mich. h. same.
Beyer, Wm. H. book-keeper Howard, Whitcomb & Co b. 430 Main.
Beyerby, Geo. lab. h. Seneca at Hydraulics.
Beyerman, August, lab. h. Pratt bet. Genesee and Sycamore.
Beyers, Wm. bl'cksmith, Main n. Puffer, h. same.
Beze, John, lab. h. White's Corners plank road, near city line.
Bhilk, Henry, tailor, at 64 S. Div. b. same.
Bibus, John, lab. h. Mulbery n. Virginia.
Bibus, Michael, milkman, h. 204 Elm.
Bibus, Valentine, lab. h. Mulberry n. Virginia.
Bichel, Geo. carp. h. 11 Roos alley.
Bichelweier, Anthony, lab. h. Pine n. Cypress.
Bichy, Henner, tailor, h. 6 Maple.
Bick, Henry, at C. R. R. h 120 William.
Bickel, Baptist, butcher, h. Batavia n. Johnson.
Bickel, John G. paints and glass, Ellicott cor. Genesee, h. same.
Bickelman, Conrad, mason, h. Mich. n. North
Bickelman, Geo. mason, h. Michigan n. North.
Bickelmann, Sebastian, milkman, h. Oak n. North.
Bickle, Geo. lab. h. Elm n. North.
Bidaman. J. ironw'ks, b. N. Wash.'n. Bird ave.
Biddalcom, Walt. mason, h. Miami n. La.
Biddell, Jos. lab. h. Ferry n. Massachusetts.
Biddle, Francis X. teamster, h Walnut, n. Wm.
Bidner, Leonhart, lab. h. Lutheran n. Bat.
Bidwell, Alfred B. book-keeper, Bidwell and Mason, h. Niagara n. Bidwell.

Bidwell, B. S. book-keeper, h. 227 7th.
Bidwell, Benj. H. Cottage cor. Muryland.
Bidwell, Charles S. firm Mason & B. h. Elk n. Hayward.
Bidwell, D. D. police justice, office 1st police station, h. 216 Niagara.
Bidwell, J. H. custom house, h. Elk ab. Ala.
Bidwell, Vincent, marine inspector, cor. Lloyd, h. 72 Seneca.
Bieber, Jacob, lab. h. Peckham cor. Emslie.
Bieber, Peter, police, h. 106 Tupper.
Biegeler, August, st'n mason, h. Watson n. Bat.
Bielhen, Fred. cooper, h. Hollister n. Spring.
Bierlem, Geo. lab. h. Goodell cor. Goodell aly.
Bierma, Hen. confectioner, 350 Main, h. same.
Bierma, Ralph, 131 Main, h. 52 Tupper.
Bierma, Rudolf, confec'ner, h. 72 E. Tupper.
Biermann, Wm. 28 Central Wharf, h 536 Mich.
Bierwert. John, butcher, h. Peckham cor. Jeff.
Biesenthal, Solomon, salesman, Altman & Co. h. 97 Ellicott.
Bigelow, Samuel A. h. 107 Niagara. *
Bigelow, Samuel O. 16 Central Wharf, b. 107 Niagara.
Bigelow, Wm. H. com. merch. 15 Central wharf, b. 107 Niagara.
Bignall, Elizabeth, Miss, music teacher, b. College n. Virginia.
Bignall, Elizabeth, widow, h. College n. Va.
Bibl, Casper, lab. h. Batavia n. Watson.
Bibl, John. lab. h. Walnut n. Batavia
Bilas, Mathias, lab. h. Sycamore n. Ash.
Billeb, Ernst, grocer, Bat. cor. Grey, h. same.
Biller, John, lab. h. Fox. n. Genesee.
Biller, Jno. M. milk peddler, h. Grey n. Gen.
Biller, John, lab. h. Fox n. Genesee.
Biller, Michael, lab. h. 443 Michigan.
Biller, M. foundryman, with Brayley & Pitts.
Billey, W. E. carp. h. 44 Court.
Billings, Amelia S. Miss, teacher No. 10 School, b. 27 Ellicott.
Billings, C. F. clerk, h. 101 Clinton.
Billings & Dickson, shipbrokers, 29 C. Wharf.
Billings, Francis P. ship agent, 29 C. Wharf, h. 111 Clinton.
Billings, Harriet, boarding, h. 27 Ellicott.
Bilz, Jos. grocer, Genesee cor. Elm, h. same.
Bimler, John, carp. h. 31 Cherry.
Bindeman, F. W. Jr. with W. S. Abbott, b. 6 Court.
Binder, David, gardener, h. Herman, N. of Gen.
Binder, John, lab. h. Hickory n. Genesee.
Binder, Marzoff, cooper shop, Tonawanda n. Hamilton.
Binder, Sebastian, lab. h. 210 Genesee.
Bindofer, Paul, shoemaker, cor. Niagara and Amherst.
Binga, John, lab. h. 10 Milnor.
Bingel, Conrad, lab. h. Genesee E. tollgate.
Bingenheimer, Philip, lab. h. 95 Cherry.
Bingerman, Jacob, lab. h. Best cor. Mich.
Bingham, Robert, plane maker, h. cor. Howard and Adams.
Bingham, Robt. tool mak'r, h. How'd n. Monroe.
Bingham, Robt. M. firm Eddy & B. h 189 Del.
Bingham, Wm. mason, h. Mich. n. High.
Binighoff, J. widow, b. Spring n. Genesee.
Bippert, George, gardener, h. Walden n. Ferry.

Birch, Elizabeth, wid. washerwoman, h. Perry n. Delaware.
Bird, John, brickmaker, h. Rase n. Clinton.
Bird, Wm. A. Sr. president Erie Co. Savings Bank, h. Niagara n. Albany.
Bird, Wm. A. Jr. firm Chase & B. h. Niagara n. Breckenridge.
BIRGE & Co. paper hanging warehouse, 174 Main.—See adv. p. 73.
Birge, Martin H. paper hanging merchant, h. 79 N. Division.
Birgler, Isodore, mason, h. Bennett n. Bat.
Birkuer, Paul, rag peddler, h. Watson n. Peckham.
Birle, Geo. brickmaker, Clinton bel. R. R. crossing.
Birnback, Jos.* shoemaker, Mich. n. S. Div. h. Walnut n. Batavia.
Birner, Christoph, lab. h. Oak n. North.
Bisantz, Magdalena, widow. h. Gen. n. tollgate.
Biscoff, Caspar, carpenter, h. Grey n. Batavia.
Biscoff, Geo. lab. h. Jefferson n. Carlton.
Biscoff, Henry, turner, h. 251 Elm.
Bisgood, Henry V. 216 Wash. h. 16 Clinton.
Bisgood, Wm. clerk, 438 Main, b. cor. Court and Pearl.
Bishop, Alex. yardman, h. Washington, under Presbyterian Church.
Bishop, Henry, turner, with S. D. Sikes.
Bishop, James, wagon maker, h. Perry n. Ala.
Bishop, Jas. D. derrick business, h. Palmer n. Virginia.
Bishop, John. b. Niagara n. Hamilton.
Bishop, Stephen. miller, h. Niag. n. Hamilton.
Bishop, Vernon B. cl'k Pratt & Co. b. 27 Ellicott.
Bishop, Vernon D. at Pratt & Letchworth, b, 29 Ellicott.
Bissel, Edward, Mrs. h. Wash. n. Chippewa.
Bissell, Arthur, student. b. Del. cor. Butler.
Bissell, Harvey, with Breed, Butler & Co. b. Michigan n. Swan.
Bissell, Jno. forwarding and com. 7 Central Wharf, h. Delaware n. Utica.
Bissell. Leavitt F. attorney, 3 Brown's Building, h. Main n. Riley.
Bissell, Sheldon & Co. com. merchants. 7 Central Wharf.
Bissinger, Francis, carpenter, h. 270 Elm.
Bissinger, Frederick, cooper, h. 407 Michigan.
Bits, Chas. at Evans' planing mill.
Bitsche, Geo. peddler, h. Grey n. Genesee.
Bittack, Wm. carpenter, h. Elm n. Genesee.
Bittel, Frank, lab. h. Walnut n. William.
Bittermann, Geo. carpenter, h. Genesee bet. Jefferson and Adams.
Bixby, J. W. clerk with C. E. Noble, h. Palmer W. Maryland.
Bixby, Robert, b. Palmer n. Maryland.
Bixby, Robert, b. 36 W. Seneca.
Bixler, Adeline, seamstress, h. Hickory n. Wm.
Black & Alexander, clothing, 10 Coml. 98 and 160 Main.
Black, Hugh, Captain, h. 66 5th.
Black, Isaac, clothing, 10 Commercial.
Black, Isaac, firm B. & Alexander, 33 S. Div.
Black, J. H. with Sherman & Barnes, b. cor. Swan and Oak.
Blackmann, Mary, wid. seamstress, h. 81 Syc.

Blackman, Geo. track master N. Y. C. R. R. b. 315 Exchange.
Blackmar & Gilbert, com. mchts. 13 Central Wharf and malt house Main cor. Ferry.
Blackmar, A. T. firm B. & Gilbert, h. 309 Franklin.
Blackmar, C. V. D. b. 309 Franklin.
Blackmond, Ed. F. grocer, Ferry cor. Adams.
Blackmond. E. F. Jr. with C. E. Felton, h. 200 Washington.
Blade, Charles, h. Michigan n. S. Division.
Bladel, Chas. wood worker, with Brayley & Pitts.
Bladen, Jacob, moulder, b. B. Bladen.
Bladen, Philip, moulder, b. B. Bladen.
Blaestegner, Michael, carp. h. n. Tifft's farm.
Blain, Jacob, agent, h. 19 N. Division.
Blakeley, Joseph, liquor dealer, h. Niagara n. Hudson.
Blakeley, J. & W. fruit store and oysters, 31 Main.
Blakeley, Robt. stone cutter, h. Md. n. Cottage.
Blakeley, Wm. firm. J. & W. B. 31 Main, h. 258 Franklin.
Blanchard, Amos A. attorney, 9 Spaulding's Exchange. h. 35 Niagara.
Blanchard, F. U. S. recruiting service. 83 Main.
Blanchard, Geo. engineer, h. Ferry n. R. R. track.
Blanchard. H. C. M. D. 290 Main cor. Eagle, h. Bloomer's.
Blanchard, William, saloon, cor. Niag. & Ferry.
Blancheit, Edward, lake capt. h. 182 Niagara.
Blanck, Charles F. shoemaker, 120 Walnut.
Blanck, Daniel, tailor, h. Maple ab. Goodell.
Blaney, James, shipwright, h. Fulton n. Red Jacket.
Blaser, Joseph, grocer, h. Sycamore cor. Pratt.
Blattner, Mary, Miss. seamstress, b. 118 Batavia.
Blatz, Melcher, cooper, h. Niagara n. Austin.
Blatz, Michael, tailor, h. Mulberry n. Goodell.
Blauvelt, Jno. A. carp. h. 61 W. Chippewa.
Blazel, Geo. blacksmith. h. Burton alley n. Va.
Bleadel, Barbara, chair bottoming, h. Hickory n. Genesee.
Bleamister, Frederick, lab. h. Spring n. William.
Blecher, Caroline, Miss. milliner, b. 152 Batavia.
Blecher, Mary, widow, seamstress, h. Cherry n. Jefferson.
Blecher, Geo. mason, h. Cherry n. Jefferson.
Blecher, John, carpenter, h. 35 Ash.
Bleiler, Casper, saloon, cor. Commercial and Water, h. same.
Bleiler, Henry, painter, 11 Swan, h. over cor. Elm and Genesee.
Bleimaster, Chas. lab. b. F. Spalman, Martin's Corners.
Bleitzer, John, shoemaker, h. 51 Chippewa.
Blendinger, Conrad, tailor, h. Goodell alley n. Burton alley.
Blendinger, John, lab. h. Peach n. North.
Blessing, Jacob, blacksmith, 392 S. Division.
Blettner, Jno. Rev. St. Michael's church.
Bleyer, Frederick, carp. h. Pratt n. Batavia.
Blicher, Geo. lab. h. Adams opp. Sycamore.
Blim, Casper, lab. h. Stephen n. Walden.
Bliss, H. L. ambrotype gallery over 293 Main, h. 295 Main.

Bliss, Madam, pattern emporium, 295 Main.
Block, Catherine. widow, h. 54 Goodell.
Blodgett & Bradford, music store, 209 Main.
Blodgett, J. R. firm B. & Bradford, b. St. James.
Blodgett, Wm. H. banker, Main cor. Terrace, h. 19 Oak.
Bloesing, Henry, lab. b. N. Hiernenz 118 Bat.
Blood, Ira D. melodeon maker, h. 10th ab. Hudson.
Blood, Wm. on N. St. R. R.
Bloom, Geo. tailor, 45 Main.
Bloom, Jacob, police, h. 126 Court.
Bloome, Robert, finisher, h. Ohio n. Wash.
Bloomer, Tooker T. Bloomer's Hotel, 1 West Eagle.
Blossom, Albert, clerk, city assessor, b. Mrs. Blossom.
Blossom, Ira A. Mrs. cor. Erie and Franklin.
Blossom, Mrs. widow, h. Niagara n. Hamilton.
Blossom, Samuel, miller, Queen Ctty Mills, b. with Mrs. Blossom.
Blossom, Thos. dept. post master, h. 10 Swan
Bloust, John, stave cutter, h. E. n. Hamilton.
Blusac, Thos. cartman, h. 11th n. Rh. Island.
Blum, Jacob, shoemaker, h. 108 Batavia.
Blum, Peter, grocer, 12 Huron, h. same.
Blum, Peter, saloon, Pine n. Clinton, h. same.
Blume, Robert, machinist, 14 Court, h. Ohio n. Main.
Blumenberg, Wm. grocer, 154 Batavia, h. same.
Blumenroeder, E. lab. h. Walnut n. Batavia.
Blumenstein, Augustus, shoemaker, h. Adams n. Genesee.
Blumenthal, Chris. carp. h. Thompson n. Hamilton.
Blumhoffer, Anton, lab. h. Hickory n. Syc.
Blundell, Peter, painter, h. Louisiana n. Perry.
Blust, Adam, cooper, h. Spring n. William.
Blust, Gustavius, cooper, h. Spring n. William.
Blust, Geo. cooper, h. Jefferson n. Batavia.
Blust, John, lab. h. East n. Hamilton.
Bly, Theodore. clothing, h. Maiden lane.
Board of Trade, 5 Central Wharf.
Boardman, Conrad, lab. h. Seneca n. Heacock.
Boardman, Geo. firm Benson & Co. 313 Main, 16 E. Eagle.
Boardman, J. M. D. 4 W. Eagle, h. same.
Boardman, J. R. S. firm Case & Co. h. 195 S. Division.
Boardman, Matthew, capt. h. Fulton n. Hayward.
BOAS, S. fine groceries, etc. 234 Main, h. same. See adv. p. 50.
Boasberg, N. second hand clothing dealer, 5 Commercial, h. same.
Boast, Matthew, moulder, h. Markham cor. Gay.
Bobach, Joseph, lab. h. Genesee n. Jefferson.
Bobach, Wm. sailor, h. Cherry n. Jefferson.
Bocard, John, shoemaker, h. W. cor. plank road n. city line.
Bochart, Horace, clerk at Wash. cor. Scott, b. same.
Bochmann, Gustavius, turner, 102 E. Genesee.
Bochmer, Henry A. carp. h. 173 Oak.
Bochner, Stephen, blacksmith, h. Cherry n. Spring.
Bock, Chas. watchman at Bush & Hayward's tannery, h. Kaene n. Genesee.

Bock, Christoph, printer, h. 191 Ellicott.
Bock, Christopher, printer, h. 191 Ellicott.
Bock, Fr. mason, h. Madison n. Batavia.
Bock, Jocob, carpenter. h. 177 Batavia.
Bock, Philip, carp. h. Green n. Batavia.
Bockstedt, Henry, cartman, h. Grey n. Batavia.
Bodamer, Frederick, blacksmith, h. 4 Maple.
Bodamer, Gottlieb,* brewer, h. Genesee n. toll-gate.
Bodamer, J. with J. Alberger, h. 5th n. Georgia.
Bodamer, John, butcher, h. Maple n. Virginia.
Bode, Wm. carp. h. 73 Maple.
Bodkin, Patrick, joiner, h. across creek.
Bodwell, Bailey, carpenter, h. 135 E. Seneca.
Bodwell, Frank, clerk, with N. Jancs, b. 135 Seneca.
Boeber, Chas. painter, h. Cedar n. William.
Boechat, Francis, shoemaker, 12 Commercial, h. same.
Boechner, Stephen, lab. h. Cherry n. Jefferson.
Boeckmann, Fred. cabinet maker, h. Jefferson n. Peckham.
Boeheim, Fred. with H. Thompson, h. Cedar n. William.
Boeheim, Henry, lab. h. Cedar n. Batavia.
Boehler, Joseph, lab. h. William n. Cedar.
Boehm, Gottfrey, leather dealer, 224 Genesee, b. same.
Boehm, Henry, carp. b. Philip Boehm.
Boehman, Christopher, turner, S. Division n. R. R. crossing.
Boehme, Philip, mason, h. Adams n. Howard.
Boebmer, Albrecht, shoemaker, h. Adams n. Genesee.
Boehmer, Henry, lab. h. Adams n. Brown.
Boehringer, Jacob, carp. h. Mulberry n. Va.
Boehringer, J. M. lab. h. Lemon n. Carlton.
Boere, Jno. lab. h. Adams n. Sycamore.
Boerner, Fred. musician, b. cor. Wash. and Gen
Boesinger, John, lab. h. Walnut n. Sycamore.
Boever, Chas. teamster, h. Carroll n. Alabama.
BOGARDUS, SAMUEL, cheese merchant, 29 Main, h. 111 E. Eagle —See adv. p. 38.
Bogendoerfer, Leonard, lab. h. Krettner n. Bat.
Bogenschentz, Adam, cabinet mcker, h. Howard cor. Jefferson.
Bogenschitz, John, shoemaker, 12 Commercial, b. same.
Bogert, Chas. C. h. 101 Seneca.
Bogert & Doolittle, merch. tailors, 164 Main.
Bogert, E. B. clerk, S. O. Barnum. b. 29 Swan.
Bogert, Jas. B. firm B. & Doolittle, 164 Main, h. 66 E. Eagle.
Bogert, Lawrence K. Sr. office at B. & Doolittle's, 164 Main, h 331 Washington.
Bogert, L. K. Jr. clerk. 164 Main, b. 29 Swan.
Boggis, Wm. Niagara House, Pearl cor. Eagle.
Bogold, John, shoemaker, h. 225 Elm.
Bohl, Henry, tailor, William n. Jefferson.
Bohl, S. Casper. lab. h. Grey n. Batavia.
Bohm, John, lab. h. Pratt n. Genesee.
Bohmert, John B. police, h. 5th ab. Hudson.
Bohn, Bernhard, carp. h. Watson n. Peckham.
Bohn, Philip, lab. h. Spring n. Sycamore.
Boice, Cornelius, moulder, 237 Main.
Boice, Wm. gas fitter, 237 Main, h. 10th n. Md.
Boick, Jacob, grinder, h. 51 Cherry.
Boillatat, F. J. lab. h. Jefferson n. Peckham.

Boire. Relph, blacksmith, Washington cor. Virginia. h. same.
Bokritz. Adam, miller, h. East n. Austin.
Boland. Francis, lab. h. Kentucky, n. South.
Boland. Michael, firm B. & Son, h. 104 Main.
Boland & Son, merchant tailors, 104 Main.
Boland. Toney, sailor, h. Louisiana. n. Elk.
Boland. William, firm B. & Son, h. 104 Main.
Bolk. Martin, lab. h. Cedar n. Batavia.
Bollemer. Geo. shoemaker. h. Elk n. Chicago.
Boler. Geo. bookbinder, 165 Main, h. Goodell n. Michigan.
Boller. Charles, carpenter, b Oak n. Carlton.
Boller. Christian, musician, b. 70 Tupper.
Boller. Christian, lab. h. Fox n. Genesee.
Boller. John, moulder, h. Cherry cor. Michigan.
Boller. Margaret, widow, h. Cherry cor. Mich.
Bolson. Harriet, Mrs. h. 427 Main.
Bolton, William, lab. h. Genesee E. tollgate.
Boltzki. Jacob, blacksmith, Seneca n. old city line. h. same.
Bolz. Conrad, lab.. h. Batavia n. Monroe.
Bolz. Geo. carpenter. h. Locust n North.
Bolz. John, sash and blind maker, h. Hickory n. Sycamore.
Bolza. Louis, book-keeper, h. 22 Goodell.
Bomberg, Conrad, cigar maker. h. 134 Spring.
Bomberg, John, shoemaker, h. Spring n. Gen.
Bomberg, John A. musician, h. Spring n. Gen.
Bomberg, John. cigar maker. h. Jeff. n. S. Div.
Bomel. F. F.* tailor, over 278 Main, h. same.
Bomgurdon, Christopher. tanner, h. Adam n. Clinton.
Bomgardt, Catharine. wid. h. Wm. n. Monroe.
Bomm. Adam, ash peddler, h. 83 Cherry.
Bomm. Adam, Jr. peddler, 83 Cherry.
Bommer. Catharine, wid. h. Camp n. Genesee.
Bommer. Cornelius, carpenter, h. 109 Pine.
Bommer Philip, shoemaker. h. 91 Cherry.
Bond, B. F. cooper, b. National Hotel.
Bond. LaForest, book-keeper, b. Fulton n. Hayward.
Bond. Martin, steward on lake, h. Perry n. Hamburgh.
Bond. Oliver, pattern maker, h. Fulton n. Hayward.
Bonen. Martin, lab. h Orange cor. Cherry.
Bonholal, Jaques. machinist, h. Tup. bel. Oak.
Bonjour, A. music teacher, b. St. James.
Bonnell, Wm. H. firm Kellogg & B. h. 315 Michigan.
Bonnell, Isaac, clerk for Wm. O. Brown, b. Commercial Hotel.
Bonner. Edward, moulder, b. Fulton n. Ala.
Bonner. Thos. sailor, h. Elk n. Hayward.
Bonner. William, lab. h. South n. Hamburgh.
Bonney, Edmund, painter, b. Dick's, Clinton bel. Michigan.
BONNEY, Z. proprietor Bonney's Hotel. Washington cor. Carroll.—See adv. p. 92.
Bontem, Louis. machinist, h. Genesee n. Pine.
Booly. —, b National Hotel.
Booker, B. W. book-keeper. American Express Company, b. 26 Johnson Place.
Booker, Jacob, brickm'r. h. Ferry W. of Main.
Booram, Cornelius, clerk of markets, h. Best E. of Jefferson.
Boorman, Richard, saloon, 52 Ohio.

Boos, Geo shoemaker. h. Swan n. Jefferson.
Booth, John. lumber dealer, Ohio n. Ohio Basin, h. Chicago n. Elk.
Booth, J. W. clerk, C. L. Seymour, h. 9 Park Place.
Booth. William, plumber. 5 Terrace, h. cor. 13th and Connecticut.
Borchert, Mary. Mrs. h. 165 Oak.
Borck, Catharine, Miss, seamstress. b. John J. Borck.
Borck, John J. mason. h. Riley n. Jefferson.
Borck. John, shoemaker, h. 50 Bennett.
Borck, John, plasterer. h. Riley n. Jefferson.
Borden. Bashti, widow. b. William. H. Wing.
Bordwell, Benj. R. tavern, Genesee n. tollgate.
Bordwell, Hudson, butcher. Gen. n. tollgate.
Borgeding, Herman. carp. h. Jefferson n. North.
Bork. Joseph, shoemaker, h. Bat. cor. Hickory.
Bork, Joseph, clerk. Lyon & Co. b. 50 Bennett.
Bork, William, clerk, 236 Main. b. 78 Bennett.
Borket, Jno. ship carp. h. N. Div. n. Jefferson.
Borme, Thomas, carpenter. h. South n. Ala.
Born, J. wood worker, with Brayley & Pitts.
Born, Anna M. widow, b Genesee n. Jefferson.
Born, Jacob, tailor, h. 4 Delaware Place.
Born's brewery. Genesee, cor. Jefferson.
Bornemann, Fred. tailor, h. n. 317 Elm.
Borst, Jno. farmer, h. Williamsville road n. Delavan avenue.
Borst, John, grocer. 159 Elk, h. same.
Borst, Joseph, cooper, h. 10 Bennett.
Bortles, Geo. P. clerk, b. 287 S. Division.
Borzler. John, lab. h. Genesee, n tollgate.
Bosch, Anton, shoem'r. 47 E. Genesee. h. same.
Bosch, Fred. lab. h. High n. Ketchum alley.
Bosch, Jacob, cooper. b. German alley n. Gen.
Bosch, Wm. lab. b. German alley n. Genesee.
Bosche, John, coach painter, h. Main n. Best.
Bosche, John, milkman, h. Best n. Main.
Bosse, Chas, liquor store, Seneca junction Swan, h. same.
Bosson, James,* watchmaker, 78 Exchange. b. same.
Bost, John, moulder. h. cor. Market and Gay.
Botemore. Jacob. lab. h. Hickory n. Clinton.
Both, A harness maker, h. Swan n. Hydraulics.
Both Jacob. lab. h. Bennett n. Batavia.
Both, John, butcher, h. Bennett n. Batavia.
Botler, Dietrich, lab. h. Dearborn n. Palmer.
Bottsmeier, Andrew. farmer. h. Walden n. Gen.
Boughton & Jackson, com. merchants, cor. Michigan and Scott.
Boulder, Jacob, tanner. h. Jefferson n. Wm.
Bourgnon, Joseph, rectifier, h. 138 Ellicott.
Bourjois, Chas. machinist, h. 11 Sycamore.
Bournegal, ——, Rev. h. junction York and North.
Bourzutchsky, Robert, sexton, h. Sycamore cor. Spruce.
Boutelle, L. hat and bonnet bleacher, 21 R. Eagle, h. same.
Bouyon, Andrew, stone cutter. h. 91 Elm.
Bouyon, Paul, confectioner. 298 Main, h. same.
Bover. Charles, teamster, Carroll n. Alabama.
Bowden, Patrick, lab. h 261 Carroll.
Bowen, Daniel, carriage factory, 209 E. Seneca. h. 216 E. Seneca.
Bowen, Daniel, finisher, h. Jefferson n. Swan.

Bowen, Daniel A. carriage painter, cor. Clinton and Union.

Bowen, Dennis, firm Rogers & B. h 122 Chippewa.

Bowen, G. J. book-keeper, Hamlin & Mendsen, h. 252 Seneca.

Bowen, Geo. lab. h. Alabama n. Mackinaw.

Bowen, —, clerk, J. Walker, b. 29 Swan.

Bowen, Hartwell, firm B. & Humason, h. Swan n. junction Seneca.

Bowen & Humason, leather dealers, 109 Main.

Bowen, Jeremiah, lab. b. Ohio n. Louisiana.

Bowen, John, foreman moulder in Buffalo Eagle Iron Works, h. Perry n. Alabama.

Bowen, R. J. firm B. & Dickey, Southern hotel.

Bowen, S. W. at Pratt & Co. b. Bonney's.

Bowen, Wm. H. firm Smith & B. b. 216 Seneca.

Bowen, Wm. blacksmith, Eddy & Bingham, h. 134 Elm.

Bower, Geo. tinsmith, b. N. William n. Va.

Bower, Henry, conductor M. St. R. R. b. Mrs J. S. Miller.

Bower, Jacob, melodeon maker, h. N. William ab. Virginia.

Bower, Louis, clerk, 318 Main, h. Batavia n. Elm.

Bower, Philip, carpenter, b. N. William n. Va.

Bowes, John, caulker, h. 22 Illinois.

Bowes, Pat. caulker, b 22 Illinois.

Bowie, George, sailor, h. 166 6th.

Bowles, John, clerk, 39 Jackson.

Bowles, Mary, widow, h. 394 S. Division.

Bowles, J. C. telegraph opp. b. Bonney's.

Bowman, Benj. J. h. Washington n. Carlton.

Bowman, F. R. captain on lake, h. 16 Union.

Bowman, G. T. b. Bonney's.

Bowman, Henry, lab. h. Lake Shore R. R. n. toll bridge.

Bowman, Louis, machinist, h. Perry n. Hamburgh.

Boy, Frederick, tailor, h. Goodell n. Michigan.

Boy, Theo. J. tailor, h. 108 Goodell.

Boyd, Hugh, trackman, h. Jackson n. Canal alley.

Boyd, James A. with Breed, Butler & Co. h. 136 E. Seneca.

Boyd, Jas. tanner, b. 37 Carroll.

Boyd, Milton A. moulder, h. Potter n. arsenal.

BOYD, R. D. prod. and com. mer. 10 Central Wharf, h. 307 Franklin.—See adv. p. 36.

Boyd, Thomas, cartman, h. Jackson n. Canal alley.

Boyd, Thomas L. engineer, N. Y. C. R. R. h. 30 W. Seneca.

Boydom, A. farmer, with Geo. Malcom, h. Main n. Cold Spring.

Boyer, Wm. lab. h. Rogers n. York.

Boyle, Bryan, lab. h. cor. Cal. and N. Adams.

Boyle, Edwin, h. 7th n Hudson.

Boyle, Ellen, widow, grocer, S. Division n. Jefferson.

Boyle, Hugh, brewery and distiller, St. Paul n. Main, h. same.

Boyle, James, sailor, h. N. Div. n. Jefferson.

Boynton, Theodore, sash and blind factory, 48 Clinton, h. 218 Pearl.

Boynton, Thomas C. prod. and com. mer. 9 Central Wharf, b. Courter.

9

BOZZE, DOMINIC, proprietor Revere House, Erie st. opp. R. R. Depot.—See adv. p. 93.

Brace, Curtiss L. firm J. R. Evans & Co. h. 48 Court.

Brace, James K. foot Commercial, b. Bonney's.

Brace, John, in iron works, h. Iron place N. Washington.

Brace, Lester, h. 180 Franklin.

Brachman, Jos carp. h. Walnut n. Batavia.

Brack, Jacob, Sr.* wagon maker, h. Genesee n. Walden.

Brack, Jacob, Jr. wagon maker, h. Genesee n. Walden.

Bradbury, Geo. H. sup. B. N. Y. & E. R. R. h. 155 Pearl.

Bradbury, W. F. machinist, b. Elk n. Chicago.

Brader, Jno. carp. h. Carroll n. Van Rensseľr.

Bradford, Wm. R. firm Blodgett & B. h. 1 Carey W. of Morgan.

Bradl, Joseph. lab. h. 113 Pine.

Bradley, D. firm B. & Toles, b. Mansion.

Bradley, Elias A. h. 171 Niagara.

Bradley, Jas. saloon, Reed's Dock. h. same.

Bradley, Philo F. Am. Ex. Co. h. 98 Folsom.

Bradley, Thomas, lab. with Pierre & Co. h. Hamburgh n. Elk.

Bradley & Toles, transporters, Marine block, Ohio.

Bradninger, Jno. coppersmith, h. Mulberry ab. Goodell.

Bradshaw, Martha, widow. h. 57 Franklin.

Bradshaw, Oscar, milk peddler, h. 186 Seneca.

Brady, Dan'l, grocer, Palmer n. Virginia.

Brady, James, peddler. h. Virginia cor. 5th.

Brady, Peter, butcher, Clinton market, h. Walnut cor. Clinton.

Brady, Thomas, nail maker, h. Hudson cor. 7th.

Braeger. Chas. carp h. Watson n. Peckham.

Braeger, Frank, bl'ksm. h. Watson n. Peckham.

Braeunlein, Stephen, tailor, h. Hickory n. Gen.

Braids, Robert, grocer, h. cor. 14th and Vt.

Braids, Wm. carriage trimmer. h. 293 Oak.

Brainard, Jos. G. flour inspt. 17 Cent. Wharf. h. 171 Terrace.

Braker, C. chairworker, with S. D. Sikes.

Braman, Edw'd. machinist, h. 130 N. Division.

Bramen, Robert, lithographer. h. 84 Clinton.

Brames, Elizabeth, Miss, seamstress, b. Pratt n. William.

Brand, John, saloon. 53 Exchange, h. same.

Brandel, Margaret, widow, h. 284 Pearl.

Brandel, Michael, lab. Genesee n. Fox.

Brandell, Peter, bl'ksm. b. cor. Wm. & Walnut.

Brandle, Philip, carp. h. School near Niagara.

Brandt, Fred. tailor, h. 96 Cedar.

Brandt, Wm. musician, h. Spruce n. Genesee.

Brandt, Wm. potmaker. h. Hickory n. Gen.

Branen, Edward. carp. h. Fulton n. Red Jacket.

Braner, Conrad. cooper, h. Grey n. Batavia.

Brank, Charles, tailor, h. Watson n. Clinton.

Brannan, Patrick, truckman, h. Hickory n. Clinton.

Branner, Fred. lab. h. 66 Hickory.

Brant, Mathias, shoemaker, h. 15 Main.

Brantener, John, helper, h. Adam n. Sycamore.

Brantne, Anton, lab. h. Adams n. Sycamore.

Braum, John, cigar maker, b. Peckham cor. Jefferson.

Braumann, Peter, blacksmith, 499 Main, h. 487 Washington.
Braun, Adam, joiner, b. 182 Batavia.
Braun, Andrew, lab. h. Hickory n. Batavia.
Braun, Conrad, cooper, b. Spring cor. William.
Braun, Fred. cabinet maker, h. Burton alley cor. Oak.
Braun, George, lab. h. Herman n. Genesee.
Braun, Henry, gardener, h. Boston alley, n. Goodell.
Braun, Jacob, cooper, h. cor. East & Amherst.
Braun, John P. tanner, h. Pratt n. Sycamore.
Braun, John, lab. h. Locust n. Carlton.
Braun, John, lab. h. Sherman n. Batavia.
Braun, John, peddler, h. Walnut n. Batavia.
Braun, John A. shoemaker, h. 99 Cedar.
Braun, Lorenz, lab. h. Adams n. Genesee.
Braun, Louis, carp. h. Spring n. Sycamore.
Braun, Louis P. b. Pratt n. Sycamore.
Braun, Paul, grocer, Gen. cor. Pratt, h. same.
Braun, Wm. furnaceman, h. 253 Elm.
Brauner, Michael, teamster, at 277 Main, h. Oak n. Genesee.
Braunlich, Chas. machinist, h. Bennett n. Wm.
Braunlich, Fred. shoemaker, h. 109 Genesee.
Braxmeir, Thomas, basket maker, h. Jeff. n. Peckham.
Bray, James, miller, b. Ferry cor. N. William.
Bray, Michael, ship carp. h. Ala. n. Mackinaw.
Brayley, James, firm B. & Pitts, agricultural works, h. 70 Niagara.
BRAYLEY & PITTS, Pitts' Agricultural Works, cor. Carolina and 4th.—*See adv. p. 70.*
Brayton, I. R. with W. H. Glenny, b. 114 Pearl.
Brazee, Caroline, wid. h. cor. Blossom & Coon's alley.
Breacher, Peter, h. cor. Pratt and Sycamore.
Brean, Wm. tailor, 231 Carroll, h. same.
BREED, BUTLER, & Co. publishers and booksellers, 188 Main.—*See adv. p. 101.*
Brechner, Fred. cigar maker, h. Bat. n. Pratt.
Brechtel, Frederick, tailor, Clinton n. Spring.
Brechtel. Geo. tailor, h. Mulberry n. High.
Brechtel, Ignatz, tanner, h. Hickory cor. Cherry.
Brechtel. John, grocer, Niag. n. Mass. h. same.
Breckwise, M. lab. h. E. Bennett opp. Market.
Breeder, Joachim, lab. h. Cherry n. Spring.
Breed, F. W. firm B. Butler & Co. h. 379 Franklin.
Breen, Dual, lab. h. Genesee n. Canal.
Breester, John, lab. h. Porter n. Van Renselaer.
Brehner, L. P. clerk, with B. Hyman, b. same.
Breier, Conrad, truckman, h. Bat. n. Monroe.
Breimger, Magdalene, wid. h. Ellicott n. High.
Breinich, Jos. shoemaker, h. Hickory n. Cherry.
Breis, Martin, cooper, b. 5 Michigan.
Breis, Mathias, lab. h. Adams n. Sycamore.
Breithaupt, Lewis, firm Schoellkopf & Co. h. cor. Carroll and Exchange.
Breitung, Amand, tailor, h. Pine cor. Cypress.
Breitweiser, Henry, cigar maker, 48 Del. place.
Breitweiser. Leonhard, h. 44 Delaware place.
Bremasin, Henry, harness maker, 355 Main, h. 29 Sycamore.
Brenchle, Chas. carp. h Elm n. Goodell.
Brenchley, Wm. soap maker, h. 12th n. Verm'nt.
Brendel, Adam, locksmith, b. Walnut n. Bat.
Brendel, Chas. carp. h. Carlton n. Michigan.

Brendel, Geo. stone cutter, h. Ash n. Sycamore.
Brendel, Jno. teamster, h. Gen. E. Williamsville road.
Brendel. Peter, lab. h. Walnut n. Wm.
Brenen, John, lab. h. Folsom n. Kinney's alley.
Brenen, Philip, lab. h. n. foot Genesee.
Brenig, Diebold, tailor, cor. Amherst & Thoma.
Brennan, Andrew, drayman, h. Wm. cor. Cedar.
Brennan, Barney, with George Brennan.
Brennan, Geo. keeper of Forest Lawn Cemetery, h. Delaware, entrance to Cemetery.
Brennan, Thos. lab. h. 5th n. Hudson.
Brennen, James, lab. h. Genesee n. Jackson.
Brennen, Martin, millinery, 302½ Main, h. Hickory n. Clinton.
Brennen, Patrick, blacksmith, h. Blossom n. Huron.
Brennen, P. & Co. blacksmiths, Genesee n. Prl.
Brenner, John, mason, h. Michigan n. Best.
Brenner, Peter, peddler, h. n. R. R. crossing South Division.
Brent, Benjamin, boiler maker. h. 99 Fulton.
Brent, Henry, daguerrean, Genesee n. Spruce. h. same.
Bresemly, Fred. cooper, h. Niag. n. Hamilton.
Bretl, Peter, shoemaker, h. Monroe n. Batavia.
Brew, William, b. Revere House.
Brewer, F. H. book-keeper, h. 17 Chestnut.
Brewer, H. H. painter, h. 137 Elk.
Brewing, Charles, moulder. h. 59 Spruce.
Brewster, Israel. ag't M. C. R. R. h. 103 Carroll.
Brewster. W. S. firm Niles & B. h. 310 Pearl.
Brick, Balthasa, engineer, h. 11 Maple.
Brick, Frederick, tailor, h. 257 Elm.
Brick, Gottfried, cooper, h. William n. Pratt.
Brick, Michael, tanner, h. 109 Pine.
Brick, Nicholas, police, h. Mortimer n. Gen.
Brick, Peter, carpenter, h. 102 Goodell.
Brick, Peter, cooper, William n. Pratt.
Brick, Valentine, tailor, h. 257 Elm.
Brick, Valentine, coppersmith, b. N. Brick.
Brickel, Anton, peddler, h. Sherman n. Gen.
Brickel. Conrad, tailor, h. Bremer n. Vermont.
Brickeli, Michael, lab. h. Adams n. Sycamore.
Bridge, Joseph Augustus, carpenter, h. White's corners plank road n. city line.
Bridger, James H. ship carpenter, h. n. Ohio street toll bridge.
Bridgman, T. H. clerk, h. 103 9th.
Bridgman, W. J. firm John Bissell & Co. h. 103 9th.
Briel, George, lab. h. Hickory n. Batavia.
Brierley, William, watchman Pitts' agricultural works, h. 106 Huron.
Brigard, Charles, tailor, h. 153 Elm.
Briggs, Frank, painter, b. cor. Market & Perry.
Briggs, G. P. clerk, 205 Main, b. 29 Swan.
Briggs, Ira C. cl'k W. T. Co. h. Nia. n. Hudson.
Briggs, Jos. A. gilder, 7 Swan, h 264 N. Div.
Briggs & Martin, stair builder, cor. Terrace & Mechanic.
Briggs, Thos. gilder 7 Swan. b. 270 N. Div.
Brigham. Thomas, b. Mrs. H. Brigham.
Brigham, H. widow, h. Michigan ab. High.
Brighton, George C. actor, b. Niagara House cor. Amherst and Niagara.
Brinan, Jno. moulder, b. Commercial.
Brinckmeier, C. H. lab. 1 Vine alley.

Brinkel, George, lab. Stanton n. Lovejoy.
Brinkworth, Francis, locksmith, h. Elk n. Mkt.
Brinkworth, John, nail maker, h. Perry n. Chicago.
Brintnall, Phineas, h. 14 Ellicott.
Brintnall, Geo. carpenter, h. Mack'w n. Ala.
Brirley, Mrs. hair-work maker, 33 Union.
Brisbane, A. b. St. James Hotel.
Bristol, Cyrenius C. h. Ellicott cor. Eagle.
Bristol, Daniel, h. 10th cor. Jersey.
Bristol, Edward firm Taunt & B. b. 209 Pearl.
Bristol, Erasmus D. h. 10th cor. Jersey.
Bristol, Henry, con. 214 Main. h. 214 Pearl.
Bristol, Moses, physician, h. Del cor. Ferry.
Bristol, Theodore M. book-keeper with Black-
mar & Gilbert, b. Main cor. Ferry.
Bristol, William, book-keeper, b 214 Pearl.
Bristow, Hearld, boatman, h. cor. N. Washing-
ton and Auburn avenue.
British Consulate, Harvey Building, cor. Main
and Swan.
Britt, James, lab. h. Clinton n. Jefferson.
Britt, Pierce, coachman with George C. White,
51 E. Swan.
Brittin, Thomas, machinist, h. Elk below La.
Britting, Nicholas. lab. h. Mortimer n. Genesee.
BRITTON, NICHOLAS, copper and tinsmith,
Commercial cor. Pearl, h. 82 Carroll.—See
adv. p. 96.
Britton, William, lab. h. Alabama cor. Fulton.
Britz, Peter, shoemaker, h. Wm. n. Monroe.
Brizoloro, Antony, h. 61 Washington.
Broadhead, N. L. private school, h. 367 Wash.
Broch, John, bell ringer in tower, h. 35 Syc.
Brock, Henry, clothing store 157 Main, b. 147
Swan.
Brock, Lewis M. clerk, 157 Main. b. 147 Swan.
Brockman, Chas. blacksmith, h. Luther alley n.
Batavia.
Brockman, Fred. lab. h. Burton n. Hydraulics.
Brockway, N. R. h. 4 6th.
Brodbeck, John G. lab. h. North cor. Mulberry.
Brodfuhrer, Jno. mason, h. Grey n. Batavia.
Brodhead, F. F. teacher of modern languages,
367 Washington.
Brodhead, Wm. W. lawyer, h. and office 367
Washington.
Brodie, Archibald, picture frames, Niagara n.
Eagle.
Brodie, Jas. at iron works, h. Clinton avenue n.
Washington.
Brodt, Peter, peddler, h. Ferry n. Waldron.
Brody, Brian, lab. h. 13th n. Hampshire.
Broezel, John, saloon, Washington cor. Seneca
h. 59 E. Seneca.
Brohsard, Charles, street insp. h. Carroll n. Red
Jacket.
Brokenburg, A. S. dyer, 193 Genesee.
Brokenburg, Jas. printer, b. 193 Genesee.
Brong, Charles, tailor, h. Watson n. Clinton.
Brouharts, John, lab. h. Genesee n. Spring.
Bronner, Andrew, lab. h. Maple n. Cherry.
Bronson, Anthony, lab. h. Blossom n. Amherst.
Bronson, Jas. H. hammersman, N. S. Forge, b.
311 E. Seneca.
Brook, T. b. Western.
Brookhaus, John, cooper, h. Amherst n. Blos.
Brooks, Alonzo, moulder, h. 34 Jackson.

Brooks, Geo. candy maker, b. 23 Seneca.
Brooks, Howard, paper hanging, 272 Main, h.
Franklin.
Brooks, H. S. atty. 150 Main, h. 207 Ellicott.
Brooks, Lest. foreman Bradley & Pitts' foundry,
h. Palmer n. Maryland.
Brooks, Sheldon, moulder, h. Palmer n. Md.
Brooms, Michael, lab. h. r. Niagara n. Hamilton.
Brosart, Chas. A. Jr. printer, Advocate, h. 289
E. Seneca.
Broso, Anthony, tavern keeper, Martin's Cor.
Brosso, Mary. widow, h. Potter n. Batavia.
Brost, Geo. cigar maker, b. 33 Genesee.
Brost, Mrs. widow, h. Milnor n. William.
Brothers, Geo. cooper, h. Pratt n. Clinton.
Brothers, Lewis, h. 274 Franklin.
Brothers, Lewis, Mrs. widow, h. 274. Franklin.
Brotz, Frank, shoemaker, h. 239 Elm.
Brotz, Valentine, cabinet maker, cor. Cherry
and Michigan.
Broughton, Michael, sailmaker, cor. Lloyd and
Prime, h. Illinois n. Ohio.
Brougham, Peter, lab. h. Hayward n. Fulton.
Browell, Jn'o. baggage N. Y. C. R. R. b. Bon-
ney's Hotel.
Brown, Adam, tailor, h. 287 Genesee.
Brown, Adam, cooper, b. Peckham cor. Monroe.
Brown, Alex. H. firm Brown & McCutcheon,
h. 109 Fulton.
Brown, Alex. flour store, 289 Seneca, h. 129
Eagle.
Brown, Alva, Main cor. Chippewa, h. 3 Edw'd.
Brown Andrew, brewer, h. Hickory n. Bat.
Brown, A. sailor, h. cor. Morgan and Mohawk.
Brown, B. F. sailor, h. Pratt n. Batavia.
Brown, B. S. dentist, 301 Washington, h same.
BROWN, C. propri'r Brown's Hotel, 125 Sen-
eca cor. Michigan.—See adv. p. 93.
Brown, Capt. J. h. College n. Allen.
Brown, Chas. H. b. 5 Franklin.
Brown, Conrad, printer, h. cor. Pine and Eagle.
Brown, Conrad, lab. h. Peckham n. Stanton.
Brown, C. E. b. Western.
Brown, Daniel, lake and canal store, old packet
dock, h. 116 Niagara
Brown, David E. cl'k. 275 Main, h. 13 N. Div.
Brown, Edward, lab. h. Ohio n. Ohio basin.
Brown, Edward, bar-keeper, 9 Commercial, b.
7 Commercial.
Brown, Erasmus, engineer, h. Fulton n. Ala.
Brown, Frank, brewer, b. J. Scheu.
Brown, Frank, clerk, 311 Main, b. 41 S. Div.
Brown & Fisher, attorneys, Fargo buil. Seneca,
over Clinton Bank.
Brown, F. L. h. 89 Huron.
Brown, George, butcher, b. 311 Washington.
Brown, Geo. saloon, Eagle cor. Pearl, h. same.
Brown, Geo. blacksmith. h. Gen. n. Harman.
Brown, Geo. drover, 151 Main.
Brown, Harriet, saloon, r. 51 Lloyd, h. same.
Brown, Jas. brick maker, b. Ferry n. Jefferson.
Brown, Henry, saloon, 1 Fly n. LeCouteulx.
Brown, H. C. mantles, grates, safes, &c. Arcade
Building, h. Franklin n. Allen.
Brown, H. J. freight N. Y. C. freight depot, h.
Summer.
Brown, Jas. C. firm B. & Fisher, h. Barker opp.
Linwood avenue.

Brown, Jas. W. Eaton's Planing Mill, h. Main n. Riley.

Brown, Jas. boat shop, across Buffalo creek, h. same.

Brown, James H. mariner, h 48 Pine.

Brown, Jas. D. cl'k C. Ramsdell, b. 129 Eagle.

Brown, James, miller, h. 100 Cedar.

Brown & Johnson, insurance agt's. Yaw's b'lds.

Brown, John, firm B. & Johnson, b. American.

Brown, John, land agent, b. Mansion.

Brown, John, gardener, b. 79 W. Chippewa.

Brown, Jno. C. boot and shoe dealer, 43 E. Seneca, h. same.

Brown, John, h. cor William n. Madison.

Brown, John, turner, 160 Elm, h. Grey n. Bat.

Brown, John, saloon keeper, line boat dock.

Brown, J. N. M. D. 79 Franklin cor. Niagara.

Brown, John, mason, h. Cherry n. Jefferson.

Brown, John, sailor. h. 418 Michigan.

Brown, John, lab. h. William n. Jefferson.

Brown, Joseph, engineer, h. 222 Clinton.

Brown, Leonard. brick maker, with P. A. Balcom, h. Ferry n. Jefferson.

Brown, S. S. agent, b. Bonney's Hotel.

Brown, L. B. b. Western.

Brown, Louis, lab. h. 125 Pine.

Brown, Mary, Miss, 40 Sycamore.

Brown. Mary Ann, Mrs. 10 Michigan.

Brown, Mary, widow, h. Alabama n. Seneca.

Brown, Miss C. teacher, school No. 24, h. Best E. Jefferson.

Brown, Myron E. master mechanic N. Y. & E. R. R. machine shop, h. 106 N. Division.

BROWN & McCUTCHEON, machinists, Elk junction Ohio.—See adv. p. 56.

Brown, Nathaniel, firm Forbush & B. boot and shoe manufacturers, 91 Main, h. 134 Swan.

Brown, O. W. 46 Main, b. 5 Franklin.

Brown, Peter, cap maker, 169 Main, h. German n. Batavia.

Brown, P. W. American Express Co.

Brown, Robt. cook on lake, h. 17 William.

Brown, Robt. apprentice, b. 230 Seneca.

Brown, Robt. grocer, Mich. bet. Elk and Ohio.

Brown, Robert, waiter, h. 10 William.

Brown, R. N. Supt L. S. R. R. b. St. James.

Brown, Rumsey R. mariner. h. 117 6th.

Brown. Samuel. gold pen manufac. 185 Main, h. Park n. Virginia.

Brown, S. S. h. 41 S. Division.

Brown, Sylvester, lum'r dealer. h. 71 E. Seneca.

Brown, Wm. veterinary surgeon, Ellicott n. Mohawk, h. same.

Brown, Wm. lithographer, with Sage & Sons, h. Perry cor. Hamburgh.

Brown, Wm S. h. 115 Seneca.

Brown, Wm. laborer, 199 Exchange.

Brown, Warren, contractor, h. Thomp. n. Ham.

Brown, Wm. sailor, h. Spruce n. Batavia.

Brown W. M. manuf. chemist, h. Main at Cold Springs.

Brown, Wm. N. mariner, h. 10 William.

Brown, Wm. O. & Co. bankers, 221 Main cor. Swan.

Brown, W. O. office on Dock ft. Washington, h. 422 Main.

Brown, W. O. Jr. ass't book-keeper, Brown & Co. b. Delaware n. Barker.

Browne, Peres E. principal Pub. School No. 31, h. 94 Clinton.

Brownell, Isaac W. prod. and com. mer. 10 C. Wharf, h. 154 Pearl.

Brownell, James, clerk A. Reynolds & Co. b. Western.

Brownell, Minerva, widow, boarding house, 105 Carroll.

Brownell, C. E. M. D. h. Elk n. Hayward.

Browner, Christian, finisher, h. 126 Oak.

Browner, Michael, h. 142 Oak. in rear.

Browning, John, clerk, W. T. Co. h. 81 N. Div.

Brownlich, A. C. machinist, h. E. Bennett, n. William

Bruce, Elijah K. ship chandler, 6 and 7 Ohio, h. 30 W. Tupper.

Bruce, Harlow, merch. tailor, over 140 Main. h. 26 Ellicott.

Bruch, Jacob, finisher. h. 217 Oak n. Tupper.

Bruch, Jno. tower bell ringer h. Syc. n. Elm.

Bruch, Louis, printer, h. Oak n. Tupper.

Bruch, Martin, tailor, h. over 231 Elm.

Brucher, Jno. lab. h. r. 116 Genesee.

Bruchner, John, tailor, h. Peach n. North.

Bruckman, Louis, clerk, 294 Main. h. 372 Mich.

Brueck, Fred. printer, 358 Main. h. 109 Maple.

Brueck, Valentine, with M. H. Tryon, h. 257 Elm.

Bruggman, Henry, clerk, h. 15 Cypress.

Brucknerm, Julius, gardener, h. Walden cor. Ferry.

Brummer, Barthol, lab, h. Best opp. Elm.

Brummer, Geo. tanner, h. Goodell alley bel. Goodell.

Brunck, Francis C. M. D. firm Brunck & Held. h. 184 Niagara.

BRUNCK & HELD, publishers Daily Democrat, 194 Washington.—See adv. p. 103.

Brunck, Lawrence. lab. h. Walnut n. Genesee.

Brunck, James. upholsterer, 120 N. Division.

Brunck, S. W. firm B. & Co. land agent. 29 Arcade, b. cor. Main and Florida.

Brundige, C. G. book-keeper, 11 C. Wharf, h. 351 Franklin.

Brunet, Joseph, bootmaker, h. 75 Sycamore.

Brunke, Augustus F. shoemaker. h. 163 Clint'n.

Brunn, Andrew, with Hamlin & Mendsen, b. 179 Ellicott.

Brunn, Chas. machinist, h. Eagle n. Hickory.

Brunner, Aloise, saloon, Monroe n. Batavia, h. same.

Brunner, Anna Mary, widow, h. Walnut n. Bat.

Brunner, Christian, lab. h. Delavan av. n. Wal.

Brunner, Frank, grocer, Walnut n. Batavia. h. same.

Brunner, Joseph, machinist, B. & S. L. R. R. h. over 136 East Genesee.

Brunner, Leopold, lab. h. Sycamore n. Spruce.

Brush, Alexander, brickmaker. b. W. C. Brush.

Brush, Hiram. firm B. & Stockton, h. 234 Pearl.

Brush, Milton A. brickmaker, Clinton n. R. R. crossing.

Brush, Nat. brickmaker. h. Clinton n. C. R. R.

BRUSH & STOCKTON, rag and paper dealers, 190 Washington.—See adv. p. 77.

Brush, William C. brickmaker, h. N. Canal n. Swan.

Bruss, Louis, carpenter, h. Hickory n. Batavia.

Bruss, John, carpenter, h. Mortimer n. Genesee.
Brusseau, Antoin. nailer, h. Forest ave. n. Niag.
Brusseau, Louis, in iron works, b. A. Brusseau.
Brutscher, John. lab. h. Sycamore n. Ash.
Bryan, Geo. J. proprietor Buffalo Evening Post, b. Mrs. Rathbun, 215 Delaware.
Bryan, W. P. captain, h. 4 10th.
Bryant, Abner H. seed store, 3 East Swan, h. Main cor. Bryant.
Bryant, Bros. & Stratton. mercantile college, Brown's buildings, cor. Main and E. Seneca.
Bryant, G. H. h. 119 Niagara.
Bryant, Godfrey, h. National Hotel.
Bryant, H. B. firm B. & Stratton, mercantile college, b. Courter House.
Bryant, H. C. h. Delaware cor. Bryant.
Bryant, J. C. firm B. & Stratton, b. Courter House.
Bryant, Reuben, attorney at law, 268 Main, h. 10th cor. Virginia.
Bryant, Warren, h. 72 Clinton.
Bryant, William C. attorney at law, 268 Main, b. 10th cor. Virginia.
Bryson, Wm. soap factory, b. Hudson n. 5th.
Bryson, Lizzie, milliner, b. Hudson cor. 5th.
Bub, Conrad. lab. h. 99 Cedar.
Bubel, Michael. milk peddler, h. 69 E. Tupper.
Bubel, J. B. lab. h. Mulberry n. Goodell.
Buch, Geo. brewer, h. 186 Genesee.
Buchamier, Jno. caulker, h. Jefferson n. Clinton.
Buchhamer, B. widow, h. William n. Pine.
Buchhamer, J. caulker, b. William n. Pine.
Buchanan, Chas, H. b. 193 Franklin.
Buchanan, R. G. painter, 15 East Mohawk, h. 193 Franklin.
Buchenan, Fred. lab. h. over 338 Genesee.
Buchheiser, Jacob, wagoner, h. 38 Walnut.
Buchheit, Chas. clerk, h. German alley n. Gen.
Buchheit, Geo. J. firm B. & Staub, b. 13 East Seneca.
Buchheit, John, clerk, 194 Main, h. German alley n. Genesee.
Buchheit, Magdalena, widow, h. German alley n. Genesee.
Buchheit & Staub, saloon, 13 East Seneca.
Buchleiter, Chas. painter, 133 Genesee.
Buck, Thomas. grocer, 257 Swan.
Buckhardt, F. lamplighter, h. 34 Union.
Buckland, ——, carriage maker, b. Nat. Hotel.
Buckland, Andrew J. circulator Morning Express, h. 145 N. Division.
Buckland, Harriet, h. 252 Ellicott.
Buckland, L. h. 14th n. Hamilton.
Buckley, Wm. ship carp. h. Fulton n. Chicago.
Budd, Thos. A. h. 3 Boston block, Niagara.
Badson, Daniel B. b. 182 Seneca.
Budt, M. blacksmith. b. Genesee n. Spring.
Buecheo, Henry, carp. h. Jefferson n. Carlton.
Buecher, Margaret, widow, peddler, h. Krettner n. Batavia.
Buecher, Phalix, carp. h. Monroe n. Sycamore.
Buechi, And. farmer, h. Delavan avenue n. city line.
Buechler, August, marble polisher, h. Watson n. Batavia.
Buechler, John, marble cutter, h. 48 Jefferson.
Bueddemeyer, Fred. carpenter. h. 315 Ellicott.
Buehl, Frank, blacksmith, h. Water n. Canal.

Buehl, Louis, boot and shoe dealer, 372 Main, h. 37 Huron.
Buell, Chas. W. photographer, 214 Main, b. 128 N. Division.
Buell, J. S. forwarding and commission merchant, cor. Lloyd and Prime, h. 86 Delaware.
Buell, M. V. B. b. 297 Washington.
Buerger, Robert, lithog'r, h. Elm n. Goodell.
Buetner: Geo. carpenter, h. Locust n. Cherry.
Buettler, Mathias, grocer, 117 Batavia, h. same.
Buffalo Agricultural Machine Works and Kirby's Harvester, Scott n. Washington, office 20 Pearl.
BUFFALO BLACKING AND INK CO. 157 Washington —See adv. p. 79.
Buffalo Car Wheel Works, Louisi'a and Canal.
Buffalo Chess Club, American Hotel.
Buffalo Christian Advocate, over 3 W. Seneca.
Buffalo City Bellows Factory, cor. Alabama and Carroll.
BUFFALO COMMERCIAL ADVERTISER, R. Wheeler & Co. proprietors, 161 Main.— See adv. p. 110.
Buffalo, Cleveland and Chicago line of Propellers, foot Michigan.
BUFFALO DAILY COURIER, 178 Washington —See adv. p. 105.
Buffalo Daily Democrat and Weltburger, 194 Washington.
BUFFALO DAILY TELEGRAPH, 358 Main. —See adv. p. 104.
BUFFALO EAGLE IRON WORKS, Perry cor. Mississippi.—See adv. p. 97.
BUFFALO EVENING POST, Washington, next door to Gothic Hall.—See adv. p. 105.
Buffalo Female Academy, Del. cor. Park Place.
Buffalo Foundling Asylum, Sisters of Charity, Lewis bet. Delaware and Morgan.
Buffalo Gas Light Co. office and works Genesee cor. Jackson.
Buffalo General Hospital, High cor. Oak.
Buffalo Hospital of the Sisters of Charity, Franklin cor. Virginia.
Buffalo Iron and Nail Works, Niagara n. Forest avenue.
Buffalo Iron Railing Works, Terrace cor. Henry.
Buffalo and Lake Huron R. R. Freight Depot, River cor. Slip.
Buffalo Medical Association, 7 S. Division.
Buffalo Medical University. Main cor. Va.
Buffalo Mercantile College, Brown's Building.
Buffalo, N. Y. & Erie R. R. machine shop, Exchange cor. Louisiana.
Buffalo Morning Express, 158 Main.
Buffalo, N. Y. & Erie Freight Depot, Ohio ab. Chicago.
Buffalo, N. Y. & Erie R. R. office, Exchange cor. Washington.
Buffalo & Niagara Falls R. R. office, Erie bel. Canal bridge.
Buffalo & Niagara Falls R. R. round house. n. foot Genesee.
Buffalo Orphan Asylum, Virginia n. Delaware.
Buffalo Savings Bank, 330 Main.
BUFFALO SENTINEL, 111 Main.—See adv. p. 103.
Buffalo & State Line R. R. Freight Depot, Alabama cor. canal.

Buffalo Scale Works, 81 Main.

Buffalo & S. L. R. R. office secretary and treasurer, cor. Main and Swan.

BUFFALO STEAM GAUGE CO. cor. Washington and Perry.—*See adv. p.* 100.

Buffalo Trust Co. 223 Main cor. Swan.

Buffalo Water Works office, Erie n. Pearl.

Buffalo White Lead Works, cor. Virginia and Delaware and 6th cor. Georgia.

Buffum, R. L. machinist, h. Aurora plank road n. Whittmore's tavern.

Buffum, H. A. wagon and carriage maker, Seneca n. Whittmore's tavern, h. Buffum n. Aurora plank road.

Bugard, Peter, butcher, h. Genesee, Williamsville road.

Bugbee, Oliver, lumber dealer, cor. Dock and Long Wharf, h. 24 W. Eagle.

Buhler, Fred. lab. h. Monroe n. Batavia.

Buhler, Henry, stone cutter, h. 39 Spruce.

Buhr, Henry, mason, h. r. 163 Elm.

Bulaib, A. waiter, b. 11 William.

Bulger, Jas. grocer, 11 Reed's dock, h. same.

Bulger, John M. mariner, h. 211 7th.

Bull, Absalom, attorney, h. Breckenridge n. Niagara.

BULL, CADWALLADER, coal dealer, River opp. Erie basin, h. 176 Niagara.—*See adv. p.* 56.

Bull, Frederick B. clerk, L. S. R. R. b. 128 Swan.

Bull, G. B. firm G. B. B. & Co. h. 70 Seneca.

BULL, GEO. B. & CO. Union Stove Works, 95 Main and 1 and 2 Quay, foundry cor. Swan and Jefferson.—*See adv. p.* 63.

Bull, George W. h. 128 Swan.

Bull, Henry, at 21 and 23 Lloyd, b. 536 Wash.

Bull, Hugh L. coal dealer, h. 31 Union.

Bull, J. B. firm J. B. B. & Co. 21 and 23 Lloyd, h. 536 Washington.

Bull, J. B. & Co. leather, oil and hides, 21 and 23 Lloyd.

Bull, Theodore, h. 70 W. Huron.

Bull, Wm. S. clerk, N. Y. C. freight office, h. 128 Swan.

Bullock, R. fruit dealer, 227 Main, b. 15 Pearl.

Bullymore, Joseph, butcher, h. 185 Ellicott.

BULLYMORE, RICHARD, meat store, Mich. n. Elk st. market, h. Main opp. Bryant.—*See adv. p.* 42.

BULLYMORE, THOMAS, butcher shop, 326 Main, h. 115 Franklin.—*See adv. p.* 42.

Bullymore, Thos. R. with Thos. Bullymore, b. 115 Franklin.

Bulsen, Geo. K. clerk, 189 Main, h. 429 Main.

Bulson, Alexander, shoemaker, h. 76 Carroll.

Bulson, Daniel, with Hamlin & Mendsen, b. 182 Seneca.

Bulson, W. B. clerk, 289 Main, h. 427 Main.

Bumberie, Elizabeth, widow, h. 10th n. Mass.

Bund, Paul, teamster, h. Best cor. Oak.

Bundrock, Charlotte, widow, h. 534 Michigan.

Bundrock, Gottlieb, cutter, h. 534 Michigan.

Bundschue, Joseph, lab. h. Hickory bet. Genesee and Cherry.

Bundschuh, Bartell, butcher, h. Pine n. Cypress.

Bundschuh, Francis, shoemaker, h. 131 Batavia.

Bundschuh, Andrew, butcher, h. Cypress n. Pine.

Bundschuh, Margaret, widow, h. 17 Cypress.

Bunker, A. B. on lake, h. 444 Washington.

Bunting, Samuel, engineer, h. across creek.

Burch, Arthur, app. b. Perry n. Alabama.

Burch. John, sawyer, h. across creek.

Burch, Wm. watchmaker, h. Perry n. Alabama.

Burch, John. gen'l ticket agent, B. & E. R. R. h. 154 S. Division.

Burchbach, Geo. carp. h. Howard n. Madison.

Burck, Michael. mason, h. Grey n. Batavia.

Burckhart, Christian, grocer, Vt. cor. 12th.

Burckhart, Samuel, blacksmith, h. Dearborn n. Amherst.

Burdett, E. H. h. cor. Niagara and Delaware.

Burdett, Frank, lab. h. Ohio n. Chicago.

Burdett, Joseph, watchman, N. Y. C. R. R. h. Miami n. Louisiana.

Burdgers, James, provisions, etc. Terrace n. Mechanic, h. same.

Bures, Michael, saloon, Canal n. Evans.

Burg, Anton, carpenter, h. Best n. Elm.

Burg, Christian, moulder, b. Genesee n. Jeff.

Burg, Christine, widow, h. Genesee n. Jeffer'n.

Burg, George, paper hanger, b. 17 Batavia.

Burg, Michael, tailor, h. 548 Michigan.

Burgard, John, butcher, h. Batavia cor. Roos alley.

Burgard, Theo. butcher, cor. Delaware and Tupper, h. 161 Delaware.

Burgard, Wm. carpenter, h. Mulberry n. High.

Burgarden, Henry, boiler maker, h. Jefferson ab. High.

Burgdorf, Henry, lab. h. Hickory n. Batavia.

Burger, Alois, dyer, h. 566 Washington.

Burger, Francis, lab. h. Madison n. Clinton.

Burger, Jos. lab. b. cor. Water & Maiden Lane.

Burger, Otto, pastor, h. 446 Washington.

Burger, R. G. W. photographic and daguerrean gallery, Genesee cor. Spruce, h. same.

Burger, William J. lab. h. 279 Genesee.

Burgess, Ann, widow, h. 36 E. Eagle.

Burgess, Henry, clerk with H. O. Cowing cor. Niagara and Bird avenue.

Burghard, Daniel, cooper, h. Dearborn n. R. R.

Burghardt, Charles, butcher, cor. Delaware and Tupper, h. 72 Tupper.

Burghardt, Jno. lab. h. Mortimer n. Genesee.

Burghardt, P. F. mcht. tailor, 82 Main. h. same.

Burgin, M. iron finisher, with Brayley & Pitts.

Burbance, Jane, Mrs. 299 Eagle.

Burk, Bridget, seamstress, h. 9 Barker's alley.

Burk, Henry, mason, h. Pratt n. Eagle.

Burk, John, lab. h. Carroll n. Heacock.

Burk, Michael, lab. h. 5th n. Virginia.

Burk, Thomas, lab. h. Ohio n. Louisiana.

Burk. Wm. ship carp. h. Tenn. bel. Mackinaw.

Burk, Wm. saloon, Hayward n. Elk, h. same.

Burke, Andrew, h. 4 Walnut.

Burke, John, lab. h. Exchange n. Heacock.

Burke, Jno. lab. h. Perry n. Hamburgh.

Burke, M. widow, washwoman, h. 42 N. Div.

Burke, Michael, sailor, h. Ohio n. South.

Burke, Patrick, carpenter, h. n. Tifft's farm.

Burke, Patrick, lab. h. Exch. cor. Hamburgh.

Burkhany, Nicholas, teamster, b. Clinton cor. Cedar.

Burkhardt, Francis, machinist, h. 301 Oak.
Burkhart, Catharine, widow, peddler, h. Ash n. Batavia.
Burkhart, Catharine, widow, h. Dearborn n. Amherst.
Burkhart, Frank, machinist, h. 301 Oak.
Burkhart, Gottfried, millwright, h. Wm. n. Mon.
Burkhart, Lawrence, mason, h. Dearborn n. Amherst.
Burkhart, Marthais, mason, h. Dearborn n. Amherst.
Burkholder, Henry, Mrs. 75 Genesee.
Burles, Geo. lab. h. military road n. Amherst.
Burley, Edward, clerk, 273 Main, h. 201 7th.
Burley, Wm. paper hanger, b. 201 7th.
Burmeister, Fred. lab. b. Jeff. n. Batavia.
Burnback, Jas. shoemaker, h. Mich. n. S.Div.
Burns, Cornelius, h. Carroll n. Alabama.
Burns, Edward, ship carp. h. Ohio n. Wabash.
Burns, Ellen, wid. of Patrick, h. Chicago n. Elk.
BURNS, GEO. L. painter and glass stainer over 82 Main, h. 62 Court.—See adv. p. 73.
Burns, Henry C. clerk with Wm. O. Brown, b. 78 Morgan.
Burns, Jas. lab. h. towpath n. round-house.
Burns, James, mariner, h. 11th n. Md.
Burns, James, salter, h. Ellicott n. Goodell.
Burns, Jas. ship carp. h. 4th n. Carroll.
Burns, John, h. 101 9th.
Burns, John, carp. h. Batavia n. Hickory.
Burns, Michael, carp. h. Miami n. Alabama.
Burns, Thomas, lab. h. Kentucky n. South.
Burns, Patrick, saloon & boarding, Long wharf n. Canal.
Burns, Patrick, lab. h. 5th n. Virginia.
Burns, Sherman, watchman, h. North n. Mich.
Burns, William H. clerk Jewett & Root, h. 78 Morgan.
Burns, William, mariner, h. across creek.
Burow, Fred. printer, h. Elm n. Genesee.
Burr, Emmett D. broker, h. 22 Johnson Place.
Burr, Sydney, h. 6 Ellicott.
Burrell, John, sailor, h. Perry n. Chicago.
Burrow, Michael, lab. h. Boston alley.
Burrows, O. churn agent, b. National Hotel.
Burrows, Orson, Erie st. dpt. h. 7th n. Hudson.
Burrows, Roswell L. attorney, 1 Brown's Building, h. 78 E. Seneca.
Burrows, Wm. boiler maker, h. Hamburgh n. Carroll.
Burrus, James S. with Burrus & Lewis, Elk n. Red Jacket.
Burrus & Lewis. Elk street cattle yards.
Burrus, J. W. clerk, b. 114 Clinton.
Burt, Calvin, mariner, h. across creek.
Burt, D. W. clerk Robinson & Co. h. cor. Court and Pearl.
BURT, H. B. justice of the peace, 147 Main, h. 148 S. Division.—See adv. p. 81.
Burt, Harriet, Mrs. h. cor. Court and Pearl.
Burt, Henry W. teller Robinson's Bank, h. cor. Court and Pearl.
Burt, Isaac, tanner, Ontario n. Tonawanda.
Burt, John, cooper, h. Dearborn n. Parish.
Burtis, Arthur, Rev. D. D. h. 48 S. Division.
Burtis, A. Jr. banker, Main cor. Exchange, b. 48 S. Division.
Burtis, Peter, clerk, b. 48 S. Division.

Burton, George W. h. 27 6th.
Burton, Joel W. h. 27 6th
Burton, Lauren, livery stable, 30 Pearl, h. 50 W. Genesee.
Burton, Moses, porter. h. 49 Cherry.
Burton, Moses, Jr. cook, b. 49 Cherry.
Burton, Wm. lab. h. Niagara n. Ontario.
Burwell, Bryant. M. D. h. 120 Franklin.
Burwell, Geo. M. M. D. 66 Pearl, h. same.
Burwick, Jno. blacksmith, h. Mich. n. Clinton.
Busch, Apolinar, carp. h. Pratt n. Sycamore.
Busch, John, beer peddler, h. Mul. n. High.
Buschman, Marian, widow, h. 133 Pine.
Bush, Adam, boarding, h. Niag. n. Hamilton.
BUSH & HOWARD, leather dealers, 91 Main. —See adv. p. 51.
Bush, John, firm John B. & Co. h. 8 Carroll.
Bush, Jno. & Co. sheep skin dealers, 29 Seneca.
Bush, Jacob, farmer, Delaware above Burt.
Bush, Myron P. firm B. & Howard, 91 Main, h. 76 Swan.
Bush, Wm. carp. h. Niagara n. Hamilton.
Bushart, Wm. music teacher, h. 161 Batavia.
Busher. Charles, h. Pennsylvania cor. 12th.
Busher, Frank, light tender, b. Pa. cor. 12th.
Busher, Frederick, with Pratt & Letchworth, b. Pennsylvania cor. 12th.
Busher, Martin, mariner, h. 137 9th.
Busher, Mrs. John, widow, h. 12th cor. Pa.
Busher, Philip, cook on lake, h. Gen. n. Spruce.
Busk, Michael, lab. h. 5th n. Virginia.
Buskard, Robt. carriage maker, b. National.
Butler, Anna, widow, F. P. ambrotypist, 293 Main, h. same
Butler, C. iron finisher, with Brayley & Pitts.
Butler, Cyrus, piano maker, h. 10th n. Va.
Butler, Ed. brickmaker, h. Wm. n. Peckham.
Butler, Emma, widow. h. Bundy alley, n. Syc.
Butler, Fred. J. with Jewett & Root, h. 337 Ellicott.
Butler, Geo. whitewasher, h. 56 Elm.
Butler, Hope, city nurse, Erie Exch. h. same.
Butler, Jas. lab. h. Van Rensselaer cor. Porter.
Butler, Jas. M. captain, h. 85 Cedar.
Butler, John L. b. Linwood ave. cor. Utica.
Butler, John, carp. h. Vine n. Elm.
Butler, Julia, saloon, Perry n. Market.
Butler, Michael, blacksmith, b. H. Wierling.
Butler, Morris, h. Utica cor. Linwood ave.
Butler, O. Jr. contractor, h. 4 Park Place.
Butler, Patrick, h. 185 Exchange
Butler, Theodore, book store, 159 Main, h. Delaware cor. Carey.
Butler, Theo. H. clerk, 159 Main, b. 76 Del.
Butler, Thos. lab. h. 99 Folsom.
Butler, Wm. L. b. 29 Swan.
Butman, Jas. at Central R. R. shop, b. 132 E. Swan.
Butman, Wm. conductor, N. Y. Central R. R. h. 98 N. Division.
Butsch, Wm. boiler maker, h. Spring n. Bat.
Butscher, Peter, carp. h. Lutheran n. Batavia.
Butterfield, Dan. baker, h. 107 Carroll.
Butterfield, George K. stave cutter, with S. F. Gelston, h. Carroll n. Heacock.
Butterfield, Jas. H. h. 70 6th.
Butters, John, h. Main n. Carlton.
Butterwech, Chas. lab. h. Spring n. Genesee.

Batterwech, Chas. Jr. clerk, 211 Main, b. Spring n. Genesee.
Butts, S. B. agent, b. Bonney's Hotel.
Byer, Geo. shoemaker, b. 6 Water.
Byer, Michael, foreman Clark's stave yard, b. Hickory bet. Sycamore and Batavia.
Byers, David, lab. h. 356 S. Division.
Byrea, Edward, peddler, b. 104 Exchange.
Byrne, James, grocer, 30 Ohio, h. same.
Byrne, James, meat packer, h. 323 Ellicott.
Byrns, Edward, saloon, Ohio st. mart block, h. 302 Swan.
Byron, B. F. clk. Am. Exp. Co. b. Mansion.
Byron, Michael, foreman H. A. Harbeck's, h. Illinois n. Perry.
Byron, Wm. currier, h. 6th n. Pennsylvania.
Bywater, Wm. cabinet maker, h. Vt. n. 12th.

C.

Cabbell, Stephen, farmer, Erie Co. poor house, Main n. city line.
Cable, Andrew, at Southern Hotel.
Cable, Andrew, moulder, 5 State, h. Pratt ab. Clinton.
Cable, Ferdinand, lab. h. Pratt n. Clinton.
Caburet, Peter, grocer, Huron cor. Ellicott, h. same.
Cadock. Isaac, mason, 15 Inn place n. Wash.
Cadwallader, M. h. 7th n. Virginia.
Cadwell, E. H. clerk, 249 Main, b. 5 Franklin.
Caely, Albert, b. across Buffalo creek.
Cagrin, M. M. meat market, 29 Central Wharf.
Cahaun, Thos. lab. h. Dearborn n. Farmer.
Cahi. Matt. lab. h. 34 N. Division.
Cahill, Jno. gasfitter, 9 W. Eagle, h. 166 6th.
Cahill, Wm. carp. h. 11th cor. R. I.
Cain, James, drayman, with Thomas Clark, Ill. n. Perry.
Cain, Martin, lab. b. Exchange n. Smith.
Cairns, Alex. sail maker, b. 7 Scott.
Caldwell, Maria, h. 133 S. Division.
Caldwell, M. ship carp. h. Elm n. Carlton.
Caldwell, Seth, tallyman, N. Y. C. R. R. h. 189 N. Division.
Callaghan, Michael, saloon keeper, 2 Erie, h. same.
Callahan, Ann, wid. huckster, h. Scott n. Ill.
Callahan, Dennis, lab. across creek.
Callahan Patrick, mariner, h. across creek.
Callahan, Phala. saloon, Evans, h. same.
Callahan, Rich. hack stable, 264 Wash. h. 87 Seneca.
Callahan, Robt. lab. h. 6th ab. Maryland.
Callahan. Timothy, lab. Marvin n. Elk.
Callan, Margaret, wid. h. Kentucky n. South.
Callanan, Cornelius, grocer, 32 Terrace.
Callard, Mary, wid. h. 1 6th.
CALLENDER, S. N. grocer, 229, Main, b. Erie n. Pearl.—See adv. p. 40.
Calligan, Michael, boatmaker, h. Hickory n. Clinton.
Callin, And. shingle maker, b. Grey n. Adam.
Cally, Albert, b. across creek.
Cally, Shelden, light-house keeper, h. across creek.
Camell, Simon, lab. h. Burwell place n. Scott.
Cameron, Eliza, milliner, h. 46 Oak.

Cameron, George, capt. on lake, b. 5 William.
Cameron, G. treasurer, B. N. Y. & E. R. R. h. Delaware n. Virginia.
Cameron, Walter A. J. engineer, 92 N. Div.
Cameron, Wm. clerk, gen. ticket office B. N. Y. & E. R. R. h. Delaware n. Virginia.
Campbell, A. N. saloon, h. 93 S. Division.
Campbell, Benj. flouring mill, 61 Ohio, h. 272 Pearl.
Campbell, Daniel. ship carpenter, h. 66 Court.
Campbell, Geo. ship carp. h. Fulton n. Ala.
Campbell, Herman P. boatman, 150 E. Eagle.
Campbell, James, clerk, h. 11th cor. Hudson.
Campbell, James, clerk, 147 Main, b. 6th ab. Hudson.
Campbell, James, peddler, h. 6th ab. Hudson.
Campbell, J. A. B. derrick, cr'k. h. 258 Seneca.
Campbell, Lucy, widow, h. 238 Pearl.
Campbell, M. A. lumber dealer, n. toll bridge. h. Delaware cor. Church.
Campbell, Robert, at B. S. Engine Works, h. 10th, n. Carolina.
Campbell, Walter, at B. S. Engine Works, h. 10th n. Carolina.
Campbell, Wm. lake capt. h. 176 Delaware.
Campbell, Wm. clerk at foundry foot Wash. h. Tenth n. Carolina.
Campin, Tobias, truckman, h. Fulton n. Hayward.
CANDE, GILBERT, flour and feed dealer, cor. Michigan and Carroll, h. 141 N. Div.— See adv. p. 80.
Candee, Dean, pile driver, h. Perry n. Hayw'd.
Candee, Fernando C. stoves and tinware, 354 Main, h. Palmer n. Maryland.
Candee, Joseph, firm R. Wheeler & Co. h. 361 Franklin.
Cane, W. grocer, Hayward cor. Perry, h. same.
Canfield, J. H. with G. R. Wilson & Co. b. 157 Seneca.
Canfield, Prucia, Miss, b. 145 Elm.
Canley, Joseph, at iron works, h. Niagara n. Bidwell.
Cannaly, Ann, widow, h. 78 Perry.
Cannell, Henry N. Frontier mills, h. T. Cannell.
Cannell, Jas. flour packer in Frontier mills, h. T. Cannell.
Cannell, John, in Frontier mills, b. T. Cannell.
Cannell, Thos. shoemaker, h. Niag. n. Bouck.
Cannon, A. lab. h. Eagle n. Hickory.
Cannon, James, omnibus driver, 81 Carroll.
Cannon, James, lab. h. 14th n. Hampshire.
Cannon, John, carp. b. 7 6th.
Cannon, Thomas, carp. b. 7 6th.
Cannon, Thos. ship carp. h. Vermont n. 14th.
Cannon, Thomas C. with Brayley & Pitts, h. 6th n. Hospital.
Cannon. Peter. policeman, h. York n. 11th.
Canty, E. blacksmith, B. & L. S. R. R. h. Hayward cor. Clinton.
Canty, John C. tailor, 1 Seneca, h. 112 Sixth.
Canty, Pat. with Brayley & Pitts, h. 7 4th.
Canty, Thos. lab. h. Elk n. Michigan.
Capeder, Xavier, brewer. h. Spring n. Gen.
Capel, Jacob, lab. h. Seneca n. Ala.
Cappeller, August, polisher, h. William. n. Cedar.
Capron, Augustus, b. 1 Scott.

Carbry. John, moulder, b. Miller's blk. Mich. foot Fulton.
Cardanell, Rock, carp. h. Perry n. Hayward.
Carey. Grace, widow, h. 13 Mechanic.
Carey, H. C. 144 Main. h. 211 S. Div.
Carey James, lab. h. Erie canal n. Peniten'ry.
Carey, James, saloon, Ohio, h. same.
Carey, John H. lab. h. 66 Cedar.
Carey, Patrick, lab. h. Genesee n. Canal.
Carey, Rich. J. grocer, Abbott n. N. Y. C. R. R. h. same.
Carey, Wm. cooper, h. 36 Liberty.
Carey, Wm. A. cooper, h. 36 Liberty.
Cary, Harvey, cor. Louisiana and Carroll.
Cary, —, lab. h. 164 Seneca.
Cary, Jerry, engineer, b. 37 Church.
Cary, Samuel, h. 275 Washington.
Cary, Trumbull, b. 68 Delaware cor. Huron.
Cary, Walter, M. D. Office and h. 68 Delaware.
Caristone. B. moulder, h. 113 William.
Carley, John. lab. h. Niagara n. Ontario.
Carlet, machinist, h. 162 Seneca.
Carlin, Lieut. b. American.
Carling. Mathias. lab. h. 21 Sycamore.
Carman. Jos. sailor, b. 6 Commercial.
Carmichael, H. S. saloon. River bel. Erie, h. same.
Carmichael, Robt. grocer, Carolina cor. Palmer, h. same.
Carmody. James. lab. h. Fulton n. Chicago.
Carnel. Philip, porter, h. 81 Cherry.
Carney, James, ship carp. h. Ohio n. Chicago.
Carney. John, mariner, h. Elk cor. Marvin.
Carney, Michael, prop. Emerald House, 104 Exchange.
Carney, Wm. lab. on dock, h. Ala. n. Elk.
Carpenter, A. S. firm W. Petrie & Co. 13 C. Wharf, h. 180 Niagara.
Carpenter, Elizabeth, widow, h. 78 Oak.
Carpenter, Geo. W. gold pen maker, 159 Main, h. 122 Folsom.
Carpenter. John H. harness maker, 285 Main, h. 39 Oak.
Carpenter, L. J. lamp maker, 41 Ohio, h. 81 W. Chippewa.
Carpenter, Mart. D. clerk, 205 Main b. 26 Ellicott.
Carpenter, Socrates W. clerk, h. 149 Ellicott.
Carpenter, Thos. R. joiner. h. ac. creek.
Carr. Carpenter, prop. Farmer's Hotel, 176 Seneca.
Carr, Chas. tailor, h. cor. Morgan and Mohawk.
Carr, Henry, sailor, h. across Buffalo Creek.
Carr, James, clerk Pratt & Co. h. 22 Swan.
Carr, Jasper. with J. Weeks, b. 380 Franklin.
Carr, John, lab. h. cor. Evans and Canal.
Carr, John, lab. h. Louisiana n. South.
Carr, Michael, sailor, h. Fulton n. Hamburgh.
Carr, Pat. lab. h. Fulton n. Red Jacket.
Carr, Peter. lab. h. Chicago cor. Fulton.
Carr, Philip, fireman on lake, h. Fulton n. Chicago.
Carr, Robert, shoemaker, 43 Seneca, b. No. 5 Erie.
Carr, Thomas. saloon, cor. Clinton and Washington, h. 128 Eagle.
Carr, Thomas, tailor, h. 40 Delaware.
Carr, Wm. plumber, h. 14 William.

Carr, W. A. plumber, 354 Main, h. William n. Milnor.
Carick, Mrs. wid. h. Elk. ab. Alabama.
Carrick, Chas. fisherman, h. Bouck n. N. Wash,
Carrick, Charles, lab. h. Blossom n. Jubilee Bridge Ditch.
Carrick, John, ship carp. Moore cor. Miami.
Carrick, Margaret, wid. Wm. h. Fulton n. Ala.
Carroll, Augustus, car inspector, h. 5th n. Geo.
Carroll, Cornelius, lab. h. Mackinaw n. Penn.
Carroll, Dennis, lab. h. 17 Mississippi.
Carroll, Ed machinist, h. 37 Church.
Carroll, Ellen, wid. saloon, 162 Exch. h. same.
Carroll, James, ship carpenter, h. across Buffalo creek, opposite Reed's dock.
Carroll, John, cooper, b. Perry n. Hayward.
Carroll, John, joiner, h. 5th n. Carolina.
Carroll, John. h. 6th n. Pennsylvania.
Carroll, Martin, mariner, h. across creek.
Carroll, Mich'l, grocer, 5th n. Carolina, h. same.
Carroll, Pat. lab. h. York n. Towpath.
Carroll, Thos. truckman, h. Exch. n. Michigan.
Carruthers, Geo. engineer, b. Farmers' Home.
Carson. John. ship carpenter, h. 113 Pratt.
Carswell. Allen, ship carp. h. Lousiana n. Elk.
Carter, Eliza A. wid. of Chas. A. h. 286 Mich.
Carter, J. G. b. 286 Michigan.
Carter, W. whitewasher, h. 446 Michigan.
Carter, Wm. whitewasher, h. 71 Elm.
Cartier, George, Jr. lithographic printer, with Sage & Sons, h. 51 Clinton.
Carton, Brian, at Gasworks, h. Morgan n. Gen.
Carty, A. Queen City Ice Co. b. Revere.
Caryl, B. C. book-keeper, 2 E. Seneca, b. 262 Washington.
Caryl, Chas. cabinet maker, b. Catlin's Coffee House.
CASE & CO. tin shop, cor. Ohio and Washington.—See adv. p. 56.
Case, J. G. firm Case & Co. cor. Ohio and Washington, b. 216 S. Division.
CASE, NEHEMIAH, leather manufacturer and dealer, Exchange cor. Washington, h. 19 Carroll.—See adv. p. 51.
Case, Niles, transportation agent, C. Wharf foot Main street, h. 279 Pearl.
Case, W. H. book-keeper at 14 Exchange, h. 152 Seneca.
Casey, Edward, proprietor Western Railway Hotel, 39 Erie.
Casey, Harry, butcher, b. E. Seneca n. Chicago.
Casey, John,* blacksmith, h. Clinton n. Walnut.
Casey, Lyman R. book-keeper, 286 Main b. 59 E. Eagle.
Casey, Mac, ship carp. h. Porter n. Bouck ave.
Casey, Thomas, printer, h. 20 Perry.
Cash, Asa W. firm C. & M. 28 Central Wharf, h. Carey n. Morgan.
Cash & Merritt, insp. of high wines, 28 C. Wharf.
Casper, Anthony, clerk, 5 Seneca, b. Geo. Gage.
Casper, Joseph, stove mounter, h. cor. Batavia and Adam.
Cassady, Alice, widow h. California n. Adams.
Cassady, Robert, agent B. & L. H. R. W. h. Niagara n. Hudson.
Cassalhon, John, lab. h. Abbott road n. Iron Bridge.
Cassidy, Edward, b. Mrs. M. Cassidy.

Cassidy, Margaret, Mrs. h. California n. Adams.
Castle, Chas. law student, 290 Main, b. Delaware n. Utica.
CASTLE, DAN. B. jeweler, 135 Main, h. Delaware n. Utica.—*See adv. p. 75.*
Castle, Jno. W. clerk, B. & L. Huron freight office, b. 155 Swan.
Cation, Jno. sailor, h. 100 Fulton.
Catlin, A. engineer, h. 232 S. Division.
Catlin, Ira, Catlin's coffee house, 25 Com'l.
Cattel, John, miller, h. Hickory n. Clinton.
Caudell. John, book agent, h. Georgia bel. 5th.
Caughey, Jno. sawyer, h. Amherst n. Thomp'n.
Caul. Richard. ship carp. h. Vincennes n. South.
Caun, John, cartman, h. Elm n. N. Division.
Cavalli, Chas. h. 7th n. Hudson.
Cavalry, Rich. butcher, h. Perry n. Louisiana.
Cavanagh, Jas. lab. h. Pennsylvania cor. 13th.
Cavanagh, Jeremiah, saloon, Ohio n. Columbia.
Cavanagh, Jno. in gas works, h. Cottage n. Md.
Caveng, Luke, Rev. rec. St. Michael's church, Washington bel. Tupper.
Cear, John, saloon, Seneca n. Jeff. h same.
Cedell, Wm. tinsmith, h. Hickory n. Clinton.
Celler, Henry, boiler maker, h. over 8 Terrace.
Certier, George, lithographer, h. 51 Clinton.
Cesch, John, cooper, h. Mortimer n. Genesee.
Chabot, Theodore J. ship carp. h. Wm. n. Pine.
Chace, E. C. treasurer Emigrant Savings B'k 347 Main, h. 58 E. Eagle.
Chadderdon, James, b. 5 Franklin.
Chamberlain. A. D. blacksmith, h. 7 Vine.
CHAMBERLAIN & CO. carriage manufacturers, Niagara cor. Mohawk.—*See adv. p. 72.*
Chamberlain, Hunting S. carriage maker, Pearl cor. Mohawk, h. Ferry ab. Delaware.
Chamberlain, Jonathan, firm Chamberlain & Co. b. 19 Morgan.
Chamberlain, Jno. building mover, h. Perry n. Chicago.
Chamberlain, John E. carpenter, b. P. A. Balcom, Main cor. Ferry.
Chamberlain, John, building mover, h. 109 S. Division.
Chamberlain, Sylvester, law student with Judge Sheldon.
Chamberlain, S. M. carriage maker, b. 19 Morg.
Chamberlayne, Edward, principal public school No. 18, h. 117 S. Division.
Chambers, Hiram, insurance agent, 179 Main, h. 203 Oak.
Chambers, Mary, widow, h. Chicago n. Elk.
Chambers, Thomas, sailor, h. Elk opp. Marine.
Chambers, Thomas, lab. b. Chicago n. Elk.
Chambers, Wm. sawyer, h. r. Dearborn n. Amherst.
CHAMOT, C. P. bootmaker, 217 Washington, h. 86 Clinton.—*See adv. p. 95.*
Chamot, Fred. carp. h. Tupper cor. Ellicott.
Chamot, Louis, machinist, h. 373 Washington.
Champlin, Capt. S. h. Main above Allen.
Champlin, O. H. P. druggist, Arcade building, b. Capt S. Champlin.
Chandler, Elizabeth, widow, dress maker, b. Mariner n. Virginia.
Chandler, Frank, b. H. Chandler.
Chandler, Henry, h. 163 Swan.
Chandler, J. b. H. Chandler.

Chandler, John, b. Mrs. Chandler.
Chandler, Mary, widow, h. Thompson n. Amherst.
Chandler, Orra, h. Mariner n. Virginia.
Chantlen, Edward, gardener. Spring n. Gen.
Chapin, Cooley S. builder, Elm n. Clinton, h. 240 Franklin.
Chapin, E. P. asst. district attorney, 7 Granite Block, b. American, room St. James.
Chapin, Heman, farmer, h. Main n. Chapin.
Chapin, L. T. clerk, b. Genesee House.
Chapin, Roswell, att'y, over 148 Main, h. same.
Chapin, Wm. M. farmer, h. Main n. Chapin.
Chappel, E. liquor dealer, h. 42s Michigan.
Chappell, Nathan, b. Carroll below Alabama.
Chappoton, S. ticket agent N. Y. & E. R. R. h. 45 Ellicott.
Chappuis, J. B. stone cutter, h. 364 Michigan.
Chapman, Geo. S. h. cor. Fulton and Alabama.
Chapman, Henry, lab. b. 11 William.
Chapman, J. Y. lake and canal store, 29 Cent'l Wharf, b. Western.
Chapman, M. with Hamlin & Mendsen, b. 61 W. Huron.
Chapman, Thos. harness maker, b. 105 Terrace.
Chard, James F. dep. comptroller, cor. Franklin and Eagle, b. Mansion.
Charick, John, lab. h. across creek.
Charel, Charles. machinist at foundry cor. Water and State, h. Seneca.
Charles, Benj. caulker, h. Louisiana n. Fulton.
Charles, Edward, millwright, h. Hayward n. Perry.
Charles, Nelson, caulker, b. La. n. Fulton.
Charles, Philip, miller, h. Elk n. Chicago.
Charles, Stephen D. civil engineer, office Prosser Buildings.
Charles, Thomas, engineer, h. Ill. n. Perry.
Charlton, Franklin B. carpenter, h. 26 Niag.
Christy, J. P. clerk, b. 194 S. Division.
Chrysler, Geo. broom manuf. Green, h. 43 E. Eagle.
Chrysler, Jacob, broom maker, with G. Chrysler, b. same.
Chase & Bird, merchants and tight bar'l manuf. Niagara cor. Amherst.
Chase, Chas. L. shoemaker, 130 Pearl, h. same.
Chase, Geo. H. cashier B. & S. L. R. R. office 3 Harvey block, b. cor. Main and Huron.
CHASE, JAMES H. tea, coffee, spice dealer, 271 Main, h. 366 Franklin.—*See adv. p. 72.*
Chase, James A. firm C. & Bird, h. Amherst n. Dearborn.
Chase, Marcellus W. firm W. C. & Son, b. 90 9th.
Chase, Wesley, firm W. C. & Son, h. 90 9th.
Chase, W. & Son, school furniture, 198 7th.
Chasseuil, Jacob, saloon, Genesee n. tollgate.
Chavel, Peter, grocer, Washington cor. Tupper, h. same.
Cheakley, Benj. lab. h. 44 Jackson.
CHEESMAN & DODGE, livery stable, 116 Pearl.—*See adv. p. 93.*
Cheesman, Wm. firm C. & Dodge. h. 23 Court.
Cheevers, Thos. saloon, opp. C. R. R. freight house.
Chemit, Genenere, h. Clinton n. Cedar.
Cheney, Daniel, canal captain, h. Carroll n. Heacock.

Cheney, E. D. fish market, h. cor. Bristol and Spring.

Cherlius, G. A. music teacher, h. Elm n. Gen.

Cherry, Hamilton, farmer, Amherst n. Tonawanda.

Chesney, Samuel, saloon, Ohio n. Mich. h. same.

Chester, Anson G. editor Commercial Advertiser, h. 125 Niagara.

Chester, A. T. Rev. principal Buffalo Female Academy, h. Delaware cor. Park place.

Chester, Chas. clerk, Pratt & Co. b. 301 Oak.

Chester, —, clerk, b. 202 Swan.

Chester, Frederick, with Howard, Whitcomb & Co. b. 202 Swan.

CHESTER, LUCAS, dyer, 18 Batavia, h. same. —See adv. inside last cover.

Chester, Thos. miller, h. Dearborn n. Amherst.

Chevalier, Edward, Rev h. junction York and North.

Chichester, James L. bookbinder, 182 Washington, h. 263 S. Division.

Chidsey, C. H. with Pratt & Co. h. 40 7th.

Chief of Police. office 12 Exchange.

Chilcott, Alfred, joiner, h. Perry n. Hamburgh.

Chilcott Robert, ship joiner, h. Hamburgh n. Perry.

Childs, Henry, h. 145 Swan.

Childs, J. B. widow, h. over 12 Sycamore.

Childs, Geo. sailor, h 342 Michigan.

Chisler, Christian, lab. Krettner n. William.

Chittenden, Chas. machinist, b. Jefferson n. Wm.

Chittenden, Geo. tallyman, H. Niles & Co. h. 3 Scott.

Chittenden, Thos. joiner, h. Jefferson n. Wm.

Choate, E. H. book-keeper with J. T. Flint, b. City.

Chobcal, Thos. tailor, h. Monroe n. Brown.

Choppe, Frank. finisher, h. Seneca n. Chicago.

CHOYER. THOS. silver plater. over 146 Main, h. 16 Folsom.—See adv. p. 77.

Chresz, Geo. painter, h. Batavia n. Lutheran.

Chretien, Chas. carp. h. Wash. n. Burton alley.

Chretien, Chas. painter and glazier, 457 Main, h. same.

Chretien, John, leather store, h. over 3 E. Gen.

Christ, Andrew, sewer maker, h. 4 Bennett.

Christ. Frederick, engineer, Evans' elevator, h. 148 9th.

Christ, Fred. engineer, h. 148 9th.

Christ, Henry, milkman, h. Hickory n. Batavia.

Christ, John, shoemaker, h. Lutheran n. Bat.

Christ, P. J. saloon, Maiden Lane, h. same.

Christbaum, August, lab. h. Sycamore n. Pine.

Christbaum, Joseph, lab. h. Sycamore n. Mich.

Christean, Wm. on C. R. R. b. Revere.

Christensen, Peter, porter, Roos' alley n. Wm.

Christey, Arthur. book-keeper, h. 34 Pine.

Christian, John. captain, h. Ferry n. Canal.

Christian, Wm. breakman, b. John Christian.

Christie, C. H. clerk, 318 Main, h. 194 S. Div.

Christoph. Eugene. 150 Main, b. 75 Batavia.

Christoph, Frederick W. carriage painter, 15 E. Eagle, h. 77 Batavia.

Christoph, Lorenz, lab. h. Sycamore n. Walnut.

Christopher, Henry, lab. h. over 188 Genesee.

Chur, Chris. milk dairy, Genesee n. Williamsville road.

Church, Alfred, in elevator, h. Watson n. How'd.

Church, Allen, watch maker, with R. Church, 9 E. Swan, b. 24 Eagle.

Church, Alvah. broker. Exchange cor. Washington, h. 213 Niagara.

Church, Henry W. book-keeper, with J. G. Dudley, b. 29 Swan.

Church, Levius S. com. of deeds, Elk cor. Louisiana, h. 217 S. Division.

Church, Merwin, book-keeper, 259 Main, h. 37 Oak.

Church, Ralph, watch maker, Swan n. Washington, h. 24 E. Eagle.

Churchill, C. P. firm C. & Parker, h. 511 Main.

Churchill, H. civil eng'r, h Palmer n. Hudson.

Churchill. Homer. clerk. b. Seneca cor. Chicago.

Churchill & Parker, grocers. 336 Main.

Churchill. W. Sumner, sign writer and painter, 157 Main, b. 14 E. Mohawk.

Churchyard, Jos. lumber dealer, cor. Clinton and Adams, h. Adams n. Clinton.

Cink, Frank. shoemaker. b. 106 Exchange.

Ciprian, Mey, tailor, h. Johnson opp. North.

Cittel, Louis, lab. b. Fulton n. Hamburgh.

Cittel. John C. miller, h. Fulton n. Hamburgh.

City Building and Loan Association, 236 Main.

City Hall Buildings, cor. Franklin and Eagle.

Clabb, Henry, carpenter, h. S. Division n. R. R. crossing.

Clabbox, Thos. carpenter, h. 63 William.

Clabbox, Peter, carpenter, h. Pine n. William.

Glabeaux, Amos, joiner, h. 52 Bennett.

Clads, John, shoemaker, b. 2 Michigan.

Claessen, C. E. clerk, h. 183 Franklin.

Claessen, Thiery, French teacher, 183 Franklin.

Clammont, John, teamster, h. Ferry n. Main.

Clanc , Wm. B. painter, over 92 Main, h. 93 9th y

Clapp, A. M. & Co. proprietors Morning Express, 158 Main.

Clapp, A. M. firm A. M. C. & Co. h. cor. 7th and Georgia.

Clapp, Charles P. upholsterer, h. 90 W. Hur.

Clapp, Harry H. firm A. M. C. & Co. b. cor. Georgia and 7th.

Clapp, Henry, carp. h. 400 S. Division.

Clapp, Mathews & Waite, steam printing house 158 Main.

Claraluna, Wm. teacher language and music, h. 225 Washington.

Clare, Mich. machinist, h. Mack'w n. Chicago.

Clark, Adam, h. 9th n. Georgia.

Clark, Alfred, blacksmith, h. Elk n. Chicago.

Clark, Alfred, Michigan n. Swan.

Clark, A. L. printer, b. 125 Michigan.

Clark, Brad. millwright, h. Adams n. Albany.

Clark, B. B. carp. h. Eagle n. Spring.

Clark, Charles A. clerk, city clerk's office, b. Seth Clark.

Clark, Daniel, engineer, h. 7th n. Pensylvania.

Clark, David, firm C. & Waterman, h. Niagara n. Vermont.

Clark, David N. cooper. Burwell Place between Scott and Perry, h. Pearl above Virginia.

Clark, Daniel, mason, h. 1 Tracy.

Clark, Delevan F. attorney, 7 Arcade Building, h. 50 N. Division.

Clark, D. L. stitching, b. 89 E. Seneca.

Clark, Edwin, clerk, b. 255 Washington.

Clark, E. A. Mrs. millinery store, 283 Main h. same.
CLARK. EDWIN, sewing machines, Kremlin block.—*See adv. opposite page.*
Clark, Elizabeth A. widow, h. 294 Ellicott.
Clark, Elizabeth b. Elk cor. Lousiana.
Clark, Erastus, Jr. freight agent N. Y. C. R. R. Co. b. 25 Ellicott.
Clark, E. W. h. 21 Pearl.
Clark, F. D. at O. H. P. Champlin's, b. 1 Tracy.
Clark, Geo. M. book-keeper, b. Oak n. Clinton.
Clark, Geo. H. mariner, h. Fulton n. Hayward.
Clark, George R. soap dealer with J. Wheeler, h. Fulton n. Alabama.
Clark, George W. Mrs. ambrotypist, 348 Main, h. same.
Clark, H. A. conductor, N. st. R. R. b. D. Clark.
Clark, H. A. painter, h. 171 Oak.
Clark, Henry, lab. h. Jeff. n. Peckham.
Clark, Henry, carpenter, b. 294 Ellicott.
Clark, H. S. Am. Ex. Co. b. 33 W. Chippewa.
Clark, J. butcher, cor. Riley and Jefferson.
Clark, Japr. with Sherman & Barnes, h. 56 6th.
Clark, John, saloon, h. 30 Scott.
Clark, John, fireman, b. Revere.
Clark, John, paper peddler, b. Clinton n. Jeff.
Clark, John, reamer, b. National.
Clark, John, boiler maker, h. South n. Ohio.
Clark, John, grocer, h. across creek.
Clark, Jno. B. saloon, 22 Exchange, h. same.
Clark, Joseph W. M. D. h. and office 283 Main.
Clark, Joseph, printer, b. 376 Michigan
Clark, Justus, 23 Central House.
Clark, L. B. attorney, 13 Spaulding's Exchange, h. 377 Franklin.
Clark, Lot, h. Ferry n. Delaware.
Clark, M. lab. h. 163 S. Division.
Clark, Myron H. at 34 Lloyd, h. 30 Chippewa.
Clark, O. A. b. Revere House.
Clark, Orange W. firm Adams & Co. h. 40 Carroll.
Clark, Orton S. with Young, Lockwood & Co. b. 35 Chippewa.
Clark, Peter, lab. h. Carroll below Heacock.
Clark, Predensia, widow, h. across creek.
Clark, R. B. boarding house, 275 Exchange.
Clark, S. A. book-keeper Palmer & Monteath, b. Courter House.
Clark, Seth, firm Sears & C. 9th n. Penn.
Clark, Stephen C. cl'k, 6 C. Wharf, h. 282 Pearl.
Clark, Stephen E. book-keeper, Michigan cor. Scott, b. 21 Pearl.
CLARK & STORMS, dealers in clothing, 308 Main.—*See adv. p. 88.*
Clark & Waterman, ice dealers, Main cor. Sen.
Clark, Striphing W. drover, Seneca n. Jeff'n.
CLARK, THOMAS, distillery, cor. Wash. and Perry, h. Main n. Barker.—*See adv. p. 49.*
Clark, W. A. machinist, h. 97 6th.
Clark, William, stove mounter, b. Swan n. Union furnace.
Clark, William, moulder, h. 391 Swan.
Clark, William, h. 10 Ellicott.
CLARK. WM. H. baker, Main cor. Huron and junc. Elk and Ohio, h. Ohio junc. Elk.—*See adv. p. 47.*
Clark, William E. clerk, b. 282 Pearl.
Clark, Zenas, cl'k. H. Stillman, h. 35 Chippewa.

Clarke, Charles E. attorney, 2 Granite block, Main, h. 259 Franklin.
Clarke, Cyrus, prod. and com. 5 Central Wharf, h. Cold Spring.
Clarke, E. H. stave dealer, 2 Main, up stairs, b. American.
Clarke, E. J. h. 22 Carolina.
Clarke, F. C. b. 22 Carolina.
Clarke, Stephen C. book-keeper, 6 Central Wharf, b. 282 Pearl.
Clarke, Walter, Rev. pastor 1st Presbyterian Church, h. 468 Main.
Clarkson, Jno. engineer, h. Perry n. Hamburgh.
Claratuna, S. B. Mrs. teacher, No. 14, h. 225 Washington.
Clary, Thomas, sailor. h. 4th n. Virginia.
CLAUDE, LOUIS, French dyers, 306 Mich. h. same.—*See adv. p. 52.*
Claus, Daniel, clothing store, 123 Genesee.
Claus, Casper, lab. h. Ash n. Sycamore.
Clausz, Geo. lab. h. Williamsville road n. Ferry.
Clawson, B. F. book-keeper, h. 64 W. Mohawk.
Clay, H. M. lithographer, h. 115 6th.
Clayton, M. Mrs. milliner, 370 Main, h. same.
Clayton, Thos. G. tinsmith, h. Terrace n. Pearl.
Clayton, T. J. tinsmith, h. next U. S. hotel.
Clebeaux, P. ship carp. h. Hickory n. Clinton.
Clement, Jno. teamster, h. Ferry n. Main.
Clemmens, Henry, h. William n. Bennett.
Clemmons, C. C. painter, h. 137 E. Seneca.
Clemons, Ann, Miss, boarding house, 436 Main.
Clemons, Jacob, grocer, on Seneca n. 13th Ward House.
Clemons, Robert, lab. h. 487 Washington.
Cleudenning, Henry, brakeman, b. 24 Chicago.
Cleovin, Philip, omnibus driver, h. 98 Carroll.
Clere, Veroni. Miss, h. Elm n. Sycamore.
Clever, Cecelia, widow, h. over 12 Sycamore.
Cleveland, Anna, school teacher, b. 87 West Huron.
Cleveland, Grover, attorney at law, Erie cor. Pearl, b. 11 Oak.
Cleveland, Henry, b. Mansion House.
Cleveland, L. lamp manufactory, cor. Washington and Perry, b. Mansion House.
Cleveland, Palmer, builder, h. 87 Huron.
Cleveland, S. Edwin, at Washington cor. Perry, h. 7 Church.
Clifford, Chas. baker, b. junction Elk and Ohio.
Clifford, G. C. b. Western Hotel.
Clifford, James, grocery and house Hudson n. Niagara
Clifford, J. C. firm Brown & Co. b. Delaware n. Barker.
Clifford, Jno. plumber, 237 Main, h. 70 Pine.
Clifton, Richard, lab. h. 103 7th.
Clifton, Wm. at Gas Works, h. 44 Jackson.
Clingon, William, machinist, LeCouteulx n. Canal, h. 3 Evans.
Clinton, Chas. A. engineer, b. 43 Pearl.
Clinton, DeWitt, attorney, 19 Arcade Building, b. 43 Pearl.
Clinton, George DeWitt, Capt. N. Y. S. V. M. h. Niagara cor. Breckenridge.
Clinton, Geo. W. Judge of Superior Court, b. 43 Pearl.
Clinton, Henry P. Lieut. N. Y. S. V. M. h. Niagara cor. Breckenridge.

Clinton, Henry, lab. h. Niagara n. Bidwell.
Clinton, Jane, wid. h. cor. Niag. and Breck'rge.
Clinton, Jane. teacher, b. Mrs. Clinton, cor. Niagara and Breckenridge.
Clinton Mills, L. Enos & Co. upper Bl'k Rock.
Clinton, Thomas R. clerk, City Clerk's office, b. cor. Niagara and Breckenridge.
Clock, Richard, lab. h. Carey bel. Morgan.
Clodal, A. brass finisher, 237 Main.
Clor, Michael, boot and shoe dealer, 133 Main, h. 72 Delaware.
Close, Thomas, brickmaker, h. Clinton n. Raze.
Close, Emery, captain on lake. h. 96 Carroll.
Close, John W. machinist, h. 309 Seneca.
Close, Patrick, mason, h. 6th n. York.
Close, Jerome B. printer, h. 176 Swan.
Closson, Benjamin F. clerk, Central Wharf, b. 62 West Mohawk.
Cluen, Peter, lab. h. Hickory n. Batavia.
Cluff, Anne, widow, Niagara n, Bouck.
Clute, A. L. widow, h. 66 S. Division.
Clute, James E. checkman, L. S. R. R. h. 66 S. Division.
Coad, Thomas, ship carpenter, h. Miami n. La.
Coak, Jos. blacksmith, Washington cor. Green, h. 7th n. Georgia.
Coan, Cyrus, h. 4 11th.
Coan, Wm. H. painter, h. 4th ab. Georgia.
Coates, Jacob, lard boiler, with R. Bullymore, h. St. Paul n. Main.
Coats, John, h. Van Rensselaer n. Carroll.
Coatsworth, Caleb, h. Elk n. Alabama.
Coatsworth, John, h. Elk n. Hamburgh.
Coatsworth, Jos. carp. h. cor. Gay and Potter.
Coatsworth, Thomas, wood yard, cor. Erie and Canal, h. 21 Union.
Cobb, A. R. farmer, h. Best E. of Jefferson.
Cobb, Carlos, firm C. & Co. h. cor. Swan and Ellicott.
COBB & CO. produce commission merchants and shipping agents, 20 and 21 Central Wharf.—*See adv. p. 36.*
Cobb, E. G. Red Jacket saloon, 182 Main.
Cobb, Francis, drayman, h. 177 Seneca.
Cobb, L. E. clerk, Red Jacket dining saloon.
Cobb, Oscar, firm C. & Co. h. 8 Church.
Cobb, Samuel, hackman, h. 111 W. Huron.
Cobb, Wm. H. firm Wm. H. C. & Co. h. Delaware ab. Allen.
COBB, WM. H. & CO. flour and grain dealers, cor. Terrace and Evans.—*See adv. p. 80.*
Coburn, T. S. clerk, 4 Exchange, b. Delaware cor. Summer.
Cochlin, Chas. lab. h. across creek.
Cochrane, A. G. C. book-keeper, American Express Company, h. 67 E. Eagle.
Cochrane, Edward C. American Express Company, b. 67 Eagle.
Cochrane, Timothy, merchant tailor, 107 Main, h. same.
Cochrane, William, b. 67 E. Eagle.
Codd, James, ship carp. h. Louisiana n. Elk.
Coe, Spencer C. attorney, over 140 Main, h. 6th n. Hudson.
Coen, Ann, widow, h. 4th n. Carolina.
Coester, J. dyer, 444 Michigan, h. same.
Coester, William, weigher, with C. W. Evans, b. 444 Michigan.

Coffall, Felix, lab. h. Ohio n. South.
Coffee, Cornelius, lab. h. Abbott.
Coffin, J. on Niagara Street R. R. b. 7th n. Vt.
Cofflin, C. A. cond'r, N. Y. C. R. R. h. 51 Oak.
Cogan, James, lab. 4th n. Carolina.
Cogswell, Henry F. h. 45 W. Genesee.
Cogswell, M. C. millwright at Eagle Iron Works, h. 64 E. Eagle.
Cohen, Charles, clerk, b. 223 Carroll.
Cohn, Samuel, peddler, h. 43 Cherry.
Coine, Michael, lab. h. 6th n. Mass.
Coit, Alfred S. b. G. C. Coit. 111 Delaware.
Coit, A. H. firm G. C. C. & Son, h. Morgan ab. Huron.
Coit, Chas. T. cashier International Bank, h. cor. Swan and Pearl.
Coit, Edgar C. clerk, G. C. C. & Son, b. G. C. Coit, 111 Delaware.
Coit, F. E. Bennett's Elevator, h. 169 Pearl.
Coit, Geo. h. Swan cor. Pearl.
Coit, Geo. Jr. asst. supt. Buff. gas light Co. h. 134 Franklin.
Coit, G. C. firm G. C. C. & Son, h. 111 Del.
Coit, G. C. & Son, wool, hides and com. 70 Main and 15 Hanover.
Colburn, Mary E. widow, h. 15 Union.
Colburn, Ransom H. civil engineer, 14 Spaulding's Exchange, b. Delaware cor. North.
Colburn, T. F. b. 15 Union.
Cole, Alexander, grocer, 163 Seneca.
Cole, D. W. vinegar and pickle factory, 8 Hanover, b. 16 Carroll.
Cole, George, shoemaker, b. 163 Elk.
Cole, Jno. H. shipwright, h. 227 Carroll.
Cole, Jno. watchman, h Mariner ab. Virginia.
Cole, Robert W. painter, h. Fulton n. Alabama.
Cole, Robert, boatman, h. 11th n. Massachusetts.
Cole, Warren, h. 16 Carroll.
Coleman, Chas. office 4 Swan, b. 303 Main.
Coleman, Chas. H. 4 E. Swan, h. 325 Wash.
Coleman, John, shoemaker, h. 97 Fulton.
Coleman, John C. bricklayer, h. Park n. Va.
Coleman, John H. drug store, glass and paints, 4 E. Swan, b. Huron cor. Main.
Coleman, Jno. lab. h. Fox n. Genesee.
Coleman, Martha A. saloon, 17 Batavia.
Coleman, Wm. picture gallery, over 4 E. Swan, h. 13 9th.
Coleman, Wm. B. mason, h. 22 Palmer.
Colerin, Wm. boatman, h. Packet dock n. Com'l.
Coles, Stephen, lab. h. Perry n. Alabama.
Colgrove, Bela H. attorney, 6 Hollister Building, h. 143 Clinton.
Colie, Edwin T. book-keeper, b. 108 Clinton.
Colie, G. W. book-keeper, b. 108 Clinton.
Colie, O. S. agent, h. 108 Clinton.
Colie, S. D. lumber dealer, Michigan bet. Seneca and Exchange, h. 352 E. Seneca.
Collamer, Charles, engineer, N. Y. C. R. R. b. Courter House.
Collamer, G. D. clerk N. Y. C. R. R. freight depot, h. 149 Pearl.
Collamer, J. supt. N. Y. C. R. R. h. Erie n. Del.
Collary, Roger, tanner, h. Ontario cor. Niagara.
Collary, Richard, farmer, h. Ontario cor. Niag.
Colleck, Wm. moulder, b. cor. Scott and Market.
Collen, S. shoemaker, h. Sycamore n Michigan.
Collette, Leon, Am. Exp. mess. h. 39 Union.

Collette, L. N. watchmaker, 39½ Union, h. same.
Colley, David D. carriage maker, Washington n. S. Division, b. 127 Chippewa.
COLLIGON, F. Eagle Brass Foundry, cor. Wash. and Perry, h. 131 Oak.—*See adv. p. 56.*
Colligon, John, brass founder, h. Walnut n. Clinton.
Colligon, John B. clerk, Perry cor. Washington, b. 131 Oak.
Colligon, L. W. engineer, b. 131 Oak.
Colligon, Peter, lab. h. Tennessee n. South.
Collingwood, Ralph, lab. b. Spring n. William.
Collingwood, Roger, engineer, b. Spring n. William.
Collingwood, Wm. clerk, h. Wm. n. Spring.
Collins, Cornelius, lab. b. Manley's, Ohio opposite freight depot.
Collins, Dan. lab. h. Fulton n. Chicago.
Collins, Dennis, policeman, h. 7th n. Hudson.
Collins, D. Jr. clerk at P. O. b. 7th ab. Hu son.
Collins, Ellen, widow, h. across creek.
Collins, Franklin, b. 25 Pearl.
Collins, James, lab. h. across creek.
Collins, Jas. lab. h. 219 Carroll.
Collins, Joannah, widow, h. n. foot Genesee.
Collins, John, baggageman, S. L. R. R. h. Folsom n. Chicago.
Collins, John, ship carpenter, Bidwell's ship yard, b. 4 Oak.
Collins, John, lab. h. N. Division n. Hickory.
Collins, John, lab. h. Carroll n. Alabama.
Collins, Laurence, switchman, N. Y. C. R. R. h. Elk n. N. Y. C. R. R. track.·
Collins, Michael, lab. h. Abbott's road n. Elk.
Collins, Michael, lab. h. Louisiana n. Ohio.
Collins, M. firm C. & McClay, h. 4 Oak.
Collins, Morris, lab. h. Mill n. Red Jacket.
Collins, Morris, Jr. blacksmith, b. 110 Exch.
Collins, Pat. lab. h. Seneca n. Hamburgh.
Collins, Pat. lab. h. Lake n. Niagara.
Collins, Pat. lab. h. Connecticut n. towpath.
Collins, Tim. lab. h. Connecticut n. towpath.
Collins, T. F. blank book manufacturer, 156½ Main, h. 25 Pearl.
Collins, Thos. shoemaker, h. 11th cor. Mass.
COLLINSON, SAM, file maker, Hospital bel. Court, h. Fulton n. Ala.—*See adv. p. 52.*
Collis, Wm. saloon, 21 E. Seneca.
Colome, Francis, cook at American, h. 104 Sycamore.
Colquhoun, John, h. Palmer n. Virginia.
Colston, Fred. moulder. b. 137 Seneca.
Colston, John, bakery, 426 Main.
Colt, Frank, fireman, S. L. R. R. h. Perry n. Hamburgh.
Colton, Frank, engineer, h. 142 Elk.
Colton, Henry, Mrs. widow, h. 202 Pearl.
Colton, Isaac C. ass't pres't Buff. N. Y. & Erie R. R. h. Eagle cor. Delaware.
Colton, Joseph, b. 13 Court.
Columbus, Alex. farmer, h. n. Lee's Corners.
Colvin, Alex. Jr. teamster, b.Walnut n. Clinton.
Colvin, Barton B. b. 163 Franklin.
Colvin, Benona, farmer, Burt n. Delaware.
Colvin, Dexter, seaman, h. Louisiana n. Elk.
Colvin, Hanan, farmer, Colvin, bet. Burt and Amherst.
Colvin, John, blacksmith, b. Walnut n. Clinton.

Colvin, Mary, widow of Alexander, Walnut n. Clinton.
Colwell, Daniel, book-keeper, 278 Main, h. 5 E. Huron.
Colyer, C. W. teacher No. 11, h. 59 Clinton.
Coman, A. B. printer, 5 W. Seneca, b. 25 Pearl.
Combs, S. M. Mrs. seamstress, b. cor. Washington and Genesee.
Comerford, Nich. lab. h. White's Cor. plank road n. city line.
Comerford, Wm. G. butcher, h. White's Cor. plank road n. city line.
Compton, Louis, carpenter, h. 203 N. Division.
Comstock, Albert L. M. D. h. Albany cor Jeff.
Comstock & Co. fancy goods, 230 Main.
Comstock, Geo. salesman, Eaton's planing mill, h. 214 Carroll.
Comstock, Jas. mariner, h. 10th n. Maryland.
Comstock, James E. mariner, h. Mariner n. Va.
Comstock, John, carpenter, h. 134 Folsom.
Comstock, Jos. miller, h. Niagara n. Hamilton.
Comstock, Martin, grocer, liquors, etc. 21 Main, h. 291 Michigan.
Comstock, M. L. hat and cap store, 202 Main, b. 29 Swan.
Comte, Frank, h. and store Niag. n. Hamilton.
Connant, Allen E. carpenter, h. Fulton n. Ala.
Condon, John, captain, h. 360 Swan.
Cone, H. dry goods, 194 Main, h. 56 N. Div.
Cone, Wm. H. waiter, Bonney's Hotel.
Cone, Wm. M. printer, Commercial Advertiser, h. Spring bet. Swan and S. Division.
Conell, Andrew, ship carp b. La. n. Miami.
Congar, H. M. M. D. 137 Pearl, h. same.
Congdon, Harriet M. widow, h. Potter n. Wm.
Conlon, John, painter, b. 257 Franklin.
Conkling, Aurelean, att'y, clerk U. S. District Court, 13 Government Building, h. 206 Pearl.
Conkling F. A. b. 206 Pearl.
Conley, Edw. saloon, h. Mackinaw cor. Ohio.
Conley, John, saloon, Ohio junction Miami.
Conley, Michael, lab. h. n. round house.
Connar, Chris. at Robert's malt house, h. Elm n. Goodell.
Connell, Jas. lab. h. Perry n. R. R. crossing.
Connell, John, lab. h. Genesee n. Jackson.
Connell, John, saloon, 21 Water, h. same.
Connell, Richard, saloon, Evans cor. Water, h. same.
Connell, Thos. lab. h. Exch. n. R. R. crossing.
Connelly, Edward, sailor, h. Louisiana n. Elk.
Connelly, James, produce dealer, Elk st. market, h. Perry n. Alabama.
Connelly, James, lab. h. S. Division n. R. R. crossing.
Connelly, John stone cutter h. Virginia n. 6th.
Connely, John, lab. Erie canal n. Ft. Porter.
Connely, Michael, saloon, h. 197 Washington.
Connely, Timothy, lab. h. Ferry n. N. Adams.
Conner, Daniel, lab. h. across creek.
Conner, Patrick, lab. h. Perry n. R. R. track.
Conner, Thos. lab. h. Columbia n. Ohio.
Connere, Peter, sailor, h. La. n. Mackinaw.
Conners, Michael, lab. h. Carroll n. Heacock.
Connor, Jno. drayman, h. Perry bet. Hamburgh and Alabama.
Connor, M. O. Rev. pastor St. Bridget's church, h. Louisiana n. Fulton.

Connors, Dennis, lab. h. 4th ab. Georgia.
Connors, John, stone mason, h. 5th n. Va.
Conover, Wm. carpenter, h. Hickory n. Eagle.
Conover, Dan. boatman, h. 37 Cedar.
Conoway, Pat. lab. h. 108 Fulton.
Conrad, Adam, blacksmith, b. Genesee cor. Oak.
Conrad, Jacob, mason, h. Jefferson n. Clinton.
Conry, Michael, lab. h. Genesee n. Erie canal.
Conry, T. J. news depot, 17½ Seneca, b. 5 Carroll.
Consdorff, Anthony J. boot fitter, h. Spruce n. Genesee.
Constantine, Jas. lab. h. across creek.
Constantine, James, cooper, h. 6th bel. Va.
Constantine, J. W. h. 140 6th.
Constantine, L. A. h. 131 Clinton.
Constantine, Patrick, lab. h. 11 Iron place, N. Washington.
Conway, Dennis, lab. h. Indiana n. Perry.
Conway, Hugh, at N. St. R. R. stable, h. 9th n. Hampshire.
Conway, John, tinsmith, b. Fulton n. Hayw'd.
Conway, Lackey Y. Jr. tinsmith, b. 6th n. Va.
Conway, John, lab. h. 5th n. Carolina.
Conway, Lackey Y. tinsmith, h. 6th n. Va.
Conway, Thomas, lab. with Henry Childs, h. Hayward n. Perry.
Conway, Thos. teamster, h. 11th n. Carolina.
Cook, Benjamin, bricklayer, h. 4 Vine.
Cook, Mrs. B. midwife, h. 4 Vine.
Cook, B whitewasher, Hoffman alley n. Ham.
Cook, Chas. L. butcher, h, 189 E. Seneca.
Cook, C. T. Mrs. h. Park n. Virginia.
Cook, E. F. teacher No. 6, h. 226 S. Division.
Cook, E. L. clerk, b. 59 Oak.
Cook, Edward, barber, Exch. h. Potter n. Wm.
Cook, Edward, clerk, cor. Eagle and Pearl, b. 105 Ellicott.
Cook, Eli, attorney, cor. Main and S. Division, h. 170 Franklin.
Cook, Frank, clerk, at 211 Main, h. Oak n. Goodell.
Cook, Fred. bakery, Seneca bel. R R. track, h. same.
Cook, Henry, shoemaker, h. Pine n. Goodell.
Cook, I. J. with Hamlin & Mendsen, b. Bonney's Hotel.
Cook, James, sailor, h. 199 N. Division.
Cook, John, joiner in Prince & Co.'s factory, h. 12th n. Connecticut.
Cook, John, shoemaker, 8 Water, h. 7. Water.
Cook, Joseph, painter, 45 Swan.
Cook, Josiah, attorney, firm Cook & Crandall, 136 Main, h. 101 Oak.
Cook, Lyman, builder, h. Oak n. Clinton.
Cook, Merritt, book-keeper, b. 226 S. Division.
Cook, P. G. missionary, h. 96 Clinton.
Cook, Patrick, lab. h. 5 Mississippi.
Cook, Patrick, warehouseman, foot Lloyd, h. same.
Cook, Peter, h. Walnut n. William.
Cook, Philip, moulder, h. 266 Adam.
Cook, W. P. baggageman, h. Georgia cor. 5th.
Cook, William, mariner, h. across creek.
Cook, Wm. teamster, b Main cor. North.
Cooke, firm John, C. & Lytle, h. 30 Oak.
Cooke & Lytle, saddles and harness, 10 Exch.
Cool, James, carver, h. N. Div. n. Grosvenor.

Cooley, Henry, paper hanger, h. 138 Oak.
Cooley, James, lab h. 170 Seneca.
Cooley, John, moulder, h. 34 Union.
Cooley, Joseph W., G. W. R. R. office, b. cor. Morgan and Chippewa.
Cooley, Lois, widow, h. 91 Oak.
COOLEY, WM. S. merchant tailor, 7 Seneca, h. Mulberry ab. Goodell.—See adv. p. 88.
Coombs, John C. clerk at B. & S. L. R. R. treasury office, 3 Harvey Block.
Coombs, Robt. rect. and vinegar fact. 53 Morgan, h. 10th cor. Pennsylvania.
Coon, Courtland. clerk, 194 Main, b. 67 Seneca.
Coon, John S. 293 Seneca.
Coon, Henry, ice peddler, h. cor. 5th and Pennsylvania.
Cooney, Geo. carp. h. 106 Folsom.
Cooney, Pat. h. 114 6th.
Cooper, Alex. confectioner, h. across creek.
Cooper, Alex. Empire Bowling Saloon, Canal.
Cooper, Alonzo, engineer B. N. Y. & E. R. R. h. 324 S. Division.
Cooper, Ann, widow, h. 7th n. Pennsylvania.
Cooper, Arthur, b. 223 N. Division.
Cooper, C. S. marble worker, r. Field's, Del. n. Virginia.
Cooper, David, police, h. 149 Eagle cor. Mich.
Cooper, James, cooper, h. Amherst n. Thom.
Cooper, Jno. well digger, h. Ill. n. Scott.
Cooper, Nathaniel, saddler, 31 Seneca, h. 2 Oak.
Cooper, Robt. lab. h Forest ave. n. N. Wash.
Cooper, T. H. cashier B. & L. H. R. R. Erie, h. 18 Carroll.
Cooper, William, h. 22 Walnut.
Cooper, Wm. stone cutter, h. r. Field's marble works.
Coots, W. A. h, Ferry n. Delaware.
Coots, Wm. A. Jr. clerk B. N. Y. & Erie freight office, b. Ferry n. Delaware.
Copeland, Alonzo P. carp. h. 312 Ellicott.
Coppings, John, painter, h. n. 9th.
Coppock, Wm. R. horticulturist, Main n. Forrest avenue, h. same.
Corbin. Geo. b. Western Hotel.
Corbin, Peter, dep. sheriff, h. 48 N. Division.
Corbit, Michael, blacksmith, Perry n. R. R. crossing, h. same.
Corbit, Bridget, widow, h. across creek.
Corcan, Martin, hack driver, b. 92 Exchange.
Corcilius, Jacob, 174 Main, h. 136 Batavia.
Corcoran, Cornelius, boarding, Columbia n. Ohio.
Corcoran, B. clerk, E. W. Doran, b. same.
Corcoran, Edward, baker, 57 Wash. h. same.
Corcoran, James, engineer, h. York n. 9th.
Corcoran, L. b. Western.
Corcoran, Martin, teamster, h. 9th n. Hudson.
Corcoran, M. shoemaker, h. 21 Lloyd.
Cornell, G. E. supt. bridge repairs, B. & E. R. R. h. 216 Swan.
Cornell, Geo. W. at 60 Main, b. Western.
Cornell, S. Douglas, White Lead Works, cor. Delaware and Virginia, h. 14 Park place.
CORNELL, SAMUEL G. sec'y Niag. White Lead Co. h. 14 Park place.—See adv. p. 103.
Corners, James, teamster, Brayley, & Pitts.
Corning, J. S. brakeman, N. Y. C. R. R. h. 421 Main.

Corning, John, N. Y. C. R. R. h. 421 Main.
Cornish, Jane, widow. h. 17 6th.
Coins, James, nailer, Bird avenue n. N. Wash.
Corns, Joseph, sup. iron nail works, h. Bidwell n Niagara.
Cornwall, S. W. Res'voir House, Niag. cor. Vt.
Cornwell, Francis E. atty. cor. Main and Court, h. cor. Franklin and Allen.
Corp. Charles R. Phœnix saloon, 181 Ellicott, h. same.
Corr. W. tailor, 198 Main. b. Bonney's Hotel.
Corridan, Jerry, saloon. Exch. n. R. R. crossing.
Corwin, Jesse. pail maker, b. S. B. Corwin.
Corwin, J. pail factory, b. J. Sloan.
Corwin. Oscar, pail factory, h. Niag. n Clinton avenue.
Corwin, S. B. pail maker, h. Niag. n Bird av.
Cosack, Herman, engraver, h. 310 Michigan.
Cosgrit, James, ship. carp. h. Vincen. n. South.
Costello, John. boiler maker. h. 5th n. Ca.
Costello, Thomas P. shoemaker, 112 Pearl, h. same.
Costello, Thomas, hostler, Franklin House.
Costello, Thos. lab. h. Exch n. R R. crossing.
Coster, Georgana, shirt maker, 273 Main, b. 444 Michigan.
Cotchison, Jno. gardener, h. 32 Court.
Cott, Jno. shoemaker, h Clinton n Hickory.
Cott, John. car insp. N. Y. C. R. R. h. 70 Hick.
Cotte, Jacob, h. r. 284 Pearl.
Cotter, Ann. Mrs. saloon, tow path n. Erie, h. same.
Cotter, James, lab. h. Vincennes n. South.
Cotter, James R. 159 Main, b. 76 Ellicott.
Cotter, James, lab. b. Ohio opp. freight depot.
Cotter, Kerns, mariner, h. across creek.
Cotter, Patrick, mariner. h. across creek.
Cotter. P. H. tailor, h. 14th n. Connecticut.
COTTER, THOMAS, prop. Globe Hotel, cor. Beak and Exchange.—*See adv. p. 92.*
Cottier, Hugh, firm Sheppard & C. h. 294 Franklin.
Cottier. Robert, gold beater, 100 Washington cor. Exchange, h. 226 N. Division.
Cotterell, Thos. lab. 77 Church.
Cottle, Octavius O. attorney, 190½ Main, h Delaware n. Allen.
Cotton, Geo. W. h. 311 Franklin.
Cotton, Jno. capt. b. Elk St. House, cor. Mich. and Elk.
Cottrall, Thomas, lab. h. Church n. Jackson.
Cottrell, Geo. Clinton cor. Ellicott.
Coughlan, Daniel, mariner, across creek.
Coughlan, Mary, milliner, b. 36 W. Seneca.
Coulent, Jaques, machinist. h. 12 William.
Cournea, Jas. musician, 197 Washington.
Courneen. R. carp. h. Steuben n. Alabama.
Court House, new, Clinton cor. Ellicott.
Court House, old, Washington n. Clinton.
Courter, A. B. h. Franklin n. Allen.
COURTER, R. prop. Courter House, cor. Erie and Terrace.—*See adv. p. 92.*
Courtney. Morris, painter, 9 Terrace, b. Globe.
Cowan, Chas. grocer, 96 Main. h. same.
Cowan, David, lab. Dr. Lord, h. Delaware n. Forest Lawn.
Cowan, C. H. firm Ribbel & C. h. American.
Cowan, Robt. joiner, h. Ellicott n. Dodge.

Cowing, Fordyce, canal stable. Canal n. Evans. h. Delaware ab. Virginia.
Cowing, H. O. store, cor. Niagara and Bird av. h. cor. Pennsylvania and 10th.
Cox, Ed. P. gardener, h. Jersey cor. Rogers.
Cox, Gustavus, surveyor, h. Main cor. Huron.
Cox, John D. lab. h. 98 Carroll.
Cox, John, tailor. b. cor. Niagara and Eagle.
Cox. John F. fruit merchant, h. 105 N. Div.
Cox, Samuel, fruit dealer, 295 Main, b. 105 N. Division.
Coy, Emeline. boarding house, 381 Michigan.
Coy, Sarah, h. 381 Michigan.
Coye, Schuyler. firm DeForest & C. h. N. W. cor. Niagara Square.
Coyle, James, lab h. 5th n. York.
Coyle, Jas. ship carp. h. 13 Walnut.
Coyle, Wm. ship. carp. b. 5th n. York.
Coyne, James. h. 5th n. Carolina.
Crabbs, Phil ship carp. h. Hickory n. Clinton.
Crabner, Fred. cooper, h. Niagara n. Amherst
Crabtree, Wm. engineer, h. Fulton n. Hamb't.
Crackenbush, J. Z. capt. h. Dearborn n. Austin.
Craghill, H. tinsmith, Niag. n. Pa. h. Ala. bet Hudson and Pennsylvania.
Craghill. T. stone mason, h. H. Craghill.
Craig. Aaron F. lumber inspector, foot Genesee. h. 78 Niagara.
Craig. F. S. lumber merchant, h. Miller's block. Michigan.
Craig, Wm. H. truckman, h. Perry n. Hayward.
Crain, B. A. canal insp'r, h. 66 W. Chippewa.
Cramer, A. foundryman, Brayley & Pitts.
Cramer, Geo. tailor, h. 535 Michigan.
Cramer, Joseph, shoemaker, b. 137 Batavia.
Cramer, Jno. farmer, town line road bet. Del. and Main.
Cramer, Michael, miller, h. Niag. n. Amherst
Cramer, Peter, saloon, 94 Batavia.
Cramer, Peter, Jr. musician, b. 94 Batavia.
Cramer, Philip, miller, h. Thomp. n. Hamilton.
Crampton, James, nailsmith, 154 Batavia.
Crampton. J. horse nail maker, h. 450 Batavia.
Crandall, DeForest, firm Cook & C. h. Western.
Crandall, Lodema, Mrs. nurse, b. Huron cor. Ellicott.
Crane, S. H. boiler maker, h. 25 Exchange.
Crary. Oscar F. clerk, custom house, h. Cottage n. Virginia.
Crate, James, watchman. h. 5th n. Hudson.
Craven, Stephen, in iron works, h. Forest ave. n. Washington.
Craw, Henry, lab. h. Amherst n. Thompson.
Crawford. Charles, hackman, h. 92 Oak.
CRAWFORD, JOHN, marble works, 84 and 85 Niagara, h. same.—*See adv. p. 94.*
Crawford, Thomas, painter. h. 411 Swan.
Creamer, Jacob, cabinet maker, h. ov. 522 Michigan.
Creamer, Martin, stove maker, h. Walnut n. Bat
Crefer, Wm. painter. h. Ash n. Batavia.
Creighton. J. A. cigar maker, h. 7th n. R. I.
Cremer, Mrs. Jno. tailoress, h. 19 Park Place.
Crewe, H. book-keeper, J. D. Roberts, b. 79 Chippewa.
Crilasque, Daniel, confectioner, h. 99 Batavia.
Crimmer, P. h. Jacob May.
Crittenden, Delia, Mrs. h. 19 E. Tupper.

Crittiden. F. clerk, 7 Seneca, b. 12 Carroll.
Croake. Wm lab. h. Erie basin n. Genesee.
Crockell, Jacob, bricklayer, h. Ellicott n. N.
Crocker, Wm. farmer, h. Delavan ave. cor Grider.
Crocker, L. & Co. cattle yard, Tifft's farm
Croker, John. lab. h. Niagara n. Ontario.
Cromer, Nathaniel, h. 282 S. Division.
Cronan, Daniel, at N. Y. & E. R. R. h. Mill n. Heacock.
Cronan, Cornelius, lab. h. Mill n. Alabama.
Cronan, Jerry, lab. h. Exch. n. Hamburgh.
Cronan, Mark, lab. h. Ohio n. Louisiana.
Cronin, Dennis, lab. h. Ohio n. Louisiana.
Cronin, J. lab. h. cor. Rhode Island and 9th.
Cronin, John, farmer, h. Ontario n. Tonawanda.
Cronin, Patrick, lab. h. Exch. n. Hamburgh.
Cronin, Timothy, lab. h. Niagara n. Farmer.
Cronyn, Eliza C. b. 2 Erie.
Cronyn, John, Dr. h. 76 Pearl.
Cronyn, Patrick, lab. h. Genesee n. Canal.
Crookdasher, Henry, white lead works, h. Krettner n. Batavia.
Crooker, Fred. tinsmith, h. 35 Sycamore.
Crooker, Geo. prop. Red Jacket Hotel, junc. Elk and Seneca.
Crooker, Henry, lab. h. Peugot n. L. S. R. R.
Crooker, John. lab. h. cor. Peugot n. L. S. R. R.
Crooks, Andrew M. salesman, 207 Main h. 138 Clinton.
Crooks, Wm. lab. h. r. Niagara n. Hamilton.
Crookston, L. W. cl'k, 316 Main, h. 5 Franklin.
Crosby, C. dealer in patent medicines, at 255 Main, h. 200 S. Division.
Croseley, James, blacksmith, h. 112 6th.
Crosier, Geo. W. clerk, b. J. M. Crosier.
Crosier, John, warden B. G. Hospital, h. same.
Crosman, John, agt. M. C. R. R. Co. h. 157 Del.
Cross, Jacob, at Evans & Co. planing mill.
Cross, Silas, cooper, h. Pratt bet. Sycamore and Genesee.
Crossan, Patrick, lab. h. across ship canal.
Crossgrove, Thomas, in Prince & Co.'s factory, h. 11th n. Connecticut.
Crossland, John F. h. 32 E. Seneca.
Crossland, Mrs. J. F. milliner, 32 E. Seneca.
Crossley, James, blacksmith, h. 112 6th.
Crossley, John T. butcher. h. Main n. North.
Crossley, Joseph, wagon maker, 10th n. Md.
Crosswaight, Wm. ship carp. h. 200 Swan.
Crowe, Pat. saloon, 5 Evans, h. same.
Crow, Wm. painter. h. Seneca n. Hamburgh.
Crowder, Eliz. Mrs. h. cor. Ferry and William.
Crowder, Jacob, alderman, Canal n. Ferry, h. Albany n. Barton.
Crowley, Catherine, seamstress, 32 Main.
Crowley, Den. h. Niagara opp. Strawberry Is.
Crowley, Edmund, lab. cor. Thompson and Austin.
Crowley, Michael, lab. h. Ohio n. tollbridge.
Crowley, Michael, melodeon maker, h. Hudson n. 9th.
Crowley, Timothy, lab. h. Bouck n. Niagara.
Crowley, Timothy, policeman, h. 7th n. Hudson.
Crowley, Timothy, clerk in post office, b. 7th n. Penn.
Crowther, Rodney, Mrs. music teacher, h. 46 6th.

10

Croxon, Richard, clerk. 23 Main, h. cor. Georgia and 7th.
Cruice, Thomas, blacksmith, b. cor. 5th and Maryland.
Cruise, L. blacksmith. h. Folsom n. Chicago.
Cruise, Thos. blacksmith, h. cor Md. and 5th.
Cruise, Thomas, Jr. blacksmith, h. cor. 5th and Pennsylvania.
Crudden, James, lab. h. Exch. n. Heacock.
Cruttenden, Charles F. with A. Root. b. 19 E. Tupper.
Cruttendon, Delia, widow, h. 19 E. Tupper.
Cuddehe, M watchman, h. 56 Folsom.
Cuff, Francis, blacksmith. h. Fulton cor. Ala.
Cuff, Sam. boiler maker, b. Fulton n. Alabama.
Cullen, James, lab. h. 12 Iron place N. Wash.
Cullen, John, saloon, cor. Illinois and Dock.
Cullen, Martin, caulker, cor. Perry and Hamburgh.
Cullen, Thos. ship carp. h. Kentucky n. South.
Cullins, James, lab. h. Terrace n. Henry,
Culver, Betsey, widow, h. 115 W. Huron.
Culver, Hobart. carp. h. Ferry n. Niagara.
Cumming, Caroline M. teacher Buffalo Orphan Asylum, b. same.
Cumming, James, blacksmith, h. 208 N. Div.
Cumming, John, sailmaker, Lloyd cor. Prime, h. Fulton n. Chicago.
Cumming, P. H. firm Murray, C. & Grant, 316 Main, b. American.
Cummings, Emory, Eastern agent B. C. & C. line, with W. T. Co. b. 79 S. Division.
Cummings, Emory, clerk, Howard, Whitcomb & Co. b. 5 Franklin.
Cummings, Morris, white lead works, h. Allen, n. Delaware.
Cummings, N. T. carp. h. 105 Fulton.
Cunnane, John, sailor, h. Fulton n. Chicago.
Cunningham, Alfred, shop keeper of penitentiary, b. H. S. Cunningham.
Cunningham, Alvah, wall guard at penitentiary, b. same.
Cunningham, Bridget, widow, h. across creek.
Cunningham, Catharine, widow, Ind. n. Perry.
Cunningham, Daniel, lab. h. Louisiana n. Ohio.
Cunningham, H. S. superintendent of penitentiary, cor. 5th and Pennsylvania.
Cunningham, James, machinist, b. Mary Cunningham, 9 Delaware Place.
Cunningham, John, lab. h. Amherst n. city line.
Cunningham, Mary, wid. h. 9 Delaware Place.
Cunningham, Pat. lab. b. E. G. Spaulding.
Cunningham, Thos. cartman, h. Ex. n. Griffin.
Cullery, J. finisher, b. r. 11 William.
Cuntz, George. lab. h. Grey n. Genesee.
Curby, Jno. sailor, h. LeCouteulx.
Curran, Andrew, lab. h. 10th n. Maryland.
Curran, Michael, flask maker, at Buffalo Eagle Iron Works, h. N. Division n. R. R. crossing.
Curran, Minerva, wid. of John F. h. 489 Wash.
Curnen, Thos. blacksmith, h. 158 Georgia.
Currey, Wm. K. clerk, 308 Main, b. Swan.
Currier, Jos. drugs, groceries, &c. 163 Main, h. 91 Niagara.
Curry A. h. Amherst cor. Tonawanda.
Curry, Francis, civil engineer, h. 132 Swan.
Curry, W. H. book-keeper, with Clark & Storms, b. 29 Swan.

Curry, Michael, sailor, h. Louisiana n. Elk.
Curson, E. b. 18 William.
Curson L. lab. b. 18 William.
Cursons, Olive, widow, h. 18 William.
Cursons, Robert D. book-keeper, with C. L. Chapin, b. same.
Curtenius, J. L. attorney, 12 Spaulding's Exchange, h. 28 W. Eagle.
Curtenius, J. Y. freight agent, N. Y. C. R. R. Erie, h. Court cor. Terrace.
Curtis & Demings, leather merchants, 72 Main.
Curtis. W. B. milk dairy, h. Batavia n. Williamsville road.
Curtiss, C. G. firm Willard & C. cor. Lloyd and Prime, b. W. Eagle n. Delaware.
Curtiss, Geo. E. with L. Pond, 198 Main.
Curtiss, Henry A. clerk, 202 Main, h. Hudson cor. 9th.
Curtiss, Lyman L. h. 24 N. Division.
Curtiss, Peter, President Buffalo Trust Company, 223 Main, h. 462 Main.
Curtiss, Sear, tallyman, W. T. Co. h. 50 E. Eagle.
Curtiss, Walter L. firm C. & Deming, b. 462 Main.
Curtiss, Wm. H. with M. L. Comstock, b. 9th cor. Hudson.
Curtpatrick, Geo. fireman, h. 1 Evans.
Cushman, Ambrose, carpenter, 117 Carroll.
Cuthbeart, John, carp. h. Jefferson n. Swan.
Cutler, Abner, h. 25 S. Division.
Cutler, Clara, Mrs. boarding house, 509 Wash.
Cutler, Chris. bar tender, Amer'n, b. 7th n. Pa
Cutler Godfreid, shoemaker, h. 119 Walnut.
Cutler, Samuel J. melodeon maker, h. Oak n. Carlton.
Cutler, William H. attorney, Main cor. Swan, h. 178 S. Division.
CUTTER & AUSTIN, elevating and commission merchants, Norton and Ship Canal.—See adv. p. 44.
Cutter, A. W. firm C. & Nims, h. 166 Franklin.
Cutter & Bailey, flour and feed store, 201 Wash.
Cutter, C. S. book-keeper, h. 166 Franklin.
Cutter, D. M. clerk, W. H. Cutter, b. 178 S. Division.
Cutter, G. W. attorney, h. 309 Washington.
Cutter, Jas. C. firm C. & Bailey, b. 67 S. Div.
Cutter & Nims, commission merchants, 6 Central wharf.
Cutting. H. S. attorney, 227 Main, up stairs, b. American Hotel.
Cutting, H. T. shoemaker, h. Parish n. East.
Cutting, Thomas S. general agent and process server, h. 88 E. Seneca.

D.

Dabzell, F. L. millwright, b. Western Hotel.
Dachent, E. widow, h. 242 Genesee.
Dachent, Jno. printer, b. 242 Genesee.
Dadman, Frederick, lab. h. Lemon n. High.
Daga, William, shoemaker, h. 222 Genesee.
Dahinten, Francis, glass stainer, b. Batavia cor. Pratt.
Dahl. Balthaser, lab. h. Sherman n. Genesee.
Dahl, Daniel, lab. h. Sherman n. Genesee.
Dahl. Henry, grocer, Genesee cor. Johnson, h. same.

Dahl, Frederick, shoemaker, b. S. Dahl.
Dahlman, L. firm L. D. & Co. 274 Main, h. 152 Ellicott.
Dahlman, L. & Co. dry goods store, 274 Main.
Dailey, Thomas, lab. h. across creek.
Dailey, Michael, mariner, h. across creek.
Dakin, Geo. coal agent, foot Gen. h. 89 S. Div.
Dale, Jas. paper ruler, h. 22 10th.
Daley, Charles, peddler, h. 4th n. Virginia.
Daley, James, engineer, h. 114 Cedar.
Daley, Lawrence, lab. b. 6 Michigan.
Daley, Patrick, h. Ohio n. South.
Daley, S. J. lab. b. Mrs. Daley, Perry n. La
Daley, Thos. ship carpenter, b. Ohio n. South.
Daley, widow. h. Niagara n. Bouck.
Daly, Catharine, wid. tailoress, h. Perry n. La
Daly, James, distiller, h. Chicago n. Ohio.
Daly, Michael, lab. h. Lake n. 6th.
Dalton, Charles, firm D. & Kingston, h. Terrace n. Court.
Dalton, John, ship carpenter, h. 22 Illinois.
Dalton & Kingston, painters, 247 Main.
Dalton, Richard, bolter, h Tennessee n. South.
Dalzell, Wm. gardener, h. Washington n. High.
Damainville, L. M. D. over 163 Main, b. 219 Delaware.
DAMAINVILLE, A. liquor dealer, 163 Main, h. 219 Delaware.—See adv. p. 49.
Dambach, Justus, grocer, h. cor. Sycamore and Hickory.
Damon. Hiram, cheese dealer, 25 Main, h. 95 E. Seneca.
Dampro, Fred. teamster, h. Maple n. Goodell.
Dana, Robert, painter, 120 Folsom.
Dandinger, Philip, h. 47 Spruce.
Dandinger, Philip, Jr. b. 47 Spruce.
Danebroch, Wm. lab. h. 294 Oak.
Danenhour, Gottfrey, lab. h. Hickory n. Gen.
Danforth, F. L. cashier, Pratt & Co. h. 15 N. Division.
Danforth, L. agent for Jas. G. Dudley, h. 101 S. Division.
Dangel, Adam, painter, h. Towpath opposite workhouse.
Danhauser, Geo. lab. h. Carlton n. Locust.
Daniel, Henry, carpenter, h. 9th n. Hampshire.
Daniel, John M. wood dealer, yard Michigan, h. 195 Swan.
Daniel, Wm. moulder, h. Pine n. William.
Daniels, Chas. att'y, cor. Lloyd and Main, b. N. Pearl n. Allen.
Daniels, Jas. Am. Express, h. 11 W. Seneca.
Danikin, Urs. silver plater, h. Elm n. Burton alley.
Danler, Peter J. painter, 9 Terrace, h. Best n. Ellicott.
Dann, H. A. b. 53 S. Division.
Dann J. C. h. 53 S. Division.
Dannele, Stephen, gardener, h. Miami n. Ferry.
Danner, Augustus, lab. h. Clinton n. Raze.
Danner. Henry, b. 126 Sycamore.
Danner, John, carpenter, h. Monroe n. Brown.
Danner, Michael, Sen. grocer, h. 126 Sycamore.
Danny, Geo. policeman, h. Kaene n. Genesee.
Dano, Geo. R. breakman, N. Y. C. R R b. Bonney's.
DANTZER & CO. soap and candle manuf. cor. Exchange and Chicago.—See adv. p. 77.

Dantzer, Morand, soap manuf. b. Exchange n. Chicago.
Dantzer, Peter M. soap manuf. Hamburgh, h. Exchange n. Chicago.
Dantzer, Chas. soap maker, b. Exch. n. Chicago.
Danzel, Jos. lab. h. Monroe n. Brown.
Danzig, A. clerk, at 280 Main, b. 52 N. Div.
Darcy, Chas. policeman, h. 88 5th.
Darcy, Daniel, mason, h. 71 5th.
Darcy, Daniel, Jr. mason, b. 71 5th.
Darcy, Eliza, widow, h. 18 6th.
Darley, Thomas, machinist, h. 5 Folsom.
Darling, A. B. carpenter, b. 171 Washington.
Darling. E. A. billiard saloon, 306 Main, h. 330 Main.
Darling, John, T. T. Bloomer's, h. 3 9th.
Darragh, John, com. merch. 14 Central Wharf, h. Main ab. North.
Darragh, Allen, clerk, J. G. Deshler, b. Main ab. North.
Darrigan, Richard, 197 Main, h. 152 Clinton.
Darrow, N. h. Delaware n. Allen.
Darrow, Robert, Mrs. h. Huron n. Ellicott.
DART & BROS. planing mill, Ohio basin cor. Mackinaw.—*See adv. p.* 86.
Dart, Erastus D. firm D. & Bros. b. cor. Niagara and Georgia.
Dart, Joseph, firm D. & Bros. h. Niagara cor. Georgia.
Darvan, David, h. 5th n. Carolina.
Dascomb, Hiram, hide dealer, h. 207 N. Div.
Datt, August, hat and cap store, 73 Genesee.
Daub, Louis, tailor Cherry n. Hickory.
Daucht, Frederick, lab. h. Cherry n. Hickory.
Davern, John, lab. h. 5th n. Virginia.
Davey, Marsden, engraver, Com'l Adv. office, h. 9 Seneca.
Davey, Ed. painter, h. Ohio n. Louisiana.
Davidson, Jas. A. carpenter, h. 5th ab. Pa.
Davidson, John B. barber, shop 23 Seneca, h. 96 N. Division.
Davidson, Margaret, widow of Alex. h. Palmer n. Maryland.
Davis, A. L. grocer, Franklin cor. Chippewa.
Davis, Asahel, Rev. h. 296 Swan.
Davis, Benj. gilder, h. 29 Clinton.
Davis, Ed. B. at Com. Adv. b. 13 Franklin.
Davis, Emerson L. cor. Prime and canal slip.
Davis, Epenetus H. druggist, 10 Terrace, h. 211 N. Division.
Davis, Geo. ship carpenter, h. Alabama n. Elk.
Davis, Geo. baggage master B. & L. H. R. R. h. 131 N. Division.
Davis, Griffith, sawyer, b. 233 Carroll.
Davis, Henry M. clerk, h. 137 N. Division.
Davis, Henry, whitewasher, h. Sycamore n. Walnut.
Davis, Humphry, foreman Fitch's shoe store, cor. Mich. and Seneca, h. same.
Davis, Jacob, lumber insp'r, h. 290 Franklin.
Davis, J. H. book-keeper Jas. Howell, h. 73 6th.
Davis, Jarvis, gunsmith, with P. Smith, h. 127 Main.
Davis, John, grocer, h. Elk bel. Louisiana.
Davis, John J. at 193 Main, b. 3 Ash.
Davis, J. T. clerk, 240 Main, b. 9 Boston Block.
Davis, Oscar B. h. Delaware n. North.
Davis, Samuel, sailor, h. 144 S. Division.

Davis, Thad. C. att'y, 14 Spaulding's Exch. h. Summer n. Delaware.
Davis, Townsend, book-keeper. D. P. Dobbins, h. Johnson Place cor. Carolina.
Davis, Wm. att'y, 3 Terrace, h. Carey bel. Morgan.
Davis, Wm. sailor, h. Perry cor. Mississippi.
Davis, Wm. D. shoemaker, South n. Niagara.
Davis, Wm. H. clerk, B. N. Y. & E. R. R. office, h. 9 Boston Block.
Davis, W. H. Jr. clerk, W. S. Abbott, b. 9 Bost. Block.
Davis & Wilke, ins. agents, Merch. Exchange.
Davison, Wm. C. mariner, h. 68 6th.
Davy, Pat. lab. h. Perry n. Canal bridge.
Daw, Alfred D. firm H. D. & Son, h. 57 Morgan.
Daw, Henry, firm H. D. & Son, h. 36 W. Eagle.
Daw, John, ship carp. h. 10 Mechanic.
Daw, Harriet, widow, b. St. Paul.
DAW, H. & SON, shipping and com. merch's, 26 Central Wharf.—*See adv. p.* 55.
Daw, Wm. farmer, h. Delaware n. Chapin.
Dawes, Wm. butcher, h. Seneca n. 13th Ward House.
Day, David F. att'y, 207 Washington, h. 15 9th.
Day, David B. carp. h. 217 7th cor. Virginia.
Day, Ebenezer, h. 444 Main.
Day, Geo. gas fitter, &c. 9 W. Eagle, h. 6th n. Ft. Porter.
Day, James, ruler, h. 22 10th.
Day, Jno. firm P. Brennon & Co. h. Mechanic n. Terrace.
Day, John G. whitewasher, h. Elm n. Vine.
Day, John, clerk, Joe Fongerore.
Day, Hiram C. attorney, 164 Main, b. 444 Main.
Day, Lester, regalia maker, h. 82 Niagara.
Day, Norris, band box maker, Niagara cor. Md. h. Day's Park ab. Cottage.
Day, Thaddeus, Am. Ex. Co. h. 215 Seneca.
Dayton, C. L. M. D. office Niag. cor. Amherst, h. Amherst cor. Thompson.
Dayton, H. M. h. Niagara n. Amherst.
Dayton, L. P. M. D. office cor. Niag. and Amherst, h. cor. Amherst and Thompson.
Deacon, Jacob. stonecutter, h. cor. Folsom and Kinney alley.
Deacon. Robt. W. Prince's melodeon factory, h. 115 9th.
Deacon, Wm. R. melodeon maker, b. 17 6th.
Deam, Chas. marble cut. h. Spruce n. Genesee.
Dean, A. M. grocer, h. 260 S. Div.
Dean, James, boarding h. 20 Washington.
Debray, Adam, 18 Lloyd, h. 10 6th.
Debus, Andrew, grocer, cistern and cooper shop, h. Batavia cor. Walnut.
Debus, Fred. lab. h. Batavia cor. Walnut.
Debus, Phil. grocer, h. cor. Monroe and Pec'm.
Decamp, Joseph, cooper, h. South n. Niagara.
Dech, Frank, carp. h. Bennett n. Batavia.
Deck, Anthony, porter, Wm. H. Glenny, h. Mariner ab. Virginia.
Deck, Geo. F. pattern maker, b. Mariner bet. Allen and Virginia.
Deck, Jacob N. machinist, h. 311 Oak.
Decker, A. J. firm J. B. Johnson & Co. b. Bonney's Hotel.
Decker, L. butcher, h. Adams bet. Clinton and Howard.

Deckett, Henry, sailor, h. 11th n. Hampshire.
Dedo, Henry, shoemaker, h. Boston alley n. Va.
Dee, Henry O. firm Holbrook, D. & Co. h. 46 Delaware.
Dee, Wm. H. firm Holbrook, D. & Co. h. 82 W. Tupper.
Deery, Thos. variety store, 408 Main b. Gen. House.
Deeves, T. S. with A. L. Griffin & Co. h. 5th n. Carolina.
Deeves, Wm. Mrs. wid. h. 5th n. Carolina.
Deffry, Peter, gunmaker, h. Niag. n. Bird av.
De Forest, Cyrus H. firm De F. & Coye. h. 56 S. Division.
De Forest, H. P. with De Forest & Coye, h. 56 S. Division.
De Forest, J. S with De Forest & Coye, b. 56 S. Division.
DE FOREST & COYE, coal dealers, Genesee and Erie basin.—See adv. p. 46.
Degenerr. Charles. mason, h. Ferry n. Jefferson.
Degenfelder, Anton, finisher, h. Hickory n. Clinton.
De Graff, James. H. printer, Republic, b. 27 Folsom.
De Graff, Jno. J. ag't propellers, h. 27 Folsom.
De Grote, Jas. lab. h. East n. Parish.
Deban, Ann, widow of Patrick, h. 58 William.
Deban, Alice, theatre performer, b. 58 Wm.
Deban, John, teacher, h. 58 William.
Dehling, Conrad, lab. h. 63 Cedar.
Dehlinger, Elizabeth. wid. h. 237 Elm.
Dehlinger, J. clerk 319 Main, b. K. Dehlinger.
Dehlinger, Katharine, widow, h. 237 Elm.
Dehlinger, Paul, bricklayer, h. 239 Elm.
Dehn. John, lab. h. Goodell alley n Tupper.
Deibold, C. saloon, and board, 3 Ohio, h. same.
Deibold, Geo. shoe store, 12 Com'l, h. Franklin ab. Edward.
Deibold, Peter, lab. h. Porter n. Van Rensselaer.
Deiler, Geo. contractor, h. Hamilton n. Dearborn.
Deinzer. Andrew, lab. h. Elm n. Burton alley.
Deitrich, Charles, cooper, h. 256 Genesee.
Delaney, Dennis, lab. 189 Exchange.
Delaney, James, ship carpenter, h. ac. creek.
Delaney, James, nailer, h. Wash. n. Forest ave.
Delaney, John, caulker, h. Ohio cor. South.
Delaney, Michael, ship carpenter, h. ac. creek.
Delaney, Pat. ship carp. h. Tennessee bel. Mackinaw.
Delany, C. D. b. Main n. Best.
Delano, James, musician, h. 19 Johnson Place.
Delany, John, lab. h. 300 Seneca.
Delany, Nicholas, caulker, Jones' yard, h. end Blackwell's slip.
Delitsch, B. with E. Seyd & Co. b. Oak n. High.
Dell, Geo. lab. h. Pratt n. Genesee.
Dell, John, engineer at Safford's factory, h. same.
Dellahite, Thomas, lab. h. South n. Hamburgh.
Dellenbaugh, Frederick, M. D. h. 87 Batavia cor. Potter.
Dellenbaugh, S. M. D. 358 Main, h. 133 Ellicott.
Deller, Jacob, lab. h. Pratt n. William.
Deller, Margaret, Miss. seamstress, b. Jacob D.
Delvecchio, Charles H. musician, 17 E. Eagle, h. same.

Demarest, James, h. 48 W. Mohawk.
Demarest, James F. office 1 Adam's Block. h. 122 Pearl.
Demarest. Wm. C. with Sherman & Barnes, h. 45 Delaware.
Demard, James, painter, h. cor. Terrace and Mechanic.
Demeretz, Wm. carpenter, h. Clinton n. Spring.
Demick, Wm. iron works, Dearborn n. R. R.
Demmer, Jacob, wagon maker, with Wm. Barker. h. Milnor bet. Batavia and Wm.
Dempsey, Chas. book-keeper. h. 169 Niagara.
Dempsey, Matthew, lab. h. Fulton n. Alabama.
Dempsey, Pat. joiner, h. Fulton n. Hayward.
Demster, Robert,* blacksmith, h. 5 Mississippi.
Demster, Wm. lab. h. Adam n. William.
Demuth, John, clerk Harvey & Allen, b. 184 S. Division.
Denbey, Jeremiah, ship carpenter, b. Ohio n. South.
Dengel, Adam, lab. foot Joy. b. same.
Dengler, John, butcher, h. Oak n. North.
Denicombe, John, shoemaker, 7 Genesee, h. same.
Dennecker, Joseph, silver plater, h. r. 140 Gen.
Dennecker, Urst, silver plater. h. 316 Elm.
Dennis, Bernard, lab. b. Lewis n. military road.
Dennis & Cottier, gold and silver leaf manufacturer, Wash. cor. Exch.
Dennis, James H. cistern maker, 265 Swan h. same.
Dennis, Maria, wid. h. Massachusetts cor. 10th.
Dennis, Robert,* boot manuf. 96 Barker's blk. E. Seneca, h. same.
Dennis, Thomas, firm D. & Cottier. h. 158 Pearl.
Denison, Timothy P. book-keeper, L. & L J. White, h. Pearl n. Virginia
Dennison, Alfred, ship carpenter, h. cor. Carroll and Chicago.
Dennison, C. G. book-keeper, 54 Main, h. 265 Pearl.
Dennison, John, tallyman, h. Perry n. Ala.
Denniston, Geo. book-keeper, h. 157 E. Seneca.
Denny, Jacob, grocer, Court cor. Hospital, h. same.
Denny, Mrs. wid. over cor. Canal alley and 6th.
Dentler, Florian, carp. h. Oak cor. Virginia.
Dentler, John J. mason, h. 292 Elm.
Dentler, Nicholas, carp. h. Locust n. North.
Denton R. piano tuner, h. 5 9th.
Denton, R Jr. music teacher, h. 5 9th.
Denz, Matthew,* watchmaker, 200 Gen. h. same.
Denzinger, Barbara, seamstress, h. 156 Bat.
Denzinger, Joseph, piano maker, b. 156 Bat.
Denzinger, Maria, wid. seamstress, h. 156 Bat.
Deott, Edward, caulker, h. 25 Mississippi.
Depher, Bartholomew, cooper, h. cor. East and Hamilton.
DePuy, Wm. H. Rev. pastor Pearl st. M. E. Church, h. 48 W. Chippewa.
Derby, Rufus, sailor, h. 407 Michigan.
Derflein, John, tailor, h. Mulberry n. Goodell.
Derhaar, Christian, cabinet maker, h. Pratt n. Sycamore.
Derhaar, John, cabinet maker, h. Pratt n. Syc.
Derks, Theodore, lab. h. 57 Cedar.
Derla, Stahles, brickmaker, h. Madison n. Clinton.

Derlin, A. Mrs. h. 511 Washington.
Dermody, E. Mrs. widow, h. 6th cor. Hudson.
Derner, Frank, lab. h. Grey n. Genesee.
Derr, Andrew, upholsterer, h. Washington n. Chippewa.
Derr, F. M. saloon, cor. Amherst and Dearborn.
Derr, John, baker, 105 Pine, h. same.
Dersey, John, lab. h. Batavia cor. Ash.
Dersman, Valentine, shoemaker, h. Cedar n. William.
Dervey, S. P. h. 92 Clinton.
Desch, George, carpenter, h. 60 Cedar.
Desch, John, joiner, h. 60 Cedar.
DeSelle, Max. lab. h. Dearborn n. R. R.
DeSelle, Philip, carp. h. Amherst n. city line.
Deshler, John G. for. and com. mer. 14 and 15 Central Wharf. h. 465 Main.
Deshler. John, printer, b. 242 Genesee.
Desmond, Timothy, ship carp. h. across creek.
Desse, Fred. cabinet maker, h. 17 Sycamore.
Deterl, Joseph, shoemaker, h. Sycamore opposite Mortimer.
Deters, John, with Sherman & Co. h. Locust above Virginia.
Detmar, Christoph, furnaceman, h. 530 Mich.
Detmers, Julius, book-keeper. h. 164 Oak.
Detombul, Anton, moulder, h. Mich. n. Tupper.
Dette, C. Mrs. widow of Louis, cook, Martin Luther college, Maple n. Virginia, h. same.
Dette, Theodore, piano maker. b. Maple n. Va.
Dettman, Charles, lab. h. Maple n. High.
Dettman, John, carp. h. Monroe n. Peckham.
Deuchler, Peter, lab. h. Exch. n. Van Renssel'r.
Deutcher, Nicholas, cooper, h. Cherry n. Spruce.
DEUTHER, GEORGE A. looking-glass store, 12 Exchange, h. Eagle n. Hickory.—See adv. p. 72.
Deuther, Louis, cabinet maker, h. Lutheran n. Batavia.
Deutscher, Conrad, tailor, h. Sherman n. Bat.
Deutschler, Joseph, mason, h. 528 Michigan.
Deuel, Albert T. clerk, Franklin House.
Deuel, Wm. peddler, Albany cor. School.
Devereux, Hugh J. b. 229 7th.
Devereux, Kate, widow, h. 229 7th.
Devening, Daniel, M. D. h. 361 Michigan.
Devening, William, b. 361 Michigan.
Devenport, Chas. Y. firm D. & Nelson, h. 231 N. Division
DEVENPORT & NELSON, boiler makers, LeCouteulx cor. Canal.—See adv. p. 55.
Deverell, Tarlton, check agent N. Y. C. R. R. h. 137 S. Div.
Devine, Francis F. piano forte tuner and manufacturer, cor. Md. and Niag. b. 35 Swan.
Devine, John, cartman, h. Exchange n. Griffin.
Devine, Owen, lab. h. 214 N. Div.
Deviney, Peter H. carpenter, h. 47 Delaware.
Devit, Edward, engineer, F. S. Gillson's stave yard, h. Perry n. Hamburgh.
Devitt, Thos. sailor, Blossom n. Koon's alley.
Devney, James P. ship carp. h. Ky. n. Mack'w.
Dewald, Henry, tailor, h. Goodell alley above Tupper.
Dewald, Louis, h. Bennett n. William.
Dewein, Fred. tanner, h. 7 Roos' alley.
Dowey, Daniel, blacksmith. b. Park n. Del.
Dewey, Norman R. h. 29 7th.

Dewis, John, mason, h. 3 Ash.
Dewis, Peter, tailor, h. Ash n. Batavia.
Dewitt, A. N. h. 193 Swan
Dewitt, John, teamster, h. Niag. n. Hamilton.
DeYoung, J. J. variety store, 147 Main, h. 201 S. Division.
Diamon, John, weighmaster, h. Ala. cor. Mac.
Diamond, Alexander, foreman Coburn Square Elevator. h. Alabama n. Seneca.
Diamond, Robert, superintendent of Wilkinson's Elevator. h. Alabama n. Seneca.
Diamond. William, engineer, b. Ala. n. Seneca.
Dibbard, Martin, watchman, N. Y. & E. R. R.
Dicfendorf, Alford, lab. h. Swan n. Jefferson.
Dick, Alexander, Rev. h. 64 W. Tupper.
Dick, Frederick, gunsmith, h. 109 E. Genesee.
Dick, L. telegraph operator, N. Y. C. R. R. b. Southern Hotel.
Dick, Jacob, brass finisher, h. 311 Oak.
Dick, Robert, Rev. h. 80 Tupper.
Dick, Robt. capt. h. Clinton n. Monroe.
Dick, William, cooper, h. Bennett n. William.
Dickenherr, Martin, carpenter, h. Locust n. Va.
Dickes, Rolf. carp. h. Maple n. High.
Dickesson, Wm. ship carpenter, h. 57 William.
Dickey, Anderson, stock agent, N. Y. C. R. R. h. 133 S. Division.
Dickey, Benjamin, firm D. & Marsh, N. Canal n. Emslie.
DICKEY & BOWEN, proprietors Southern Hotel.—See adv. p. 93.
Dickey, John, stock agent, n. N. Y. C. R. R. b. Southern Hotel.
Dickey, J. P. firm D. & Bowen, Southr'n Hotel.
Dickey & Marsh, flour and feed dealers, 212 Washington.
Dickie, James G. office 6 Brown's Buildings, b. 62 E. Swan.
Dickinson, Ann, widow, h. over 344 Main.
DICKINSON, THOMAS. jeweler, 270 Main, h. same.—See adv. p. 76.
Dickinson, Thomas, Jr. b. Thos. Dickinson, Sen.
Dickinson, Wm. moulder, h. 4th n. Carolina.
Dickman, Fr. lamplighter, h. 11 William.
Dickman, G. & C. 2 and 4 Elk st. Market.
Dickman, Geo. firm G. & C. D. h. Carroll n. Chicago.
Dickson, A. B. firm Billings & D. 29 Central Wharf, h. 188 S. Division.
Dickson, Agnes, widow, h. 21 Clinton.
Dickson, Catharine, h. 454 Michigan.
Dickson, Geo. B. capt. on lake, h. 100 N. Div.
Dickson, Hiram, painter, h. Bowery n. Allen.
Dickson, James, engineer, h. 77 Church.
Dickson, John, saddler, n. cor. Va. and Niagara.
Dickson, Robt. works Wardwell, Webster & Co. b. 77 Church.
Dickson, William, h. 225 N. Division.
Dickson, William, capt. h. 177 Eagle.
Dickson, Wm. capt. h. Barker cor. Linwood avenue.
Dickson, Wm 5th n. Hudson.
Diebold, Andrew, merchant tailor, 11 Com'l. h. same.
Diebold, August, shoemaker, b. 173 Batavia.
Diebold, B. grocer, cor. Canal and Maiden lane, h. same.
Diebold, Casimer, tailor, h. 128 Michigan.

Diebold, Geo. lab. h. Shumway n. Peckham.
Diebold, Geo. shoemaker, 12 Com'l. h. Franklin n. Edward.
Diebold, Jacob, tanner, h. Walnut n. Genesee.
Diebold, Jas. with J. Adams. b. Mary Diebold.
Diebold, Joseph, grocer, Batavia cor. Adams, h. same.
Diebold, Mary, widow, h. Walnut n. Genesee.
Diebold, Michael. tanner, b. Walnut n. Batavia.
Diebold, Sebastian, flour and feed store, 133 Batavia, h. same.
Diebolt, A. feed store, Canal ab. Maiden lane, h. Franklin n. Edward.
Diegelmann, Andrew, carp. h. 312 Elm.
Diegelmann, L. shoemaker, h. Niagara n. Pa.
Diehl, Adam, joiner, h. Ferry n. Walden.
Diehl, Adolph, tailor, h. Goodell n. Mulberry.
Diehl, Conrad, mason, h. 2¦6 Pearl.
Diehl, Conrad. clerk. 402 Main, b. 296 Pearl.
Diehl, Fred. lab. h. Hickory n. Sycamore.
Diehl, George. lab. h. Best n. Michigan.
Diehl, Henry,* tobacco store, 322 Main, b. 296 Pearl.
Diehl, Henry, carp. h. Cedar n. Batavia.
Diehl, Jacob, fluid peddler, h. Walnut n. Bata.
Diehl. Jacob W. clerk, b. 296 Pearl.
DIEHL, JOHN P. druggist, 402 Main, b. 264 Pearl.—See adv. p. 74.
DIEHL & PARKER, liquors, 263 Main.—See adv. p. 49.
Diehl, Peter, cooper, h. Goodell cor. Oak.
Diehl, Peter, carp. b. Maple n. High.
Diehl, Philip, engineer, B. &. S. L. R. R. h. 27 Walnut.
Diehl, Wm. peddler, h. Vermont cor. Brayton.
Diehr, Mathias, bricklayer, h. 317 Ellicott.
Dieling, Daniel, shoemaker, h. 238 Elm.
Diemker, David, milkman, h. Grey n. Genesee.
Diepforth, Bartholomew, cooper, h. Hamilton n. East.
Dieping, Geo. milkman, b. N. Div. n. Hickory.
Dier, Christ. grocer, Canal n. Erie.
Diesel, Peter, lab. h. East n. Hamilton.
Diestel. Ernst, shoemaker, Ohio n. Wabash, h. same.
Dietcer, Daniel, carp h. 167 Clinton.
Dietcer, G. H. carp. h. 167 Clinton.
Dietcer, John, carp. h. 167 Clinton.
Dieterle, Geo. lab. h. Genesee n. Jefferson.
Diethigh, P. constable, h. over 39 Erie.
Diethomble, Anthony, moulder, h. Michigan n. Genesee.
Diethomble, E. moulder, h. Michigan n. Gen.
Diethomble, Nicholas, lab. Michigan n. Gen.
Dietley, Anton. bricklayer, h. Locust n. High.
Dietrich. Andrew, carp. h. Washington n. Burton alley.
Dietrich, Chas. lab. with Pierce & Co. h. Heacock n. Carroll.
Dietrich. Chas. bakery, Jeff. n. Clinton, h. same
Dietrich, Charles. lab. h. Carroll n. Heacock.
Dietrich, Christian, blacksmith, h. 405 Mich.
Dietrich, Geo. S. clerk, 124 Main, h. Oak cor. Genesee
Dietrich, John. carp. Spring n. William.
Dietrich, Nicholas, mason, h. Bennett n. Bat.
Dietrich, Paul, lab. h. 214 Elm.
Dietz, Leonard, lab. h. Herman n. Genesee.

Dietz, Martin. tailor, h. 410 Batavia.
Dietzel, Frederick, lab. h. Sherman n. Genesee.
Dietzel, Henry, whip maker, h. cor. Goodell and Michigan.
Diflin, John, woodworker, Brayley & Pitts.
Dighton, John, b. National.
Dihl. Frank, dry goods, Clinton n. Walnut.
Dilcher Christopher, mason. h. Grey n. Bat.
Dilcher, Henry, mason, h. Grey n. Batavia.
Dilger, And. lab. h. Genesee n. Sherman.
Dilger, Xavier, watchman, Genesee n. Spruce, h. same.
Dill, Isaac S. mariner, h. 11th n. Virginia.
Dill, Reuben, shipping agt. and marine insp. 2 Ohio, h. 30 7th.
Dillan, Jno. with Stewart & Efner, h. Folsom n. Chicago.
Diler, Nicholas, blacksmith, b. 293 Oak.
Diller, Jno. foreman Richmond's Elevator, h. 370 Franklin.
Dillett, Andr. cooper, h. Dearborn n. Hamilton.
Dillon, Catharine, widow, h. Dangherty's alley.
Dillon, James,* shoemaker, h. Elk n. La.
Dillon, Martin, sailmak'r with Provoost & Newkirk. h. Chicago n. Elk.
Dillsworth, Sarah J. widow, seamstress, h. 188 Genesee.
Dimery, Maria, dressmaker, 117 Pearl, h. same.
Dimmick, M. mariner, h. 6 Terrace.
Dimond, Henry S. painter, 3 S. Division, h. 9th n. Vermont.
Dingbaum, Ann, widow, h. William n. Hickory.
Dingeldein, Wm. lab. h. Krettner n. Batavia.
Dingeldey. J. blacksmith, 55 Exch. h. same.
Dingens, Frank L. b. 33 Genesee.
Dingens, J. A. clerk, 356 Main, h. same.
Dinger, Geo. shoemaker, h 7 Cypress.
Dinwoodie, Wm. C. firm D. & Co. Michigan cor. Clinton, h. 38 Clinton.
Dircks, Matilda, Mrs. h. 288 Elm.
Dirk, Nicholas, lab. h. 501 Michigan.
Dirlfren, Jno. Brayley & Pitts, h. Goodell n. Mulberry.
Dirnberger, Joseph, finisher, h. 137 Elm.
Dirr, Mathias, tanner, h. at Bush & Howard's tannery.
Dischler, Michael, lab. h. Fox n. Genesee.
Dish, Peter, lab. h. S. Division n. Emslie.
Dishinger, Jacob, carpenter, h. 69 Maple.
Dishmur, Christian, organ maker, h. Smith's alley n. Jefferson.
Distel, Chas. shoemaker, h. 17 Cherry.
Ditlon, Anton, gardener, h. High n. Locust.
Ditmar, Frederick,* cooper, h. German alley n. Sycamore.
Ditmar, Geo.* tinsmith, Genesee n. Hickory.
Dittl, Jos. lab. h. Krettner n. Lovejoy.
Ditto, John A. civil engineer, City Surveyor's office, h. 98 9th.
Ditzel, Birnhart, ship carpenter, h. 28 Bennett.
Diump, Jno. lab. h. Hickory n. Batavia.
Diump, Martin, filer, b. Jno. Diump.
Divine, Andrew, h. Pearl cor. Terrace.
Divotto, Vincienzo, prof. of the crank, r. Hospital n. Niagara.
Dix, Charles, saloon, Fly n. State.
Dix, Jno. saloon. 6th n. Court, h. same.
Dix, Jos. lab. h. Batavia n. Adams.

Dixon, Geo. farmer, 40 Sycamore.
Doane, B. F. watchman, h. over office, Washington n. Ohio.
Doat, Jas. farmer, Best n. Jefferson.
Dobbins, Charles H. clerk with S. Dobbins, b. 120 Swan.
DOBBINS, D. P. insurance agent, 4 Thompson Bl'k, Prime, h. 7 Niag.—*See adv. opp. name.*
Dobbins, James, lab. h. Abbott road n. Iron bridge.
DOBBINS, SAM. grocer, Swan cor. Michigan, h. 120 Swan.—*See adv. p. 41.*
Dobinson, Hannah K. widow, h. 146 Ellicott.
Dobinson, Wm. A. firm Klein & D. cor. Evans and Water, h. Ellicott ab. Huron.
Dobinson, Wm. A. block maker, h. 146 Ellicott.
Dobmeier, Adam, mason, h. Herman n. Gen.
Dobmeier, Felix, teamster, h. 61 Cedar.
Dobmeier, John, lab. h. Hickory n. Batavia.
Dobson, Sam. boiler maker, h. Fulton cor. Red Jacket.
Dochler, A. G. Rev. h. M. L. College, Maple n. Virginia.
Dodd, Martha J. milliner, 8 S. Div. h. same.
Dodd, Wm. saloon, 25 E. Seneca, h. 5 S. Div.
Dodds, Stephen V. mason, h. 11th n. Virginia.
Dodds, Thomas, mason, h. Patten n. William.
DODGE, A. L. grocer, 17 Main.—*See adv. p. 38.*
Dodge, Clark, porter, Am. Hotel, h 32 Carroll.
Dodge, George. cl'k, 17 Main, b. Courter House.
Dodge, Hampton, firm Cheesman & D. h. 23 Court.
Dodge, John, h. Clinton n. Madison.
Dodge, John W. clerk, Pratt & Letchworth.
Dodge, Jno. student, b. 56 Pearl.
Dodge, Lewis, M. D. 56 Pearl, h. same.
Dodge, R. C. Mrs. widow, h. 257 Franklin.
Dodge, Thomas, clerk, cor. Seneca and Washington. b. cor. Erie and Pearl.
Dodge, Willis, clerk, P. O. b. 52 E. Swan.
Dodsworth, John. book-keeper, Buffalo Scale Works, b. cor. Michigan and Folsom.
Dodsworth, Charles, book-keeper, 106 Main, b. cor. Michigan and Folsom.
Dodsworth, Wm. merchant tailor, 106 Main, h. cor. Michigan and Folsom.
Dodsworth, Wm. Jr. 106 Main, h. Michigan cor. Folsom.
Doerffell, Hermann, cigar manufacturer, 84 E. Genesee, h. same.
Doerk, Conrad, shoemaker, Monroe n. Batavia.
Does, Jno. lab. h. Fox n. Genesee.
Doffey, Barney. lab. h. Terrace n. Canal.
Doghany, Patrick, butcher, Mich. cor. Carlton.
Dohartz, Wm. saloon, under Revere House.
Dohl, Geo. boiler maker, h. Grey n. Genesee.
Dolan, Jas. grocer, Niagara cor. Breckenridge.
Dolan, John, lab. h. Mill n. Heacock.
Dolan, Michael, lab. h. Hudson cor. Cottage.
Dolan, Michael, lab. h. Otto n. Hayward.
Dolan, Patrick, mason. h. cor. Miss. and Perry.
Dolan, Pat. cartman, h. Peddlers all. n. Seneca.
Dolan, Patrick, grocer, 122 Exchange, h. same.
Dolan, Philip, ship carp. h. Van Rensselaer.
Dolan, Philip, walter, Mansion, h. 9 Beak.
Dolan, Wm. finisher, b. Mill bet. Heacock and Hamburgh.

Dolbert, Kate, wid. b. Batavia opp. Milnor.
Dold, Jacob, butcher, 8 and 10 Elk st. market, h. White's Corners pl'k road bel. iron bridge.
Dold, Jno. J. h.White's Corners bel. iron bridge.
Dole, Thomas D. agent N. Y. C. R. R. propellers, h. cor. Swan and Erie.
Doll, Antony, butcher, h. Niagara n. Virginia.
Doll, Frank, blacksmith, h. Aurora n. Whittmore's tavern.
Doll, Fred. milk dairy, h. Genesee n. Williamsville road.
Doll, Jacob, lab. h. Mulberry n. High.
Doll Sebastian, grocer, Canal cor. Evans, h. 23 Canal.
Dolsen. William, machinist, b. Ala. n. Elk.
Domedion, Fred. lab. h. 18 Cherry.
Domedion. Jacob. printer, h. 24 Sycamore.
Domeny, Edward, whitewasher, h. Grey bet. Genesee and Batavia.
Dompfen, Jno. teamster, h. Johnson n. North.
Donahan, John, sailor. h. 13 Mississippi.
Donahue, Daniel, lab. h. Chicago n. Ohio.
Donahue, Daniel, lab. h. Perry n. R. R. track.
Donahue, Edward, caulker, b. 11 Carroll.
Donahue, Ellen. widow, h. 49 Clinton.
Donahue, James, lab. h. Clinton ave. n. N. Washington.
Donahue, Lawrence, flagman, h. Gen. cor. R. R.
Donahue, Mary, widow, h. cor. Carroll and Red Jacket.
Donahue, Simon, shoemaker, E. Paige, h. 1 Eagle.
Donahue, Thomas, at L. S. R. R. h. Perry cor. Red Jacket.
Donald, William, stereotyper, Commercial Advertiser office, h. Porter n. Van Rensselaer.
Donaldson, Br's, shipsmiths, cor. Ind. and Ohio.
Donaldson, David, firm D. & Bros. h. 121 6th.
Donaldson, John, firm D. & Bros. h. 117 6th.
Donaldson, Oliver, shipsmith, h. 121 6th.
Donaldson, Wm. firm D. & Bros. h. 119 6th.
Donavan, Daniel, lab. h. 5th n. Maryland.
Donavan, Daniel, lab. b. York n. towpath.
Donavan, Dennis, lab. h. cor. Carroll and Jeff.
Donavan, Peter, lab. h. Tenn. n. Mackinaw.
Donavan, Richard, lab. h. Tecumseh n. Hamb'g.
Donevan, Michael, lab. h. across creek.
Donevan, Mrs. widow, h. across creek.
Donovan, Dan'l, M. S. R. R. b. Mrs. J. S. Miller.
Donkin, Louis, caulker, h. across creek.
Donlon, Jas. cartman, h. 13th n. Massachusetts.
Donn, Nicholas, wood seller, h. Jersey cor. 11th.
Donnath, August, tailor, h. Sherman n. Gen.
Donner, Henry L. book-keeper, with Sherman & Co. h. 307 Oak.
Donner, Nebamuck, carpenter, h. Burton alley n. Michigan.
Donelly, Edward, blacksmith, h. Terrace n. Mechanic.
Donnelly, Edward J. electrotypist, b. Western.
Donnely, Catharine, widow, h. Daugherty's alley n. Folsom.
Donoghue, Hugh, rope maker, h. and ropewalk Vermont n. Brayton.
Donohoe, Denis, British consulate, 6 Harvey Block, h. 137 W. Huron.
Donohou, Michael, clerk, Hamlin & Mendsen.
Doohan, Mary, widow, h. across creek.

Doolan. Morris, waiter, Courter House, h. foot Court.

Doolittle, Jno. J. firm Bogert & D. h. 63 Eagle.

Dooley, Pat. hostler, 47 Delaware.

Dooly, Jno. coachman, h. on alley bet. Niagara and 7th.

Dopf, Geo. lab. h. Schmitt's alley n. Jefferson.

Dopp. H. W. machinist, h. 13th n. Connecticut.

Doppel. Geo. tailor, h. cor. Tupper and Va.

Doran, Edward W. grocer. Niagara n. Pa.

Doran, James, lab. h. cor. Jackson and Wilson slip.

Dorer. Catherine, seamstress, h. r. 449 Mich.

Dorer, Henry, coppersmith. h. 436 Michigan.

Dorkney. Pat. salter. h. Michigan n. Carlton.

Dorn, Philip, tailor. h. 112 Tupper.

DORR, E. P. President board lake underwriters, gen'l. agt. Ætna insurance co. Hartford, agt. N. Y. board underwriters, office cor. Prime and Lloyd, h. 161 Niagara cor. Carolina.—See adv. opp. 1st cover inside.

Dorr, Ed. surveyor, h. Walnut n. Clinton.

Dorr. Felix, lab. h. Adams n. Batavia.

Dorr, Jos. W. clerk, Bush & Howard, h. cor. Staats and Niagara.

Dorr. Margaret, seamstress, 112 Batavia.

Dorsey. James, machinist. h. State.

Dorsey, Owen, blacksmith, h. Carolina bel. 5th.

Dorsheimer, Jacob, lab. h. Sherman n. Genesee.

Dorsheimer, Phil. lab. h. Johnson n. Genesee.

Dorsheimer, Wm. attor'y, 7 Court, b. Mansion.

Doshmer. Philip, boiler maker, h. Genesee n. Johnson.

Dorst, Fred. grocer. Niag. cor. Huron, h. same.

Dorst. Jacob, clerk, b. F. Dorst.

Dorst. Jacob, baker, with L. Rodenbach, b. Hickory cor. William.

Dorst. Margaret. widow of Conrad, saloon, Oak cor. Koon's alley, h. same.

Dorst. Phil. grocer, Main cor. Allen, h. same.

Dort, John, lab. h. 6 Maple.

Dorty. Thomas, lab. h. Carroll n. Hamburgh.

Dory. A. wood worker, with Brayley & Pitts.

•Dury. D. Mrs. midwife, h. Vermont n. 11th.

Dose. Chas. sawyer, h. Amherst n. Blossom.

Doslinger. And. shoemaker. h. Johnson n. High.

Dossert. John, music teacher, h. St. Paul cor. Ellicott.

Dotterl. Geo. shoemaker. h. 125 Pine.

Doty. John, engineer, h. cor. Carroll and La.

Doty, Rufus, engineer, h. 213 7th.

Doty. Steward W. brakeman, N. Y. C. R. R. h. 222 Carroll.

Dotzlee. Jacob, lab. h. Grey n. Genesee.

Dotzler. John, blacksmith, Goodell, cor. Elm, h. same.

Dougherty. Chas. lab. h. across creek.

Dougherty, Chas. tanner, b. 201 N. Division.

Dougherty, Jno. moulder, h. 47 Oak.

Dougherty, Alex. h. 201 N. Division.

Dougherty, Geo. clerk, 4 Exc'g. b. 201 N. Div.

Dought, John, commission merchant, 4 Central Wharf, h. 456 Main.

Douglas, John T. captain, h. 7th n. Hudson.

Douglas. W. H. contractor, office 214 Main, b. Bloomer's.

Douglass, Darius E. Mrs. widow, h. Virginia below 11th.

Douty, Jane, saloon, cor. Exc'ge and Heacock.

Douw, P. J. att'y, ov. 146 Main, h. same.

Douw. G. engineer, h. 159 S. Division.

Dow, William K. h. 144 6th n. Virginia.

Dowd, Barney, lab. h. Marvin n. Elk.

Dowd, Elizabeth, widow of John, h. 183 Swan.

Dowling, Peter R. agent, b. New Eng. Hotel.

Downing. John, truckman, h. Va. cor. 6th.

Downey, Barney, lab. h. across creek.

Downey, James, mariner, h. across creek.

Downey, Dennis, laborer, h. across creek.

Downs, David, shoemaker, h. cor. Ohio and La.

Downs, Francis, farmer, h. Batavia n. school house No. 25.

Downs, Pat. blacksmith, h. 10 Barker's alley.

Doyl, John, lab. h. Elk n. Marvin in rear.

Doyle, Edward, ship carp. h. Ohio n. Wash. sq.

Doyle, Henry J. clerk, with Thomas Dole, h. Clinton below Cedar.

Doyle, Hugh, lab. h. 26 Mississippi.

Doyle, Jerry. lab. h. Van Rensselaer n. Porter.

Doyle, Jno.* shoemaker, h. Hay'rd cor. Fulton.

Doyle, John, lab. h. Elk n. Michigan.

Doyle, Larry, lab. h. cor. Gen. and Jackson.

Doyle, Lawrence, lab. h. Gen. n. Jackson.

Doyle, Margaret, wid. h. Gen. n. Jackson.

Doyle, Mary, widow, h. towpath n. Genesee.

Doyle, Michael, mason, h. Carroll cor. Ala.

Doyle, Moses, lab. h. 14th n. Vermont.

Doyle, Patrick, stone mason, h. Carolina n. 5th.

Doyle, P. C. book-keeper, Courier Office, h. 36 6th.

Doylo, Peter. ship carp. h. Vincennes n. South.

Doyle, Thomas, lab. h. Genesee n. Jackson.

Doyle, Timothy, silk agent, b. 109 Carroll

Doyle, Timothy, sailor. h. Abbott road bel. R. R.

Doyle, William L. auditor, B. N. Y. & E. R. R. h. 36 6th.

Drake, Ebenezer H. lumber agt. h. 172 9th.

Drake, James, on lake, h. 6th n. Pennsylvania.

Drake, Saphrona, widow, b. 55 Ellicott.

Drake, — telegraph operator, b. 29 Swan.

Drambert, Adam, lab. h. Grey n. Genesee.

Draper, Fred. cooper, h. Lewis n. Amherst.

Draper, J. W. painter, 118 Pearl, h. 4 9th.

Draper, O. H. firm D. & Rathbun, h. 160 S. Division.

Draper & Rathbun, boot & shoe dealers, 253 Main.

Dras, Henry, tailor, h. over 157 Cherry.

Draum, Philip, shoemaker, h. Syc. n. Hickory.

Draves, Joachim, tailor, h. Cherry n. Hickory.

Dray, John, lab. h. Folsom n. Kinney's alley.

Dray, Thomas, ship carp. h. La. n. South.

Drecher, Frederick, firm D. & Co. h. Elm cor. Batavia.

Drecher & Co. lumber dealers, cor. Batavia and Elm.

Drescher, Casper I. band box maker. h. 117 Pine.

Drescher, Jacob, lab. h. Mulberry n. High.

Drescher, William. tailor, h. 378 E. Genesee.

Dreher, Chas. C. cigar maker, h. 153 Syc.

Dreher, Charles, firm D. & Co. h. Tupper bel. Oak.

Drehr, Frederick, cooper, h. East n. Hamilton.

Dreibus, Jacob, cooper, h. Grey n. Genesee.

Dreier, Henry, tailor, h. Burton alley n. Oak.

Dreier, William, tailor, h. Mulberry n. Carlton.
Dreiss, Frederick, carpenter, h. Pratt n. Wm.
Drenkhahn, Frank, ship carpenter, h. cor. Howard and Watson.
Drenkhahn, Wm. shoemaker, h. Monroe n. Bat.
Dres, Henry, Mrs. widow, h. 215 Ellicott.
Dress, Benhardt, carp. b. 215 Ellicott.
Dreshler, Geo. lab. h. Camp n. Sycamore.
Dreves, Christ. lab. h. Ketchum alley n. High.
DREW, EDWARD, designer and carver, 136 Main. h. Caroline n. Niag.—*See adv. p. 89.*
Drew, George H. carver, h. 40 N. Division.
Drew, James T. engineer, h. 153 S. Division.
Drew, Mary E. dressmaker, h. 40 N. Division.
Drew, W. H. Major 21st regiment N. Y. S. V. M. h. cor. Pearl and Tupper.
Drewis, Charles, mason, h. 262 Elm
Drewis, Frederick, mason, h. 556 Michigan.
Drewis, Henry. carpenter, h. 264 Elm.
Drewis, John, laborer, h. 262 Elm.
Drexelius, Anthony. policeman, h. 62 William.
Drexelius, August, moulder, b. 60 William.
Drexelius, August, moulder, b. 8 Bennett.
Drexelius, Frank, laborer, b. 60 William.
Drexelius, Henry, moulder, b. 60 William.
Drexlius, Carolina, widow, h. 18 Bennett.
Drexler, Geo. woodsawyer, h. Spring n. Wm.
Drexler, Jno. cooper, h. Mortimer n. Peckham.
Drexler, John, street inspector, h. Hampshire n. 11th.
Dreyer, Conrad, tailor, h. Grey n. Batavia.
Dreyer, Fred. tailor, h. Grey n. Batavia.
Driller, Richard, carpenter, h. 80 Sycamore.
Driscall, Cornelius, lab. b. La. n. Perry.
Driscall, Cornelius, laborer, h. across creek.
Driscall, Cornelius, laborer, h. Ohio n. Chicago.
Driscall, Dan. lab. h. towpath n. round house.
Driscall, Michael, lab. h. Carroll n. Heacock.
Driscoll, Charles, lab. h. n. Mile square Niag.
Driscoll, Julia, widow, h. O'Connor's yard.
Driscoll, Timothy, lab. h. Ohio below South.
Driscoll, Timothy, laborer, h. across creek.
Drinen, Pat. lab. h. Terrace n. Mechanic.
Drinnon, Edward, lab. b. Elk n. Ohio.
Dripensea, Fred. cooper, b. Mary Frost.
Dripensea, Jos. cabinet maker, b. Mary Frost.
Droegmoeller, Jno. tinsmith, b. Elm cor. Va.
Drowish, Augustus, carpenter, h. 63 Maple.
Druar, John, grocer, Niagara n. Amherst.
Druar, John, Jr. clerk Chase & Bird.
Drullard, Geo. Chief Police, h. 313 Michigan.
Drullard, R. N. Y. C. R. R. h. 76½ N. Division.
Drullard, Solomon, freight agent, N. Y. C. R. R. h. 256 Seneca.
Drummer, Augustus, clerk, Elk cor. Louisiana, h. same.
Drummer, Andrew, book binder, h. 48 Walnut.
Drummer, Peter, moulder, h. Wm. n. Stanton.
Drummer, Margaret, widow, h. 48 Walnut.
Drummer, George, carpenter, h. Main cor. Va.
Dubois, Jos. joiner, h. 102 Elm.
DUBOIS, J. B. tailor, 149 Main, h. 22 Oak cor. N. Division.—*See adv. p. 88.*
Dubois, Philo, silversmith, 11 E. Swan, h. 24 Oak.
Dubois, Samuel, b. 22 N. Division.
Duborn, A. M. tinware manufacturer, 29 Commercial, h. same.

Duckene, Michael, carpenter, h. Burton alley n. Goodell.
Dudley, Bros. tin and coppersmiths, 57 Main.
Dudley, Edward, firm J. Parker & Co. b. 32 Ellicott.
Dudley, George B. b. 266 Pearl.
Dudley, Geo. E. clerk 271 Main, b. 49 Ellicott.
Dudley, H. P. book-keeper, cor. Peacock and Norton, b. 18 Ellicott.
Dudley, James G. dealer in scales, bells, &c. 93 Main, h. 9 Oak.
Dudley, John E. agent, John R. Fero, h. 49 Ellicott.
Dudley, J. D. firm J. D. D. & Co. 3 State, h. 44 W. Eagle below Delaware.
Dudley, J. D. & Co. Globe Brass Foundry, 3 and 5 State.
Dudley, Joseph P. 5 State, h. 16 6th.
Dudley, M. T. firm Dudley Brothers, b. 44 W. Eagle.
Dudley, Thomas J. h. 266 Pearl.
Dudley, Wm. H. with G. B. Bull, h. 119 S. Div.
Duehnige, J. wood-worker, Brayley & Pitts.
Duehringer, Jno. lab. Grey n. Batavia.
Duell, Fanny, dressmaker, b. 43 Elm.
Duemuelin, Anton. locksmith, b. 550 Michigan.
Duenkel, Thomas, lab. h. Hinckley n. Spring.
Duerenberger, Joseph, soap maker, h. Spruce n. Sycamore.
Duerrenberger, Jacob, gardener, h. Best E. of Jefferson.
Duerrenberger, Jacob, Jr. h. Best E. of Jeff'n.
Duerenberger, John, lab. h. Spruce n. Syc.
Duerfeldt, Frederick. cigar maker, 263 Main, h. Hickory n. Clinton.
Duerfeldt, Gustavus, piano maker, A. & J. Keogh, h. Johnson n. Batavia.
Duering, Casper, laborer, h. 302 Elm.
Duerk, Egidius, laborer, h. Elm n. Carlton.
Duerr, Augustus, mason, h. 24 Walnut.
Duerr, John M. carpenter, h. Pratt n. Sycamore.
Duerscher, Wolfgang. lab. h. Hickory n. Bat.
Duewiger, Francis, tailor, h. over 138 Elm.
Duff, A. M. horse shoeing, cor. Terrace and Henry, h. 8 6th.
Duff, M. 19 Water, h. same.
Duffy, James, carp. b. Moore cor. Miami.
Duffy, Joseph, mason, h. 348 Michigan.
Duffy, Martin, teamster, with H. Gardner, h. Clinton n. Emslie.
Duffy, Martin, ship carpenter, h. Tennessee below Mackinaw.
Duffy, William, warehouseman, with Evans, h. Fulton n. Chicago.
Duffy, Wm. keeper Buffalo Cemetery, North n. Lemon.
Dufner, Michael, lab. h. Adams n. Brown.
Dufrind, Henry, carp. h. Alabama n. Mack'w.
Duga, Charles, musician, h. 1 J Maple.
Dugan, David, blacksmith, b. 50 5th.
Dugan, Patrick, iron works, h. alley between East and Thompson.
Dugan, Patrick, watchman, N. Y. C. R. R. h. Perry n. Alabama.
Dugan, P. mariner, h. across creek.
Dugan, R. lab. h. Burwell n. Scott.
Dugan, Timothy, lab. h. 11th n. R. I.
Dugan, William, lab. 9th n. Hampshire.

Duggan, Daniel, blacksmith, Elk n. Louisania, h. Perry below Louisania.
Duggan, Mary, widow, h. Niagara n. Virginia.
Duggan. Patrick M. grocer, 169 E. Seneca, h. same.
Duke. Chas. carpenter, h. Spruce n. Batavia.
Dukes, John, shoemaker, h. Mich. n. High.
Dulenty. Patrick. lab. h. across creek.
Dulenty. Thos. lab. h. Marvin n. Elk.
Duler, George, sawyer, h. Ohio n. Louisiana.
Dulitz, Louis, D. D. h. William cor. Milnor.
Duman, Francis, lab. h. Walnut n. Batavia.
Dumman, Joseph, lab. h. 10 Bennett.
Dryer. William R. with W. J. Keays & Co. b. 279 Pearl.
Drynan, Elizabeth, widow, h. 5th cor. Carolina
Dunbar, Albert, clerk, b. 283 Pearl.
Dunbar, Edward, steward, Terrapin Lunch, b. 5 Franklin.
Dunbar, Geo. H. ass't teller N. Y. & E. Bank, b. 8 Park place.
DUNBAR & HOWELL, Eagle Iron Works, cor. Mississippi and Perry.—*See adv. p.* 97.
Dunbar. Jewett J. book-keeper, Jewett & Root, b. Courter.
Dunbar, W. J. book-keeper with Dunbar & Howell, b. 8 Park place.
Dunbar, L. Mrs. widow. h. 283 Pearl.
Dunbar, Robert, firm D. & Howell, Eagle Iron Works, h. 8 Park place.
Dunbar. Thos. h. 119 6th.
Duncan, Edward, steersman, h. 163 Seneca.
Duncan, Geo. lab. h. Elk n. Chicago.
Duncan, Robt. ship carpenter, h. Va. n. 6th.
Duncan. Jas. ship carp. h. 11th n. Virginia.
Duncan, Thomas, theatre, h. 35 Swan.
Duncan, Jno. teamster for Jason Parker.
Duncan. Robt. iron finisher, Brayley & Pitts.
Dunbach, Geo. F. tailor, h. 253 Elm.
Dunchel, Jacob A. carp. h. Fulton n. Chicago.
Dunckhorst, William, lab. h. Ash n. Batavia.
Dunker, John, lab. h. Locust n. Carlton.
Dunker, Maria, nurse, h. Locust n. Carlton.
Dunlap, Robt. joiner, h. Carolina cor 10th.
Dunlap. Robt. Jr. grocer, 10th ab. Carolina, h. 1 Haddock Block, cor. 10th and Carolina.
Dunlap, Thos. engineer, h. 92 Folsom.
Dunlop, James. carp. h. 20 Johnson Place.
Dunlop, James, Jr. carp. b. 20 Johnson Place.
Dunn, Daniel, sailor, h. 5th n. Georgia.
Dunn, Jane, widow, teacher, h. 99 Clinton.
Dunn, Joseph, ship carp. h. Hamburgh n. Elk.
Dunn, Sam'l, lumber dealer, h. Ohio n. Chicago.
Dunn, V. R. contractor. h. Niagara cor. Va.
Dunn, V. spile driver, h. Perry n. Hamburgh.
Dunn, Wm. tinsmith, b. cor. Eagle and Cedar.
Dunne, Mary, Mrs. grocer, cor. Eagle and Cedar.
Dunnavan, Timothy, lab. b. 38 Ohio.
Dunnivan, Michael, lab. h. Miss. n. Ohio.
Dunnovan, John, lab. h. 9th cor. Jersey.
Dunow, Ludwig, machinist, b. Exch. n. Mich.
Dunphy, Thos. paper hanger, 270 Main, h. 296 Franklin.
Dupon, Geo. A. tailor, b. Western.
Dupp, Wm. machinist, h. 13th n. Connecticut.
Darcey, Jno. clerk, h. Delaware place n. Del.
Durfee, Philo, prod. com. merch. 2 Central Wharf, h. Georgia n. Niagara.

Durfee, Jas. cigar maker, b. J. Schaller.
Durfield, Frederick, cigar maker, h. Hickory n. Clinton.
Durick, Lavina, wid. h. 413 E. Seneca n. Jeff.
Durk, Adam, lab. h. 199 Ellicott.
Durk, Martin, clerk, 155 Main. h. 117 Pine.
Durken, Wm. blacksmith, 15 E. Eagle, h. Court opp. Niagara Market.
Durkin, Thos. boarding, 6 Commercial.
Durkin, Thos. grocer, h. Folsom cor. Chicago.
Durland, L. H. conductor N. Y. & E. R. R. b. 54 Swan.
Durling, Wm. R. miller, h. 256 Carroll.
Durnin, Wm. J. L. S. R. R. office, h. 11 Church.
Durr, Catharine, widow of John, h. Clinton n. Pratt.
Durr, John, moulder, 6 Clinton n. Pratt.
Durr, Louisa, widow, h. 13 Genesee.
Durr, Margaret, machine stitching, 6 Clinton n. Walnut.
Durr. Mary Ann, machine stitching, 6 Clinton n. Walnut.
Durrey, Thos. lab. h. 5th n. Carolina.
Dursch, Wm. lab. h. Milnor n. Batavia.
Durshordwe, Fred. carp. h. 292 Elm.
Durst, John, butcher, h. Hamilton n. Jefferson.
Dusel, Andreas, carp. h. Mulberry n. Virginia.
Dusel, Sebastian, blacksmith. h. Mulberry n. Va.
Dusenbery, Benj. h. 152 S. Division.
Dusenberry, Erastus F. tinsmith, 259 Main, h. 152 S. Division.
Dusenberry, Hiram, capt. b. Michigan cor. Elk.
Dusenberry, Hiram. tinsmith. b. 152 S. Div.
Dusenberry, W. R. tinsmith, 259 Main, h. 152 S. Division.
Duston, Henry, with Brayley & Pitts. b. 7 6th.
Duthie, Jas. lumber dealer, Niagara cor. Ga. h. 87 9th.
Dutton, Colton, h. 15 E. Tupper.
Dutton. E. H. stave dealer, office 2 Main, h. 47 E. Eagle.
Duval, Jno. boiler maker. h. Wash. n. Perry.
Duygan, Thomas, lab. h. Exchange n. Smith.
Duzen, Fred. stone mason, h. Palmer n. Md.
Duzen, William, fisherman, b. F. Duzen.
Dwire, Thos. sailor, h. Louisiana n. Tennessee.
Dwyer, Edward, ship carp. h. 334 Seneca.
Dwyer, Matthew, carp. h. Tenn. n. Mackinaw.
Dwyer, M. 3 Rock, h. 18 10th.
Dwyer, Mary, grocer, cor. 4th and Georgia.
Dye, Peleg E. teacher, h. Niagara cor. R. I.
Dyer. Chas. joiner, h. Hickory n. Clinton.
Dyer, Henry, boiler at iron works, h. Forrest avenue n. Niagara.
Dygert, Claud W. clerk, express office, h. 57 Ellicott.
Dygert, J. W. express office, h. 57 Ellicott.
Dygert, Walls, clerk, Int. Bank, b. 57 Ellicott.
Dykeman, Geo. tanner, h. Clinton n. Jefferson.

E.

Eagan, John, clerk, 56 Main, b. Staats n. Niag.
Eagen, Edward, blacksmith, h. 50 5th.
Eagen, John, stewart, h Ohio n. Michigan.
Eagen, M. lab. h. across creek.
Eager, Jos. shoemaker, b. over 218 Genesee.

Eagle, Jno. blacksmith, h. cor. Courtland and Maple.

Eakins, Peter, clerk, Sherman & Barnes.

Eames, E. W. book-keeper, 20 Cen. Wharf, b. 26 S. Division.

Eames, M. R. com. mer. 20 Cen. Wharf, h. 26 S. Division.

Earhardt, Andrew, blacksmith, h. 202 Ellicott.

Earl. Ira. b. 74 Chippewa.

Earle. Helen, dressmaker, ov. 12 Niag. h. same.

Earsmein, Martin, printer, h. 38 Dela. place.

Eary, John, sailor, h. Perry cor Hayward.

Eastabrooks. E. H. printer, Morning Express office. h. 145 Virginia.

Eastman, George, sailor, h. Miami n. Louisiana.

Eastman, Sandford, M. D. b 24 W. Genesee.

Eaton, Anna M. widow of Louis, h. Main opp. Bryant.

EATON, BROWN & CO. planing mill.—*See adv. p. 85.*

Eaton, Charlotte, widow, b 35 Niagara.

Eaton, C. S. clerk, Hamlin & Mendsen, h. 28 Carolina.

Eaton. John B. at planing mill, h. 675 Main opp. Bryant.

Eaton, Lewis L. at plan'g mill, h. 135 Franklin.

Eaton, Mark, machinist, h. r. Perry at R. R. crossing.

Eaton, P. B. h. 28 W. Tupper.

EATON'S PLANING MILL, Hospital cor. Court.—*See adv. p. 85.*

Eatons, Richard, barber, Mansion House, b. 38 Michigan.

Ebbs. Maria L. h. 6th n. Pennsylvania.

Ebele, F. lab. Spring cor. Champlin.

Ebeling. Fred. blacksmith, h. Wm. n. Krettner.

Ebenezer Land Office. 330 Main.

Eberhard, Caroline, widow, h. 262 Elm.

Eberhard, Geo. brewer, h. Bata. cor. Hickory.

Eberhard, John, lab. h. S. Division bel. Jeff.

Eberhardt, B.* shoemaker, cor. Ohio and Ind.

Eberhardt, Christian, b. J. Eberhardt.

Eberhardt, Jacob, lab. b. J. Eberhardt.

Eberhardt, John, machinist, h. 309 Oak.

Eberhart, Jno. lab. h. Walnut n. Sycamore.

Eberle, Casper, lab. b. Boston al. bel. Burton al.

Eberlein. Fred. Ch. brush maker, h. Mortimer n. Sycamore.

Ebert, Michael, musician, h. 70 Tupper.

Ebling, John,* cooper, h. Lewis n. Amherst.

Echardt, Fredinand, Batavia plank road n. city line.

Echart, Martin, shoemaker, h. Main n. Ferry.

Eck. Leon, marble cutter, h. 57 Maple.

Eck. Lewis, brewer, h. 118 Cedar.

Eckel, Elizabeth, widow, h. Ash n. Sycamore.

Eckel. Jacob. moulder, h. Locust n. Cherry.

Eckel, John, teamster, h. Sycamore n. Pratt.

Eckel, Louis, clerk, 277 Main, h. 204 E. Eagle.

Eckel, Martin, lab. h. Fox n. Genesee.

Eckert, Conrad, lab. h. 57 Cedar.

Eckert. E. widow, h. Sycamore cor. Spring.

Eckert, F. foundryman Brayley & Pitts.

Eckert, Frederick. lab. h. Ash n. Batavia.

Eckert, George, lab. h. Fox n. Genesee.

Eckert, Jacob, blacksmith, h. Grey n. Batavia.

Eckert, John, lab. h. German alley n. Genesee.

Eckert, Joseph, h. 312 Elm.

Eckert. Leopold, lab. 38 Cherry.

Eckert, Peter, lab. h. Mortimer n. Sycamore.

Eckert, Sebastian, shoemaker, h. Wm. n. Bata.

Eckert, Thomas. shoemaker, h. 344 Michigan.

Eckhardt, Geo.* leather deal. 246 E. Genesee.

Eckhardt, John, harness maker, 148 Seneca, h. 38 Ash.

Eckhart. Adam, shoemaker, h. over 105 Gen.

Eckles, James, fisherman, h. Niag. n. Amherst.

Eckles, Stephen, grocery, opp. guard lock.

Eckley, J. S. office 68 Main, h. 3 Palmer.

EDDY & BINGHAM, Clinton Iron Works, Jackson cor. Church.—*See adv. p. 55.*

Eddy, Robert, M. firm E. & Bingham, h. 179 Terrace.

Edgar, Oliver, joiner, Virginia n. 4th.

Edge, Ed. landlord, h. Forest av. n. Niagara.

Edmonds, Richard, clerk, with Pratt & Co. h. 127 E. Eagle.

Edmonds, Thomas, tinsmith, h. 11 Illinois.

Edmondson, Andrew, painter, h. r. 285 Swan.

Edmons. John, tailor, b. 153 Genesee.

Edmunds, James J. M. D. office Michigan foot of Fulton, h. same.

Edstrom, Andrew, nailer, Pooley Place, Clinton Forest.

Edstrom, Andrew, at iron works, h. Pooley n. N. Washington.

Edwards, Jno. grocer, Louisiana n. Tennessee.

Edwards, Rich. H. agent Geo. Parr, h. Virginia n. Niagara.

Edwards, Samuel, American Express Co. h. Folsom n. Chicago.

Edwards, T. sailor, h. 20 Illinois.

Edwards, Wm. lab. h. Fulton n. Alabama.

Eeles, James A. plumber, b. 208 Eagle.

Eeles, Kate, widow, h. 208 Eagle.

Eeles, Wm. A. coppersmith, b. 208 Eagle.

Eels, Edward, on N. St. R. R. b. 7th n. R. I.

Effner, Henry, printer, 11 Cedar.

Efner, B. C. firm Stewart & E. 44 W. Eagle.

Efner, Elijah D. pres't Buff. Savings Bank, 330 Main, h. Connecticut cor. 7th.

Efner, Geo. B. livery, 8 Ellicott, b. Ct. cor. 7th.

Egan, Michael, carp. h. Ohio n. Louisiana.

Eger, Anthony, shoemaker, Ohio, h. Genesee bet. Walnut and Hickory.

Egerter, Anna M. widow, h. Weaver alley n. Burton alley.

Egether, Jno C. waiter, Bonney's Hotel.

Egge, Jacob, tailor, Sycamore n. Hickory.

Egger, S. shoemaker, h. Wm. bet. Bennett and Cedar.

Eggers, G. C. h. Batavia plank road n. Williamsville road.

Egloff. Francis, blacksmith, b. P. Egloff.

Egloff, Peter, lab. h. Watson n. Clinton.

Ehlers, Herman W. saddler, h. William cor. Adams.

Ehlers, Louis, patent yeast maker, h. Watson n. William.

Ehresman, Martin, lab. h. Elm n. Virginia.

Ehret, Martin, lab. h. Genesee n. Jefferson.

Ehrhardt, Casper, lab. h. Watson n. William.

Ehrhoff, J. G. shoemaker, b. 126 Elm.

Ehrlich, Francis, bookbinder, h. Ellicott cor. Carlton.

Ehrlinger, Michael, lab. h. Adams n. Sycamore.

Ehrnpforth, Chas. G. h. 76 Chippewa.
Eibell, Jos. bookbinder, with J. M. Johnson, b. 125 Michigan.
Eich, Gottleib, h. Grey n. Batavia.
Eich, Sebastian, lab. h. Herman n. Genesee.
Eicheldoerfer, M. tailor, h. 13 Maple.
Eichelkraut, John, lab. h. Sherman n. Genesee.
Eichenbroet, John, tailor, h. 106 Goodell.
Eichhamer, Michael, lab. h. Fox n. North.
Eichhorn, Leonhardt, peddler, h. Monroe n. Brown.
Eichier, Gottlieb,* hatter, h. Genesee n. Sherman.
Eichner. Peter, veterinary surgeon, h. 23 Hur'n.
Eimel, John, lab. h. Adams n. Genesee.
Einsfeld, John G. lab. h. Goodell n. Maple.
Eirich, Gottlieb, lab. h. 552 Michigan.
Eisel, —, lab. b. Elm n. Genesee.
Eisele, Andrew, tanner, with A. B. Platt, h. Monroe n. William.
Eisele, Edward, jeweler, h. Clinton n. Adams.
Esenhardt, Barbara, wid. h. Jeff. n. William.
Eisenhardt, John, shoemaker, h. r. 244 Gen.
Eisenholt, John, blacksmith, Niag. n. Amherst.
Eisert, Michael, carp. h. 42 Maple bel. Virginia.
Eisinger, Michael, carp. h. Mulberry n. Carlton.
Eislinger, Sebastian, cooper, h. Jeff n. Peckham.
Eismann, Felix, lab. h. Batavia n. Jefferson.
Eiss, Geo. h. Sycamore n. Walnut.
Eissner, Bernhard, h. Batavia cor. Grey.
Eiuler, Catherine, wid. 309 Genesee.
Ekel, Jacob, moulder, h. Locust n. Cherry.
Ekman, Henry, cabinet maker, b. Stowe's bl'k. Canal.
Elcheser, Andreas, wagoner, h. William n. Madison.
Elder, John, cabinet maker, h. 7th n. Pa.
Elder & Stearns, paper hanging and upholstering, 270 Main.
Elder, Stewart. firm E. & Stearns, 270 Main, h. 150 Delaware.
Eldridge, Benj. paper hanger, h. 129 Franklin.
Eldridge, Delos, moulder, B. S. engine works, h. 142 Elk.
Eldridge, G. C. clerk, 384 Main, b. Franklin House.
Eldridge, John P. truckman, b. Phœnix Hotel.
Eldridge, Samuel, clerk, W. T. Co. h. 90 North Division.
ELDRIDGE, ZOETH, prop. Franklin House, Seneca cor. Ellicott.—See adv. p. 92.
Elebeck, Junius H. barber, Arcade block, h. 50 Oak.
Eley, John, h. 19 7th.
Eley, Mary, wid. h. Main n. Buffalo Plains.
Eley, Philip, farmer, b. Samuel Eley.
Eley, Sam'l, grocer, Main cor. Eley R. h. same.
Eley, Samuel, Jr. farmer, with Samuel Eley.
Elgas, Peter, moulder, h. Goodell alley bel. Goodell.
Elhardt, M. lab. h. across creek.
Eller, Louis, tailor, 108 Tupper, h. same.
Ellicot, Pat. blacksmith, h. Folsom n. Chicago.
Ellig, Gottlieb, carp. h. Ferry n. Massachusetts.
Ellig, Peter, tinsmith, 137 Clinton.
Eliot, John D. paymaster, N. Y. C. R. R. Exchange, h. 69 S. Division.
Elliot, Wm. lab. h. Terrace n. Canal.

Elliott, Bernard, cartman, h. 6th n. Penn.
Elliott, John, lab. Clinton Forest.
Elliott, John, health inspector, h. Delaware n. North.
Elliott, John, saloon, Peacock n. Evans, h. same.
Elliott, Thomas, joiner, h. Palmer ab. Maryland.
Elliott, Wm. teamster, h. Delaware n. North.
Ellis, A. D. com. merch. 9 Central Wharf, h. 16 Delaware.
Ellis, Caroline, Miss, music teacher, Courier House.
Ellis, Geo. Canal, h. 4 Carroll.
Ellis, Henry Wm. mariner, h. 52 Palmer.
Ellis, H. F. blacksmith, h. cor. Carroll and Ala.
Ellis, Isaac, salesman, 99 Main, h. same.
Ellis, Robt. A. W. canal stable, Canal, h. 4 Carroll.
Ellis, Thomas, saloon, h. 34 Scott.
Ellis, Thos. h. 27 Scott.
Ellis, Wm. teamster, h. Clinton n. Ravine.
Ellis, Wm. pattern maker, h. 75 Oak.
Ellis, Wm. carp. h. 95 Oak.
Ellsworth, Henry, typefounder, h. 153 N. Div.
Eloghsky, Itzick, peddler, h. 13 Eagle.
Elsworth, A. B. teacher No. 20, h. Amherst n. East.
Elseasser, Wm.* shoemaker, cor. Kaene and Genesee, h. same.
Elser, Sebastian, butcher, b. 115 Batavia.
Elsesser, John, shoemaker, h. Dearborn n. Amherst.
Elsheimer, Geo. grocer, Genesee cor. Johnson, h. same.
Elsinghorst, John H. tinsmith, h. 134 Batavia.
Ely, Elizabeth, Mrs. h. ov. 536 Michigan.
Emerick, Charlotte, wid. h. 39 State.
Emerick, Christiene, seamstress, b. Jn. Emer'k.
Emerick, Jacob, dep. sheriff, h. 124 Oak.
Emerick, John, carp. 103 Pine.
Emerick, Louis, whisky manuf. 44 E Genesee, h. same.
Emerick, Philip, butcher, h. Walnut n. Batavia.
Emerson, C. A. Pratt & Co. h. 39 W. Eagle.
Emerson, Nelson, gate keeper, h. Ohio st. toll-bridge.
Emerson, Thomas E. clerk, b. 81 S. Division.
Emery, Christ, iron works, h. cor. military road and Philip.
Emery, C. K. h. 5th n. Pennsylvania.
Emig, Emil, printer, b. 25 Genesee.
Emig, Jno. hat store, 385 Main, h. same.
Emka, Henry, shoemaker, h. 106 Exchange.
Engel. A. rag peddler, b. 146 E. Genesee.
Emmerling, Henry, lab. h. Ferry n. Mass.
Emmerling. Ph. grocer, h. Batavia cor. Monroe.
Emmons, Wesley, carp. h. 96 S. Division.
Emrich, Gottfreid, butcher, h. Jefferson n. Bat.
Emrick, Chas. liquor dealer, h. Cherry cor. Maple.
Emsfeldt, J. P. printer, h. 533 Michigan.
Emslie, Geo. foreman Corn Dock Elevator, h. Virginia n. 11th.
Emslie, Peter, city surveyor, cor. Franklin and Eagle. b. St. James.
Ende, Jno. harness maker, h. Clinton n. Jeff.
Endel, Chas.* blacksmith, Genesee n. Walden.
Enders, Ferdinand, grocer, Batavia cor. Monroe, h. same.

Endicott, S. W. h. Forest ave. n. DeWitt.
Endras, Barbara, widow, h. 177 Genesee.
Endres, Andrew, lab. h. Boston al. bel. Va.
Endres, Geo. grocer, 80 E. Genesee, h. same.
Endres, Jno. cooper, h. Adams n. Batavia.
Endres, Jno. lab. h. Mulberry n. High.
Engal, A. wood workor, Brayley & Pitts.
Engel, August. ship carp. h. Ellicott cor. Va.
Engel, Balthasser, beer peddler, h. 234 Elm.
Engel, Balzar, brewer, b. G. Roos.
Engel, Chas. lab. b. 72 Tupper.
Engel, Frank, firm Nauert & E. h. Emslie cor. Lovejoy.
Engel, Jacob, lab. h. Grey bet. Gen. and Bat.
Engel, John, shoemaker, h. 245 Elm.
Engel, Nicholas, lab. h. Krettner n. Batavia.
Engel, Wendel, carp. h. Virginia n. Tupper.
Engelskirchen, T. 135 Main, b. Clinton cor. Ellicott.
Enger, Nicholas, with Pratt & Co. h. Mulberry n. Virginia.
Engerer, John, teamster, b. Watson n. Batavia.
Engler, Jno. lab. h. Walnut n. Batavia.
Englehard, Geo. lab. h. Maple n. High.
Englehard, Geo. lab. h. Eagle n. Jefferson.
Englehard, Geo. warehouseman, h. Batavia cor. Madison.
Englehard, John, lab. h. Maple n. High.
Englehard, Jno. tailor, h. Monroe n. Batavia.
Englehaupt, John, lab. h. Grey n. Genesee.
English, Charles, watchmaker, Erie st. depot, b. Revere House.
English, John, with Job Alberger. h. Locust n. Spring.
Enis, Albert, waiter, h. 16 Clinton.
Enos, L. & Co. com. merchants and millers, 17 Central Wharf.
Enos, Lawrence, com. mer. 22 Cent. Wharf, h. North n. Delaware.
Enright, D. M. printer, h. 6 4th n. Georgia.
Ensign, Chas. People's line propellers, Marine dock, b. 212 Pearl.
Ensign, Edward. clerk, b. 212 Pearl.
Ensign, Elisha W. stone merchant, Main cor. Virginia, b. 212 Pearl.
Erb, John. mason, h. Camp n. Genesee.
Erb, Mariah E. milliner, h. 69 Genesee.
Erb, Peter. wood peddler, h. 106 Genesee.
Erban, Julia, wid. h. Clinton n. Jefferson.
Erbes, Jacob, shoemaker, 6th cor. Hospital, h. cor. Court and 6th.
Erdman, Frank, trimmer, with Pierce & Co. h. William n. Jefferson.
Erenst, Henry, at Evans' planing mill.
Erfenbeck, Clemens, teamster, h. 294 Oak.
Erfenbeck, Fred. tinsmith, h. Weaver alley n. Virginia.
Erfurt, Peter, lab. h. 19 Bennett.
Erickson, Elling. carp. h. 224 N. Division.
Erie Basin Elevating Co. n. foot of Genesee.
Erisman, John, shoemaker. h. 98 Cedar.
Erisman, Martin, pressman. h. 38 Del. place.
Erisman, Mary, widow, h. Watson n. Clinton.
Erlbacher, Michael, lab. h. Walnut n. Batavia.
Erlbacher, Peter, gas fitter, h. 135 Sycamore.
Erie, Ignatz, blacksmith, h. Pine n. William.
Erlenbach, Adam, carp. b. 369 Michigan.
Erlich, Frederick, lab. h. Pratt n. Batavia.

Ermann. Deitrich, blacksm. h Wm. n. Walnut.
Erness, Peter, lab. h. Adams n. Clinton.
Ernewine, John. chair maker, b. I. Ernewine..
Ernst, Albert, Main st. R. R. h. Va. n. Cottage
Ernst, Gabriel, lab. h. Spring n. Genesee.
Ernst, Gottfrey. at 358 Main, h. 89 Elm.
Ernst, Henry, grocer, h. Eagle cor. Pratt.
Ernst, Jacob. carp. h. Monroe n. Brown.
Ernst, J. F. Jr. firm J. Fleeharty & Co. 27 Central Wharf, h. 230 Pearl.
Ernst, John F. Rev. select school, cor. Mohawk and Pearl, h. Pearl cor. Chippewa.
Ernst, Jno. tailor, h. 409 Michigan.
Ernst, Joseph, lab. h. 28 Spruce.
Ernst, M. tailor, h. 89 Elm.
Ernst, Peter, carp. h. Kaene n. Genesee.
Ernst, Phillip, lab. h. Park n. Virginia.
Ernst, V. printer, Morn. Ex. h. 47 Del. place.
Errman, Michael, carp. h. Krettner n. Peckham.
Ersheit, Nich. carp. h. Spruce n. Sycamore.
Ersing, Andrew, lab. h. Cedar n. William.
Ertel, Michael, lab h. Madison n. Batavia.
Ertz, Geo. lab. h. Camp n Genesee.
Ertz, Geo. mason, h. Sycamore n. Kaene. ·
Erwin, Charles, b. Western.
Erwin, Thomas, tinsmith, with N. Britton, h. 30 Green.
Esander, Ernst. cooper, h. Thompson n. Parish.
Eschenfelder, Wm. mason, 26 Ash n. Sycamore.
Esperiment, John, saloon, r. 41 Ohio, h. same.
Esser, John, retailer, Globe Mills, h. Thompson n. Amherst.
Essig, Henry, shoemaker, h. Boston alley ab. Tupper.
Essinberg, Wm. pattern maker h. cor. 9th and Jersey.
Esslinger, Charles, baker, Batavia n. Hickory, h. same.
Ester, David, barber, Elk st. market.
Estes, C. M. Mrs. dressmaker. 131 Chippewa.
Etchingham, James, rafter, b. across creek.
Etchingham, John, lab. h. across creek.
Etinne, Frank, barber, 78 Exchange, h. same.
Etman, D. blacksmith, h. William n. Hickory.
Etzel, Michael, grocer, h. High cor. Locust.
Euscher, Frederick, lab. h. Watson n. William.
Eustaphieve, A. A. sec'y Buff. Mutual Ins. Co. h. cor. Georgia and 7th.
Eustaphieve. A. E. clerk, Mutual Ins. Co. h. Georgia cor. 7th.
Eva, Adam, hotel, 110 Exchange, h. same.
Eva. John, cooper, h. cor. Parish n. Tonawanda.
Evans, Anthony, lab. h. across creek.
Evans, E. B. boiler iron works, h. Pooley place, n. Bird ave.
EVANS, CHAS. W. prop. Evans' Elevator, Norton cor. Water, h. 273 Wash.—See adv. p. 44.
Evans, E. T. h. 26 6th.
Evans, Edwin T. ford. and com. merch. cor. Water and ship canal, h. 272 Washington.
Evans, Evan, at iron works, h. Pooley place. n. N. Washington.
Evans, Geo. warehouseman, h. cor. Erie and Norton.
Evans, James C. ford. and com. merch. cor. Water and ship canal, h. 272 Washington.
Evans, Joseph, cabinet maker, h. Perry n. Mich.

Evans, John R. firm J. R. Evans & Co. h. 31 Ellicott.

EVANS, JOHN R. & Co. props. planing mill, Mechanic n. Terrace.—*See adv. p.* 86.

Evans, Lewis E. clerk, Water cor. ship canal, h. cor. Mohawk and Ellicott.

Evans, Lewis M. atty. b. 31 Ellicott.

Evans, Margaret, wid. of Wm. h. 273 Wash.

Evans, Matthew, clerk, b. cor. Erie and Norton.

Evans, O. B. daguerrean, Main cor. Erie.

Evans, Richard, glue maker, Abbott road n. iron bridge.

Evans, Robt. warehouseman, h. cor. Erie and Norton.

Evans. Steven, clerk, b. cor. Erie and Norton.

Evans, Thomas, Buff. Iron and Nail Works, h. Forest ave. n. N. Washington.

Evans, Wm. A. firm J. R. E. & Co. h. 35 E. Eagle.

Everding, Wm. harness maker, 31 Seneca, b. 2 Oak.

Evers, John P. capt. h. 108 6th.

Everson, John, lab. h. 72 Bennett.

Every, Stephen M. Hamlin & Mendsen, h. 12 7th.

Eves, John, engineer, N. Y. & E. R. R. h. 324 S. Division.

Ewalt, Peter, tailor, h. 313 Oak.

Ewart. Wm. sailor, h. across Buffalo creek.

Ewig, Peter, grocer, h. Goodell n. Michigan.

Exelby, R. millwright, Miami n. Shepard's iron works.

Exelby, Wm. millwright, h. Van Rensselaer n. Carroll.

Exstein, Hiram, book-keeper, 194 Main, b. 56 North Division.

Ey, Charles, Seneca n. Whittmore's tavern.

F.

Faber, Henry, blacksmith, h. Eagle n. Hickory.

Faber, Jacob, grocer. h. Abbott road bel. Smith.

Faber, Jacob, locksmith, h. Exchange n. Van Rensselaer.

Faber, Theobald,* bakery, h. Genesee n. Pratt.

Faerber. Christian, carp. h. Batavia n. Madison.

Fagan, M. foundryman, Brayley & Pitts.

Fahay, Jas. blacksmith, h. Exch. n. Louisiana.

Fahey, John, hostler, 303 Main, h. Oak n. Bat.

Fahey, Thos. blacksmith, h. 189 Exchange.

Fahl, John, h. Peckham n. Jefferson.

Failing, L. C. carp. h. Terrace n. Mechanic.

Fair, Catherine, Miss, seamstress, b. 16 Pratt.

Fairbanks, A. sailor, h. Scott n. Washington.

Fairchild, Maria, wid. nurse, h. 75 Delaware.

Fairchilds, F. O. printer, Courier, h. 40 E. Sen.

Fairchilds, John, teamster, Am. Ex. Co. b. 98 Folsom.

Fairchilds, Joseph L. atty. and special dep. co. clerk, b. 285 Pearl.

Fairfield, Jamin, pattern filer, h. 105 Carroll.

Fairman, F. F. h. 213 Delaware.

Fairman, J. P. teller Manuf. and Traders' Bank, 228 Pearl.

Falck, Abraham, with Altman & Co. h. 238 Carroll.

Falk, John, lab. h. Mulberry n. Virginia.

Falka, Henry, teamster, h. 38 Maple.

Falkenhahn, Charles, tailor, h. Spring n. Wm.

Falkner, Susan, Mrs. h. Chippewa n. Main.

Faller, John, h. 121 Pine.

Faller, Martin, h. Pratt n. Cl'nton.

Faller, Matt. blacksmith, h. Clinton cor. Pratt.

Faller, Wm. chair finisher, b. 125 Pine.

Fallis, Janet, grocer, Chippewa cor. Franklin h. same.

Fallon, James, merchant tailor, 224 Main, h. Courter House.

Fallon, Michael, 5th n. Virginia.

Falvey, Michael, carp. b. Ohio n. South.

Farber, Henry, bl'ksmith, h. Eagle n. Hickory.

Fargo, J. F. firm W. F. & Co. h. 45 E. Eagle.

Fargo, Willett, Maj. U. S. A. b. Rising Sun.

Fargo, Wm. G. director Am. Ex. office. h. Niagara cor. Franklin.

Farley, Jas. at iron works, h. Adams n. Albany.

Farley, Mathew, lab. h. Jackson n. Genesee.

Farmer, Alex. teamster. b. Wm. Farmer.

Farmer, Terrance. truckman, h. Perry n. La.

Farmer, Wm. h. Niagara n. Hamilton.

Farmer, Wm. Jr. b. Wm. Farmer.

Farnham, Chas. S. b. 459 Main.

FARNHAM & HODGE, coal yard, Erie cor. River.—*See adv. p.* 46.

Farnham, H. N. Jr. cor. Dock and Dock, b. 23 Church.

Farnham, Leroy, b. N. Pearl.

Farnham, Thos. firm F. & Hodge, coal yard, cor. Erie and River, h. 459 Main.

Farnlacher, John, lab. h. r. 19 Pratt.

Faron, Jos. stone cutter, h. Wash. cor. Va.

Farron, James, cabinet maker, h. 493 Wash.

Farr, Chilleon, foreman Shepard's Iron Works, h. Morgan n. Carey.

Farr, Geo. hostler, 303 Main, b. Court cor. Pearl.

Farrar, Frank M. engineer. h. 31 7th.

Farrel, Daniel, h. 5th n. Virginia.

Farrell, Andrew, lab. h. towpath bel. Genesee.

Farrell, Christopher, carp. h. Fulton n. Ala.

Farrell. Cornelius, cartman, h. cor. Heacock and Carroll.

Farrell, Jas. peddler. h. Perry n. Hamburgh.

Farrell, John, lab. h. towpath n. round house.

Farrell, John, lab. h. Exchange n. Griffin.

Farrell, John, lab. h. 91 5th.

Farrell, John, optician, with Andrews & Son, h. 9th, 2 doors from York.

Farrell, Laurence, lab. h. Exch. n. Hamburgh.

Farrell, Pat. stone mason, h. 6th cor. Maryland.

Farrell. Wm. sailor, h. Louisiana n. Elk.

Farringer, Thomas, mason, h. 139 Oak.

Farrington, Jno. printer, h. Louisiana n. Ohio.

Fartheringham, Alex. h. 1 Church.

Farthing. Geo. butcher, 12 Elk st. market, h. Cazenovia n. Seneca.

Farthing, James, firm J. & J. F. meat store, 291 Main, h. 311 Washington.

Farthing, John, butcher, 291 Main, h. Seneca n. Farthing.

Farthing, John, boatman, b. — Church.

Farthing, Thomas, butcher, stall No. 1 Elk st. market, h. White's Corners plank road.

Farver, C. widow, h. Mortimer n. Hollister.

Farver, Peter, grocer, cor. Ellicott and Huron.

FARWELL, E. & H. D. coffin warerooms, Niagara cor. Pearl.—*See adv. p.* 94.

Farwell. Henry D. firm E. & H. D. F. coffin maker, 13 and 15 Niagara, h. 56 Chippewa.
Farwell, William, b. Carey bel. Morgan.
Fassnacht, John, brewer. h. 176 Oak.
Faster, Amos, rope maker, h. Forest avenue n. N. Washington.
Fatty, Geo. L. butcher. h. Elk n. R. R. track.
Faude, Chas. gardener, h. Smith's alley n. Jeff.
Faul, Jacob, cooper, h. Parish n. Thompson.
Faul, Michael, miller, h. Parish n. Thompson.
Faust, John, lab. h. Pratt n. Sycamore.
Faust, John, lab. h. Sycamore n. Kaene.
Faust, T. painter. 164 Exchange, h. 83 Pine.
Faude, Jacob, melodeon maker, h. Hick. n. Bat.
Faxlanger, Frank, saloon, under 117 Main, h. 168 Elm.
Faxon, Henry, printer, b. over 157 Main.
Faxon, Jas. printer, h. 27 Niagara.
Fay, Amos F. firm S. Shepard & Co. 54 Main, h. 38 Carroll.
Fay, C. M. Mrs. widow, h. 137 Delaware.
Fay. John, lab. h. 5th n. Georgia.
Featherstone, Wm. H. printer, h. 5th n. Hud.
Fawsit, Wm. brewer, h. Carroll n. Van Rens'r.
Faxon, Daniel E. printer, over 157 Main.
Fecher, Jos. moulder. Bennett n. Batavia.
Fecher, Elizabeth, widow, h. Bat. cor. Pratt.
Federlein, Fred. musician, b 82 E. Genesee.
Fee, Alex. lab. h. Dearborn n. Amherst.
Fee, Thos. lab. h. Austin n. Tonawanda.
Feeney, John, lab. h. Michigan foot Fulton.
Feennfgeld, Chs. lab. cor. 10th and Virginia.
Feeney, John, boiler maker, h. Mich. cor. Elk.
Feeney, Pat, ship carp. h. Elk n. Hayward.
Feez, Philip, barber, b. 45 Genesee.
Fein, Jacob, glover, 27 Seneca, h. 181 Gen.
Feith, Nicholas, grocer, Syc. n Spruce, h. same.
Foegen, John, lab. h. Ash n. Sycamore.
Foegen, John, Jr. moulder. h. Ash n. Sycam'e.
Foegen, Matthias, b. John Foegen.
Fegher, Joseph, moulder, 5 State, h. Bennett n. Batavia.
Feige, Henry, shoemaker, h. Gen. n. Sherman.
Feigel, John, carp. h. Cherry n. Jefferson.
Feil, Gottlieb, h. Niagara n. Amherst.
Feist, Matthias, mason, h. 53 Cedar.
Feizel, Chas.* butcher, Genesee cor. Spruce, h. same.
Felten, Christian, lab. Mulberry n. Carlton.
Feldman, Henry, Rev. h. Mulberry n. Virginia.
Feldmann, Anthony, farmer, h. Delavan ave. n. Williamsville road.
Feldmann, Anthony, Jr. farmer, h. Delavan ave. n. Williamsville road.
Feldmeyer, Jno. G. lab. h. Sherman n. Genesee.
Felganmacher, Jos. A. M. D. h. 140 Batavia, office same.
Felgenmacher, A. organ builder, b. 140 Batavia.
Felgenmacher, Julius, jeweler. b. 140 Batavia.
Felker, Fred. shoemaker, 36 Maple.
Fell, A. agent, B. & L. H. R. R, b. 205 7th.
Fell, Geo. at cor. Com'l and Canal. b. 15 Com'l.
Fell, Edward, tailor, h. Spruce n. Batavia.
Fell, William, b. Western Hotel.
Feller, Adam, lab. h. Adams n. Batavia.
Fellger, John, lithographer, h. Hickory n. Bat.
Fellner, Godfred,* shoemaker, h. 10th n. Hampshire.

Fellner, Lewis, clerk, P. O. h. Syc. n. Mich.
Fellows, Chas. M. mariner, h. 392 Swan.
Fellows, E. W. b. Western Hotel.
Fellows, James H. sailor, h. Miami cor. La.
Fellows, Jeremiah C. printing ink and lamp-black, 227 Main, h. 72 E. Swan.
Fellows, Jno. O. captain, h. St. Paul n. Main.
Fellows, John, sailor, b. capt. Jno. O. Fellows.
Felser, Peter, blacksmith, h. Adams n. Batavia.
Feltes, Nicholas, saloon, Elk street market, h. same.
Felthousen, H. C. firm Russell & F. h. 113 Main, h. 24 7th.
Felthousen & Russell, tinsmiths, 113 Main.
Felthousen, Robert T. coppersmith, b. Carolina n. Niagara.
Felton, Benj. F. news depot, 205 Washington, b. cor. Clinton and Ellicott.
Felton, Chas. E. printer, 7 E. Seneca, up stairs, h. 128 6th.
Felton, Christene, widow, h. 4 Maple.
FELTON, JOHN, stationer and gold pen manufacturer, 159 Main, h. 89 Clinton.—See adv. p. 95.
Felton. William, piano maker, h. 4 Maple.
Felz, John, finisher, h. Watson n. Batavia.
Fenerstein, P. Mrs. midwife, h. 150 Clinton.
Fenerstein, Peter, at N. Y. C. R. R. shop, h. 150 Clinton.
Fenstermacher, William, grocer, Seneca n. junction Swan, h. same.
Fenzl, Florian, coffin maker, Niag. cor. Pearl, h. Mulberry n. Carlton.
Ferber, Christina, widow, h. Mortimer n. Bat.
Ferber, Peter, lab. b. Mortimer n. Batavia.
Ferguson, C. lab. h. Mrs. S. Ferguson.
Ferguson, Eli, h. 100 6th.
Ferguson, James, at Gas Works, h. Wilkeson slip n. Jackson.
Ferguson, John, in Niagara steam forge, h. 368 S. Division.
Ferguson, Jno. clerk, A. Fallon, b. Jeff. n. Bat.
Ferguson, Susan, widow, boarding house, Ohio n. Columbia.
Ferguson, T. tailor, h. Jefferson n. Batavia.
Ferguson, William, b. 6th n. Pennsylvania.
Ferkel, Martin, boot and shoe store, 394 Main, h. same.
Ferkel Philip, shoemaker, Ohio n. Chicago, h. same.
Fernald, G. W. H. C. clerk, S. Enos & Co. b. 170 Main.
Fernbach, Stephen, farmer, Steel n. Walden.
Fero, A. clerk, J. R. Fero, b. 7 Ellicott.
Fero & Barnard, grocery and Canal stable, Canal n. Evans.
Feron, Jas. stone cutter, h. Burton alley n. Weaver alley.
Fero, John, firm F. & Barnard, h. 72 Niagara.
Fero, John R. liquor store, Terrace, h. 83 Franklin.
Fero, Robert, machinist, b. 7 Ellicott.
Ferrick, Martin, ship carp. b. Perry n. Hayw'd.
Ferris, Christopher, h. Carolina bet. 9th and Niagara.
Ferris, Edward L. at 58 Arcade Buildings, b. 4 Edward.
Ferris, Hester A. widow, h. 4 Edward.

Ferris, Margaret, widow, h. 36 E. Eagle.
Ferris, P. J. coffee and spice mills, cor. Hanover and Canal, b. Western Hotel.
Ferris, W. W. book-keeper, 174 Main, b. Carolina n. Niagara.
Ferron, Thos. porter, b. National Hotel.
Fertig, John, carp. h. Weaver al. n. Burton al.
Fesler, Henry D. clerk, Dinwoddie & Shulz, b. cor. Swan and Ellicott.
Fester, John, lab. h. Camp cor. Genesee.
Festner, Bernard, clerk, 364 Main, h. 56 Clint'n.
Festus, Peter, grocer, 247 Seneca, b. same.
Feszler, Andrew, lab. h. Maple n. North.
Fete, Geo. machinist, h. N. Div. n Jefferson.
Feth, Adam, carpenter, b. 4 Bennett.
Feth, Engelhard, carp. b. Lovejoy n. Emslie.
Feth, Jacob, carpenter, b. 113 Pine n. Batavia.
Fetzer, Fred. lab. h. Adams n. Peckham.
Feuchter, Philip, varnisher, h. over 389 Main.
Feuerbach, Adam, brewer, h. 296 Elm.
Feuerbach, Geo. gardener, h. Locust n. North.
Feuerbach, Joseph, lab. h. Mulberry n. High.
Feuerstone, John, mason, Walnut n. Genesee.
Feuerstone, Mrs. widow, h. over 3 Cherry.
Fick, Chas. maltster, h. Elm ab. Goodell.
Fick, Francis, carpenter, h. 42 Maple bel. Va.
Fick, John H. saloon, cor. Canal and Erie, h. same.
Fickel, C.* shoemaker, h. Clinton bel. Mich.
Fickel, Chas. shoemaker, h. 173 Batavia.
Fickert, Louis, saloon, Kaene n. Genesee.
Fickel, N. shoemaker, h. Clinton bel. Michigan.
Fickes, Benjamin F. ambrotypist, 324 Main, h. 23 Clinton.
Ficks, John, lab. h. Brayton n. Vermont.
Ficks, Peter, lab. h. Brayton n. Vermont.
Ficks, Rosina, widow, h. Sherman n. Genesee.
Fickley, F. lab. h. Michigan n. Elk.
Fideng, John, mason, h. Krettner n. Batavia.
Fidler, John, cooper, East n. R. R.
Fiedler, Francis, music teacher, h. 159 Elm.
Fiedler, Gottfried, lab. h. Walnut cor. Syc.
Field, Henry, greenhouse, h. 68 Huron.
Field, Joseph, C. foreman, Howard Agricultual Works, b. 99 Delaware.
Field, Norman S. marble works, Del. ab. Va.
Field, Matthew, lab. h. Clinton n. Raze.
Field, M. D. machinist, b. 63 S. Division.
Field, M. H. barnkeeper, b. Louisiana n. Elk.
Field, Thomas C. shoe dealer, h. 82 E. Seneca.
Fields, Eli, with Stimpson & Matthews, 6 C. Wharf. h. 6 Commercial.
Fields, John, lab. h. Porter cor. Bouck.
Fields, Lucius, lab. b. 204 N. Division.
Fields, Emma, Mrs. washerwoman, h. 74 Oak.
Fields, Robert, h. 203 Swan.
Fields, S. H. builder, h. 296 Ellicott.
Fields, William, b. 203 Swan.
Figerwith, Wm. lab. h. Clinton n. C. R. R.
Fiiz, Christian, peddler, h. 182 Genesee.
Fiiz, Julia, widow, h. Cherry n. Genesee.
Fiiz, Philip, saloon, Genesee n. Spruce, h. same.
Filbert, Louis E. teacher, h. 143 Elm.
Fildmier, Geo. boiler maker, Norton n. Evans, h. German n. Genesee.
Filer, Geo. musician, h. Maple n. Goodell.
Filer, John, Wash. market, b. Walnut n. Wm.
Fill, Michael, shoemaker, 12 Com'l, b. same.

Fillbauer, Henry, lab. h. 352 Genesee.
Fillmore, Millard, ex-president, office 7 Court, h. N. E. cor. Niagara square and Delaware.
Fillmore, Millard P. firm Sprague & F. b. Niag. square.
Fillo, Francis, blacksm. h. N. Canal n. Emslie.
Filner, Lewis, clerk, P. O. h. 61 Sycamore.
Fine, Jacob, glove maker, 27 Seneca, h. 180 Gen.
Finegan, Frank. b. 5 Ellicott.
Finegan, Jas. carp. h. Genesee n. gas works.
Finegan, Mary, Mrs. board'g house. 5 Ellicott.
Finegan, Mary, Miss, clerk, b. 5 Ellicott.
Finegan, Pat. lab. h. 14th n. Hampshire.
Fingwend, Louis, lab. h. Jefferson n. Seneca.
Finigan, Pat. tinsmith, h. Genesee n. Terrace.
Finch, Hiram, wheat buyer, h. W. Seneca n. Franklin.
Finck, Christ. sailor, h. Sherman n. Batavia.
Finck, Daniel, shoemaker, h. Swan n. Spring.
Finck, Jacob, boarding house, 184 Batavia.
Fink, Anton, tailor, William n. Cedar.
Fink, Chs. brewer, b. 209 Oak.
Fink, Frank, mason, h. Locust n. High.
Fink, Henry, brewer, b. 209 Oak.
Fink, John, lab. b. East n. Hamilton.
Fink, John,* stave cutter, h. East n. Hamilton.
Fink, John, mason, h. 40 Cherry.
Fink, John, grocer, 199 Batavia, b. same.
Fink, John, brewer, b. Haefner's Brewery.
Finkler, John, milkman, h. 321 Elm n. Va.
Finland, Robt. millwright, h. Niag, n. Parish.
Findley, Geo. engineer, h. 9 Walnut.
Finley, Jas. engineer, h Hickory n. Clinton.
Finley, Jas. grocer, Carolina cor. 9th, b. Palmer ab. Virginia.
Finley, Jas. M. fireman, L. S. R. R. h. 386 Sen.
Finley, James, with Sternberg & Co. h. Perry n. Hayward.
Finley, Jane, widow, h. Perry n. Hayward.
Finley, John, Jr. weighmaster. h. 106 Fulton.
Finley, Robert, clerk, b. Exchange cor. Beak.
Finn, Catharine, widow, h. Jackson n. Gen.
Finnegan, Owen, clerk, b. Genesee n. Terrace.
Finnegan, Pat. drayman, b. 86 5th.
Finnerty, John, waiter, Emerald House, 104 Exchange.
Finnfgeld, Theadore, lab. h. 44 Bennett.
Finster, John, lab. h. Grey n. Batavia.
Finsterback, Frank, boiler mak'r, h. 290 N. Div.
Firbeck, Adam, malter, h. Elm n. Goodell.
Firmenich, Jos. M. D. 302 Main, h. 177 Oak.
Fisch, Michael, lab. h. 112 Hickory.
Fischer, Caroline, over 94 E. Genesee.
Fischer, Chas. firm J. & G. F. h. 180 Oak.
Fischer, Christian, farmer, h. Genesee E. Williamsville road.
Fischer, Conrad, lab. h. Weaver's al. n. Good'l.
Fischer, Francis, grocery, Elm cor. Tupper, h. same.
Fischer, Frank. firm F. & Weiland, h. Elm cor. Tupper.
Fischer, Frederick, carp. h. 500 Michigan.
Fischer, Fred. butcher, h. Fox n. Genesee.
Fischer, Geo. lab. h. Jefferson n. William.
Fischer, Geo. firm J. & G. F. h. 74 E. Genesee.
Fischer, Geo. Sr. basket maker, h. 258 Elm.
Fischer, Gottlieb,* baker, Genesee cor. Johnson, h. same.

Fischer, Henry.* butcher, h. Gen. cor. Hick'y.
Fischer, Henry, shoemaker, h. Pratt n. Syca.
Fischer, Jacob P. firm Geo. Urban & Co. h. 92 E. Genesee cor. Oak.
Fischer, Jacob, lab. h. Steel n. Walden.
Fischer, Jno. firm J. & G. F. h. 74 E. Genesee.
Fischer, John, lab. h. Fox n. North.
Fischer, John B. lab. h. Genesee n. Herman.
Fischer, John, mason, h. Grape n. High.
Fischer, John. lab. h. Goodell alley n. Goodell.
Fischer, J. & G. flour, feed and lumber, 74 E. Genesee.
Fischer, John J. mason, h. Grey n. Batavia.
Fischer, Justus, lab. h. Johnson n. Genesee.
Fischer, Louis, carp. h. Locust n. Cherry.
Fischer, Michael, lab. h. Cypress n. Michigan.
Fischer, Michael, tailor, b. 240 Elm.
Fischer, Paul, carver, h. Ellicott cor. Huron.
Fischer, Paul, carp. h. over 37 Huron.
Fischer, Peter, butcher, b. Monroe n. Syca.
Fischer, Roman, painter, h. Batavia cor. Pine.
Fischer, W. lab. h. Elm ab. Genesee.
Fischer & Weiland, Buff. Novelty Ag'l Works, 520 Michigan.
Fischer, Wolfgang, carp. h. Monroe n. Wm.
Fish & Armstrong, insurance agts. 44 Main.
Fish & Avery, prod. and com. 18 Cent. Wharf.
Fish, H. J. clerk, Pratt & Co. b. 87 Franklin.
Fish, Henry H. clerk, 18 Cent. Wharf. b. 156 Delaware.
Fish, J. M. Mrs. widow, 129 S. Division.
Fish, L. G. tallyman, N. Y. C. R. R. b. 163 S. Division.
Fish, Silas H. prod. and com. 18 Cent. Wharf. h. 156 Delaware.
Fish, Willis R. with J. Weeks. b. 380 Franklin.
Fish, S. H. & Co. Union Line, 18 Cent. Wharf.
Fisher, A. C. paper hanger, h. Mariner n. Va.
Fisher, Charles, b. Revere House.
Fisher, Geo. B. clerk, F. S. Fitch, b. Seneca cor. Michigan.
Fisher, Henry, shoemaker, b. cor. Terrace and Church.
Fisher, James H. att'y at law, firm Brown & F. h. 153 E. Seneca.
Fisher, James, h. 153 E. Seneca.
Fisher, J. G. barkeeper, Bonney's Hotel.
Fisher, Jno. mason, h. 9th n. Hampshire.
Fisher, Jno cigar maker, h. Spruce n. Batavia.
Fisher, Jno. tailor, h 405 Michigan.
Fisher, Jno. laborer, h. Maiden lane.
Fisher, Jno. Jr. lab. h. Monroe n. Batavia.
Fisher, John. Jr. tinsmith, h. Monroe n. Batavia.
Fisher, Louis, lab. h. N. Wash. n. Bird ave.
Fisher, Martha A. widow, 5 Carroll.
Fisher, Martin, shoemaker, h. 282 Franklin.
Fisher, Martin, Jr. tinsmith, b. 282 Franklin.
Fisher, Nicholas, tailor, h. 135 Oak.
Fisk, Harvey, with Pratt & Co. h. 87 Franklin.
Fisk, H. C. supt. N. Y. & E. R. R. b. Mansion.
Fisk, Sylvanus, b. Maid n. Utica.
Fiske, E. boatman, h. 11 William.
Fiske, Edward. b. 466 Main.
Fiske, F. W. firm G. S. Hazard & Co. h. 49 Del.
Fiske, Geo. M. book-keeper, R. Williams, h. 466 Main.
Fiske, William, h. 466 Main.
Fitch, H. S. painter, h. 21 Pearl.

Fitch, Augustus B. attorney, 5 Weed's Block, h. 5 Niagara.
FITCH, F. S. dry goods and groceries, cor. Mich. and E. Seneca, h. Mich. n. Seneca.— *See adv. p. 41.*
Fitch, Hannibal F. painter, Palmer ab. Va.
Fitch, William. h. 5 Niagara.
Fitch, William, clerk. b. Summer n. Delaware.
Fitch, Wm. C law-office, 14 Spaulding's Exchange. b. T. C. Davis.
Fithian, Freeman J. district attorney, 7 Court, h. 161 Franklin.
Fitzgerald, Betsey, widow, h. Elk cor. Moore.
Fitzgerald, Daniel, lab. b. Van Rensselaer n. Porter.
Fitzgerald, Dennis, tailor. b. Cotter's Exch.
Fitzgerald, Garrett, lab. Van Renssel'r n. Exch.
Fitzgerald, Jas. lab. h. York n. towpath.
Fitzgerald, Jno. lab. h. n. Mason's ship yard.
Fitzgerald, John, lab. h. Emily bel. Delaware.
Fitzgerald, John, lab. h. 10th n. Maryland.
Fitzgerald, Percy, cutter, 11 Commercial, b. 7th n. Pennsylvania.
Fitzgerald, Peter, lab. h. 137 Pine.
Fitzgerold, Thos. clerk, h. 10th bet. Maryland and Hudson.
Fitzgerald, Thos. lab. h. Chicago cor. Elk.
Fitzhenry, Edward, blacksmith, h. Fulton n. Alabama.
Fitzmorris, Dan. lab. h. Heacock n. Elk.
Fitzmorris, Mary, widow, h. 6th n. Maryland.
Fitzmyer, Fred. h. 136 9th.
Fitzpatrick, Francis, switchman, N. Y. C. R. R. h. Mill n. Heacock.
Fitzpatrick, Jerry, sailor, h. 382 Swan.
Fitzpatrick, Michael, lab. Niagara n. Parish.
Fitzpatrick, Thos. painter, at 15 Eagle, h. 240 Seneca.
Fitzpatrick, Wm. sailor, h. Perry n. Hayward.
Fitzpatrick, Wm. stove moulder, b. cor. Scott and Market.
Fitzroy, Emma, wid. h. Virginia n. Garden.
Fitzroy, Jos. book-keeper, b. Va n. Garden.
Fitzsimons, —, boarding house. Elk n. Marvin.
Fix, Bernhard, carpenter, h. Maple n. High.
Fix, Ferd. blacksmith. h Herman n. Genesee.
Fix, Geo. lab. h. Mulberry n. High.
Fix, Geo. grocer, h. 555 Seneca.
Fix, Jacob, lab. b. Brayton n. Rhode Island.
Fix, Margaret, Mrs. h. Elm cor. Tupper.
Fix. Matthew, tailor, h. Grey n. Genesee.
Fix, Nicholas, teamster, h. 95 Goodell.
Fix, Valentine, lab. h. Genesee n. German al.
FLACH, B. & BRO. locksmiths, 17 Mohawk. —*See adv. p. 89.*
Flach, Julius E. grocer. Sycamore cor. Oak.
Flach, Richard, grocer, Ellicott cor. Clinton, h. 19 Clinton.
Flacht, Philip,* tailor, Ash n. Syc. h. same.
Flagenstine, Peter, cabinet maker, 241 Main, h. Monroe n. William.
Flagg, Jno. L. sailor. h. Ohio n. Wabash.
Flagg, S. D. 11 Central Wharf, h. cor. Franklin and Allen.
Flagg, Samuel D. Jr. м. р. 294 Main, b. cor. Franklin and Allen.
Flaig, Mathew. lab. h. Adams n. Peckham.
Flaherty, Jeremiah, lab. b. Smith's Block, Exch.

11

Flaherty, Michael, lab. h. Genesee n. Erie can'l.
Flammer, Matthew, umbrella maker, h. Adams n. Batavia.
Flanagan, Jno. ship carp. b. Wm. Flanagan.
Flanagan, Patrick, tinsmith, b. Wm. Flanagan.
Flanagan, Wm. lab. h. Terrace n. Genesee.
Flanagan, Wm. Jr. tinsmith, b. Wm. Flanagan.
Flanagan, Margaret, wid. h. Lock n. Terrace.
Flannagan, Michael, teamster, h. 5 Evans.
Flannigan, Jas. lab. Peacock n. Norton.
Flannigan, John, joiner, h. 284 Swan.
Flannigan, Patrick, blacksmith, h. Daugherty alley n. Folsom.
Flannigan, Patrick, grocer, cor. Elk and Marvin.
Flannigan, Patrick, watchman, b. Elk opp. Marvin.
Flannigan, Wm. saloon, Evans cor. Peacock.
Flare, Andrew, cooper, h. Dearborn n. Parish.
Flare, Fred. cooper, h. Dearborn Tonawanda.
Flatau, Ferdinand, book-keeper, h. over 18 Gen.
Flaudung, Henry A. moulder, h. Maple n. Goodell.
Flechenstein, Peter, cabinet maker, h. Monroe n. William.
FLEEHARTY, J. & CO. prod. shipping and com. merch. 27 Central Wharf, h. 24 Delaware.—See adv. p. 37.
Fleeharty, James, lab. h. Ohio n. Chicago.
Fleleh, Peter, shoemaker, h. Boston alley ab. Tupper.
Fleischauer, Theodore, saloon, 153 Main, h. 138 Main.
Fleischhauer, Fred. lab. h. Sycamore n. Jeff'n.
Fleischman, Mathias, carp. h. 68 Pine.
Fleischman, Michael, brewer, h. Batavia cor. Hickory.
Fleischman, Michael, brewer, b. G. Roos.
Fleischmann, Margaret, widow, h. Delaware avenue n. Walden.
Fleishman, Michael, lab. h. 98 Cherry.
Fleischmaur, Matthew, cabinet maker, h. Pine n. Clinton.
Fleist, Conrad, at J. M. Hutchinson's, h. Clinton n. Jefferson.
Fleming, Edward, printer, b. 9th n. Hudson.
Fleming, Ernst, tailor, h. William n. Pine.
Fleming, Frank, machinist, h. 19 Bennett.
Fleming, John, h. 201 Oak.
Fleming, John, Jr. b. 201 Oak.
Fleming, John, lab. h. 388 Swan.
Fleming, Mary, widow, h. 9th n. Hudson.
Fleming, Robert, engineer, b. 201 Oak.
Fleming, Thomas, printer, h. 201 Oak.
Fleming William, tailor, h 535 Michigan.
Fleming, William, deputy collector of customs, h. 108 W. Huron.
Flerl, Christopher, tanner, h. Krettner n. Wm
Flersheim, G. B. clerk, 275 Main, h. 306 E. Seneca.
Flersheim, Lem. H. at 275 Main, h. 105 Ellicott.
Flesch, Peter, lab. h. Goodell alley ab. Tupper.
Fletcher, Theresa, h. Hickory n. Eagle.
Fletcher, Wm. sailor, h. Abbott road n. R. R.
Fletcher, William. lab. h. Kentucky n. South.
Fleury, Francis, finisher, 9 Water, h. E. Bennett ab. William.
Flexsing, Elizabeth, widow, h. 134 Spring.
Flick, Philip, cooper, h. Watson n. Peckham.

Flink, Joseph, lab. h. Walnut n. William.
Flinn, David, lab. h. lake shore road n. Tiff's farm.
Flinn, Jno. shoemaker, 4 Canal, h. same.
Flinn, Lucy, dress making, b. cor. Exch. & La
Flinn, Stephen, saloon, 6 Commercial.
Flinn, Thomas, lab. h. Palmer ab. Maryland.
Flynn, Jas. lab. h. Palmer n. Maryland.
Flynn, John, lab. h. Exch. at N. Y. C. R. R.
Flynn, Stephen, currier, 5 Ohio.
Flynn, Thomas, sailor, h. 155 Walnut.
Flynn, Thomas, lab. h. across creek.
Flint, Charles G. lessee St. James Hall, h. 77 6th.
Flint, J. T. ticket ag't N. Y. C. line propellers, foot Michigan, h. 46 Ellicott.
Flint, Oscar T. book-keeper, E. P. Dorr, b. 46 Ellicott.
Flint, William B. firm Howard, Whitcomb & Co. b. 29 Swan.
Flinteowitz, Markus, cigar maker, Genesee n. Johnson.
Flore, George, lab. h. Ash n. Sycamore.
Flos, George, cooper, Mortimer n. William.
Fludder, James, joiner, h. 68 Tupper.
Fluette, George, carp. h. Louisiana n. Elk.
Fobes, William D. h. 445 Main.
Foedy, Michael, lab. h. Louisiana n. Elk.
Foel, Christian, baker, h. over 140 Genesee.
Foell, George G. clerk, Commercial Hotel.
Foell, John, baker, Ellicott above Chippewa, h. same.
Foelker, Philip, lab. h. 130 E. Genesee.
Foertsch, George, Rev. St. Michael's Church.
Foesh, Henry, lab. h. Jefferson n. Peckham.
Foester, Baptist, Gen. n. Spruce, h. same.
Fogarty, John, grocer, Perry n. Hayward, h. same.
Fogerty, James, grocer, Clinton n. Montgomery.
Fogel, Carl, shoemaker, h. 105 Genesee.
Fogel, John E. cooper, h. Syc. n. Hickory.
Fogle, John, lab. h. Seneca n. Whittmore's tavern.
Foglesang, Geo. lab. h. Pratt n. William.
Fogt, Wm. joiner. h. Eagle n. Jefferson.
Foley, Daniel, printer, b 9th n. Hudson.
Foley, Ellen, widow, h. across creek.
Foley, G. capt. h. Fulton n. Alabama.
Foley, John, lab. h. across creek.
Folger, E. F. h. 349 Washington.
Folger, Jno. blacksmith, h. 85 9th.
Folk, Leopold, h. Dearborn n. Hamilton.
Folk, Sophia, widow, h. Mulberry n. Goodell.
Folkman, Christ. h. 2 Vine.
Follett, Joseph E. h. 61 Seneca.
Foller, Nicholas, lab. h. rear 24 Cherry.
Folsom, Oscar, clerk, h. 83 S. Division.
Fonster, Adam, shoemaker, h. over 26 Spruce.
Fontaine, Elic. policeman, h. Watson n. Clinton.
Foot, Henry, teamster, h. Clinton n. Rrze.
Foote, Albert W. foreman Union furnace, h. 55 5th n. Georgia.
Foote, Delia, Miss, h. North cor. N. William.
Foote, Geo. C. carp. h. Genesee n. 5th.
Foote, Lewis C. clerk, b. Western.
Foote, R. S. clerk canal collector, b Mansion.
Foote, Thomas M. law student, 180 Main, h. North cor. William.

Foote, Wm. canal collector, Merchants' Hotel Building, Com'l and Canal, h. 17 Carroll.
Foote, William. Jr. clerk at canal collector's office, b. 17 Carroll.
Foote, William, firm Morton, F. & Co. h. 35 W. Seneca.
Footet, Thos. grocer, Abbott plank road n. Elk.
Foran, Mary, dress maker, b. 119 Batavia.
Foran, Mary, widow, h. 119 Batavia.
Forbes, Joseph D. fire brick manufacturer, h. 4 Tracy.
Forbes, Jno. h. 57 Washington.
Forbs. Martin, b. 57 Washington.
FORBUSH, ELIAKIM B. attorney, Main cor. Swan, h. 66 Mohawk.—See adv. p. 83.
Forbush, J. C. firm F. Brown & Co. 91 Main, h. 74 E. Eagle.
Forbush, Walter H. mechanical draughtsman, 8 Weed's Block, b. 66 Mohawk.
Ford, Elijah, attorney, firm F. & Son, 216 Main, h. Delaware cor. Chippewa.
Ford, E. W. h. cor. South and Dearborn.
Ford, H. E. lab. h. East n. Hamilton.
Ford, Henry, cabinet maker, h. 122 6th.
Ford, Jacob, express driver, h. over 48 E. Genesee.
Ford, James E. attorney, firm F. & Son, 216 Main, b. Delaware cor. Chippewa.
Ford, Mathew, baggage master, N. Y. C. R. R. b. 117 Seneca.
Ford, Michael, boarding. Columbia n. Ohio.
Ford, Rensselaer D. b. 116 S. Division.
Ford, Richard, wagon maker and blacksmith, 312 Michigan, h. 232 Carroll.
Ford, William A. porter, Bonney's Hotel, h. Seneca cor. Ellicott.
Foreman, A. printer, b. 29 Pearl.
Forest, Andrew, ship carp. h. Fulton n. Chicago.
Forester, Fred. carriage maker, h. 23 Spruce.
Forester, Oliver O. saloon, Carroll cor. Michigan, h. William n. Pine.
Foster, Clarissa, Miss, h. 209 Ellicott.
Forr, J. S. clerk. with B. M. Howard.
Forrester, Henry, firm Quinn & F. h. 11th n. Jersey.
Forrester, Jas. clerk, 100 Exchange, b. same.
Forrester, Wm. saloon, 100 Exchange, h. same.
Forshler, Henry, finisher. h. Walnut n. Batavia.
Forster, Fred. coach maker, h. 23 Spruce.
Forster, Jas. lab. h. 312 Elm.
Forster, Jos. tailor, h. Weaver alley n. Va.
Forster, Martin, tailor, b. Beaver alley n. Va.
Forster, Michael, harness maker, with Kolb & Co. h. Oak n. Burton alley.
Forsyth, Ed. carpenter, h. 128 Clinton.
Forsyth, Jas. carver and gilder, h. 117 Walnut.
Forsyth, Jas. G. clerk 54 Main. b. 408 Main.
Forsyth, Jos. h. Ellicott n. Carlton.
Forsyth, Robt. shoemaker. 51 Seneca, b. same.
Forsyth, Thos. grocer, Main n. Ferry, h. same.
Forsyth, Wm. clerk, h. Cottage n. Maryland.
Fort. I. M. h. 20 Oak.
Fortier, Chas. G. insp. Home Ins. Co. h. 11th.
Fortier, Jas. P. h. Jersey n. North.
Fortier, L. B. with Rounds & Hall, h. 21 Park place.
Fortier, P. J. sailor. h. Maryland n. 10th.
Fortune, Thos. h. 6 Tracy.

Fosdick, Chas A. teacher No. 27, b. 329 Ellicott.
Fosdick, John S. teacher No. 14, h. 329 Ellicott.
Fost. M. moulder, h. 50 William.
Foster, Andrew, clerk, Howard, Whitcomb & Co. h. 18 Chestnut.
Foster, Chas. H. with G. R. Wilson.
Foster, Mrs. widow, h. 206 Seneca.
Foster, Daniel. b. Western.
Foster, D. G. clerk, 267 Main. h. 26 N. Div.
Foster. D. W. tallyman, N. Y. & E. R. R. h. 96 Carroll.
Foster. George E. clerk Foster & Co. b. 30 W. Eagle.
Foster, H. Mrs. h. 45 Cedar.
Foster. Henry, with T. D. Dole, b. Wadsworth.
Foster. Jas. H. with Sherman & Barnes, h. 281 Pearl.
Foster, Joseph, shoemaker, h. over 7 Genesee.
Foster, Martin, lab. h. 567 Washington.
Foster, Robert, lab. b. Chicago n. Elk.
Foster, Sebastian, with Jewett & Root, h. Sycamore n. Pratt.
Foster, Thomas, ship carp. h. Cedar n. N. Div.
Foster. W. C. firm W. C. F. & Co. h. 30 W. Eagle.
Foster, W. C. & Co. shipping and com. merch. 20 Central Wharf.
Foster, Wm. b. Revere.
Foth, John, tailor. h. Spruce n. Sycamore.
Fotheringham, Alex. clerk, 318 Main, b. 11 Church.
Fougeron, Joseph, grocer, Niagara cor. Mohawk, h. same.
Fougeron, Mary A. widow, h. 375 Washington.
Foundling Asylum, Edward n. Delaware.
Fountaine, Eli, ship carp. h. Watson n. Clinton.
Fowler, Chas. F. conductor N. st. R. R. h. 9th n. Rhode Island.
Fowler, Geo. L. Terrapin Lunch, cor. Main and Terrace. h. 35 Ellicott.
Fowler, Henry, weighman, h. Perry n. Hamburgh.
Fowler, Samuel, blacksmith, h. Canal alley n. Jackson.
Fowler, Seymour. horse dealer, h. Seneca n. Red Jacket hotel.
Fox, A. R. Com. Adv. office, b. 128 Pearl.
Fox, Chas. R. b. Bloomer's, room St. James.
Fox, Esther, widow of Augustus C. h. 90 S. Div.
Fox, Geo. farmer, h. Genesee E. Williamsville road.
Fox, Geo. iron finisher, Brayley & Pitts.
Fox, Hiram, machinist, h. Carroll n. Alabama.
Fox, Mary, huckster, h. Hickory n. Batavia.
Fox, Michael, sailor, h. 63 5th n. Court.
Fox, Orrien, sailor, h. 11 William.
Fox, Peter, watchman, h. 93 5th.
Fox, Samuel, mariner, h. Palmer ab. Virginia.
Fox, Watson A. firm Gardner, Ritt & F. h. 49 W. Eagle.
Fox, W. G. proprietor billiard rooms, 208 Washington, h. 14 Carroll.
Fraas, Christoph, lab. h. Mulberry n. High.
Fraehers, John, lab. h. German alley n. Gen.
Fralick, F. G. clerk, H. Wing & Co. b. 304 Pearl.
Frame, Alexander, butter, cheese, etc. Elk st. market, h. Fulton n. Hamburgh.
Francis, Alex. 18 Water, h. same.

Francis, Brigdon, teamster, h. Hayward n. Elk.
Francis, Daniel, h. 13 Oak.
Francis, Geo. sailor, h. Root n. 5th.
Francis, Henry, carpenter, h. 38 William.
Francis, H. F. ship carpenter, h. 16 Mississippi.
FRANCIS, JULIUS E. drug store, 268 Main, b. cor. Swan and Ellicott.—See adv. p. 94.
Francis, Lyman, lab. h. 135 Carroll.
Francis, Lyman, h. Fulton n. Hamburgh.
Franger, Henry, saloon, 4 Canal, h. same.
Franinger, Paul, barber, 4 Com'l, h. same.
Franck, Jacob, Merchts. Disp. h. 186 Niagara.
Frank. A. H. machinist, h. 13th n. R. I.
Frank, Anton, musician, h. 84 Batavia.
Frank, Casper, lab. h. 232 Elm.
Frank & Co. machine shop, Eaton's planing mill, Hospital.
Frank, Chas. tanner, h. Hickory n. William.
Frank, Edward, blacksmith, b. J. Barth.
Frank, Edward J. clk. 178 Main, h. 186 Niag.
Frank, Florian, lab. b. Revere.
Frank, Fred. lab. h. Peckham n. Monroe.
Frank. Geo. furnaceman, h. Tupper cor. Boston alley.
Frank, Geo. lab. h. Adams n. Batavia.
Frank, Geo. mason, h. Washington n. Chip'wa.
Frank, Geo. iron finisher, with Brayley & Pitts.
Frank. Job. carp. b Walnut n. Sycamore.
Frank, John. musician. h. 84 Batavia.
Frank, John, milk peddler, h. Steele n. Walnut.
Frank, John L. mason, h. Cedar n. Clinton.
Frank, Martin, grocer, h. cor. Best and Mich.
Frank, Michael, blacksmith, h. 110 Tupper.
Frank. Peter, with Jewett & Root, h. Cherry n. Virginia.
Frank, Peter. marble cutter, h. Best n. Mich.
Frank. Peter, carp. h. Watson n. William.
Frank, Sam. embroiderer, h. over 119 Genesee.
Frank. Theodore, gardener, h. N. Washington n. Auburn.
Frank. Valentine, shoemaker, h. Sherman n. Batavia.
Frank, Valentine, huckster, b Best n. Mich.
Frankenburgher, Frank, blacksmith, h. Batavia n. Hickory.
Frankenstein, Fred. upholsterer, h. over 96 E. Genesee.
Frankenstein, John, lab. h. 500 Michigan.
Franklin, Ann, widow, h. 293 Swan.
Franklin, Benj. D. tinsmith. h. 3 Folsom.
Franklin, Dan'th, millwright, h. Main n. Utica.
Franklin, Edmond, sail maker, h. 293 Swan.
Franklin, James, milk dairy, h. Walden n. Bat.
Franklin, Jane, washer, h. cor. Coon and Blossom alley.
FRANKLIN & RAND, sailmakers, Marine block.—See adv. p. 47.
Frantz, Jos. carp. h. Mortimer n. Genesee.
Franz, Casper, shoemaker, 277 Main, h. Hickory n. Sycamore.
Franz, Maria, widow, b. 119 Pratt.
Fraser, David, firm D. F. & Bro. h. Michigan n. High.
Fraser, D. & Bro. horse collar manufacturers, 28 Terrace.
Fraser, Donald, marble cutter, h. 25 7th.
Fraser, Simon, dealer in boots and shoes, 340 Main.

Fraser, Wm. machinist, b. over 1 Niagara.
Fraser, Wm. T. sailor, h. Fulton n. Alabama.
Fraser, Margaret, Mrs. h over 1 Niagara.
Fraser, John, firm D. F. & Bro. b. Globe Hotel.
Frask, A. iron finisher, with Brayley & Pitts.
Frauenknecht, A. lab. h. Pratt n. Clinton.
Frauenknecht, Joseph. lab. h. 59 Cedar.
Fraunreiter, Anton, shoemaker, h. Walnut n. William.
Frawley, Daniel, lab. h. Church n. Terrace.
Frawley, Jas. lab. h. cor. Scott and Illinois.
Frawley, Mary, M. widow, h. Georgia n. 4th.
Frawley, Wm. lab. h. cor. Virginia and 4th.
Frazee, H. U. Lake and Canal store, 29 Cent. Wharf, b. Western.
Frecker, Peter, switchman, C. R. R. h. Hickory n. Batavia.
Fred, Michael, teamster, h. Hospital n. Niag.
Fredenburgh, Julius, clothier, 124 Main, h. 9 Main.
Frederich, Chas. mason, h. Cherry n. Spruce.
Frederick, Jno. tailor, h. 102 Hickory.
Frederick, John, paver, h. Mortimer cor. Hollister.
Frederick, Jno. carp. b. 2 Peacock.
Frederickson, Geo. sailor. h. 100 9th.
Freedlawd, D. b. capt. F. Wolf.
Freehold, Conrad, brickmaker, h. Jefferson n. Clinton.
Freeman, Adam, firm Smith & F. h. Dearborn n. Parish.
Freeman, Augustus, carp. h. 37 Cherry.
Freeman, Lewis, h. 98 6th.
Freeman, Margaret, wid. h. Parish n. East.
Freeman, Martin, carp. h. 37 Cherry.
Freeman, Oscar, drover, h. over cor. Ellicott and Huron.
Free Masons' Hall, cor. Court and Main.
Freer, Elizabeth, wid. teacher, h. 20 10th.
Frehrs. Frank, cabinet maker, h. Jeff. n. Wm.
Frei. Anthony, stone mason, h. Johnson n. Batavia.
Frei, Anthony, Jr. cigar maker, h. Johnson n. Batavia.
Frei, John, paver, h. Spring n. Sycamore.
Freiberger, Fred. lab. h. Exch. n. Heacock.
Freidel, Thomas, watchman, h. Thompson n. Hamilton.
Freidle, Jacob. baker, h. 44 Michigan.
Freidenburgh, Philetus, miller, h. Niagara n. Hamilton.
Freidman, A. h. Main n. Buffalo Plains.
Freidman, C. B. night watch, h. 6 6th.
Freidman, Xavier, butcher, h. Mich. n. Best.
Freier. Fred. cooper, h. Spring cor. William.
Freiert, Fred. C. cigar maker, h. 95 E. Seneca.
Freimiller, Susanna, wid. h. Wm. n. Bennett.
Freind, Adam, lab. h. Sycamore n. Walnut.
Freischlag. Fred. butcher, Hickory.
Freitag, John, millstone maker, h. Michigan n. Carlton.
French, E. F. firm F. & Co. h. 99 Swan.
French, F. C. blacksmith, h. R. I. n. 14th.
French, Harlow, blacksmith, 374 Washington, h. 41 Clinton.
French, H. J. teacher No. 33, b. 112 S. Div.
French, Henry, soap maker, h. 15 Hudson.
French, Jno. S. clerk, h. 168 S. Division.

French, J. H. prin. school No. 15, h. over .cor. Ellicott and Huron.
French & Husted, flour and feed. 204 Wash.
French, T. B. blacksmith, h. 41 Clinton.
French, William L. teacher No. 19, b. Mrs. Ludlow.
French, Wm. W. firm F. & Husted, b. 14 Oak.
Frenz, Henry, lab. h. Clinton n. Emslie.
Fresh, Elizabeth, basement, 95 Seneca.
Freshom, Geo. W. capt. on lake, h. Palmer n. Maryland.
Freund, Andrew, shoemaker, h. Bat. n. Jeff.
Frey, Anthony, shoemaker, h. 139 Walnut.
Frey, Barbara, wid. h. Genesee E. Herman.
Frey, Christ. carp. h. Peckham cor. Shumway.
Frey, Geo. shoemaker, b. cor. Water & Maiden lane.
Frey, John, shoemaker, h. L. Buehl.
Frey, John, saloon, h. Main n. Ferry.
Frey, Thomas, butcher. b. cor. Elm and Clinton.
Freytag, Ferdinand, basket maker, b 113 Gen.
Freytag, Michael, lab. h. over 342 Genesee.
Freytag, Wm. Com'l Adv'r, b. ov. 342 Genesee.
Frick, Fred. carp. h. Pratt n. Sycamore.
Frick, Mart. lab. h. Maple bel. Virginia.
Friday, Geo. horse dealer, Kaene n. Genesee.
Fridey, John, stone cutter, h. Mich. n. High.
Friebis, Peter, saloon, cor. Batavia and Oak.
Friedenberger, Catharine, seamstress, b. Sycamore n. Ash.
Friedenberger, Francisca, seamstress, b. Sycamore n. Ash.
Friedenberger, John, h. Sycamore n. Ash.
Friedenberger, Rosina, widow, seamstress, h. Sycamore n. Ash.
Friederich, Henry.* brewer, Spruce n. Cherry.
Friederich, Valentine, carp. h. Jeff. n. William.
Friederichs, John, shoemaker, h. 401 Michigan.
Friedman, John,* cooper, h. Amherst n. East.
Friedmann, Joseph. painter, h. 6 Union.
Friedrich, John. shoemaker, h. Spruce n. Bat.
Friedrich, Fred. h. Michigan n. High.
Friedrich, Fred. mason, h. Stanton n. Batavia.
Friedsch, Henry, lab. h. Grape n. High.
Frienkstine, John, lab. h. Michigan n. Goodell.
Fries, Charles, peddler, h. Grey n. Genesee.
Fries, Elizabeth, wid. h. Monroe n. Batavia.
Fries, Henry, lab. h. Oak cor. Virginia.
Fries, Jacob, shoemaker, h. 12 Sycamore.
Fries, John, bricklayer, h. 279 Oak.
Fries, John, with John Felton, b. 200 Elm.
Fries, John, lab. h. 240 Elm.
Fries, Joseph, lab. h. Weaver alley n. Va.
Fries, Marx, lab. h. Ash n. Batavia.
Fries, Mrs. h. 200 Elm.
Frieschlag, Fred. cooper, b. Clinton n. Jeff'n.
Frieschlag, Jacob & Bro.* coopers, Clinton n. Jefferson.
Frieze, Jos lab h. Clinton ave. n. N. Wash.
Frieze, Jos. Jr. in iron works, b. Jos. Frieze.
Frink, H. A. & Co. stave and lumber dealers, 2½ C. Wharf, h. 131 Niagara.
Frink, Lyman, joiner, h. 153 Eagle.
Frisch, Anton, lab. h. Fox n. North.
Fritaze, John, shoemaker, h. Clinton n. Spring.
Fritcher. August, painter, h. 12 Bennett.
Fritz, Geo. tailor, h. 120 Walnut n. William.
Fritz, Louis, painter, h. Fox n. Genesee.

Fritz, Martin, lab. h. Fox n. Genesee.
Fritzenschaf, August, lab. h. Walnut n. Clinton.
Frolich, John, prop. Maiden Lane House.
From, Jacob, shoemaker, h. 34 Chippewa.
Fromm, Louis, upholsterer, h. Potter n. Gay.
Frommel, Ed. piano maker. b. Clinton n. Spring.
Frommer, Chas. music teacher, b. Clinton n. Spring.
Frommer, Ed. piano maker, b. Clinton n. Spring.
Frommer, Fred. h. Clinton n. Spring.
Frommholz, Sebastian, lab. h. Bat. cor. Bennett.
Frommholz, Peter, barber, 265 Main, up stairs, h. 43 Cherry.
Frost, C. A. Evans' planing mill.
Frost. F. J. beater, N. S. forge, h. cor. Perry and Hayward.
Frost, J. foreman, H. Childs, h. Perry cor. Hayward.
Frost, Mary, wid. boarding, h. Palmer n. Md.
Frost, N. Mrs. widow, boarding, 137 E. Seneca.
Frost. Ransom M. conductor, h. 127 Michigan.
Frowley. Dan. at gas works, h. Church n. Jackson.
Frowley, Jas. lab. h. Perry n. Ohio basin slip.
Frt, Michael, lab. h. 85 Mohawk.
Frueh, H. painter, h. 559 Michigan.
Fruel, Jacob, cooper, h. Parish n. East.
Frutig. Philip, tailor, h. Sycamore n. Jefferson.
Fuch, Fred lab. h. Walnut n. Sycamore. ·
Fuchs, Augustus. firm F. Bro's. h. 137 Ellicott.
FUCHS, BROTHERS, grocers, 390 Main.— See adv. p. 49.
Fuchs, Charles, lab. h. Burton n. Hydraulics.
Fuchs, Conrad, lab. h. Boston alley, bel. Va.
Fuchs, Edward, firm F. Bro's. h. 28 Huron.
Fuchs, Geo. lab. h. Camp n. Genesee.
Fuchs, Geo. lab. h. Genesee n. Walden.
Fuchs, Gustavus, cl'k. 390 Main, h. 137 Ellicott.
Fuchs, Henry, lab. h. Walnut n Sycamore.
Fuchs, John, tailor, h. 100 Hickory.
Fuchs, Joseph, lab. h. Seneca n. Alabama.
Fuchs, Julius, firm F. Bro's. h. 139 Ellicott.
Fuchs, Lenhard, lab. h. Cedar n. Batavia.
Fuchs, Peter, lab. h. Grey n. Genesee.
Fuchs, Ulric, lab. h. Walnut n. William.
Fuell, John, tailor, 352 Main, b. same.
Fues. Conrad, butcher, h. Oak n. Best.
Fug, Andrew, laborer. h. 34 Bennett.
Fuge, Wm. sailor, h. Ohio n. Wabash.
Fuhr, Mary. widow, h. over 51 Delaware place.
Fuhrmann, Philip J. barber, 45 E. Genesee, h. same.
Fuhs, Jacob, lab. h. Walnut n. Batavia.
Full, Michael, mason, h. Fox n. Genesee.
Fullam, John W. M. D. h. Niagara cor. Breckenridge.
Fullem, Edward, joiner, h. Maryland n. Palmer.
Fuller, George, painter, b. Elk n. Alabama.
Fuller, James, R. R. agent, b. Brown's Hotel.
Fuller, Wm. painter, h. Perry n. Hayward.
Fuller, William, in saw mill. b. Niagara n. Forest avenue.
Fullerton, William, tinsmith, h. Ga. below 6th.
Fullington, Eben'r, carp. h. Ferry n. Adams.
Fullington, Geo. engineer, b. E. Fullington.
Funck. John. teamster, h. 370 Genesee.
Funk, Conrad, lab. Best cor. Michigan.

Funk, George, painter. h. Genesee n. Grey.
Funk, Margaretta, widow, h. Mich. n. High.
Funk, Valentine, mason, h. Mich. n. North.
Funk, Valentine, with Jewett & Root.
Funke, Christopher, shoemaker, b. 116 Exch.
Furcht, Chas. carp. h. Cedar n. William.
Furcy, William.* shoemaker, h. 103 Eagle.
Furgeson, Geo. lab. h. 13th n. Conn.
Furgeron, George H. h. Walden N. of Best.
Furgeron, Mary A. widow, h. Walden N. Best.
Furguson, John, sailor, h. Pine n. Batavia.
Furlong, Peter, ship carp. h. Va. cor. 4th.
Furlonge, Joseph, M. D. Dudley Hall, h. 5th above Pennsylvania.
Furness, Ignatius, teamster, h. Niagara n. Hamilton.
Furniss, Amelia R. widow of Jno. h. 93 Ellicott.
Fursman, E. deputy sheriff, h. 131 Clinton.
Furthneller, William, shoemaker, h. Clinton below R. R.
Fussell, Thomas, mariner, h. Perry n. Chicago.

G.

Gabriel, Martin, sailor, b. 4 Water.
Gackla, George, laborer, h. 310 Genesee.
Gackla, John, laborer, b. 310 Genesee.
Guckle, John, paper box maker, 273 Main, h. cor. Genesee and Spruce.
Gaeber, George, laborer, h. 40 Maple.
Gaertner, Mathias, weigher, Washington opposite Market, h. 249 Oak.
Gaertner, Peter, b. 249 Oak.
Gaertner, Valentine, wagon maker, 273 Main, h. cor. Genesee and Spruce.
Gaettelman, John, saloon, 74 Washington.
Gaetz, Chas. clerk, h. 33 E. Huron.
Gaetz, George, firm P. Becker & Co. 384 Main, h. Howard n. Monroe.
Gaetz, Geo. at cor. Canal and Evans, h. same.
Gaetz, John, gardener, h. 9th above Jersey.
Gaetz, Michael, Sr. grocer, Canal cor. Evans, h. 33 E. Huron.
Gaetz, Michael, saloon, cor. Main and Ohio.
Gage, George, grocer, 5 E. Seneca, h. North W. Delaware.
Gage, William, millwright and pattern maker, h. 3 Scott.
Gager, Charles L. capt. h. 205 Pearl.
Gager, John C. book-keeper, S. Shepard & Co. 54 Main, h. 258 Pearl.
Gager, the Misses. h. 258 Pearl.
Gager, S. N. leather dealer, b. 255 Washington.
Guire, John, machinist, h. Walden n. Genesee.
Galagher, John, butcher, h. cor. Porter and Van Rensselaer.
Galagher, John. h. Niagara n. Pennsylvania.
Gallager, Patrick, blacksmith, h. Burwell place n. Scott.
Gallagher, Jas. truckman, h. Fulton n. Ala.
Gallagher, Mort. watchman N. Y. C. R. R. b. Otto n. Hayward.
Gallagher, Patrick, lab. h. Fulton n. Alabama.
Gallagher, Jas. tinsmith, b. capt. W. H. Stark.
Gallagher, Edward, firm Jameson & Co. canal inspector, h. 171 N. Division.
Galavan, Martin, engineer, h. 14 Missouri.
Galbraith, James H. machinist, h. Ala. n. Elk.

Gale, George A. printer. h. 16 E. Eagle.
Gall, Jac. book-keeper. Erie Co. Savings Bank, 244 Main, h. 248 Ellicott.
Gall, Martin, carpenter. h. 248 Ellicott.
Galle, Henry, mason, Heacock n. Seneca.
Galle, John, carp. h. Mulberry n. Goodell.
Galleler, Michael, lab. Sycamore n. Ash.
Gallenbach, Frantz, lab. h. 575 Main.
Galley, Ann, widow, washer, h. 51 Church.
Galley, Thomas, ship carpenter, h. 51 Church.
Galligan, Jas. lab. h. military road n. Amherst.
Galligan, Michael, capt. h. 6th n. Maryland.
Galligan, Richard, teamster, h. Mulberry n. Goodell.
Galligan, William, furniture dealer, 34 and 36 Ellicott, h. 55 Ellicott.
Gallivan, Timothy, lab. b. Ohio opp. frt. depot.
Gallman, Philip, carp. h Spring n. Clinton.
Gallmeier, Barbara, widow, washerwoman, h. Harmon n. Genesee.
Galloway, James, prop. Whittmore's Tavern, Aurora plank road.
Galvin, Martin, engineer, h. 14 Mississippi.
Galvin, Mary, widow, boarding. 50 Ohio.
Gamblee, David, cook, h. Pine n N. Division.
Gamkus, Frederick, lab. h. 120 Pine.
Gamm, Christian, lab. h. Walnut n. Sycamore.
Gammel, Jacob, upholst'r, Chamberlain Bros. b. Cold Spring House.
Gandelhomme, C. F. cabinet maker, h. Gen. n. toll gate.
Gank, Nicholas, lab. h. Hickory n. Clinton.
Ganner, Adam, mason, Walnut n. Clinton.
Ganson, Christina, wid. washer. h. 284 Pearl.
Ganson, Geo. H. ass't. cash. Marine Bank, h. 5 Palmer.
Ganson, John, att'y, 18 Spaulding's Exch. h. 102 Delaware.
Ganson, John S. president N. Y. and Erie Bk. h. Delaware cor. Chippewa.
Ganter, Michael, mason, h. 559 Michigan.
Gantzer, Xavier, machinist, h. 7 Monroe.
Garahan, Patrick, miller, b. cor. Ohio and Mich.
Garbe, Jacob, cooper, h. East n. Hamilton.
Garber, Frank G. tanner, h. 228 E. Eagle.
Garber, Jno. lab. h. cor. Carroll and Van Rens.
Gardie, Anthony, shoemaker, h. Delaware av. n. Williamsville road.
Gardner, A. lab. b. 288 N. Division.
Gardner, capt. R. P., U. S. A. b. Church cor. Franklin.
Gardner, Chas. brakeman, L. S. R. R. b. Nat'nal.
GARDNER, CHAS. Justice of the Peace, 150 Main, h. Church cor. Frank.—*See adr. p. 81.*
Gardner, Chas. F. clerk, b. 12 Church.
Gardner, Ferdinand, shoemaker at 20 S. Div. h. 106 Clinton.
Gardner, Gayer, student. b. 12 Church.
Gardner, Henry, at 39 Seneca, h. Franklin n. Edward.
Gardner, Jas. confectioner. 39 Exch. h. Pearl.
Gardner, James, lab. h. 5th n. Maryland.
Gardner, John M. firm G. Ritt & Fox, h. 135 Pearl.
Gardner, Jno. M. att'y, 153 Main. h. 156 Niag.
Gardner, Matthew, lab. h. 9 Mississippi.
Gardner, Noah H. firm Palmer & G. h. Seneca cor. old city line.

1861.

GARDNER, RITT & FOX,

Insurance Agency

No. 10 Main St., and 5 Central Wharf.

FIRE, MARINE AND CANAL
INSURANCE.

Policies Issued on Cargoes and Hulls of Steam and Sail Vessels, Cargoes and Hulls of Canal Boats, Buildings, Merchandise, and other Insurable Property.

CORN EXCHANGE OF NEW YORK.

Capital and Surplus,..$300,000

WASHINGTON MARINE OF NEW YORK.

Capital and Surplus,..$275,000

NEW ENGLAND OF HARTFORD, CONN.

Capital and Surplus,..$250,000

NORTHERN ASSURANCE OF LONDON, ENG.

Capital and Surplus, ...$2,200,000

ALBANY CITY OF ALBANY, N. Y.

Cash Capital, ...$100,000

Jno. N. Gardner.   M. Leo Ritt.   Watson A. Fox.

GARDNER. RITT & FOX. insurance agents, 5 C.Wharf and 10 Main.— *See adv. opp. name.*
Gardner, Thos. boatman. h. 13th n. Vermont.
Gardner, Willis. at 5 C. Wharf, b. 135 Pearl.
Gardner, Wm. Jr. book-keeper, Pratt & Co. h. 134 Ellicott.
Gardner, Wm. hardware, Terrace, h. 134 Elli't.
Gardner. Wm. at 5 Cent. Wharf, b. 135 Pearl.
Garity, Timothy, finisher, b. Elm n. Sycamore.
Garland, Saml. tailor. J. Fallon. h. 13 Huron.
Garlock. A. D. engineer. h. 205 N. Division.
Garnautt, Philip, gardener, Butler n. Dela.
Garonell. Adam, shoemaker. b. 12 Commercial.
Garono. Henry, clerk, 54 Main, b. 74 Bennett.
Garono. Lorenz, huckster, Clinton market, h. 74 Bennett.
Garratt, Lawrence. at Evans & Co. plan'g mill.
Garret, Jno. whitewasher. h. 176 Oak.
Garrett, C. land agt. office Granite Buildings, Main, up stairs, b. 254 Pearl.
Garrigan, Matthew, grocer, cor. 6th and Pa. h. same.
Garsons, George, sailor, h. Elk cor. Ohio Basin slip.
Garvey, James, lab. b. Otto n. Alabama.
Garvin. H. D. M. D. 1 Hart Block, Erie
Garvin, Joseph, ship carp. b. across creck.
Garvin. Patrick, lab. h. Ohio n. R. R.
Gary. Frank, boiler maker, b. Tennessee bel. Mackinaw.
Gary, Patrick. carp. h. Tenn. n. Mackinaw.
Gascoigne. James, moulder, b. 130 S. Division.
Gaskell, Thomas, sailor, h. 201 Washington.
Gaspar. John, lab. h. r. 4th n. Genesee.
Gass. Adam. engineer, h. Wm. bel. Jefferson.
Gass, Peter, milkman, h Ferry E. of Walden.
Gastel, Anthony, shoemaker, b. 269 Pearl.
Gastel. Geo. shoemaker, h. 269 Pearl.
Gastel. Geo. lab. h. Herman n. Genesee.
Gastel. Jas. grocery. cor. Goodell and Mulberry.
Gaston, C. b. Western.
Gatcviler, Gustavus. engraver, h. ov. 92 Gen.
Gates. Abel, patent lamp maker, b. 16 E. Eagle.
Gates, D. F. clerk, N. Y. C. R. R. b. 77 S. Division.
Gates, George B. sleeping car, h. 77 S. Div.
Gates. Joseph, marble cutter, b. 24 Del. place.
Gates, Louisa. cap maker, h. Rose alley.
Gates, Michael, Jr. b. cor. Gen. and Morgan.
Gates, Mrs. widow, h. 24 Delaware place.
Gates. N. marble cutter, b. 24 Delaware place.
Gattie, Adam, printer, h. 27 Walnut.
Gattie, Jos. h. Seneca n. N. Y. & E. R. R. track.
Gattner, J. H. lab. h. Grey n. Batavia.
Gauch. Jacob, drover. h. Spruce n. Sycamore.
Gauchat, Auguste, saloon, cor. Elm and Syc.
Gauger, William, piano maker, b. 549 Michigan.
Gauger, John, peddler, h. 549 Michigan.
Gavin, John, proprietor Shamrock House, Exchange n. Michigan.
Gavin. Pat. caulker, h. Fulton cor. Ohio Basin.
Gay. Chas. C. F. M. D. Main cor. Mohawk, h. 180 Pearl.
GAYLORD, H. M. steam marble works. Erie cor. Terrace. h. 442 Main.— *See adv. p. 96.*
Gazlay, Dickinson, capt. b. Ferry n. Adams.
Geagan & Sherwood, saloon, 8 Swan.
Geagan, Wm. butcher, h. Wash. cor. High.

Geagan, William. firm G. & Sherwood, h. cor. High and Washington.
Gearns, Pat. lab. h. 73 5th.
Geary. James. firm W. G. & Co. 59 Main, h. Washington n. Perry.
Geary, W. firm W. G. & Co. h. over 59 Main.
Gebhard, Lorenz, h. 538 Michigan.
Gebhard, Nicholas, on lake, h. 521 Washington.
Gebhaner, Casper, blacksmith, h. Niagara n. Amherst.
Geblaur, Chas. machinist, h. 206 Eagle.
Geckler, Godfreid, carp. b. Pratt n. Sycamore.
Gegla, John, lab. h. Genesee n. Spruce.
Gegla. Jno. Jr. box maker, b. J. Gegla, Sr.
Geh. John, shoemaker, h. Steele n. Walden.
Gehbauer, Conrad. joiner, h. Adams n. Bat'a.
Gehee, Andrew, lab. h. Perry n. Elk st. market.
Geher, Geo. blacksmith, h. Watson n. Batavia.
Gehring. Geo. P. Elk street market, h. Walnut n. William.
Gehrung, Fred. carpenter, h. Elm n. Genesee.
Geib, Fred. bricklayer, h. 211 Oak.
Geib, Louis, varnisher, h. 248 Genesee.
Geier, John, grocer, 109 Pine.
Geier, Louis, shoemaker, h. 324 Ellicott.
Geier, Peter. saloon, h. Sycamore cor. Pratt.
Geiershofer, Isaac. firm L. Dahlman & Co. 274 Main, b. Georgia cor. Niagara.
Geirshofer, Abram. firm Loewi & G. 306 Main, h. Niagara n. Maryland.
Geigand, Joseph, lab. h. Locust n. North.
Geiger, Anton. cooper. h. r. Dearb'n n. Amherst.
Geiger, Jacob, mason, h. r. 136 E. Genesee.
Geiger, Fritz, clerk, P. O. b. 178 Ellicott.
Geiger, Michael, lab. h. Steele n. Walden.
Geiger, Regina, Mrs. milliner, 178 Ellicott, b. same.
Geil, Adam, cooper, h. Lewis n. Amherst.
Geimer, Adam. machinist, h. York n. 13th.
Geimer, Christian, lab. h. Best n. Michigan.
Geiner, Catharan, widow, h. Lutheran n. Wm.
Geiner, Wm. Jr. printer, h. Catharan Geiner.
Geis, Valentine G. h. 16 Walnut.
Geise, John. lab. h. Sycamore n. Ash.
Geisen. Andrew, teamster, h. Kaene n. Genesee.
Geisendorfer, Michael, cooper, h. Mulberry n. High.
Geiser, Bernhard, lab. h. 80 Monroe.
Geiser, Christopher, lab. h. William n. Jeff.
Geiser, Frederick, butcher. h. 49 Cedar.
Geiser, John. lab. h. Jefferson cor. William.
Geiser, John, lab. h. 80 Monroe.
Geller, Anton, carpenter, h. Adams n. Syc.
Gellwahler, Sebold, carp. h. Mulb'y n. Goodell.
Gemmel, Mathias, produce dealer, Clinton market, h. cor. Watson and Batavia.
Gemuth, John. tailor. h. Main opp. St. Paul.
Gender, Wm. lab. h. Hickory n. William.
Gener, John, lab. h. 38 Hickory.
Genguagen, Mathias. mason, h. 567 Washingt'n.
Genoar, Aug. ship carp. h. Mathew n. Mortimer.
Genoar, Francis. ship carpenter. b. 2 Canal.
Genoar, Henry, brass finisher, 237 Main, h. 111 Pratt.
Gensler, Adam, joiner, b. 182 Batavia.
Gensler, Casper, mason, h. 16 Maple.
Gensler, Fr. cigar mak'r, h. 16 Maple n. Cherry.
Gensler, John, lab. h. 16 Maple.

Gensler, Samuel, 4 Com'l, h. 100 E. Seneca.
Gentleman. Ed. carpenter, h. Mich. n. Batavia.
Gentsch, Bernard, vinegar maker, b. Batavia n. Walnut.
Gentsch, Gottleib, tailor, h. 140 Genesee.
George, Chas. clerk, b. Waverly House.
George, Chas. clothier, b. Revere House.
George, G. clerk, 54 Main, b 170 6th.
George, Henry, turner, h. Maple ab. Goodell.
George. Lorenz, Jr. shoemaker, b. 171 Batavia.
George, Peter, ash peddler, h. Johnson n. Gen.
George, Peter, blacksmith, h. 165 Clinton.
George, Robert, lab. b. Hamilton n. Dearborn.
George, Wm. R. at Waverly House, cor. Erie and Canal.
Georgen, Peter, tanner, h. Adams n. William.
Georger, Chas. hatter, 388 Main, h. 9 E. Gen.
Georger, Frank, hat and cap store, 382 Main, h. 241 Ellicott.
Georger, F. A. & Co. dry goods, 400 Main.
Georger. F. A. firm F. A. G. & Co. h. Main cor. Utica.
Georger, Ignatz, helper, h. Wash. n. Chippewa.
Georger, Lewis, saddler, junc. Ohio and Elk, h. cor. Hickory and Clinton.
Georgie, Nick. lab. Spring n. William.
GERARD, A. H. printer's furniture maker. Mechanic n. Terrace, h. same.—See adv. p. 70.
Gerard, Angeline, widow, h. Dearborn n. R. R.
Gerard, Mrs. widow, h. 27 Huron.
Gerard, Peter, tailor, h. Ash n. Batavia.
Ce·ber, Chas. printer, b. cor. Elm and Goodell.
Gerber. Chas. brewery, Main n. Va. h. same.
Gerber, Donies, shoemaker, b. Weaver alley cor. Burton alley.
Gerber, F. G. with Howell & Smith, h. 228 E. Eagle.
Gerber, Henry, barber, 2 Water, h. same.
Gerber, Henry, Jr. b. 36 Ash.
Gerber, Henry, gardener, h. 36 Ash.
Gerber, J. at Pratt & Letchworth's.
Gerber, Louis, at White's, b. 36 Ash.
Gerber, Sigmund, butcher, Main cor. Burton alley.
Gerber, Wm. silver plater, 201 Wash. b. 1 Gay.
Gerber, Wm. b. 36 Ash.
Gerbrach, Conrad, butcher, h. r. 150 E. Gen.
Gerg. Peter. lab. h. Clinton n. Hickory.
Gergen, Nicholas, at Prince & Co's, h. Mulberry n. High.
Gerhard, August, stone cutter, h. Boston alley n. Goodell.
Gerhard, Geo. shoemaker, b. Court cor. 6th.
Gerhard, Jacob, tanner, h. 543 Michigan.
Gerhard, John, lab. h. Goodell bet. Oak and Elm.
Gerhard, Joseph, brewer, h. Boston alley n. Goodell.
Gerhard, Theobald, teamster, h. 390 E. Genesee.
Gerhardt, Fr. lab. h. 81 Spruce.
Gerhardt, John P. grocer, h. cor. Elk and Ala.
Gerhrurg, F. wood worker, Brayley & Pitts.
Gerig, Geo. P. lab. h. Sycamore n. Jefferson.
Gerlach, Christ'n, builder, h. Pratt n. Genesee.
Gerlach, Fred. cabinet maker, firm Sturm & G. 132 E. Genesee, h. 141 Oak.
Gerlach, Henry, lab. h. Watson n. Peckham.
Gerlach, Jacob,* painter, h. 233 Genesee.

Gerlach, Jacob H. lab. h. 20 Walnut n. Bat.
Gerlach, Mary, millinery, 233 Genesee. b. same.
Gerlach, Phil. cigar maker, h. Johnson n. Bat.
Gerlach, Wm. cabinet maker, 132 E. Genesee, h. 162 Elm.
Germain, C. C. carp. h. Genesee cor. Walden.
Germain, Elizabeth, widow of Louis, washerwoman, b. 445 Pine.
Germain, Geo. P. clerk, with Hamlin & Mendsen, b. 232 Ellicott.
Germain, James, carpenter, b. Maple n. High.
Germain, Reuben J. Rev. h. Dearborn n. Amherst.
Germain, Rollin, att'y, 7 Court, h. 136 E. Eagle.
German, John C. tailor, h. 232 Ellicott.
German, Michael, boatman, h. 76 Carroll.
Germann, John, tailor, b. Kaene n. Genesee.
Germann, Peter, carp. h. Kaene n. Sycamore.
German, Phil. grocer, Batavia cor. Bennett, h. same.
Gerner, Andrew, lab. b. Walnut n. William.
Gerold, B. Mrs. h. over 12 Sycamore.
Gerold, Charles, carpenter, h. 398 Michigan.
Garre, John. iron finisher, Brayley & Pitts.
Gerretson, John, moulder, h. 14 Bennett.
Gerring, Chas. b. Walnut n. William.
Gerring, Geo. J. butter and egg dealer, 32 Elk st. market, h. 316 Seneca.
Gerspack, Joseph, lab. h. Jefferson n. Carlton.
Gerst, Jacob, grocer. h. Niagara n. Amherst.
Gerst, Louis, lab. h. Spring n. Sycamore.
Gerstner, M. A. harness maker, b. 39 Oak.
Gertes, Albert, at gas factory, h. 11 Sycamore.
Gertner, John, lab. h. Sherman n. Genesee.
Gertner. Ferdinand, bootmaker, h. 106 Clinton.
Gerttalcer, Jacob, furniture finisher, 307 Main, h. Adams n. Batavia.
Gesber, H. carpet weaver, Main n. Eley road.
Gese, Julius, ext. of coffee manuf. h. 68 Wm.
Gese, J. G. ext. of coffee manuf. h. 68 Wm.
Gese. Louis, M. D. h. 421 Michigan.
Gesellgen, John. joiner, h. Madison n. Batavia.
Gesellgen, Melchior, joiner, h. Batavia n. Jeff.
Gesse, Chas. brewer, h. St. Paul n. Ellicott.
Gessel, John, teamster, h. Forest av. E. Walden.
Gessel, Joseph, lab. h. Forest av. E. Walden.
Gessel, Simon, lab. h. Walden n. Steele.
Gestel, Margaret, widow, h. Goodell n. Mulberry.
Gester, Anna M. Mrs. h. 40 Sycamore.
Gestermeyer, Geo. cooper, h. Sycamore n. Ash.
Gethoefer, Geo. bookbinder, h. 59 William.
Gethoeffer, Wm. printer, h. 3 Milnor.
Getrost, John,* watch maker, 501 Michigan, h. same.
Gettelmenn, Chas. shoemaker, h. Sherman n. North.
Getz, J. lab. h. 108 Goodell.
Getzinger, Geo. at 6 and 8 Hanover, h. 5 Scott.
Getzmyer, Jos. lab. h. 7th cor. Hudson.
Geyer, Adam, Sr. lab. h. Camp n. Sycamore.
Geyer, Chris. prop Geyer's hotel. 6 Comm'l.
Geyer, C. H. M. cigar maker, b. 342 Main.
Geyer, C. W. E. cigar maker, b. 342 Main.
Geyer, F. W. M. cigar maker, b. 342 Main.
Geyer, F. C. W.* cigar maker, 342 Main, h. same.
Geyer, Geo. milk dairy, Gen. n. Wm'sville R.

Geyer, Gustaf, h. Shumway n. Lovejoy.
Geyer, Henry, grocer, Burton al. cor. Ellicott.
Geyer, Henry. lab. h. Sycamore n. Pratt.
Geyer, J. shoemaker, h. 148 Clinton.
Geyer. Wm. lab. h. Spring n. Clinton.
Ghantium, Theo. glass stainer, h. Milnor n. Bat.
Gibbins, John J. druggist, 129 Main, b. Mrs. Otis Allen.
Gibbons, Chas. sailor, h. Perry n. Ohio basin slip.
Gibbons, Chas. firm G. & Hager, h. 9th n. R. I.
Gibbons, Chas. W. Star brewery, St. Paul n. Main, h. same.
GIBBONS & HAGER, ginger wine, syrups, &c. 57 Exchange.—See adv. p. 50.
Gibbons, Michael, lab. h. 6th n. Virginia.
Gibbs, James S. att'y, 164 Main, h. 260 Franklin.
Gibbs, Hevin, boot and shoemaker, h. Watson n. Peckham.
Gibhard, Lorenz, saloon, opp. Elk St. Market.
Giblawr, Ferdinand, machinist, Eagle n. Cedar.
Gibson, Bro's. forwarders, 28 Central Wharf.
Gibson, Caroline. widow, h 73 N. Division.
Gibson, Chas. H. book-keeper, 6 Cent. Wharf, h. 73 N. Division.
Gibson, Elijah B. sailor, h. Fulton n. Hamb.
Gibson, Ellen, widow, nurse, h. 6N William.
Gibson, Geo. carpenter, h. 136 Elk.
Gibson, Hugh. lab. h. Mississippi n. Elk.
Gibson, Isa. Miss, dressmaker, b. 63 Chippewa.
Gibson, John A. clerk, A. Gibson, 2 Scott, b. Mary Gibson.
Gibson, John, shoemaker, h. Perry n. La
Gibson, John G. book-keeper with C. W. Evans, b. 220 Pearl.
Gibson, Jno. lab. h. Iron place n. N. Wash.
Gibson, Mary, widow, h. 10th n. Virginia.
Gibson, Robert, cooper, h. Evans.
Gibson, Robert, mariner, h. 175 Seneca.
Gibson, William L. ford. and com. merch. 28 Central Wharf, h. 220 Pearl.
Giddings, A. H. b. 11th n. Hampshire.
Giebler. Augustus, clerk, h. over 113 Genesee.
Giehs, John, lab. h. 202 Sycamore.
Giekele, Christian, butcher, Mulb. n. Carlton.
Gierner, Michael, lab. h. Adams n. Sycamore.
Gies, Adam, weaver, h. 351 Michigan.
Gies, Casper, peddler. h. 351 Michigan.
Gies, Elizabeth, seamstress, b. Bat. cor. Pratt.
Gies, John, lab. h. Batavia cor. Pratt.
Giesen, Reinhart, lab. h. Grey n. Genesee.
Giesendorfer, Michael, carriage trimmer, h. 78 W. Tupper.
Giesler, Gabriel, cutter, 65 Gen. h. 63 Gen.
Giesz, Ignatz. grocer, h. Sycamore cor. Jeff.
Giesz, F. M. carpenter, b. 429 Michigan.
Giesz, Mary Ann, widow, h. 429 Michigan.
Giffing, Isaac H. dentist, 203 Main, b. same.
Giffing. W. H. canal captain, h. n. Virginia.
Gifford, E. lab. h. lake shore road n. toll bridge.
Gifford, E H. wood worker, Brayley & Pitts.
Gifford, Frank, conductor L. S. R. R. b. Amrc'n.
Gifford, T. S. Mrs. widow, b. 29 Swan.
Gilbert, A. D. grocer, h. 100 Chippewa.
Gilbert, Chas. peddler, h. Wm. n. Mortimer.
Gilbert, Chas. sailor, h. Carolina n. 5th.
Gilbert, Edwin, firm Blackmar & G. h. 72 S. Division.

Gilbert, David, joiner, h. Park n. Virginia.
Gilbert, Eliphalet, engineer, h. ac. creek, opp. Reed's Dock.
Gilbert, H. Roy, book-keeper, Frontier Mills, h. Ferry n. Adams.
Gilbert, J. E. teacher No. 3, b. David Gilbert.
Gilbert, Jno. M soap and candle factory, h. Delaware n. Barker.
Gilbert, Samuel, carp. h. College n. Allen.
Gilbert, Sarah J. wid. dress maker, h. 471 Mich.
Gilboy, Wm. lab. h. Forest ave. n. N. Wash.
Gilchrist, Jno. mariner, h. Elk opp. Moore.
Gill, David, puddler, Buff. Iron and Nail Works, h. Dewitt n. Bird avenue.
Gill, Michael, engineer, h. 28 Chicago.
Gill, Pat. grocer, Ohio n. Michigan, h. same.
Gillan, Paul, clerk. 6 Terrace.
Gillard. Edward, ship smith, h. 375 Michigan.
Gillespie, Albert A. book-keeper, E. H. Clark, b. 134 S. Division.
Gillespie, Geo. W. clerk on propeller, h. 134 S. Division.
Gillespie, Jas. book-keeper, Pratt & Co. b. 65 E. Eagle.
Gillespie, W. C. engineer. b. 134 S. Division.
Gillet, Albert A. book-keeper, b. 114 E. Eagle.
Gillet, Augustus N. lieut. b. 63 Seneca.
Gillet, E. J. gristmill, Michigan at canal, b. 63 S. Division.
GILLETT, HENRY T. distiller, 18, 20 and 22 Lloyd, h. 114 E. Eagle.—See adv. p. 48.
Gillett, W. H. at 1N Lloyd, b. 114 E. Eagle.
Gillig, Frank L. prop. Cold Spring Hot. h. same.
Gillig, Lorenz, asses'r, h. 159 and 161 Genesee.
Gillig's Hall, 159 and 161 E. Genesee.
Gilligan, Daniel. lab. h. 9 Mississippi.
Gillman, Alfred W. saloon, Washington, h. 174 Delaware.
Gilman, Albert, boat builder, h. 101 Seneca.
Gilman, Alfred, prop. Union House, 197 Wash.
Gilman, Henry J. clerk, h. 21 E. Tupper.
Gilman, John, boat builder, b. 103 E. Seneca.
Gilmartin, Catherine, wid. h. North n. Hampshire.
Gillmore, Hubert, clerk, h. 151 N. Division.
Gilpin, Joseph, printer, with Sage & Sons, b. 5th n. Hudson.
Ginier. F. W. lab. h. Clinton cor. Pratt.
Ginn, Michael, ship carp. h. Hayward n. Fulton.
Ginther, Jacob, foundry, Washington cor. Chippewa, h. Cedar n. Batavia.
Girard, A. joiner, h. 13 Mechanic.
Girard, Joseph, ship caulker, 85 Carroll.
Gisel, John, pump maker, h. Genesee n. Jeff.
Gitener, John, lab. h. Sherman n. Genesee.
Gittere, Jacob A. with S. V. R. Watson, b. 406 Michigan.
Gittere, Jacob H. 406 Michigan.
Gittere. Joseph, turner, h. 12 Sycamore.
Gittere, Joseph, blacksmith, b. 406 Michigan.
Gittere, Nicholas, mason, h. cor. Cedar & Bat.
Gittere, Peter, stereotyper. h. 44 Cedar.
Given, James, wood worker, Brayley & Pitts.
Given, James, h. Auburn ave. n. N. Wash.
Glantz, Ered. gunsmith, 16 E. Gen. h. same.
Glantz, Henry, chair maker, with S. D. Sikes, h. Hickory n. Clinton.
Glas, Nicholas, lab. h. Krettner cor. Lovejoy.

Glasey, Sam. tailor, h. Hickory n. Clinton.
Glass, Adam, gardener, h. Elm n. Carlton.
Glass, Jacob, lab. h. Sycamore n. Spruce.
Glass, John, lab. h. over 183 Pratt.
Glass, Wm. lab. h. Steuben n. Alabama.
Glasser, Jacob, baker, b. Ellicott n. Chippewa.
Glasser, John, baker, Sherman n. Genesee.
Glasser, John, farmer and blacksmith, cor. Delaware and Burton.
Glassert, John, blacksmith, h. Pratt n. Gen.
Glassford, T. h. 91 Clinton.
Glassman, Charles, h. Pratt n. Sycamore.
Glauber, John B. lab. h. Mulberry n. High.
Glaze, Elizabeth C. dressmaker, h. r. 171 Elm.
Gleason, A. Will. student at law, b. 43 Oak.
Gleason, Burns, Com'l Adv'r office, b. cor. Niag. and Virginia.
Gleason, Hugh, peddler, h. 12th n. R. I.
Gleason, James, shoemaker, h. 9 Terrace.
Gleason, Jas. lab. h. Exch. n. R. R. crossing.
Gleason, John, engineer, h. 98 N. Division.
Gleason, John, lab. h. 69 Main.
Gleason, John, lab. h. Exch. n. Griffin.
Gleason, Lorenzo, carp. h. 13th n. Connecticut.
Gleason, Phil. W. cl'k, 120 Main, h. 221 Carroll.
Gleason, S. h. Virginia cor. Niagara.
Gleason, Tim. lab. h. Exch. n N. Y. & E. R R.
Gleeson, Ed. teamster, h. alley bet. Niagara and 7th.
Gleeson, John, lab. h. Carroll n. Jefferson.
Gleis, Elizabeth, widow, b. Hickory cor. Bat.
Glen, Owen, truckman, h. 37 Blossom.
Glen, Wm. rope maker, h. Forest ave. n. N. Washington.
Glendingin, H. fireman, b. 324 S. Division.
GLENNY, WM. H. crockery, 162 Main, h. 464 Main.—See adv. p. 83.
Gleser, John, mason, h. Cedar n. William.
Glesner, Martin, at White & Wardwell's, h. Hickory n. William.
Glinbeck, Jn. marble polisher, h. 78 W. Tupper.
Glitz, Eursula, wid. h. Niagara n. Amherst.
Glock, Geo. carp. h. Lemon n. High.
Glogan, F. lab. h. 44 Cherry.
Glore, Geo. Jr. cooper, b. Peter Glore.
Glore, Peter, cooper, b. East n. Parish.
Gmile, Barney, upholsterer, h. Bat. n. Monroe.
Gnaun, Adam, brewer, b. Batavia cor. Cedar.
Gnann, Mathias, saloon, 22 Main, h. same.
Godfrey, Lucius, with A. J. Rich.
Godwin, C. E. b. 227 7th.
Godwin, D. C. carriage-maker, 15 E. Eagle, h. 293 Washington.
Goehrig, Jacob, lab. h. Spring n. Sycamore.
Goehrig, John, lab. h. Spring n. Sycamore.
Goehrig, John J. lab. h. Spring n. Sycamore.
Goehring, Geo. lab. h. Adams n. Batavia.
Goehrung, Christoph, tailor, h. Hickory n. Gen.
Goeller, Andrew, carpenter, Grey n. Batavia.
Goembel, Paul, butcher, 63 W. Chippewa, h. Batavia cor. Spruce.
Goender, Gottfrey, lab. h. German alley n. Gen.
Goerner, August, tailor, h. Goodell alley n. Tupper.
Goesel, John, stone deal'r, h. Forest av. n. Main.
Goettellman, Philip, saloon, 2 Commercial.
Goettley, Jacob, cabinet maker, h. Elm ab. Genesee.

Goetz, Chas. butcher, h. Michigan n. North.
Goetz, John, mason, h. Michigan n. Carlton.
Goetz, John, tailor, h. Adams n. Batavia.
Goetz, Joseph, grocer, Gen. cor. Spruce, h. same.
Goetz, Rosina, widow, h. Roos alley n. Wm.
Goewe, Dean D. saloon, 31 Exchange. h. same.
Goff, A. machinist, h. 262 S. Division.
Goff, James, lab. h. across creek.
Goffe, Joseph, mason. Clinton n. Smith.
Goffe, Wm. mason, h. Clinton n. Smith.
Gogel, Michael, barber shop. Niagara n. Mohawk, h. cor. Niagara and Maryland.
Goitan, John L. book-keeper, h. Washington n. Carlton.
Gold, Anthony, shoemaker. h. 410 S. Division.
Gold, C. R. Mrs. widow, h. 446 Main.
Gold, Henry, tailor, h. Carlton n. Elm.
Gold, John, distiller. h. Elm ab. Genesee.
Gold, John. shoemaker. b. Walnut n. Sycamore.
Goldbeck, — peddler, h Goodell n. Elm.
Goldberg, J. S. M. D. h. 79 Ellicott.
Goldberger, Isaac S. M. D. 239 Ellicott. h. same.
Golden, Ira, ship carp. h. 13 Mechanic n. Terrace.
Golden, Martin, lab. h. Niagara n. Breckenridge.
Goldey, John, h. 266 S. Division.
Golding, D. S. with Howard, Whitcomb & Co. h. 105 S. Division.
Goldman, D. h. 21 William.
Goldschmit, Joseph, lab. h. Johnson n. Bat.
Goldschmit, L. cigar manuf. b. 13 Carroll.
Goldstein, Xavier, lab. h. Spring n. Genesee.
Goldstone, Jno. helper, h. Spring n. Genesee.
Goldthorp, Jemima, Miss, b. Batavia n. Walnut.
Goliat, Peter, mason, h. 405 Michigan.
Goll, George, cabinet maker, h. Monroe n. Clinton.
Gollan, John, blacksmith, h. 7 9th.
Gollner, John, lab. h. Hollister n. Spring.
Gollop, James, fisherman, h. 29 Spring.
Gollwitzer, Christoph, lab. h. Spring n. Syc.
Gollwitzer, Geo. lab. h. cor. Milnor and Wm.
Gollwitzer, Michael, grocer, h. cor. Michigan and Sycamore.
Gologly, Eugene, sailor, h. Chicago cor. Fulton.
Gonyo, Louis, caulker, h. Carroll n. Louisiana.
GOOD, ADAM, brass and bell foundry, 21 Ohio. b. Oak n. Carlton.—See adv. p. 57.
Good, Adam, Jr. clerk, Good's bell foundry, h. Oak between High and Carlton.
Good, George C. engineer, h. 43 Del. place.
Good, J. A. grocer, h. 277 Genesee, h. same.
Good, Jacob, clerk, with J. A. Good, 277 Gen. cor. German alley.
Good, John, machinist, b. 21 Ohio.
Good. Philip, shoemaker, b. 171 Batavia.
Goodbread, Jacob, shoemaker, h. Seneca bel. rail road track.
Goodell, Maria B. b. 7th n. R. I.
Goodenough, Wm. fireman, h. 46 6th.
Goodfellow, John, brakeman, h. 195 N. Div.
Gooding, Rodney, h. 76 Ellicott.
Goodman, Stephen F. machinist, b. 153 9th.
Goodrich, James A. moulder, h. 280 Swan.
Goodrich, E. H. watchmaker and jeweler, 183 Washington, h. cor. 7th and Carolina.

Goodrich. Edson H. clerk, 183 Washington, b. cor. 7th and Carolina.

Goodrich, Guy H. land agent, 2 Weed's Building. h. Franklin n. Allen.

Goodrich, William J. carpenter, h. Carroll cor. Red Jacket.

Goodwin, Frank, Main St. R. R h. Main n. Ferry.

Coodwin, John, shoemaker, h. r. 72 Tupper.

Goodwin, Manvielett, brick-maker, h. Ferry opposite race course n. Jefferson.

Goodwin. Patrick, saloon, h. cor. Scott and Elk street market.

Goodwin. Patrick, grocer. Elk opposite Moore.

Gooley, Stephen B. steward. 11th n. Mass.

Goosman, James. lab. h. Amherst n. City line.

Gootwasser, Philip, carpenter, h. Hickory n. Genesee.

Gorbet, Adam, carp. h. cor. La. and Seneca.

Gorder, Edward, lab. h. towpath, bel. Genesee.

Gordon, Anna, widow, h. 13 Elm.

Gordon. George, warehouseman, 13 Central Wharf, h. Elm n. High.

Gordon, Henry, shirt and collar manufacturer, over Hamlin & Mendson, b. 14 Oak.

Gordon, Joseph, caulker, h. Folsom n. Jeff'n.

Gordon, Patrick, brickmaker, h. Exchange below Van Rensselaer.

Gore, Ralph, brick maker, h. Ellicott, below Tupper.

Gore, P. wood worker, Brayley & Pitts.

Gorge. Louis, saddler, h. Hickory n. Clinton.

Gorges, John. mason, h. Pratt n. Genesee.

Gorley. Charles, sailor. h. Evans.

Gorman, Dennis, lab. h. Lock n. Terrace.

Gorman, Jas. ship carp. b. Tenn. n. Mack'w.

Gorman, Jno. lab. b. Marvin n. Elk.

Gorman, Matthew, lab. h. Michigan cor. Elk.

Gorman, Michael, lab. h. La. n. Ohio.

Gorman, Michael, lab. h. Bird av. n. DeWitt.

Gorman, Patrick, lab. h. Barton cor. Arkansas.

Gorman, Patrick. b. John Gorman.

Gorman, Robt. bricklayer, h. Carolina n. Efner.

Gorom, Nelson, ship carpenter, h. Adams n. Clinton.

Gorren, Nancy, widow, h. 139 N. Division.

Gorris, Frank, machinist, 14 Court, h. 27 Pine.

Gorris, James, machinist, h. 97 6th.

Gorris, Hubbard, shoemaker, b. Mich. n. Wm.

Gors. Sebastian, lab. h. Monroe n. Sycamore.

Goscho, August, lab. h. Bennett n. William.

Gorton, H. W. firm G. & Matteson, 208 Main.

Gorton, Job, city assessor, h. Dearborn n. Amherst.

Gorton & Matteson, shirt and collar manufacturers, 208 Main.

Goscho, August, lab. h. Bennett n. William.

Goslin, Alexander, keeper at Erie County Penitentiary, b. H. S. Cunningham.

Goss, Adam, lab. h. William n. Jefferson.

Gosset, William L. whitewasher, h. over 24 Walnut.

Gotthelf, Mat. drover. h. Batavia n. Monroe.

Gotthelf, Moses, drover, b. Munroe n. Batavia.

Gottman, Henry, grocer, h. Gen. n. Mortimer.

Gottschalk, Henry, tailor, h. Pratt n. William.

Gottschalk, William, lab. h. Maple n. Cherry.

Gottschall, Peter, lab. h. end St. Paul.

Gottstein, Dominic, tailor, 573 Main, h. same.

Gotzemer. John, lab. h. 292 Elm.

Goudnoudh, Edward, lab. h. 41 Jackson.

Goul, Conrad, tanner, h. Steuben n. Heacock.

Goul, Mary, widow, b. Cedar n. William.

Gould, E. O. salesman, with E. Corning & Co. b. Washington cor. S. Division.

Gould, E. S. steward, Bonney's Hotel, b. 26 W Genesee.

Gould, Frank, b. Southern Hotel.

Gould, James, sail maker. b. 5th n. Georgia.

Gould, L. D. builder. 36 Carroll, h. 25 Carroll.

Gould. Michael, lab. h. cor. Spring and Swan.

Gould, Phares, produce merchant 8 Central Wharf. h. Washington cor. S. Division.

Gould, Sylvanus O. attorney, 19 Arcade Buildings, h. 41 Court.

Gould, Thomas T. with U. S. Express, h. Eagle below Spring.

Gould, William. M. D. 125 Pearl, h. same.

Goulden, Christopher, gardener, h. 14th n. Ct.

Goulden, Martin, lab. h. 12th n. R. I.

Gowans, Andrew, with Gowans & Beard, b. Chicago n. Perry.

Gowans & Beard, soap and candle factory, Chicago cor. Perry.

Gowans, James S. N. Y. S. V. M. 21st Reg't, b. 5 Johnson place.

Gowans. John, book-keeper, with G. & Beard. h. 17 Johnson place.

Gowans, Peter, firm G. & Beard, h. 5 Johnson place.

Gowans, William, with Gowans & Beard, b. 5 Johnson place.

Gowey, Wm. clerk, with C. G. Irish, jr. b. Red Jacket saloon.

Grabbit, Jno. teamster, h. 9 Roos alley.

Grabau, J. A. A. pastor, h. cor. Goodell and Maple.

Graber, Andrew, clerk, 316 Main, b. Genesee House.

Graber, Geo. carp. h. Kaene n. Sycamore.

Grabenstatter, Frank, gardener, h. Best n. Mich.

Grabenstatter, Frank. Jr. barber, 31 E. Seneca, b. Best n. Michigan.

Grabenstatter, John, barber, 31 E. Seneca, b. Best n. Michigan.

Grace, Thomas, fireman, b. National.

Grace, Wm. H. engineer, h. 276 N Division.

Graeber, Peter, machinist, h. Batavia h. Hick.

Graeber, Jno. lab. h. Spruce n. Sycamore.

Graebner, Geo. butcher, High n. Michigan, h. same.

Graef, Geo. carp. h. 158 Genesee.

Graefe, Chas. cigar maker, h. 11 Cypress.

Graefer, Catherine, widow, h. Kaene n. Syca.

Graefer, Wm. carp. h. Kaene n. Sycamore.

Graefesmuehl, Fred. cab. maker, h. 42 Maple.

Graefin, Peter Jas. lab. h. Sherman n. Genesee.

Graess, C. G. shoemaker, h. 35 William.

Graesser, Chas. C. tailor, h. Potter n. William.

Graf, Andrew, bl'ksmith, h. Watson n. Peck'm.

Graf, G. grocer, Batavia n. Hickory, h. same.

Graf. Herman, lab. h. Camp. n. Sycamore.

Graf, Jacob, moulder, h. Syca. n. Jefferson.

Graf, John, lab. h. 268 Elm.

Graf, John G.* wagoner, Genesee cor. Michigan, h. 158 Genesee.

Graf. Louise, Mrs. h. 526 Michigan.
Graf, Philip, grocer, Oak cor. Tupper, h. same.
Graf. Wenzel, lab. h. Krettner n. Batavia.
Graff, Andrew, harness maker, 31 E. Seneca, b. 2 Oak.
Gruff. A. comb maker, h. 53 Cherry.
Graff. Chas. rope maker, h. 130 Tupper.
Graff, H. woodworker, Brayley and Pitts.
Graff, Thomas, h. Palmer n. Maryland.
Grafferd, —, peddler, h. Genesee n. Jefferson.
Gragabob, John, lab. b. Pratt n. Genesee.
Gragabob, John, Jr. h. Pratt n. Genesee.
Graham, Amasa, 22 Cent. Wharf, h. 42 Court.
Graham, Charles, boat builder, h. N. Wash. n. Clinton avenue.
Graham, Eliza, nurse, Buff. Orphan Asylum, h. same.
Graham, Geo. shoemaker, 20 Batavia, h. same.
Graham. Jas. exch. broker, Wadsworth House, h. 55 Carroll.
Graham, James, carp. h. Steuben n. Alabama.
Graham, John, gardener. h. Main n. North.
Graham, Mary, widow, Park Coffee House, 2 Clinton. b. Boston House.
Graham, Thomas, blacksmith, h. 273 Exch.
Graham. Thomas, clerk, 318 Main, b. Batavia n. Oak.
Graham, W. C. barber. 25 Exchange.
Graham, Wm. machinist, h. Mineral Spring st. n. Aurora plank road.
Graham, Wm. tailor, h. 418 Michigan.
Grahling, Fred. flour and feed store, 76 E. Genesee, h. same.
Grahling, Jacob, wagoner, h. Potter n. Wm.
Graihling, Jacob, farmer, h. Walden N. of Best.
Gram. Chas. crockery store, 344 Main, h. 366 Michigan.
Gram. F. C. clerk. 344 Main, h. 366 Michigan.
Gram. Louis, harness maker, h. 39 Oak.
Gramby, John, waiter, h. Milnor n. Wm.
Granacher, Lorenzo, cabinet maker, h. 137 Genesee.
Grandin, H. M. agent, h. Washington n. High.
Grandison, Jas. L. brass founder, 27 Exch.
Grandison, William, waiter, Bonney's Hotel, b. same.
Granger, Casper, farmer, h. Delaware n. Forest Lawn.
Granger. Warren, city surveyor's office, b. Del n. Utica.
Granger. Wm. farmer, h. Delaware n. Utica.
Granniss & Co. oyster depot, 315 Main.
Grant, Angus, firm Murray & G. b. 408 Main.
Grant, Chas. E. saloon, Wm. n. Bennett.
Grant. David M. clerk, Sherman & Barnes, h. 30 S. Division.
Grant, Jas. lab. h. Carolina n. 9th.
Grant, Patrick, blacksmith, h. 4th n. Genesee.
Grant, Robert, firm Murray, Cumming & G. b. 5 Franklin.
Grant, Wm. ship carp. h. 4 Hayward.
Grase, John, ship carp. N. Div. n. Grosvenor.
Graser, Christian, farmer, h. Bat. plank road n. Williamsville road.
Graser, Chris. baker, b. 34 Seneca.
Graser, Henrietta, widow, h. 28 Bennett.
Graser, Jno.* shoemaker, 139 Batavia, h. same.
Grass, A. grocer, h. cor. Wm. and Hickory.

Grass, Leonard J. tailor, h. Sherman n. Bat.
Grass, Philip, clerk, b. Wm. cor. Hickory.
Grass, W. Mrs. widow, h. 168 Elm.
Grassel, John, finisher, h. Ash n. Sycamore.
Grasser. Andrew, clerk. Murray, Cumming & Grant, b. Genesee House.
Grat, Anthony, rag peddler, h. Watson n. Bat.
Gratz, Chas. sash and blind maker, h. Monroe n. William.
Gratz, Chas. piano maker, with A. & J. Keogh.
Grau, Francis, milliner, b. Oak cor. Gen.
Graumel, Lenhard, shoemaker. h. 177 Gen.
Graus, Jno. artist, h. Spring cor. Hollister.
Grauss, J. J. hair work. 328 Main, h. 28 Gen.
Graves, Jno. tailor, h. Revere.
Graves, Quartus, printer, Express office, h. 31 N. Division.
Grawits, Chas. saloon, Huron cor. Ellicott, h. same.
Gray, David, associate ed. Courier: b. 65 Eagle.
Gray, E. P. M. D. office 6 W. Swan, b. 32 E. Swan cor. Ellicott.
Gray, Jos. box maker, h. 174 Franklin.
Gray, Jos. Jr. joiner, h. Palmer ab. Maryland.
Gray, Sarah R. teacher No. 6, b. 14 E. Eagle.
Gray, Wm. carp. h. Pooley Place n. N. Wash.
Gray, Wm. clerk, 171 Main. b. 125 Swan.
GREAT WESTERN RAILWAY, office on Washington n. Exchange.—See adv. p. 98.
Grebner, Chas. lithographer, with Sage & Sons, h. Pratt n. Sycamore.
Green, Anthony, caulker, h. Va. cor. Niagara.
Green, Chas. light house inspector, Brown's Buildings, b. Mansion House.
Green, Christiana, widow, h. 392 Franklin.
Green, Elias, h. 200 Pearl.
Green, Elzade, wid. h. Carroll bel. Alabama.
Green, E. T. Rev. h. Seneca n. Whittm're's tav'n.
Green, H. engineer, cor. Pine and Eagle.
Green, Henry, joiner. h. 119 Oak.
Green, H. T. cl'k, S. O. Barnum, b. 30 Morgan.
Green, Horace H. clerk, in county clerk's recording office, h. 217 Niagara.
Green, Jas. lab. h. Root n. Penitentiary.
Green, Jas. sailor, h. across creek.
Green. Jas. rectifier and liquor dealer. Niagara n. Pennsylvania.
Green, Jas. W. engineer, h. Hampshire n. 11th.
Green, Jno. saloon, ac. creek, opp. Reed's dock.
Green, John, sailor, h. Chicago n. Elk.
Green, Lawrence, sailor, h. Perry n. Illinois.
Green, Manly C. clerk, in county clerk's office, b. 138 Eagle.
Green, Mary, widow, carpet weaver, h. Smith's block, Seneca.
Green, O. J. county clerk, h. 138 Eagle.
Green, Sam'l, fisherm'n, h. Niag. n. Hampshire.
Green, Samuel C. b. 39 Court.
Green, Starr, milkman, h. 91 S. Division.
Green, Wm. shoemaker, Chippewa opp. Mark't.
Greene, J. W. japanner, h. 29 Union.
Greene, Wm. H. attorney, firm G. & Stevens, 3 N. Division, h. 270 Washington.
Greener, Chas. artist, h. 95 Genesee.
Greenhalgh, Rowley, sawyer, h. Gay cor. Mark.
Greenland, Jas. plasterer, b. Mrs. A. Cooper.
Greenshield, John, firm G. & Laux, h. 75 N. Division.

Greenshield & Laux, clothing store, Commercial cor. Canal.
Greenvault & Co. commis'n merch'ts, 73 Main.
Greenvault, Henry V. firm G. & Co. h. 134 N. Division.
Greenwood, Henry, h. Elk n. Smith.
Greenwood, Thos. carp. h. Military n. Amherst.
Greger, Jos. shoemaker, h. Ferry opp. Rogers.
Gregory, Benjamin P. b. 100 E. Eagle.
Gregory, E. V. costumer, h. 50 Clinton.
Gregory, Geo. W. telegraph operator, N. Y. C. R. R. h. 16 Chestnut.
Gregory, Jos. G. clerk, 6 Main, b. 35 W. Swan.
Gregory, V. R. firm V. R. G. & Co. h. 224 N. Division.
Gregory, V. R. & Co. marble works, Washington n. S. Division.
Gregory, William, clerk, Michigan cor. Scott, h. 16 Chestnut.
Grehling, Jacob. wagon maker, h. Potter n. Wm.
Greifenstein. John, carpenter, Grey n. Batavia.
Greigg, Geo. lab. h. German alley n. Genesee.
Greigg, Harris H. book-keeper, Merchant's Dispatch, b. 73 S. Division.
Grein, Ernst, blacksmith, h. at Hydraulics.
Grein, Conrad, blacksmith. h. at Hydraulics.
Greiner, Chas. book-keeper, 28 Main, b. cor. Oak and Clinton.
Greiner, Edward, upholsterer, b. 114 Exch'ge.
Greiner, Fred. baker, 458 Michigan, h. same.
Greiner, H. shoemaker, 116 Exchange, h. same.
Greiner, Jno. Sr. Spruce n. Sycamore.
Greiner, John, locksmith, 186 Elm, h. same.
Greiner, Jno. firm Miller & G. h. 20 Clinton.
Greiner, Theo. lab. h. Adams n. Genesee.
Greisen, J. P. att'y, 136 Main, h. Palmer n. Va.
Gressel, Jno. lab. h. r. 41 Cherry.
Gresslein, N. lab. h. Spruce n. Ash.
Greter, Peter. gardener, h. Michigan ab. High.
Gretzler, Fred. lab. h. 321 Elm.
Gretzler, John, shoem'r, h. Mulberry n. High.
Grey, Albert, machinist, h. cor. Chestnut and Swan.
Grey, Ernst G. h. 135 Ellicott.
Grey, William, sawyer, Pulley place.
Gribber, Chas. b. 252 Genesee.
Gribber, Jno. lab. h. Porter n. Van Rensselaer.
Gribor, John. lab. h. 94 Cedar.
Gridley, Clement, contractor, h. 260 Franklin.
Gridley, Frederick, cashier, White's Bank, h. North n. York.
Gridley. Geo. H. book-keeper, Attica Bank, b. 260 Franklin.
Grien, Henry, clerk, 329 Mich, b. 30 Clinton.
Gries, Alfred, lab. h. 149 Swan.
Griesenger, Jos. lab. h. Steele n. Walden.
Griesert, Wm.* shoemaker, 300 Seneca.
Griesman, Jacob, lab. h. 1 Walnut.
Griest, Chas. painter, b. Tremont.
Griestmacher, Andrew, at lead works, h. Utica n. Jefferson.
Griffen, A. L. prod. com. merch. 23 Central Wharf. h. 29 E. Swan.
Griffen, B. lab. h. Terrace n. Mechanic.
Griffen, Colman, cook, h. Bundy n. Sycamore.
Griffen, Jacob, sailor, h. 115 Oak.
Griffen, M. lab. b. 6 Michigan.
Griffen, Pat. sailor, h. Perry n. Ohio basin.

Griffin, Harmon, land broker, over 427 Main, h. 455 Main.
Griffin, Hiram, farmer, h. Main n. Chapin.
Griffin, John, grocer, Hudson cor. 7th.
Griffin, J. B. firm G. & McDonald, 17 Central Wharf, h. 50 W. Tupper.
Griffin & McDonald, prod. and com. merchs. 7 Central Wharf.
Griffin, Matthias, carp. h. Church bel. Sloan.
Griffin, Mrs. widow, h. 6th n. Pennsylvania.
Griffin, P. Rev. h. 46 E. Swan.
Griffis, Benj. F. lab. h. Carolina n. 9th.
Grimard, Gustavus, liquor dealer, 356 Main, h. 183 Oak.
Grimm, Eliz. Mrs. h. r. 234 Elm.
Grimm, Geo. ship carp. h. Walnut n. Sycamore.
Grimm, John C. at Bloomer's, h. 251 Franklin.
Grimm, Mich. carpenter, h. 199 Ellicott.
Grimmer, Chas. cigar maker and music teacher, h. Elm cor. Tupper.
Grimmer, Geo. blacksmith, h. Cedar n. Wm.
Grinberg, Harris, dry goods, 400 Seneca, h. same.
Grisjeun, Eugene, stone cutter, h. Goodell cor. Washington.
Grissim, John, Mrs. widow, h. 36 E. Eagle.
Griswold, A. S. M. D. oculist and aurist, 23 Church.
Griswold, Frank S. clerk, Sherman & Barnes, b. Franklin.
Griswold, Walter, keeper ft. Porter, h. 6th n. Rhode Island.
Grobe, Christian. lab. h. Ketchum n. Carlton.
Grobe, Jacob, peddler, h. Adams n. Heacock.
Groben, Chas. dealer oil, paints, Bennett cor. William, h. same.
Groben, Jacob, chair maker, h. 127 Spring n. Batavia.
Grober, Nicholas, lab. h. Goodell n. Michigan.
Groehrich, Chas. Wm. lab. h. Lutheran n. Bat.
Groening, N. C. R. with Sherman & Barnes, b. 82 Pratt.
Groes, John. shoemaker, h. Niag. n. Hampshire.
Groesbeck, J. L. h. 354 Washington.
Groestein, Morris, peddler, h. 102 E. Seneca.
Groetzinger, John, distiller, h. Spring n. Wm.
Groff, Jacob, cooper, h. Niagara n. Hamilton.
Grogan, Mary, widow Jas. h. Green cor. Beak.
Groger, David L. merchant, h. 471 Michigan.
Groh, John, tailor, h. Krettner n. Lovejoy.
Grollmitz, Fred. W. cabinet maker, h. 273 Elm.
Groning, Chas. carpenter, h. Pratt n. William.
Gros, J. D. att'y, 152 Main, h. 5 10th.
Groshans, Godfred, tanner, h. 378 Michigan.
Groshans, Wm. machinist, b. 378 Michigan.
Groshaw, Eugene, stone cutter, h. Washington n. Goodell.
Gross, Bernhard, firm Kunz & G. h. 444 Wash.
Gross, Chas. tinsmith, h. Sycamore cor. Kaene.
Gross, Daniel, att'y, 152 Main, h. 10th n. Va.
Gross, Elizabeth, widow, b. 166 Clinton.
Gross, Frederick, lab. h. Oak cor. Tupper.
Gross, George,* grocer, Hickory n. Sycamore, h. same.
Gross, Henry. moulder, h. William n. Cedar.
Gross, Henry, tailor, h. towp'th n. round-house.
Gross, Jacob, carp. h. Genesee n. Carlton.
Gross, John, lab. h. Cherry cor. Hickory.

Gross, John, joiner, h. Clinton n. Jefferson.
Grosse H. at Evans & Co's planing mill.
Grossen, Henry, teamster, h. Miller's block, Michigan.
Grossman, George, distiller, h. Dearborn n. Hamilton.
Grossman, John, tailor, h. over 77 Genesee.
Grosvenor, Lucien, switchman, h. Perry n. Hamburgh.
Grosvenor, S. B. firm G. & Brown, ins. office, h. Franklin n. Allen.
Grosvenor, Seth H. office 37 Pearl, h. 207 Pearl.
Grote, Henry, lab. b. 73 Swan.
Grotendorst, John, lab. h. William n. Cedar.
Grotsch, Leonard, lab. h. Monroe n. Peckham.
Grubel, Martin, lab. h. Ferry E. Jefferson.
Gruber, Christian, lab. h. Genesee n Jefferson.
Gruber, Geo. lab. h. Walnut n. Batavia.
Gruber, Jacob, saloon, Market cor. Perry, h. 2 Court.
Gruber, Kolinbarth, tailor, h. 114 Cedar.
Gruber, Michael, blacksmith, h. 62 Bennett.
Gruhler, Bernhard, cooper, h. Hamilton n. Dearborn.
Grunholzer, I. J. M. D. 136 E. Genesee, h. same.
Gruner, Valentine, grocer, Chicago cor. Ohio, h. same.
Grupp, John, boiler maker, h. 122 Walnut.
Gruss, John, carpenter, h. Clinton n. Jefferson.
Guck, Michael, mason, h. Ketchum alley n. High.
Guembel, Hall, butcher, h. Batavia cor Spruce.
Gueneman, Chas. carpenter, b. Maple n. High.
Guenther, Andrew, with Geo. Scott, h. 199 Genesee.
Guenther, Anthony, 160 Elm, h. Cherry n. Jeff.
Guenther, August, cooper, h. Hickory n. Syc.
Guenther, Christian, baker, Niag. n. Hamilton.
Guenther, F. H. Rev. D. D. h. Hickory n. Wm.
Guenther, Jacob, moulder, h. Cedar n. Wm.
Guenther, John G. h. 114 E. Eagle.
Guenther, Mary, widow, h. 9 Cherry.
Guenther, N. J. R. clerk, Pratt & Letchworth, h. 47 Ellicott.
Guenther, Valentine, wagon maker, h. Hickory bet. William and Batavia.
Guenther, Wm. peddler, h. Cherry cor. Orange.
Guenther, Wm. lab. Best n. Michigan.
Guerner, Geo. lab. h. 141 Walnut.
Guessnewald, Fred. shoemaker, h. Carlton n. Jefferson.
Gugeler, Andrew, shoemaker, h. Bat. n. Pine.
Guide, Frederick, lab. with Pierce & Co. h. N. Division n. Jefferson.
Guier, Adam, h. 275 Elm.
Guild, E. T. bootmaker, 52 Exch. h. 1 Union.
Guild, Harrison, clerk, with R. Bullymore, h. 441 Seneca.
Guild, Harrison, Jr. printer, b. 441 Seneca.
Guillard, J. Rev. pastor, Church of Holy Angels, b. cor. York and North.
Guiltner, James, lab. h. Jefferson n. Clinton.
Guitteau, John L. book-keeper, h. Washington n. Carlton.
Gundlach, Charles, b. American.
Gundlach, Elizabeth, Mrs. h. 546 Michigan.
Guman, John, tailor, h. Best n. Michigan.
Gumber, L. Mrs. widow, h. 49 Cedar.

Gunn, Daniel, drover, h. Genesee junc. Best.
Gunold, Rudolf, shoemaker, Ohio n. Chicago, h. same.
Gurney, Wm. H. atty. with Humphrey & Parsons, old P. O. bld'g, b. cor. Seneca and Mich.
Gurr, Ed. gardener, h. Walden n. Ferry.
Gusen, Andrew, lab. h. Kaene n. Genesee.
Gusset, Wm. L. whitewasher, h. 24 Walnut.
Gust, Ignatz, saloon, 8 Commercial, h. Maiden lane n. Canal.
Guster, A. piano maker, h. Eagle cor. Hickory.
Gutekunst, Jno. tin worker, h. Milnor n. Wm.
Gutekunst, John, works cor. Pearl and Seneca, b. Milnor n. William.
Guth, Geo. carp. h. Maple n. Virginia.
Guth, Louis, surgeon, h. Batavia n. Walnut.
Guthrie, E. B. sec'y Western Elevating Co. h. 99 Niagara.
Guthrie, Mary, widow, h. across creek.
Guthrie, S. S. prod. com. mer. 11 Cent. Wharf, h. 49 W. Genesee.
Gwinn, J. M. teller N. Y. & E. Bank, h. 160 Delaware.
Gwinn, Wm. R. h. 160 Delaware.
Gyer, Wm. shoemaker, 36 Chippewa.
Gygli, Francis, h. Clinton cor. Walnut.
Gygli, Fred. grocer, Clinton cor. Walnut.

H.

Haag, Fred. painter, h. Hickory n. Genesee.
Haag, John, tailor, h. 31 Sycamore.
Haag, Jos. tailor, h. Boston alley n. Tupper.
Haag, Leonard, mason, h. Adams n. Batavia.
Haakey, Frederick, teamster, h. North Canal n. Jefferson.
Haas, Abraham, peddler, h. 167 Batavia.
Haas, Adam, lab. h. Walnut n. Batavia.
Haas, Chas. shoemaker, H. Argus. b. William n. Pine.
Hass, Chas. lab. h. Exch. n. Van Rensselaer.
Haas, Chas, Wm. printer at Dem. and Weltberger. h. Lovejoy n. Stanton.
Haacker, Jno. cooper, h. 10 Scott.
Haas, Christian, carp. h. 238 Elm.
Haas, Conrad, lab. h. Spring n. Sycamore.
Haas, Conrad, lab. h. Adams n. Genesee.
Haas, Daniel, lab. h. 238 Elm.
Haas, David,* brewer, Spring cor. Cherry, h. same.
Haas, Geo. engraver, b. 117 Clinton.
Haas, John, baker, 571 Main, h. same.
Haas, J. L. printer, b. 117 Clinton.
Haas, John, lab. h. Ash n. Sycamore.
Haas, John, tailor, h. Johnson n. Batavia.
Haas, John, mason, h. 52 E. Tupper.
Haas, Margaretha, widow, h. 117 Clinton.
Haas, Nicholas, bootmaker, 2 Canal, b. Revere House.
Haas, Nicolaus, Sr. shoemaker, h. Cypress n. Michigan.
Haas, Philip, shoemaker, h. Jefferson n. Genesee.
Haberkorn, George, lab. h. Herman n. Gen.
Habermann, Casper, stone mason, h. Bat. cor. Stanton.
Haberstro, John F. clerk, b. 401 Main.
Haberstro Jos. L. & Co. brewery, High n. Main.

Haberstro, Joseph L. firm Jos. L. H. & Co. h. High n. Main.
Hack. B. blacksmith, h. Ash n. Sycamore.
Hacker, Adam, mason, h. 133 Walnut.
Hacker, Martin.* butcher, 342 Main, h. same.
Hackett, Patrick, patent roofer, Folsom n. Kinney alley.
Hackett, William, lab. h. 10th above Jersey.
Hackland, John, saloon, Ash n. Gen. h. same.
Hackmer, Charles, teamster, h. 2 ! Ash.
Haddock. Henry H. book-keeper, 336 Main, b. 511 Main.
Haddock, Lorenzo K. attorney, 8 Spaulding's Exchange, b. American.
Haden, B. ship carpenter. h. 5th n. Carolina.
Hader. Grace, Miss, b. 126 Batavia.
Haderer, John, grocer, Gen. cor. Fox. h. same.
Haderer, Michael, lab. h. Fox n. Genesee.
Hadfield, Robt. clerk. h. 10th above Hudson.
Hadley. Elijah, firm H. & Husted, h. 107 E. Swan.
Hadley, George. м. ɒ. h. Main n. Utica.
Hadley & Husted, hardware dealers, 119 and 27 Main.
Hadley, James, м. ɒ. h. Main n. Utica.
Haefner. Aloys, firm H. & Bros. h. High cor. Michigan.
Haefner. Bros. brewery, High cor. Michigan.
Haefner, Conrad. lab. h. William n. Jefferson.
Haefner, Francis, bookseller, 222 Ellicott, h. same.
Haefner,Geo. grocer, High n. Ketchum, h. same.
Haefner, Margaret, widow, h. Monroe n. Syc.
Haefner, Michael, firm H. & Bros. h. High cor. Michigan.
Haefner. Philip, tanner, h. Clinton n. Madison.
Haefner. Stephen, 203 Main, h. Spring n. Bat.
Haebring. John. grocer, h. Bat. cor. Emslie.
Haene. Magdalena, Mrs. h. Burton al. n. Oak.
Haennel, Alexander, barkeeper, Main cor. Clinton, b. 401 Main.
Haering. Conrad. tailor, Bundy alley n. Syc.
Haescher. Anna E. wid. h. High cor. Ketchum.
Haffa, John, tailor, h. William n. Cedar.
Haffeld, Andrew, lab. h. Krettner n. Lovejoy.
Haffer, Michael, shoemaker, Lewis n. Amherst.
Hafley, Henry, h. Dearborn n Amherst.
Hafner, John, turner, h. 41 Sycamore.
Hafner, Fred. lab. h. Clinton cor. Pratt.
Haft, Anton, carp. h. n. Tifft's farm.
Haften, Alex. cigar maker, b. 23ᵈ Elm.
Hagel. Michael, hackman, h. 13 Pearl.
Hagelin, Adolph, grocer, William n. Pine.
Hageman, Jno. A. h. Edward opp. Park school.
Hagemann, Henry, lab. h. Delavan avenue opposite Grider.
Hagen, Christ. teamster, h. Sycamore n. Pine.
Hagen, Henry, shoemaker, h. cor. Tonawanda and Amherst.
HAGEN, MICHAEL, proprietor Buff. Sentinel, 111 Main, h. same.—See adv. p. 103.
Hagar. Raymond, doper, S. L. R. R. h. Jefferson n. Seneca.
Hager, Charles, ornamental painter, 231 Main, b. Spring n. William.
Hager, Christ. lab. h. Grey n. Genesee.
Hager, John, cap maker, 290 Main. h. Genesee cor. Elm.

Hager, John W. ship carpenter, h. Peckham n. Monroe.
Hager, Philip, printer, h. Eagle n. Hickory.
Hager. Philip, stone cutter, h. Eagle n. Hick'y.
Hager, Robert. book store, 364½ Main, h. 243 Ellicott n. Tupper.
Hagermer, Jacob, machinist, h. Jefferson n. Peckham.
Hagerman. Norman, blacksmith, Chicago cor. Miami, h. Hydraulics n. Emslie.
Haggart, J. L. capt. ferry boat, b. cor. Niagara and Ferry.
Haggerer, John, G. lab. h. Maple n. Carlton.
Haggerty, M. sailor, h. Columbia n. Ohio.
Hagmeier, Louis, grocer, 162 Oak, b. same.
Hague. Gordon, painter, 66 Lloyd, h. N. Div. n. Pine.
Hague. Jos. boiler maker, h. Elk below Smith.
Hahman, Fred. lab. h. Hollister n. Mortimer.
Hahn, Conrad. Mrs. h. Summer n. Rogers.
Hahn, Engelhard. lab. h. Davis n. Genesee.
Hahn, Frederick W.* saw filer, 4 Court, h. 90 Clinton.
Hahn, Henry, joiner, h. 73 Goodell.
Hahn, Henry, joiner. 115 Ellicott.
Hahn, Louis, baker, h. Monroe cor. Howard.
Hahn. Marie, widow, washerwoman, h. Monroe n. Batavia.
Hahn. R. stone cutter. h. Spruce n. Sycamore.
Hahn, Sebastian. blacksmith, h. 318 Genesee.
Haight, Edgar, h. 44 Oak.
Haight, M. C. watchmaker, 266 Main, b. 161 Swan.
Haines, Emmor, lumber merch. h. High n. Oak.
Haines, E. W. com. merch. 147 Main, h. 165 Franklin.
Haines, Nathan, grocer, 145 S. Division cor. Chestnut. h. same.
Haines, Samuel. h. 301 Michigan.
Halbert, Norton A. firm Hopkins & H. h. Main n. Riley.
Halbert, Sanford, h. 263 Swan.
Halblaub, Michael, cooper, h. East n. Parish.
Halburd, James, ship carpenter, h. 162 6th.
Haldane, Jas. gardener, 2 Scott. h. Best n. Jeff.
Haldsch, G. wood worker, Brayley & Pitts.
Hale. Henry, tinsmith, with Hadley & Husted, b. William.
Hale. Henry H. stave dealer, Marine Block, Ohio, h. 127 Niagara.
Hale. Jacob. lab. h. Vermont n. Rogers.
Hale, Jno. C. ice dealer, 190½ Main, h. cor. Niagara and Auburn.
Hale, J. H. conductor, Niagara St. R. R. b. 9th n. Vermont.
Hale, Lovina, widow, tailoress. h. 103 Clinton.
Halech, Peter, fence maker, h. 442 Michigan.
Hale, Simeon, prop. Buff. Plains House, Main n. Buff. Plains.
Hale, Wm. C. milk dealer, 203 S. Division.
Hale, Z. J. b. Buffalo Plains House.
Haley, Jas. peddler, h. Adams cor. Arkansas.
Haley, Jas. mariner, h. across creek.
Haley, John, lab. h. across creek.
Haley, Jno. lab. h. Genesee n. canal.
Haley, Jno. grocer, h. Evans cor. Fly.
Haley, Michael, lab. across creek.
Haley, P. H. blacksmith, h. 29 Exchange.

Haley, Thos. lab. h. Niagara n. Breckenridge.
Haley, Thos. lab. h. Genesee n. canal.
Halifax, Nathaniel, melodeon maker, h. Virginia cor. Palmer.
Hall, A. G. clerk, b. 103 Clinton.
Hall, Albert G. b. 29 E. Swan.
Hall, Andrew A. Am. Ex. Co. h. Va. n. Niag.
Hall, Chas. B. with Sherman & Barnes, b. 29 E. Swan.
Hall, C. W. heeler, h. 325 Washington.
Hall, Harvey, capt. on lake, h. 186 N. Division
Hall, Henrietta, seamstress, b. 28 Cypress.
Hall, H. W. b. Niagara n. Bidwell.
Hall, Jacob, milkman, h. Maryland ab. Cottage.
Hall, Jas. sailor, h. Elk cor. Michigan.
Hall, Jas. mechanic, h. Elk n. Smith.
Hall, Jas. H. b. 302 Franklin.
Hall, Jas. Q. overseer, h. 292 Fulton.
Hall, Jas. W. milkman, Main n. Ferry.
Hall, Joel, lumber and wire work dealer, 115 Main, h. 302 Franklin.
Hall, John, waiter, b. 11 William.
Hall, Josie, Miss, b. 28 Cypress.
Hall, Lydia M. widow of Morris, h. 61 6th.
Hall, Nathaniel, firm Rounds & H. ins. agt's, 2 Brown's Building, h. 49 E. Eagle.
Hall, N. K. judge of U. S. Cir. Court, h. 144 Franklin.
Hall, Richard, furniture, 6 Quay, h. 74 Main.
Hall, Robert W. book-keeper, Lyon & Co. b. 29 Swan.
Hall, Sylvester, mariner, h. Pratt n. Eagle.
Hall, Wm. lab. h. Sycamore n. Ash.
Hall, Wm. lab. h. 438 Michigan.
Hall, W. B. h. 171 Elm.
Hallennen, Michael, blacksmith, h. ac. creek.
Hallennen, Patrick, lab. across creek.
Haller, Cris. lab. h. Adams S. of Batavia.
Haller, Fred. grocery, Eagle cor. Hickory.
Haller, Fred. C. shoemaker, h. 442 Michigan.
Haller, John, carpenter, b. 29 Ash.
Haller, J. F. shoemaker, h. 440 Michigan.
Haller, John, tailor, h. 95 Oak.
Haller, John G. shoemaker, h 50 E. Tupper.
Haller, Martin, grocer, h. Walnut n. Batavia.
Halley, Myron B. Mrs. h. Dearborn n Amh'rst.
Halley, Wm. book-keep'r. b. Mrs. M. B. Halley.
Hallmann, Edward, clerk, 434 Main, b. 238 Pearl.
Halloran, David, lab. h Emslie n. Clinton.
Halpin, Martin, lab. 160 Exchange.
Halpin, Henry, lab. h. cor. Exch. and Hamb.
Halsey, Henry H. law student, 7 Arcade buildings, b. 4 Union.
Halsey, T. G. Mrs. h. 4 Union.
Haltey, Jno. blacksmith, Gulf cor. Del. h. same.
Hambleton, Aaron, engineer, h. Miami n. Ala.
Hameister, Henry, lithographer, with Sage & Sons, 20 Delaware place.
Hamelman, Chas. blacksmith, b. 171 Genesee.
Hamill, David, cartman, b. J. Hamill.
Hamill, Eliz. seamstress, b. J. Hamill.
Hamill, Jno. cartman, b. Jefferson n. Howard.
Hamilton, A. M. painter, h. Abbott n. Martin's Corners.
Hamilton, Chas. J. foreman Eaton's planing mill, h. 54 6th.
Hamilton, Jas. M. firm Ensign & H. h. 212 P'rl-

Hamilton, Margaret, Mrs. h. 500 Michigan.
Hamilton, Patrick, h. 46 5th.
Hamilton, R. S. carp. h. Wash. n. Goodell.
Hamilton, Theodore B. atty. b. 6 S. Division.
Hamilton, Thos. sailor. h. 7 Scott.
Hamilton, Wm. h. 58 6th.
Hamlich, Philip, flour and feed, 191 N. Division. h. same.
Hamlin, Charles W. law student, 190½ Main. h. 147 Franklin.
Hamlin, C. J. firm H. & Mendsen, h. Franklin cor. Virginia.
Hamlin, D. R. h. 147 Franklin.
Hamlin, Frederick N. clerk. H. & Mendsen, b. cor. Virginia and Franklin.
Hamlin, John S. book-keeper, h. 6th cor. Carolina.
Hamlin & Mendsen, dry goods, carpets, and paper dealers, 206, 208 & 212 Main.
Hamm, Paul, tinsmith, h. Pratt n. Genesee.
Hamman, Peter, turner, h. 159 Batavia.
Hammer, Jacob, carp. h. Monroe n. Batavia.
Hammerschmidt, Charles, farmer, h. Seneca n. tollgate.
Hammerschmidt, Peter, farmer, h. Seneca n. tollgate.
Hammond, A. Mrs. wid. housekeeper, Boaney's Hotel.
Hammond, Benj. capt. on lake, h. High n. Oak.
Hammond, E. D. with Jason Parker, h. 66 Huron.
Hammond, Fred. V. painter, b. 121 Clinton.
Hammond, G. W. clerk. b. 121 Clinton.
Hammond, John, ship carpenter, h. Fulton n. Louisiana.
Hammond, Julia, widow, h. 121 Clinton.
Hammond, Mary, dressm'r. 346 Main. h. same
Hammond, Mary A. wid. William S. h. 146 S. Division.
Hammond, W. W. law student, b. cor. Mich and Seneca.
Hammond, Wm. lab. h. 15th n. Commercial.
Hamper, John, butcher, 96 Niagara. h. same
Hampton, C. L. wid. h. 7th n. Pennsylvania
Hanavan & Albro, flour and feed store, 36 E. Seneca.
Hanavan, Anna, widow, h. acr. Buffalo creek.
Hanavan, John, firm H. & Albro, b. Hayward n. Fulton.
Hanaky, Andrew. lab. h. Clinton bel. Raze.
Hanascy, Patrick, engineer, h. 11th cor. Va.
Handcock, H. G. coppersmith, b. 11 Walnut
Handcock, Jas. coppersmith, b. 11 Walnut
Handley, John, mariner, h. Louisiana n. Elk.
Handlin, John, lab. h. 5th n. Virginia.
Handrahan, Jn. grocer, Elk n. Moore, h. same
Handrich, Adam, shoemaker, b. John Handrich.
Handrich, Jacob, marble cutter, h. Mulberry n. North.
Handrich, John,* shoemaker, h. 10th n. Md.
Handson, Wm. sailor, h. South n. Vincennes
Handy, John, lab. h. Fulton n. Chicago.
Hanegan, Mary, stalls 35 & 37 Elk st. h 15 Mississippi.
Hanes, Charles, turner, b. F. Hanes.
Hanes, Fred. turner, 122 Sycamore, h. same
Hanes, Fred. Jr. turner, b. 122 Sycamore

Hangen, P. wagoner, 318 Genesee. h. Kaene n- Sycamore.
Hankes, John, pattern maker, LeCouteulx n. Canal, h. 36 Watson.
Hankins, John, boat builder, ac. creek.
Hanks, Wm. engineer, L. S. R. R. h. 330 S. Division.
Hanley, Edmond, switch tender, h. n. Erie st. depot.
Hanley, Michael, watchman, Buff. Ag. Mach. Works, h. Perry n. Hamburgh.
Hanley, Thomas, clerk at 104 Exch. b. same.
Hanley, Hannah, wid. h. Marvin n. Elk.
Hanley, Mary, wid. h. Ohio n. Chicago.
Hanlin, Mary, saloon, Seneca n. Heacock.
Hanlon, James, sailor, h. 5th n. Carolina.
Hanlon, John, sawyer, ac. creek.
Hanly, Cornelius, lab. ac. creek.
Hann, Jas. carp. Louisiana n. South.
Hann, John, tinsmith, h. Walnut n. Genesee.
Hannat, Rich. peddler, h. Smith blk. Carroll.
Hannon, Frank, breaksman, N. Y. C. R. R. b. National Hotel.
Hanna, John, moulder, h. 75 Spruce.
Hanour. Peter J. saloon, Commercial n. Terrace, h. 394 Main.
Hanovan, Patrick, lab. h. Hamburgh n. Perry.
Hanovan, John, lab. h. Elk n. Marvin.
Hanrahan, John, lab. h. William n. Pine.
Hansel, Wm. upholsterer, h. 226 Oak.
Hansell, Mathias, tailor, h. Adams n. Peckham.
Hansen, Christ, shoemaker, h. Clinton n. Raze.
Hanson, Abr. carrriage trimmer, h. 16 Park pl.
Hanson, J. A. 163 Eagle.
Hanson, John, grocer, Jackson cor. Wilkeson slip, h. same.
Hanson, Kate R. school teacher, b 16 Park pl.
Hanson, Mary Ann, widow, h. Roos alley n. William.
Hanson, Thomas, grocer, h. Jackson cor. Wilkeson slip.
Hansman, Louis, printer, Express office, h. 203 Genesee.
Happ, Bartell, tailor, h. 401 Michigan.
Happercorn, John, butcher, cor. Hudson and 7th, h. Herman n. Genesee.
Harbaur, John, shoemaker, h. 142 Batavia.
Harbeck, H. A. stave dealer, office 1 C. Wharf.
Harbourne, Henry, shoemaker, at 236 Main, h. 53 Cedar n. William.
Harch, Henry, lab. h. Ferry n. Waldron.
Hard, Sam. B. atty. 20 Spaulding's Exchange, b. American.
Harder, Geo. lab. h. Mulberry n. Virginia.
Harder, P. wood worker, Brayley & Pitts.
HARDIKER & TOYE, plumbers and gas-fitters, cor. Pearl and Eagle.—See adv. p. 71.
Hardiker, Wm. firm H. & Toye, h. 272 N. Division bel. Spring.
Hardison, Geo. b. Western.
Hardman, Michael, tailor, h. 118 Michigan.
Hardt, Wm. shoemaker, h. Grey n. Batavia.
Hardy, Chas. W. clerk. 316 Main, b. 35 E. Swan.
Hardy, Ed. J. cab. maker, h. Carey n. Morgan.
Hardy, Hugh, ship carpenter, h. Hayward n. Fulton.
Hardy, James, lab. h. Efner n. Carolina.
Hardy, Peter, peddler, h. 221 7th n. Georgia.

12

Hare, Chas. farmer, h. Elk n. Red Jacket Hotel.
Hare, James, printer, Courier. b. 95 Seneca.
Hare, Richard, printer, Courier, b. 95 Seneca.
Hargrave, Jas. tailor, h. 168 6th.
Hark, Theodore, lab. h. Walnut n. Batavia.
Harkness, Stephen, dairyman, h. Exchange n. Heacock.
Harland, Chs. sailor, h. cor. Chicago and Elk.
Harman, J. tailor, h. 108 Exchange.
Harman, Frederick, lab. h. Madison n. Peck'm.
Harmon, Cyrus, salesman, J. H. Evans & Co. h. 58 6th.
Harmon, F. P. master miller, h. Dearborn n. Amherst.
Harmon, Judson, Mrs. h. 174 Pearl.
Harmer, Thos. porter, h. 48 William.
Harmes, Christopher, ship carp. with Mixer & Smith, h. Louisiana n. Sandusky.
Harms, Wm. tailor, h. 322 Elm.
Harolt, Gustof, joiner, h. Spring n. William.
Harper, Leonard, agt. h. Mariner n. Virginia.
Harper, David, b. Western.
Harper, Thos. tallyman, b. Ohio n. Wash. sqr.
HARRADEN. JAMES, builder, h. 3 Elm.— See adv. p. 57.
Harrer, Jno. lab. h. Fox n. Genesee.
Harries, Ann, widow, b. 87 Clinton.
HARRIES, EDWARD, groceries, drugs and dye stuffs, 180 Main, h. 87 Clinton.—See adv. p. 40.
Harrington, Amanda, Mrs. h. 11 Court.
Harrington, Brigham, telegrapher, b. 7 Johnson place.
Harrington, Chas. brakesman, S. L. R. R. b. 137 Seneca.
Harrington, Daniel, farmer, Ontario n. Tonawanda.
Harrington, James, agt. Detroit and Milwaukee R. R. h. 7 Johnson place.
Harrington, James, barkeeper, National.
Harris, Abraham, clothing, &c. 7. Commercial.
Harris, Asa P. h. 126 N. Division.
Harris, Chas. blacksmith, h. Fulton n. Ala.
Harris, Charles D. grocer, 27 Commercial, b. 6 Park place.
Harris, Charles, grainer, h. 62 Elm.
Harris, Chauncey, policeman, h. Palmer n. Hudson.
Harris, D. P. firm D. P. H. & Co. h. 25 Johnson place.
Harris, D. P. & Co. livery stable, cor. Terrace and Lock.
Harris, Edward, teamster, h. 135 Carroll.
Harris, Frances, Miss, b. B. Harris.
Harris, George J. farmer, h. Abbott n. iron bridge.
Harris, James W. proprietor Cold Spring Cottage, Main n. Ferry,
Harris, Jesse, firm H. & Preston, h. Clinton n. Raze.
Harris, John, hostler, London Hotel, b. same.
Harris, Joseph, livery stable, Perry n. Washington, h. n. iron bridge.
Harris, J. H. saloon, Long Wharf n. Com.
Harris, Levi, peddler, h. 4 Scott.
Harris, Linus E. office 214 Main, h. 25 Carolina.
Harris, Peyton, renovator, h. 379 Michigan.
Harris, Robert, caulker, h. Folsom n. Jeff'n.

Harris, R. W. proprietor Elk Street House, Elk cor. Michigan.
Harris, S. W. b. Linus E. Harris.
Harris, widow, dressmaker, h. 382 Washington.
Harris, Walter S. b. Main n. Perry.
Harris, William, with Newman & Scovill, h. Washington n. Scott.
Harrison, Jane, widow, washerwoman, h. 5th n. Virginia.
Harrison, J. C. supt. Cleveland steamers, Long Wharf, h. 453 Main.
Harrison, R. B. caulker, h. Alabama n. Fulton.
Harrison, Richard, 39 Seneca.
HARRON, ROBERT, stone yard, Erie opposite Courter House, h. 63 Mohawk.—See adv. p. 69.
Harrison, Samuel, h. 388 Seneca.
Harrison, Thos. iron finisher, Brayley & Pitts.
Harrop, James, blacksmith, h. Court n. Erie canal.
Harroun, G. K. firm Sandford, H. & Co. h. 360 Franklin.
Harsch, Jacob, lab. h. Madison n. Peckham.
Hart, Anon, gunsmith, h. 180 S. Division.
Hart, Austin S. firm H. Ball & H. h. 14 Johnson place.
HART, BALL & HART, plumbers, 237 Main. —See adv. p. 71.
Hart, Ellen, widow, h. Sandusky n. Louisiana.
Hart, H. variety store, 275 Main.
Hart, Henry, farmer, h. White's Corners plank road below iron bridge.
Hart, Henry, clothing store, 171 Main, h. 74 Pearl.
Hart, Henry S. printer, h. Palmer n. Carolina.
Hart, John, cigar maker, b. 7th n. Rhode Island.
Hart, Johnson, painter, b. Car. n. Virginia.
Hart, Luther, engineer, N. Y. C. R. R. h. 12 Chicago.
Hart, Robert, b. Niagara n. Albany.
Hart, Thomas, shoemaker, h. Hamburgh n. Fulton.
Hart, Wm. A. firm H. Ball & H. h. 14 Johnson place.
Hart, William B. farmer, Aurora plank road n. city line.
Hart, W. J. tobacconist, b. National Hotel.
Hartel, Geo. shoemaker, h. Johnson n. Gen.
Hartell, Martin, lab. h. 2 River.
Hartfelder, John, carp. h. Mich. n. High.
Hartfurt, Gerhard, joiner, h. 184 Batavia.
Hartigan, Wm. blacksmith, h. 104 Exch.
Hartinger, Albert, lab. h. Walnut n. Batavia.
Hartington, William, lab. h. 104 Exchange.
Hartley, James, joiner, h. Carolina below 5th.
Hartley, Timothy, Main St. R. R. h. Ferry n. Main.
Hartlieb, Louise, widow, h. Jefferson n. Wm.
Hartman, A. lab. h. r. 447 Michigan.
Hartman, Adam, sailor, h. Louisiana n. Elk.
Hartman, Barbara, wid. 195 Gen. up stairs.
Hartman, Casper, shoemaker, Locust n. Cherry.
Hartman, Catherine, widow. h. Mich. n. Best.
Hartman, Francis, lab. h. 230 Elm.
Hartman Frederick, book-keeper, S. C. Woodruff, b. 35 Swan.
Hartman, Henry, lab. h. Jefferson n. William.
Hartman, John, lab. b. 142 E. Genesee.

Hartman, John, lab. h. Grey n. Genesee.
Hartman, John, lab. h. Clinton n. Jefferson.
Hartman, Joseph, scavenger, h. 27 Sycamore.
Hartman, S. F. book-keeper, L. C. Woodruff, b. cor. Swan and Ellicott.
Hartman, Valentine, lab. h. Adams n. William.
Hartmann, Chas. F.* groc'r, 64 Goodell. h. same
Hartmeyer, Lucas, carpenter, h. 237 Oak.
Hartnett, Daniel, lab. Ohio n. Chicago.
Hartnett, Timothy, lab. h. Ohio n. Chicago.
Hartnett, John, lab. h. Alabama n. South.
Hartsheim, Eliz. wid. peddler, h. 72 Bennett.
Hartzell, J. Hazard, Rev. h. 81½ Clinton.
Hartzer, Xavier, shoemaker, h. Spruce n. Gen.
Harvey & Allen. flour and feed dealers, 206 Washington and 23 Central Wharf.
Harvey, Alexander W. firm Marshall & H. 330 Main, h. 171 Pearl.
Harvey, Charles W. M. D. dentist, h. S Division cor. Washington.
Harvey, D. clerk, Harvey & Allen, b. 34 W. Seneca.
Harvey, Egbert, h. 454 Main.
Harvey, Horace J. firm H. & Allen, b. 32 W. Seneca.
Harvey, John, blacksmith, h. Carolina n. 5th.
Harvey, John C. firm H. & Wallace, h. 187 Sen.
Harvey, Leon F. dentist, b. 5 S. Div. cor. Wash.
Harvey, Thos. L. drover, h. Genesee n. Walden.
Harvey & Wallace, carriage manuf. Lock n. Courter House.
Haselton, Leonard, carriage maker, 18 Exch. b. Western.
Hasenfratz, Peter, furnaceman, 268 Elm.
Hasenhzal, Fred. shoemaker, 10 Terrace, h. 177 E. Swan.
Haskal, Joseph, farmer, Niagara n. city line.
Haskins, Monroe, carriage painter, b. Bonney's Hotel.
Haskins, R. W. h. Michigan n. Swan.
Haskins, Wm. musician. h. Canal n. Evans.
Haslam, James, with E. Corning & Co. b. Ill. n. Ohio.
Hasselbach, Anton, meat market, cor. N. Div. and Pine.
Hassinger, Jacob,* hatter. h. Batavia n. Adams.
Hassinger, Wm. painter, Batavia cor. Adams.
Hasted, Fred. circulator of a paper, h. 66 Hick.
Hastings, Chancey J. real est. agt. 3 Brown's Building, h. 9th ab. Virginia.
Hastings, J. B. with B. H. King. b. 12th n. Vt.
Hastings, Thomas B. joiner, h. 12th n. Vt.
Hastings, Wm. manuf. sea grass, h. Dearborn n. Amherst.
Hastings, W. J. book-keeper, b. cor. Morgan and Chippewa.
Hatch, Eleazer P. h. 13 Court.
Hatch, E. N. conductor N. St. R. R. b. Niagara cor. Albany.
Hatch. E. N. dept. coll'tr customs, b. S. Lyons.
Hatch's Elevator n. foot Washington, ac. creek.
Hatch, Israel T. h. Cottage cor. College.
Hatch, Junius H. atty. b. cor. Niagara and Alb.
Hatch, J. H. Jr. law student, b. Niagara n. Albany.
Hatch, Wm. clerk, b. J. H. Hatch.
Hathaway, Chas. carp. Palmer ab. Carolina.
Hathaway, J. T. h. 292 Pearl.

Hathaway, J. W. mariner, h. 11th n. Maryland·
Hathaway, N. C. clerk, E. R. Jewett & Co. b· 292 Pearl.
Hatter, William W. saloon, 8 Canal.
Hattig, Jno. lab. h. 562 Michigan.
Hatwell, Geo. lab. h. 254 Ellicott.
Hatz, Fred. whitesmith. h. Pine cor. Cypress.
Hau, Nicholas, lab. h. Grape n. Cherry.
Hauck. Adam, firm H. & Kiefer, h. Oak n. Tup.
HAUCK, A. & J. KIEFER, copper, tin and sheet iron, 395 Main.—*See adv. p. 96.*
Hauck, Conrad, groceries and dry goods, 226 Batavia cor. Pratt, h. same.
Hauck, John, carp. h. ov. 173 Batavia.
Hauck, Joseph, turner, h. 126 Pine.
HAUCK & KIEFER, hardware and tinsmithing, 393 Main.—*See adv. p. 96.*
Haudis, M. lab. h. East cor. Farmer.
Hauenstein, Geo. grocer, High cor. Michigan.
Hauenstein, Henry, clerk, b. Tupper n. Oak.
Hauenstein, John G. lab. h. Locust n. North.
Hauenstein, John, M. D. 357 Wash. h. 257 Oak.
Hauer, Jno. lab. h. Herman n. Sycamore.
Hauf, Jacob,° baker, 110 Sycamore n. Ash, h. same.
Haug, John, lab. h. cor. Farmer and East.
Hanise, Henry, lab. h. cor. Terrace and Mech.
Hauk, Anton, lab. b. cor. Water and Maiden lane
Haukins & Johns, boat builders, ac. Buff. creek.
Haul, Henry, barber, h. 11 Sycamore.
Haupt, Albert, clerk, 320 Main, b. 450 Wash.
Haupt, Frederick, h. 450 Washington.
Hausenges, J. G. shoemaker, h. Hick. n. Syc.
Hauser, Jno. cigar m'r. h. Monroe n. Peckham.
Hauser, Michael, cook, h. Pine n. Batavia.
Hauser, Tho. tailor, h. Adams n. Sycamore.
Hauser, Wendelin, shoemaker, h. 245 Oak.
Hauser, Xavier, carp. h. Sycamore n. Spring.
Haushahn, John, lab. h. Camp n. Sycamore.
Haushahn, Leonard, moulder, h. Camp n. Syc.
Haushammer, Peter, shoemaker, 178 Oak.
Hausle, F. clerk, 399 Main, b. 146 Genesee.
Hausle, Jno. A. firm H. & Son, b. 146 E. Gen.
Hausle, Matthias, firm H. & Son, h. 133 Gen.
Hausle, Paul, firm Bettinger & Co. b. 146 Gen.
Hausle & Son, hardware and dry goods, 146 and 148 E. Genesee.
Hausler, George, carp. h. 65 Maple.
Haven, Solomon G. att'y, 7 Co'rt, h. 34 W. Gen.
Havens, E. S. h. 2 Park place.
Havens, J. S. county trea. office, b. 5 Franklin.
Havens, Leander, stove-mounter, h. 2 Chestnut.
Havens, Seely W. pattern-maker. 141 Clinton.
Hawes, S. W. firm Atwater & H. b. 29 7th.
Hawk, Wm. Thos. harness maker, b. Canada House.
Hawkins, E. W. joiner, h. Fulton n. Red Jack.
Hawkins, Geo. clerk, with Wm. Hawkins, b. 59 S. Division.
Hawkins, Isaac, ship carp. h. Abbott n. Elk.
Hawkins, John W. b. 59 S. Division.
Hawkins, John, barber, Southern Hotel, h. 52 Bennett.
Hawkins, Mrs. L. boarding house, 36 W. Sen.
Hawkins, Wm. lumber dealer, River n. Erie basin, h. 59 S. Division.
Hawks, Thos. S. news depot, 10 E. Seneca, h. 41 Franklin.

Hawley, E. J. firm M. S. H. & Co. b. Bonney's Hotel.
Hawley, E. S. sup't. B. L. and N. Works, h. 287 Pearl.
Hawley, Lucien, sec'y Buff. Ag'l M. Works, h. 292 Ellicott.
Hawley, Lucinda, widow, b. Niag. n. Bouck av.
Hawley, Mary A. widow, h. Seneca cor. Hea'k.
Hawley, M. S. pres. Int. Bank, h. Niagara sqr.
HAWLEY, M. S. & CO. com. merchants, 18 and 19 C. Wharf.—*See adv. p. 35.*
Hay, Isabella, wid. of Jno. h. Gen. n. Terrace.
Hay, M. W. milkman, 28 Carroll.
Haycraft, H. J. musician, b. 44 Pearl.
Hayden, Benj. h. Niagara cor. Clinton avenue.
Hayden, James, hostler, 144 Exchange.
Hayden, John, tallyman, h. Mackinaw n. Ala.
Hayden, Marg't, widow, h. Clinton n. Emslie.
Hayden. Sevilla, widow, b. 180 Franklin.
HAYEN, JACOB F. dealer in tob. and cigars, 5 Terrace, h same.—*See adv. p. 74.*
Hayes, Geo. E. dentist, 247½ Main, h. 1 S. Div.
Hayes, James, machinist, h. 158 Carroll.
Hayes, James A. painter, 293 Seneca.
Hayes, John, lab. h. Louisiana n. South.
Hayes, Robt. P., U. S. Ex. office, h. 165 Pearl.
Hayes, Teddy, fireman, h. Ohio cor. Illinois.
Hayes, Pat. lab. h. Chicago n. Elk.
HAYFORD, RILEY, firm G. O. Vail & Co. Wash. Dock, foot of Chicago, b. North W. of Delaware.—*See adv. p. 61.*
Hayward, Chs. firm H. & Selmser, h. 33 Niag.
Hayward, C. firm Selmser & Co. h. 33 Niagara.
Hayward, Emma, widow, h. Abbott n. Martin's Corners.
Hayward, G. W. firm Beard & H. h. 32 E. Swan.
Hayward & Selmser, prod. com. 16 Central Wharf.
Haywood, Geo. F. clerk, h. Virginia n. 11th.
Haywood, G. F. clerk, Marshall & Harvey, h. Virginia n. 10th.
Hazard, Ed. foreman, W. E. Co. h. 58 E. Swan.
Hazard, Geo. S. & Co. prod. com. mer. 25 Central Wharf, h. 71 Delaware.
Hazard, John H. ass't foreman, W. E. Co. h. Cold Spring.
Hazard, John R. firm G. S. H. & Co. b. 71 Delaware.
Hazard, Morris, 1 Central Wharf, h. Main opp. Barker.
Hazard, Morris, clerk, b. Main cor. Northampton.
Hazell, Eli, machinist, h. 153 Eagle.
Hazell, John, engineer, b. 174 N. Division.
Hazell, Thos. with Pratt & Letchworth, h. 26 Hickory.
Hazell, Wm. clerk, b. 26 Hickory.
Hazell, Wm. baggage master N. Y. C. R. R. b. City Hotel.
Hazteck, Henry, carpenter, h. Elm n. Genesee.
Hazy, John, lab. Iron place, N. Washington.
Heacock, E. S. Mrs. widow, b. 35 Pearl.
Heacock, R. B. Mrs. widow, h. 35 Pearl.
Heacock, Grosvenor W. pastor, h. Main ab. High.
Heacock, Samuel, h. Main n. Delavan avenue.
HEAD, JOSEPH A. prod. com. and cheese mer. 60 Main, h. Johnson pl.—*See adv. p. 38.*

Healy, Dennis, plumber, h. 89 Carroll.
Healy, John, lab. h. 5th n. Carolina.
Healy, Mary, widow, h. Albany n. School.
Hearne, Henry, clerk, 131 Main, h. Folsom n. Chicago.
Heath, John, type founder, b. 117 Seneca.
Heath, Richard, shoemaker, h. 55 Exchange.
Heather, R. W. saloon, Canal n. Commercial.
Heather, Wm. painter, h. 41 Union.
Hebard, J. F. engineer. h. 162 9th.
Hebard, J. H. engineer, h. Clinton n. Monroe.
Hebenstreit, G. John, watchmaker, 186 Main, h. Genesee n. Ellicott.
Heber, Joseph, brickmaker, h. Clinton n. Smith.
Hebron, James, currier, 187 S. Division.
Hebron, Mary, Miss, dressmaker, h. 187 S. Div.
Hebron, Stephen, join 'r, h. 187 S. Division.
Heceler, G. piano maker, with A. & J. Keogh.
Heck, Geo. lab. h. 10th n. Massachusetts.
Heck, Peter, J. Head. b. Mrs. Seeber, Batavia.
Heckel, Conrad, brewer, h. 290 Elm.
Heckel, Gottlieb, clerk, 28 Main, h. cor. Pine and William.
Heckel, G. A. grocer, cor. Fulton and Hamburgh, h. same.
Heckel, John, lab. h. Locust n. Carlton.
Hecker, Charles, clerk, b. Wash. n. High.
Hecker, widow, h. Washington n. High.
Hecker, John, cap maker, over 119 Genesee.
Hecker, Joseph, carriage maker, h. 22 7th.
Heckl, J. lab. h. Locust n. Carlton.
Heckl, Peter, barber, Main cor. Swan, h. 60 S. Division.
Heckler, Catharine, widow, h. over 75 Cherry.
Heckler, John, ship carp. h. Main cor. North.
Heckler, Peter, musician, h. 122 E. Genesee.
Heckler, Peter, lab. h. North n. Main.
Hecox, W. H. att'y, h. 261 Franklin.
Hederwick, John, h. Perry n. Hayward.
Hedge, Chas. L. book-keeper, b. 28 S. Division.
Hedges, Edwin, organ maker, h. Eagle n. Walnut.
Hediger, Henry, cap maker, h. over 138 E. Genesee.
Hediger, Jacob, shoemaker, 10th cor. Maryland.
Hediger, M. b. 10th cor. Maryland.
Hedzel, Aug. h. Hickory n. William.
Heeb, John M. blacksmith, h. Genesee cor. Herman.
Hefferton, Wm. lab. h. 157 Elk.
Heffler, John, lab. h. Jefferson n. William.
Hefford, Thos. builder, Elm n. N. Division, h. 19 Oak.
Hefrin, Catharine, widow, b. 97 Hospital.
Hegel, Gottlieb, baker, Locust n. Virginia.
Hegen, John, carpenter, h. 56 Bennett.
Hehr, Wm. porter, 205 Main, h. Batavia opp. arsenal.
Heibach, Edw'd, butcher, h. Batavia n. Watson.
Heibach, Geo. butcher, Peckham cor. Watson, h. same.
Heidelbach, Geo. grocer, h. Clinton n. Cedar.
Heidenreich, Andrew, saddler, 167 Batavia.
Heider, Philip, lab. h. Madison n. Batavia.
Heighton, Wm. saloon, 7 Revere Block, h. same.
Heihl, Deibold, chair maker, h. 120 Pratt.
Heilback, Susan, widow, h. Cherry n. Va.
Heilig, Geo. lab. h. Adams n. Brown.

Heilmann, Barb. widow, h. Potter opp. arsenal.
Heim, Jos. lab. h. Grey n. Batavia.
Heimann, Nicholas, basket maker, h. Genesee n. city line.
Heimann, Michael, lab. h. Jefferson n. Gen.
Heimentz, Ad. saloon, Ohio n. Mich. h. same.
Heimerle, Chas. warehouseman, h. 133 Elm.
Heimerle, Catharine, widow, h. 50 Bennett.
Heimerle, Henry, saw filer, 78 William.
Heimerle, Michael, finisher, h. 18 Mortimer n. Genesee.
Heimler, Jos. stone cutter, h. Goodell n. Mich.
Heimlich, C. hardware and stoves, 348 Main, h. Genesee n. Hickory.
Heimlich, Geo. lab. h. 92 Hickory.
Heimlich, H. Chris. match manuf. 234 E. Genesee, h. same.
Heimlich, Louis, at 12 Central Wharf, h. 191 N. Division.
Heimlich, Michael, varnisher, h. Mortimer n. Genesee.
Heimlich, P. J. Jr. prod. and com. 12 Central Wharf, h. 191 N. Division n. Cedar.
Hein, And. tool maker, h. Batavia n. Spruce.
Hein, Catharine, Mrs. h. 485 Washington.
Hein, Geo. mason, h. Grey bet. Genesee and Batavia.
Hein, Geo. carpenter, h. Parish n. Thompson.
Hein, Michael, cooper, h. Goodell n. Oak.
Hein, Valentine, lab. h. Monroe n. Batavia.
Heine, Gottfried, porter, h. Tupper cor. Oak.
Heinold, Michael, lab. h. Williamsville road n. Batavia plank road.
Heinold, Michael, Jr. brewer, b. Genesee E. toll gate.
Heinrich, Aug. tailor, h. Wm. n. Cedar.
Heinrich, Barnard, saloon, 3 Canal.
Heinrich, Chas. peddler, h. Spruce n. Genesee.
Heinrich, Cris. lab. h. Hickory n. Clinton.
Heinrich, John, lab. h. Pratt n. William.
Heins, Diebold, carpenter, h. Sycamore n. Ash.
Heintz, Geo. moulder, h. Pratt n. William.
Heintz, Jas. carpenter, b. 117 Pratt.
Heintz, Jno. carpenter, h. 109 Pratt.
Heintz, Martin, carpen er, h. Pratt n. Wm.
Heinz, Adam, painter, h. Pratt n. Clinton.
Heinz, Chas. clerk, 28 and 30 Main, h. Franklin n. North.
Heinz, Henry, lab. h. Watson n. Peckham.
Heinz, Jacob, lab. h. 16 Ash.
Heinz, John, carpenter, h. 119 Pratt.
Heinz, Jos. moulder, h. Spring n. Chamberlain.
Heinz, Marzolf, tailor, h. Boston alley n. Va.
Heinz, Peter C. moulder, h. Peckham n. Watson.
Heinz, Peter, painter, b. 242 Ellicott.
Heinze. Adolpho C. with J. H. Chase, h. Oak cor. Tupper.
Heinze, Chas. G. book-keeper, Dart Bros. h. 181 N. Division.
Heinzer, Jas. lab. h. 102 Batavia.
Heinzman, Ernst, cooper, h. Syc. opp. Keens.
Heiser, Frank, blacksmith, h. Bennett.
Heiser, Peter blacksmith, h. 7th n. Hospital.
Heiser, Wm. mach'st, b. Seneca opp. Hamb'gh.
Heisler, Wm. tailor, h. over 94 E. Genesee.
Heisner, Jos. carp. h. Boston al. n. Burton al.
Heistend, Christian, ship carp. h. Hayward n. Perry.

Heiszler. Jac. grocer, Main n. Ferry, h. same.
Heit, Henry, teamster, h. Dearborn n. Farmer.
Heitz, Eustachius, shoemaker, h. Spring n. Syc.
Heitzhous, Henry, boiler maker, b. 155 Elm.
Heitzhous, Mary, wid. tailoress, h. 155 Elm.
Heitzman, Conrad, milkman, Gen. n. Jeff.
Heitzman, Jno. cooper, German al. n. Sycamore, h. Mortimer n. Sycamore.
Heitzman, Leopold, farmer, h. Dearborn n. Amherst.
Heitzman, Louis, cooper, h. Genesee n. Jeff.
Hekman, Jacob, lab. Cherry n. William.
Helbling, Jos. stone cutter, h. Mulberry n. Vi.
Held, Bernhard. lab. h. Genesee n. Adams.
Held, Fred. firm Brunck H. & Co. b. Mansion.
Heldebrandk, B. lab. h. High n. Johnson.
Helfer, Chas. blacksmith, h. 59 Cedar.
Helfrich, Barbara, wid, h. Pratt n. Sycamore.
Hellenbrecht, Catharine, wid. Wal. n. Clinton.
Hellenbrecht, Wm. b. Walnut a. Clinton.
Heller, Christ.* wagon maker, h. Monroe n. Bat.
Heller, Jno. wagon maker, 562 Seneca, b. same.
Hellinger, Geo. carp. h. Monroe n. Sycamore.
Hellriegel, Conrad, h. Batavia cor. Pratt.
Hellriegel, Conrad, clerk. Howard, Whitcomb & Co. h. Genesee cor Elm.
Hellriegel, Henry, shoe store, 8 Com'l, h. same.
Hellriegel, Henry, grocer, h. 576 Main.
Hellriegel, John, Jr. clerk, Post-office, b. Batavia cor. Ellicott.
Hellriegel, Marg. widow, h. 349 Genesee.
Hellriegel, Philip, Mrs. grocer, h. cor. Genesee and Elm.
Hellriegel, Philip L. with Sherman & Barnes, h. 351 Genesee.
Hellriegel, Wm. H. with Sherman & Barnes, b. 349 Genesee.
Hellriegel, Wm. bakery, 356 E. Gen. h. same.
Hellwic, Marg. widow, h. 258 Franklin.
Helm, Morris, h. 153 N. Division.
Helmuth, Jno. carpenter, h. Wm. n. Monroe.
Helpeau, Joseph, lab. iron works, 4th ave. n. N. Washington.
Helstonn, Thos. lab. Exch. n. N. Y. & E. R. R.
Helt, Peter, shoemaker, b. L. Buehl.
Helwig, J. organ maker, h. Watson n. Peckh'm.
Helz, Jos. Sr. shoemaker, h. Adams bel. Syc.
Helz, Jos. Jr copper smith, b. Adam n. Bat.
Heman, Fred. lab. b. Spruce n. Batavia.
Hemann, Jac. tanner, h. S. Div. n. N. Y. C. R.R.
Hemborg, Joseph, lab. h. 99 Oak.
Hemenway, Edwin, conductor, N. St. R. R. b. 155 Delaware.
Hemenway, Emily, widow, h. 234 Ellicott.
Hemenway, H. B. clerk, b. 23 Ellicott.
Hemenway, Israel, butcher, h. Conn. n. 13th.
Hemenway, Silas, h. Georgia n. 7th.
Hemming, R. firm Wheeler, H. & Co. chromotypers and relief engravers, 161 Main, h. 33 Eagle.
Hemphling, Michael, cooper, h. Military road n. Amherst.
Hemstreet, Abr. mechanic, h. 14 E. Mohawk.
Hemstreet, B. F. house mover, h. 14 Mohawk.
Hemstreet, John, lab. h. Seneca n. Heacock.
Hemstreet, Wm. ship carp. h. Alabama n. Elk.
Henaner, Margaret, widow, h. Grey n. Gen.
Henderson, Alex. h. Delaware ave. E. Main.

Henderson, Albert N. electrician, 186 Main, h. 66 Swan.
Henderson, Chas. H. clerk, b. 12 Eagle.
Henderson, Edward, Jr. with A. M. Clapp & Co. b. 12 Eagle.
Henderson, Henry, agent Ontario steamers, cor. Erie and Canal, h. cor. Va. and Terrace.
Henderson, Jno. barber, b. Spruce n. Batavia.
Henderson, Rich. mason, h. 171 Elm.
Hendler, Matthias, lab. h. Stanton n. Batavia.
Hendrick, Herman, lab. h. cor. Wm. and Cedar.
Hendrick, John, iron works, h. Thompson n. Amherst.
Hendryck, Geo. sailor, h. 5th n. Georgia.
Hendry, James, sailor, b. 5th n. Georgia.
Heneage, Robert, machinist, 4 7th.
Henize, Adolpho C. with J. H. Chase, b. Oak cor. Tupper.
Henkel, Henry, cap store, 125 Main, h. same.
Henkes, John, carp. h. Watson n. Peckham.
Henkin, Christian, gardener, h. Utica n. Jeff.
Henking, Ernest, gardener at Prospect Hill, cor. York and 6th, h. same.
Henking, E. Mrs. pattern emporium, 370 Main.
Henn, Chas. P. engineer, h. Pratt n. Clinton.
Henn, Charles, tailor, h. 57 Exchange.
Hennebach, John, farmer, Amherst n. city line.
Henneberger, Daniel, cabinet maker, Genesee n. Kaene.
Henner, Joseph, grocer, 5 Sycamore.
Hennerberger, Philip, mason, h Mich. n. High.
Hennes, Adam, laborer, h. Best cor. Elm.
Hennesay, Mich. warehouseman, h. 27 Scott.
Hennesey, Dan. mason, h. Clinton n. Ravine.
Hennesey, John, boatman, h. 100 6th.
Hennesse, Thomas, grocer, Smith Block, Exch.
Hennesy, Pat. shoemaker, at 43 E. Seneca, h. 91 Hospital.
Hennig, Herman, grinder, h. 3 Tupper.
Henning, G.* boot-maker, 20 S. Div. h. same.
Henning, Michael, cooper, h. Dearborn n. Amherst.
Henricks, G. H. laborer, h. Walnut n. William.
Henry, Abigail, Mrs. h. 443 Main.
Henry, F. J. clerk, 207 Main, h. 322 Ellicott.
Henry, Jacob, miller, h. Niagara n. Hamilton.
Henry, James, barber. 204 Washington, h r. Wash. St. Baptist Church.
Henry, Nicholas, grocer, cor. Spruce and Gen.
Henry, S. H. Vulcan foundry.
Henschel, Julius, sailor, h. Walnut n. Batavia.
Hensel, John G. lab. h. 239 Elm.
Hensen, John, cab. maker, h. Bat. n. Sherman.
Henshaw, C. H., U. S. Exp. Co. b. Bloomer's.
Hessy, Dan. boiler maker, b. Michigan n. Ba'.
Hentz, — finisher, h. Michigan n. Sycamore.
Henz, Nicholas, finisher, h. Monroe n. Syc.
Hepp, Matthias, cooper, h. Locust ab. Cherry.
Hepp, Michael, lab. h. Adams n. Genesee.
Hepp, Otto, machinist, h. 70 Bennett.
Heppel, Leonhardt, lab. h. Locust n. High.
Heppner, August, lab. h. 53 Cherry.
Hepworth, Jos. cab. maker, h. 90 Franklin.
Hepworth, Wm. H. with Hamlin & Mendsen, h. 6 W. Huron.
Herbach, Auguste, Mrs. milliner, 83 E. Gen.
Herbach, Daniel, carp. h. 83 E. Genesee.
Herbein, Joseph, barber, 295 Main, h. 1 Wm.

Herbein, Michael, shoemaker, h. cor. Carolina and 5th.
Herberg, Augustus, Jr. instrument maker, h. Elm cor. Genesee.
Herberg, Gustave, piano maker, A. & J. Keogh, h. 115 Genesee.
Herbert, Thos. cartman, b. Walnut n. Wm.
Herbert, Theresa, widow, h. 119 Batavia.
Herberg, Emil, music teacher, ov. 113 Gen.
Herbold, Fred. grocer, 142 Genesee, h. same.
Herbold, Geo. gardener, h. Delaware n. Allen.
Herbold, Martin, baker, 188 Elm, h. same.
Herbst, Conrad, lab. h. Maple n. High.
Herbst, Geo. tailor, h. Michigan n. Best.
Herbst, Michael, lab. h. Peach n. High.
Herbst, Ulrich, blacksmith, N. Y. C. R. R. works, h. Monroe n. Peckham.
Herbst, Wolfgang, lab. h. Monroe n. Batavia.
Herd, B.* tinsmith, 235 Genesee, h. same.
Herdel, John, cooper, h. Thompson n. Amherst.
Herger, Chas. clerk, 299 Main, h. Washington n. High.
Hering, Peter, carp. h. Kaene n. Genesee.
Herkel, Fred. lab. h. Watson n. Peckham.
Herlan, John J. wagoner, Genesee cor. Spring, h. Mulberry n. Goodell.
Herlan, John J. wagoner, h. Pine n. Batavia.
Herlan, Wm. clerk, 21 E. Eagle, b. Pine n. Bat.
Herland, Jacob, wagoner, h. 112 Pine.
Herle, Alois, shoemaker, h. 401 Michigan.
Herle, Annie, widow, h. Sycamore n. Spruce.
Herle, Geo. tailor, Main cor. Swan, h. Spruce n. Batavia.
Herle, Henry, shoemaker, h. 23 Ash.
Herle, Michael, lab. h. Best n. Oak.
Herlein, —, wagoner, h. 142 E. Genesee.
Herman, Christian, teamster, h. Adams n. Syc.
Herman, Geo. lab. h. Clinton bel. Emslie.
Herman, Jacob, moulder, German al. n. Gen.
Herman, John, clothing store, 2 Genesee, h. 439 Michigan.
Herman, John, blacksmith, h. German alley n. Genesee.
Herman, John, blacksmith, h. Arsenal.
Herman, Laney, wid. h. Peckham n. Watson.
Herman, Louis, with Hollister & Laverack, h. 203 Ellicott.
Hermann, Chas. with C. E. Felton, b. 52 Delaware place. *
Hermann, Christian, shoemaker, Hickory n. Clinton.
Hermann, Jacob, gardener, h. Gen. n. Jeff.
Hermann, John, clothing store, 2 W. Genesee, h. 410 Michigan.
Hermann, Jos. grocer, h. cor. Clinton and Pine.
Hermann, Louis, carpenter, 18 Maple.
Hermann, Michael, tailor, h. Hickory n. Gen.
Hermatte, Jacob, lab. h. Camp n. Sycamore.
Hermen, Anna M. widow, h. 52 Del. place.
Herniman, Henry, joiner, h. 13th n. Ct.
Herniman, Robt. carp. h. 12th n. Vermont.
Herold, Adam, carp. h. Hickory n. Sycamore.
Heron, Ed. firm Prothais & H. h. 12 Main.
Heron, P. R. saloon, 2 and 4 Main. h. same.
Herr, Francis J. grocer, Best n. Oak.
Herr, Fred. lab. h. 225 Elm.
Herr, George, baker, Maple opp. Burton alley n. Goodell.

Herr, Jacob, shoemaker, h. 139 Genesee.
Herr, Vitas, peddler, h. 55 Maple bel. Va.
Herrick, James, lab. b. cor. Scott and Elk St. Market.
Herring, Adam, carp. h. Genesee opp. Grey.
Herring, John H. truckman, h. 256 S. Division.
Herring, Wm. carpenter, h. 311 E. Seneca.
Herrington, Anna, seamstress, b. 119 Batavia.
Herrington, Jane, widow, h. 119 Batavia.
Herrman, Jos.* butcher, Vermont n. 13th.
Herrmann, Christopher, keeper of arsenal, h. same.
Herrmann, J. H.* shoemaker, h.* Mich. n. Bat.
Herron, John, foreman. gas works, h. 43 Jack'n.
Herrop, James, engineer, gas works, h. 14th n. Hospital.
Herscher, Michael, lab. h. Watson n. Batavia.
Herschler, Henry, machinist, b. Clinton n. Spring.
Herschler, Jacob, engineer, h. Clinton n. Spring.
Herschler, Mary, Mrs. wid. b. Clinton n. Spring.
Hersee, Benj. cabinet maker, b. 344 Wash.
Hersee, Harry, cabinet maker, 241 Main, h. 344 Washington.
Hersee, James, chair maker, 241 Main, h. 344 Washington.
Hersee, James, Mrs. dressmaker, h. Wash. cor. Chippewa.
Hersee, Martha, Mrs. h. 344 Washington.
Hersee, Thompson, firm H. & Timmerman, h. 371 Washington.
Hersee & Timmerman, furniture dealers, 307 and 309 Main.
Hersee, Thomas, engineer, b. 2 Marvin.
Hersee, Wm. book-keeper, 307 Main, b. 344 Washington.
Herth, John, lab. h. Bundey alley n. Sycamore.
Hertel, Ferdinand,* dyer, h. Syc. n. Michigan.
Hertel, Fred. dyer, 6 Court, h. Sycamore n. Michigan.
Hertil, Geo. lab. h. 215 Elm.
Hertkorn, Ambrose, cabinet maker, h. 170 Oak.
Herttell, John C. b. Louisiana n. Carroll.
Herttsough, Martin, lab. h. Batavia cor. Mad.
Hertzberger, Jno. carp. h. Mulberry n. Goodell.
Herzberg, Martin, carp. h. 95 Goodell.
Hesler, Conrad, lab. h. Cherry n. Virginia.
Hess, Francis, colporteur, h. Carlton n. Oak.
Hess, Frank, shoemaker, 182 S. Div. h. same.
Hess, Geo. shoemaker, h. Locust n. Carlton.
Hess, Geo. shoemaker, 14 Main, h. Tupper n. Elm.
Hess, Geo. h. Monroe n. Sycamore.
Hess, Henry, carp. h. Utica n. Rhode Island.
Hess, Henry, engineer, h. Eagle n. Walnut.
Hess, Jacob, lab. h. Mackinaw n. Alabama.
Hess, Jacob, grocer, Fulton n. Chicago.
Hess, John, type founder, h. Hickory n. Syc.
Hess, John, blacksmith, with John Weeks, h. William n. Pine.
Hesse, Charles, baker, 175 Elm, h. same.
Hesse, E. umbrella maker, h. 103 Genesee.
Hesse, Fred. carpenter, h Batavia cor. Jeff.
Hesse, M. Mrs. milliner. 368 Main, h. 103 Gen.
Hesse, Peter F. umbrella maker, 368 Main, h. 103 Genesee.
Hesselschwerdt, Jacob, lab. h. 38 Hickory.
Hessinger, John, lab. h. Lemon n. Carlton.

Hester, Thomas. lab. h. 5th n. Virginia.
Heszler, Gottlieb, piano maker, with A. & J. Keogh, h. Johnson n. Batavia.
Hettick, C. clerk, Erie Co.; Savings Bank, h. Exchange n. Michigan. ·
Hettinger, Henry, lab. Forest ave. E. Walden.
Hettinger, Jn. cooper. h. Smith's alley n. Jeff.
Hettinger, John, clerk. b. J. Walker.
Hetto. John. lab. h. Thompson n. Parish.
Hettrich, John, lab. h. Adams n. Sycamore.
Hettrichs, Peter, tailor, 10s Exchange, h. same.
Hettrick, Christian, carp. h. Pine n. Batavia.
Hetzel. August, joiner. h. Hickory n. William.
Hetzel. Caroline, h. 405 Sycamore.
Hetzel, John, lab. h. Hickory n. William.
Hetzel, Saloma, h. Hickory n. William.
Heubach, H. butcher, h. Grape n. North.
Heuser. M. J. cooper, h. 575 Main.
Heusle, Chris. h. Walnut n. Batavia.
Hewett, Henry, lab. Exch. n. Alabama.
Hewitt, Delos, h. Vandalia n. Mackinaw.
Hewitt. Henry, moulder, b. 105 Carroll.
Hewitt, Sarah A. wid. h. 231 Pearl.
Hewson & Miller, carriage makers, 48 Exch.
Hewson. Wm. firm H. & Miller, h. Abbott road n. Whittmore's tavern.
Hey, John.* tailor. 15 Sycamore, h. same.
Heyer, Ferd'nd, tanner, h. Grange n. Chicago.
Heymann, Joachim, D. D. St. Mary's Church, h. same.
Heywood, R. H. flour merchant. h. 81 Seneca.
Hibbard, Andrew, caulker, h. Perry n. Ala.
Hibbard, A. C. merchant tailor, b. Delaware ab. Allen.
Hibbard, D. J. G. book-keeper, 19 C. Wharf, h. Breckenridge n. N. Washington.
Hibbard, Daniel. h. Breckenridge n. Carlton.
Hibbard, Geo. B. atty. ov. International blk. h. 307 Pearl.
Hibbard, Henry, scale maker, b. Clinton n. Jefferson.
Hibbard, Levi, sailor, h. Canal bet. Lloyd and Hanover.
Hibbard, L. D. h. Delaware ab. Allen.
Hibbard, Sarah. milliner, h. 45 Clinton.
Hibbard. L. b. Western.
Hibsch, Michael, grocer, Eagle cor. Union.
Hibsch, Peter, carp. h. Cherry cor. Virginia.
Hickey, Andrew P. clerk, 334 Main, b. 210 Pearl.
Hickey, Chas. lab. h. East n. Bird.
Hickey, Hugh, lab. h. York n. Erie canal.
Hickey, James, lab. h. Ohio n. Chicago.
Hickey, John, printer, b. 28 Folsom.
Hickey, John L. clerk, 268 Main, b. 168 E. Seneca.
Hickey, Pat. carman, h. 168 Seneca.
Hickey, Pat. joiner, b. 111 Folsom.
Hickey, Pat. lab. h. Perry n. Chicago.
Hickey, Thos. grocer, cor. Perry and Indiana.
Hickey, Wm. carp. h. 36 Liberty.
Hickley, Geo. tailor, 27 N. Division, h. same.
Hickman, Ambrose, blacksmith, b. 68 Tupper.
Hickman, Arthur, blacksmith, Illinois n. Ohio, h. Carroll n. Chicago.
Hickman, Isaac, blacksmith, B. & S L. R. R. b. 131 N. Division.
Hickman, Thomas, machinist, h. 271 N. Div.

Hickmann, Wm. hostler, h. 10th n. Hampshire.
Hicks & Bro. boat shop, across creek.
HICKS D. CLINTON, Com'l Col. ov. 194 Main, h. 10th ab. Md.—See adv. opp. second cover inside.
Hicks, Geo. shoemaker, 55 Exchange, h. same.
Hicks, John, boatman, h. 144 9th.
Hield, Martin, carp. h. Hickory n. Sycamore.
Hieling, Philip, chairmaker, with S. D. Sikes.
Hiemenz, Nich. brewer, 118 Batavia, h. same.
Hiemenz, Teresia, widow. h. 118 Batavia.
Hiemluz, Martin, lab. h. Madison n. Sycamore.
Hiente, Christian, lab. h. Pratt n. William.
Hiente, Jacob, painter, h. Pratt n. William.
Hiente, Jno. moulder, h. Pratt n. William.
Higgins, B. ship carp. b. Wm. Barker, Com'l.
Higgins, C. D. & Co. fish merchants, cor. Lloyd and Canal.
Higgins, C. D. firm C. D. H. & Co. h. 47 Frank'n.
Higgins, DeWitt. auction and commission merchant, 225 Main, b. Western Hotel.
Higgins, Edmond, saloon. Union basin, b. Ll'd.
Higgins, Edward, engineer, h. Cedar n. Eagle.
Higgins, Geo. C. book-keeper. b. Carroll n. Ala.
Higgins, John, clerk, 4 Exchange, b. St. James.
Higgins, Jno. C. N. Y. C. freight house h. 7th n. Carolina.
Higgins, Martin, lab. h. Mackinaw cor. Ky.
Higgins, Mat. gardener, h. towpath opp. work house.
Higgins, Mathew, joiner, h. 346 S. Division.
Higgins, Michael, lab. h. Michigan n. Carlton.
Higgins, Thos. sailor, h. 185 Terrace.
Higgins, Zenas, firm C. D. H. & Co. h. cor. Carroll and Alabama.
Higgins, Pat. drayman, h. cor. Terrace and Mechanic.
Higgins, Thos. lab. h. Perry cor. Indiana.
Higham, John B. h. 82 E. Seneca.
Higham, Mrs. h. 350 Seneca.
Highgate, Jno. currier, h. Hudson n. 6th.
Highland, Margaret, widow, h. across creek.
Highland, P. mariner, across creek.
Hikal, Jacob, gardener, h. r. Ferry n. Delaware.
Hil, Diebold, chairmaker, with Sam'l D. Sikes, h. Sycamore n. Ash.
Hilbert, John, tailor, 10 Maple.
Hilbert, John N. tinsmith, h. Oak n. Carlton.
Hilbert, Sylvester, brewer. b. J. Jost.
Hilburger, Tobias, lab. h. Herman n. Genesee.
Hildebrandt, Henry, shoemaker, 386 Main, h. 353 Michigan.
Hildebrant, Mich. lab. h. Monroe n. Peckham.
Hildreth, O. carp. h. cor. Church and Terrace.
Hilf, Henry, miller, Niagara n. Hamilton.
Hilfinger. Henry, shoemaker, b. 160 Clinton.
Hilfinger, John, moulder, h. Batavia n. Madis'n.
Hilfinger, Martin, watchmaker, h. Clinton n. Adams.
Hilgenack, Jno. joiner, h. 430 Michigan.
Hilgenberg, Wm. cigar maker, h. 277 Elm.
Hill, Annie G. washerwoman, h. 9 Terrace.
Hill, Anthony, blacksmith, h. Ash n. Sycamore.
Hill, Augustus, printer, Eveinng Post, h. William cor. Pine.
Hill, Chas. moulder, h. 280 Swan.
Hill, Chas. book-keeper, with O. H. P. Ramsdell & Co. h. 193 7th.

Hill, Davidson, salesman, 410 Main, b. 193 7th.
Hill, E. A. b. 217 Franklin.
HILL, F. C. tinsmith and stove dealer, 269 Main, h. 266 Washington.—*See adv. p. 62.*
Hill, Geo. at R. R. station, b. Globe Hotel.
Hill, Geo. iron works, h. Niagara n. Amherst.
Hill, H. F. lumber dealer, h. 217 Franklin.
Hill, Jas. cartman, h. Bristol n. Spring.
Hill, Jos. coppersmith, h. Adams n. Batavia.
Hill, Joseph, lab. h. ov. 8 Court.
Hill, J. F. firm J. F. H. & Co. h. 5 Union.
Hill, J. F. clerk, 269 Main, b. 266 Washington.
HILL, J. F. & CO. book store, 201 Main.—*See adv. p. 95.*
Hill, J. D. m. d 2 W. Eagle, h. 70 Delaware.
Hill, J. H. b. Western Hotel.
Hill, M. W. bot. phys. 245 Main, h. 93 N. Div.
Hill, Marcus, boarding house, 83 Carroll.
Hill, Martha, widow, h. Jefferson n. Howard.
Hill, Mary, mantilla maker, b. Mrs. Martha Hill.
Hill, Matilda, dressmaker, b. Mrs. Martha Hill.
Hill, Robert, with Jewett & Root, h. Perry n. Hamburgh.
Hill, Sam'l, potash maker, h. Jeff. n. Howard.
Hill, S. G. book-keeper, h. 104 6th.
Hill, Thomas, messenger American Express Company, h. 173 S. Division.
Hill, William, lab. h. 47 Jackson.
Hill, William, omnibus driver, h. 90 Carroll.
Hill, William, h. 128 Clinton.
Hillam, Wm. printer, Express office, h. 9 Vine.
Hillard, Avery, clerk, Noyes & Robey, h. Palmer ab. Virginia.
Hiller, Nicholas, tanner, h. 67 Hickory.
Hillman, Auguste, lab. h. La. bel. Mackinaw.
Hillman, F. sailor. b. Cypress n. Michigan.
Hills, Horace, broker, 247 Main, h. Washington cor. Lafayette.
Hills, John, woodworker, Brayley & Pitts.
Hills, Misses, ladies school, cor. Washington and Lafayette.
Hilt, Peter, lab. h. Amherst n. Lewis.
Hilton, A. W. printer, h. Morgan n. Niagara.
Hilton, Jno. P. at Jno. Weeks, h. York n. 15th.
Hilz, William, lab. h. 14th n. Vermont.
Himburg, Fred. bl'ksmith, h. Hickory n. Clint'n.
Himelsbach, Joseph, joiner and grocer, 11th cor. Virginia, h. same.
Himgardner, Jno. lab. h. 54 Cedar.
Himlington, David. b. Revere House.
Himmele, Geo. carpenter, h. Grey n. Batavia.
Himmelreich, Henry, lab. h. Tupper n. Oak.
Himminghofen, Chas. P. clothing store, 15 E. Genesee, h. same.
Hinde, Joseph G. mariner, h. 140 9th.
Hinder, Jacob, h. Maple n. Goodell.
Hinderberger, Peter, blacksmith, h. German alley n. Genesee.
Hindermeir, Jacob, lab. h. Grey n. Batavia.
Hindermeir, Jno. lab. h. Watts n. Batavia.
Hinderskirch, Alois, grocer, 569 Main, h. same.
Hines, Martin, Evans & Co's planing mill.
Hingston, Edward, ship carp. h. Miami n. La.
Hingston, John T. boat builder, foot Hudson. h. 6th n. York.
Hingston, Wm. boat builder, foot Hudson, h. 6th n. York.
Hinkley, A. S. m. d. homœopathist, 51 Ellicott.

Hinman, George W. 144 Main, b. 211 S. Div.
Hinman, R. W. captain, b. Western.
Hinnan, John, carp. h. n. Tifft's farm.
Hinson, George, attorney, over 152 Main, h. 11 Carroll.
Hintz, A. D. printer, b. 99 Swan.
Hinway, Michael, lab. towpath n. round house.
Hinze, Fred. firm Kurtzman & H. h. 437 Mich.
Hipbocher, John, painter, h. Bundey alley n. Sycamore.
Hipch, Annie, widow, h. 45 Cherry.
Hipch, George, moulder, b. 45 Cherry.
Hipch, Jacob, moulder, h. 45 Cherry.
Hipchen, Anth. moulder, h. Hickory n. Sya.
Hiple, Franz, bricklayer, h. 247 Elm.
Hipple, F. G. with Sherman & Barnes, h. 180 Cherry.
Hirn, John, lab. h. 4th n. Genesee.
Hirner, Christian, engineer, h. 22 Ohio.
Hirsch, Adolph,* tinsmith, 344 Gen. h. same.
Hirsch, A. S. b. 502 Washington.
Hirsch, Benjamin, tinsmith, b. 344 Genesee.
Hirsch, Josephine, Mrs. h. 502 Washington.
Hirsch, Magdelene, Mrs. h. 502 Washington.
Hirsch, Nicholas, locksmith, h. 502 Wash.
Hirsekorn, William, miller, Evans elevator, h. cor. Maiden lane and Fly.
Hirsh, Charles, brass finisher, h. 112 Mich.
Hirsh, Chris. C. clerk, h. 49 Delaware place.
Hirshbeck, Xavier, lab. h. 124 Elm.
Hirshberger, Michael, lab. h. Johnson n. North.
Hirt, Jacob, cooper, h. William n. Pine.
Hirtzel, John, lab. h. Stanton n. Batavia.
Hirzel, Lewis, grocer, Seneca n. Red Jacket.
Hiselwert, J. lab. h. r. 38 Hickory.
Histe, Joseph, miller, h. Thompson n. Amherst.
Hitchcock, F. b. Western.
Hichler, Henry," cooper, Spring above Gen. h. same.
Hitchler, Henry, b. H. Hitchler, Jr.
Hitchler, Michael, moulder, h. Mortimer n. Gen.
Hittler, George, farmer, h. Delavan avenue n. Williamsville road.
Hitzel, Jacob, mason, h. Carlton n. Jefferson.
Hitzel, Jacob,* butcher, h. 237 Gen. n. Hickory, h. same.
Hitzel, Jacob, tanner, h. Cedar n. William.
Hitzer, Adam, lab. h. Spring cor. Batavia.
Hitzer, Emily, dressmaker, b. Spring cor. Bat.
Hoag, Allen, hackman, b. 13 Pearl.
Hoag, D. fish dealer, h. 30 Pine.
Hoag, F. wood worker, Brayley & Pitts.
Hoag, Frank, farmer, Delavan avenue n. Williamsville road.
Hoag, Jacob, Sr. h. Delavan avenue n. Kraster road.
Hoag, Jacob, Jr. h. Delavan avenue n. Kraster road.
Hoag, Jos. farmer, h. Elk n. Red Jacket Hotel.
Hoag, Margaret, milliner, h. cor. Perry and Hayward.
Hobacre, Louis, teamster, b. Niagara n. Breck.
Hobein, Adam, lab. h. Pratt n. Clinton.
Hobson, Thomas, tinsmith. Adams n. Clinton.
Hoch, John, brewer, h. German alley n. Syc.
Hoch, John, lab. Samuel Eley, b. same.
Hoch, Julius, lab. h. Hickory n. Batavia.
Hochheiner, Nicholas, lab. h. Adams n. Brown.

Hochraeder, John, lab. h. Walnut ab. Batavia.
Hochreiter, Jno. lab. h. Hickory n. Batavia.
Hochstaetter, Nicholas, moulder, h. Pine n. Batavia.
Hochstater, Christian, pastor, Lutheran Church, h. same.
Hock, Frederick, clerk, with Sherman & Co. h. 39 Spruce.
Hock, John, butcher, 115 Batavia, h. 10 Bennett n. Batavia.
Hock, Patrick, lab. h. off Elm n. Louisiana.
Hocker, Jno. cooper, h. cor. Scott and Burwell.
Hockin, G. boatman, h. 11 William.
Hoddick, Fred. melodeon maker, h. 227 Oak.
Hodge & Baldwin, joiner shop and lumber yard, Delaware ab. Allen, h. Niag. cor. Carolina.
Hodge, Benj. pomologist, h. Main cor. Utica.
Hodge, Jasper, policeman, b. cor. Utica and Maryland.
Hodge, Lyman D. attorney, 8 Spaulding's Exchange, b. Main cor. Utica.
Hodge, Philander, firm Farnham & H. h. 187 Franklin.
Hodge, P. A. attorney, 7 Seneca, b. 29 Swan.
Hodge, V. builder, firm H. & Baldwin, h. Delaware n. North.
Hodge, William, Mrs. h. Main cor. Utica.
Hodge, Wm. h. Delaware n. Utica.
Hodge. Wm. lab. h. Ferry E. Walden.
Hodgekins, Ellen, b. Mrs. M. Hodgekins.
Hodgekins, Mary, wid. h. Bidwell n. Niagara.
Hodgekins, Thomas, clerk, H. O. Cowing, b. Mary Hodgekins.
Hodges, Hillary, butcher, h. 11th n. Virginia.
Hodges, Lewis L. proprietor American Hotel.
Hodges, Preston L. clerk American, b. same.
Hodgkins, Jas. mechanic, b. Mrs. M. Hodgekins.
Hodgson, George, tallyman B. N. Y. & E. R. R. h. South n. Hamburgh.
Hodgson, Mathew, tallyman, B. N. Y. & E. R. R. b. Exchange cor. Michigan.
Hodgson, Robert, clerk, B. N. Y. & E. R. R. b. Exchange cor. Michigan.
Hoefeller, Lewis, firm H. & Bros. h. 174 Swan.
Hoefeller, Nathan, firm H. & Bros.
Hoefeller, S. & Bros. clothing, 140 Main.
Hoefeller, Segmund. firm H & Bros. h. 174 Swan.
Hoefler, George, lab. h. Cedar n. Batavia.
Hoeffler, Conrad, with Thomas Clarke, h. Wm. below Jefferson.
Hoefle, George, cabinet maker, 160 Elm, h. Goodell n. Oak.
Hoefle, John,* cooper, William cor. Spring, h. Davis n. Sycamore.
Hoeffner, John, plasterer, h. 248 Elm.
Hoefner, Barbara, widow, h. Cedar n. Batavia.
Hoefner, Jacob, lab. h. Hickory n. Batavia.
Hoefner, Vincence, lab. b. Hickory n. Bat.
Hoehl, Valentine, barber, h. and shop Niagara n. Amherst.
Hoehn, Anna M. widow, h. Elm n. Best.
Hoehn, Fred. mariner, h. r. 184 Oak.
Hoein, Casper, lab. h. Shumway n. Park ave.
Hoellerer, Andrew, potter, h. Best n. Oak.
Hoenes, George, tailor, h. Locust n. Carlton.
Hoenes, Henry,* turner shop, h. Madison cor. Batavia.
Hoepfner, H. A. printer, h. 11 Cedar.

Hoepner, Frederick, chair maker, h. Maple cor. Virginia.
Hoernlein, John, turner, h. 239 Oak.
Hoernlein, Jacob, turner, b. 239 Oak.
Hoernlem, Wm. turner, b. 239 Oak.
Hofer, John, tailor, b. Boston alley n. Jeffn.
Hoff, August, carp. h. Adams n. Batavia.
Hoff, Christian, lab. h. 61 Maple.
Hoffer, Fred.* butcher, 374 Main, h. 85 Elm.
Hoffer, Fred. Jr. clerk, b. 85 Elm.
Hoffer, George, butcher, 155 Ellicott.
Hoffer, George, butcher. h. Smith's alley n. Jefferson.
Hoffer, J. S. saloon, cor. Water and Maiden lane.
Hoffer, Michael, shoemaker, h. Amherst above Niagara.
Hoffer, Peter, lab. h. Vine alley n. Elm.
Hoffman, Abraham, at 40 Pearl, h. Delaware bel. Virginia.
Hoffman, Adam, saloon, 6 State n. Canal.
Hoffman, Augustus, lab. h. Bristol n. Spring.
Hoffman, C. wood worker, Brayley & Pitts.
Hoffman, Chas. teacher, h. 83 Elm.
Hoffman, Christian, blacksmith, h. German alley n. Genesee.
Hoffman, Conrad, carp. h. Ketchum n. Carlton.
Hoffman, Daniel. h. Hamilton n. Thompson.
Hoffman, Frank, lab. h. Goodell n. Maple.
Hoffman, Frank, nailsmith, Genesee cor. Spruce, h. same.
Hoffman, Frank, machinist, b. Hickory n. Wm.
Hoffman, Fred. butcher, h. Vine alley n. Mich.
Hoffman, Fred. weaver, h. 39 Cherry.
Hoffman, Florian, lab. h. S. Division n. Emslie.
Hoffman, Henry, barber, 85 E. Genesee, h. same.
Hoffman, Jacob, bricklayer, h. Mulberry n. Carlton.
Hoffman, Jacob, tailor, h. Walnut n. William.
Hoffman, Jas. lab. h. 438 Michigan.
Hoffman, John, lab. h. Goodell n. Cherry.
Hoffman, John, gardener, h. Hamilton n. Thompson.
Hoffman, John, lab. h. Goodell n. Elm.
Hoffman, John, gas fitter, h. 14 Bennett.
Hoffman, John, piano maker, b. Goodell cor. Elm.
Hoffman, Joseph, mason, h. 94 Hickory.
Hoffman, Jos. lab. h. 553 Michigan.
HOFFMAN, JULIUS, variety store, 294 Main, h. 147 Ellicott.—See adv. p. 79.
Hoffman, Leonard, grocer, h. cor. Adams and Peckham.
Hoffman, Mary, h. r. Virginia garden.
Hoffman, Michael, lab. 115 Pratt.
Hoffman, Michael, milkman, h. William cor. Roos alley.
Hoffman, Michael, lab. Clinton n. Smith.
Hoffman, O. iron finisher, Brayley & Pitts.
Hoffman, Peter, turner, 160 Elm, h. Vermont n. Rock.
Hoffman, Peter, lab. h. Hickory n. Batavia.
Hoffman, Peter, clerk, W. G. Fox, 195 Main.
Hoffman, Philip, lab. h. Maple n. High.
Hoffman, Phocian, attorney, 2 Exchange, h. 38 Goodell.
Hoffman, S. grocer, h. Forest avenue n. R. R. track.

Hoffman, Valentine, brewer, h. Main cor. St. Paul.
Hoffman, Wm. shoemaker. h. Pratt n. Syc.
Hoffman, Wm. lab. h. Mulberry n. High.
Hofman, Louis, shoemaker, h. 53 Walnut.
Hofman. Sam. peddler, h. 64 Spring n. Batavia.
Hoffmeier, John, mason, h. 407 Michigan.
Hoffmeyer, —, student, M. L. College, h. Maple n. Virginia.
Hoffmeyer, Caspar, h. Niag. n. Forest avenue.
Hoffmier, Lewis, grocer, Niagara cor. Mass.
Hofhaltz, Chas. lab. h. Locust n. Mulberry.
Hofheins, A. huckster, h. 192 Seneca.
Hofheins, Alex. tinsmith, 190 Seneca.
Hofheins, Chas. lab. h. Locust n. Virginia.
Hofheins, Elias, bricklayer, h. Locust n. Va.
Hofheins, George F. milk dairy, h. Genesee n. tollgate.
Hofheins, Michael, lab. h. Locust n. Virginia.
Hofner, Anselm, firm Ritt & H. h. Van Rensselaer n. Exchange.
Hog, Jos. bookstore, Batavia n. Arsenal place.
Hog, Jos. Jr. b. Jos. Hog, Sr.
Hogg, John, cooper, h. Perry n. Alabama.
Hogan, Chas. b. 83 Elliott.
Hogan, Chas. ruler, 94 Tupper.
Hozan. Jas. confectioner, h. 91 Hospital.
Hogan, Jas. lab. h. Perry n. Hamburgh.
Hogan, Margaret, widow, h. 2 Elk.
Hogan, Michael, painter, h. Carolina n. 5th.
Hogan, Pat. boarding, Ohio n. River.
Hohenstein, Chris. car maker, 15 E. Eagle, h. Goodell n. Oak.
Hohenstein, Henry, blacksmith, b. Goodell n. Oak.
Hohl, Emil, 129 Genesee, h. same.
Hohler, Julius, brewer, with P. Welsh, b. Clinton n. Cedar.
Hohman, John, blacksmith, h. Locust n. Va.
Hohmann, Geo. gas factory, h. 512 Michigan ab. Tupper.
Hoist, John, farmer, Military road, bet. Philips road and city line.
Holbrook, Anthony, tanner, b. cor. 7th and Hudson.
Holbrook, Dee & Co. dry goods, 320 Main cor. Swan.
Holbrook, Edwin A. firm H. Dee & Co. h. 113 Delaware.
Holbrook, H. b. Western.
Holbrook, Wm. clerk, b. 66 S. Division.
Holchar, Henry, lab. h. r. 92 Sycamore.
Holden, Chas. blacksmith, h. Eagle bel. Spring.
Holden, Christiana, widow, h. 142 S. Division.
Holder. John, barber, 4 Water, h. 1 Water.
Holf, Christian, lab. 61 Maple.
Holfelner, Mathias, grocer and carp. h. Batavia cor. Pine.
Holl, Jacob, lab. h. Watson n. William.
Holl, John, lab. h. Pine n. Batavia.
Holl, Philip, wagon maker, 131 Sycamore n. Spruce.
Holl, Wm. cigar maker, h. Batavia n. Pratt.
Holland, Dennis, mariner, h. 92 6th.
Holland, Otis, carpenter, h. 10th n. Virginia.
Holland, Tim. lab. h. Erie canal n. Fort Porter.
Holledreher, John, grocer, Batavia n. Jefferson, h. same.

Holleran, Ellen, widow. h. South n. creek.
Holleran, Pat. lab. h. Thompson n. Amherst.
Hollerieth, Mathias, grocer, 405 Main, h. same.
Hollerith, Geo. bonnet rooms, 272 Main, h. same.
Holley, Chas. lab. b. 54 E. Swan.
Hollfelder, John, carp. h. Michigan n. North.
Hollfelder, Stephen, lab. h. Adams n. Sycamore.
Hollister, James, flour dealer, Central Wharf, h. 128 Franklin.
Hollister, John. h. 488 Main.
HOLLISTER & LAVERACK. grocer, drugs, etc. 202 Washington.—See adv. p. 40.
Hollister, Robert, firm H. & Laverack, h. 450 Main.
HOLLOWAY. ISAAC. stone yard, Michigan and canal. h. Del. n. North.—See adv. p. 68.
Holloway, John, Mrs. widow, h. Franklin n. Allen.
Holly, Allen, horse bucket manuf. h. Bristol n. Spring.
Holm, Ludwig, tailor. h. 531 Michigan.
Holman, E. D. grocer, 145 Main, b. 400 Franklin.
Holman, Wm. confectioner, 136 Main, h. cor. Hayward and Otto.
Holmes, B. firm E. & B. H. h. 63 S. Division.
Holmes, Daniel W. school teacher, b. 127 Chippewa.
Holmes, Edward, firm E. & B. H. h. 63 S. Div.
Holmes, Elizabeth, widow, h. 66 Ellicott.
Holmes, Emmet, lab. Prospect hill vineyard.
HOLMES, E. & B. lumber and planing mill, Michigan n. C. R. R.—See adv. p. 90 and 91.
Holmes, Henry S. printer, h. 2 Court.
Holmes, Isaac, lab. h. lake shore road n. Tiff's farm.
Holmes, J. B. book-keeper, h. 71 William.
Holmes, Mary, widow. shirt maker, b. 36 Franklin.
Holmes, Mary, Mrs. h. r. 435 Main.
Holmland, Wm. carp. h. Madison n. Howard.
Holsch, John, cabinet maker, h. Maple n. Va.
Holschar, Henry, with Hodge & Baldwin, b. 82 Sycamore.
Holschue, Mary, widow, h. Mich. n. Genesee.
Holser, Jno. J. japanner, h. 365 Michigan.
Holshau, John, lab. h. Marvin n. Elk.
Holsiag, John, moulder, h. Oak n. Goodell.
Holst, M. A. lab. h. Cedar n. William.
Holt, A. F. tobacco peddler, h. Ct. n. 13th.
Holt, A. J. com. merchant, 14 and 15 C. Wharf.
Holt, J. ship carp. b. Western Railway House.
Holt, John, brewer, h. Grey n. Batavia.
Holtz, Fred. tailor, h. Clinton bel. Pratt.
Holtz, John, cooper, h. East n. Austin.
Holtz, Wm. lab. h. cor. East and Hamilton.
Holtzschub, Jacob, lab. h. 60 Bennett.
Holzborn, Louis, grocer, Elk cor. Louisiana.
Holzhausen, August, blacksmith, Genesee cor. Oak, h. same.
Holzler, Margaret, widow, h. Boston alley n. Tupper.
Holzworth, C. hay and grain dealer, Market cor. Fulton, h. same.
Homan, Benjamin, h. 37 N. Division.
Homan, Phineas, asst. editor Daily Republic, b. 28 Carolina.

Hombe, Fred. tailor, h. 130 Sycamore.
Hombe, Fred. Jr. tailor, b. 130 Sycamore.
Homelius, Henry, shoemaker, b. 407 Michigan.
MOMER & CO. crockery merchants, 175 Main.
—See adv. p. 83.
Homer, Peter, piano maker, b. 512 Michigan.
Hommalaars, P. P. bl'ksmith, h. Exch. n. Mich.
Homsberger, John, lab. h. Grey n. Batavia.
Hon. Henry, tailor, h. 299 Ellicott.
Honeck, Adam, mason, h. 220 Genesee.
Honeck, Fred. chair maker, 160 Elm, h. 136 Genesee.
Honer, Frank, soap maker, h. Keane n. Gen.
Hong, Samuel, lab. h. Carroll n Heacock.
Hoodenbacher, Wm. tailor, b. 2 Water.
Hook, Henry, milkman, b. r. 338 Genesee.
Hook, Thos. blacksmith, Terrace cor. Henry, h. Ash n. Genesee.
Hooker, Grace, widow, with Sherman & Barnes, b. 83 Franklin.
Hoole, Joseph T. h. 223 Niagara.
Hooper, John, lab. h. Tonawanda n. Niagara.
Hoople, James, baggageman, h. 6th n. Md.
Hootlocker, Wm. Mrs. widow, h. Delaware n. Barton.
Hopfel, Barbara, widow, h. Monroe n. Syca.
Hopfel, Geo. lab. h. Monroe n. Sycamore.
Hopkins & Co. com. merch'ts, 8. Cent. Wharf.
Hopkins, Chas. A. firm H. & Co. b. Huron cor. Main.
Hopkins, Charles M. h. 3 E. Mohawk.
Hopkins, Evan, h. Forest avenue n. Dewitt.
Hopkins & Halbert, attorneys, 2 Exchange.
Hopkins, James A. finisher, b. 56 Folsom.
Hopkins, John, saloon, h. Water cor. Erie.
Hopkins, John O. policeman, h. Jefferson cor. S. Division.
Hopkins, Jos. clerk, 249 Main, b. 3 E. Mohawk.
Hopkins, Josiah, lab. h. cor. Swan and Elm.
Hopkins, Nelson, under sheriff, h. 210 Frank.
Hopkins, Nelson K. firm H. & Halbert, h. Linwood avenue n. Bryant.
Hopkins, Sarah A. widow, 36 7th.
Hoppman, H. marble polisher, h. Spring n. Wm.
Hora, Mary, widow, h. Adams n. Genesee.
Horan,Wm. C. printer, Courier office, b. 20 Pine.
Horch, Peter, carp. h. Grey n. Genesee.
Horin, Jas. watchman, at Wood & Co. h. Scott n. Washington.
Horlzer, Jacob, moulder, h. 338 Michigan.
Hormell, Geo. tanner, b. Carroll n. Van Renss'r.
Horn, Ann M. widow, h. 104 Cedar.
Horn, Francis, lab. h. Mulberry n. Virginia.
Horn, Leonhard, lab. h. German alley n. Gen.
Horn, Louis, shoemaker, h. Madison n. Peck'm.
Horn, Michael, lock maker, h. Keane n. Gen.
Horn. Philip, moulder, h. 2 Bennett.
Hornbeck, Jas. clerk, b. Perry n. Chicago.
Hornbeck, Maria, widow, h. Perry n. Chicago.
Hornbecker, C. sawyer, with A. & J. Keogh.
Hornberger, Conrad, cabinet maker, h. 50 Del. place.
Hornbuckle, Richard, brick maker, h. Batavia n. toll gate.
Hornburg, Wm. bootmaker, 20 S. Div. h. 34 Maple.
Hornecker, Jos. saloon, 319 Genesee, h. same.
Horneye, Conrad, tailor, h. 156 Cherry.

Hornick, S. N. clerk. 172 Main, b. 23 Church.
Horning, Wm. tinsmith, h. ov. 3 Court.
Hornung, Andrew, tailor, h. 296 Elm.
Hornung, Chas. street paver, Genesee cor. Elm.
Hornung. John. blacksmith, h. Mortimer n. Gen.
Horrell. Howell, farmer, Main n. Chapin.
Horrigan, Sarah, wid. h. Chicago n. Merrimack.
HORTON, A. W. prod. com. mer. 10 Central Wharf, h. 287 S. Division—See adv. p. 35.
Horton, C. M. agt. E. Corning, 30 and 32 Pearl, h. 33 W. Seneca.
Horton, Jas. shoemaker, 278 Main, h. 6 Cedar.
Horton, Jno. M. with E. Corning & Co. b. 38 W. Seneca.
Horton, Jno. lab. h. Delavan avenue n. Main.
Horton, Wm. farmer, h. 10th n. Maryland.
Horvitz, T. clothing, 99 Main, h. same.
Hosford, A. b. 32 Union.
Hosford, J. h. 32 Union.
Hosford, William, b. 32 Union.
Hosmer, Alb. keeper Fort Porter, h. 2 Carol'a.
Hosmer, Chas. G. cabinet maker. Niagara cor. Virginia, h. Virginia n. Niagara.
Hosmer, E. J. with Robt. Thomas, b. 83 Niag.
Hosmer, Geo. H. with Pratt & Letchworth, b. 83 Niagara.
Hosmer, Geo. W. Rev. h. 83 Niagara.
Hosmer, L. L. shoemaker. h. Carolina n. Niag.
Hosmer, Park S. upholsterer, b. 165 Niagara.
Hosmer, Silas, upholsterer, h. 165 Niagara.
Hossong, L. cooper, h. 34 Union.
Hotchkiss, Fred. A. grocer, Maryland cor. Palmer, h. same.
Hotchkiss, Hiram, jeweler, 210 Main, h. 2 Car'y.
Hotchkiss, J. W. jeweler,* 189 Main, h. 364 Franklin.
Hotchkiss, Margaret, Mrs. b. 478 Michigan.
Hotchkiss, Mary, widow, h. Pooley place n. Bird avenue.
Hotchkiss, Thos. b. with Mary Hotchkiss.
Hotchkiss, T. W. lumber dealer, River n. basin, room 6, over Mathews & Talman.
Hotchkiss. Wheeler. h. 7th cor. Carolina.
Hott, Ernst, teamster, h. Best E. Jefferson.
Hotter, Jacob, carpenter. h. r. 99 Pine.
Hottinger, And. mason, h. Brown n. Adams.
Hottinger, Jos. stone quarry, h. Bat. n. city line.
Hottinger, J. M. clerk, b. 15 Main.
Hottinger, Martin, saloon, 15 Main, h. same.
Hottum, Jno. G. carp. h. Spring n. Sycamore.
Hottum, Jno. G. capt. h. Bat. n. Mortimer.
Houck, Gabriel, b. P. Houck.
Houck, Jno. saddler, at 285 Main, h. Vermont bet. 9th and 10th.
Houck, Philip, flour store, h. 91 Genesee.
Houck, Valentine, machinist, h. 13th n. Conn.
Hougbataling, John W. conductor, L. S. R. R. h. 91 N. Division.
Houghton, Geo. W. firm Talcott & H. h. 447 Main.
Houghton, Henry, painter. h. 107 Eagle.
Houley, Michael, lab. h. Exch. n. R. R. cross'g.
Houlighan, Thos. blacksmith, h. r. 119 Bat.
Houschld. John, lab. h. 44 Krettner.
House, Abner, mariner, h. 197 7th.
HOUSE, GERRITT, organ builder, Clinton opp. new court house, h. 43 Ellicott.—See adv. p. 72.

Houser, Chs. lab. h. bet. Clinton and William on city line.

Houser, Geo. carpenter, h. Park n. Allen.

Houser, Matthias, lab. h. Clinton n. Raze.

Houser, Michael, peddler, h. Jeff. n. Howard.

Hovey, D. A. jeweler, 266 Main, h. 346 Wash.

Hovey, Josiah, h. 346 Washington.

How, Nich. lab. h. 46 Grape.

Howard, A. h. Staats cor. Howard.

Howard, Austin A. attorney, ov. 279 Main, h. North n. Delaware.

Howard, Daniel, pump and block maker, Evans cor. Water, h. 49 Oak.

Howard, Ethan H. firm H. Whitcomb & Co. h 45 W. Genesee.

Howard, Geo. firm Bush & H. h. 88 E. Swan.

Howard, Gibson F. ass't book-keeper, with R. L. H. b. 99 Delaware.

Howard, Harry, lab. b. 111 Carroll.

Howard, Henry, sec'y Buffalo Sav. Bank, h. 443 Main.

Howard, H. E. cash'r Marine Bank, h. 440 Main.

Howard, John, lab. h. 11 William.

Howard, R. L. prop. Howard's Agricultural Works, Chicago n. canal, h. 99 Delaware.

HOWARD, WHITCOMB & CO. dry goods merchants, 207 Main and 216 Washington. —See adv. p. 87.

Howard, Wm. rope maker, h. Pooley place.

Howard, W. S. com. merch. 9 Cent. Wharf, h. 309 Pearl.

Howard, Wm. b. 49 Oak.

Howard, Wm. H pump maker, b. 49 Oak.

Howard's Agricultural Works, Chi. n. Canal.

Howcutt, John, storage and commission, store warehouse foot Washington.

Howe, Henry H. prod. and com. merch. Lloyd cor. Prime, h. 29 Swan.

Howe, Joseph H. painter, h. 12th n. Pennsl'va.

Howe, Joseph H. boarding house, 27 Ohio.

Howe, Mary E. widow, h. 107 9th.

Howe, O. B. com. merch. 13 Prime, b. Mans'n.

Howell, Daniel, Jr. tailor, h. 209 N. Div.

Howell, Jas. G. Supt. Wilkeson's Elevator, b. 62 E. Swan.

Howell, Jas. R. carver and gilder, 439 Main, h. Virginia n. 11th.

Howell, John, firm H. & Smith, h. 276 Ellicott.

Howell, Luther, gardener, h. 11th n. Pa.

Howell, Porter A. tallyman, B. & L. S. R. R. h. 28 N. Division.

HOWELL & SMITH, bottling establishment, and vinegar manufacturers, 35 E. Seneca.— See adv. p. 50.

Howell, S. W. firm Dunbar & H. merch. miller, cor. Dearbon and Amherst.

Howell, Wm. carver and gilder, 439 Main, h. 11th n. North.

HOWELLS, JAMES, contractor, and stone dealer, h. 169 S. Division.—See adv. p. 69.

Howland, Hannah, widow, h. High n. Peach.

Howland, Chas. ice dealer, 4 Brown's Buildings, h. 181 Niagara.

Howland, Holder, policeman, 151 Franklin.

Howland, Marcus, h. 181 Niagara.

Howland, Theo. 4 Brown's Build. h. 181 Niag.

Howland, Thos. capt. on lake, h. 259 N. Div.

Howley, Edward, grocer, 231 E. Seneca.

Hoy, John, boarding house, 49 Ohio.

Hoy, Louis, tailor, h. 14 Bennett.

Hoyer, F. F. M. D. Erie County Poor House, residence Tonawanda.

Hoyer, Lorenz, tailor, h. Alabama n. Elk.

Hoyt, Benjamin, foreman car shop, N. Y. C. R. R. h. 184 N. Division.

Hoyt, Bradley, lumber contractor, h. Bird ave. n. Washington.

Hoyt, Gabriel, lumber dealer, cor. Genesee and River, h. 112 E. Eagle.

Hoyt, James G. attorney, cor. Court and Main, h. 176 Pearl.

Hoyt, John G. mechanic, h. Elk n. Hayward.

Hoyt, John G. joiner, h. Louisiana cor. Allen.

Hoyt, N. B. saw mill, h. Bird ave. n. DeWitt.

Hoyt, Orson C. M. D. h. 498 Washington.

Hoyt, Polly, widow. h. Niagara cor. Rhode Is.

Hoyt, Seth, ag't N. Y. C. R. R. h. 101 Folsom.

Hoyt, Wm. B. with Morton. Foot & Co. h. 2 6th.

Hoyt, William H. with E. F. Cromwell, h. 176 Pearl.

HUBBARD, CHAS. J. Globe Foundry, cor. Carroll and Chicago, h. 151 E. Swan.—See adv. p. 61.

Hubbard, Geo. L. insurance agent, 5 Spaulding's Exchange and 15 Central Wharf, h. 119 Delaware.

Hubbard, Jas. G. foreman B. N. Y. & E. repairing shop, h. 255 E. Swan.

Hubbard, J. S. Am. Ex. Co. h. 92 W. Huron.

Hubbard, Linus P. book-keeper, 239 Main, h. 70 S. Division.

Hubbard, Milton R. station master, N. Y. C. R. R. h. Parish n. Dearborn.

Hubbard, Ozias, wood yard, h. 132 6th.

Hubbard, Robt. A. clerk, with G. L. Hubbard, b. 119 Delaware.

Hubbard, S. J. book-keeper, L. S. R. R. b. 126 Swan.

Hubbell, Alfred S. firm Wood, H. & Co. h. Mansion House.

Hubbell, Dan. V. bar tender, Carr's saloon, h. Genesee House.

Hubbell & Davis, atty's, 14 Spaulding's Exch.

Hubbell, H. S. firm Wood, H. & Co. h. Mans'n.

Hubbell, Jno. firm H. & Davis, h. 272 Pearl.

Hubbell, Orrin M. hostler, h. 109 Clinton.

Hubbell, Selim B. ship carp. h. 159 S. Div.

Hubbell, William C. b. 159 S. Division.

Hubbers, Henry, peddler, h. Bat. n. Sherman.

Hubel, Joseph, tailor, h. 139 Batavia.

Hubel, R. lab. h. 139 Batavia.

Hubele, F. shoemaker, h. 180 N. Division.

Huber, Benedict, lab. h. William n. Cedar.

Huber, Emil, A. book-keeper, h. 414 Ellicott.

Huber, Gottlieb, peddler, h. Walnut n. Syca'e.

Huber, Jno. cooper, h. Dearborn n. R. R.

Huber, John, tailor, h. Walnut n. Batavia.

Huber, Joseph, carp. h. Walnut n. Batavia.

Huber, Marcus, peddler, h. Genesee n. Grey.

Huber, Marcus, lab. h. Rogers n. Vermont.

Huber, Mary A. widow, h. 249 Elm.

Huber, Mary, widow, h. William n. Cedar.

Huber, Mary, Miss, h. 110 Batavia.

Huber, Mathias, lab. h. 70 E. Tupper.

Huber, Michael, moulder, h. Hickory bet. Clinton and William.

Huber, Miss, music teacher, h. 6 Court.
Huber, Stephen, watchman, h. Hickory bet. Clinton and William.
Huber, Victor, lab. h. Walnut cor. Batavia.
Hubert, Ludwig, lab. h. 581 Washington.
Hubner, Jno. tailor, h. 113 Pine.
Huck, Jacob, lab. h. Niagara n. South.
Huck, John, ship carpenter, h. 8 Bennett.
Huck, Philip J. saloon, 184 Oak, h. same.
Hucker, Nathaniel, manager telegraph, Spaulding's Exchange, h. 11 Johnson place.
Huckerby, Jas. maltster, h. North n. Ellicott.
Hucksted, Thomas, lab. with P. A. Balcom, h. Ferry n. Jefferson.
Hudson, A. C. clerk, Niagara steam forge, b. 29 E. Swan.
Hudson, B. lab. h. Washington n. Clinton.
Hudson, Geo. tallyman, h. South n. Hamburgh.
Hudson, John T. attorney, old P. O. buildings, b. American Hotel.
Hudson, Jos. W. paper hanger, h. 89 E. Seneca.
Huddleston, Thomas, lawyer, b. 283 Pearl.
Huebel, Ferdinand,* shoemaker, Niagara cor. Morgan, h. same.
Huebsch, Geo. carp. h. Sherman n. Batavia.
Huelmantel, Bernhard, tailor, h. Bat. n. Hick'y.
Huenfeld, F. butcher, cor. 5th and Ca. h. same.
Huetter, Chas. lawyer, 4 Arcade Buildings, h. Tupper n. Ellicott.
Huff, Maria, dressmaker, 2 W. Eagle, h. same.
Huff, Oliver W. grocer, 7th cor. Ca. h. same.
Huff, Silas, ship carpenter, h. 169 Elk.
Huff, Valentine,* blacksmith, Genesee n. Walden. h. same.
Huffman, Wm. lever man. h. Mulb'y n. High.
Hufnagel, Mich. lab. h. Smith alley n. North.
Huggins, Wm. H. painter, b. 262 Seneca.
Hughes, Dominic, lab. h. Exc. n. R. R. cross'g.
Hughes, Edward, lab. h. Exchange n. Smith.
Hughes, J. H. M. D. h. Michigan n. Carroll.
Hughes, John W. painter, 47 Seneca, h. 324 Michigan.
Hughes, Jno. sailor, h. Hickory n. Batavia.
Hughes, John, hackdriver, h. 137 Elm.
Hughes, Jno. pattern maker, h. 100 Hickory.
Hughes, John, lab. h. Hayward cor. Fulton.
Hughes, Jno. E. piano maker, h. 6th cor. Md.
Hughes, Mich'l, lab. h. Exc. n. R. R. crossing.
Hughes, Pat. ship carpenter, h. Miss. n. Perry.
Hughes, Pat. lab. h. Exchange n. Griffin.
Hughes, Pat. grocer, 19 Mississippi, h. same.
Hughes, Thos. engineer, cor. 5th and Pa.
Hughes, William, grocer, 274 Seneca cor. Kinney alley.
Hughes, Wm. butcher, Ohio n. swing bridge, h. same.
Hughs, Phelix, grocer, cor. ship canal and Water.
Hughson, George H. book-keeper, with R. L. Howard, h. 75 Carroll.
Hughson, Wm. peddler, h. cor. Vt. and 10th.
Hugron, Catherine, widow, Francis, h. Swan n. R. R. crossing.
Hugron, Lewis, engineer, N. Y. C. R. R. h. Seneca n. Spring.
Huijung, Herman, tailor, h. Pine n. Batavia.
Huk, Anton, blacksmith, h. Ash n. Genesee.
Hulbert, Ruth, widow, h. 11 Oak.

Hulbert, M. A. proprietor Niagara House, lower Black Rock.
Hulbert, Samuel, agent, office Niagara Falls depot, h. 74 Tupper.
HULL, D. B. proprietor of Western Hotel, Terrace cor. Pearl.—See adv. p. 92.
Hull, Ed. C. h. 329 E. Seneca.
Hull, J. Jr. wood worker, Brayley & Pitts.
Hull. Jacob, wood worker, Brayley & Pitts.
Hull. Jas. D. with Pratt & Letchworth, h. over 88 E. Seneca.
Hull, John, foundryman, Brayley & Pitts.
Hull, R. B. book-keeper, Roger & Co. b. 352 S. Division.
Hull, Robt. cartman, h. 352 S. Division.
Hull, Martin, mason, h. 14 E. Eagle.
Hull, Willard, farmer. Ontario n. Tonawanda.
Hulse, Andres D. machinist, h. cor. Hamburgh and Elk.
Humason, W. J. printer, Courier, b. 114 S. Division.
Humason, G. firm Bower & H. h. 114 South Division.
Humberger, George, lab. 38 Cherry.
Humberstone, Eliz. dressmaker, h. 1 Church.
Humberstone, John, h. 1 Church.
Humble, John, ship carpenter, h. 44 Pine.
Hume, Stevenson, h. 74 Perry.
Humell, J. clerk, 60 Niag. b. 69 6th.
Hummel, George, clerk, 400 Main, b. Genesee House.
Hummel, J. F. porter, 34 Lloyd, b. Hickory above Batavia.
Hummel, Mich'l, milkman, h. Clinton n. Pratt.
Hummel, Robt. carp. b. Moore n. Elk.
Hummel, Wm. carp. b. Moore n. Elk.
Hummel, William, varnisher, h. Lovejoy n. Krettner.
Humphrey, Arnold L. receiver, Niagara Falls depot, h. 15 6th.
Humphrey, Geo. cor. Canal and Evans.
Humphrey, Henry, saloon, 4 Lloyd, h. same.
Humphrey, James M. firm H. & Parsons, h. 294 Franklin.
Humphrey, James, with John Stevenson.
Humphrey, Jos. b. Lloyd opp. Sailors' Home.
Humphrey, M. T. clerk, American Express Co. b. 29 E. Swan.
Humphrey & Parsons, attorneys, old post office building.
Hungenger, Jacob, policeman, h. Hickory n. Genesee.
Hunn, Calvin B., U. S. Express office, h. Utica n. Main.
Hunn, D. L. Rev. h. Utica n. Main.
Hunn, Geo. clerk, at 147 Main, b. 139 S. Div.
Hunsche, Henry, lab. h. Boston alley n. Burton alley.
Hunsche, Henry, Jr. lab. b. Boston alley n. Burton alley.
Hunsche, William on R. R. h. 210 Elm.
Hunsenger, Michael, wagon maker, Niagara n. Hamilton, h. same.
Hunsinger, Charles, butcher, Niagara n. Parish, h. same.
Hunt, Horace, b. N. Pearl n. Virginia.
Hunt, John, with J. Adams & Co. b. Bonney's Hotel.

Hunt, Sandford, Rev. h. 76 Perry.
Hunt, Sanford B. m. d. editor Express and supt. of schools, h. N. Pearl above Virginia.
Hunter, Geo. prod. and com. mcht. 42 Main, h. 176 9th.
Hunter, George E. grocer, 2 Birkhead Building, h. same.
Hunter, John B. dealer in leather, hides and oil, 2 Birkhead Building, h. same.
Hunter, James, oil distiller, h. 77 Church.
Huntz, John, saloon, 6½ Commercial, h. same.
Huntziker, John, carp. b. Pratt n. Batavia.
Hup, J. blacksmith, Brayley & Pitts.
Huppman, Henry, marble cutter, h. Spring n. William.
Huppuh, Joseph, painter, 3 S. Division, h. 9th n Hudson.
Hurlbert, Edwin, wood dealer, Green rear N. Y. C. depot, h. 152 Franklin.
Hurley, James, lab. h. Ohio n. South.
Hurley, Lawrence, carp. b. Ct. n. 13th.
Hurley, Michael, lab. h. Ct. n. Erie canal.
Hurley, Timothy, blacksmith, h. 160 George.
Hurley, Timothy, lab. Ohio n. R. R.
Hurley, William, lab. h. 13th n. R. I.
Hurst, Jas. sawyer, h. Perry n. R. R. crossing.
Hurst, John, gardener, h. Waldron N. Best.
Huss, A. carp. between Genesee and Syc.
Huss, Anton, h. East n. Berry.
Huss, Florence, cooper, h. Pratt n. Genesee.
Huss, Louis, cigar maker, h. Wm. cor. Cedar.
Huss, Michael, cigar maker, h. Walnut n. Gen.
Husser, Wm. Mrs. widow, wax flower maker, h. 60 6th.
Hussey, John, policeman, h. Staats n. Court.
Hussy, Peter, blacksmith, h. 7th n. Hospital.
Hussong, Fred, baker, h. Clinton n. Spring.
Hussong, Louis, cooper, h. 12 Cypress.
Hussongs, C. grocer, h. Seneca n Dole.
Husted, Charles, tinsmith, b. 43 Union.
Husted, E. S. flour and feed, 41 Seneca, h. 45 Union.
Husted, Emeline T. widow, h. 99 Clinton.
Husted, E. piano tuner, b. 7th n. Pennsylvania.
HUSTED, E. & G. sash and blind, 142 Seneca. —See adv. p. 95.
Husted, Frank H. b. 115 Clinton.
Husted, Giles, sash and blind manufacturer, 140 Seneca, h. 38 Pine.
Husted, J. H. firm Hadley & H. 115 Clinton.
Husted, Samuel, clerk, D. M. Woodward, h 43 Union.
Husted, S. tinsmith, with Hadley & H. b. 43 Union.
Husted, Wm. H. painter, h. 276 Oak.
Husted, William H. h. 115 Clinton.
Husted, W. L. firm French & H. b. 115 Clinton.
Huster, Albert, tailor, h. Clinton n. Raze.
Hutchings, W. A. foreman, Shepard's boiler shop, h. Carroll n. Chicago.
Hutchins, C. B. m. d. office 238 Main, b. Mansion
Hutchinson, Elisha, m. d. h. 43 7th.
HUTCHINSON, JOHN M. leather dealer, 40 and 42 Lloyd, b. Chippewa cor. Georgia.— See adv. p. 43.
Hutchinson, William H. teller, White's Bank, h. 7th n. Georgia.
Huth, Francis, wagon maker, h. 12 Bennett.

Hutter, Sepher, butcher, with Richard Bullymore, h. cor. Ellicott n. Hampton.
Hutterer, Joseph. lab. h. over 171 Batavia.
Huyck, Gerritt, h. 117 Clinton.
Huyck, John H. clerk, 202 Washington, h. Southern Hotel.
Hutzler, Geo. lab. h. Johnson n. Genesee.
Hutzler, Joseph, lab. h. Johnson n. Genesee.
Huzzey, John, lab. h. towpath below Genesee.
Hyatt, Gilbert, clerk, street commissioner's office, h. 92 Clinton.
Hyatt, John, carp. h. Krettner n. Peckham.
Hyer, Francis, carp. h. 556 Michigan.
Hyman, B. & Son, 120 and 154 Main, h. 37 W. Seneca.
Hyman, B. firm B. H. & Son, h. 37 W. Seneca.
Hyman, Fred. lab. h. Spruce n. Batavia.
Hyman, H. firm B. H. & Son, b. 37 W. Seneca.
Hyman, Henry, clk. 154 Main, h. 37 W. Sen.
Hyman, Isaac, clothier, 122 Main. h. 4 Scott.
Hyman, Isaac. clk. b. 102 E. Seneca.
Hyman, Nicholas, clk. B. Hyman & Son, h. 33 Main.
Hynes, Michael. lab. b. 15 Mechanic.
Hynes, Owen, lab. h. 15 Mechanic.
Hynes, Peter, ship carpenter, b. 15 Mechanic.
Hyzer, L. H. 5 Central Wharf, b. 20 Carroll.

I.

Idrich, Conrad, dyer, 144 Batavia.
Ignatz, Andrew, tailor, h. Monroe n. Batavia.
Ignatz, Christ. carp. h. Monroe n. Sycamore.
Ihde, Fred. tailor, b. Walnut n. William.
Ihrig, Christian,* bakery, 374 Genesee, h. same.
Ihrig, Conrad, dyer, b. 142 Batavia.
Ihrig, Marg. E. wid. h. Herman n. Genesee.
Ihrig, Peter, stocking weaver, h. 247 Elm.
ILLINOIS CENTRAL R. R.—See adv. inside first cover.
Imel, Henry, lab. h. 106 Tupper.
Imlay, Louis, h. Moore n. Elk.
Ingalls, David S. grocer, 346 Main, h. same.
Ingalls, Geo. W. firm I. & Lamphier, h. 34 5th.
Ingalls & Lamphier, painters, 107 Main.
Ingersoll, Edward, Rev. h. 7 E. Mohawk.
Ingersoll, Edward S., U. S. Express Office, b. Rev. E. Ingersoll.
Ingersoll, Geo. cond. N. St. R. R. b. 9th n. Vt.
Ingersoll, M. paper and rag warehouse, 196 Washington, h. 36 Delaware.
Inglesant, Mary, widow, b. 140 Franklin.
Inglesant, Wm. K. with Altman & Co. b. 140 Franklin.
Inglis, Jas. book-keeper, comptroller's office, h. 10 Johnson place.
Ingman, Jas. cooper, h. Niagara n. Austin.
Ingram, Thos. h. N. Washington n. Forest ave.
Ingram, W. H. porter, 44 Main, h. Fulton n. Chicago.
Inman, Clarinda, Mrs. Ontario n. Tonawanda.
Inman, Geo. H. clerk, b. 43 Oak.
Inman, Geo. boiler maker, 260 Carroll.
Inman, Henry. foreman, Moores & White, 7 Swan, h. 43 Oak.
Inman, Henry, baggageman, N. Y. C. R. R. h. 23 6th.
Innes, Geo. clerk, 316 Main, b. 11 Oak.

Innes, Dan. clerk, Murray, Cumming & Grant, b. 5 Franklin.

Insenhoff, John, lab h. Johnson n. North.

Institution Deaf and Mute, Edward bet. Delaware and Morgan.

Iobe, John P. lab. h. Peckham n. Krettner.

Iresh, Robt. lab. b. cor. Perry and Elk st. mar.

Irish, B. G. clerk, with A. L. Mathews, h. Carolina bet. 6th and 7th.

Irish, C. G. clerk, h. 355 Michigan.

Irish, C. G. Jr. auction rooms, 5 and 7 W. Seneca, h. 126 E. Eagle.

Irlbacher, Geo. butcher, h. Monroe n. William.

Irlbacher, Jno. firm Irr & I. h. Oak n. Syc.

Irlbacher, Peter, gas fitter, h. Syc. n. Walnut.

Irmler, August, tailor, h. 106 Elm.

Irr, Geo. firm I. & Irlbacher. h. Oak n. Syc.

Irr & Irlbacher, plumbers and gas fitters, 1, 2, and 3 Mohawk.

Irvin, Francis, with Hamlin & Mendsen.

Irvin. James S. Jr. with S. & G. Husted, h. 16 Union.

Irvin, Jno. ship carp. b. 6th n. Maryland.

Irving, W. Jas. ship carp. h. Pratt n. William.

Irwin, Charles, dealer in sewing machines, J. Benton & Co. b. 35 Swan.

Irwin, Jas. S. shoemaker, h. Walnut n. Wm.

Isaac, Thomas, lab. h Ohio n. Chicago.

Isham, J. H. with Hamlin & Mendsen, b. 145 Pearl.

Isham. John, with Hamlin & Mendsen, b. Pearl ab. Court.

ITJEN, HENRY, Wash. Hotel, 15 Com'l.— *See adv. p. 92.*

Iuler, Balthaser, lab. h. Kaene n. Genesee.

Iuler. Jacob, carpenter, h. Kaene n. Genesee.

Iunemann, Fred.* carpenter, Del. n. North, h. Boston Alley n. Virginia.

Ives, J. H. gardener, Utica n. Michigan.

Ives, Wm. librarian, Y. M. A. h. 3 Park place.

J.

Jackle, C. wood worker. Brayley & Pitts.

Jackman, Jennie, Miss. teacher, b. 39 Oak.

Jackson, A. broker, 5 Exchange b. Mansion.

Jackson, A. chair maker. h. 220 S. Division.

Jackson, C. Mrs. widow, h. r. 447 Michigan.

Jackson, D. D. 27 Central Wharf, b. Western Hotel.

Jackson, J. exch. broker, 5 Exch. h. 130 Swan.

Jackson, Jas. sailor, h. Exchange n. Alabama.

Jackson, Jno. boot and gaiter fitter, ov. 7 Swan.

Jackson, John, sailor, h. Fulton n. Alabama.

Jackson, John, butcher, h. Summer n. Rogers.

Jackson, Josiah, chair maker, b. 220 S. Div.

Jackson, Josua, waiter, b. 11 William.

Jackson, Mat. paper hanger, h. Eagle n. Spring.

Jackson, Sam. chair maker, h. 220 S. Div.

Jackson, Wm. Cedar cor. Clinton.

Jackson, Wm. whitewasher, h. 95 Oak.

Jackson, Wm. lab. h. St. Paul n. Main.

Jacky, Frederick, lab. h. 236 Elm.

Jacob, Fred. drover, h. Genesee cor. Grey.

Jacob, Fridrich, lab. h. Genesee n. Mortimer.

Jacob, Louis, carp. h. Boston alley n. Tupper.

Jacob, Rudolph, b. 83 Elm.

Jacob, Rudolph, pattern maker, b. 214 Bata.

Jacob, Wm. keeper toll gate, McAdam road.

Jacobi, Herman,* shoemaker, 6 Water, h. same.

Jacobi, Henry, carp. h. 201 Genesee.

Jacobs, Gustav, clerk. h. 74 Tupper.

Jacobs, B. clerk, b. 33 S. Division.

Jacobs, Wm. lab. h. Adams n. Sycamore.

Jackson, Wm. butcher, h. St. Paul n Main.

Jaegel, Christ. butcher, h. Mulberry n. Carlton.

Jaeger, George, grocer, 145 Batavia, h. same.

Jaeger, Henry. cooper, h. Grey n. Genesee.

Jakla, Fred. shoemaker, b. E. Flacht.

Jainer, Wm. printer, b. Lutheran alley.

James, F. Rev. asst. pastor St. Patrick's Church, h. S. Division n. Emslie.

James, John, h. 217 Oak.

James, Nelson, grocer, 409 Seneca, h. same.

James, Richard, copper smith, h. Folsom n. Kinney's alley.

James, Susan, widow, h. 201 Carroll.

Jameson, Wm. W. teamster, with R. L. Howard, h. 3 William.

Jamison, Chauncey, farmer, h. Elk n. R'd Jack.

Jamison, Isaac, truckman, h. 126 Tupper.

Jamison, Jas. & Co. canal store and stables, 23 Canal.

Jamison, Jas. firm J. & Co. h. 28 Folsom.

Jamison, Jno. lab. h. 10 Tracy.

Jamison, J. A. sailor, h. Ohio n. Michigan.

Jamison, Wm. clerk, h. S. Div. n. Chestnut.

Jammison, S. Brooks, h. 42 N. Division.

Janaka, Henry, tailor, h. Locust n. Carlton.

Janes, Nelson, land agent, 2 Hollister Block, h. 111 E. Seneca.

Jangraw, Nicholas, saloon, 2 Canal.

Jann, Adam, lab. h. Sherman n. Genesee.

Jann, Barbara, midwife, h. Sherman n. Gen.

Jann, Mary Ann, widow, h. 139 Oak.

Jann, Michael, lab. h. Johnson n. High.

Janseu, Henry, harness maker, 6 Canal, h. Pine n. William.

Jarrett, James A. clerk, h. 136 S. Div.

Jarvis, Ralph L. engineer, h. Mariner n. Allen.

Jarvis, Roman, shoemaker, h. 23 Illinois.

Jarvis, William, cook, h. 66 Clinton alley.

Jaster, Louis, printer, h. Michigan n. North.

Jauman, Geo. lab. h. Bennett n. Batavia.

Jax, Frances, Miss, b. 110 Batavia.

Jax, John, mason, h. 110 Batavia.

Jax. John, mason, h. Jefferson n. Batavia.

Jearger,Chr. huckster, h. Spring n. Genesee.

Jefferson, Michael, firm M. J. & Son, tinsmith, Mohawk n. Niagara, h. same.

Jefferson, Thos. M. firm M. J. & Son, tinsmith, b. Michael Jefferson.

Jeffrey, Wm. carp. h. 6th n. Pennsylvania.

Jeffrey, Thos. blacksmith, h. St. Paul n. Main.

Jegel, Philip, carp. h. Carlton n. Lemon.

Jehle, Edward, clerk, with S. Boas, 224 Main.

Jenkins, J. L. clerk, Sherman & Barnes, b. 14 Clinton.

Jenkins, Lewis, b. 79 E. Swan.

Jenkins, R. Jr. Am. Exp. Co. h. 14 Clinton.

Jenkins, Sophia, Mrs. dressmaker, b. 54 6th.

Jenks, N. lab. h. Hickory n. Clinton.

Jenner, R. druggist, 438 Main, b. 436 Main.

Jennings, Thomas, sailor, b. 6 Commercial.

Jenrich, Fred. milkman, h. Fox n. Genesee.

Jensen, Thos.* cooper, Wash. cor. Perry, h. ov. P. Stanton, Washington.

Jerome, L. D. constable, h. 9th n. Vermont.

Jerrard, Peter, tailor, h. Ash n. Batavia.

Jerret, Henry, exp. messenger, Chicago n. Exch.

Jessamine, Jas. sail maker. h. 5th n. Georgia.

Jetter, Jacob, file cutter, 118 E. Genesee, h. same.

Jeubeau, Jos. boatman, Blossom n. Amherst.

Jeudevine, Charles B. printer, b. 124 Carroll.

Jeudevine, H.* shoemaker, h. 316 Michigan.

Jeutter, John C. clothing store, 497 Wash. h. same.

Jewell, Darius, painter, h. 71 N. Division.

Jewell, Harriett, widow, h. 124 Swan.

Jewell, James A. with Hollister & Laverack, b. 71 N. Division.

Jewett, E. M. firm E. R. J. & Co. 161 Main, b. Bonney's Hotel.

JEWETT, E. R. & CO. stationers and paper warehouse, 161 Main.—See ad. colored leaf opp. name.

Jewett, E. R. firm E. R. J. & Co. 161 Main, b. American.

Jewett, Henry C. clerk, Jewett & Root, b. 100 Delaware.

JEWETT, JOHN C. housekeeper's emporium, 259 & 31 Main, h. 102 E. Eagle.—See adv. colored leaf opp. name.

Jewett, J. J. L. C. firm Taylor & J. h. 21 Church.

JEWETT & ROOT, stove works, Miss. bet. Oak and Perry.—See adv. p. 43.

Jewett, S. S. firm J. & Root, h. 100 Delaware ab. Chippewa.

Jingerech, Conrad, firm G. Renner & Co. 281 Main, h. Ellicott cor. Burton.

Job, Dora, widow, h. 153 Sycamore.

Jobst, Chris. lab. b. Burton alley, n. Goodell.

Joeger, Maria, wid. h. cor. Cherry and Locust.

Joels, Nathan, peddler, h. 71 E. Tupper.

Joergers, Ignatz, blacksmith, b. 487 Wash.

Johan, Peter, engineer, h. Mulberry n. Carlton.

Johannes, Francis,mason, h. Ketchum n. High.

Johannes, Mich'l, mason, h. Ketchum n. High.

Johans, Peter M. painter, h. 34 Bennett.

Johe, Henry, cooper, b. Peckham n. Emslie.

Johe, Jacob,* baker, h. Batavia n. Spring.

Johe, William, cooper, h. Peckham n. Emslie.

John, Henry, wagon maker, b. Goodell n. Mich.

Johnson, Almer, engineer, h. 185 Eagle.

Johnson, Alonzo C. moulder, b. 113 Seneca.

Johnson, And. baker, h. Monroe n. Batavia.

Johnson & Bros. fish market, Lloyd n. canal.

Johnson, Boliver, prod. dealer, h. 95 Barker's block, E. Seneca.

Johnson, Carr, gardener, h. Maryland n. 6th.

Johnson, Chas. renovator, Pearl cor. Terrace, h. Bundy alley n. Sycamore.

Johnson, Chas. cook, h. cor. Hamburgh and Carroll.

Johnson, Chas. fisherman, b. N. Washington n. Auburn avenue.

Johnson, Chas. saloon, foot of Erie.

Johnson, Chas. E. clerk, at P. O. b. 16 E. Eagle.

Johnson, Chas. C. b. O. F. Presbrey.

Johnson, Chas. N. b. J. S. Johnson.

Johnson, C. H. book-keeper, b. Courter.

Johnson, D. shoemaker. 2 Commercial, h. Maiden lane cor. Fly.

Johnson. D. machinist, h. 346 Seneca.

Johnson, Edward, Frontier mills, b. N. Washington n. Auburn avenue.

Johnson, Elenor, Mrs. widow, 102 6th.

Johnson, Elenor, Mrs. widow, h. N. Washington n. Auburn avenue.

Johnson, Elizabeth, widow, h. 312 Ellicott.

Johnson, Frank, packer, Frontier mills, b. N. Washington n. Auburn avenue.

Johnson, Fry & Co. publishers, 190½ Main.

Johnson, Geo. fisherman, h. Porter n. Auburn avenue.

Johnson, Geo. glass stainer, 82 Main, b. 106 W. Huron.

Johnson, Geo. confectioner, 40 Pine.

Johnson, Geo. W. Am. Ex. Co. b. 157 E. Sen.

Johnson, Geo. W. attorney, office and h. 27 E. Eagle.

Johnson, Geo. P. M. Black Rock, h. Niagara n. Bouck avenue.

Johnson, Gerard, h. 63 6th.

Johnson, Guy, carpenter, h. 264 Seneca.

Johnson, Hamilton, sailor, b. 6 Commercial.

Johnson, Henry, carriage trimmer, h. 163 Cedar.

Johnson, Hiram, banker, h. 457 Main.

Johnson, James N. clerk, Chicago cor. Scott, b. 63 6th.

JOHNSON, JAS. M. book-binder, 161 Main, h. 45 Franklin.—See adv. p. 102.

Johnson, James E. mariner, h. Folsom n. Kinney alley.

Johnson, Jno. B. & Co. prod. and com. merch. Bullymore Block, opp. Elk st. market.

Johnson, J. B. firm J. B. J. & Co. Bullymore Block, h. 369 Franklin.

Johnson. John, carpenter, h. Hudson ab. 12th.

Johnson, John, truckman, h. Perry n. La.

Johnson, John, att'y, b. Delaware n. Allen.

Johnson, J. Girard, att'y, 3 Hollister building, b. L. D. Hibbard.

Johnson, J. S. firm Brown & J. h. 67 Pearl.

Johnson, J. W. engineer, h. 104 Walnut n. William.

Johnson, L. C. engineer, h. 102 Walnut n. William.

Johnson, L. F. blacksmith, h. 2 Cedar.

Johnson, Louis, lab. h. S. Division bel. R. R. track.

Johnson, Lucy, widow, h. 58 Lloyd.

Johnson, Mary, widow, nurse, h. 47 Delaware.

Johnson, Mathias, peddler, 104 Exchange.

Johnson, Michael, tailor, h. La. bel. Elk.

Johnson, N. B. tailor, 5 Beirnheimer Block, h. 156 Pearl.

Johnson, Peter, lab. h. on White's Corners plank road n. city line.

Johnson, Peter, boiler maker, b. Ohio n. River.

Johnson, Rebecca W. Miss, teacher, b. 9th n. Vermont.

Johnson, Renix, shoemaker, 16 Exch. h. same.

Johnson, Richard, b. N. Wash. n. Auburn ave.

Johnson, Robt. firm Young, Lockwood & Co. h. Utica n. Main.

Johnson, R. R. with W. O. Brown, h. Elk n. La.

Johnson, Samuel, machinist, h. 5th n. Hudson.
Johnson & Steward, wholesale grocers, Market n. Perry.
Johnson, Taylor, musician, h. 47 Genesee.
Johnson, Wallace, com. mer. 89 Main, h. 381 Franklin.
Johnson, Wallace, firm W. J. & Co. b. Franklin ab. Allen.
Johnson, Wells, eating house. Elk St. Market.
Johnson, Wm. blacksmith, b. cor. Ferry and N. William.
Johnson, William, lab. h. on White's Corners plank road n. city line.
JOHNSTON, ANDREW M. grocer, 52 Main, h. 161 S. Division.—*See adv. p.* 38.
Johnston, G. W. wood worker, Brayley & Pitts.
Joles, A. J. widow, h. Hudson n. 6th.
Jonas, John. lab. h. Batavia cor. Jefferson.
Jones, Adam, constable, h. 342 S. Div.
Jones, Albert, book-binder, at 196 Wash. b. 287 Michigan.
Jones, Chas. R. b. 108 E. Eagle.
Jones, Chas. S. agt. N. Y. associated press, h. 29 Johnson place.
Jones, Chapin W. with Miles Jones, h. Carey bel. Morgan.
Jones, Fred. ship builder, h. Del. n. Barker.
JONES, GEO. Buffalo Iron Railing Works, cor. Terrace and Henry, h. 108 E. Eagle.—*See adv. p.* 55.
Jones, Geo. H. with Geo. Jones, h. 20 7th.
Jones, Henry, lab. h. Goodell n. Michigan.
Jones, H. P. mer. tailor, 20 Arcade buildings, opp. American, h. 201 Franklin.
Jones Isaac A. for. and com. 10 C. Wharf, h. Del. n. Bryant.
Jones, Isabella, widow, nurse, h. Staats cor. Niagara.
Jones, James, peddler, h. 171 Elm.
Jones, James, lab. h. Conn n. Erie canal.
Jones, John, fish dealer, h. 165 S. Division.
Jones, John, gardener, Seneca junction Exch.
Jones, Jno. F. conductor N. Y. C. R. R. h. 268 E. Seneca.
Jones, Marsh N. cor. Dayton and Prime, h. cor. Georgia and Chippewa.
Jones, Mary, widow, h. Porter n. Bouck.
Jones, Mary Ann, widow, h. 203 7th.
Jones, Merlin, with Miles Jones. h. 8 9th.
Jones, Michael, milkman, h. Wm. n. Spring.
JONES MILES, pork dealer and inspector. Prime cor. Dayton, h. cor. Chippewa and Georgia.—*See adv. p.* 42.
Jones, Nathaniel, builder, h. 74 N. Division.
Jones, Peter, engineer, h. Mulberry n. Carlton.
Jones, Peter, gardener, h. North n. Ellicott.
Jones, Richard P. machinist, h. 75 6th.
Jones, Richard R. whitewasher, h. 137 N. Division.
Jones, Robert A. captain on lake, h. Cedar n. Eagle.
Jones, Stephen, sailor, b. Elk n. Louisiana.
Jones, S. Mrs. midwife, h. Wm. n. Spring.
Jones, Theodore, tailor, h. 10 Maple.
Jones, Thos. grocer, Fulton cor. Alabama.
Jones, Wm. blank book manuf. over 196 Washington, h. 287 Michigan.
Jones, Wm. G. butcher, h. Niag. n. Parish.
13

Jones, Wm. carp. h. Bundy alley n. Syc.
Jones, Wm. with Miles Jones, h. Carey bel. Morgan.
Jones, W. W. sign painter, h. Milnor n. Wm.
Jontion, Theodore, glass stainer, h. Milnor n. Batavia.
Jopp, F. H. silversmith, h. Batavia bet. Elm and Michigan.
Jopp, John. pattern maker, b. 27 Sycamore.
Jordan, Chas. sailor, h. Elk n. Louisiana.
Jordan, David. lab. 219 Carroll.
Jordan, Lydia E. widow, b. 10 Morgan.
Jordan, Martin, lab. h. 4th n. Genesee.
Jordan, Mathew, clerk, N. Y. C. R. R. h. Elk n. Smith.
Jordan, Patrick, ship carpenter, h. Tennessee n. Mackinaw.
Jordan, Samuel S. clerk, h. 131 Huron.
Jordon, Thos. sailor, h. Elk n. Smith.
Jordon, Thos. moulder, h. 33 Scott.
Jordon, John A. engineer, h. Hayward n. Elk.
Jorre, John, lab. h. Spruce n. Genesee.
Joseph, Jos. painter, 47 E. Seneca, h. 113 Carroll.
Joset, Frederick, engineer "City of Buffalo," h. Clinton cor. Oak.
Joset, Joseph, mason, h. Spring bet. Genesee and Sycamore.
Joslin, Caroline, widow, h. Hudson n. 9th.
Joslyn, Chauncey, stock agent, h. Seneca n. Dole.
Joslyn, George, proprietor 13th Ward House, Seneca n. Dole.
Josselyn, H. B. saloon, 7 Comm'l, h. same.
Josslin, Samuel, cistern maker, h. High cor. Elm.
Jost, Jos. brewer, Batavia cor. Pratt, h. same.
Joy, Lewis B. firm Wardwell, Webster & Co. b. 6 Delaware.
Joy, Thaddeus, Mrs. h. 12 Delaware.
Joy, Walter, coal dealer, office over 180 Main, h. 12 Delaware.
Joyce, D. W. book-keeper, b. 143 Swan.
Joyce, Wm. lab. h. Otto n. Hayward.
Judd, Orvan K. Am. Exp. Co. h. 4 Carey.
Judge, Alfred, b. 233 Carroll.
Judge, Henry, teamster, with Richard Bully-more, b. S. Hutter.
Judge, Jos. butcher, b. 233 Carroll.
Judson & Avery, prod. com. merchs. and for-warders, 24 Central Wharf.
Judson, J. S. A. atty. cor. Court and Main, b. 120 Pearl.
Judson, Libeus, grocer, h. 113 E. Seneca.
Judson, Maria, widow, b. 415 Swan.
Judson, W. H. firm J. & Avery, h. 143 Franklin.
Juenemann, August, cigar maker, b. 264 Elm.
Juenemann, F. carp. h. Boston alley n. Va.
Juenemann, Rosina, widow, h. 264 Elm.
Juengart, Jno. saloon, Spring n. Gen. h. same.
Juengerich, Conrad, tailor, h. Ellicott cor. Bur-ton alley.
JUENGLING, HENRY F. jeweller, 3 Niag-ara, h. 128 Clinton.—*See adv. p.* 75.
Juerges, A. shoemaker, h. 544 Michigan.
Juliard, Lewis, blacksmith, h. Sen. cor. Ala.
Julier, H. S. express messenger, b. Revere.
Jung, Anton, brewer, h. 208 Batavia.

Jung. Chas. mason, h. Mortimer n. Genesee.
Jung. Jacob, teamster, h. Oak n. Best.
Jung. Jacob, book-binder, h. 211 Ellicott.
Jung. John, trunk maker, h. 239 Ellicott.
Jung. John, cooper, h. William cor. Spring.
Jung, John, lab. h. 175 Batavia.
Jung. Jos. farmer, h. Herman N. of Genesee.
Jung. Michael, match manuf. h. 228 Oak.
Jung. Theobold, cigar maker, h. 194 Elm.
Jungken, Herman, lab. h. Walnut n. Batavia.
Jungman, Peter, cooper, h. 153 Walnut.
Jungman, John,* cooper, Pratt n. Sycamore, h. same.
Junkert, Albert, moulder, h. Mulberry n. High.
Junkes, Mary, widow, h. 133 Batavia.
Junkes, Joseph, teamster, h. 91 Pine.
Junkes, Jacob, lab. b. Pine cor. Batavia.
Junkes, Michael, lab. b. Pine cor. Batavia.
Junkes, Anthony, moulder, b. Joseph Junkes.
Justin, A. A. wagon maker and blacksmith, Niagara n. Hamilton, h. same.
Justin, G. machinist, h. Niagara n. Hamilton.
Justin, Reuben, h. Dearborn n. Parish.
Justin, Thos. carp. h. Parish cor. East.

K.

Kabel, Martin, farmer, cor. Main n. Amherst.
Kaert, Geo. lab. h. Cedar n. William.
Kager, Geo. lab. h. Hudson n. 11th.
Kaicher, Gustof, Evans & Co.'s planing mill.
Kain, Pat. salter, h. St. Paul n. Main.
Kairus, J. finisher, Brayley & Pitts.
Kaiser, Andrew, bricklayer, h. 104 Cedar.
Kaiser, Anna M. widow, b. Andrew Kaiser.
Kaisar, B. saloon, 7 Peacock, h. same.
Kaiser, Chas. clerk, 205 Main, b. Batavia bel. Jefferson.
Kaiser, Fred. plasterer, h. Maple n. High.
Kaiser, John, bricklayer, h. Maple n. High.
Kaiser, John, lab. h. Johnson n. Genesee.
Kaiser, John, shoemaker, h. High cor. Maple.
Kaiser, Ludwig, butcher, h. Ellicott n. Dodge.
Kaiser, Peter, h. Batavia n. Jefferson.
Kaler, Alexander, book-keeper, P. S. Stevens, h. 119 N. Division.
Kalsow, John, lab. h. Goodell alley n. Tupper.
Kaltenbach, Xavier T. brewer, Lutheran n. Batavia.
Kam, George, lab. h. Maple n. High.
Kam, John, bakery, Spring cor. Gen. h. same.
Kam, Philip, tailor, h. Spruce n. Genesee.
Kamarer, Matthew, blacksmith, cor. Terrace and Henry. h. Walnut n. Batavia.
Kamer, Casper, Main St. R. R. stable, h. Main n. Ferry.
Kamerling, S. A. cutter, h. 25 Cedar.
Kamiller, Mier, harness maker, b. 2 Genesee.
Kamm, Baptist, bakery, Hickory n. Batavia, h. same.
Kamm, Christian, lab. h. Locust n. North.
Kamman, Henry, farmer, h. White's Corners plank road n. city line.
Kammon, Henry, butcher, Sen. n. Jeff. h. same.
Kammon, John, butcher, junc. Swan and Sen.
Kamnerer, Francis, lab. h. Hickory n. Syc.
Kamper, Chas. liquor dealer, 112 Exch. b. N. Division cor. Spring.

Kampf, Wm. carpet weaver, h. Williamsville road n. Ferry.
Kamprath, Fred. shoemaker, h. 214 Batavia n. Hickory.
Kandel, Fred. cooper, b. A. Debus.
Kane, Andrew, lab. h. bet. Fulton and Perry.
Kane, Henry, sailor, h. Louisiana n. Mackinaw.
Kane, Peter, blacksmith, h. 5th ab. Carolina.
Kane, William, jeweller, h. 64 Court.
Kankelwitz. Chas. cigar maker, h. cor. Ellicott and Chippewa.
Kantz, Chas. cutter, H. Hart, h. 206 S. Div.
Kanzow, Chas. cigar maker, h. Bat. n Walnut.
Kanzow, Rudolph, cigar maker, h. Hickory n. Cedar.
Kappel, August, brewer, b. Batavia cor. Cedar.
Kappel, Jno. shoemaker, h. Monroe n. William.
Kappenmann, Joseph, stone cutter, h. 17 Monroe n. Batavia.
Kappo, Christian, plasterer, h. 15 Maple above Goodell.
Kappo, John, watchman, with Pierce & Co. h. Hickory n. William.
Karausky, Alex. cap maker, h. 414 Michigan.
Karback, John, tailor, h. Hospital n. Niagara.
Karch, Matthias,* mason, Adams n. Brown, h. same.
Kark, John. tailor, h. Hollister n. Spring.
Karl, Andreas, turner, 12 Batavia.
Karl, Cecelia, millinery, Emslie n. Lovejoy, h. same.
Karl, John, stone mason, h. Adams n. Brown.
Karl, Lorenz, lab. h. Emslie n. Lovejoy.
Karle, Chr. stone cutter, h. Genesee n. toll gate.
Karlein, Michael, mason, h. 550 Michigan.
Karlmeier, Charles, peddler, h. 411 Michigan.
Karn, Adam, Jr. trunk maker, h. Maple cor. Carlton.
Karnatz, Chris. brewer, h. Elm n. Goodell.
Karney, John M. with Geo. L. Fowler, h. 13 Palmer.
Karney, J. W. saloon, 33 Exchange.
Karnte, John, butcher, Cherry n. Maple.
Karr, Corydon, with Pratt & Co. h. 152 E. Swan.
Karr, Jas. N. with Pratt & Co. h. 222 E. Swan.
Karr. John, lab. h. Pine n. William.
Kassler, John. hatter. 152 Batavia, h. same.
Kasson, C. H. with Howard, Whitcomb & Co. b. 144 Pearl.
Kasson & Co. locomotive office, 93 Main.
Kasson, William M. firm K. & Co. 93 Main, h. 26 E. Swan.
Kastner, Geo. wagoner, 220 Batavia, h same.
Kastner, Mary, wid. h. Batavia cor. Jefferson.
Kastner, Michael, carp. h. Maple n. North.
Katzat, Geo. watchman, h. Grey n. Batavia.
Katzenberger, Andrew, lab. h. Spruce n. Gen.
Kauber, Fred. lab. h. Krettner n. Batavia.
Kauer, Jacob, shoemaker, h. 99 Batavia.
Kaufmann, Anton, on lake, h. 564 Michigan.
Kaufmann, Geo. blacksmith, h. 197 Ellicott.
Kaufmann, Louis, lab. h. Wm. n. Walnut.
Kaufmann, Louis, lead works, h. Wm. n. Cedar.
Kaufmann, M. baker, b. Burton alley n. Wash.
Kaumeyer, Chas. policeman, h. 164 Cherry.
Kauner, Peter, carp. h. Monroe n. Sycamore.
Kautz, John, lab. h. Niagara n. Mass.

Kautzmann, Adam, h. Michigan n. North. ·
Kavanagh, James, printer. b. 111 Main.
Kavanagh, James, tinsmith, h. r. 228 Seneca.
Kavanagh, John, lab. h. across creek.
Kavanas, Hugh, porter, with Wallace Johnson, h. 83 Carroll.
Kavery, Michael, h. 6th n. Maryland.
Kay, H. milkman, h. Niagara n. Bouck.
Kayser, August, cabinet maker, h. Pratt n. Syc.
Kayser, C. F. F. printer, h. Bennett n. Batavia.
Keahnen, Nicholas, moulder, h. Adams n Park avenue.
Keal, Wm. mason, h. over 16 Cherry.
Kean, J. G. cutter, J. B. Dubois, 149 Main, b. American.
Kean, James, foreman, E. Clark's stave yard, h. 84 Carroll.
Kean, Patrick, lab. h. St. Paul n. Main.
Kean, Thos. editor and proprietor Buffalo Daily Republic, b. 54 Swan.
Keaner, John, milkman, h. Cherry n. Jefferson.
Kearney, James, ship carp. h. Ohio n. Wabash.
Kearney, John, caulker, b. Ohio n. Wabash.
Kearney, William A. caulker, h. Ala. n Elk.
Kearny, Bridget, widow, b. across creek.
Kearns, Hugh, porter, 24 Prime, h. Jackson above Genesee.
Keating, Robert, book-keeper, Jewett & Root, b. 78 N. Division.
Keays, W. J. & Co. com'l line propellers, foot Washington.
Keays, Wm. firm W. J. K. & Co. 11 Ohio, h. 120 6th.
Keefe, Simon, painter, h. Palmer above Md.
Keefer, Michael, lab. h. 11th cor. Carolina.
Keegan, Ellen, widow, h. Virginia between Palmer and 9th.
Keel, Charles A. green grocer, h. Bullymore's Block.
Keel, James O. farmer, h. Elk n. Red Jacket.
Keeler, James, carp. b. Ash cor. Sycamore.
Keeler, W. J. resident engineer, office 2 Prosser Block, b. Mansion.
Keelp, Joel, mariner, h. Market n. Perry.
Keelty, Michael, h. 398 S. Division.
Keely, James, saloon, 1 Peacock, h. same.
Keen, G. B. cutter, h. 32 W. Seneca.
Keen, James, machinist, h. 10 Virginia.
Keena, Michael, sailor, h. 54 5th.
Keena, Peter, Jr. moulder, h. Perry cor. Ill.
Keena, Peter, grocer, Perry cor. Ill. h. same.
Keenan, Chas. lab. h. Elk n. Hayward.
Keenan, John, bricklayer, h. Virginia n. 6th.
Keenan, M. gas fitter, h. 5th n. Virginia.
Keenan, Patrick, lab. h. r. Carolina n. Palmer.
Keene, Wm. lab. h. Porter n. Bouck.
Kehl, Peter, mason, h. Walnut n. Batavia.
Kehn, Catharine, widow, h. Best cor. Ellicott.
Kehr, Ferdinand, grocer, b. R. I. n. Chenango.
Kehr, Peter, stone cutter, h. Utica n. Rogers.
Keiber, Fred. lab. h. Krettner cor. Lovejoy.
Keiber, Geo. cooper, h. Batavia cor. Walnut.
Keicher, John, with Sage & Sons, h. Peacock.
Keiffer, S. wood worker, Brayley & Pitts.
Keifer, Mathew, coppersmith, h. Spring n. Bat.
Keflem, Michael, carp. b. Johnson n. Gen.
Keil, Philip, joiner, Eaton's plaining mill, h. Watson n. William.

Keil, Casper, cigar maker, b. Watson n. Wm.
Keim, Geo. butcher, h. 135 Genesee.
Keim, Henry, h. Sycamore opposite Camp.
Keim, Joseph, lab. h. 79 Spruce.
Keim, Michael, tailor, h. Lutheran n. Bat.
Keipner, Charles, lithographer, h. Pratt n. Syc.
Keipper, Anton, moulder, h. Johnson n. Bat.
Keiser, Benjamin, lab. h. 81 Monroe.
Keiser, Christian, lab. h. Clinton n. Jefferson.
Keiser, Gottlieb, sash maker, h. Peck'm n. Jeff.
Keiser, John, marble polisher, h. Johnson n. Genesee.
Keiser, Leopold, clothing, 41 Main, h. same.
Keiser, Wm. lab. h. Clinton n. Jefferson.
Keisterberger, Nicholas, painter, h. cor. Clinton and Jefferson.
Keitch, Henry, gardener, h. Jeff. n. North.
Keith, Alex. sailor, h. Michigan n. Fulton.
Keith, Chas. P. ship carp. h. Elk n. Moore.
Keith, John, ship carp. h. Elk n. Moore.
Keith, Wm. ship carp. cor. Ohio and Elk, h. Perry n. Louisiana.
Keits, Conrad, tailor, h. 12 Maple.
Keitz, Louisa, h. 124 Walnut.
Keitz, Mary, widow, h. 124 Walnut.
Kelch, John, clerk, h. 79 Sycamore.
Kelch, Peter. lab. h. 62 Bennett.
Kelderhouse, Jeremiah, with J. Kelderhouse, h. 10th n. Rhode Island.
KELDERHOUSE, JNO. wood dealer, Court opp. gas works, h. Cottage cor. Virginia.— See adv. p. 45.
Kelderhouse, Reb'ca, Mrs. b. Jno. Kelderhouse
Kelderhouse, Samuel, boatman, h. 10th n. R. L
Kelderhouse, Thos. boatman, h. 70 5th.
Kelliker, Jeremiah, lab. h. Carrol n. Van Rens.
Kellar, Chas. painter, b. 250 Genesee.
Keller, Chas. lab. h. White's Cor. plank road n. city line.
Keller, Christian, shoemaker, h. Gen. n. Adams.
Keller, Conrad, tanner, h. Hickory n. Genesee.
Keller, Edward, foreman Shaw & Kibbe, h. Pine n. Clinton.
Keller, H. H. artist, b. 295 Main.
Keller, Maria, widow, h. 33 Cherry.
Keller, Matt. blacksmith, b. 115 Cedar.
Keller, Michael, lab h. South Division n. R. R.
Keller, Michael, tanner, h. Genesee n. Grey.
Keller, Michael, printer, h. 196 Elm.
Keller, Nicholas, moulder, h. Cedar n. Batavia.
Keller, Philip, lab. h. Walnut n. William.
Keller, Sylvester, gardener, h. Jeff. n. High.
Keller, Stephen, h. 120 Michigan.
Keller, Wallace, artist, h. 183 Terrace.
Kellerman, Fred. lab. h. Maple n. Carlton.
Kellermann, G. farmer, h. Genesee n. Walnut.
Kelley, Geo. butcher, h. White's Corners plank road n Peugeot.
Kelley, H. S. carpenter, h. 42 Bennett.
Kelley, James, shoemaker, b. 25 Ohio.
Kelley, Jas. with W. T. Co. b. 41 Church.
Kelley, John M. printer, b. 7 Walnut.
Kelley, John, lab. h. Perry n. Chicago.
Kelley, Jos. lab. h. 2 Iron place, N. Washington.
Kelley, Richard, printer, Courier. b. 7 Walnut.
Kelley, Robt saloon, h. Ohio n. Washington.
Kelley, Thomas J. pressman, Courier, b. 7 Walnut.

Kelley, William S. h. 7 Walnut.
Kelling, Frederika, widow, h. 321 Elm.
Kellogg, A. J. clerk, Canal n. Evans, h. Palmer n. Virginia.
KELLOGG & BONNELL, dealers in hardware, &c. 178 Main.—*See adv. p. 45.*
Kellogg, Charles, clerk, Hadley & Husted, b. 29 E. Swan.
Kellogg, D. W. finisher, 3 State, b. 31 N. Div.
Kellogg, Oscar, at S. P. Wisner's, h. 7th n. R. I.
Kellogg, S. S. att'y, 152 Main. h. 9th n. Pa.
Kellogg, Walter P. firm K. & Bonnell, 178 Main, h. Delaware cor. Bryant.
Kellogg, Wm. stove mounter, b. cor. Mississippi and Scott.
Kellner, John, lab. h. Sherman n. Genesee.
Kelly, A. dress maker, h. 62 Oak.
Kelly, Bernard, hostler, b. Globe Hotel.
Kelly, Catharine, wid. h. Louisiana n. Ohio.
Kelly, Daniel, cooper, h. Burwell place.
Kelly, Daniel, lab. h. Chicago n. Ohio.
Kelly, Daniel, land agent, h. Breckenridge n. N. Washington.
Kelly, Dennis, lab. h. Green n. Beak.
Kelly, E. S. foreman Atwater & Haws, h. 5th ab. Pennsylvania.
Kelly, James, moulder, b. 104 Exchange.
Kelly, James, station keeper, W. T. Co. b. 41 Church.
Kelly, John, hostler, h. Nicholas alley.
Kelly, John, gardener, h. Cal. plank road n. toll gate.
Kelly, John, Jr. butcher, h. n. toll gate, Cal. plank road.
Kelly, John P. machinist, h. 1 Hamburgh.
Kelly, Julia, milliner, b. 24 6th.
Kelly, Michael, carp. h. Massachusetts n. d 2th.
Kelly, Michael, lab. h. 108 Fulton.
Kelly, Mich. lab. h. towpath n. Breckenridge.
Kelly, Murty, h. 13 Church.
Kelly, Pat'k, gardener, h. R. I. cor. Chenango.
Kelly, Patrick, machinist, b. 36 W. Seneca.
Kelly, Pat. brass finisher, b. 36 W. Seneca.
Kelly, Thomas, saloon, 144 Main, h. same.
Kelly, Thomas, lab. h. 4th ab. Georgia.
Kelner, F. lab. h. 350 Genesee.
Kelsey, J. b. 295 Swan.
Kembel, Henry, ship carp. h. Perry n. Hamb'h.
Kemm, John, carp. h. Jefferson n. Sycamore.
Kemnerer, Jacob, lab. h. Stanton n. Batavia.
Kemnitz, Theo. carp. h. 409 Michigan.
Kemp, D. F. clerk, 156 Main, b. 65 5th.
Kemp, George A. carp. b. 65 5th.
Kemp, John, on lake, h. Walnut n. Clinton.
Kemp, Thomas, carp. cor. Fly and Le Couteulx, h. 65 5th.
Kemp, Wm. painter, 49 Seneca, h. cor. Eagle and Union.
Kempen, Jas. mill-saw'r, h. Niag. cor. Hamil'n.
Kempff, Fred. clerk, 390 Main, b. 139 Ellicott.
Kempke, Geo. carp. h. Goodell n. Michigan.
Kempson, John, clerk, L. S. R. R. h. ft. Erie.
Kemter, George, tailor, h. 229 Pearl.
Kendall, A. machinist, h. Louisiana n Perry.
Kendall, C. pastor Wash. St. U. P. h. 26 Oak.
Kendall, Fred. clerk, h. 118 Swan.
Kendall, J. Milton, cashier, Manchester & Rich. h. N. Pearl n. Virginia.

Kendrick, Jane, widow, dressmaker. h. 47 Del.
Kenedee, Michael, lab. h. across ship canal.
Kenell, Valentine, harness maker, h. Clinton n. Spring.
Kennedy, A. H. auctioneer, Exch. cor. Main, h. Morgan bel. Niagara.
Kennedy, Chas. E. with Dudley Bros. 57 Main, b. 152 9th.
Kennedy, Chas. machinist, b. 7 Scott.
Kennedy, James, grocer, h. 343 Seneca.
Kennedy, Jno. lab. h. towpath n. round house.
Kennedy, Jno. saloon, Virginia n. Niagara.
Kennedy, Jno.* shoemaker, Georgia bel. 5th.
Kennedy, Jno. R. office D. P. Dobbins, h. cor. N. Washington and Bird.
Kennedy, Jno. saloon, Evans n. Water. h. same.
Kennedy, Lester, engineer, L. S. R. R. h. cor. Spring and Seneca.
Kennedy, Pat. lab. h. Louisiana n. Ohio.
Kennedy, Perry, gate-keeper at Penitentiary, b. same.
Kennedy, S. G. book-keeper. Manuf. and Trader's bank, b. 29 E. Swan.
Kennedy, Thomas, clerk, 27 Commercial, h. 6 Park place.
Kennedy, Thos. h. Seneca n. Heacock.
Kennedy, Wm. cartman, h. 138 W. Huron.
Kennedy, Wm. B. mariner, h. bet. Van. Rensselaer and Heacock on Seneca.
Kennedy, Wm. miller, h. Niag. n. Brekenr'dge.
Kennel, Henry, brick maker, h. Pratt n. Gen.
Kennel, Jacob, carriage maker, b. 67 Hickory.
Kennel, Valentine, saddler, 362 Main, h. Clinton n. Pratt.
KENNETT, THOS. merchant tailor, 183 Main, h. 57 E. Swan.—*See adv. p. 88.*
Kennett, Thos. Jr. b. 57 E. Swan.
Kennett, Wm. H. clerk, 183 Main, b 57 Swan.
Kenney, Bryan, gardener, h. Ala. n. Hamp.
Kenney, Jno. W. ship joiner, h. Hudson cor. Cottage.
Kenney, Kearn, Mrs. h. Maryland cor. 4th.
Kenngott, Jno. finisher, h. Spring n. Sycamore.
Kennington, John, blacksmith. h. Rog. n. Sum.
Kennington, Jno. huckster. h. Rogers ft. Sum.
Kent, Arthur, clerk, 54 Main, h. 148 6th.
Kent, Edwin, clerk, at 37 Seneca, h. 40 Carroll.
Kent, Wm. blacksmith. b. cor. Va. and Niag.
Kent, W. J. works Prince & Co. h. cor. Virginia and Niagara.
Kenton. N. W. hatter, h. 257 N. Division.
Kenyon, Darrion, book-keeper, h. 169 Swan.
Kenyon, H. F. book-keeper, B. & L. S. R. R. office, cor. Swan and Main, h. 169 Swan.
Kenyon, L. M. firm K. & Wright, h. 262 Wash.
Keogh, Augustine, firm A. & J. K. h. 22 Ellicott.
KEOGH, A. & J. piano forte manufactory, 257, 259 and 261 Washington —*See adv. p. 66.*
Keogh, Austin, clerk, 257 Wash. b. 22 Ellicott.
Keogh, Elizabeth, widow, h. 9 Mortimer.
Keogh, John, firm A. & J. K. h. 22 Ellicott.
Keogh, John, lab. h. Ellicott n. North.
Keogh, Lawrence, pattern maker, h. 100 Fol'm.
Keogh, Patrick, piano maker, b. 5 Ellicott.
Keogh, Paul, cooper, b. 9 Mortimer.
Keogh, Timothy, plasterer, h. Smith n. York.
Keough. Thos. shoemaker, b. Perry, Spaulding's Exchange.

Kepel, Wolfgang. mason, h. Sycamore n. Kaene.
Kepell, Sebastian. lab. h. Adams n. Sycamore.
Kepler. Gottfrey, lab. h. 84 Sycamore.
Keppel. Fred. clerk, Lanning & Miller, b. 60 S. Division.
Kepplut, Jno. lab. h. Bat. cor. Jefferson.
Kerbel, Peter. shoemaker, h. Elm cor. Va.
Kerber, John, mason, h. Adams n. Sycamore.
Kerber, Jos. blacksmith, Genesee cor. Adams, h. same.
Kercher, Fred. finisher. h. 11 Sycamore.
Kerchmeyer, Lorenz, blacksmith, h. 101 God'l.
Kerdel, Jno. jeweller, h. cor. S. Div. and Pine.
Kerdel, Jos. jeweller, b. 181 S. Division.
Keren, John, lab. h. Monroe n. Clinton.
Kerher, Joseph. painter, h. Jeff. n. Peckham.
Kerigan, J. tailor, 2 1st, h. same.
Kerker, Henry, mason, h. Jeff. cor. Peckham.
Kerker, Jacob, bricklayer, h. Goodell cor. Mich.
Kerling. Andreas. lab. h. Walnut n. Wm.
Kern, Anthony, carp. h. 44 Delaware place.
Kern, Frank, carpenter. b. 44 Del. place.
Kern, Louis, brewer, h. Best n. Main.
Kernaham. John, varnisher, h. 73 Spruce.
Kernan, Michael, brick maker, N. Div. n. R. R.
Kerney, John M. bar-tender, Terrapin, h. Palmer ab. Carolina.
Kernig, Gottleib, lab. h. Burton alley n. Mich.
Kernig. John, farmer. h. Abbott plank road n. iron bridge.
Kerns, Alice, widow, b. 37 N. Division.
Kerns, Nicholas, mariner. h. 46 N. Division.
Kerr, A. T. firm K. & Laing, 53 Main, b. Batavia n. Elm.
Kerr, James, machinist, b. 10th n. Virginia.
Kerr, John, machinist, h. 112 Folsom.
Kerr, John, lab. b. 6 Michigan.
Kerr & Laing, wholesale liquor store, 53 Main.
Kerr, Marian, widow, h. 10th n. Virginia.
Kerr, Robt. engineer, h. Terrace n. Mechanic.
Kerr, Thomas, engineer, h. Terrace n. Eric.
Kerschel, John, lab. h. Hickory n. Batavia.
Kersher. Henry, brewer, h. J. Weppner.
Kerst, F. A. tailor, Ohio n. Mackinaw.
Kerst, Elizabeth, widow, h. 117 Pine.
Karsten, C. grocer, Mulberry n. Va. h. same.
Kertz, Matthias, painter, h. 221 Ellicott.
Kertz, M. wood worker, Brayley & Pitts.
Kese, Jno. lab. h. Madison n. Batavia.
Kesler, Eeibholt, carp. lake shore road n. Tift's farm.
Kesner, Wm. cabinet maker, h. 251 Elm.
Kessel, John, shoemaker, h. Batavia n. Grey.
Kessener, F. h. Green opp. Central depot.
Kessler, John, clerk, h r. 160 Oak.
Kessler, Wm. bar-tender, h. 536 Michigan.
Kester, Ann, nurse, h. 435 Main.
Kester, Irving, clerk, W. Johnson, h. 136 W. Huron.
Kester, Levi, brakesman, N. Y. C. R. R. h. Carroll n. Alabama.
Kestler, Geo. lab. h. Swan at R. R. crossing.
Kesz, Peter, carpenter, b. Spruce n. Batavia.
Ketcham, A. P. clerk, Buffalo water works, b. 286 Pearl.
Ketchum, A. R. supt. water works, h. 286 Pr'l.
Ketchum, George B. firm Peter & K. h. 236 Franklin.

Ketchum, Jesse, h. North opp. Mariner.
Ketchum, Wm. h. 109 Delaware.
Ketchum, Wm. F. h. Delaware cor. Mohawk.
Kettelhol, Sophia, wid. h Mortimer n. Wm.
Kettler, John, cabinet maker, h. 15 Bennett.
Kettner. Philip, lab. h. Spring n. Genesee.
Keuer, Daniel, h. Pratt n. Clinton.
Keuper, Christian, tailor, h. Pratt n. Clinton.
Keys, Chas. H. clerk, 8 Seneca, b. 88 Clinton.
Keys, Louis R. jeweler, 8 Seneca, h. 88 Clin'n.
Khem, Wm. carp. h. Bat. beyond toll gate.
Kibbe, Geo. R. firm Shaw & K. h. Morgan cor. Carey.
Kibbon, Samuel, trackman, h. Carlton n. Mich.
Kick, Jno. tanner, h. Swan n. Grosvenor.
Kick, Jno. policeman, h. Syc. cor. Walnut.
Kiebler, Frederick, b. Moses Baker.
Kief, Jas. lab. h. W. Genesee.
Kief. William, carpenter, h. Illinois n. Ohio.
Kiefer, Fred. porter, b. 1 Delaware.
Kiefer, Geo. shoemaker, h. 161 Batavia.
Kiefer. Gertrude, widow, h. 119 Cedar.
Kiefer, Henry, lab. h. 451 Michigan.
Kiefer, Joseph, cooper. h. 97 Pine.
Kiefer, Martz. tinsmith, b. Spring n. Peckham.
Kiefer, Nicholas, sailor. b. Spring n. Peckham.
Kiefer, Peter, lab. b. Spring n. Peckham.
Kieffer, Chas. firm K. & Klein, h. 519 Wash.
Kieffer & Klein, paint shop, Gen. n. Sycamore.
Kiefhaber, Adam, tailor. h. Hickory n. Clinton.
Kiefhaber, Peter, lab. h. Sycamore n. Pratt.
Kiehner, Peter. carp. h. Michigan n. Virginia.
Kiener, Jas. lab. h. Pine n. William.
Kiepe. Wm. carpenter, h. Clinton n. Spring.
Kierner, John, lab. h. Johnson n. Genesee.
Kiesel, Conrad, with Thos. Clark, h. Clinton n Spring.
Kihlberg, Jno. trunk m'kr 219 Main, h. 3 Com'l.
Kihll, Geo. grocer, h. 300 Seneca.
Kilderhouse, James, farmer, town line road n. Delaware.
Kile. P. sash and blind m'kr, h. Watson n. Wm.
Kilheney, Jno. lab. h. 7th n. Maryland.
Kilheney, Patrick. painter, b. 7th n. Maryland.
Kilhofer, Jno. insurance agt. h. 32 E. Tupper.
Killan, N. printer, Com'l Adv. b. 5 Carroll.
Killcoyne. Catharine, saloon, Michigan n. Ohio.
Killinger, Mathias, frame maker, h. William n. Walnut.
Killy, Daniel, mariner, across creek.
Kilpeck, Bartlay, steward, h. 61 William.
Kilty, Michael, hostler, h. 206 N. Division.
Kilty, Michael, constable, h. 396 S. Division.
Kimball, Conrad, saloon, Terrace n. Genesee.
Kimball, Elvira, widow, h. 6th ab. Hudson.
Kimball, Geo. F. drover, 102 Swan.
Kimball, Hiram A. law student, 164 Main, b. 201 Terrace.
Kimball, L. T. with H. C. Walker, b. 105 Niag.
Kimberly, Edward, clerk. Western Transportation Company, b. 329 Washington.
Kimberly, Jacob, painter, h. 18 Cherry.
Kimberly, Jacob, Jr. painter, 9 Terrace, h. 18 Cherry.
Kimberly, John L. President Buffalo City Bank, h. 329 Washington.
Kimberly, John L. Jr. book-keeper in Buffalo City Bank, b. 329 Washington.

Kimmick, Jacob, lab. h. Vermont n. Bristol.
Kimmit, Francis, rope maker, h. 29 Carolina.
Kimmit, Rosa, widow, h. cor. 5th and Virginia.
Kinane, Pat. finisher. 233 Main.
Kincade, Thos. teamster, b. Wash. cor. Scott.
Kindel, John, mason, h. 19 Hickory n. Syc.
Kinderman, Martin, student, b. Martin Luther College.
Kinellck, John, carpenter, h. 11th n. Mass.
King, A. H. with B. H. King, h. 248 S. Div.
KING, B. H. jeweler, over 202 Main, h. 317 Michigan.—See adv. p. 75.
King, Charles, barber, h. 6 Vine.
King, Charles, tinsmith, b. 57 Fulton.
King, E. S. student, b. 93 N. Division.
King, Geo. mason, h. cor. Ferry and Michigan.
King, Henry, clerk at 161 Main, b. 155 Pearl.
King, J. E. M. D. ov. 8 E. Seneca, h. 37 Niagara.
King, John, shoemaker, b. 5 Water.
King, M. engineer, b. Fulton n. Alabama.
King, Mary T., N. Y. millinery store, 5 S. Div.
Kingnal, Matilda, widow, h. Maple n. Cherry.
King, Peter, silver plater, h. 104 Tupper.
King, Phil. silver plater, b. 106 Tupper.
King, Rufus S. com mer. 12 Central Wharf, h. N. W. cor. Niagara Square.
King, Samuel, millinery, 5 S. Division, h. 25 Niagara.
King, Sidney B. office 67 Seneca, b. same.
King, Wm. saloon, Canal n. Evans.
KING, WM. Jr. druggist, 249 Main, b. 29 Swan.—See adv. opp. name.
King, W. H. machinist, Brayley & Pitts.
Kingman, A. T. b. 67 E. Eagle.
Kingman, Charles, carpenter, b. Maple n. High.
Kingman, Geo. Mrs. Delaware n. North.
Kingman, Leenaert, peddler, h. Walnut n. Clinton.
Kingman, Wm. carp. h. Spring n. Batavia.
Kingot. John, finisher, cor. Terrace and Henry, h. Spring n. Sycamore.
Kingsbury, Lucy, widow, h. 139 Huron.
Kingscott, Wm. butcher, h. Seneca junc. Exch.
Kingsley, A. S. key maker, with G. A. Prince & Co. h. 6 9th.
Kingsley, Martin, watchman, Brayley & Pitts.
Kingsley, Martin, h. 234 Delaware.
Kingsley, Silas, h. 81 Franklin.
Kingston, Geo. painter, h. Hudson cor. Palmer.
Kink, Albert, mason, h. Genesee n. Walnut.
Kinkade, Dennis, mail carrier, h. 7 Folsom.
Kinlne, Michael, lab. h. Howard n. Monroe.
Kinne, H. M. firm Lockwood & K. h. 196 Pearl.
Kinne, James, b. Carolina bel. 5th.
Kinne, John, h. Carolina bel. 5th
Kinne, Michael, lab. h. 79 Church.
Kinne, Richard, plumber, b. Carolina bel. 5th.
Kinnear, Sylvester, ship smith, 14 Water, h. Park n. Virginia.
Kinnear, Wm. H. ship smith, foot Water, h. 18 Swan.
Kinney, G. P. h. 6 7th.
Kinney, James, lab. h. Fulton n. Hayward.
Kinney, John, bar tender, h. Perry n. Mich.
Kinney, Michael, lab. h. Van Rens. n. Porter.
Kinney, Patrick, mason, h. Terrace n. Genesee.
Kinnlus, Dorothy, wid. h. Grey n. Batavia.
Kinsky, Anthony, engraver, b. 199 Franklin.

Kinsky, B. stone cutter, h. 40 Delaware place.
Kinsky, B. Jr. marble worker, b. 40 Delaware place.
Kinsky, Charles M stone cutter, h. 53 Delaware place.
Kinsky, Geo. foreman, Field's marble works, b. 40 Delaware place.
Kinsky, Geo. pattern maker, h. 199 Franklin.
Kinstler, C. machinist, h. Maple n. Virginia.
Kinyon, G. W. M. brakesman, h. 100 Carroll.
Kip, Henry, sup. U. S. Ex Co. h. 270 Pearl.
Kirby, A. mail agent, b. Courter House.
Kirby, Thos. lab. b. 38 Exchange.
Kirby, Wm. A. patentee Kirby's mowing reaper, h. 11 Park place.
Kirch. John, grocer. Niagara n. Austin.
Kirch, Peter, grocer, Niagara n. Hamilton.
Kirchberger, Joseph, carp. h. Pine n. Cypress.
Kirchenbower. John, cabinet maker, h. Terrace n. Genesee.
Kirchgasser, Christ. cabinet maker, h. Watson n. William.
Kirchgesner, John, blacksmith, h. Pine n. Bat.
Kirchgessner, Jos. lab. h. Hollister n. Mortimer.
Kirchemeyer, Franz, lab. h. Shumway n. Bat.
Kirchmeyer, John, truckman, h. Walden n. creek.
Kirchmeyer, M. lab. h. Walnut n. Batavia.
Kirchmeyer, Philip, lab. b. John Kirchmeyer.
Kirchner, Adam, mason, h. Kaene n Sycamore.
Kirchner, Geo. peddler, h. Boston alley bel. Virginia.
Kirchner, Jacob, hostler, h. Kaene n. Genesee.
Kirckholder, Frederick, h. Grey cor. Potter al.
Kirhhoff, John, saloon, cor. Water and Lloyd.
Kirk, Anna, widow, h. 181 Swan.
Kirk, Mary, h. Blossom n. Koon's alley.
Kirk, Robert, painter, with H. G. White, h. 5 Beek.
Kirk, Thomas, butcher, h. Elk n. Hayward.
Kirker, Francis, mason, 202 Genesee.
Kirkholder, Eugene, clerk, 145 Main, b. cor. Gay and Potter.
Kirkholder, W. H. clerk, 150 Main, h. cor. Gay and Potter.
Kirkhover, Lewis,* brick maker, h. 420 Seneca.
Kirkover, Oliver, mason, h. Seneca n. Red Jacket.
Kirkpatrick, J. book-keeper, U. S. Dispatch, b. Mansion.
Kirn, Anthony, carp. h. 44 Delaware place.
Kirsch, Emanuel, grocer, cor. Seneca and Michigan, h. 370 Michigan.
Kirsch, Geo. lab. h. Best n. Oak.
Kirsch, Peter, grocer, h. 119 Seneca.
Kirst, Joseph, cooper, h. Mortimer n. Genesee.
Kiser, Fred. mason, h. Maple n. High.
Kisker, Adam J. carp. h. 29 Hickory.
Kissinger, John, clerk, h. Mulberry ab. Goodell.
Kissock, David, fire marshal, h. 87 Niagara.
Kitson, John, carp. h. Fulton n. Alabama.
Kitzinger, Peter, engineer, h. Walnut n. Gen.
Kitzner, Peter, engineer, h. Walnut n. Syc.
Klaein, Jacob, shoemaker, h. Pratt n. Clinton.
Klaes, Philip, lab. h. 8 Ash.
Klaes, Peter, firm Behringer & K. h. 298 N. Division.
Klaholz, Francis, D. D. St. Mary's Church.

Klaholz, Bernhard, school teacher, h. Mulberry n. Carlton.
Klaiber, Jno. F. carp. h. Mortimer n. Genesee.
Klanc, Peter, gunsmith, 139 Main, h. Pratt n. Clinton.
Klapp, Nicholas, boiler maker, h. Michigan n. Cypress.
Klas, Jno. at Elk St. Market. h. Seneca.
Klasset, John, blacksmith, White's tool shop, h. Pratt n. Genesee.
Klauck, Dorrothea, widow, h. Locust n. High.
Klauck, Henry, turner, b. Clinton cor. Hick'y.
Klauck, John, mason, h. Camp n. Genesee.
Klausman, Chas. lab. h. Mulberry n. Virginia.
Klee, F. C. shoemaker, 22 Main,' h. same.
Klee, Jos. lab. h. Monroe n. Sycamore.
Klehn, Mary C. widow, h. 263 Elm.
Kleiber, Fred. lab. 160 Elm, h. Mortimer n. Gen.
Kleiber, Jos. furnaceman, h. 243 Elm.
Kleibz, Mich. ash peddler, h. Jeff. n. Carlton.
Klein, Augustus, chair maker, S. D. Sikes, h. 41 Spruce.
Klein, Caroline, h. over 5 E. Genesee.
Klein, Chas. Jr. painter, b. 43 Spruce.
Klein, Chas. E. cooper. h. Goodell cor. Mich.
Klein, Chas. firm Kieffer & K. h. 41 Spruce.
Klein, Charles, carp. h. Pratt n. Sycamore.
Klein, Chas. farmer, h. Williamsville road n. Ferry.
Klein, Chas.* painter, 43 Spruce, h. same.
Klein, Conrad, N. Y. C. R. R. h. Wm. cor. Jeff.
Klein, Conrad, tanner, 4 Quay, h. Morgan n. Court.
Klein & Dobinson, pump and block makers, Evans cor. Water.
Klein, Frank, tailor, h. Carlton n. Locust.
Klein, Fred. moulder, h. over 396 Michigan.
Klein, George, clerk, 430 Main, b. same.
Klein, Gottfried, shoemaker, h. 484 Michigan.
Klein, Hawley, firm K. & Dobinson. h. 27 7th.
Klein, Henry, cooper, h. Seneca n. Jefferson.
Klein, Jacob, grocer and turner, Clinton cor. Spring, h. same.
Klein, Jacob, cooper. h. Mulberry n. Goodell.
Klein, Jacob, blacksmith, Grey n. Batavia.
Klein, John, foreman, Hausle & Son, 146_E. Genesee, b. same.
Klein, Jno. clerk, b. 484 Michigan.
Klein, Jno. chair maker. 160 Elm, h. 181 Bat.
Klein, John, tailor, h. Monroe n. Batavia.
Klein, John, upholsterer, h. Michigan n. Va.
Klein, Jos. cooper, h. Tonawanda n. East.
Klein, Louis, butcher, 102 Tupper, h. same.
Klein, Michael, lab. h. Mortimer cor. Hollister.
Klein, Michael, ship carp. h. Peckham n. Kret.
Klein, Nicholas, lab. h. Adams n. Batavia.
Klein, Peter, blacksmith, h. Pine n. William.
Klein, P. J. meat store. 61 Exch. h. same.
Klein, —. lab. Pine n. Clinton.
Klein, Peter, moulder, h. Spring n. William.
Klein, Peter, tailor, 2 Main, b. same.
Klein, Philip, saddler, h. Mich. n. Burton alley.
Klein, Philip, blacksmith, b. cor. Del. and Bart.
Klein, Philip G. saloon, cor. Vt. and 13th, h. same.
Klein, Philip, lab. h. cor. Mulberry and Goodell.
Klein, Theobold, teamster, h. Spring n. Gen.
Kleindenz, Roslia, h. 489 Washington.

Kleineidan, Robt. D. D. St. Mary's.
Kleinhanb, Peter. shoemaker, h. Camp n. Gen.
Kleinhans, Christian, shoemaker, h. Kaene n. Genesee.
Kleinschmidt, Chas. saw filer, h. Seneca n. Jeff.
Kleinschmidt, Ernst. lab. b. Oak cor. Va.
Kleinschmidt, Mary, widow, h. Oak cor. Va.
Kleinvogle, Wm. shoemaker, 20 S. Division, h. 418 Michigan.
Kleisz, Peter, lab. h. 118 Cedar.
Klemitz, Henry, shoema'r. h. Cherry n. Orange.
Klemm, Andrew, h. Monroe n. Peckham.
Klemm, Jacob, lab. h. Cypress n. Michigan.
Klepser, Geo. clerk, b. Amherst n. Tonawanda.
Kleyman, Henry, carp. h. Pine n. Batavia.
Kliber, Geo. lab. h. River n. W. T. Co.
Klicker, Jacob, gardener. h. Jeff. n. Genesee.
Klier, Andrew. carp. h. Krettner n. Peckham.
Klier, Andrew. lab. h. Adams n. Sycamore.
Klier, Justin, lab. h. 104 Pine.
Klies, Peter, barber, 25 Genesee, h. same.
Klim, Jno. upholster, h. Mich. n. Burton alley.
Kline, Hiram, moulder, h. Folsom cor. Chicago.
Kling, Christ, butcher, h. Seneca n. junc. Exch.
Kling, David, lab. h. 104 Batavia.
Kling, Geo. lab. h. Locust bet. High & Carlton.
Klingenbiehld, Wm. mason, h. Adams opp. Brown.
Klinger, Carl W. shoemaker, h. Elk ab. Ala.
Klink, Geo. coachman, J. F. Fargo, b. same.
Klink, Tobias, bricklayer, h. Mulberry n. Va.
Klinkhammer, Clem'ns, liquor dealer. b. 127 N. Division.
Klinsbeck, Jno. marble cutter, h. 178 Tupper.
Klipfel, Casper, Shepard's foundry, h. Mulberry n. Carlton.
Klipfel, Chas. vinegar manf. 231 Elm, h. same.
Klipfel, John, blacksmith, h. 321 Elm.
Klippel, Valentine,* grocer, Gen. cor. Hickory.
Klippel, Philip, farmer. h. Mich. n. North.
Klock, Jno. lab. h. 20 Vine alley.
Kloeber, G. D. lab. h. Niagara n. Farmer.
Kloser, Augusta, b. Mrs. C. Kloser.
Kloser, Caroline, widow, h. Milnor n. Wm.
Kloser, Chas. E. bootmaker, b. Mrs. C. Kloser.
Klotz, J. M. North Buffalo Hotel, Niag. cor. Hamilton.
Klotz, Wm grocer, h. Niagara n. South.
Klouse, John, lab. h. Adams n. Peckham.
Klub, Nicholas, h. Michigan bet. Bata. and Syc.
Klug, Joseph, saloon, 204 Genesee, h. same.
Kluth, Elvine, Mrs. h. 258 Elm.
Knab, Geo. blacksmith, Washington n. Va.
Knahu, Michael, tailor, h. Walnut n. Syc.
Knaller, John, teamster, b. James Doat.
Knapp, Geo. clerk, b. I. S. Newton's.
Knapp, Jacob, mason, h. Mulberry n. Goodell.
Knapp, Joseph, lab. h. Locust n. High.
Knapp, Lyman, h. 89 N. Division.
Knapp, Nicholas, shoemaker, h. Ash n. Syc.
Knapp, Nicholas, moulder, Terrace cor. Henry, h. Delaware place n. Delaware.
Knapp, S. L. builder, h. 250 Seneca.
Knapp, Stephen L. builder, h. 253 E. Seneca.
Knaub, Anton, cooper, h. Amherst opp. Lewis.
Knauert, Stephen, shoemaker, h. Walnut n. Batavia.
Knaup, Peter, moulder, h. Mich. n. Genesee.

Knauper, Michael, grocer, h. Goodell cor. Mulberry.
Knaus, Andrew, blacksmith, h. 275 Elm.
Knauss, John, butcher, h. Goodell alley n. Tupper.
Knecht, Catharine, widow, h. Camp n. Genesee.
Knecht, Geo. tailor, h. 57 Cedar.
Knecht, Jacob, lab. h. Spring n. Genesee.
Kneeland, E. Y. furnace builder, 36 Clinton, h. same.
Knell, Louis, boiler maker, b. J. Frink.
Knell, Peter, carp. h. German alley n. Syc.
Kneller, C. C. widow, h. Spring n. Genesee.
Knetch, August, tailor, h. 412 Michigan.
Knettel, Christopher, cabinet maker, 161 Bat.
Kneus, John, lab. h. Carroll n. Van Renssel'r.
Kney, Geo. tailor, h. 130 Elm.
Knickenberg, Henry, iron peddler, h. 496 Mich.
KNIGHT, J. wine and spirit dealer, 324 and 330 Main, h. 172 Delaware.—See adv. p. 50.
Knight, Jacob, sailor, h. William n. Bennett.
Knight, Theodore C. engineer, h. Clinton n. Madison.
Knight, T. M. carriage maker, 214 Elk, h. Fulton n. Alabama.
Knight, Wm. lab. h. Canal alley n. Jackson.
Knight, W. M. daguerrean artist, 2 Arcade Building, h. 35 N. Division.
Knippel, August, lab. h. Maple n. Carlton.
Knippel, Catharina, widow, h. Mortimer n. Genesee.
Knippel, Geo. shoemaker, h. Walnut n. Bat.
Knobloch, Charles, shoemaker, h. 20 Bennett.
Knobloch, Charles, firm J. L. Haberstro & Co. High n. Main.
Knobloch, John, with Forbush, Brown & Co. h. 24 Bennett.
Knobloch, John, brewer, b. Haberstro & Co.
Knoch, Godfrey, lab. h. Adams n. Sycamore.
Knodel, Henry, printer, b. 480 Michigan.
Knodel, M. widow, dress maker, h. 480 Mich.
Knoedler, John, baker, b. Batavia n. Hickory.
Knoehnen, Nicholas, moulder, h. Adams n. Peckham.
Knoell, Jacob, carp. h. Wm. cor. Jefferson.
Knole, Christian, lab. h. S. Division n. R. R. crossing.
Knoll, Christian, tailor, h. Roos alley n. Wm.
Knoll, Henry, peddler, h. Maryland n. College.
Knollhove, —, gas fitter, h 159 Sycamore.
Knopf, Francis, mason, h. Pine n. William.
Knorl, Christ. lab. h. 406 S. Division.
Knorr, Bernard, tanner, h. Van Rensselaer n. Carroll.
Knorr, Chas. tailor, h. Adams n. William.
Knorr, Henry, grocer, h. Brayton n. R. L
Knorr, Martin, saddler, b. 167 Batavia.
Knower, Chas. tailor, h. Adams n. Peckham.
Knower, Timothy,* bakery, under Western.
Knowles, E. finisher, Brayley & Pitts.
Knowles, Thos. ship carp. b. Ohio n. South.
Knowles, Wm. sawyer, h. South n. Hamburgh.
Knox, John, joiner, h. N. Division n. Grosvenor.
Knox, Pat. lab. h. Louisiana n. Ohio.
Knox, Rebecca, corset maker, h. 40 Delaware.
Knupfer, Pelagius, lab. h. 223 Elm.
Kobb, Jos. grocer, Batavia cor. Emslie.
Kobele, Jacob, dockman, h. Clinton cor. Jeff.

Kobler, Daniel, carpenter, h. Monroe n. Wm.
Koch, Charles, lab. h. 2 Vine.
Koch, Geo. teamster, b. L. Roth's brewery.
Koch, Geo. lab. h. North cor. Oak.
Koch, Henry, carp. h. Maple n. Goodell.
Koch, Henry, shoemaker, h. 109 Pine.
Koch, Jacob, gardener, h. Best opp. Oak.
Koch, Jacob, tinsmith, with Shepard & Co. h. 76 Bennett.
Koch, Jacob, baker, 116 E. Genesee, h. same.
Koch, John, shoemaker, h. 71 Maple.
Koch, John, lab. h. 553 Michigan.
Koch, John, lab. h. Michigan n. High.
Koch, Joseph, tailor, h. 68 E. Tupper.
Koch, Matthias, shoemaker, b. Johnson n. Gen.
Koch, Peter, mason, h. Adams n. Sycamore.
Koch, Wm. lab. h. Best n. Elm.
Koch, Xavier, sailor, h. 10 Bennett.
Kochems, Adam M. printer, b. 26 Spruce.
Kochems, Anna M. widow, h. Spring n. Bat.
Kochems, John A. tailor, h. 26 Spruce.
Kochems, John, moulder, h. Spruce n. Syc.
Koebler, Bernhardt, h. Bond n. R. R. crossing.
Koegel, Chas. ambrotypist and photographist, 34 E. Genesee, h. same.
Koehersberger, Philip, boiler maker, h. Sycamore cor. Pratt.
Koehler, David, lab. h. Genesee n. Spruce.
Koehler, Emile, h. over 123 Genesee.
Koehler, Frank, bakery, 138 Batavia, h. same.
Koehler, Henry, carpenter, h. Goodell alley ab. Tupper.
Koehler, Sophie, widow, h. Hickory n. Gen.
Koehn, August, tailor, h. 264 Elm.
Koehn, John, carpenter, h. Burton alley n. Ellicott.
Koelmel, Lucas, wagoner, h. 448 Michigan.
Koenig, Catharine, widow, h. Fox n. Genesee.
Koenig, Chas. lab. h. Cherry n. Virginia.
Koenig, Chris.* grocer, 331 Genesee, h. same.
Koenig, Geo. tanner, h. Walnut n. Batavia.
Koenig, John, shoemaker, h. Mulberry bel. Virginia.
Koenig, Joseph, blacksmith, h. Ash n. Syc.
Koepke, August, wagon maker, h. Sycamore n. Michigan.
Koepler, John, lab. h. North cor. Oak.
Koeppen, August, carpenter, h. Ellicott n. Virginia.
Koeppen, Christian, lab. h. n. Exchange on R. R. track.
Koffman, Geo. blacksmith, h. Elm ab. Gen.
Kohl, Geo. shoemaker, h. Ketchum n. High.
Kohl, John, mason, h. 271 Oak.
Kohl, Martin, lab. h. Adams n. Sycamore.
Kohl, Mary, widow, h. William n. Pine.
Kohl, Wolfgang, lab. h. Fox n. Genesee.
Kohlbach, Frederick, mason, h. Mulberry n. Goodell.
Kohlbacker, Adam, shade painter, 231 Main, h. 125 Walnut.
Kohlbacker, Henry, varnisher, A. & J. Keogh, b. 125 Walnut.
Kohlbrenner, Casper, lab. Ferry n. Main.
Kohlbrenner, Ferd. h. Mulberry n. Goodell.
Kohlbrenner, Jacob, grocery, Maple cor. Goodell.
Kohler, Adam, carp. h. r. 19 E. Huron.

Kohler, Christ. tailor, h. Lutheran n. Wm.
Kohler, Michael, lab. h. Michigan n. High.
Kohlgruber, Frederick H. grocer, h 155 Bat.
Kohlis, John, lab. h. Stanton n. Peckham.
Kohlman, Francis, cooper, h. Maple n. High.
Kohlman, Henry, moulder, h. Adams n. Syc.
Kohlmorgen, C. shoemaker, h. cor. Perry and Mississippi.
Kohn, George, shoemaker, h. 72 E. Tupper.
Kohn, John, with Jewett & Root, h. Monroe n. Batavia.
Kohnle, Alois, at Gilbert's soap factory, h. Oak n. Batavia.
Kohnus, Chas. shoemaker, b. 1 Water.
Kohoe, Richard, lab. h. Tupper cor. Ellicott.
Koin, M. lab. h. Carroll n. Michigan.
Kolb, Charles A. harness maker, 355 Main, h. same.
Kolb, Edward, lab. h. Genesee n. Carlton.
Kolb, Geo. M. & Co. harness dealers, 117 Main.
Kolb, Geo. M. firm G. M. K. & Co. h. 355 Main.
Kolb, Jacob, firm G. M. K. & Co. h. 175 Oak.
Kolb, John, lab. h. 256 Genesee.
Kolb, Maria, h. 160 Oak.
Kolb, Michael, moulder, h. Johnson n. Batavia.
Kolbmeier, Henry, mason, h. 112 Pine.
Kollasik, Matthias, tailor, h. 16 Michigan.
Kollaski, Alex. hatter, 80 Main, h. 440 Mich.
Koller, John, carp. h. Adams n. Batavia.
Kollert, Charles, lab. h. Maple n. High.
Kollert, Michael, lab. h. Michigan n. High.
Kolleschan, George, shoemaker, h. cor. Spring and Sycamore.
Kolman, J. H foundryman, Brayley & Pitts.
Kolmorgan, Fred. cooper, h. cor. Scott and Burwell.
Kolp. Frank. moulder, h. Pratt n. William.
Kolpflesh, Hendrich, gardener, h. 11th n. Vt.
Kolz, Nicholas, shoemaker, h. 96 Hickory.
Komas, Arnst, butcher, h. Wm. n. Madison.
Kommer, Geo. finisher, h. 238 Elm.
Konaff, Philip, lab. h. Clinton cor. Pratt.
Konrad, Wm. baker, b. 124 Seneca.
Kontz, John, stove mounter, h. S. Division n. city line.
Koon, Henry, sailor, h. Cedar n. Eagle.
Koonce, Michael, finisher, Brayley & Pitts.
Koons, Henry, lab. h. Niagara n. Bouck ave.
Kopf, Charles, cooper, h. Amherst n. Thompson.
Kopf, J. P. printer, h. over 51 E. Tupper.
Kopf, John, cooper, h. East n. Hamilton.
Kopp, John, lab. h. Burton alley n. Wash.
Korber, Geo. lab. h. Batavia n. Emslie.
Korber, Michael, mason, h. Monroe n. Syc.
Korfmann, Lewis, carpenter, h. Sherman n. Batavia.
Kormornus, Fred. lab. h. Mulberry n. Virginia.
Korn, Charles, shoemaker, b. 77 Genesee.
Korn, Charles, blacksmith, h. 136 E. Genesee.
Korn, Conrad, turner, h. German alley n. Syc.
Korn, Geo. lab. h. Monroe n. Batavia.
Korn, Philip, shoemaker, h. Exch. n. Jeff.
Kornbrobst, John, lab. r. 151 Oak.
Kortz, A. clerk, b. 109 Seneca.
Kortz, Godfrey, lab. h. William n. Watson.
Kortz, John, carpenter, h. cor. Goodell & Oak.
Korzelius, Jacob, clerk, 174 Main, b. Batavia n. Pine.

Korzelius, John, vinegar factory. Batavia cor. Pine, h. same.
Koslowski, Charles, blacksmith, h. Michigan cor. Carlton.
Kossouss, John, mason, h. Abbott plank road n. iron bridge.
Kottner, Henry, lab. h. Spring n. William.
Kowall, Henry, carpenter, h. Ellicott cor. Burton alley.
Kraemer, Adam, blacksmith, h. 319 Ellicott.
Kraemer, Andrew, milkman, h. German alley n. Genesee.
Kraemer, Henry, butcher, h. Michigan n. Burton alley.
Kraemer, Jacob, pattern maker, h. Cherry n. Spruce.
Kraemer, Lewis, lab. h. 121 Cherry.
Kraener, Peter, b. 252 E. Genesee.
Kraengell, Fred. carp. h. Bennett n. Batavia.
Kraetz, Adolph, carp. h. 41 Sycamore.
Kraetz, Christ, mason, h. Amherst n. city line.
Kraetzer, Lenhard, Mrs. h. cor. Goodell and Cherry.
Kraffert, Jacob, carp. h. High n. Smith alley.
Krafft, Fred. Wm. carp. h. Wm. cor. Lutheran.
Kraft, Anthony, carp. h. 293 Ellicott.
Kraft, Christ. cooper, h. Hamilton n. Delaware.
Kraft, Conrad, lab. b. H. Kraft.
Kraft, Francis J. undertaker, 29 E. Huron, h. same.
Kraft, Henry, lab. h. r. 47 Delaware place.
Kraft, Henry, tinsmith, h. 367 Michigan.
Kraft, Henry, lab. h. Kaene n. Sycamore.
Kraft, John, lab. b. H. Kraft.
Kraft, J. peddler, b. 7th n. R. I.
Kraft, Michael, gardener, h. Breckenridge n. Rogers.
Kraghot, Geo. night watch, for R. L. Howard.
Kramer, A. stone mason, Cherry cor. Spruce.
Kramer, Conrad, shoemaker, h. Pine n. Wm.
Kramer, H. iron finisher, Brayley & Pitts.
Kramer, John, peddler, h. 59 Cedar.
Kramer, Michael, lab. h. German alley, n. Syc.
Kramer, Valentine, lab. h. Pine n. Batavia.
Kranichfeldt, Albert, moulder, h. Oak n. Carlton.
Kranichfeld, Henry, barkeeper, 25 Commercial, b. same.
Kranichfeld, John, moulder, b. Oak n. Carlton.
Kranichfeld, John A. lab. h. Oak n. Carlton.
Kranigfeld, Gottlieb, tailor, h. Camp n. Gen.
Kranz, John M. saloon, 7 Canal, h. same.
Krapp, Frederick, boat builder, h. Clinton n. Walnut.
Krapp, Henry, saloon, 5 Commercial. h. same.
Krathwohl, John, grocer, 448 Wash. h. same.
Kratz, Lorenz, carp. h. Mulberry n. Goodell.
Kratz, Martin, lab. h. Locust n. Virginia.
Kratz, Michael, carp. h. Clinton n. Madison.
Kratzenstein, Sophia, widow, Pratt n. Syc.
Kraus, Andrew, fireman, Ketchum alley n. High.
Kraus, Christian, 211 Main. h. 577 Washington.
Kraus, Fred. tailor, h. 17 Huron.
Kraus, Geo. mason, h. Clinton bel. R. R. crossing.
Kraus, John, clerk, h. 577 Washington.
Kraus, John, lab. h. Adams n. Brown.

Kraus, John, shoemaker, h. Elm n. High.
Krause, Wm. J. barber, Commercial, h. 495 Washington.
Krauss, Marg. widow, h. Grey n. Batavia.
Krausskopf, Wm. music teacher, h. 36 Goodell.
Kreamer, Charles, carp. h. Maple n. North.
Kreamer, Henry, butcher, h. Michigan n. Burton alley.
Kreamer, Matthias, tailor, h. 36 Bennett.
Krech, Charles, tinsmith, 72 E. Gen. h. same.
Kreft, Frederica, wid. h. Locust n. Carlton.
Kreher, Adam,* shoemaker, 195 Genesee, h. same.
Kreher, Lawrence, carp. h. Hickory n. Gen.
Kreher, Michael, lab. h. Grey bet. Genesee and Batavia.
Kreier, Chris. mason, h. Cedar n. William.
Kreiger, A.* tailor, ov. 255 Gen. h. same.
Kreiger, Benj.* boot and shoemaker, 341 Gen. h. same.
Kreiger, Christopher, lab. h. Spruce n. Gen.
Kreiger, Conrad, lab. h. Camp n. Genesee.
Krein, Chas. boat builder, h. Niagara n. South.
Krein, Joseph, printer, h. Watson n. Wm.
Kreiner, Geo. firm G. K. & Co. h. 106 Exch.
Kreiner, Geo. Jr. firm G. K. & Co. h. 22 Folsom.
Kreiner, G. & Co. boot and shoe dealers, 106 Exchange.
Kreiner, Jacob, shoemaker, h. 22 Folsom.
Kreinheder, J. carpenter, h. Grey n. Batavia.
Kreinheder, Jno. H. h. Grey n. Batavia.
Kreis, Chas. upholsterer, 307 Main, h. Walnut n. Sycamore.
Kreis, Geo. carpenter, h. Hick'y n. Sycamore.
Kreise, Lewis, lithographer, Sage & Sons, b. 2 Canal.
Kreiss, Geo. saloon, h. Main n. Ferry.
Kreitz, Jacob, saloon, Chippewa opp. market, h. same.
Kreitzbender, Jas. tanner, h. Bat. n. Lutheran.
Kreitzburg, Valentine, watchman, h. Hamilton n. Niagara. .
Krenheder, Henry, piano maker, h. Grey n. Batavia.
Kress, Fred. firm K. & Warren, h. cor. Ellicott and Carlton.
Kress, Valentine, grocer, Amherst cor. Lewis.
Kress & Warren, hardware, 383 Main.
Kressman, Jacob, mason, h. Lemon n. Va.
Kressmen, Phil. mason, h. Cherry n. Spring.
Krettner, Jacob, commissioner of deeds and insurance agent, 281 Main.
Krettner, J. Jr. clerk, 281 Main.
Krettner, Louis, clerk, 281 Main, b. same.
Kretz, Michael, tailor, h. 249 Oak.
Kreutz, Jos. carpenter, h. Clinton n. Madison.
Kreuzen, John, lab. h. Locust n. High.
Krick, Adam, engineer, h. Mortimer n. Gen.
Krick, Nicholas, moulder, h. over 138 Genesee.
Krick, Philip, tailor, h. Mortimer n. Genesee.
Krieg, B. shoemaker, h. 179 Batavia.
Kriegbaum, Jno. Jr. lab. h. Locust n. High.
Kriegbaum, John, lab. h. Mulberry n. High.
Kriegbaum, Lenhardt, bricklayer, h. Locust n. Virginia.
Krieger, Fred. tailor, h. Kaene n. Sycamore.
Krieger, M.* cabinet maker, 218 Gen. h. same.
Krieger, Michael, Jr. cabinet maker, b. 218 Gen.

Krieger, Wm. painter, h. Genesee n. Walnut.
Kries, Annie M. widow, seamstress, h. Spruce n. Genesee.
Krietner, Fred. flagman, h. Van Rensselaer n. Exchange.
Kriter, Jacob, tailor, h. 169 Clinton.
Kritzberger, Conrad, clerk. Elk n. La. b. same.
Kroetsch, Geo. carp. h. Mulberry n. Virginia.
Krohnenfeldt, W. shoemaker, h. 11 Sycamore.
Kroll, John, tailor, h. Jefferson n. William.
Krollman, John. cabinet maker, h. 169 Clinton.
Krollman, John, tanner, h. 2 Bennett.
Kromer, Jno. book store, 98 Pine, h. same.
Kron, Jacob, lab. h. Pratt n. Genesee.
Kron, John, saloon, Ellicott cor. Chippewa.
Krost, Jacob, lab. h. 413 Michigan.
Krost, Louis, moulder, b. Bennett n. William.
Krost, Louis, h. Bennett n. William.
Krueger, August, blacksmith, h. Hick'y n. Wm.
Krueger, John F. W. hardware dealer, 23 E. Genesee, h. 35 Sycamore.
Krueger, John, lab. h. Walden n. William.
Krug, Geo. shoemaker, h. Genesee n. Grey.
Krug, Gottleib, cooper, h. 468 Michigan.
Krug, Vit, tailor, h. Seneca n. R. R. crossing.
Kruger, Fred. joiner, b. 49 N. Division.
Krumholz, Ferdinand, h. 287 Oak.
Krumholz, Jos. clerk, gas works, b. 287 Oak.
Krupp, Geo. A. firm Theobald & K. 352 Main, h. same.
Krupp, Geo. grocery, 147 Batavia cor. Bennett.
Krupp, Joseph, mason, h. Michigan n. Best.
Kruse, Henry C. grocer and wood dealer, 23 Canal, h. 31 William.
Ksall, Stephen, tanner, h. William n. Madison.
Kuchler, John, miller, h. Hamilt'n n. Thomps'n.
Kuchler, Michael, moulder, h. 578 Washington.
Kuebeller, Phil. G. saloon, 31 Mohawk, h. same.
Kuebler, John,* butcher, h. Genesee cor. Grey.
Kuechenmeister, John, b. 496 Michigan.
Kuehmund, F. lab. h. Spring bet. Syc. and Bat.
Kuehn, Otto F. W. musician, b. cor. Huron and Genesee.
Kuempel, Louis, grocer, Pratt n. Batavia.
Kughler, G. D. M. D. 126 Pearl, h. same.
Kughler, Andrew, lab. h. Lutheran n. Batavia.
Kugler, Wm. shoemaker, h. Hickory n. Wm.
Kuhl, Henry, lab. h. William n. Jefferson.
Kuhn, Abraham, Evans & Co. planing mill.
Kuhn, Charles, baker, b. 225 Ellicott.
Kuhn, Conrad, milkman, h. Locust n Cherry.
Kuhn, Fran. A. tailor, Goodell cor. Goodell al.
Kuhn, F. dep'ty sheriff, h. Genesee n. Williamsville road.
Kuhn, G. lithograph'r, Sage & Sons, h. 133 Oak.
Kuhn, Henry, lab. h. Amherst n. city line.
Kuhn, John, tinsmith, h. William cor. Pratt.
Kuhn, Michael, lab. h. 57 Cedar.
Kuhn, M. farmer, h. Amherst n. city line.
Kuhn, Magdalene, widow, b. 16 Goodell.
Kuhn, Peter, painter, h. 133 Oak.
Kuhn, Wm. cabinet maker, h. Cypress n. Mich.
Kuhner, Frederick, blacksmith, Main n. Buffalo Plains.
Kull, Frederick, grocery and provision store, cor. Lloyd and Prime.
Kulow, John, boot maker, with G. Henning, h. 106 Clinton.

Kulow, Michael, lab. h. Ketchum alley n. High.
Kulzer, Geo. lab. h. Johnson n. North.
Kumann, Jacob, lab. h. Gen. cor. Walnut
Kumarr Mathias, blacksmith, h. Walnut n. Bat.
Kumf, Peter, boiler maker, h. Kaene n. Syc.
Kumpf, Geo. lab. h. Kaene n. Genesee.
Kumpf, Geo. Jr. boiler maker, b. Kaene n. Syc.
Kummer, Walpurja, widow, b. 554 Mich.
Kunty, John. lab. h. S. Div. below Jeff.
Kuntz, Christian. shoemaker. h. Tupper n. Elm.
Kuntz, David, lab. h. Mortimer n. Genesee.
Kuntz, Gregory, carpenter, h. Goodell alley n. Goodell.
Kunz, Meirad, peddler, h. Gen. n. Fox
Kunz & Gross, marble factory, Main n. Chip.
Kunz, Wm. firm K. & Gross. h. 14th.
Kunze, Jno. lab. h. Bat. n. Pratt.
Kunzman, Phil. lab. b. 127 Pine.
Kuper, Rich. H. express mess'ngr. b. 69 S. Div.
Kurst, Chas. lab. h. 16 Maple.
Kurtz, Aug. wagon maker, h. William below Hickory.
Kurtz, Daniel, blacksmith, h. William below Hickory.
Kurtz, Henry, tanner. h. Pratt n. William.
Kurtz. John, carp. h. Goodell cor. Oak.
Kurtz, Nicholas, paver, b. Mulberry above Goodell.
Kurtzman. Christ. piano maker, 213 Eagle.
Kurtzman & Hinze. piano forte manufactory, Staats cor. Mohawk.
Kurtzwart, Baptist, mason, h. 265 Elm.
Kurtzwart, Frank, carp. h. 296 Elm.
Kurtzwart, John, lab. h. 239 Elm.
Kurz, Francis, liquor dealer, h. Madison n. Batavia.
Kuster, C. A. watch maker, h. 158 Batavia.
Kuster, Gotfried, h. Bat. n. Pratt.
Kuster, Jos. butcher, 7 Canal n. Maiden lane.
Kutzlapp, Ernst. lab. Bat. n. Pratt.
Kutzlett, Jacob, shoemaker, h. Shumway n. Batavia.
Kyle, Alice, boarding house, 200 Washington.
Kyle, Hannah, wid. h. Clinton n. Emslie.

L.

Laahceil, Mrs. Indian doctress, cor. Washington and Carroll.
Labby, Chas. carp. h. South n. Sycamore.
Labby, Charles, carpenter, h. Fulton n. Ala.
Labby, Joseph, ship carp. h. Ala. n. Mackinaw.
Lachner, Geo. grocer. 577 Main, h. same.
Lacy, Clark B. American Express Company, b. 122 E. Eagle.
Lacy, E. D. book-keeper, Farmers and Mechanics' Bank, h. 442 Main.
Lacy, John T. cashier, American Express Company. h. 122 E. Eagle.
Lafferty, Pat. sailor, h. Perry n. Hamburgh.
Lafiam, Joseph, boarding house, Ohio cor. Wabash.
Laganhadir, H. joiner, h. Carroll bet. Red Jacket and Heacock.
Laheny, Bridget, widow, h. 5th n. Virginia.
Laher, George, milkman, h. Watson n. Bat.
Lahman, John, farmer, Del. n. town line road.
Laible, Christopher, grocer, Amherst cor. Ton.

Laible, Nicholas, blacksmith, h. Lewis n. Amherst.
Laing, Abraham, firm A. L. & Co. h. cor. Mass. and Chenango.
Laing, A. & Co. groceries and liquors, 71 Main.
Laing, Daniel, firm A. L. & Co. h. Niagara below Virginia.
Laing, David N. moulder, h. 7 Scott.
Laing. Jacob, grocer and provision dealer, 51 Main, h. Batavia bet. Oak and Elm.
Laing, I. H. clerk, 51 Main, b. Batavia n. Elm.
Laing. J. P. book-keeper, 51 Main, b. Batavia n. Elm.
Lake, S. secretary Farmers' Mutual Insurance Co. agt. 1 Hollister Block. h. 253 Franklin.
Lake Shore and Michigan Southern R. R. office, 147 Main.
Laly, Michael, saloon, Canal dock.
Lamb, Henry, butcher, 1 Birkhead Buildings, Commercial, b. same.
Lamb, Margaret, Mrs. h. 405 Michigan.
Lamb, Michael, carp. b. Clinton n. Hickory.
Lamber, Augustine, stone cutter, h. Washington cor. Virginia.
Lambert, Francis, barber, h. 200 Oak.
Lambert, James, book-keeper, Altman & Co. h. 260 Swan.
Lamberton, Wm. cl'k, Great Western Dispatch, h. Eagle n. Michigan.
Lambrix, Henry, plasterer, h. r. 258 Franklin.
Lemerer, Catharine, wid. h. 528 Michigan.
Lamey, Margaret, widow, grocer, Perry cor. Mississippi.
Lamey, Patrick, lab. h. Elk n. Louisiana.
Lamie, John, lab. h. Carroll n. Louisiana.
Lammy, Peter, tailor, h. 160 Genesee.
Lamon, Mrs. widow, h. Cherry n. Spruce.
Lampert, James L. cashier, with Altman & Co. h. 206 Swan.
Lamphear, Hiram H. melodeon maker, b. 178 Niagara.
Lamphear, Joseph, teamster, h. cor. Hamilton and Thompson.
Lamphier, Charles, firm Ingalls & L. h. Hudson cor. 12th.
Lamphier Thomas, melodeon maker, h. 10th n. Carolina.
LAMPMAN, WARREN, Justice Peace, 142 Main. h. 16 Perry.—See adv. p. 81.
Lana, Elizabeth, widow, h. 11th cor. Virginia.
Lana, John, blacksmith. h. 11th cor. Virginia.
Lanaghen, Patrick, brick maker, h. Canal n. Grosvener
Lancer, John lab. b. 38 Ohio.
Lancer, John, mariner, h. Hudson n. 10th.
Landefield, C.* shoemaker, h. Clinton above Hickory.
Lander. James, boot and shoe manufactory, 156 Main, h. 3 6th.
Landerer, Martin, coop'r, h. Hampshire n. 10th.
Landgraf, Geo. tanner, h. Clinton n. R. R. crossing.
Landgraf, John, lab. h. Monroe n. Brown.
Landschuft, Christian. peddler, h. Burton n. Hydraulics.
Landschuft, Wm. wagoner, h. 136 Batavia.
Landsman, John, lab. h. Johnson n. Genesee.
Landwher, Frank, mason, h. 41 Hickory.

Lane, Geo. A. express messenger, h. Chestnut cor. Swan.
Lane, G. C. b. 30 Chippewa.
Lane, John, harness maker, Evans n. Canal, h. 175 Terrace.
Lane, John, lab. h. Tennessee n. Mackinaw.
Laneyon, John, joiner, h. 14th n. Vermont.
Lang, Adam, grocer, h. Walnut cor. Sycamore.
Lang, A. wagon maker, cor. Chicago and Perry, h. same.
Lang, C. F. car inspector, N. Y. C. R. R. h. 24 William.
Lang, Chas. silver plater, cor. Niagara and School.
Lang, Christian. wagon maker, h. Clinton n. Spring.
Lang, Christian, mason, h. 500 Michigan.
Lang, C. W. piano finisher with A. & J. Keogh.
Lang, Daniel, melodeon maker, h. 62 Cedar.
Lang, Frank, butcher, 97 Genesee n. Oak. h. same.
Lang, Geo. lab. h. 172 Oak.
Lang, Geo. F. brewer, h. Genesee cor. Grey.
Lang, Henry, wagoner. h. Clinton n. Spring.
Lang, Jacob, butcher, 126 Batavia.
Lang, John, gardener, h. Michigan n. Best.
Lang, M. lab. h. Mulberry n. Goodell.
Lang, Michael, lab. h. 261 Elm.
Lang, Michael, tool maker, h. Batavia cor. Ash.
Lang, Michael, carpenter, b. Michigan n. Best.
Lang, Michael, baker, b. 188 Elm.
Lang, Mrs. widow, h. Delaware ave. n. Walden.
Lang, Susanna, midwife, h. 500 Michigan.
Lang, Victor, printer, 358 Main, h. cor. Washington and Huron.
Lang, Wm. lab. h. Michigan cor. Goodrich.
Langa, Fred, shoemaker. h. Spring n. William.
Langdon, Charles H. ass't teller Clinton Bank, b. 53 Ellicott.
Langdon, Geo. P. firm L. & Sears, h. Franklin n. Virginia.
Langdon, James, engineer, b. S. Hutter.
Langdon, Jno. Mrs. b. 52 E. Seneca.
LANGDON & SEARS. pork dealers and inspectors, 22 and 24 Han'er.—See adv. p. 42.
Lange, August, peddler, h. Camp n. Sycamore.
Lange, Chas. William, piano maker, 259 Washington, h. 16 Peckham.
Lange, Elizabeth, widow. h. Mich. n. Carlton.
Lange, William C. shoemaker, h. 273 Elm.
Langenbach, Gottlieb, lab. h. Del. av. n. Wald'n.
Langfeld, John,* shoemaker, Genesee cor. Camp, h. same.
Langfeld, Jacob, shoemaker, h. Camp cor. Gen.
Langfeld, Jno. N. shoemaker. h. Camp n. Gen.
Langgood, J. h. Hickory n. Clinton.
Langheienrich, Henry, locksmith. h. 206 Oak.
Langheir, Andrew, mason. h. Adams n. Syca.
Langlo, Christian, lab. h. Elm n. Carlton.
Langlo, Fred. lab. h. Elm n. Carlton.
Langmeyer, Frank. shoemaker, b. 99 Oak.
Langmeyer, John, works Evans & Co.'s planing mill.
Langmeyer, Mary, widow, h. 99 Oak.
Laning, A. P. firm L. & Miller, h. 238 Franklin.
Laning & Miller, att'ys. 6 Brown's Buildings.
Lankes, John. lab. h. Monroe cor. Sycamore.
Lankes, Michael, lab. h. Adams n. Batavia.

Lannan, Thos. farmer, h. Best E. of Jefferson.
Lannen, Jas. ship carp. h. Hamb. n. Fulton.
Lannen, Pat. bricklayer. h. Oak n. High.
Lannein, Thos. lab. h. 4th ab. Maryland.
Lannigan, Mary, widow, h. Vt. n. 15th.
Lannon, Edward, bricklayer, b. Fred. Dadman.
Lannon, Jas. lab. h. Main n. North.
Lannon, Joseph, printer, Express, b. Walnut n. Clinton.
Lannon, Mary, widow, h. Walnut n. Clinton.
Lannon, Thos. ship carpenter. Ala. n. Carroll.
Lansing, Garrett, foreman, Jewett & Root, h. 214 E. Swan.
Lansing, Henry L. treasurer. B. & S. L. R. R, 3 Harvey Block, h. 106 Del. cor. Johns'n pl.
Lansing. Livingston, clerk, B. & S. L. R. R. freight office, b. Delaware n. Park place.
Lansing, Stephen, stove mounter, h. cor. William and Pine.
Lansing, S. A. widow, b 50 Pine.
Lansittel, Anthony, whitewasher, h. 208 Gen.
Lanz, Ferdinand, tailor, h. Cherry n. Maple.
Lapach, Frank, sailor, h. 12th n. Massachusetts.
Lapierre, Jos. stone cutter. h. 318 Ellicott.
Lapoint. Lawrence. ship carp b. Ohio n. Chi.
Lapp, Christian, lawyer, h. 98 Oak.
Lapp, Isaac. miller, h. Ferry cor. Washington.
Lapp, Jacob, grocer, Mart Block, Ohio, h. 112 Elm.
Lapp, Susan K. teacher No. 15, b. 98 Oak.
Lappin, Robt. boarding house, 46 Ohio.
Lapple, Peter, tailor, b. 45 Spruce.
Lapple, Peter. Jr. clerk, b. 45 Spruce.
Lapsley, Geo. printer, Courier office, h. 6 Gay.
Larau, Oliver, lumberman, h. 393 Seneca.
Larch, Lewis, boarding house, Niag. n. Parish.
Larkin, John, picture frame maker, 37 Cedar.
Larkin, L. H. widow, h. 78 Niagara.
Larkin, Mary, h. 78 Niagara.
Larkins, Philip, h 73 5th n. Court.
Larned, J. N. local editor, Morning Express, h. 138 9th.
Larner, Jas. lab. h. Exchange n. Smith.
LARREAU, ANDREW N. prop. National Hotel, 91 and 92 Exchange.—See adv. p. 93.
Larreau, Jno. A. clerk, National Hotel.
Larreau. L. D. attorney, 4 Arcade Buildings. b. National.
Larrow, Noah, mason, h. Math'w n. Mortimer.
Larrug, Jno. mason, b. Spruce n. Genesee.
Lasser, Casper, h. 28 Maple.
Latham, T. W. clerk, 318 Main. b. City Hotel.
Lathbury, E. T. machinist, h. R. L n. 12th.
Lathrop, Laura C. widow of Herman F. h. 75 Clinton.
Latta, Robt. grocer, Niag. n. Mohawk, h. same.
Lattau, Michael, grocery, 7 Canal, h. same.
Lattimore, John, boatman, h. across creek.
Latz, Jacob, lab. h. Walnut n. Batavia.
Latz, John. lab. h. 262 Elm.
Lau, Jno. mason, h. Davis n. Genesee.
Laub, Adam. firm L. & Bros. h. 11 E. Genesee.
Laub & Brothers, leather store, 11 E. Genesee.
Laub, Fred. firm L. & Bros, 11 E. Genesee.
Laub, Geo. firm L. & Bros, h. 11 E. Genesee.
Lauber, Frank, carpenter. h. Mich n. North.
Lauber, Geo. house mover, h. Elm n. Burt'n al.
Lauber, Matthias, shoemaker, h. 11 Spruce.

—See adv. p. 42.
—See adv. p. 93.

Laudenbacher. Fred. britannia ware, cor. Pearl and Seneca, h. 105 Eagle.
Laudon. Chas. lab. h. Adams n. Genesee.
Lauer, F. V. gas fitter, h. Michigan n. High.
Lauer, Geo. warehouseman, h. Church n. Ter.
Lauer, Ludwig. shoemaker, h. 296 Elm.
Lauer, Martin, Rev. h. 295 Oak.
Lauer, Nicholas, shoemaker, h. Mich. n. High.
Laughlan, Martin, lab. h. across creek.
Laughlin. Pat. h. Exchange n. Red Jacket.
Lauinger, Theo. engineer, h. Hickory n. Bat.
Launschbach, Wm.* shoemaker, Com'l Hotel Block, h. Pratt n. Genesee.
Lauser, Martin, lab. h. Adams n. Batavia.
Laut, Frid. cooper h. Keane n. Genesee.
Laut, Geo. cooper, h. Keane n. Genesee.
Laut, Henry, lab. h. Keane n. Genesee.
Laut, Peter, lab. h. Keane n. Genesee.
Lautenslager, Fred. saloon, Main cor. Clinton, h. 401 Main.
Lautenbach, Fred. blacksmith, h. Wm. n. Pine.
Lauth, Philip, lab. h. 181 Batavia.
Lautz, Wm. soap and candle factory, Batavia n. Spring, h. same.
Laux, Adam, lab. h. 170 Elm.
Laux, Barbara, widow, h. Hinkley n. Mort.
Laux, Elizabeth, widow, Mulberry n. Good'l.
Laux, Jacob, tailor, b. Peckham n. Stanton.
Laux, John, teacher, h. Wm n. Mortimer.
Laux, Martin. firm Greenshield & L. Com'l. cor. Canal, h. 105 Seneca.
Lavin, Mary, wid. grocer, 407 Seneca. h. same.
Larin, Peter, farmer, Del. n. town line road.
Lavender, Geo. sail maker, h. 20 Perry.
Laverack, Wm. firm Hollister & L. h. 80 Del.
Laverack, Wm. A. clerk at 202 Washington, b. 80 Delaware.
Laverty. Henry, book-keeper, 291 Main, b. 311 Washington.
Lavery, Wm. J. clk. 163 Main, h. 176 Franklin.
Lavictaire, Samuel, caulker, h. Fulton.
Lavort, Eli, lithographer, h. 89 Cedar.
Lavy, Bridget, milliner, b. 6th n. Maryland.
Law. James, millwright, 179 Swan.
Lawler, Jno, with R. L. Howard, h. 13th n. Ga.
Lawler, Robert, machinist, LeCouteulx n. Canal, h. 4th n. Georgia.
Lawless, Thos. grocer, Elk opp. Moore.
Lawlor, J. D. machinist, b. 14th n. York.
Lawlow, Edward, sailor, h. Ala, opp. Carroll.
Lawrance, B. pail maker, h. Amherst n. Lewis.
Lawrance, Seier, lab. h. Amherst n. city line.
Lawrence, B. painter, h. Walnut n. Clinton.
Lawrence, Chas. Wm. lab. h. Clinton ave. n. N. Washington.
Lawrence, Joseph, policeman, Elk n. Chicago.
Lawrence, Richard, telegraph repairer, h. 6th n. Hudson.
Lawson, Conrad, tinsmith, h. Pratt cor. Wm.
Lawson, Edward, blacksmith, b. 46 Ohio.
Lawson, Richard. bird stuffer, h. Wash. n. Perry.
Lawson, Peter, Sr. sailor, h. Pratt n. William.
Lawson. Peter, ship carp. h. Roos al. n Wm.
Lay, Chas. Mrs. h. 168 Swan.
Lay, Frances, widow, h. 94 Oak.
Lay, Leo'd, shoemaker, h. Chip'wa opp. market.
Laycock, Thos. farmer, h. n. junction Seneca and Exchange.

Lazarus, Elizabeth, widow, Batavia cor. Ash.
Lazarus, Ephraim.* clothier, 38 Main, h. same.
Lazarus, Jos. clothier, 38 Main, h. same.
Lazarus, Nathan, tanner, h. 81 Elm.
Leach, J. W. ship carp. Alabama opp. Carroll.
Leader, John J. grocer, cor. Perry and Illinois.
Leake, W. J. M. D. 18 Mart Bl'k, Ohio, b. same.
Leamann, F. shoemaker, h. Syc. n. Hickory.
Learned, Sam. M. D. 22 S. Division, h. same.
Leary, Catharine, widow, h. Marvin n. Elk.
Leary, Cornelius, lab. b. Exch. n. Red Jacket.
Leary, Dan. lab. h. Mill n. Heacock.
Leary, Hamphrey, lab. h. Elk n. Michigan.
Leary, James, lab. b. Ohio n. R. R. track.
Leary, Jerry, lab. h. Mill n. Red Jacket.
Leary, Timothy, lab. h. Mill n. Heacock.
Leaton, Jno. lumber mer. b. 6th n. Ft. Porter.
Leavey, Mart. porter, h. 6th n. Hudson.
Leavey, Michael, clerk, A. Reynolds & Co. h. 6th n. Maryland.
Leavitt, James S. blank book manufacturer, 70 Lloyd. h. 46 Court.
Lebenbruk, Nicholas. lab. h. Pratt n. Eagle.
Leber, John, tailor, ov. 112 Batavia.
Leberer, John. brewer, h. Lutheran n. William.
Lebert, Christian, machinist, Court cor. Pearl, h. r. 34 Batavia.
Lebert, Martin, tailor, h. Bennett n. Batavia.
Lebert, Philip, lab. h. Hollister n. Spring.
LeBoutillier, G. T. b. 52 E. Swan.
Lechard, Lewis, lab. h. Walden n. Genesee.
Lechleiter, Fred. lab. h. Ferry n. Massachusetts.
Leck, William. plasterer, h. 14th n. Mass.
LeClear, L. attorney, 3 Terrace, b. Bonney's Hotel.
Lecomte, Louis, h. 355 Washington.
Ledebor, Henry,* wagoner, Adams n. Sycamore, h. same.
Lederdorf, Chris. lab. h. Cherry n. Spring.
Lederdorf, Michael, lab. h. Chicago n. Hickory.
Lederer, Charles, cabinet maker, 160 Elm, h. Kaene n. Genesee.
Lederer, Chas. Jr. carver, h. Kaene n. Genesee.
Lederer, Lenhard, butcher, cor. Michigan and Goodell.
Lederer, Wm. chairmaker, h. Kaene n. Gen.
Lederman, Elizabeth, widow, washer, h. Grey n. Genesee.
Ledger, John, sailor, h. Elk n. Hayward.
Lee, Bryan, lab. California n. Adams.
Lee, Chas. T. jeweler, h. 17 Park place.
Lee, Cyrus P. secretary Erie Co. Savings Bank, h. North n. Franklin.
Lee, E. h. Niagara cor. Virginia.
Lee, E. H. Miss, millinery. 279 Main, h. same.
Lee, Jas. H. clerk in P. O. h. 279 Main.
Lee, Jas. I. lab. h. Elk n. R. R.
Lee, John R. agent Manhattan life insurance company. 37 Pearl, h. 113 Franklin.
Lee, Patrick, clerk, 199 Wash. b. Globe Hotel.
Lee, Richard, mariner, h. Hudson n. Cottage.
Lee, Stephen, carpenter, h. Perry n. Chicago.
Lee, Strange Jas. lab. h. LeCouteulx.
Lee, Thos. teamster, h. Hampshire cor. 9th.
Lee, Uriah D. h. 44 Delaware.
Lee, W. A. cabinet maker, h. N. Wash. n. Bouck.
Leech, J. H. stationer, cor. Main and Exchange, 3d story.

Leech, John W. grocer and ship carpenter, cor. Niagara and Pearl.
Leech, Philip, shoemaker, 9 Commercial, h. cor. Maiden lane and Canal.
Leech, William, waiter, h. 103 Clinton.
Leen, Thos. lab. h. 231 Carroll.
Lees, David C. blacksmith, b. Seneca opp. Heacock.
Lees, Jno. butch'r, 23 Elk st. mark't, h. 176 6th.
Leetsch, John, saloon, Pearl, h. 4 Centre.
Legel, Fred. blacksmith, h. Hickory n. Clinton.
Leggett, Alex. weigher, h. Virginia n. 11th.
Leggett, Peter, ship carp. h. Carroll n. Ala.
Lehman, Fred. ship carp. b. Walnut n. Bat.
Lehman, John, lab. h. 37 Elm.
Lehman, Jos. saloon, 149 Elm.
Lehman, Meyer, wagoner, h. William n. Pine.
Lehmann, Chas. lab. h. Ash n. Sycamore.
Lehmann, Charles, at Union ticket office, 443 Washington.
Lehmann, Jos. shoem'r, h. Watson n. Peckh'm.
Lehmann, Nicholas,* shoémaker, 7 S. Division, h. 110 6th.
Lehmann, Philip, millwright, h. 90 Bennett.
Lehner, Andrew, tailor, h. 253 Elm.
Lehner, Casper, butch'r, h. Abb't n. iron bridge.
Lehner, Mich'l, lab. h. Monroe n. Sycamore.
Lehnhardt, Andrew, mason, h. Walnut n. Bat.
Lehr, Geo. ship carp. h. Pine n. Cypress.
Lehr, Henry, ship carp. h. Milnor opp. arsenal.
Lehr, Jacob, farmer, Military road n. city line.
Lehr, Peter, foreman, h. 13 Van Rensselaer.
Leibel, John, shoemaker, h. Boston alley ab. Goodell.
Leiber, Christian, painter, 269 Elm.
Leiber, Geo. finisher, h. Mich. n. North.
Leibinger, Aloise, lab. h. Spring n. Sycamore.
Leibl, Albert, shoemaker, h. Hickory n. Bat.
Leibly, Ernst, moulder, h. 70 Bennett.
Leichtnam, Jno. grocer, 407 Main, h. same.
Leichtnam. Joseph, Eley road n. Main.
Leighton, Edward, saloon, r. 43 Ohio.
Leighton, R. boatman, Niag. n. Hamilton.
Leikhart, Henry, shoemaker, Niagara n. Hamilton, h. same.
Leininger, Chas. carp. h. Jeff. cor. Carlton.
Leininger, Geo. painter, h. Mulberry n. High.
Leipold, Geo. tailor, h. Mich. n. North.
Leis, Daniel, mason, h. Johnson n. Genesee.
Leisser, Jno. ship carp. h. Bennett n. Bat.
Leist, Jacob, carriage trimmer, 303 Main, h. Batavia cor. Walnut.
Leitch, Wm. lab. h. Amherst n. Tonawanda.
Leman, John H. moulder, h. 30 Scott.
Lemberger, F. blacksmith, Brayley & Pitts.
Leminger, Christ. shoemaker, h. 38 Cherry.
Lemky, Gottleib, joiner, h. Maple n. Carlton.
Lemle, Christ. cooper, h. Military road n. Am.
Lemme, Chas. tailor, h. Mich. n. High.
Lemmon, John C. book-keeper, h. 93 Clinton.
Lemont, Rollin, engineer, Dearborn n. Ham.
Lender, Geo. fireman, h. Wash. n. Goodell.
Lenen, Barnard, engineer, Buff. Elevator, h. across creek.
Lenen, Philip, lab. b. Ohio n. R. R. track.
Leney, Henry, plasterer, h. Perry n. Ala.
Leniberg, Daniel, tailor, h. Herman n. Gen.
Lenhard, Mary, widow, h. Niag. n. Hamilton.

Lenhart, And. grocer, 232 Seneca. h. same.
Lenhart, Margaret, widow, h 240 Elm.
Lenk, George, grocer, Mulberry cor. Carlton, h. same.
Lenk, Simon, helper, h. Ind. n. Ohio.
Lent, J. M. with Breed, Butler & Co. b. West'n.
Lenz, Gottfr. shoemaker, h. Adams n. Bat.
Lenz, Magdalena, Mrs. h. Adams n. Batavia.
Leo, Michael, mason, h. Mass. n. 10th.
Leonard, C. O. grocer, Ohio cor. Ill. b. 3 Ill.
Leonard, David, carp. h. Hamburgh n. Fulton.
Leonard, G. F. b. 3 Illinois.
Leonard, John, ship carp. h. 13 Illinois.
Leonard, Lurana, widow, h. 3 Illinois.
Leonard, Norman, mittens and gloves, 27 Seneca, b. Western.
Leonard, Patrick B. grocer, Genesee n. bridge. h. same.
Leonard, Wm. saloon-keeper, 8 Canal dock.
Leonhard, Adam R. clerk, b. 2 Water.
Leonhard, Louis, turner, Swartz & Rebman, h. Walnut n. Sycamore.
Leonhardt, Chas. lab. h. German al. n. Sycam.
Leons, D. painter, h. 38 Hickory.
Leopold, George, lab. h. Spring n. Genesee.
Leopold, Jos. stone cutter, Spring n. Genesee.
Lerch, John, carp. h. Carlton n. Locust.
Leroque, Jas. ship carp. h. 4th n. Carolina.
Lerquemain, Jno. E. awning maker, h. Walnut cor. Clinton.
Lescher, Herman, lab. h. Military n. Amherst.
Leser, John H. mason, h. 403 Michigan.
Leslie, John, mason, h. Grey n. Batavia.
Leslie, Wm. carp. h. 354 Michigan.
Lessner, John, lab. h. Hickory n. William.
Lesswing, Jacob, blacksmith, h. Clinton n. Spring.
Lesswing, Peter, blacksmith, B. & S. L. R. R. h. Stanton n. Peckham.
Lester, Joseph, porter, 180 Main, h. Van Renselar n. Exchange.
Lester, Joseph. h. Del. n. Delavan ave.
Letchworth, Ed. H. at Pratt & L. h. 99 S. Div.
Letchworth, Josiah. firm Pratt & L. b. Mansion.
Letchworth, Wm. P. firm Pratt & L. b. Mansion
Lettnin, August, lab. h. 522 Michigan.
Letterman, Wm. bl'ksmith, h. Palmer cor. Md.
Letts, Wm. lab. h. Miami n. Louisiana.
Leubold, Jno. lab. h. North n. Michigan.
Leueker, Wm. peddler, h. 133 Pine.
Leuterky, Chas. cooper, h. ov. 48 Sycamore.
Levi, Emanuel, clothier, Gothic Hall, 184 Main. h. 223 Michigan.
Levi, Felix, peddler, h. Monroe n. Batavia.
Levi, Harris, clerk, 153 Main, b. 30 Exchange.
Levi, Isaac, peddler, h. 30 Exchange.
Levi, Lewis, ship carp. h. La. n. Elk.
Levi, Moses, drover, h. Batavia n. Monroe.
Levi, Sigfried N. upholsterer, 24 Exchange, h. Maiden lane.
Levigner, Jno. ship carp. h. Hayward n. Elk.
Levin, Thos. A. saloon, 3 Peacock.
Levyn, Segmund, firm Phillipp & Co. 192 Main. b. 6 Carroll.
Lewin, Wm. finisher, h. Genesee n. Jeff.
Lewis, Albert, h. 46 Virginia.
Lewis, C. E. lithographer, 200 Main, h. cor. Morgan and Niagara.

Lewis, C. E. saloon, Canal n. Commercial.
Lewis, C. Mrs. dressmaker, h. 431 Sycamore.
Lewis. Franklin, carp. h. 8 Union.
Lewis, George W. homœopathic physician, 131 Pearl, h. same.
Lewis, Henry, mariner, h. towpath opp. workhouse.
Lewis, Jas. machinist. h. 431 Michigan.
Lewis, John, Sr. dentist, ov. 278 Main.
Lewis, Levi, engineer, h. 258 S. Division.
Lewis, Loron L. attorney, 4 Arcade Buildings, h. 249 Franklin.
Lewis, Peter, mariner, h. 12 Illinois.
Lewis, Rebecca, widow, 73 Elm.
Lewis, R. H. carp. b. 8 Union.
Lewis. Samuel, Mrs. boarding, h. 52 E. Swan.
Lewis, T. C. firm Burrus & Lewis.
Lewis, Thos. barber, b. 34 Clinton.
Lewis, William, stock agent, B. & E. R. R. h. 185 N. Division.
Lewis, Wm. clerk, B. N. Y. & E. R. R. h. 100 E. Eagle.
Ley, Clara, widow, h. Bennett n Bat.
Ley, Michael, tailor, h. Genesee n. Hickory.
Ley, Paul, carp. h. 592 Washington.
Leydeker, Geo. cabinet maker. h. 168 Clinton.
Liard, Francis. teacher, h. 114 Tupper.
Libby, Jas. saloon and fruit store, 182 Wash. h. 11th ab. Virginia.
Liberenz, Frautz. lab. h. Burton n. Hydraulics.
Libertrau, Geo. F. lab. h. Johnson n. North.
Lichten, A. peddler, h. 223 Carroll.
Lichten, Rudolph, clerk, b. 223 Carroll.
Lichtenberger. Jos. carp. h. Maple n. Carlton.
Lichtenstein, Ed. clothing, 13 Main, h. same.
Lichtenstein, John, Rev. h. Oak cor. Carlton.
Lichtenstein, Jos. B. clerk, 13 Main, h. same.
Lichtenthal, Matthias, tailor, h. Ash n. Syc.
Lichtenthal, Nicholas, h. Adams n. Bat.
Lieb, Leopold, farmer, h. Delavan ave. n. Walden.
Lieber, Geo. blacksmith, h. Mich. n. North.
Liebetrut, Mrs. widow of Julius, h. Tupper n. Oak.
Liebl. Jno. grocer, 94 Goodell cor. Elm. h. same.
Liebl, Michael, lab. h. Watson n. Batavia.
Liebler, John, lab. h. Fox n Genesee.
Liebler, John J. grocer, 7 J William. h. same.
Liebler, Margareth, milliner. h. 70 William.
Liebrich, Geo. tailor. h. 72 Mulberry.
Lied, Chris. saloon, 114 Exchange, h. same.
Liedersdorf, Chs. lab. Cherry n. Jefferson.
Liekner, Francois, gardener, h. Grey bet. Batavia and Genesee.
Lienert, John, mason, h. North n. Ellicott.
Lienert, Joseph, mason, h. Oak n. North.
Lienert, Louis, mason, h. Michigan n. North.
Lies, George, lab. h. n. Peckham.
Liestner. Jno. barber, Main cor. Scott.
Lighthall, E. boatman, h. 9 Terrace.
Lighton, Robt. lab. h. Porter n. Beak.
Lilia. August, clerk, h. over 163 Batavia.
Limberger, Fred. blacksmith, h. 563 Michigan.
Linamen. Frank, h. Michigan ab. Batavia.
Linberger, Michael, lab. h. Pratt n. Sycamore.
Linch, Bridget, h. 554 Michigan.
Linch, Sophia, widow, h. 301 Ellicott.
Lincoln, Calvin, fisherman, b. Niag. n. Parish.

Lincoln, Barney, grocer, cor. N. Division and Michigan.
Lincoln, Pat. ship carp. h. 15 Mechanic.
Lincoln, Preston M. Niagara n. Parish.
Linda, J. R. engineer, 11th ab. Jersey.
Linde, W. wood worker, Brayley & Pitts.
Lindemann, August, butcher, h. Michigan n. Burton alley.
Lindenberg, Cornelius, lab. h. 201 Genesee.
Lindenberg, Marie E. midwife. h. 201 Gen.
Linder, Wm. carpenter, h. 67 Maple.
Lindner, Fred. lab. h. Locust n. High.
Lindner, Frederick, lab. h. Best n. Oak.
Lindner, Geo. furnaceman. h. 559 Washington.
Lindner, Geo. mason, Cherry n. Spruce.
Lindner, Geo. cigar maker, b. 277 Elm.
Lindner. John, lab. h. Oak n. Best.
Linemann, Tory, shoemaker. 6 Water.
Link, Jacob F. lab. h. Batavia n. Pratt.
Linke, Henry, gardener, h. Williamsville road n. Batavia plank road.
Linn, Hamilton, lab. h. Amherst n. Florida.
Linnebon, Adam, painter, h. Pratt n. Batavia.
Linnemann, Henry Chr. mason, h. 129 Pine.
Linsenhuber, Jno. lab. h. Clinton n. N. Y. C. R. R.
Linnenkohl, Wm.* shoemaker, 75 Ellicott, h. same.
Linninger, Saul, gardener, h. Genesee n. Williamsville road.
Linsenmau. Jno. carpenter, h. Locust n. High.
Lints. J. J. book-keeper. Breed, Butler & Co. h. 3 Fitch Block. Michigan.
Lints, R. M. with Breed, Butler & Co. b. 3 Fitch Block, Michigan.
Lipe. Jas. baggageman, N. Y. C. R. R. h. 105 Clinton.
Lipp, Jno. A. stone cutter. h. Bat. n. Hickory.
Lipp, John, tinsmith. h. 29 Spruce.
Lipp, Philip, stone cutter, h. Walnut n. Bat.
Lippe, Martin, painter, h. Hickory n. Genesee.
Lippert, Margarette, widow. h. 466 Michigan.
Lippmann, Chas. A. wagoner, 268 Elm.
Lipsey, Thomas, brass moulder, b. Emerald Hotel.
Lipsey, Wm. moulder, b. 4 Elk.
Liser, Jacob, b. Ferry n. Jefferson.
Lisle, Barbara, widow, h. Batavia n. Lutheran.
Lisstenburger, Peter, lab. h. Jeff. n. William.
Littig. Jos. organ maker, h. Schmitt's alley n. Jefferson.
LITTLE & ARNOLD, for. and com. mers. foot Commercial.—See adv. p. 37.
Little, James. lab. b. Jas. Holdene.
Little, S. C. firm L. & Arnold. h. 55 E. Eagle.
Littlefield, John, conductor, N. Y. C. R. R. h. 308 Seneca.
Littlefield, L. breakman, N. Y. C. R. R. h. 230 S. Division.
Littlefield, Silas, baggageman. h. 37 Cedar.
Littlejohn, —. lab. h. Sycamore n. Ash.
Litz, Jno. tailor, h. Pratt n. Genesee.
Litz, John, 170 Main, h. 6 Huron.
Lloyd, Alfred A.* cigar manufacturer, over 263 Main, b. Bonney's
Lobee, Dirk, tailor, h. 213 Ellicott.
Lobstein, Edward, with J. Denny. h. same.
Loby, Faring, baker, h. Cedar n. Clinton.

Lochner, Jacob, beer peddler. b. S. Roths.
Lochner, Jacob, brewer, h. 290 Elm.
Lochta, Andrew, lab. h. Cherry n. Spring.
Lochte, Henry, bakery, 180 Genesee, h. same.
Lock. Chas. H. builder, h. 185 Delaware.
Lock, C. L. Am. Ex. Co. h. 125 Franklin.
Lock, John, mason, h. 185 Delaware.
Lock, John E. with M. S. Hawley & Co. h. 185 Delaware.
Lock, Wm. H. mason. h. 68 11th n. Maryland.
Locke, Wm. C. auctioneer, 138 Main, h. 3 Swan.
Lockrow, Harman M. tobacconist, 229 Ellicott.
Lockrow, Thomas, M. D. Adams Block, Wash. b. 229 Ellicott.
Lockwood, Chas. actor, h. Seneca n. Chicago.
Lockwood, D. J. salesman, 275 Main, b. Del. ab. Chippewa.
Lockwood, E. M. clerk P. O. h. 154 Clinton.
Lockwood, Geo. G. pressman, Com'l Ad'v. h. 61 Oak.
Lockwood, Harmon M. agt J. Adams & Co. h. 229 Ellicott.
Lockwood, John A. firm Young, L. & Co. h. 224 Niagara n. Maryland.
Lockwood, John F. firm L. & Kinne, h. 148 Pearl.
Lockwood, & Kinne, prod. and com. 11 Central Wharf.
Lockwood, N. S. M. D. over 266 Main cor. Niag.
Lockwood, Orrin. h. 92 Eagle.
Lockwood, Stephen, firm Sawin & L. Hollister Building, b. Mansion.
Lockwood, Thomas, M. D Adams Block, Wash. b. 229 Ellicott.
Lockwood, Tim. T. M. D. 21 Niagara. h. same.
Lockwood. Wm. cor. Washington and Carroll.
Lodwick, John, teamster, with Dickey & Marsh, h. cor. Genesee and German.
Loeb. Jacob,* grocer, Cherry n. Jeff. h. same.
LOEBERICK, CHARLES A. watchmaker, 382 Main, h. 526 Mich.—See adv. p. 75.
Loebig, Michael,* tinsmith, Genesee n. Hickory, h. same.
Loebrick, August, joiner. b. Watson n. Clinton.
Loebrich, George, confectionery, 127 Genesee. h. same.
Loebrick, Henry, clerk, 294 Main, b. 127 Gen.
Loegier. Valentine, brick maker, Genesee n. Walden.
Loenhard, Dora, widow, h. 133 Pine.
Loeper, J. C. M. D. h. Goodell n. Michigan.
Loerch, F.* brewer, 200 Gen. h. same.
Loerch, Peter, brewer, b. 198 Genesee.
Loerch, Philip, M. D. h. 198 Genesee.
Loerd, Morris, cramper, b. 346 Genesee.
Loerd, John, Jr. 156 Main. b. 346 Gen.
Loerr, Henry, lab. h. Mortimer n. Gen.
Loerr, Jacob, marble polisher. h. 163 Cherry.
Loersch, J. P. insurance agent, cor. Sycamore and Oak, h. same.
Loesch, Frank, carp. h. 241 Oak.
Loesch, N. shoemaker, 565 Main.
Loesch. Philip, cigar maker, h. Krettner n. Lovejoy.
Loesch. Peter, sawyer, Spruce n. Sycamore.
Loescher, Abram, finisher, h. Spring n. Syc.
Loew John, cramper, h. 346 E. Genesee.
Loewenthine, Hyman, Rev. h. 118 Pearl.

Loewi, Samuel, firm L. & Geirshofer, h. Niag. n. Maryland.
Loewi & Geirshofer, dry goods, 306 Main.
Loeffler, Crescens, Miss. h. 489 Washington.
Loff, Margaret, widow, h. Hickory n. William.
Loft, Wm. h. 27 N. Division.
Loftus, Daniel, mariner, h. Perry n. Elk street market.
Loftus, John, teamster, h. cor. Va. and Tupper.
Loftus, Michael, Sternberg elevator, h. Heacock cor. Exchange.
Logan, B. h. 22 6th.
Logan, David, foreman, Sloan's brewery, h. Exchange n. Alabama.
Logel, George, carpenter, h. 275 Elm.
Login, David, peddler, h. Exch. n. Heacock.
Loh, John, lab. h. Elm n. Carlton.
Lohmann, John, lab. h. Johnson n. Gen.
Lohner, Jacob, stone cutter, h. St. Paul n. Rosebach alley.
Lohouse, F. W.* shoemak'r, 3 Clinton, h. Potter n. William.
Lohs, Sebastian, lab. h. Hickory n. Gen.
Lokker, A. shoemaker, h. Spring n. Bristol.
Lomer, John, bar-keeper, b. Mich. n. Tupper.
Lommer, F. C. carriage painter, Mulberry ab. Goodell.
Londagan, Wm. blacksmith, h. Peacock.
Loner, Jacob, stone cutter, h. St. Paul.
Long, Chris. stone cutter, h. Eagle n. Hickory.
Long, David, lab. b. Ohio n. R. R. track.
Long, Ed. on N. St. R. R. b. J. Schaller.
Long, Geo. mason, h. Monroe n. Howard.
Long, Jacob, mason, h. 27 Cherry.
Long, James, blacksmith, Spring n. Gen.
Long, John, mason, b. 27 Cherry.
Long, John, saloon, 45 Exch. h. same.
Long, John, at 131 Main, h. Ellicott n. Chip.
Long, John, confectioner, b. 215 Ellicott.
Long, Magdalen, confectioner, h. 215 Ellicott.
Long, Margaret, widow, h. 12 Elm.
Long, Michael, coppersmith, h. Pine n. Wm.
Long, Michael, lab. 280 N. Division.
Long. Sarah, widow, h. Vermont n. 14th.
Long. William, piano maker, with A. & J. Keogh, h. 149 9th.
Long, Wm. confectioner, h. 215 Ellicott.
Long, Wm. lab. h. S. Div. n. Grosvenor.
Long, Wm. on N. St. R. R. b. J. Schaller.
Long, Wm. sail maker, h. Western.
Longheim, William H. with J. Felton, b. cor. Elm and Tupper.
Longman, Jacob, lab. h. Mass. n. 10th.
Longstreet, Chris. builder, b. 22 Delaware.
Longtine, Veston, blacksmith, h. Louisiana n. Carroll.
Lonnigan, James, saloon, Ohio n. Michigan.
Loomis, Chas. B. student, b. 79 Franklin.
Loomis, C. K. general fre'g't agent L. S. R. R. h. 95 S. Division.
Loomis, Erastus, joiner, h. 56 Morgan.
Loomis, Harvey, b. 79 Franklin cor. Niagara.
Loomis, Horatio N. M. D. 79 Franklin n. Niag.
Loomis, John, Mrs. washer, h. 119 Oak.
Loomis, Thomas, L. S. R. R. ft. office, h. 29 Swan.
Looney, James, cabinet maker. h. 137 Elm.
Loos, John, tailor, Batavia n. Johnson.

Loosen, Frederick, grocer, Batavia cor. Spruce.
Loosen, Fred. Jr. b. 170 Batavia.
Loper, M. sailor, 12 Chestnut.
Loran, Wm. moulder, h. 569 Main.
Lord, And. machinist, h. Folsom n. Jeff'n.
Lord, Chas. B. book-keeper, b. 162 Seneca.
Lord, F. A. builder, Eaton's planing mill, h. Delaware n. Barker.
Lord, John C. Rev. h. Del. n. Forest Lawn.
Lord, Luke. shoemaker, h. 26 Palmer.
Lord, Thomas, policeman, h. across creek.
Lorenz, Anthony, saloon, 3 Court, h. same.
Lorenz, Baptist, lab. h. Stanton n. Batavia.
Lorenz, Chas. cooper, h. Orange n. Cherry.
Lorenz, John, Sr. lab. h. 97 Pine.
Lorenz, John, Jr. painter, h. 191 Pine.
Lorenz, John, lab. h. Spring cor. Kinney.
Lorenz, Lewis, tinsmith, b. Ash n. Batavia.
Lorenz, Michael, tinsmith, h. Michigan n. Bat.
Lorenz, Philip, lab. h. Gen. cor. Kaene.
Lorenz, Philip G. dry goods, 31 E. Genesee, h. same.
Lorich, John, moulder, h. Mulberry n. Good'll.
Lorich, Nicholas, lab. h. 554 Michigan.
Lort, Caspar R. livery stable, h. 388 Seneca.
Losehand, Barnhardt, printer, h. William n. Bennett.
Losehand, Wilhelmina, widow, h. William n. Bennett.
Loskarn, Nicholas, lab. h. Adams n. Bat.
Loson, Nicholas, harness maker, h. 59 Gen.
Loson, S. saddler, b. 69 Genesee.
Loss, Jacob, teamster, Madison n. Syc.
Lossing, — lab. h. 11 William.
Loszy, J. G. tailor, h. over 6 Maple.
Loth, P. cutter, 204 Main, h. 148 E. Eagle.
Lotheridge, A. L. book-keeper, C. J. Mann's, h. 31 N. Division.
Lothrop, Joshua R. M. D. Wash. cor. Swan.
Lothrop, Thomas, M. D. Niagara n. Clinton av. h. same.
Loton, Jalez, chair maker, h. 73 Oak.
Lotridge, F. A. h. 44 Clinton.
Lotterman, Phl. lab. h. Ketchum alley n. High.
Lotz, Melchior, painter, h. 116 Cedar.
Lotz, Phil. lab. h. Monroe n. Batavia.
Louacy, John, lab. Bennett's elevator, h. across creek.
Loupe, Frances M. widow, h. 75 W. Chippewa.
Love, A. B. grocery, 191 Niagara, b. 13th n. Vermont.
Love, David, grocer, cor. Perry and Wash.
Love, G. M. printer, b. 13th n. Vermont.
Love, George M. major, N. Y. S. V. M. h. 131 Franklin.
Love, Ilvia, widow, h. N. Wash. n. Auburn.
Love, James B. printer, h. 13th n. Vermont.
Love, Jas. cartman, h. 93 9th.
Love, John W. with Clapp, Matthews & W. h. 13th n. Vermont.
Love, John, marble polisher, h. 13th n. R. I.
Love, John, foreman, Isaac Holloway, b. 3 6th.
Love, M. shoemaker, h. Clinton n. Cedar.
Love, Thos. C. Mrs. h. 131 Franklin.
Love, Thos. Frontier mills. b. Mrs. I. Love.
Love, Wm. machinist, h. 14th n. R. I.
Lovejoy, G. L. scale maker, 81 Main, h. Park n. Virginia.

Lovejoy, Henry, civil engineer, h. 96 E. Swan.
Lovejoy, Sarah, widow, h. 171 E. Seneca.
Lovell, Geo. V. stable foreman, N. st. R. R. h. Niagara n. School.
Lovell, Wm. engineer, h. Eagle n. Spring.
Loveridge, A. A. h. 6 Mohawk.
Loveridge, Ed. D. liquor merch. 176 Washington, h. 105 Niagara.
Lovering, Alice R. Miss, b. 30 E. Eagle.
Lovering, Chas. F. 22 Central Wharf, h. 30 E. Eagle.
Lovering, Wm. M. b. 30 E. Eagle.
Lovett, Michael, joiner, h. Kinney alley n. Swan.
Lowack, Anton, lab. h. Grey n. Genesee.
Lowe, Lewis, sailor, h. 47 Delaware.
Lowe, Robert, saloon, Court n. 7th, h. same.
Lown, Geo. cooper, h. across creek.
Lowry, George, prop. Metcalf's Tavern, h. Abbott road n. junction Elk.
Loyd, William, porter, Erie st. depot, h. Potter n. Gay.
Luackar, Andrew, tailor, h. 28 Ash.
Lubban, Fred. shoemaker, 82 Main, b. Comm'l bel. Canal.
Lucas, L. D. carp. b. 193 E. Eagle.
Lucey, Timothy, moulder, b. 104 Exchange.
Luckemeyer, Catharine, widow, h. Grey n. Genesee.
Luckly, John, lab. h. Pratt bet. Genesee and Sycamore.
Luckly, Thos. with Jewett & Root, h. Pratt n. Sycamore.
Lucy, Julia, widow, h. across creek.
Ludlow, A. J. Mrs. widow, h. Niagara n. Clinton avenue.
Ludlow, E. clerk, 162 Main.
Ludlow, Myron M. clerk, 180 Main, b. Niagara n. Clinton avenue.
Ludtka, William, peddler, h. Gen. cor. Spruce.
Ludwick, H. teamster, h. Main n. Amherst.
Ludwig, Conrad, peddler, h. Johnson n. Gen.
Ludwig, Geo. carp. h. Maple n. Virginia.
Ludwig, Henry, carp. h. Sycamore n. Kaene.
Ludwig, John, pattern maker, h. over 25 E. Genesee.
Ludwig, Jno. A. lab. h. Genesee cor. Sherman.
Ludwig, Nicholas, moulder, h. Adams n. Wm.
Luedecke, Henry, saloon, h. 133 Genesee.
Luedtke, Geo. lab. h. Rogers n. Connecticut.
Luehmann, Christian F. cabinet maker, 98 E. Genesee.
Luesenhop, Adolf, cabinet maker, h. 219 Ellicott.
Luex, Martin, drayman, h. 40 Ash.
Luigart, Matthias, boarding house, 32 E. Gen.
Luipold, Dorothea, widow, h Jefferson n. Wm.
Luippold, Martin, grocer, Wm. cor. Jefferson.
Luke, Sarah, Mrs. h. 523 Washington.
Luman, Fred. lab. h. Connecticut n. 15th.
Lumpp, Martin, lab. h. 144 Oak.
Lund, Edward, clerk, E. Corning & Co. h. 4th n. Court.
Lund, Wm. tinner, Court cor. 4th.
Lung, Anton,* shoemaker, Mortimer n. Syc. h. same.
Luony, Honora, widow, washer, h. Exchange n. Hickory.

14

Luscher, A. finisher, h. Spring n. Genesee.
Lusk, Julia H. h. 69 Clinton.
Lustig, Magdaline, widow, h. Best n. Main.
Luther, Sidney A. shoemaker, h. 165 Seneca.
Lutz, Abraham. farmer. h. Main n. Eley road.
Lutz, Eberhardt, cooper, h. Monroe bet. Batavia and William.
Lutz, Frederick, butcher, b. 176 Oak.
Lutz, G. A. brewer, b. Walnut n. William.
Lutz, Jacob. tailor, b. Wm. Schneider.
Lutz, John, lab. h. Adams n. Peckham.
Lutz, John, lab. h. Brayton n. R. I.
Lutz, John, ship carp. h. 214 Genesee.
Lutz, John, saloon, Ohio cor. Michigan, h. Hayward cor. Perry.
Lutz, Matthias, carp. h. 210 Genesee.
Lutz, Rudolph, carp. h. Elm cor. Tupper.
Lux, Chs. h. 314 Ellicott.
Lux, Henry, shoemaker, 215 Ellicott.
Lux, John, brewer, b. Haberstro & Co.
Lux, Joseph, wagon maker, h. Main n. Buffalo Plains.
Lux, Ludwig, Rev. h. junc. York and North.
Lym, Rob't, gardener, h. Main n. Best.
Lyman, Burke, type founder, with N. Lyman, h. 103 N. Division.
Lyman, C. Mortimer, clerk, Peabody's, h. 305 Franklin n. Edward.
Lyman, D. R. druggist, h. 2 Johnson Place.
Lyman, E. B. clerk, 44 Main, b. 3 Johnson place.
Lyman, John L. type founder, with N. Lyman, h. 41 Oak.
Lyman, J. S. at 44 Main, b. 3 Park place.
Lyman, John, type founder, h. Ga. bel. 5th.
Lyman, Loomis, porter Fire Marshal's, Franklin cor. Eagle, h. Pearl n. Court.
Lyman, N. type founder, 18 W. Seneca. h. 23 Ellicott.
Lyman, N. B. type founder, h. 375 Franklin.
Lyman, P. Stephen, type founder, h. 119 E. Eagle.
Lyman, R. W. clerk, D. Brown, b. Western.
Lyman, Wm. E. type founder, h. Franklin n. Edward.
Lymburner & Torrey, sheepskin factory, Granger n. Main and Hamburgh canal.
Lymburner, H. M. firm L. & Torrey, h. 24 Ellicott.
Lynch, Andrew, joiner, h. Perry n. Chicago.
Lynch, Ann, widow, washerwoman. h. 84 5th.
Lynch, Charles, mariner, h. ac. creek.
Lynch, D. lab. h. ac. creek.
Lynch, Dennis, lab. h. South n. creek.
Lynch, Edward, with Alex. S. Anderson & Co. h. cor. 6th and Maryland.
Lynch, Jno. varnisher, h. Hudson n. 5th.
Lynch, Jas. saloon, Evans cor. Canal.
Lynch, John, carpenter, h. Fulton. n. Chicago.
Lynch, John, lab. h. Ohio n. Louisiana.
Lynch, Michael T. sailor, h. Abbott bel. R. R.
Lynch, Michael, hostler, at Harris' Hotel.
Lynch, Michael, lab. h. Abbott Plank road n. iron bridge.
Lynch, Michael. joiner, h. Moore n. Elk.
Lynch, Thos. lab. h. Canal n. Commercial.
Lynchan, Daniel, at 196 Main, h. Carolina, n. 9th.

Lynde, A. L. h. Wadsworth park n. North.
Lynn, David, sailor, Perry cor. Louisiana.
Lynn, Patrick, grocer, h. Exch. n. Hamburgh.
Lynn, Wm. watchman, N. Y. C. R. R. depot, h. Seneca n. Alabama.
Lyon & Co. land agents, Brown's Buildings.
Lyon, E. R. jeweler, h. N. Pearl n. Virginia.
Lyon, H. E. Mrs. boarding house, 29 Swan.
Lyon, Jas. S. firm Lyon & Co. h. Michigan cor. Eagle.
Lyons And. butcher, h. Genesee n. Walden.
Lyons, James, Queen City Ice Co. b. Revere.
Lyons, John, miller, h. 11th n. Rhode Island.
Lyons, Michael, lab. h. Ferry n. Adams.
Lyons, Pat. Queen City Ice Co. b. Revere.
Lyons, Pat. lab. h. 16 Morgan n. Genesee.
Lyons, Richard. printer, h. 83 E. Seneca.
Lyons, Rich'd B. printer, Com'l Adv. h. 85 Seneca.
Lyons, S. W. prop. R. R. House, Ferry n. Erie canal.
Lyons, Timothy, ship carp. h. 16 Morgan n. Genesee.
Lyons, Timothy, lab. h. 18 Perry.
Lyport, David, h. 27 Clinton.
Lytle, Charles P. clerk, 10 Exch. b. 45 Oak.
Lytle, John S. firm Cook & Lytle, h. 45 Oak.

M.

McAcron, H. capt. h. 52 William.
McAllester, E. b. Franklin n. Virginia.
McAlny, Lot, shoemaker, h. 49 Exchange.
McAloon, Jno. lab. h. 5th n. Virginia.
McAndy, Thos. lab. h. Elk n. Moore.
McArthur, Alex. capt. lake, h. 7th n. Penn.
McARTHUR. J. J. confectioner, 297 Main. h. same.—See adv. p. 79.
McAuley, Bernard, actor. h. Pal'er n. Hudson.
McAvoy, Thos. lab. h. 99 Hospital.
McAvoy, Wm. A. cigar manufacturer, b. Globe Hotel.
McBean, Charles, book-keeper, h. 33 Ash.
McBean, Henry, sailor, b. 33 Ash.
McBride, Alex. grocer, Erie canal n. Genesee, h. same.
McBride, Ed. lab. h. Louisiana n. South.
McBride, Henry, b. Alex. McBride.
McBride, Wm. Jewett & Root, h. Miller Block, Michigan.
McBurney, Wm. ship carpenter h. Miami n. La.
McCabe, Patrick, lab. h. ac. creek.
McCabe, Bartholomew, sail maker, h. n. Clark's stave yard.
McCabe, Francis, lab. h. Elk n. Moore.
McCabe, Henry, blacksmith, h. La. n. Exch.
McCabe, Hugh, Traveler's Home. 118 Exch.
McCabe, Jos. grocer, h. Elk n. Marvin.
McCabe, Michael, sawyer, h. Elk n. Moore.
McCabe, Pat. carpenter, h. Fulton n. Chicago.
McCall, Hugh, ship carp. h. cor. Jefferson and Carroll.
McCall, Louisa, widow, h. Amherst n. Tonawanda.
McCarack, Pat. lab. h. LeCoutenlx.
McCarney, Neil, sailor, h. 178 N. Division.
McCarney, Simon, clerk, N. Y. C. freight office, b. 72 6th.

McCarney, Peter, sailor, h. 72 5th.
McCartey, Charles, lab. h. towpath n. Genesee.
McCarthy, Ann, h. 103 Clinton.
McCarthy, Charles, clerk, b. 21 Illinois.
McCarthy, Charles, ship carp. h. Fulton n. Ala.
McCarthy, Charles, engineer, h. Perry n. Chicago.
McCarthy, Cornelius, lab. h. 11th n. Carolina.
McCarthy, Ellen, widow, h. Ohio n. Elk.
McCarthy, Frank. ship carp. h. Fulton n. Ala.
McCarthy, Jeremiah, machinist, 11th n. Car.
McCarthy, John, grocer, h. 260 Seneca.
McCarthy, John, lab. h. Chicago n. Ohio.
McCarthy, Jno. lab. h. 21 Scott.
McCarthy, Lawrence, lab. b. Ohio n. R. R. track.
McCarthy, Louis, printer, b. 103 Clinton.
McCarthy, Mary, Mrs. h. 217 Ellicott.
McCarthy, Mary, widow, washer, h. Louisiana n. South.
McCarthy, Thos. lab. h. Terrace n. Mechanic.
McCarty, Anthony, saloon, Ohio n. Michigan, h. same.
McCarty, lab. h. ac. creek.
McCarty, James, cooper, h. 11 Mississippi.
McCarty, James, lab, h. Ohio n. R. R. track.
McCarty, John, lab. h. Louisiana n. Ohio.
McCarty, Michael, lab. h. Mill n. Heacock.
McCarty, Thomas, blacksmith, h. 5th n. Va.
McCarty, Thomas, porter, St. James, b. same.
McCarty, Timothy, lab. Ohio n. R. R. track.
McCarty, Thos. sailor, h. Louisiana n. Ohio.
McCarty, Tim. milk peddler, h. 186 Seneca.
McCay, John, conductor. h. 30 Carolina.
McCern, Daniel. lab. h. Ohio n. Wabash.
McChristall, Rosanna, wid. h. 97 Hospital.
McCibben, Robert, 16 Long Wharf, h. Eagle.
McClannan, Serena, h. 105 Delaware.
McClanty, Markam, joiner, h. Palmer n. Md.
McCleary, Barnard, on Niagara st. R. R. h. Hospital n. 7th.
McClennon, Andrew, mariner, h. Elk opp. Monroe.
McCloud, Robert, h. Iron place, N. Washington.
McCloud, John, saloon, 48 Ohio.
McCloy, J. G. b. Western.
McClure, James, cooper, h. 17 Palmer.
McClure, Jos. spar maker, h. Perry n. Ala.
McCollom, J. C. book-keeper, h. 15 Pearl.
McCollom, T. P. h. 15 Pearl.
McCollum, Alex. com. merch. b. Bonney's Hotel.
McCollum, Otis, paper warehouse, 24 and 26 Pearl, h. 50 Pearl.
McComb, Matthew, salesman, h. 567 Wash.
McCombs. Eliz. wid. confectioner, 410 Main.
McCombs, Robert, ship carp. h. Miami n. La.
McConkey, John, shoemaker, Ohio n. Illinois, h. same.
McConnell, Mary, Mrs. b. Massachusetts n. 12th.
McConvee, John, ship carp. h. 64 5th.
McConvell, John, tinsmith, h. 32 Union.
McConvey, James, carp. h. 328 N. Division.
McCooll, James, hatter, 80 Main, h. same.
McCora, G. W. M. D. cor. Commercial and Water, b. Bonney's Hotel.
McCord, Andrew, on Niagara st. R. R. h. Hospital n. 7th.

McCord, Andrew, lab. h. Terrace n. Mechanic.
McCormack, Chas. M. St. R. R. h. Ferry n. Main.
McCormick, E. lab. h. 5th n. Georgia.
McCormick, Eliza, widow, h. 12th n. Vermont.
McCormick, Frank.* blacksmith, 115 Pearl, h. 32 Green.
McCormick, Pat. lab. h. Exch. n. Alabama.
McCormick, William T. h. 350 S. Division.
McCoy, John, conductor, h. 30 Carolina.
McCoy, Martin. saloon. packet dock n. Canal.
McCoy, Mary E. widow, h. 452 Michigan.
McCrary, Erastus, keg maker, h. 9 7th.
McCray, Guildford W. M. D. druggist, Com'l cor. Water, b. Bonney House.
McCrea, Chas. lake capt. h. N. Div. n. Jeff.
McCready, And. tinsmith, 269 Main, h. Court.
McCready, Anna Maria, h. 33 Court.
McCready, Caleb C. painter, h. 116 Folsom.
McCready, Jennie, teacher, b. 149 S. Division.
McCready, Maria, widow. h. 149 S. Division.
McCredie, J. book-keeper and cashier, D. Richmond, h. 193 Delaware.
McCrogan, Margaret, milliner, b. 32 E. Seneca.
McCue, Ann, widow, h. 5th n. Georgia.
McCully, Henry, h. 210 Seneca.
McCumber & LeClear, atty. at law, 3 Terrace.
McCumber, Orlando, atty. 3 Terrace.
McCutcheon, S. coppersmith, 13 Elk, h. 11 Walnut.
McDearmot, John, h. Folsom n. Kinney's alley.
McDearmott, Dan. drayman. h. Burwell place.
McDermot, Eliza, teacher No. 19, b. Gulf n. Niagara.
McDermot, Peter, Frontier mills, h. Gulf n. Niagara.
McDermott, Hugh, gardener, h. Best n. Main.
McDermott, Michael, lab. h. 21 Mississippi.
McDeroth, Wm. lab. h. Virginia n. 4th.
McDonald. Chas. saloon, Elk n Michigan.
McDonald, Chas. C. prod. com merch. 17 C. Wharf, h. Abbott 4 miles from Main.
McDonald, David, clerk. b. 287 Michigan.
McDonald, Donald, ship carp. h. La. n. Ohio.
McDonald, Hector, atty. with Welch & Dundas, b. Bloomer's.
McDonald, James, grocer, h. 99 Exch.
McDonald, Jane, widow, h. 287 Michigan.
McDonald, Jno. shoemaker, Ga. n. 6th, h. same.
McDonald, Martin, grocer, h. N. Div. n. Jeff.
McDonald, Wm. clerk, 346 Main.
McDonald, William, clerk, 287 Michigan.
McDonell, Dan. lab. h. Fulton n. Alabama.
McDonnel, Michael, blacksmith, Blossom n. Huron.
McDonnell, Doughin, gardener, h. Michigan n. Carlton.
McDonnell, Margaret. widow, h. Elk n. Mich.
McDonhue, Michael, lab. h. Clinton ave. n. N. Washington.
McDonnough, Luke, policeman, h. 192 9th n. Hudson.
McDonnough, Thos. joiner, h. 9th n. Hudson.
McDougal, John, mariner, h. Moore n. Elk.
McDougal, John C. machinist, h. 11th n. Mass.
McDougal, Margaret, Mrs. b. 13 Elm.
McDougal, Ronald, saloon, 17 E. Sen. h. same.
McElvaney, Chas. engineer, h. Carroll n. La.
McEvoy, Mellick, lab. h. Otto n. Hayward.

McEwen, Barney, truckman, h. Wash. n. Scott.

McEwen, Wm. B. clerk, Hamlin & Mendsen, h. Park n. North.

McFarland, James, cutter, 106 Main, h. Walnut n. Clinton.

McFarland, Levi, h. Dearborn n. Hamilton.

McFarlane, Jas. h. 94 Walnut.

McFarlane, Wm. L. b. Walnut n. William.

McFaul, A. B. firm Dunn & McF. 60 Goodell.

McFaul, Daniel F. agt. Revere House. b. same.

McFayden, Jane, wid. boarding house, cor. Columbia and Elk.

McFee, Allan, blacksmith, b. 322 Seneca.

McFee, Peter, h. 5th n. Carolina.

McFeely, Fred. P. with R. L. Howard, h. 5 Folsom.

McGarry, Jas. miller, h. Miami n. Alabama.

McGary, Margaret, wid. h. Bouck n. Niagara.

McGean, Jas. truckman, h. Wm. n. Cedar.

McGean, Wm. clerk, Evan's elevator, b. Wm. n. Cedar.

McGee, James, carp. h. Virginia n. 11th.

McGee, John, switchman, N. Y. C. R. R. foot York, h. same.

McGee, Pat. carp. h. Wm. n. Walnut.

McGee, Pat. engraver, Sage & Sons, h. Virginia cor. 11th.

McGerge, Michael, stone cutter, h. Jefferson n. Clinton.

McGill, John W. clerk, 46 Main, b. Mrs. Warren.

McGill, John, at custom house, b. 35 E. Swan.

McGill, Wm. cl'k, Wm. H. Glenny, b. 62 Swan.

McGilliese, Anges, carp. h. 243 Elm.

McGillivray, Donald, founder, b. 95 N. Div.

McGillivray, Wm. clerk, Hamlin & Mendsen, h. 95 N. Division.

McGilvray, Duncan,* ship carp. 125 6th.

McGinniss, —, wid. h. Niagara n. Breck'ge.

McGivern, Patrick, h. Elk opp. Marvin.

McGlinn, Jas. bakery, Niagara cor. Pa. h. same.

McGloin, Francis, b. 75 S. Division.

McGloine, Barnard, ship carp. h. Exchange n. Hamburgh.

McGory, John. lab. h. 9th n. Pa.

McGovern, Barney, at Evan's elevator, h. Evans n. Water.

McGovern, Jno. carp. Evans.

McGowan, Frank, hackman, b. 56 Carroll.

McGowan, Henry, carp. h. 140 W. Huron.

McGowan, James, brickmaker, h. S. Div. bel. R. R.

McGowan, James, blacksmith, Elk n. La. h. Hamburgh n. Perry.

McGowan, J. S. weighman, b. 74 E. Seneca.

McGowan, Mary, widow, h. 74 Seneca.

McGowan, Michael, moulder, h. 27 Scott.

McGowan, Robt. joiner, b. Moore n. Elk.

McGowan, Steward, blacksmith, b. Hamburgh n. Perry.

McGowans, Pat. ship carp. h. 15 Mechanic.

McGrath, Dan. lab. h. towpath n. round house.

McGrath, Michael, lab h. Elk opp. Moore.

McGratta, Thos. clerk, 17 Main, h. 7 Elk.

McGravey, Pat. sailor, h. Ill. n. Scott.

McGraw, Pat. lab. h. Gen. n. Jackson.

McGraw, Mike, b. Smith Block, Exchange.

McGraw, Pat. lab. b. Smith Block, Exchange.

McGriffin, Jno. sailor, h. r. 97 Fulton.

McGuerk, Robt. engineer, h. cor. 5th and Caro.

McGuigan, Owen, undertaker, h. Elk n. Chic.

McGuire, Barnard, lab. b. G. T. Williams.

McGuire, D. tavern, Ohio cor. South.

McGuire, Jas. lab. h. Fulton n. Chicago.

McGuire, Jas. grocery, Otto n. Hayward.

McGuire, John, carp. h Clinton n. James.

McGuire, John, with J. F. Noyle, h. Louisiana n. Fulton.

McGuire, Michael, lab. h. across creek.

McGuire, Pat. milkman, h. Clinton n. Emslie.

McGuire, Pat. blacksmith, h. Hayward n. Fult.

McGuire, Stephen, shoemaker, 145 Exch.

McGuire, Thos. lab. h. N. Canal n. Emslie.

McGurk, Edward, ship carp. h. La. n. Fulton.

McGwigan, Owen, Jr. ship carp. b. Elk n. Chic.

McGwigen, Pat. truckman, h. 11 Huron.

McHenry, Jas. h. 42 5th.

McHenry, John, lab. h. 11th n. R. I.

McHenry, Jno. grocer, 4th n. Ga. h. same.

McHenry, Jno. carp. b. Revere.

McHoney, Thos. machinist, h. 50 Pine.

McInery, Lot, shoemaker, h. 49 Exchange.

McIlvany, Sarah, widow, h. Watson n. Peck'm.

McIlvenia, Jno. painter, b. 49 Clinton.

McIntyre, Jas. scroll sawing, bel. Terrace, h. cor. Howard and Adams.

McIntyre, Jane, seamstress, b. 179 Swan.

McIntyre, Michael, lab. h. 104 Carroll.

McKay, Alexander, clerk, post-office, h. 197 Terrace.

McKay, Donald D. paper-hanger, h. 64 6th.

McKay, Garlis, book-keeper, b. 266 S. Div.

McKay, Robt. h. 88 Pearl.

McKay, William, clerk, 31 Main, h. Perry n. Hayward.

McKay, Wm. blacksmith, h. 11th n. Hampshire.

McKee, Jas. W. engineer, h. Va. cor. Garden.

McKeen, John, glue factory, h. Martin's Cor.

McKoever, Rich. sawyer, h. Amherst n. Blos'm.

McKenna, James, moulder, b. 98 9th.

McKenna, Jerry, moulder, b. 98 9th.

McKenna, Jno. moulder, h. Jeff. cor. Folsom.

McKenna, Jno. sailor, h. 27 Carolina.

McKenne, Sarah, widow, h. 10 Boston Block.

McKenney, Jas. lab. h. 117 Carroll.

McKeown, Hugh, cartman, h. Carey n Morgan.

McKernan, Margaret, Miss, dress maker, h. 31 Clinton.

McKernan, Pat. h. Fly.

McKibbin, Hugh, h. 106 E. Eagle.

McKibbin, Hugh, Jr. salesman, b. 106 E. Eagle.

McKibbin, R. H. at J. C. Harrison's, Reed's Dock, h. 106 E. Eagle.

McKinlay, Robt. joiner, h. 7 7th.

McKinley, Jno. G. book-keeper, Scott n. Wash. b. 7 7th.

McKinnon, W. R. b. Western.

McKnight, F. A. book-keeper, 16 Cent. Wharf, b. 52 Pearl.

McKnight, Geo. F. book-keeper, J. M. Hutchinson, b. 158 Pearl.

McKnight, James, h. Franklin n. North.

McKnight, Theo. W. 12 Cent. Wharf, h. Franklin cor. North.

McLane, Chas. H. clerk, b. Niagara n. Breckenridge.

McLane, Henry, civil constable, h. 17 7th.

McLane, John, whitewasher, h. 104 Oak.
McLane, Pat. melter, Shepard's iron works, h. Fulton n. Hayward.
McLaren, Chas. H. printer, b. 2 Carroll.
McLaren, Jas. ship carp. b. n. Elk St. market.
McLaren, Willard, printer, b. 2 Carroll.
McLaughlin, L. teamster, h. 5th cor. Virginia.
McLaughlin, Pat. teamster. h. 138 Elk.
McLaughlin, Robt. lab. h. Evans.
McLean, John. h. Niagara cor. Albany.
McLeish, Arch. clerk. 14 Exch. h. 16 7th.
McLeish. C. Mrs. h. Main n. Ferry.
McLeod, J. blacksmith, h. 43 Church.
McLeon. Robt. clerk, Cutter & Hustin, b. Genesee House.
McLinn, H. barber, 74 Elm.
McLochlin, James, grocery, across creek.
McMahon, John. lab. b. 6 Michigan.
McMahon, John E. firm Tillinghast & McM. h. 74 Delaware.
McMahon, Jno. lab. h. Perry n. Elk St. market.
McMahon, —, widow, h. across creek.
McMan, Jno. cooper, h. Ohio n. swing bridge.
McMann, Michael, truckman, h. 86 Carroll.
McMann. Thos. bl'ksmith, h. Hamilton n. Niag.
McManus, Jas. hostler, 303 Main, h. Terrace n. Church.
McMaster, Catharine, widow, h. 52 W. Tupper.
McMennis, Jas. lab. Mechanic n. Terrace.
McMerrick, C. P. conductor, N. Y. C. R. R. b. 20 6th.
McMichael, Jas. clerk, h. Niagara n. Amherst.
McMillen, Hugh, Mrs. widow, h. 70 Chippewa.
McMullen, Jas. saloon. Mich. Central Dock.
McMullen, James, cartman, h. 128 Tupper.
McMullen, John, saloon, Com'l cor. Water.
McMullen, William, Main st. R. R. b. Mrs. J. S. Miller.
McNally, Chas. lab. h. Niagara n. Bird ave.
McNally, James, hackman, h. 13 Pearl.
McNally, James, fish market, Lloyd, h. Canal cor. Lloyd.
McNamara, Dennis, lab. h. Perry n. Chicago.
McNamara, Jas. lab. h. Folsom n. Kinney al.
McNamara, Pat. lab. h. Tenn. cor. Mackinaw.
McNamara, Pat. lab. h. Louisiana n. R. R.
McNamara, Thos. lab. h. La. n. R. R. crossing.
McNamara, John, lab. h. La. n. Tennessee.
McNamarah, Hubbert, drayman, Exchange n. Van Rensselaer.
McNaughton, Dan'l, bl'ksmith, Water, h. 71 6th.
McNAUGHTON. JOHN, commission merch't, 58 Main, h. 73 E. Seneca.—*See adv.* p. 39.
McNaughton, Gilbert, engineer, h. Palmer n. Hudson.
McNeal, Elias, clerk, county treasurer's office, h. 131 9th.
McNeal, Norman B. treasurer Erie county, 11 Spaulding's Exchange, h. Lancaster.
McNeal, Andrew, mariner, h. 16 Mississippi.
McNeal, Peter, candle maker, h. Perry bel. La.
McNeil, Louis, sailor, h. Carey bel. Morgan.
McNeil, Hector, sailor, b. 6 Commercial.
McNemerney, P. cooper, h. Mortimer n. Wm.
McNeringheny, Peter, shoem'r, b. 160 Clinton.
McNerney, Jno. cooper, b. Mortimer n. Wm.
McNesbit. Thos. h. cor. N. Div. and Chestnut.
McNicholas, Walter, sailor, h. 12 Mississippi.

McNish, David clerk, b. Globe Hotel.
McNish, Wm. pattern maker, b. Globe Hotel.
McNoe, Geo. clerk, B. & S. L. R. R. h Seneca n. opp. Heacock.
McNorton, Daniel, blacksmith, cor. Michigan and Ohio.
McNorton, Gilbert, engineer, b. Palmer n. Md.
McNorton, John, commission merchant. 58 Main, h. 73 Seneca.
McNorton, Rebecca, Mrs. h. Palmer, ab. Md.
McNulty, J. h. cor. Perry and Indiana.
McMurchie, A. sailor, b. 6 Commercial.
McMurray, Thomas, tailor, Main cor. Eagle, h. 84 W. Huron.
McMurtry, Jno. machinist, h. Miama n. Ala.
McPhail, Gilbert, sailor, h. 136 Elk.
McPhelney, Wm. lab. h. Porter n Van Rens'lr.
McPherson, A. with J. M. Fish, b. 64 Court.
McPherson. And. fireman, N. Y. C. R. R. b. Revere House.
McPherson, Angus, butcher, 11 and 13 Elk st. market, b. Seneca cor. Dole.
McPherson, John, clerk, h. 157 Pearl.
McPherson, John, at Elk st. market, h. Seneca cor. Dole.
McPherson, R. C. butcher, 11 and 13 Elk street market, b. Dole cor. Seneca.
McPherson, Sam'l, produce deal'r, h. 3 Carroll.
McQuade, S. wood worker, Brayley & Pitts.
McQueen, John, with Prince & Co. h. 6th ab. Hudson.
McQuen, Geo. musician, h. 54 Pine.
McQuester, S. B. com. mer. b. Bonney's Hotel.
McQuin, Alex. saloon, Canal cor. Maiden lane.
McQuoin, Geo. W. musician, h. 54 Pine.
McRobert, John, h. 207 Seneca.
McShannock, Duncan, lab. h. Mich. n. Fulton.
McTagart, Philip, 92 Main.
McVean, Sarah, widow, h. 9th n. Vermont.
McVeen, Robert, book binder, h. Chestnut cor. S. Division.
McVetty, Thos. sailor, h. Clinton bel. Spring.
McVicker, Jas. cartman, h. Niagara n. Georgia.
McWade, Barnard, lab. h. 4th ab. Virginia.
McWade, S. h. cor. Carolina and 5th.
McWhorter. George, baggage master, Erie st. depot, h. Carolina bel. 6th.
McWhorter, Jno. news dealer, N. Y. C. R. R. depot, h. 85 Clinton.
McWilliams, A. clerk, S. Shepard, b. 515 Main.
McWilliams. Francis, Sr. shoe store, 310 Main, h. 515 Main.
McWilliams, Francis, Jr. firm McW. & Sons, b. 515 Main.
McWilliams, R. firm McW. & Sons, b. 515 Main.
McWilliams & Sons," shoe store, 310 Main.
Maar, John G. carp. h. Sycamore n. Jefferson.
Mabb, Thomas, lab. h. 11 William.
Mabbatt, James, blacksmith, h. Fulton n. Ala.
Mabbatt, Jno. boiler maker, h. r. Perry n. Ala.
Mabie, Moses T. shoe store, 278 and 410 Main, h. 39 Ellicott.
Mabie, William, lab. h. 44 Virginia.
Mabis, John, grocer. Niagara n. Parish.
Mabis, Mrs. widow, b. with John Mabis.
Macartney, G. B. capt. h. 10th n. Maryland.
Macdonell, Allan, attorney, 5 Harvey building, up stairs.

Macdonell, D. daguerrean gallery, 232 Main, h. 58 Chippewa.
Macdonell, Dennis, lab. h. Elk n. Chicago.
Macdonell, R. daguerrean rooms, 275 Main, entrance on N. Division.
Mace, James C. boarding stable, 217 Washington, h. 44 Carroll.
Machbet, Mary, A. widow, h. Washington n. Burton alley.
Machemer, Peter, farmer, h. Jefferson n. Best.
Machinier, Adam, lab. h. Monroe n. Peckham.
Machmer, Peter, lab. h. Jefferson n. Best.
Machold, Frank, carpenter, h. Heacock n. Elk.
Machold, Godfred, carp. h. Heacock n. Elk.
Machwirth, Ed. confect'nr, 409½ Main, h. same.
Mack, David, carpenter, h. Folsom n. Chicago.
Mack, James, lab. h. Michigan n. Elk.
Mack, Patrick, printer, b. 113 Folsom.
Mack, R. W. book-keeper, b. 118 Franklin.
Mack, S. lab. h. across creek.
Mack, Wm. shoemaker, h. Hickory n. William.
Mack, William J. ship chandler, 22, 23 and 24 Long Wharf, h. 118 Franklin.
Mackay, Edward, M. D. 123 Pearl, h. same.
Mackay, John, hackman, No. 11, h. 80 Eagle.
Mackay, Michael, hackman, No. 40, b. 3 Centre.
Mackeldon, Thos. plasterer, h. 3 Walnut.
Mackenzie, C.* hatter, 4 Terrace, h. Seneca n. Alabama.
Mackenzie, C. Jr. hatter, b. C. Mackenzie.
Mackenzie, James, hatter, at* Comstock's, b. C. Mackenzie.
Mackie, Alex. Mrs. b. Bowery n. North.
Mackintire, Jno. lab. h. 5th n. Virginia.
Mackintosh, James, boiler maker, h. Hayward n. Fulton.
Maclern, Anna, saloon, 40 Exchange, h. same.
Macloy, Jno. G. with A. L. Griffin & Co. b. Bonney's Hotel.
Macomber, Chas. S. attorney, 152 Main, h. 41 Ellicott.
Macy, S. H. h. 217 Seneca.
Madden, Chas. E. cl'k for E. Madden, b. 44 5th.
MADDEN, EDWARD, coal dealer, Erie and ship canal, h. 44 5th.—See adv. p. 46.
Madden, John, trackmaster, N. Y. & E. R. R. h. Seneca n. N. Y. & E. track.
Maderer, Geo. lab. h. Peach n. High.
Madgett, Thos. foreman, Geo. Parr, h. 23 Court.
Madigon, M. lab. b. Hoffman alley n. Hamilt'n.
Madison, Jas. N. butcher, h. Weaver al. n. Va.
Madison, J. H. assistant cashier, White's Bank, h. 23 S. Division.
Maer, Geo. boiler maker, h. North n. Locust.
Mafleva, Robt. lab. h. 137 Oak.
Magee, J. H. foreman, Wood, Hubbell & Co. h. 105 Clinton.
Mager, Elijah, book-keeper, h. Com'l Hotel.
Magill, A. J. clerk, 162 Main, b. 63 Franklin.
Magill, Wm. clerk, 164 Main.
Magin, Wm. lab. h. Jackson n. Genesee.
Mahama, T. H. & Co. ins. agt's, &c. 7 S. Div.
Mahama, T. H. firm T. H. M. & Co. h. 92 W. Tupper.
Mahan, Andy, lab. h. Exch. n. Hamburgh.
Mahanan, Jeremiah, sailor, h. Kentucky n. Pa.
Maharg, John, cartman, h. Carey bel. Morgan.
Maharg, John W. 68 Main, b. J. Maharg.

Mahar, John, lab. h. 231 Carroll.
Maher, James, plumber, 237 Main, h. Folsom n. Kinney's alley.
Maher, Jas. cartman, h. Ohio n. South.
Maher, Jerry, saloon, Ohio n. Chicago.
Maher, John, plumber, 237 Main, h. Folsom a. Kinney's alley.
Maher, Lawrence, cartman, h. La. n. South.
Maher, Martin, tallyman, N. Y. & E. R. R. h. Ohio n. Washington square.
Maher, Pat. saloon, dock, h. Perry n. R. R.
Maher, Wm. lab. h. 4th n. Virginia.
Mahl, Geo. lab. h. over 177 Genesee.
Mahl, Henry, shoemaker, h. 116 Sycamore.
Mahn, Fred. mason, b. 24 Maple.
Mahon, Elam A. clerk, C. & H. C. Tucker, h. Niagara n. Albany.
Mahon, Wm. rope maker, Clinton Forest.
Mahoney, James, lab. h. Elk n. Marvin.
Mahony, Anora, widow, h. r. 41 Nicholas al.
Mahony, Catherine, widow, h. across creek.
Mahony, Cornelius, lab. b. 38 Ohio.
Mahony, Cornelius, 11th Ward House, cor. Rhode Island and 11th.
Mahony, Daniel, mariner, b. 11th n. R. L.
Mahony, Daniel, lab. h. 41 Jackson.
Mahony, Daniel, lab. h. Aub. ave. n. N. Wash.
Mahony, Dennis, grocer, 318 E. Sen. h. same.
Mahony, Dennis, lab. b. 38 Ohio.
Mahony, Dennis, maltster, h. Wadsworth n. North.
Mahony, Ellen, widow, h. Miss. n. Elk.
Mahony, Jerry, sailor, h. on flats n. Louisiana.
Mahony, Jno lab. h. Morgan n. Genesee.
Mahony, John, lab. b. across creek.
Mahony, John, lab. 44 Ohio.
Mahony, Julia, widow, h. across creek.
Mahony, Martin, lab. h. St. Paul cor. Main.
Mahony, P. blacksmith, h. 191 Exchange.
Mahony, Patrick, lab. b. Smith Block, Exch.
Mahony, Patrick, lab. h. 318 Seneca.
Mahony, Pat. lab. h. Louisiana n. Ohio.
Mahony, Thos. mariner, h. across creek.
Mahony, Tim. lab. h. Jackson cor. Canal al.
Mahony, Wm. lab. h. Exchange n. Smith.
Mahr, Pat. J. Main St. R. R. stable, b. Mrs. J. S. Miller.
Maier, Isaac, milkman, h. Howard cor. Monroe.
Maier, Jacob, turner, h. Adams n. Batavia.
Maier, Jno. lab. h. Spring cor. Sycamore.
Maiers, Stephen,* shoemaker, 125 Pine, h. same.
Maillefert, Chas. teacher, h. 29 Maple.
Maillefert, Samuel, teacher, h. 29 Maple.
Maine, Chauncey, cooper, h. Niag. n. Hamilton.
Maine, Jno. cooper, Niagara n. Austin.
Maischoss, Jno. stove mounter, h. 68 E. Tup'r.
MAJOT, A. wig maker and hair dresser, 173 Main, h. 175 Delaware.—See adv. p. 83.
Mala, Alfred, wagon maker, h. Ala. n. Fulton.
Malcom, Geo. malt house, Main cor. Ferry and Wash. dock, Ohio, h. Delaware 3d ab. Ferry.
Malcom, John, last finisher, h. 250 Carroll.
Malhoubie, Chas. prof. h. Delaware ab. Va.
Mallens, Theo. lab. White's Corners plank road n. Martin's Corners.
Mallon, C. Mrs. h. Spruce n. Genesee.
Mallon, Daniel, carp. h. Spruce n. Genesee.
Mallon, Hugh, mariner, h. York n. 11th.

Malone, Ant'y. ship. carp. b. Perry n. Ohio basin slip.
Malone, John, lab. h. Ferry n. Chicago.
Malone, Pat. saloon, 68 Exchange, h. same.
Malone. Thos. drayman, b. 86 5th.
Maloney, David, lab. h. Otto n. Alabama.
Maloney, Jas. bar-keeper, B. Scott. b. 8 Scott.
Maloney, Jno. C. bar-keeper, h. Scott.
Maloney, John, mariner, h. across creek.
Maloney, Michael, saloon, 3 Erie, h. same.
Malony, Jas. umbrella maker, h. Scott cor. Mississippi.
Maltby, Mrs. widow of Isaac F. h. 71 Oak.
Malzer, Geo. carp. h. Sycamore cor. Mortimer.
Mamro, Wm. lab. h. Ketchum alley n. High.
Managhan, Pat. lab. h. cor. Carroll and Heacock.
Manchester, Bradford A. firm M. & Rich, h. 17 Court cor. Pearl.
Manchester & Rich, bankers and exch. brokers, Main cor. Seneca.
Mane, Henry. machinist, h. Virginia n. 10th.
Maag, Geo. shoemaker. h. Hickory n. Genesee.
Mang, Wm. shoemaker, 28 Niagara Square, h. same.
Mange, Nicholas, farmer, Burton n. Delaware.
Mange, Peter, farmer, Burton n. Delaware.
Mango, Adam, carpenter, h. r. 16 Cherry.
Mango, Catherine, wid. h. Mich. n. Genesee.
Mangold, Conrad, brewer, h. G. Roos.
Mangold, Jacob, blacksmith, h. Ferry n. Jeff.
Mangold, Jacob, Sr. h. Ferry E. of Jefferson.
Manham, Jas. mariner, h. across creek.
Manhard, Anthony, lab. h. 143 Batavia.
Manhard, Frank.* boot and shoe store, cor. Exchange and Chicago.
Manhard, Jno. tailor, h. 141 Batavia.
Manher, John, mariner, h. across creek.
Manich, Valentine, carp. h. Madison n. Bat.
Manin, Wm. lab. h. Burwell place bel. Scott.
Maning, Mary, widow, h. Ohio n. Louisiana.
Mank, Lewis, tailor, h. Walnut cor. Sycamore.
Mank, Peter, farmer, cor. Delaware and town line road.
Manleer, James, b. E. J. Palmer.
Manleer, Nicholas, lamp maker, b. E. J. Palmer.
Manley, Adin T. with Wood, Hubbell & Co. b. 93 Niagara.
Manley, D. S. Buffalo nursery, Utica bet. Delaware and Rogers, h. same
Manley, James, iron finisher, Brayley & Pitts.
Manley, James A. engineer, h. Virginia n. 11th.
Manley, John, lab. h. Louisiana n. Ohio.
Manley, Tim. lab. h. Ohio n. Michigan.
Mann, Chas. J. prod. and com. merch. 15 Central Wharf, h. 109 E. Swan.
Mann, James, blacksmith, h. 199 7th.
Mann, Mary, widow, seamstress, h. Virginia n. Niagara.
Mann, W. B. firm W. B. M. & Co. 17 Central Wharf, h. Barker cor. Main.
Mann, W. W. attorney and counselor, 216 Main, h. 29 Ellicott.
Mannahan, Pat. lab. h. Connecticut n. towpath.
Manning. J. h. Ohio n. Mart.
Manning, John B. 6 Main, b. 5 Main.
Manning, Mrs. h. 100 E. Eagle.
Manning, S. machinist, h. 103 E. Seneca.

Manning, Thos. spar maker, b. Ohio n. La.
Manny, John. lab. h. 248 Seneca.
Manser, Fred. turner, at Prince & Co's, h. 14th n. Jersey.
Manser, Thomas, h. 14th n. Jersey.
Mansfield, John, machinist, b. 157 E. Seneca.
Mantel, George, lab. h. Jefferson bet. Genesee and Sycamore.
Manwiler, Jacob, wagon maker, h. 81 Carroll.
Mara, Jas. lab. h. Exchange n. Van Rensselaer.
March, Francis, fireman, b. 234 S. Division.
Marchant, Jacob, stone cutter, 77 Sycamore.
Marchant, Ursula, widow, washer, h. 138 Ellicott.
Marcus, Julius. tailor, 157 Main, h. 147 Swan.
Marer, Patrick, carman, Perry n. Alabama.
Marhover, Jacob, peddler, h. 20 Potter.
Marhover, Jacob, Jr. lab. h. 20 Potter.
Maristone, M. carpenter, h. 62 Pine.
Mark, John, lab. h. Palmer n. Maryland.
Mark, Joseph, machinist, b. John Mark.
Markay, Wm. plasterer. h. Walnut n. William.
Marker, Michael, miller, h. Thompson n. Hamilton.
Markey, Jas. lab. b. Mackinaw n. Kentucky.
Markham, Geo. maltster, Ohio n. Washington square, h. Cold Spring.
Markle, Jacob, cooper, h. Farmer n. East.
Markle, John J. engineer, h. Fulton n. Ala.
Marks, J. iron finisher, Brayley & Pitts.
Marks, John, foundryman, Brayley & Pitts.
Marks, Martin, theatre saloon, b. r. 74 Chippewa.
Maron, Geo. A. joiner, h. 191 E. Eagle.
Maroney, Michael, lab. h. Michigan n. Ohio.
Maroney, Pat. lab. h. Sandusky n. La.
Maroney, Timothy, lab. h. Marvin n. Elk.
Marr, John, carp. b. 56 Oak.
Marsdorf, John, blacksmith. h. Ash n. Gen.
Marsh, E. weighman, h. Mason n. Breckenridge.
Marsh, Eugene, firm Dickey & M. b. 167 E. Sen.
Marsh, Geo. J. canal insp. with H. C. Walker, b. Bonney's.
Marsh, Joseph, boarding stables, Green n. Michigan, b. Wadsworth.
Marsh, Joseph, N. Y. C. R. R. b. Wadsworth.
Marsh, P. S. sup. Mer. Dispatch, h. 120 S. Div.
Marshall, A. J. book-keeper, h. cor. Amherst and Dearborn.
Marshall, B. D. Rev. h. 156 Seneca.
Marshall, C. D. student at law, b. 78 Pearl.
Marshall, Charles R. book-keeper, Palmer & Gardner, h. Seneca n. junc. Swan.
Marshall & Harvey, attorneys, 330 Main.
Marshall, J. E. Mrs. b. 78 Pearl.
Marshall, Jas. ship carpenter, h. Vandalia n. Mackinaw.
Marshall, John, lab. h. Mulberry n. Virginia.
Marshall, Orsamus H. firm M. & Harvey, h. 78 Pearl.
Marshall, Wm. carriage maker, h. Carroll cor. Michigan.
Marsland, R. S. cashier, 318 Main, h. 65 S. Div.
Martell, Jas. h. Fulton n. Louisiana.
Martell, John, firm M. & Bro. h. Ala. n. Perry.
Marter, Peter, lab. h. Kaene n. Genesee. .
Martial, John, glazier, h. 281 Oak.
Martin, Aaron, tavern, Martin's Corners.
Martin, Amelia, Mrs. dress maker h. 217 Oak.

Martin, Daniel, lab. h. East n. South.
Martin, David, carp. b. 74 Chippewa.
Martin, Dominick, grocer, cor. Penn. and 5th.
Martin, Ernestine M. clerk, 323 Main, b. same.
Martin, Francis, teamster, h. Niag. n. Bird.
Martin, Frederick, cabinet maker, h. over N. E. cor. Carolina and 9th.
Martin, Henry, drayman, h. Potter opposite arsenal.
Martin, Henry H. cashier, Manufactures and Traders' Bank, h. 483 Main.
Martin, Henry, president, Manufacturers and Traders' Bank, h. 470 Main cor. Tupper.
Martin, Horace, h. Lee's Corners.
Martin, Jacob, grocer, Batavia cor. Hickory.
Martin, J. C. printer, h. Elm n. N. Division.
Martin, Joseph, truckman, b. Genesee House.
Martin Luther College, Maple n. Virginia.
Martin, Mary, widow, b. 5th above Pa.
Martin, Michael, caulker, h. Perry n. Ala.
Martin, Owen, drayman, b. cor. 5th and Pa.
Martin, Philip, blacksmith, 186 7th.
Martin, Robt. sailor, h. Hampshire n. 10th.
Martin, Stephen, porter at Western.
Martin, Thos. lab. across creek.
Martin, Wm. carpenter, h. 132 Ellicott.
Martin, Wm. lab. h. Monroe n. Batavia.
Martin, Wm. joiner, h. 11 10th.
Martin, Simon, carp. h. Locust n. Cherry.
Martindale, Thomas, blacksmith, h. Van Rensselaer n. Porter.
Martine, F. Z. paper hanger, h. 224 Eagle.
Marvel, Chas. policeman, h. Carlton n. Oak.
Marvell, Henry, boat builder, h. towpath opp. work house.
Marvin, Chas. E. clerk, cor. Seneca and Wash. b. cor. Franklin and Court.
Marvin, Edward G. 155 Main, b. Franklin cor. Court.
Marvin, Eurotas, with A. Reynolds & Co. cor. Court and Franklin.
Marvin, F. C. cl'k 155 Main, h. 93 Franklin.
Marvin, Geo. sailor, h. across creek.
Marvin, Geo. L. firm Le Grand & G. L. M. h. 58 W. Mohawk.
Marvin, James, stone cutter, b. Mary Frost.
Marvin, Le Grand, firm Le Grand & G. L. M. h. 461 Main.
MARVIN, LE GRAND & G. L. attorneys, over 156 Main.—See adv. p. 83.
Marvin, Sarah L. Mrs. h. 80 Huron.
Maser, William, cigar maker, h. Michigan n. Genesee.
Maskill, Robt. lab. h. 4th n. Carolina.
Masman, J. F. grocer, cor. La. and Exch.
Mason, Addison P. 19 William, h. cor. Morse and Perrin.
Mason, A. G. clerk, h. 110 Clinton.
Mason, Andrew S. firm Mason & Bidwell, h. Swan n. Hickory.
MASON & BIDWELL, ship builders, at Buffalo marine railway.—See adv. p. 64.
Mason, Chas. printer, h. Fox n. Genesee.
Mason, Dan. farmer, Delevan ave. E. Main, h. Washington below Tupper.
Mason, E. J. works for Bush & Howard, h. 5th n. Hudson.
Mason, Eliza, widow, Fox n. Genesee.

Mason, Ezra, b. 102 9th.
Mason, F. B. clerk, with Jno. Bush, 29 Seneca, b. 27 Seneca.
Mason, James, ship carp. h. 10 S. Division.
Mason, James D. lab. h. Elm n. High.
Mason, J. B. with Young, Lockwood & Co. h. r. 9 Huron.
Mason, John, hostler, Bonney's Hotel.
Mason, John B. painter, h. 102 9th.
Mason, Seth L. clerk, at 29 E. Seneca, h. 27.
Mason, Wm. H. with Jewett & Root, 43 Elm.
Mason, Wm. W. Mrs. h. 43 Elm.
Masse, M. clerk, 274 Main, b. 26 Chicago.
Masses, S. foreman wood workers, Brayley & Pitts.
Massing, Wm. wood worker, Brayley & Pitts, h. Vermont n. Rogers.
Massmann, Mathias, grinder, h. 192 Elm.
Mast, Daniel, lab. h. Wm. n. Monroe.
Masten, Frederick H. firm Jos. Warren & Co. h. 307 Washington.
Masten, J. G. Judge Supreme Court, h. 443 Main.
Masten, John, b. 448 Main.
Master, Frances, Miss, teacher No. 2, b. Batavia n. Walnut.
Master, Jane, widow, h. Bat. n. Walnut.
Masters, John, engineer, h. Fulton n. Ala.
Masters, Samuel, pattern maker, b. Louisiana n. Elk.
Materer, John, lab. h. Adam n. Sycamores.
Math, John M. bakery, Walnut n. Batavia h. same.
Mathas, Conrad, bakery, Genesee n. Spruce, h. same.
Mather, John, clerk, city treasurer, b. Bonney's Hotel.
Mathers, Eliza, Miss, h. 52 Clinton.
Mathes, Philip, carp. h. 144 Huron.
Mathews, A. L. druggist, 255 Main, h. 181 Del.
Mathews, Ephraim, confectioner, h. Monroe n. Clinton.
Mathews, Harry, sawyer, h. cor. Elk and Ala.
Mathews, Henry, engineer, h. Ferry n. Erie canal.
Mathews, J. M. 6 C. Wharf, b. Mansion.
Mathews, Louis, firm M. & Talman, h. 211 Pearl.
MATHEWS & TALLMAN, grocers, 334 Main.—See adv. p. 39.
Mathews, William, mail agent, b. Courter House.
Mathias, Christopher, organ maker, with G. House, h. Michigan n. High.
Mathus, Thomas, brick maker, h. Genesee E. tollgate.
Matterson, Wm. boiler maker, N. Y. & E. R. R. h. 107 Fulton.
Matteson, E. L. book-binder, 165 Main, b. 287 Michigan.
Matteson, Harry H. dealer in boots and shoes, 256 Main, h. 291 Oak.
Matteson, S. A. attorney at law, b. 116 6th.
Matthaes, Christian G. dealer in carpet and hose, 222 Genesee, h. same.
Matthews, Harry, printer, b. 45 S. Division.
Matthews, J. N. firm Clapp, M. & Waite, h. 97 S. Division.
Matthews, T. C. carp. h. 312 Michigan.

Matthews, Thos. lab. h. Carroll n. Red Jacket.
Mattice, Fred M. drain tile manufacturer, h. 10th ab. Jersey.
Mattice, Ruth A. teacher, b. F. M. Mattice.
Mattison, Chas. Z. firm Gorton & M. h. 4 Ellicott.
Mattison, Hiram, driver, h. 116 6th.
Matzedorf, Christ. blacksmith, h. 538 Michigan.
Matzedorf, Louis, lab. h. Clinton n. Adams.
Matzen, P. wood worker, Brayley & Pitts.
Maue, Christena, wid. h. Ferry E. of Jeff'n.
Mauer, John, mason, 178 Oak.
Mauer, Jos. lab. h. Sherman n. Batavia.
Mauerer, John, lab. h. Herman n. Genesee.
Mauerer, Peter, sailor, h. Lutheran n. Batavia.
Mauerman, Francis, varnisher, h. Oak n. Best.
Mauerman, John, plasterer, h. St. Paul n. Ellicott.
Mauerman, Stephen, h. Oak n. Best.
Maul, Conrad, lab. h. Oak n. North.
Maul, Geo. moulder, h. Goodell al. n. Goodell.
Maul, John, lab. h. Adams n. Sycamore.
Maurer, Geo. brewer, h. Elm cor. Tupper.
Maurer, Nicholas, musician, h. Hickory n. William.
Maurer, Rudolph, tailor, b. 410 Michigan.
Maurer, Wm. carp. h. Grape n. North.
Mautz, Jacob,* grocer, Genesee cor. Spring, h. same.
Mavaus, Joachim, tailor, h. 176 Genesee.
Maxon, Alanson, clerk, Bradford & Chase, h. 44 Niagara.
Maxwell, Joshua, h. 32 S. Division.
May, Jacob, tanner, h. 55 Cedar.
May, James, at International, b. 6th n. York.
May, Michael, musician, h. 138 Batavia.
May, William, mariner, h. ac. creek.
Maycock, Thomas, painter, h. 20 Steuben.
Mayer, Christopher, cooper, h. Syc. n. Spruce.
Mayer, Francis, mason, h. Michigan n. High.
Mayer, Geo. C. cashier, Sherman & Barnes, h. Madison n. Howard.
Mayer, J. wood worker, Brayley & Pitts.
Mayer, Jacob, carp. h. Seneca n. Heacock.
Mayer, John, lab. h. Johnson cor. North.
Mayer, Jos. peddler, h. Walnut n. Genesee.
Mayer, Martin, M. D. office and h. 85 Franklin.
Mayer, Peter,* shoemaker, 23 Genesee, h. same.
Mayes, Geo. L. joiner, h. 139 Clinton.
Mayher, John, h. Cherry n. Michigan.
Mayhew, Jonathan, firm Buffalo Steam Guage Co. office 1 Brown's Building, h. 64 Mohawk.
Maynard, E. A. h. 56 E. Seneca.
Maynard, F. H. engineer, N. Y. & E. R. R. h. 32 Carroll.
Maynard, Robert H. land broker, office and h. 67 E. Seneca.
Meach, S. L. flour and feed, h. 166 Swan.
Meacham, George, coffin maker, h. Carey bel. Morgan.
Mead, Chas. M. D. 159 Elk, h. same.
Mead, Geo. R. E. at 340 Main, b. 348 Main.
Meadows, Chas. engraver, h. Pearl cor. Seneca.
Mealig, Louis, blacksmith, h. Walnut n. Bat.
Meatt, Jas. billiard saloon, 9 Commercial, b. 7 Commercial.
Meder, Joseph, carp. h. 245 Elm.
Meech, Asa B. land office, over 223 Main, h. 359 Franklin.

Meech, Elizabeth, Miss, teacher, b. Delaware ab. Virginia.
Meech, H. L. prop. Wadsworth House.
Meech, James, steward, Wadsworth House.
Meech, John H. b. Wadsworth House.
Meech, Sam. L. firm W. H. Cobb & Co. h. 166 Swan.
Meech, Wellington, prop. Metropolitan Theater, b. Wadsworth.
Mehan, Pat. flagman, N. Y. & E. R. R. h. Hamburgh n. Carroll.
Meehan, Pat. rope maker, h. Pooley place.
Meeker, Henry N. machinist, h. 261 Swan.
Mega, G. J. fence maker, b. Western R. W. House.
Mehegan, Chas. lab. h. across creek.
Mehen, Mary, wid. nurse, h. Ct. n. 12th.
Mehler, John, lab. h. Grey bet. Gen. and Bat.
Mehltreter, Chas. tailor, h. Spring n. Hickory.
Mehnard, L. J. harness maker, b. Pine n. Wm.
Meidel, Nicholas, lab. h. Adams n. Batavia.
Meidl, Martin, lab. h. Shumway n. Peckham.
Meidenbauer, John Geo. malt house, Mich. n. High, h. same.
Meidenbuer, Geo. farmer, h. Peach n. High.
Meier, Andrew, teamster, h. 106 Cedar.
Meier, Antone, lab. h. Adams n. Sycamore.
Meier, Ernst, lab. h. Stanton n. Batavia.
Meier, Jacob, lab. h. Batavia n. Jefferson.
Meier, Jacob, finisher, h. Pratt n. Batavia.
Meier, John, lab. h. Krettner n. Lovejoy.
Meier, John G. shoemaker, h. Hickory n. Bat.
Meier, John, varnisher, h. 26 Pine.
Meier, John, lab. h. Oak n. North.
Meier, Stephen, makes fireworks, h. 8 Maple.
Meierle, Jos. tailor, h. 233 Oak.
Meiers, Henry, carp. h. Pine n. Batavia.
Meinel, Geo. mason, h. Weaver's alley n. Va.
Meinhardt, Fred. lab. h. Sycamore opp. Kaene.
Meisel, Jno. lab. h. Sherman n. Genesee.
Meissner, Ernst G. private school, 136 E. Gen. h. same.
Meissner, Julius, carp. h. W. Wm. ab. Va.
Meissner, Wm. E. G. carpenter, h. Amherst n. Thompson.
Meister, Adam, wagoner, h. foot Water.
Meister, Adam, lab. h. over 254 Genesee.
Meister, Edward, tailor, h. Mortimer n. Syc.
Meister, Wm. shoemaker, h. Mulberry n. Va.
Meister, Wm. grocery, Tonawanda n. Niag.
Meitz, Geo. blacksmith, h. Cherry cor. Maple.
Meixler, Philip, milkman, h. Pratt n. Wm.
Melancon, Oliver, painter, firm M. & Courtney, h. Sycamore n. Spring.
Melin, John, tailor, b. Genesee House.
Melling, Jas. Am. Exp. Co. h. 96 E. Eagle.
Melling, John, Am. Exp. Co. b. 96 E. Eagle.
Melloth, Peter, lab. h. Monroe n. William.
Melvins, Jno. cooper, h. Elk cor. Ala.
Menard, Irena, tailoress, h. Carolina n. Efner.
Menard, Joseph, ship carp. h. Fulton n. Ham.
Mench, Philip, lab. h. 206 Genesee.
Mench, Wm. b. Genesee n. Hickory.
Mendsen, T. H. firm Hamlin & Mendsen, h. 145 Pearl.
Menge, Edward, carp. h. Bennett n. Batavia.
Menge, Jacob, E. teamster, h. 318 Elm.
Menger, Martin, cooper, h. Dearborn n. R. R.

Menges, Adam, carp. h. Spruce n. Genesee.
Menges, Wm. lab. h. 179 Batavia.
Menick, Conrad, lab. h. Goodell cor. Mulberry.
Menig, Jos. carp. h. 13 Cypress.
Menik, Jno. lab. Monroe n. Batavia.
Mennig, Adam, carp. h. Jefferson n. Peckham.
Mennig, C. R. cider vinegar, h. Bat. n. Walnut.
Mensch, Catharine, widow, h. Cedar n. Wm.
Mensch, Catharine, widow, h. Gen. n. Hickory.
Mensch, Chas. F. clerk, Hamlin & Mendsen, b. Genesee n. Hickory.
Mensch, Fred. lab. h. Genesee n. Hickory.
Mensch, Fred. moulder, b. Cedar n. Wm.
Mensch, Jno. moulder, b. Cedar n. William.
Mensch, Margaret, widow, h. 171 Elm.
Mensch, Wm. h. 18 E. Genesee.
Mensch, Wm. printer, b. Gen. n. Hickory.
Mercer, Geo. carriage painter, h. Wash. n Chip.
Mercer, J. L. sail maker, h. Western.
Mercer, Joseph, capt. mariner, 7 5th.
Merchant's Dispatch, La. n. R. R. track.
Merchfelder, Jacob, mach. h. Syc. n. Walnut.
Meredith, Richard, boarding house, 160 Exch.
Mergenhagen, J. & Bro. props. City Hotel, Exchange cor. Michigan.
Mergenhagen, John, firm M. & Bro.
Mergenhagen, Peter, firm M. & Bro.
Mergi, Jno. gardener, b. 57 Grey.
Mergler, Bartol, carp. h. Mulberry n. Va.
Meriem, Frank, capt. h. 29 N. Division.
Merk, Wm. shoemaker, h. Hickory n. Wm.
Merkel, Jno. shoemaker, b. High n. Lemon.
Merker, Julius, at Pratt & Co. 424 Michigan.
Merker, Julius, clerk, Pratt & Co. h. 428 Mich.
Merkla, Lenhard, cabinet maker, h. Hickory n. Sycamore.
Merkle, Wm. F. F. clerk, J. G. Gerhardt, cor. Elk and Alabama.
Merkling, Geo. lab. h. Hickory n. Sycamore.
Merkling, John, shoemaker, 151 Oak, h. same.
Merkt, Gregory, lab. h. 179 Genesee.
Merrick, Samuel, breakman, h. alley bet. 6th and 7th.
Merrill, Albert S. lawyer, 148 Main, h. 35 Ced.
Merrill, E. T. iron finisher, b. 35 Cedar.
Merrill, H. Lee, kook-keeper, h. 384 Delaware.
Merrill, Henry L. h. 384 Franklin.
Merrill, Ira, h. Niagara n. Jefferson.
Merrill, Jerome B. h. 250 Ellicott.
Merrill, Silas L. book-keeper, 273 Main, h. 225 Delaware.
Merriles, Wm. machinist, h. 6th n. Virginia.
Merrilles, W. iron finisher, Brayley & Pitts.
Merring, Augustus, lab. h. Bundy's alley n. Syc.
Merring, Chas. h. Bundy's alley n. Sycamore.
Merritt, George H. tallyman, N. Y. C. R. R. h. 48½ Oak.
Merritt, Jas. M. firm Cash & Merritt, h. 156 N. Division.
Merritt, Peter, cooper, h. 120 Chippewa.
Merry, Henry J. machinist, b. Va. n. Niag.
Mertz, Conrad, carp. h. Walnut n. Sycamore.
Mertz, Jacob, milkman, Williamsville road n. Ferry.
Merwin, H. R. clerk, 318 Main.
Merzig, M. blacksmith, h. Lutheran n. Wm.
Mesler, Isaac C. boat builder, h. Palmer n. Hud.
Mesmer, Mich. flour dealer, 277 Main, h. same.

Mesmer, Peter, tailor, 217 Elm.
Mesnard, John, confectioner, 75 Gen. h. same.
Mesner, Anthony, brewer, h. Clinton n. Emslie.
Mesner, Joseph, lab. h. Heacock n. Carroll.
Mesner, Peter, furniture dealer, 243 Main, h. 78 Genesee.
Messer, Adam, lab. h. Oak n. Virginia.
Messer, D. Mrs. wid. h. cor. Niag. and Austin.
Messer, Mathias, lab. h. Elm n. Virginia.
Messing, Conrad, mason, h. Vt. n. Rogers.
Messing, Henry, lab. h. R. I. n. Chenango.
Messing, H. J. clerk, over 156 Main, b. 189 Gen.
Messing, Jacob, stone cutter, h. Rogers n. Vt.
Messing, Lewis, with Jewett & Root, h. Utica n. Rhode Island.
Messing, Peter, h. Utica n. Rogers.
Messing, Wm. painter, h. Vt. n. Rogers.
Messing, Wm. Jr.* grocer, 189 Gen. h. same.
Messing, William, Sr. capt. No. 4 police, h. 189 Genesee.
Messinger, John, lab. h. Seneca n. Chicago.
Messinger, John, carp. b. 70 Bennett.
Messmer, Anthony, carp. h. Shumway n. Lovejoy.
Messmer, L. lab. h. Bat. n. Hickory.
Metat, Joseph, carp. h. Howard n. Emslie.
Metcalfe, Clarance H. h. junc. Elk and Abbott.
Metcalfe, James H. drove-yard junc. Elk and Abbott road, h. 94 E. Swan.
Metcalfe, John C. conductor, B. & L. H. R. R. h. 109 N. Division.
Metka, Fred. mason, h. 557 Michigan.
Metler, G. Fr. tailor, h. Spring n. Sycamore.
Metler, George, at C. Cobb & Co's, cor. Terrace and Evans.
Metropolitan Theater, Main above Seneca.
Metz, Abram, deputy supt. Erie Co. Penitentiary, b. same.
Metz, Adam, lab. h. 44 Bennett.
Metz, Apollonia, widow, h. 44 Bennett.
Metz, Charles, saloon, cor. Main and Exch. h. 564 Washington.
Metz, Christian, firm M. & Rathbone, h. St. James.
Metz, Fred. lab. h. 547 Michigan.
Metz Geo. lab. h. Walnut n. Batavia.
Metz, Geo. J. lab. h. 4 Bennett.
Metz, Jacob, brass moulder, h. cor. Lovejoy and Krettner.
Metz, John, lab. h. 73 Goodell.
Metz, Joseph, lab. h. Spring n. Bat.
Metz, Ottille, widow. h. 259 Elm.
Metz, Peter, shoemaker, h. 78 Monroe.
Metz & Rathbone, att'ys at law. 334 Main.
Metz, Valentine, carp. h. 4 Bennett.
Metzdorf, John, lab. h. 23 Ash.
Metzen, Peter, cabinet maker, h. Sycamore n. Walnut.
Metzger, A. moulder, h. W. Bennett n. Wm.
Metzger, Frank, saloon, Ohio n. Chicago.
Metzger, George, livery stable, 326 Washington, h. 371 Michigan.
Metzger, Jacob, merchant tailor, 34 Main, h. same.
Metzger, John, saloon, Exch. n. Mich.
Metzger, Jno. mason, h. Mulberry n. Goodell.
Metzger, John P. tailor, h. Peckham n. Jeff.
Metzger, Mrs. wid. h. R. I. n. 11th.

Metzler. John, mason, h. Clinton n. Jeff.
Meurer, Charles, cabinet maker, h. Walnut n. Batavia.
Meuret, Lewis, boiler maker, h. Van Rensselaer.
Mexner, Fred. cooper, h. Spring cor. Wm.
Mey, Fred. millwright, h. Seneca n. Heacock.
Meyer, Amelia, Miss, East n. Farmer.
Meyer, Andrew, mason, h. 265 Elm.
Meyer, Arnold, lab. h. 119 Walnut.
Meyer, Casper. mason, h. 136 Sycamore.
Meyer, Chas. provisions, 22 Wash. market, h. 314 Ellicott.
Meyer, Chas. tailor, h. North n. Lemon.
Meyer, Chas. blacksmith, h. Gen. n. Spring.
Meyer, Christopher, lab. h. Pratt cor. Syc.
Meyer, Conrad, lab. Boston alley n. Tupper.
Meyer, Conrad, teacher school at Church, Ellicott above Washington market.
Meyer, Conrad, blacksmith, h. Peach n. North.
Meyer, Dietrich, farmer, h. Elm n. Best.
Meyer, F. widow, h. Spring n. Sycamore.
Meyer, F. blacksmith, William cor. Hickory, h. Pratt n. Clinton.
Meyer, Franz, lab. h. Herman n. Gen.
Meyer, Fr'd. butcher, 221 Oak, h. same.
Meyer, Fred. pastor Baptist Church, Spruce, h. 30 Walnut.
Meyer, Fred. grocer, Wm. opp. Potter.
Meyer, Frederick, clerk 146 Gen. b. same.
Meyer, Frederick, cooper, Spring cor. Syc.
Meyer, Frederick, rag peddler, h. Walnut n. Sycamore.
Meyer. Frederick G. cabinet maker, h. Locust n. High.
Meyer, Frederick, book-binder, h. 107 Gen.
Meyer, Geo. engineer, b. 142 Oak.
Meyer, Geo. lab. h. Genesee E. Williamsville road.
Meyer, Geo. boiler maker, h. North n. Locust.
Meyer, Geo. lab. h. Johnson n. Genesee.
Meyer, Geo. painter, h. Best n. Oak.
Meyer, George lab. h. Batavia n. Williamsville road.
Meyer, George M. shoemaker, h. Michigan n. Best.
Meyer, Gottlieb, painter, h. Amherst n. East.
Meyer, Helene, widow, h. 558 Michigan.
Meyer, Henry, farmer, b. Elm n. Best.
Meyer, Jacob, locksmith, h. 69 Hickory.
Meyer, Jacob, carriagesmith, b. Locust n. High.
Meyer, Jacob, carp. h. Locust n. High.
Meyer, James, carp. h. Military road n. Lewis.
Meyer, J. painter, Brayley & Pitts.
Meyer, John G. stone cutter, h. Carlton n. Jeff.
Meyer, John, lab. h. Monroe between Batavia and Sycamore.
Meyer, Jno. bakery, Clinton n. Emslie, h. same.
Meyer, John, boiler maker, h. r. 206 E. Gen.
Meyer, John, lab. h. Cherry n. Spring.
Meyer, Jno. wagon maker, Niag. n. Austin.
Meyer, John, bricklayer. h. Elm n. North.
Meyer, John, turner, b. Bat. n. Mortimer.
Meyer, John, boiler maker, h. Maple n. High.
Meyer, Jos. lab. h. Cherry n. Spruce.
Meyer, Jos. Jr. printer, h. Cherry n. Spruce.
Meyer, J. W. A. grocer, Batavia cor. Walnut h. same.

Meyer, Joseph, lab. h. 43 Ash.
Meyer, Louis, carp. h Howard n. Watson.
Meyer, Louis, lab. h. Pine n. Bat.
Meyer, Louisa, wid. h. Madison n. Howard.
Meyer, Magnus, painter, h. 571 Washington.
Meyer, Mary, widow, b. 35 Milnor.
Meyer, Mary, widow, h. 174 Oak.
Meyer, Michael, lab. h. 557 Michigan.
Meyer, Michael lab. Mich. n. Best.
Meyer, Olive, dress maker, b. 129 Franklin.
Meyer, Peter, lab. h. Mortimer n. Batavia.
Meyer, Philip, tinsmith, h. 54 Goodell
Meyer, Philip, carp. Niag. n. Hamilton.
Meyer, Simon. cooper, h. Bat. n. Mortimer.
Meyer, Theodore, machinist, h. 145 Oak.
Meyer, Wendelin, farmer. h. Gen. n. Walden.
Meyer, Wm. clerk, h. 64 William.
Meyer, Wm. cabinet maker, h. 94 Goodell.
Meyer, Xavier, mason, h. Locust n. High.
Meyers, Chs. cook, h. Cypress n. Pine.
Meyers, Daniel, lab. h. Milnor n. William.
Meyers, Geo. stone cutter, h. Bristol n. Emslie,
Meyers, Jos. sailor, h. Bristol below Spring.
Meyers, Lena. seamstress, b. Bat. cor. Milnor.
Meyers, Mary, widow, h. Bat. cor. Milnor.
Meyers, Nicholas, mathamatical instrument manufacturer, b. Bat. cor. Milnor.
Meyers, William, warehouseman, 21 Lloyd, h. Wm. above Pine.
Michael, Fred. painter, b. 43 N. Division.
Michael, Jacob, moulder, b. 43 N. Division.
Michael, John, h. 121 Pearl.
Michael, John, h. 121 Pearl.
Michael, Lorenz, moulder, h. Pine n. Bat.
Michael, Morris, h. 121 Pearl.
Michael, Nicholas, cartman, b. 43 N. Division.
Michaelis, Wm. peddler, b. Hickory n. Bat.
Michaels, August, carp. h. Maple n. Goodell.
Michel, John, lab. h. Adams n. Batavia.
Michel, J.* shoemaker, h. Vt. n. 13th.
MICHIGAN CENTRAL RAIL ROAD.—See adv. p. 99.
Mickel, John, ship carp. h. 5th n. Carolina.
Mickens, Wm. lab. h. Niagara n. Sloan.
Mickley. Thos. distiller, b. Austin n. Niagara.
Middleidich. Franklin, h. 194 N. Division.
Middleton, Geo. sail maker, h. 12 5th.
Middleton, Wm. sailor, h. 4th n. Virginia.
Miesel, Catharine, widow, b. Walnut n. Bat.
Miesel, Christian, lab. h. Walnut n. Batavia.
Mignery, Geo. F. clerk, 1 Clinton, b. 110 Elm.
Mignery, Nicholas, lab. h. 110 Elm.
Mignery, Nicholas, Jr. machinist, h. 110 Elm.
Mignery, Peter F. clerk, b. 110 Elm.
Miland, James, sail maker, h. 7th. cor. Hudson.
Milborn, Mary. widow, h. across creek.
Miles, Geo. breakman L. S. R. R. b. National.
Miles, —, clerk, b. 255 Washington.
Milgam, Moritz, boiler maker, h. 18 Ash.
Millan. Adam, packer, 162 Main, h. Carlton n. Michigan.
Millar, A. P. firm Welch & M. b. Miss Clemons, 436 Main.
Millar, R. W. Merch. Disp. b. 219 E. Seneca.
Millard. Geo. nailer, h. Sloan n. Niagara.
Millard. Jas. teamster, h. Niagara n. South.
Millard, Samuel, land proprietor, h. Niagara n. Forest avenue.

Millard, Thos. h. Niagara n. Bird.
Miller, Adam, tanner, h. William n. Cedar.
Miller, Adam, musician, h. 88 Cherry.
Miller, A. C. M. D. h. 42 William.
Miller, A. D. A. firm M. & Greiner, h. 400 Franklin.
Miller, Alex. h. Cottage cor. Maryland.
Miller, A. M. printer, b. 467 Michigan.
Miller, Andrew, mason, Pratt n. William.
Miller, And. brewer, b. X. Kaltenbach.
Miller, Barbara, widow, h. 68 Delaware place.
Miller, Bennett & Co. Buff. Mower and Reaper, 14 Water cor. LeCouteulx.
Miller, Bernhert,* grocer, 505 Michigan, h. same.
Miller, Carl, hostler. h. Hamilton n. Niagara.
Miller, Chas. F. firm D. P. Harris & Co. h. 45 Pearl.
Miller, Chas. G. office 6 Brown's Buildings, h. 214 Franklin.
Miller, Chas. sup. Main st. R. R. b. Main n. Ferry.
Miller, Chas. b. Genesee n. Spring.
Miller, Charles, butcher, b. P. J. Murphy.
Miller, Chas. lab. h. William n. Krettner.
Miller, Chris. stone cutter, h. Best n. cor. Mich.
Miller, Chr. mason, h. Walnut n. William.
Miller, Chris. lab. h. 72 Tupper.
Miller, Chris. book-binder, h. Clinton n. Spring.
Miller, Christian, lab. h. Roos alley n. Wm.
Miller, Christian, butcher, h. Batavia n. Hickory.
Miller, Conrad, ship carp. h. 115 Walnut.
Miller, Conrad, ash peddler, h. S. Division n. Emslie.
Miller, Conrad, lab. h. Best n. Michigan.
Miller, Conrad, lab. h. Alabama n. Mackinaw.
Miller, Conrad, lab. h. Pine n. Cypress.
Miller, Dan. mason, h. Walnut n. William.
Miller, Dan. h. 61 Genesee.
Miller, David, mason, h. Walnut n. William.
Miller, E. grocer, h. cor. Monroe and Howard.
Miller, E. A. clerk, N. Y. C. R. R. freight office, b. Franklin.
Miller, Emanuel, foreman, shoe shop, Erie Co. poor house.
Miller, Francis, cap maker, b. cor. Genesee and Ellicott.
Miller, Fred. lab. h. Maple n. Carlton.
Miller, Fred. lab. h. High n. Maple.
Miller, Fred. carp. h. Maple n. Goodell.
Miller, Fred. carp. 123 Genesee.
Miller, Fred. lab. h. Shumway n. William.
Miller, F. S. capt. h. 112 S. Division.
Miller, Geo. lab. h. Walnut n. Batavia.
Miller, Geo. tailor, with J. Small, h. 43 Niag.
Miller, Geo. lab. h. Best n. Elm.
Miller, Geo. ship carp. h. Walnut n. Batavia.
Miller, George, blacksmith, h. East n. Amherst.
Miller, Gottlieb, lab. h. N. Canal n. Grosvenor.
Miller & Greiner, wholesale grocers, 28 and 30 Main.
Miller, Harry B. h. North opp. Wadsworth Park.
Miller, Harry, h. Franklin cor. Erie.
Miller, Henry, mason, h. Grey n. Genesee.
Miller, Henry H. cooper, h. Niag. n. Hamilton.
Miller, Henry, marble polisher, h. 114 Syc.
Miller, Henry, shoemaker, h. 155 Cherry.

Miller, Henry, tinsmith, b. Genesee n. Spring.
Miller, Henry, finisher, h. over 136 Genesee.
Miller, H. B.* distiller, Spring n. Batavia, h. North opp. Wadsworth Park.
Miller, Jacob, shoemaker, b. 7 Commercial.
Miller, Jacob," cooper, h. East n. South.
Miller, Jacob, tanner, h. cor. William and Jefferson.
Miller, Jacob. with Tweedy & Smith, h. Genesee cor. Ellicott.
Miller, Jacob, carp. h. Spring n. Sycamore.
Miller, Jacob, carp. h. Clinton n. Pratt.
Miller, Jacob, gardener, h. Utica cor. Chenango.
Miller, Jacob, keeper pest house, Rogers n. North.
Miller, James, com. of deeds, 181 Main, h. 380 Main.
Miller, James, rigger, h. Elk n. Hamburgh.
Miller, John, carpenter, h. Ash n. Genesee.
Miller, John, butcher, Palmer n. Va. h. same.
Miller, John, with H. Utley, h. Genesee n. Jefferson.
Miller, John, last maker, h. Wm. n. Cedar.
Miller, John, painter, h. 9th n. Maryland.
Miller, John, carp. h. Fulton n. Alabama.
Miller, John, tailor, over 215 Ellicott.
Miller, John, moulder, h. Maple bet. High and Carlton.
Miller, John, lab. h. Batavia n. Williamsville road.
Miller, John, wagoner, h. Genesee n. Walnut.
Miller, John, lab. h. Roos n. William.
Miller, John, mason, h. 9 Cherry.
Miller, John, h. Walden N. of Best.
Miller, John, tailor, h. r. 178 Genesee.
Miller, John, ship carp. h. Perry n. Alabama.
Miller, John, carp. h. Roos alley n. Wm.
Miller, John, on canal, h. 172 Oak.
Miller, John, lab. h. Walnut n. Batavia.
Miller, John, porter, h. 386 Genesee.
Miller, John, cooper, 12 Cypress.
Miller, John, cooper, b. 398 Michigan.
Miller, John, tailor, h. 418 Michigan.
Miller, John, gardener, h. Ferry n. Delaware.
Miller, John, gardener, b. Utica n. Delaware.
Miller, John, tanner, h. Hickory n. Batavia.
Miller, John, moulder. h. Genesee cor. Spruce.
Miller, John F. barber, 9 Com'l, h. Maple st. Goodell.
Miller, John, lab. h. Ellicott bet. Chippewa and Tupper.
Miller, John, lab. h. Spring n. Genesee.
Miller, John, lab. h. Sycamore n. Keene.
Miller, John,*daguerrean gallery, 505 Mich. h. same.
Miller, John, saloon, 133 Genesee, h. same.
Miller, John, lab. h. Best n. Mich.
Miller, John, tailor, h. r. 178 Genesee.
Miller, John, moulder, h. Gen. cor. Spruce.
Miller, John, shoemaker, h. W. Gen. n. Morgan.
Miller, Joseph, lab. h. 46 Delaware place.
Miller, Jos. mason, h. Mortimer n. Hinckley.
Miller, L. saloon, 92 Exchange.
Miller, Lena, milliner, b. Bat. cor. Ash.
Miller, Louis, ship carp. h. Pratt n. Eagle.
Miller, Louis, at J. D. Roberts, h. Mulberry cor. Carlton.
Miller, Ludwig, lab. h. Mulberry n. Carlton.

Miller, Luman A. stove and tin dealer, 354 Main. b. 93 N. Division.
Miller, Margaret, widow. h. Grey n. Genesee.
Miller, Martin. lab. h. Locust n. Va.
Miller, Mary P. nurse, h. 213 N. Division.
Miller, Mathias, shoemaker, h. 56 Bennett.
Miller, Michael, firm Hewson & Co. h. Hickory n. Batavia.
Miller, Michael, carp. h. 382 Genesee.
Miller, Nelson, h. Vt. cor. 7th.
Miller, Nicholas, bricklayer, h. 313 Ellicott.
Miller, Octavia, wid. b. Boston.
Miller, Otto, carp. h. Spring n. Batavia.
Miller, Peter, engineer on lake, h. 37 Carroll.
Miller, Peter, mason, h. 119 Batavia.
Miller, Philip, stone cutter, h. Gen. n. Pratt.
Miller, Philip. lab. h. Mortimer n. Genesee.
Miller, Philip B. porter, 207 Main, h. Genesee n. Spring.
Miller Polhemus J. breakman, b. Boston.
Miller, Richard, ship carp. h. 5 Milnor.
Miller, Richard, printer. Com. Adv. b. 467 Mich.
Miller, Richard, tailor, h. 1 Mark.
Miller, Robt. h. 219 Seneca.
Miller, Rosina, widow, grocery, h. 467 Mich.
Miller, Sebastian, lab. h. Watson n. William.
Miller, Sebastian, with Pratt & Co. h. cor. Mortimer and Hollister.
Miller, Simon, lab h. 30 Spruce.
Miller, Tobias, lab. h. Pratt n. Sycamore.
Miller, Wm. A. 30 Main, b. 400 Franklin.
Miller, Wm. gardener, h. Utica n. Rogers.
Miller. Wm. salesman, 183 Main, h. 203 Ell'c't.
Miller, Wm. F. att'y, office 6 Brown's Building, and firm Lanning & Miller. h. 188 Pearl.
Miller, Wm. H. Seward, breakman, b. Boston.
Miller, Wm. W. clerk. A. T. Co. b. Western.
Millhaupt, Gregor, shoemaker, h. 121 Pine.
Millhiser, Jno. cabinet maker, h. S. Div. n. R. R. crossing.
Millhiser, John. carpenter, 404 S. Division.
Milliken. C. A. grocer and com. merch. 68 Lloyd. b. 420 Main.
MILLINGTON, EDWIN H. gent's furnishing store, 314 Main, h. 100 Clinton.—See adv. p. 80.
Millington, Jos. roller, Buff. I. & Nail Works, h. N. Wash. n. Bird ave.
Millington, Thos. roller, Buff. I. & Nail Works. h. Niagara n. Auburn.
Milring, Henry, grocer, b. 104 Tupper.
Milring, Wm. grocer, 104 Tupper, h. same.
Mills, A. firm A. M. & Son, h. 56 Eagle.
Mills, A. & Son, carriage spring manufactu'rs, 20 and 22 Elm.
Mills, Geo. C. baggage master, L. S. R. R. h. 76 N. Division.
Mills, Henry, turner, h. 7th n. Hudson.
Mills, H. H. at Farmers' and Mechanics' Bank, b. 7th n. Hudson.
Mills, Jas. A. machinist. b. 15 Pearl.
Mills, Jas. H. firm A. M. & Son, h. 23 Union.
Mills, John, Sternberg & Co. elevator, h. 52 William.
Mills, Jno. painter, h. 9th n. Massachusetts.
Mills, Jno. h. 14 6th.
Mills, Josiah A. lawyer, over 268 Main, h. 72 E. Eagle.

Mills, Mary, widow, h. Hickory n. Batavia.
Mills, Robt. firm M. Walsh & Co. h. 50 6th.
Mills, Walsh & Co. Buff. Sectional Dock, Blackwell canal n. Mason & Bidwell's.
Mills, W. I. office 213 Wash. h. 133 Pearl.
Mills, Wm. saloon, cor. Canal and Evans.
Millva, Catharine, widow, h. Illinois n. Ohio.
Milnor, G. A. h. Milnor n. William.
Milnor, Wm. baggage master. h. 135 Elm.
Milsom. Wm. ornamental plasterer, h. Carroll n. Red Jacket.
Milson, George, engineer, h. 17 Church.
Milzer, G. shoemaker, 7 Com'l, h. same.
Mincer, Jno. carpenter, h. Stanton n. Wm.
Minch, Henry, tailor, h. 23 Walnut.
Minch, Jno. carpenter, h. Monroe n. Syc.
Miner. Jas. 17 Exchange.
Miner, Julius F. M. D. h. 15 Ellicott. office same.
Mingen, P. blacksmith, b. 284 Pearl.
Minger, Jno. tanner, with Rumsey & Co.
Mings, Jas. hostler, for W. I. Mills, h. 47 Del.
Mings, Wm. h. Washington n. Virginia.
Mink, Matthias, carpenter, h. 261 Elm.
Minkel. Ditman, shoemaker, 84 Main, b. Washington Hotel.
Minkel. Adam, cabinet maker, 132 Genesee, h. Locust n. Virginia.
Minkle, Adam, painter, h. 75 Cherry.
Minkle, Adam. carp h. Locust n. Cherry.
Minkler, Louisa, embroidery, etc h. 41 N Div.
Minkler, Peter, saloon, La. cor. Exch. h. same.
Minnis, Chs. lab. h. Burwell place.
Minnia, Robt. cartman, b. Walnut n. William.
Minnis, Wm. cartman, h. Walnut n. William.
Minnoton, Thos. caulker, h. Elk opp. Marvin.
Mintis, Fred. cabinet maker, h. 56 Pine.
Minzer, Jno. carpenter, h. Stanton n. Wm.
Mirdes, Jno. lab. h. Cypress n. Michigan.
Mirtell, Mrs. widow, h. across creek.
Mischka, Adelbert, cabinet maker, h. Main cor. Burton alley.
Mischka, Jos. clerk, 209 Main, b. Main cor. Burton alley.
Mischo, Jacob, dyer, with S. Chester, h 249 Elm.
Mischo, Jno. grocer, Batavia cor. Pine, h. same.
Misho, Jno. lab. h. Mulberry n. High.
Mislin, Jno. shoemaker, h. 5 Cypress.
Missert, Jacob, shoemaker, h. 572 Washington.
Mitchell, David. lab. h. cor. Fly and State.
Mitchell, David, machinist. b. 220 Seneca.
Mitchell, Ed. stone cutter, h. Palmer n. Md.
Mitchell, Francis, shoemaker, with G. Hicks, b. same.
Mitchell, Francis, b. Palmer n. Maryland.
Mitchell, Frank, clerk at 163 Main. b. 3 Green.
Mitchell, Geo. brewer, 174 6th, h. same.
Mitchell, Geo. B. constable, h. 11th ab. Md.
Mitchell, G. N. law student, h. 75 11th.
Mitchell, James, fish rod manuf. h. 155 Del.
Mitchell, John D. carpenter, b. 155 Delaware.
Mitchell, Joseph, mason, h. St. Paul n. Main.
Mitchell, Michael, capt. h. Perry n. Hayward.
Mitchell, Nancy, widow, h. 220 Seneca.
Mitchell, Robt. warehouseman, h. Ship canal and Water.
Mitchell, Sam'l, gardener, Bowery n. North.
Mitchell, Thomas, engraver, b. Palmer n. Ind

Mitchell, Thos. joiner, h. 101 6th.
Mitchell, Wm. gardener, h. St. Paul n. Main.
MITCHELL, WM. J. designer and engraver on wood, 136 Main, h. Palmer n. Maryland.
—*See adv. p. 89.*
Mittag, Henry, shoemaker, Hickory n. Cherry.
Mittle, Peter, M. S. S. R. h. Main n. Ferry.
Mittler, Jno. painter, h. Grey n. Genesee.
Mittler, Lawrence, lab. h. Johnson n. Genesee.
Mixer, H. B. firm M. & Smith, b. Mansion.
Mixer, L. W. h. Lancaster village.
Mixer, L. W. & Co. lumber dealers and shippers, Marine Block, Ohio.
Mixer & Smith, lumber merchants, 6 Mart Block. Ohio.
Mixer, S. F. M. D. 74 E. Swan, h. same.
Mochel, Henry, carp. h. Main n. Buff. Plains.
Mochel, Lany, widow, h. Main n. Buff. Plains.
Mock, John, stone cutter, h. Lemon n. High.
Moehl, Hartman, butcher, Clinton n. Madison, h. same.
Moehring, Louis, shoemaker, h. Bat. n Cedar.
Moeller, Edward, music teach. h. 225 Ellicott.
Moendele, Mathias, cooper, h. Locust n. Cherry.
Moerschfelder, Nich. cutler, 397 Main, h. same.
Moerschfelder, Nicholas, Jr. cutler, 397 Main, b. same.
Moesel, Michael, lab. h. Maple n. High.
Moeser, Frank, plasterer, h. Cypress n. Mich.
Moesser, Jacob, peddler, h. Kaene n. Genesee.
Moessinger, Geo. grocer. 120 Genesee, h. same.
Moest, John, shoemaker, 215 Ellicott.
Moest, Mathew, tailor, b. 34 Main.
Moffat, Alex. lab. h. 6th n. Penn.
Moffat, James, brewer, Mohawk cor. Morgan, h. Main n. tollgate.
Moffat, William, with James M. h. 61 Mohawk.
Mohk, John, lab. h. Adams n. William.
Mohne, Henry, lab. h. Walnut n. William.
Mohr, Edw'd, firm M. & Schlag, h. 299 Ellicott.
Mohr, Frederick, shoemaker, h. r. 54 Bennett.
Mohr, Fred. lab. b. Ferry n. Main.
Mohr, Jacob, cooper, h. East n. Tonawanda.
Mohr, Martin, cigar maker, h. Maple n. Good'll.
Mohr & Schlag, clothing store, 382 Main.
Mohr, Wm. organ builder, 297 Ellicott.
Moll, Joseph, teamster, h. Adams n. Peckham.
Molloch, Chas. carp. h. William n. Monroe.
Molloch, Gottl. lab. h. Shumway n. Peckham.
Molloy, Matthew, salesman, h. 20 Illinois.
Molo, Geo. lab. h. Walden n. Ferry.
Molter, Chas. b. Sycamore n. Pratt.
Molter, Jacob, lab. h. Sycamore n. Pratt.
Molter, Jacob, butcher, h. Genesee n. Johnson.
Molter, Lewis, painter, h. Cherry n. Spring.
Monaghan, M. saloon, Fly cor. State, h. same.
Monaghan, Martin, saloon, Fly n. State.
Monforte, Joseph C. glazier, 157 Main, h. Best n. Oak.
Moninger, Peter, saloon, Wash. n. Chippewa.
Monnatin, Wenzel, blacksmith, Bat. n. Monroe, h. Monroe n. Sycamore.
Monneir, Geo. F. lumber dealer, b. 110 Elm.
Monnin, Chas. machinist, 9 Water, h. 18 Oak.
Monnin, Geo. shoemaker, h. 100 Elm.
Monroe, Daniel F. capt. on lake, h. Perry n. Hayward.
Monroe, J. cooper, h. Niagara n. Austin.

Monroe, Melissa, wid. boarding house, 7 6th.
Montague, M. O. clerk at 7 Sen. b. 12 Carroll.
Monteath, Wm. firm Palmer, M. & Co. h. Del. ab. Allen.
Montgomery, H. M. with Birge & Co. h. 108 9th.
Montgomery, James, cutter, h. Bundy's alley n. Sycamore.
Montgomery, John H. capt. on lake, h. 149 N. Division.
Montgomery, Rev. Wm. White, rector St. Luke's church, h. 211 Niagara.
Montillon, Mary, Mrs. h. Elm cor. Tupper.
Montinia, John, lab. h. Miami n. Louisiana.
Moodie, Wm. H. engineer, b. 7th n. Rhode Is.
Moody, Henry, b. 105 Carroll.
Mooken, Charles, lab. h. Folsom n. Carroll.
Mooklen, John, lab. h. Amherst n. Tonawanda.
Mooley, Isadore, farmer, cor. Delaware and Amherst.
Moon, Merrill A. grocer, 11 Seneca, b. Franklin.
Mooney, Alex. lab. h. towpath n. Genesee.
Mooney, Frank, farmer, Delaware ab. Burton.
Mooney, Hugh, cooper, h. Elk opp. Moore.
Mooney, James, firm Paul & M. h. 81 Ellicott.
Mooney, John, lab. h. Marvin n. Elk.
Mooney, John, carp. h. 81 Ellicott.
Mooney, John, lab. h. Ohio n. Chicago.
Mooney, John, saloon, foot Washington.
Mooney, John, blacksmith, 146 Seneca, h. Van Rensselaer n. Exchange.
Mooney, John, lab. h. Louisiana n. Ohio.
Mooney L. engraver, 200 Main, h. 53 Oak.
Mooney, Pat. blacksmith, h. Main n. Louisiana.
Mooney, Peter, saloon, 4 Terrace, h. Chicago cor. Seneca.
Mooney, Robt. grocer, Elk n. Marvin, h. same.
Mooney, Thos. saloon, cor. Seneca and Chicago.
Moora, Michael, flagman, N. Y. & E. R.R. h. Exchange n. Hamburgh.
Moore, A. C. 68 Main, h. 263 Elk.
Moore, Brad. with R. Tifft, milkman, 124 S. Div.
Moore, Chester, book-keeper, h. 150 E. Swan.
Moore, Charles, fisherman, h. ac. Buffalo creek.
Moore, David, Jr. Rev. h. 17 Oak.
Moore, Eli, machinist, b. 137 Seneca.
Moore, E. R. prod. and com. Central Wharf, h. 213 Delaware.
Moore, Geo. A. Hamburgh cheese, 68 Main, h. 145 Elk.
Moore, George H. book-keeper, E. Corning & Co. b. 62 Swan.
Moore, James W. sailor, h. 140 Elk.
Moore, James, lab. h. Perry n. Ohio basin slip.
Moore, Jas. building mover, h. Exch. n. Ala.
Moore, James, sailor, h. Perry n. Chicago.
Moore, Jane, Mrs. h. 136 Ellicott.
Moore, J. O. Mrs. boarding house, 62 E. Swan.
Moore, John, shoemaker, b. Niagara. n. Sloan.
Moore, John O. student, b. 62 E. Swan.
Moore, John H. h. 115 Niagara.
Moore, L. P. cigar manufac. 12 E. Seneca. h. 137 E. Seneca.
Moore, Margaret, milliner, 29 Oak, h. same.
Moore, Mark B. attorney, firm Babcock & M. h. 149 Delaware.
Moore, Phelix, ship sawyer, h. La. n. Ohio.
Moore. Theo. M. book-keeper, Geo. A. Moore, b. 145 Elk.

Moore, U. D. grocer, Morgan n. Mohawk, h. same.

Moore, U. H. clerk, U. D. Moore, h. cor. Morgan and Mohawk.

Moore, Wm. H. com. mer. Central Wharf, h. 213 Delaware.

Moore, Wm. miller, h. Dearborn n. Hamilton.

Moore, Wm. at D. Bell's, b. 18 Palmer.

Moores, W. P. firm M. & White, h. 204 Swan.

Moores & White, boots and shoes, 218 Main.

Moosgrubber, Geo. lab. h. Adams n. Sycamore.

Moot, Martin S. piano maker, 259 Washington, h. 35 Swan.

Moran, Jas. peddler, h. 104 Exchange.

Moran, John, lab. h. Peugeot n. L. S. R. R.

Moran, John. boarding house, Exch. n. Mich.

Moran, John, lab. h. 11th n. R. I.

Moran, Lawrence, turner, h. 5th n. Va.

Moran, Martin, broom maker, b. 40 N. Div.

Moran, Mary, saloon, h. across creek.

Moran, Mrs. h. Staats n. Genesee.

Moran, Pat. warehouseman, 25 Cent. Wharf, h. 225 N. Division.

Morehead, Isaac, moulder, h. 5th ab. Carolina.

Morehouse, F. B. agent, h. 71 Chippewa.

Morehouse, Harry, blacksmith, h. 159 6th.

Morehouse, Wm. at Parr's awl factory, b. 17 6th.

Morey, Chas. P. capt. h. 25 Palmer.

Morey, Henry G. capt. on lake, h. 174 9th.

Morey, J. R. h. Niagara n. Bird avenue.

Morgan, A. G. forwarding and com. merchant, h. 73 S. Division.

Morgan, Amos, builder, 35 and 37 Elm, h. 67 S. Division.

Morgan, Barney, lab. h. Canal n. Albany.

Morgan, B. L. keeper insane dept. Erie Co. poor house.

Morgan, D. E. clerk, Sherman & Barnes, b. 82 N. Division.

Morgan, Frank. blacksmith, h. Main n. Green.

Morgan, Geo. b. Revere.

Morgan, G. P. clerk, h. 30 N. Division.

Morgan, James G. firm Shuttleworth & Co. b. 51 E. Swan.

Morgan, Jas. R. clerk, W. T. Co. h. 39 W. Sen.

Morgan, Jas. W. mariner, h. Milnor n. Wm.

Morgan, L. S. Hanover cor. Prime, h. cor. Franklin and Tupper.

Morgan, Philip, at Brayley & Pitts foundry, h. 150 9th.

Morgan, Rosell, clerk, M. & Root, Erie basin, b. 30 N. Division.

Morgan, Thos. cabinet maker, h. 150 9th.

Morgan, Thos. wood worker, Brayley & Pitts.

Morgan, Wm. iron and nail works, N. Wash. n. Forest avenue.

Morgan, Wm. E. carp. h. Fulton n. Hamburgh.

Morgan, Wm. F. machinist, h. 238 S. Division.

Morgenstein, Daniel, moulder, b. 28 Walnut.

Morgenstein, F. clerk, 180 Main, b. 30 Walnut.

Morgenstein, Jacob, hatter, b. 39 E. Genesee.

Morganstein, Philipina, widow, h. Cherry cor. Michigan.

Morgott, John. lab. h. Fox n. North.

Morhart, Frank. wagon maker, h. Ash n. Syc.

Morlemer, Geo. breakman, N. Y. C. R. R. b. National.

Morley, Chas. lab. h. Ferry n. Jefferson.

Morley, Jas. P. tailor, h. ov. 352 Washington.

Morley, Thos. brick maker, h. Ferry n. Mich.

Morlock, Ignatz, lab. h. 82 Batavia.

Morlock, E. lab. h. 10 Bennett.

Morman, Daniel, lab. h. 37 Cherry.

Moroney. Michael, saloon, 7 Evans, h. same.

Morony, Pat. lab. h. 5th ab. Virginia.

Moriaty, L. farmer, h. Ontario n. city line.

Morrill, Isaac, lab. h. Elm ab. Genesee.

Morris, Andrew, blacksmith, b. Carroll n. La.

Morris, Chas. firm J. S. M. & Son, h. School n. 10th.

Morris, E. J. book-binder, J. M. Johnson, b. Carroll bel. Louisiana.

Morris, John, bolt maker, h. 256 Elm.

Morris, John, teacher, Niagara n. R. I.

Morris, John S. firm J. S. M. & Son, fireworks manufacturer, Niagara n. 10th.

MORRIS, J. S. & SON, fireworks manufact. Niag. bel. water works.—*See adv. p.* 103.

Morris, Wm. towpath n. round house.

Morriss, Ed. clerk, post office, h. 277 Franklin.

Morrisey, Mich. grocer, Chicago n. Mackinaw.

Morrisey. Patrick, lab. h. Perry n. Illinois.

Morrissey. Mich. blacksmith, h. Perry n. Ill.

Morrison, Caroline, widow, h. 5 Wm.

Morrison, Chs. A. clerk, 207 Main, b. 46 Del.

Morrison, Geo. sailor, b. 6 Commercial.

Morrison, John, lab. h. 36 Jackson.

Morrow, And. hackman, No. 8, h. 118 Niag.

Morrow, Hugh, grocer, 129 Chippewa, h. same.

Morrow, Jas. teamster, h. 94 Carroll.

Morse, Alanson, grocery, 27 Central Wharf, b. 44 Pearl.

Morse, C. B. overseer of poor, office Green opp. Beak, h. 160 9th.

Morse, Chas. E. coml. editor Courier. b. 160 9th.

Morse, C. H. salt dealer, 22 Cent. Wharf, h. 42 Niagara.

Morse, D. R. firm M. & Perrine, h. 192 Pearl.

Morse, Geo. clerk, 58 Main, h. Park ab. Allen.

Morse, Harlow, b. cor. Scott and Washington.

Morse, Henry, firm M. & Nelson, h. 72 Niag.

Morse, Lansing, saloon keeper, b. 44 Pearl.

Morse & Nelson, com. merchants, 28 C. Wharf.

MORSE & PERRINE, ship chand. cor. Lloyd and Erie canal.—*See adv. p.* 43.

Morselow, Chas. messenger, b. 60 Del. place.

Morselow, John, lab. h. 60 Delaware place.

Morselow, John Jr. clerk, 5 E. Seneca, b. 68 Delaware place.

Mortin, Jas. fireman, b. Revere House.

Morton. Alfred, teamster, h. cor. Sen. and Ala.

MORTON, FOOTE & CO. forwd. & com. mer 7 C. Wharf and 32 and 36 Lloyd.—*See adv. p.* 39.

Morton, J. A. b. 76 Ellicott.

Morton, J. F. firm M. Foote & Co. h. 4 N. Pearl.

Morton, Pamelia, widow, h. 342 Michigan.

Mory, Elizabeth, widow, h. 5th n. Georgia.

Mosbach, Walburger, h. 128 Elm.

Mosbucher, Jos. h. Sycamore n. Walnut.

Mosburger, Jacob, lab. h. Monroe n. Batavia.

Mose, Abraham, peddler, h. Vine n. Elm.

Moseler, Casper, engineer, h. Wm. h. Cedar.

Moser, Geo. sea grass maker, Dearborn n. Ham.

Moser, Matthias, cabinet maker, h. 194 Oak.

Moses, John, blacksmith, b. 58 Clinton alley.

Moses, Wm. engineer, h. 33 5th n. Georgia.
Mosgeller, John, cabinet maker, h. Adams n. Peckham.
Mosher, Chris. teamster, n. Crooker's tavern.
Moshey, Abraham, tailor, 54 Main, b. same.
Mosier, Ed. engineer, b. 13th n. Rhode Island.
Mosier, Geo. sailor, h. 10 E. Eagle.
Mosier, Jas. liquor store, 100 Bat. h. same.
Mosier, John B. tinsmith, h. 100 Batavia.
Moss, Chas. R. student, b. Main n. Utica.
Moss, Elvira E. widow. h. Main n. Utica.
Moss, Lewis, lab. h. Military road n. Amherst.
Mossack, John, lab. h. Pratt n. Clinton.
Moton, Daniel, whitewasher, 69 Cedar.
Motsch, Louis, carp. h. Chippewa cor. Ellicott.
Motsch, Mary, widow, h. North n. Oak.
Mott, E. M. b. Western.
Mott, Wm. capt. on lake, h. Madison n. Clinton.
Motz, W. A. clerk, Canal, b. same.
Mouerer, Louis. clerk, h. 146 Oak.
Moulder, Jacob, lab. h. 567 Michigan.
Moulton, Jas. b. with John Moulton.
Moulton, John, lab. h. across creek.
MOUNT, FORMAN, livery stable, Terrace n. Evans, b. Bonney's.—See adv. p. 93.
Mountney, Wm. lab. 9 Terrace.
MOVIUS, JULIUS, general ticket agent G. W. R. W. h 7ᵈ Del.—See adv. p. 98.
Moxley, Henry, barber shop, 188 Main, h. cor. William and Union.
Moxx, John, blacksmith, Syc. n. Pratt.
Moyer, Levy. clerk. 56 Main, h. 5th n. Ga.
Moylan, Jas. boiler maker, Exch. n. Mich.
Moynihen, Michael, h. Hudson n. 6th.
Moyr, Wm. lab. 9 Cedar.
Muckler, William, stove mounter, h. Fulton n. Chicago.
Muehlhaupt, Michael, shoemaker, h. 190 Pine.
Mueblinch, Louis, blacksmith, h. Walnut n. Batavia.
Muelenkamp, John C. mason, h. r. 409 Mich.
Muelenkamp, Morris, boiler maker, h. Ash n. Sycamore.
Mueler, Henry, shoemaker, h. Jerry n. Spring.
Mueller, Augustus, musician, h. 88 Cherry.
Mueller, Christ'r. mason, h. Carlton n. Locust.
Mueller, Chs. saloon, 3 Michigan.
Mueller, Conrad, lab. h. Elm n. North.
Mueller, Conrad, musician, h. 100 Cherry.
Mueller, Erhardt, wagon maker, h. Monroe n. Peckham.
Mueller, Fred. lab. h. 321 Elm.
Mueller, Geo. tailor, h. 258 Elm.
Mueller, Henry, lab. h. Batavia n. Monroe.
Mueller, Jacob, carp. h. Jeff. n. Genesee.
Mueller, Jacob, lab. h. Main cor. Burton alley.
Mueller, Jacob, shoemaker, h. Gen. n. Johnson.
Mueller, John, brewer, h. 197 Ellicott.
Mueller, John, lab. h. 215 Elm.
Mueller, John B. civil engineer, h. 511 Wash.
Mueller, John, wagoner, h. 571 Washington.
Mueller, Joseph, cooper, h. 42 E. Genesee.
Mueller, Lenhard, blacksmith, b. 571 Wash.
Mueller, Mary, Mrs. h. 546 Michigan.
Mueller, Michael, firm F. A. George & Co. h. 400 Main.
Mueller, Robt. carp. h. Best n. Oak.
Mueller, Rosa, widow, h. Mich. n. High.

Mueller, Sybilla, widow, h. 213 Elm.
Muench, Anthony, lab. h. Milnor n. Batavia.
Muench, Emil, book-binder, h. Bat. n. Jeff'n.
Muench, Henry, carp. h. Monroe n. Brown.
Muench, Hugo, beer peddler, h. Walnut n. Bat.
Muench, John, lab. h. Hinckley n. Spring.
Muenich, Geo. mason, h. 42 Cherry.
Muer, — clerk, b. 111 Clinton.
Muer, William, with Howard, Whitcomb & Co. b. 67 S. Division.
Muering, Chas. lab. h. 103 Cedar.
Mugler, Chris. engineer, h. Wm. n. Cedar.
Mugler, Philip, grocer, h. 380 Seneca.
MUGRIDGE, GEORGE, steam bakery. Ohio n. Wash. h. Miami n. Ala.—See adv. p. 47.
Mugridge, James, grocer, h. cor. Louisiana and Carroll.
Mugridge, Jas. A. clerk. b. Geo. Mugridge.
Mugridge, Jos. grocer, 92 E. Seneca, h. same.
Muirhead, Simeon, engineer, h. 212 S. Div.
Mulchback, A. grocer and shoemaker, Virginia cor. 6th.
Muldie, Jos. lab. h. Grape n. High.
Muldon, Gerald, grocer, N. Division cor. Cedar, h. same.
Mull, Fred. U. S. A. h. Maple n. Goodell.
Mullarky, Patrick, clerk, B. N. Y. & E. R. R. b. 202 Swan.
Mullen, A. moulder. h. Perry n. Alabama.
Mullen, Alexander, foreman lumber yard, b. Elk n. Louisiana.
Mullen, Geo. ship carp. h. 78 5th.
Mullen, James, sailor, h. Alabama n. Perry.
Mullen, Kearn, lab. b. 67 5th.
Mullen, Keirn, lab. h. 5th n. Georgia.
Mullen, Margaret, b. P. Mullen.
Mullen, Peter, with Niagara Ice Co. h. Mass. n. 12th.
Mullen, Roger, sawyer, h. Elk n. Moore.
Mullen, Wm. conductor, N. Y. C. R. R. h. 88 N. Division.
Mullett, John, milkman, h. Niagara n. Clinton avenue.
Mulligan, Gregory H. clerk, N. K. Hall, b. 13 Park place.
Mulligan, Jas. S. printer, b. 13 Park place.
Mulligan, Sallie C. widow, h. 13 Park place.
Mullihan, Edmund, lab. h. La. n. Tenn.
Mullihan, Edward, lab. h. La. bel. Mackinaw.
Mullineer, John, city line n. Ontario.
Mumm, Philip, gardener, h. Best n. Mich.
Munce, Jas. clerk. 52 Main, h. 40 Jackson.
Munce, John, b. 51 Church.
Munderback, J. S. forwarder, h. 130 6th.
Munger, E. D. clerk, 318 Main, b. Pearl.
Munger, J. M. clerk, Sherman & Barnes, b. cor. Court and Pearl.
Munkel, Ernst, tailor, h. Batavia cor. Sherman.
Munroe, Oliver, marketman, b. 104 Exchange.
Munroe, Wm. C. whip manufac. 359 Main, h. 142 9th.
Munroe, Wm. C. Jr. engineer, b. 142 9th.
Muns, Charles, 2 Hanover, h. 11 Oak.
Munsch, Geo. bakery, Mich. n. Syc. h. same.
Munschauer, Elizabeth, widow of John, h. 23 Sycamore.
Munshauer, Geo. J. clerk, 163 Main. b. 23 Syc.
Munshauer, Geo. grocer, Elm cor. Sycamore.

Munschauer, John P. h. 37 Sycamore.
Munshauer, Mary, Miss, h. 23 Sycamore.
Munson, Luther, ag't G. Palmer, b. Delavan ave. E. Main.
Munson, M. T. Mrs. boarding house, 60 S. Div.
Murdoch, David, Bennett's elevator, h. 64 Michigan.
Murnam, John, lab. h. 40 N. Division.
Murdoch, Robt. capt. b. G. W. Baskett.
Murphy, Ed. E. blacksmith, El'cott n. Moh'wk.
Murphy, Ellen, widow, h. Ohio n. Chicago.
Murphy, James, lab. h. Carroll n. Hamburgh.
Murphy, James, lab. h. Jackson cor. Genesee.
Murphy, John, blacksmith, Vine n. Elm.
Murphy, John W. att'y. 174 Main, h. 350 Wash.
Murphy, Jos. ship carp. h. Mack. n. Hamburgh.
Murphy, Jno lab. h. Genesee cor. Jackson.
Murphy, John, milkman, h. 251 Seneca.
Murphy, John D. h. 58 5th.
Murphy, Julia, widow, h. towpath, bel. Gen.
Murphy, Lawrence, carpenter, h. 330 N. Div.
Murphy, Ellen, widow. h. 4th n. Carolina.
Murphy, Pat. lab. h. Exch. n. Hamburgh.
Murphy, Thos. butcher, h. Perry n. Mississippi.
Murphy, T. J. grocer, cor. Franklin and Tupper, h. 272 Franklin.
Murphy, Wm. flagman, N. Y. C. R. R. h. Otto n. Alabama.
Murphy, Wm. saloon, Terrace n. Henry.
Murphy, Michael, mason, h. Clint'n cor. Waln't.
Murphy, Pat. lab. h. Spring n. Clinton.
Murpy, Jno. h. Terrace n. Mechanic.
Murphy, Jas. * shoemaker, 88 E. Seneca, h. same.
Murphy, Wm. L. confectioner, h. 2 Center.
Murray & Bro. importer wines and liquors, 7 Terrace.
Murray, Cornelius, ship carpenter, h. Beak.
Murray, Cumming & Grant, dry goods dealers, 316 Main.
Munz, Jacob, cooper, h. Dearborn n. Amherst.
Munz, John G. lab. h. Pratt n. Sycamore.
Munzert, Nich. grocer, h. Batavia n. Monroe.
Murraky, P. telegraph operator, b. 202 Swan.
Murray, Anna. Mrs. h. Chippewa n. Wash.
Murray, David S. printer, 196 Wash. h. over 41 Seneca.
Murray, H. firm M. & Bro. b. Carolina cor. 9th.
Murray, Henry, drayman, b. 199 Exchange.
Murray, Henry, agent, V. R. Gregory & Co. b. 224 N. Division.
Murray, Honora, widow, h. Jackson n. Gen.
Murray, Hugh, firm M. & Grant, h. 97 Clinton.
Murray, James, capt. on lake, h. Hayward n. Perry.
Murray, James, ship carpenter, h. 14 6th.
Murray, John A. agent, h. 327 Michigan.
Murray, John C. clerk, b. Courter.
Murray, Michael, lab. h. 160 6th.
Murray, Nathaniel, shoemaker, h. Cypress n. Pine.
Murray, Pat. joiner, h. 11th n. Carolina.
Murray, Robt. clerk at 104 Exch. b. same.
Murray, Sam'l, shoemaker, h. Cypress n. Pine.
Murray, T. firm M. & Bro. b. Carolina cor. 9th.
Murray, Wm. firm M. Cumming & Grant, b. American.
Muschal, Anton, brewer, A. Ziegele.
15

Muschel, Gustavus, shoemaker, b. 173 Batavia.
Musel, Jacob, carp. h. Batavia n. Shumway.
Muth, Adam, lab. h. Mortimer n. William.
Mutimer, J. saloon, 53 Lloyd, h. same.
Mutter, Fuetell, turner, h. 123 Walnut.
Mutter, Meinsock, lab. cor. Blossom & Amherst.
Mutz, Wm. lab. h. alley n. Hamilton.
Muzzy, Asa, machinist, 156 9th.
Muzzy, Chas. O. machinist, h. Perry n. Ala.
Muzzy, John, machinist, h. 158 9th.
Myer, F. R., R. R. and steamboat agent, 65 Exchange, h. 5th ab. Pennsylvania.
Myer, Jacob, machinist, b. Pratt n. Batavia.
Myer, John, cabinet maker, 241 Main, h. Hickory n. Batavia.
Myer, John, lab. h. Walnut bel. Sycamore.
Myer, Louis, cl'k, A. S. Anderson, h. Ga. n. 6th.
Myers, Andrew, b. Niagara n. Virginia.
Myers, E. H. sand dealer, b. cor. Erie and Peacock.
Myers, Francis H. saloon, cor. Peacock and Erie, h. same.
Myers, Fred. A. W. carpenter, h. 94 Folsom.
Myers, J. locksmith, h. 69 Hickory.
Myers, Joel W. carpenter, h. 89 9th.
Myers, John, locksmith, h. Chicago n. Perry.
Myers, John H. sup't Evans' elevator, h. Cherry bel. Spring.
Myers, Thomas, lab. h. Perry cor. Hamburgh.
Myers, Victor, sailor, b. Evans cor. Peacock.
Myers, Wm. H. glass stainer, over 79 Main, b. 215 Niagara n. Virginia.
Myers, William, lab. h. Gen. n. gas works.
Myre, J. wood worker, Brayley & Pitts.

N.

Nabb, Jacob, cooper, h. Hickory n. Eagle.
Nabholz, Jacob, coppersmith, b. Wm. n. Pine.
Nachtrieb, Chs. miller, h. 581 Washington.
Nachtrieb, Geo. teamster, h. Main bel. Allen.
Naegel, Michael, cooper, h. 11th n. Virginia.
Nagel, Caroline, midwife. h. 77 Hickory.
Nagel, Chas. F. clerk, 220 Main, b. 11th n. Va.
Nagel, Christopher, lab. h Stanton n. Peckham.
Nagel, Constantine, carp. h. Sycam'e n. Hick'y.
Nagel, Francis, cooper, Herman n. Best, h. same.
Nagel, Frank, clerk, Hamlin & Mendsen, b. 11th n Virginia.
Nagel, F. Fred. lab. h. 77 Hickory.
Nagel, F. Mrs. h. Davis n. Genesee.
Nagel, Geo. lab. h. Milnor n. Batavia.
Nagel, John C. with Hamlin & Mendsen, b. 11th n. Virginia.
Nagel, Lorenz, boiler maker, h. Sycamore n. Hickory.
Nagel, Lorenz, grocer, Cherry n. Lemon, h same.
Nagel, Louis, messenger. 205 Main, b. 11th n. Virginia.
Nagel, Louis, moulder, h. Sycamore n. Pratt.
Nagel, Mary, widow, h. 40 Hickory.
Nagel, Wm. boiler maker, h. 37 Hickory.
Nagle, Thomas, sailor, h. Illinois n. Ohio.
Nairn, Wm. cl'k with Howard, Whitcomb & Co. h. 103 Ellicott.
Nalbach, Peter, lab. h. Jefferson n. Sycamore.
Nalbach, Sebastian, lab. N. Y. & E. R. R. h. Jefferson n. Batavia.

Napp, Jacob, lab. b. 9 State.
Nardin, E. Miss, select boarding school, 27 and 29 S. Division.
Nash, E. S. printer, b. 25 Pearl.
Nash, George, carp. h. 11th n. R. L.
Nash, George, lab. b. 34 Scott.
Nash, Jas. grocer, cor. Genesee and Terrace.
Nash, Jas. ship carpenter, h. 28 Exchange.
Nash, Jas. engineer, h. cor. Gen. and Terrace.
Nash, Samuel W. firm H. Wing & Co. leather dealers, h. 307 E. Seneca.
Nash, Thos. Mrs. boarding, 20 Exchange.
Nesson, James, saloon, 101 Hospital, h. same.
Nassoy, Dominic, on R. R. h. 235 Oak.
Nastor, Jno. mason, h. Exchange cor. Smith.
Nastor, John, mason, b. cor. Exch. and Smith.
Nastor, Peter, boatman, b. cor. Exchange and Smith.
Nauert, Henry, firm N. & Engel, h. 143 Bat.
Nauert, Jacob, baker, h. 102 Batavia.
Nauert & Engel, book-binders, 178 Wash.
Naun, Cornel, basket maker, h. 220 Ellicott.
Naurt, Julius,* tin shop, Michigan cor. N. Division, h. same.
Naughton, James, sailor, h. Ala. n. Mackinaw.
Naughton, John, blacksmith, b. Ohio n. River.
Nauman, Peter, lab. h. Batavia n. Spring.
Nauwich, J. lab. h. Pratt n. Genesee.
Neabainrill, J. at gas works, h. Canal alley.
Neal, Jno. wood peddler, h. 35 Elm.
Near, J. A. cabinet maker, h. 5th n Pa.
Neave, John, farmer, Seneca n Smith.
Nebe, Jno. at gas works, h. Canal alley.
Neber, Valentine, shoemaker, 16 10th, h. same.
Nebergab, Jacob, gas works, h. Locust n.Cher'y.
Nebrich, Chas. P. h. Milnor n. Batavia.
Nebrich, Conrad, finisher, b. Spring n. Gen.
Nebrich, Henry, moulder, b. Spring n. Gen.
Nebrich, Peter, moulder, b. Spring bet. Genesee and Sycamore.
Nebrich, Wm. moulder, b. Spring n. Genesee.
Neeb, H. wood worker, Brayley & Pitts.
Neeb, Henry, grocer, Mich. n. High, h. same.
Neeb, P. wood worker, Brayley & Pitts.
Neeb, Peter, carpenter, h. Wm. n. Cedar.
Needam. Jno. mason, h. Ohio n. Louisiana.
Needham, George F. agricultural house, 247 Main, h. Walnut n. Clinton.
Needham, Joseph P. seeds and agricultural implements, 293 Main, h. 358 Washington.
Neele, Samuel W. with J. W. Mack, h. Fulton n. Hamburgh.
Neff, A. fish dealer, Lloyd n. Canal, h. cor. Lloyd and Canal.
Neff, Jacob, farmer, h. Delavan ave. n. Walden.
Neff, Louis, policeman, h. 16 Ash n. Sycamore.
Neff, Nicholas, lab. h. Elm n. Burton alley.
Neff, Simon, boot and shoe maker, h. 41 7th.
Nefel, Chs. musician, h. Goodell n. Elm.
Nefzer, Fred. brewery, Goodell cor. Goodell alley.
Negus, Geo. E. clerk, b. 94 Eagle.
Negus, James, clerk, b. 94 Eagle.
Negus, Jno. G. with Merch. Dispatch, h. 94 Eagle.
Nehaus, Christine, widow, washer, h. Adams n. Sycamore.
Nehaus, Jno. cooper, h. Thomp. n. Hamilton.

Neher, Jno. porter, American Hotel, h. Pine n. Cypress.
Neibeck, Jno. lab. h. Delavan ave. n. Walden.
Neiderhoff, Jno. warehouseman, 22 Central Wharf, h. 41 Ash.
Neidhardt, Lewis, bl'ksmith, b. Niag. n. Parish.
Neidhardt, Louis, turner, 108 Cedar.
Neill, Nicholas O. blacksmith, Main cor. Chippewa, h. same.
Neilou, Dennis, lab. b. 6 Michigan.
Neilson, Wm. trunk maker, 244 Main, h. 144 Seneca.
Neiner, Geo. joiner, h. Monroe n. Sycamore.
Neipbusch, Peter, carp. h. Spring n. Genesee.
Neiseus, Michael, lab. h. Pratt n. Genesee.
Nellany, Jno. with Jewett & Root. b. 18 6th.
Nellany, Michael, b. 18 6th.
Nellany, Owen, h. 18 6th.
Nellis, L., U. S. A. b. Western.
Nelson, A. firm H. Morse & Co. 28 Ct. Wharf, h. Elk n. Hayward.
Nelson, Chas. firm Davenport & N. b. 263 N. Division.
Nelson, E. paper.warehouse, cor. Washington and Exchange, h. 177 Washington.
Nelson, Hallett M. machinist, b. 61 Court.
Nelson, Wm. carp. h. Perry cor. Hayward.
Nemeschy, Jno. mason, h. 553 Michigan.
Nen, Conrad, h. White's Corners plank road bel. iron bridge.
Nennin, Wm. tanner, h. Wm. n. Hickory.
Nesbet, Alex. engineer, h. 58 Oak.
Nesbitt, Samuel,* blacksmith, Ohio n. Michigan, h. 32 5th.
Nesen, Chas. clerk, 318 Main, h. Va. n. Niag.
Neswalt, Vincent, blacksmith, 163 Elm.
Neswitch, Brindel, lab. h. Watson n. Peckham.
Netcher, Christian, cooper, h. Gen. n. Kaene.
Netcher, Geo. liquor dealer, Ellicott ab. Chippewa, h. same.
Neu, Geo.* cigar maker, Bat. cor. Ash. h. same.
Neu, Leon, glazier, h. Hickory n. William.
Neu, Nicholas, moulder, Sycamore n. Hickory.
Neubeck, Fred. painter, h. Lutheran n. Wm.
Neuber, Catharine, widow, h. Adams n. Gen.
Neuberger, Jos. carp. h. Lutheran cor. Wm.
Neuert, Wm. mason, h. Morton n. William.
Neukirchen, Jno. clerk, with L. & I. J. White, Ohio cor. Ind. h. 11 Milnor.
Neukirchen, Jos. 271 Main, h. 4 Boston alley.
Neukircher, Jos. engineer, h. Boston alley ab. Tupper,
Neuland, Christian, carp. h. 140 Oak.
Neuman, Jno. shoemaker, h. Maple n. Cherry.
Neunder, Clemens, teamster, h. Goodell cor. Boston alley.
Neunder, Fred. shoemaker, h. Mulberry n. Va.
Neuner, Geo. carp. h. Adams n. Sycamore.
Neunder, Henry, teamster, h. Goodell cor. Boston alley.
Neupert, Anthony, with H. Thompson & Co. h. Pine n. Batavia.
Neupert, Jno. lab. h. Clinton n. Raze.
Neusel, Chs. printer, h. Camp n. Sycamore.
Neuss, C. E. finisher, h. Pratt, n. Sycamore.
Nevill, Daniel, sailor, h. flats n. Louisiana.
Nevill, William, lab. h. across creek.
Newbigging, Thos L. b. with J. A. Chase.

Newbould, F. W. hardware, 23 Main, b. Amer.
Newbrook, Geo. 54 Main, h. 148 6th.
Newcomb, Patrick, heater, Buff. Iron and Nail Works, h. Niagara n. Bird avenue.
Newell, Bridget, wid. boarding h. 189 Exch.
Newell, Augustus, law student, 164 Main, b. 201 Terrace.
Newell, B. F. ship carp. h. 234 S. Divison.
Newell, H. G. firm V. C. N. & Bro. h. 18 7th.
Newell, Lorenzo, cooper. b. National Hotel.
Newell, Robt. telegraph operator, h. 115 6th.
Newell, V. C. firm V. C. N. & Bro. h. 21 10th.
Newell, V. C. & Bro. pork and beef inspectors, Dayton n. Main.
Newheiser, Geo. carp. b. 546 Michigan.
Newhouse, H. miller, h. Amherst n. Thompson.
Newkirk, John S. firm Provoost & N. h. 91 W. Huron.
Newland, M. A. Mrs. h. Virginia cor. 11th.
Newman & Bros. Acron water lime works, cor. Ship canal and Water.
Newman, Christopher, shoemaker, 6 Water.
Newman, Christoper, lab. Bonney's Hotel.
Newman, Emanuel, clothing, Ohio n. Columbia.
Newman, Eugene, sailor, h. Perry n. La.
Newman. Fred. saw-filer, Mowhawk cor. Main, h. 39 Sycamore.
Newman, George E. dealer in crockery, 162 Main, h. Puffer E. of Main.
Newman, Gilbert, ship carp. h. Hickory n. Gen.
Newman, G. G. electrotyper, h. 343 Seneca.
Newman. George H. salesman, 410 Main, b. Maple n. Goodell.
Newman, George L. firm N. & Scovill h. 8 Delaware.
Newman, Jno. proprietor Phœnix Iron Works, h. 55 Delaware.
Newman, John, carp. h. Illinois n. Perry.
Newman, Lonisa, widow. h. Cypress n. Mich.
Newman, Mrs. widow, William, h. Clinton n. Hickory.
Newman. Peter, cleaner. Spring cor. Bat.
Newman, Peter, blacksmith. h. 116 Cedar.
NEWMAN & SCOVILL, ship chandlers, cor. Lloyd and Prime.—See adv. p. 43.
Newman, Thomas, h. 314 Michigan.
Newman. W. H. H. dealer in rubber and leather belting, &c. 46 Main, h. 51 Delaware.
Newman, Wm. H. bar-keeper, h. 76 Clinton.
Newman, W. O. L. with Sherman & Barnes, b. 408 Main.
Newman, W. W. teacher, h. 34 Goodell.
NEWTON, ISAAC S. lumber dealer, h. Georgia n. 7th.—See adv. p. 86.
Newton, Robert, boat yard, Green, h. 113 9th.
Newton, Robt. h. 141 Oak.
Newton. Robt. G. saloon, 12 Niag. h. same.
New York State Arsenal, Batavia bet. Potter and Milnor.
Ney, E. with Oebrich. 295 Main, b. 181 Seneca.
Niagara Ice Co. office 190½ Main.
Niagara Mills, S. W. Howell, foot of Amherst.
Niagara Pail Co. on Scajaquada creek n. Tonawanda, Francis Wood agent, h. 82 Huron.
NIAGARA STEAM FORGE.—See adv. p. 60.
NIAGARA WHITE LEAD COMPANY, manufactory cor. Delaware and Virginia, office 33 Lloyd.—See adv. p. 103.

Nials, Hugh B. clerk, h. 66 Oak.
Nials, J. C. printer, b. 66 Oak.
Nibecker. John P. firm N. Pendleton, h. 292 Franklin.
Nibecker & Pendleton, carriage manufacturers, Washington above Genesee.
Nice, Chas. agent Buffalo machine works, h. Pratt n. Sycamore.
Nichell. Henry, M. D. h. 58 Sycamore.
Nichol, Mial, clerk, 275 Main, b. 255 Wash.
Nicholas, Fred. lab. h. Riley n. Jefferson.
Nicholdson, D. G. clerk, b. 32 W. Seneca.
Nicholis, C. C. book-keeper, with Hadley & Husted, b. 29 Swan.
Nicholls. C. P. engineer, L. S. R. R. b. Courter.
Nichols, Asher P. attorney, 3 Hollister Block, h. 3 Johnson place.
Nichols, Maze, gardener, h. Utica bel. Del.
Nicholson, D. H. book-keeper, h. 183 N. Div.
Nicholson, John, cracker peddler, h. Eagle n. Spring.
Nicken, Hubuert, shoemaker, h. 153 Batavia.
Nickerson, A. capt. h. 19 Palmer.
Nickerson, Jas. E. painter, b. 120 Exch.
Nickerson, Vincent, capt. h. 10th n. Maryland.
Nicklas, Sebastian, lab. b. Elm n. Best.
Nickles, Reinhard, clothing, 94 E. Gen. h. same.
Nicklin, Fred. pattern maker, h. 3 Scott.
Nicklin, James, wagon maker, 221 Pearl.
Nicklis, Jacob, with Altman & Co. b. 27 Main.
Nicklis, Wm.* tailor, 27 Main, h. same.
Nickolus, George, lab. h. Adams n. Sycamore.
Niederbild, Charles, painter, h. Spring n. Syc.
Niederbrum, Nicholas, tailor, h. Pine n. Bat.
Niederhofer, John, lab. h. 41 Ash.
Niederlander, John, firm Chretien, N. & Co. h. 130 Ellicott bet. Mohawk and Huron.
Niedhof, Chs. fisherman, h. East n. Terrace.
Niedman. Ernst, carp. h. Mulberry n. Carlton.
Niehoff, Henry, tailor, h. Mortimer n. Gen.
Nieland, F. widow, meat market, junction Seneca and Swan.
Nieman, Fred. lab. h. Ketchum n. High.
Nieman, John, lab. h. Ketchum alley n. Carlton.
Nienhaus, Henry, distiller, h. 124 Walnut.
Nienhaus, John, engineer, b. 58 Bennett.
Nierbauer, M. milk peddler, h. Adams n. Bat.
Nierschel. Anthony, lab. h. Walnut n. Bat.
Nies, Fred. carp. h. Mulberry n. Goodell.
Niese, Carolina, dressmaker. h. 204 E. Eagle.
Niesence, Michael,* nailer, Gen. cor. Spruce, h. Cherry n. Spring.
Nieser, John, shoemaker. h. 245 Elm.
Niess, Geo. clerk, post office, b. 367 Main.
Nil, Christopher, lab. h. Stanton n. William.
Niles, Barton C. engineer, h. Fulton n Hamburgh.
Niles & Brewster, insurance agents, 5 C. Wharf and 10 Main.
Niles, H. & Co. forwarding merchants, Marine Block and foot Washington.
Niles, Hiram, firm N. & Brewster, h. Delaware cor. Allen.
Niles, Mahala, widow, h. 4 Ellicott.
Niles, S. H. ship carp. h. 3 Mechanic.
NIMBS, A B. artist and photographist, 303 Main, h. Washington n. Carlton.—See adv. p. 78.

Nims, Ozias L. firm Cutter & N. h. Georgia n. Niagara.
Niquet, Henry C. wagon maker, h. 100 6th.
Nisbet, Alex. engineer, h. 58 Oak.
Nisle, David, lab. h. Sycamore n. Ash.
Nispel, John C. saloon, h. River.
Nissel, Mrs. widow, h. Arkansas n. Adams.
Nitzchke, Henry, carpet weaver, h. 142 Elm.
Nitzchke, J. G. carpet weaver, h. 146 Elm.
Noack, Augustus, tailor, h. 75 Cherry.
Noah, R. Mrs. widow, h. 6 Carroll.
Noal, Henry, lab. h. Ash n. Batavia.
Noble, Chas. B. 140 Franklin.
NOBLE, CHAS. E. agent M. C. R. R. 15 Exchange, h. 26 E. Eagle.—See adv. p. 99.
Noble, Edward, brakeman, N. Y. C. R. R. b. National Hotel.
Noble, Mary, boarding house, r. 74 Chippewa.
Noble, R. P. firm Van Buren & N. b. Bonney's Hotel.
Noble, Usual S. printer, h. cor. 6th & Caroline.
Noble, Sam'l, canal inspector, h. Oak cor. High.
Noblet, John B. joiner, h. Miami n. La.
Noelle, Henry, butcher, h. 239 Elm.
Noeller, Fred. cutter, 142 Main, h. 128 Elm.
Noeller, Geo. grocer, Gen. n. Sherman, h. same.
Nois, John, mail agent, b. Courter House.
Nolan, Christopher, sailor, h. Ohio n. Miss.
Nolan, Edward, lab. h. Mill n. Red Jacket.
Nolan, James, teamster, b. 231 Carroll.
Nolan, John, trunk maker, h. Carroll n. Ala.
Nolan, Michael, boarding house, 111 Carroll.
Noland, Bartholomew, book-keeper, h. 14th n. Vermont.
Noll, L. shoemaker, h. 164 Genesee.
Nolt, Fred. tailor, h. Mulberry n. Carlton.
Noon, Martin, lab. h. Exchange n. Griffin.
Noon, Michael, book-keeper, h. 10 W. Swan.
Noonan, Jas. cartman, h. cor. Fulton and Ala.
Noonan, Wm. grocer, Clinton n. R. R. h. same.
Norcott, Moses, lab. h. Niagara n. Clinton ave.
Normington, Mark, stone cutter, b. 233 Carroll.
Norman, Peter, lab. h. Cedar n. Batavia.
Norris, A. shipping business, h. 300 Swan.
Norris, John, att'y, over 146 Main, b. Bonney's Hotel.
Norris, Thomas, lab. h. Vincennes n. South.
North Buffalo Mills, Bauer & Schoelkopf, lower Black Rock.
North, Peter, musician, h. 9 State.
Northrop, W. H. clerk, 265 Main, b. 31 S. Div.
Northrup, A. Mrs. widow, h. cor. Court & Pearl.
Northrup, Wilbur, painter, h. 130 Carroll.
Norten, F. E. engineer, h. Terrace n. Church.
Norton, Chas. D. attorney, 3 Weed's block, h. Huron cor. Franklin.
Norton, Harry, machinist, h. Perry n. Ala.
Norton, Jas. N. lab. h. 2 Scott.
Norton, J. G. Mrs. widow, h. 139 Delaware.
Norton, Mary, milliner, 279 Main, b. cor. Chippewa and Pearl.
Norton, Pat. lab. h. Perry n. Louisiana.
Norton, Thomas, sailor. h. Vandalia n. Mack'w.
Norton, W. H. h. 5th n. Carolina.
Norton, Z. J. keeper in penitentiary, h. cor. 6th and Pennsylvania.
Noss, John, lab. h. 7 Cherry.
Nothnagel, Peter, gardener, Michigan n. Best.

Nothnagel, Philip, undertaker, h. Ash cor. Bat.
Nothnagel & Pfeifer, coffin rooms, Ash n. Bat.
Notley, Wm. sailor, h. cor. Chicago and Fulton.
Notter, George, firm Van Slyke, N. & Co. h. 124 6th.
Notter, Thomas, ship carpenter, b. 7 6th.
Noughs, Jno. lab. h. Amherst n. Thompson.
Nowak, Jno. shoemaker, h. Monroe n. Brown.
Noxon, Eliza, boarding house, 44 Pearl.
Noxon, Mary E. b. 107 9th.
NOYE, J. T. mill manufac'g and furnishing, Wash. cor. Scott, h. 182 Franklin.—See adv. outside cover.
Noye, Richard, h. 527 Washington.
Noye, R. K. with J. T. Noye, b. 188 Franklin.
Noyes, G. M. att'y, 190½ Main, b. head of Franklin.
Noyes, J. S. lumber, and forwarder, 5 River, b. cor. Huron and Main.
Nueken, Hubert, shoemaker, 12 Commercial, h. Batavia n. Bennett.
Nugent, Jerry, lab. h. Ohio n. toll bridge.
Nugent, Richard, lab. h. Kentucky n. South.
Nunolt, Philip, carpenter, h. 81 Sycamore.
Nye, Monroe, tinsmith, Niagara n. Amherst.

O.

Oakley, Jas. S. with T. D. Dole, h. 88 Franklin.
Oakley, J. W. with T. D. Dole, b. City Hotel.
Oakley, Sarah, Mrs. h. 6 Carroll.
Oaks, Samuel D. clerk, b. Saunders' Exch.
Oatman, George E. printer, Com. Adv. b. 60 W. Mohawk.
Oatman, Walter G. at 161 Main, h. 60 W. Mohawk.
Oberderfer, Chas. butcher, b. Gen. cor. Elm.
Oberduer, Marg't, wid. h. Monroe n. Peckham.
Oberholzer, J. Mrs. b. Carlton n. Oak.
Oberist, Caroline, widow, h. Davis n. Genesee.
Oberist, Chas. clerk, Main cor. Huron, b. J. J. Sidway.
Oberist, Henry, clerk, 336 Main, h. 26 Folsom.
Oberst, John P. carpenter, h. Mariner ab. Va.
Oberist, Samuel, clerk, 222 Main, h. 26 Folsom.
Oberist, Samuel J. tinsmith, b. 26 Folsom.
Oberkirker, Christian, with Bush & Howard, h. Mortimer n. Genesee.
Obermier, Ernst, lab. b. Walnut n. Batavia.
Obermier, Frank. shoemaker, h. Adams n. Sycamore.
Obermier, Joseph, lab. h. Pine n. Cypress.
Obermier, Victus. lab. h. Walnut n. Batavia.
Obertrifter, Eberhard, gas fitter, h. Genesee n. Herman.
Obertrifter, Wm. peddler. h. Gen. n. Herman.
Obre, Jacob, farmer, h. Del. ave. n. Williamsville road.
O'Brian, Daniel, coppersmith, h. 185 Exch.
O'Brian, D. lab. h. ac. creek.
O'Brian, Ed. b. 12 Perry.
O'Brian Henry, clerk, with T. C. Riley, b. 9 Niagara.
O'Brian, Mary, widow, h. Commerc'l n. canal.
O'Brian, Michael, boiler maker, h. La. n. South.
O'Brian, James, h. 213 Swan.
O'Brian, John, h. 209 E. Swan.
O'Brian, Thos. sailor, h. Elk n. Chicago.

O'Brian, Thomas. lab. h. 9 Mississippi.
O'Brian, Tim. saloon. Fly cor. Le Couteulx, h. same.
O'Brian, Timothy, lab. h. ac. creek.
O'Brian, T. J. lab. h. 12 Perry.
O'Brian, Wm. grocer, ac. creek.
O'Brien, Catherine. Mrs. grocery, 56 5th.
O'Brien, Charles. lab. Illinois n. Scott.
O'Brien, Dennis, lab. h. South n. Louisiana.
O'Brien, James, dry goods, h. 185 Exchange.
O'Brien, John H. h. cor. 5th and Carolina.
O'Brien. Kate, milliner. 142 Eagle.
O'Brien. Margaret. milliner, 142 Eagle.
O'Brien, Mart. Ohio n. Columbia.
O'Brien, Matthew, freight master, L. S. R. R. h. 207 Swan.
O'Brien. Michael, fireman, B. & S. L'. R. R. b. 356 Seneca.
O'Brien, Michael, clerk. 21 Main, h. 24 Ill.
O'Brien, Pat. hostler, Elk n. Michigan.
O'Brien, Pat. engineer. h. Perry n. Alabama.
O'Brien, Thos. tailor, h. Van Rensselaer n. Porter.
O'Brien, Thos. saloon, 126 Exch. h. same.
O'Brine, Dennis, b. Revere.
O'Brown, A. W. capt. b. Revere.
Ochsenkehl, Wm. lab. b. 150 Genesee.
O'Connell, Bridget, widow, grocery, Elk bel. Hayward.
O'Connell, C. lab. h. Louisiana n. Ohio.
O'Connell, Daniel, lab. h. 5th n. Virginia.
O'Connell, Daniel, clerk on dock, b. cor. Jackson and Genesee.
O'Connell, John, watchman, gas works, cor. Jackson and Genesee.
O'Connell, Jno. Jr. at gas works, h. 40 Jackson.
O'Connely, Wm. grocery, Niagara n. Farmer.
O'Conner, B. shoemaker, 64 Court.
O'Conner, Chs. sailor, h. 10 Mississippi.
O'Conner, — mariner. h. Jeff. n. N. Division.
O'Conner. J. lab. h. 32 N. Division.
O'Conner, John, truckman, h. 15 Illinois.
O'Conner, Margaret, wid. saloon, ac. creek.
O'Conner, Patrick, lab. b. 5th n. Virginia.
O'Connor, Catharine, h. 235 Ellicott.
O'Connor, Wm. tailor. h. Clinton n. Cedar.
O'Connor, Wm. plumber, b. 32 N. Division.
O'Day, James, b. 24 Illinois.
O'Day, Patrick, saloon, Dock n. Evans.
O'Dee, Mary, wid. h. ac. creek.
O'Donnall, Timothy, carp. h. Perry n. Ala.
O'Donnell, James, h. Ohio n. Indiana.
O'Donnell, John, carp. b. Perry n. Ala.
O'Dwyer, Ellen, Mrs. 18 10th.
O'Dwyer, Mary, Mrs. widow, h. 78 6th.
O'Dwyer, Michael. 3 Lock, h. 18 10th.
O'Dwyer, Thos. b. 78 6th.
Oelber, John P. shoemaker, h. Fox n Gen.
Oelhiemer, John, boiler maker, h. 525 Mich.
Oelklaus, Clemens R. R. h. 324 Ellicott.
Oelrich. Fred. jeweler, 295 Main, h. 181 Sen.
Oelsciger, Jacob, grocer, River n. Erie, h. same.
Oertel, Martin, paver. h. Ketchum al. n. High.
Oeser, Chas. locksmith. h. Walnut n. Wm.
Oessew, Fred. cigar maker, h. Clinton cor. Elm.
Oesterle. Lorenz, h. Best n. Oak.
Oestreicher, Franz, lab. h. Maple n. Carlton.

Oestreiker, John, lab. h. Cherry n. Maple.
Oettinger, Joseph, lab. h. Mulberry n. Va.
Offenbecher. Valentine. tanner, h. 6 Bennett.
Ofner, Peter, mason. h. Cypress n. Michigan.
Ofner, Peter, mason, h. 120 Sycamore.
Ogden, Fred. miller, h. East cor. Hamilton.
O'Grady, Edmund, saloon, 5 Peacock, h. same.
O'Grady, James, lab. h. ac. creek.
O'Grady, James, lab. h. Elk opp. Moore.
O'Grady, James, saloon, Evans, h. same.
O'Grady, Thomas, grocer, cor. Exch. and Heacock, h. same.
O'Grady, Thomas, shoemaker, h. Mary bet. Indiana and Illinois.
O'Hara, James, painter, b. National Hotel.
O'Hara, John, grocer, N. Div. cor. Elm, h. r. 37 N. Division.
O'Hara, Thomas, lab. h. Abbott road bel. R.R.
O'Hare, John, beer peddler, at W. W. Sloan's, b. Green n. Washington.
O'Harrow, John. lab. h. 93 5th.
O'Hayra, George, mason, h. 3 Mark.
Ohlenschlaeger, Jos. gardener, h. Ferry n. Delaware.
Ohler. F. S. stone cutter, h. 50 Jefferson.
Ohlmer, Herman, saloon, 3 Market Block, h. same.
Ohnesorge, Anna, midwife, h. 12 Potter.
O'Hora, Thomas, teamster, School n. 10th.
O'Keefee, John, teacher, b. S. Division bel. Emslie.
O'Kene, E. Mrs. wid. h. 5th n. Virginia.
Olborn, Jacob, blacksmith, h. 145 Batavia.
Olcott, Earl, b. Maiden lane.
Olcott, M. Mrs. saloon, Canal ab. State, h. same.
Olcott, Nelson, saloon and stable, Maiden lane.
Oldman, Wm. boiler maker, h. Fulton n. Hamburgh.
Olds, Geo. freight agent, B. & L. H. R. R. h. 6 6th.
O'Leary, J. mariner, h. ac. creek.
Olebeims, A. foundryman, Brayley & Pitts.
Olerich, John, lab. h. Massachusetts n. Utica.
Oliver, F. M. D. dentist, 2 Erie, h. same.
Oliver, Geo. W. b. 11 Niagara.
Oliver, John N. joiner, h. 169 Delaware.
Oliver, John, carp. h. 9th n. Massachusetts.
Oliver, Joseph, engineer, h. 10 Chicago.
Oliver, Martha, washerwoman, h. Carroll n. Jefferson.
Oliver, Wm. G. dentist, 11 Niagara, h. same.
O'Loughlan, Thos. lab. b. 6 Michigan.
Olman, Wm. boiler maker, h. Fulton n. Hamburgh.
Olmar, Fred. finisher. Terrace cor. Henry, h. Michigan n. Goodell.
Olschge, John, stone mason, h. Camp n. Gen.
Olson, Gadtseherk, contractor, h. Wadsworth n. North.
Olver, Elizabeth, widow, Eagle n. Jefferson.
Olver, Horatio C. iron works. Niagara bet. Franklin and Pearl, h. Eagle n. Jefferson.
Olver, John, carp. b. Vermont n. Utica.
Olver, Thomas, painter, h. Eagle n. Jefferson.
Olver, Wm. B. painter. h. 68 Chippewa.
Om, Sophia, wid. h. Ketchum al. n. High.
O'Mara, Patrick, tallyman, b. Ohio cor. South.

O'Mara, Wm. lab. h. Terrace n. Church.
O'Meara, P. tailor, 5 Commercial, h. same.
O'Meara, M. caulker, h. ac. creek.
Omphalius, Geo. saloon, Ellicott cor. Chippewa, h. same.
Ompleman, Olive, wid. h. ac. creek.
O'Neil, Edward, carp. h. 62 5th.
O'Neil, Frank. h. 4th n. Carolina.
O'Neil, James, lab. h. Perry n. Illinois.
O'Neil, John. lab. h. Louisiana n. Elk.
O' eil, John, lab. h. Virginia cor. 10th.
O'Neil, John, iron finisher, Brayley & Pitts.
O'Neil, Matthew, salesman, Homer & Co. b. 29 Swan.
O'Neil, N. blacksmith, h. 244 Pearl.
O'Neil, P. ship carpenter, h. ac. creek.
O'Neil, Patrick, sailor, h. 46 N. Division.
O'Neil, Wm. iron worker, Brayley & Pitts.
O'Neil, William, saloon, 5 Commercial.
O'Neil, William, grocer, 44 Ohio, h. same.
Onnink, Chas. J. stereotyper, h. 31 Milnor.
Onnink, Wm. J. teamster, h. 105 Oak.
Openheim, David, peddler, h. Mulberry n. Va.
Opitz. Augustus, cap maker, 80 Main, h. 179 Ellicott.
Oppenheimer, Herz, lab. h. Maple cor. North.
Opper, Geo. harness maker, cor. Evans and Canal, h. Virginia n. Delaware place.
Ord. Robert, blacksmith, Carolina n. Louisiana.
Ordner. John, with M. Hausle & Son, h. 16 Goodell.
Ordner, John, tinshop, 149 Genesee, h. same.
Ordner, John, lab. h. Steele n. Walden.
Ordway, J. M. conductor N. st. R. R. b. Mrs. A. J. Ludlow.
O'Rielly, Daniel, plumber, b. Maryland n. 11th.
O'Rielly, Sylvester J. firm O'R. & Valentine, lock manuf. 14 Court, h. Park ab. Va.
O'Rielly. Timothy, truckman, h. Maryland.
O rigel, G. cooper, h. Hamilton n. East.
Orms, Richard, machinist, h. 25 Exchange.
Ormsby, Wm. coach painter, b. 110 Exchange.
O'Rourk, Jas.* shoemaker, Ohio n. Mississippi.
O'Rourk, Pat.* shoemaker, 25 Ohio, h. same.
ORR, ALEX. B. com. merch. 58 Main, h. Niag. bel. Pennsylvania.—See adv. p. 37.
Orr, Geo. dep. sheriff, h. Abbott road.
Orr, Isaac, caulker, h. across creek.
Ort, Andrew, lab. h. Steele n. Walden.
Ort, John, blacksmith, h. Walden n. 4 mile creek.
Ort, John, teamster, h. North n. Ellicott.
Ortel, August, tailor, h. Goodell.
Osborne, Jas. shoemaker, b. 45 Tupper.
Osburne, Edward, engraver, Commercial office, h. 6th.
O'Shea, Daniel, grocer, 6th cor. Virginia, h. same.
Oshuetz, F. carp. h. Peckham n. Monroe.
Osman, Emanuel, ship carp. h. across creek.
Oster, Mathias, blacksmith, h. Monroe.
Ostheim, Conrad, tanner, b. Hickory n. Gen.
Ostheim, Henry, tanner, h. Cherry n. Hickory.
Ostrom. Oliver J h. 9 6th.
Ostwald, John, polisher. h. Sycamore n. Camp.
O'Sullivan, D. grocer, 11th n. Vermont.
Oswald, Adam J. upholsterer, b. Pratt n. Wm.
Oswald, Frederick, teamster, h. Ferry n. Main.

Oswald, Henry, butcher, b. Ohio n. swing bridge.
Oswald, John, watchmaker, h. r. 555 Seneca.
Oswald, Jos. lab. h. Jefferson n. Sycamore.
Oswald, Mathias, teamster, h. Niagara n. Breckenridge.
Oswald, Sebastian. lab. h. 173 Batavia.
Otis, C. N. architect, 5 Hollister Block. b. Am.
OTIS, H. H. bookstore, 226 Main, h. 306 Pearl. See adv. p. 100.
Otis, Levi, clerk. 226 Main, b. 306 Pearl.
Otis, Mary, widow, h. Vermont n. 10th.
Ott, Coony, lab. b. Maiden Lane House.
Ott, Dora, Miss, dress maker, b. 106 Batavia.
Ott, John, tanner, h. Spring n. Eagle.
Ott, John, lab. b. Fred. Grabenstaetter.
Ott, Samuel, tanner, b. 369 Michigan.
Otto, Adam, lab. h. Breckenridge n. Canal.
Ottenot, Nicholas, grocer, 425 Main, h. same.
Otterbein, Geo. sailor, h. Bennett n. W m.
Ottinger, Erherdt, brewer. h. 244 Genesee.
Ottinger, Joseph, basket maker, h. over 12 Sycamore.
Ottman, Lewis, lab. h. Dearborn n. Parish.
Ottmeyer, Catharine, widow, h. East n. Berry.
Otto, Chs. L. shoemaker, h. Bat. opp. Milnor.
Otto, Jas. W. clerk; city treas. b. 351 Wash.
Otto, John, firm Pickering & O. h. 351 Wash.
OTTO, LEWIS, constable, h. 117 Folsom.— See adv. p. 81.
Otto, Louis, tailor, h. Grey n. Genesee.
Ottowitz. Jos. lab. h. Johnson n. Genesee.
Ovens, Robert, baker, 31 E. Seneca. h. same.
Ovens, Robert B. bakery and confectionery, 50 Niagara, h. same.
Ovens, W. S. baker, b. 34 E. Seneca.
Overfield, Frank, cooper, h. 14th n. Vermont.
Overfield, John, lab. h. Utica n. Mass.
Ovington, Wm. H. firm Dart & Bros. h. North n. Delaware.
Owen, Jos. carp. h. Pooley n. N. Washington.
Owens, Alfred, draughtsman, Erie Exchange. b. Western.
Owens, Peter, carriage trimmer, b. 5 Franklin.
Ownwood, O. saloon, h. cor. 4th and Georgia.

P.

Packard, Samuel, mariner, h. Va. cor. 10th.
Packwood, Mary A. widow, dress maker, h. 98 Eagle.
Page, Albert, h. East cor. Parish.
Page, Edward H. daguerrean, with O. B. Evans, b. 47 Exchange.
Paige, Henry, firm T. & H. Paige, b. Western.
Paige, Timothy, boot and shoe dealer, 238 Main. b. 62 Swan.
Paige, Wilkinson, salesman, 238 Main, h. Western.
Paine, Francis, clerk, b. American.
Painter, John. carpenter, h. R. 1. cor. 9th.
Paldensberger, Philip, carp. h. 15 Cherry.
Paley, Benj. blacksmith, Terrace, h. 115 Carroll.
Palmer, Alanson, b. 7 Church.
Palmer, Archie, ship carp. h. 15 Mechanic.
Palmer, Barbara, widow of Philip, h. Jefferson n. Folsom.
Palmer, Chas. W. melodeon tuner, b. 11 Court.

Palmer, David, clerk, 278 Main, b. 22 Swan.
Palmer, Edward W. attorney, cor. Niagara and Virginia. h. 69 Maryland.
Palmer, E. J. huckster, h. 20 William.
Palmer, Elias W. gen. collector, h. 24 Morgan.
Palmer, Everard. h. Goodell cor. Oak.
Palmer, Geo. president Marine Bank, and firm J. B. Bull & Co. 21 and 23 Lloyd, h. Washington cor. Goodell.
Palmer, George, on lake, h. 161 Batavia.
Palmer, Hiram. joiner, h. cor. Chicago and Elk.
Palmer, Jas. H. with D. P. Dobbins, h. 12 Park place.
Palmer, John, caulker, h. 77 Church.
Palmer, J. C. carpenter, h. 7th n. Carolina.
Palmer, Joseph, clerk, at 278 Main, h. 22 E. Swan.
Palmer, Monteath & Co. 21 Central Wharf.
Palmer, R. C. firm Monteath, P. & Co. h. 4 Johnson place.
Palmer, Robert T. h. 165 Swan.
Palmer, Sarah H. Miss, b. E. J. Palmer.
Palmer, Wm. J. gardener, h. 13th ab. Penn.
Palmer, Wm. Mrs. widow, h. 13th ab. Penn.
Palmer, Wm. ship carp. h. 5th n. Carolina.
Palmer, W. M. works Brayley & Pitts, h. Summer n. Roger.
Paradis, Peter, shoemaker. b. Fox n. Genesee.
Paradise, B. blacksmith, at Brayley & Pitts.
Pardee, Myron J. with R. L. Howard, h. 293 Michigan.
Pardridge, Charles W. firm C. W. & E. P. h. 65 S. Division.
Pardridge, C. W. & E. dry goods, 318 Main.
Pardridge, Edward, firm C. W. & E. P. b. 65 S. Division.
Parezo, James P. saloon, Canal n. State.
Parish, Wm H. grocer, h. cor. Elk and La.
PARK, PAUL, lumber dealer, office and yard Genesee cor. 4th, h. 303 Franklin ab. Edward.—*See adv. p.* 85.
Parke, James B. book-keeper, G. R. Wilson & Co. h. 305 Michigan.
Parker, A. J. hostler, 264 Washington, b. R. Kallahan.
Parker, Andrew, book-keeper, Sears & Clark, h. 38 Delaware.
Parker, Anthony, lab. h. 383 Michigan.
Parker, E. Chas. Niag. St. R. R. h. 9th n. R. I.
Parker, E. H. firm Diehl & P. h. 75 Ellicott.
Parker, Geo. carpenter, h. Jeff. n. Carroll.
Parker, Henry, grocer, Erie n. bridge, h. cor. Blossom and Koon's alley.
PARKER, JASON, & CO. coal merchants, Norton cor. Ship canal.—*See adv. p.* 46.
PARKER, JASON, prod. and com. merch, 23 Cent Wharf, h. 32 Ellicott.—*See adv. p.* 37.
Parker, Jason, Jr. 23 Cent. Whf. b. 32 Ellicott.
Parker, Orville. book-keeper, b. 32 Ellicott.
Parker, P. G. att'y, cor. Eagle and Main, h. cor. Oak and High.
Parker, Robt. ship carp. h. Ohio n. Michigan.
Parker, Thos. L. mariner, h. 24 Carolina.
Parker, Jas. S. piano turner, h. 64 W. Chippewa.
Parkinson, Jas. cutter, W. P. & P. C. Stambach. h. 297 Michigan.
Parkinson, Virginia, teacher No. 4, b. 297 Michigan.

Parkhill, J. J. capt. b. cor. Elk and Michigan.
Parks, Geo. lab. h. Utica n. Massachusetts.
Parks, Horace, drayman, h. 187 N. Division.
Parks, Jas. S. piano tuner, 209 Main, h. 60 Chippewa.
Parmalee, Arthur W. with H. C. Walker, b. Delaware n. Main.
Parmalee, E. S. bar-tender, Revere House.
Parmalee. T. N. b. American.
Parmelee, Horace, h. Delaware ab. Utica.
Parmele, S. stave dealer, 2 Main, h. 116 Eagle.
Parmlee. A. sawyer, h. Dearbou n. Hamb.
Parmeme, C. b. 116 E. Eagle.
Parmeme, S. lumber dealer. 116 E. Eagle.
Parment, Jos. painter, h. 124 Elm.
Parr, Ellen, widow, h. 11 7th.
PARR, GEO. awl manuf. office 5th cor. Court, h. 6th n. Carolina.—*See adv. p.* 97.
Parrard, Thos. with Howell & Smith, h. 100 Elm.
Parrzeran, Christopher, lab. h Wm. n. Bennett.
Parsons, Galusha, firm Humphrey & P. att'ys, Seneca cor. Washington, h. 185 Franklin.
Parsons, John H. Amer. Exp. Co h. 295 Frkl'n.
Parsons, Sam. V. ship carp. h. 319 Michigan.
Parsons. Silas, com. merch, 17 Prime, h. 229 Franklin.
Parsons, Thos. G. book-keeper, Buff. Trust Co. b. 52 E. Swan.
Parsons, Wm. W. 60 Main, b. 2 Park place.
Partridge, Jos. h. Seneca, old city line.
Paschke, Michael, tailor, h. Abbott road bel. iron bridge.
Pascal, Martha, washerwoman, h. 403 Mich.
Passennau. J. sailor, h. Thomp. n. Amherst.
Patchin, A. D. pres't B. N. Y. & E. R. R. b. American.
Patchin, A. D. Jr. clerk N. Y. & E. R. R. b. 5 W. Eagle.
Patchin, A. T. farmer, h. White's Corners plank road n. city line.
Patchin, E. A. joiner, h. over 427 Main.
Patchin, Rich. J. pattern maker, h. Ga. n. 4th.
Patchin, T. D. office Wash. cor. Exchange, h. Delaware n. Allen.
Patchin, Thad. W. freight agent N. Y. & E. R. R. h. 5 W. Eagle.
Patee, E. F. engineer, h. Elk n. R. R.
Patrick, Thos. sailor, b. Smith's Block, Seneca.
Patschke, Fred. tailor, h. 337 Michigan.
Patscho. Christian, lab. b. La. n. Mackinaw.
Patten, David, maltster, h. Main n. Ferry.
Patterson, A. H. printer, b. 104 Exchange.
Patterson, David, at 6 Dayton, b. Carlton n. Washington.
Patterson, F. W. prod. and com. merch. 13 Cent. Wharf, h. 388 Franklin.
Patterson, H. lab. h. Hamilton n. Dearborn.
Patterson, H. teacher, ov. 383 Main.
Patterson, Jas. F. mariner, h. Wm. n. Watson.
Patterson, James, Mrs. h. 58 E. Seneca.
Patterson, Jno. cartman, b. Carlton n. Wash.
Patterson, Jno. tanner, with N. H. Gardner, h. Potter n. Van Rensselaer.
Patterson, Robt. blacksmith, b. 47 Exchange.
Patterson, Robt. boiler maker, Norton n. Water, h. junc. Elk and Ohio.
Patterson, Robert, lab. h. Carlton n. Wash.

Patterson, Thos. engineer, h. Ohio cor. Ill.
Patterson, Wm. cartman, b. Carlton n. Wash.
Patterson, Wm. sailor, h. Wm. n. Watson.
Patterson, W. W. b. F. G. Pattison.
Pattison, F. G. 43 Cedar.
Pattison, James, 181 Main, b. 126 E. Eagle.
Patzer, Adam. lab. h. 79 Hickory.
Paufner, Charles, lab. h. 218 N. Division.
Paul, Augustus, firm P. & Mooney, 11 Arcade Buildings, h. 229 Oak.
Paul, Fred. farmer, n. Ontario and city line.
Paul, John, potter, h. 394 Michigan.
Paul, Lewis, lab. h. Camp n. Sycamore.
Paul, M. harness maker, 116 Pearl, h. Pratt n. Genesee.
Paul & Mooney, Queen City land office, 11 Arcade Buildings.
Paul, Paul, lab. h. 160 Sycamore.
Paul, Peter, clerk, R. Bullymore, h. Genesee opp. Grey.
Paul, Richard, gardener, h. 72 Chippewa.
Paula, John, lab. h. Mulberry n. Virginia.
Paule, Mathias, tailor, h. 114 Cedar.
Pauli, Jacob, blacksmith, h. Spring n. Syc.
Pauli, Peter, carp. h. 114 Cedar.
Paulsackel, Chs. moulder, h. 50 William.
Paulsackel, Geo. carp. h. 50 William.
Paulus, Michael, lab. h. 12 Cypress.
Pauly, Daniel, carp. h. Exchange n. Heacock.
Pauly, Daniel, tanner, b. Exch. n. Van Rensselaer.
Pauly, Jacob, tanner, h. Exch. n. Van Rensselaer.
Pax, Casper, melodeon maker, h. Lutheran bet. Wm. and Batavia.
Pax, John, shoemaker, h. 21 Sycamore.
Pax, Tony, with Bergman & Co. h. Sycamore n. Oak.
Payne, Andrew, clerk at 290 Main, b. Genesee House.
Payne, Charles, saloon, 7 State, h. same.
Payne, C. T. h. 186 Franklin.
Payne, Fred. b. 186 Franklin.
Payne, George, boiler maker, h. Spring cor. N. Division.
Payne, Samuel, saloon, 7 State, h. same.
Peabody, J. M. h. 26 Chippewa.
Peabody, Joseph W. book-keeper, H. Niles & Co. h. 54 N. Division.
Peabody, W. H. druggist, 251 and 432 Main, b. 26 Chippewa.
Peacock. Wm.W. civil engineer, office 268 Main, h. 26 W. Eagle.
Peacock, Wm. boiler maker, h. Jefferson n. Carroll.
Pearce, J. B. clerk, Hamlin & Mensden, h. 19 N. Division.
Pearce, Samuel, carpet fitter, over 207 Main, h. 26 Union.
PEASE, F. S. manufacturer and dealer in oils, 61 Main, h. Hudson n. Niagara.—See adv. opp. name.
Pease, John, firm P. & Trowbridge, foot Lloyd, h. 73 Delaware.
Pease, John, Jr. with P. & Trowbridge, b. 73 Delaware.
Pease, Sheldon, managing agent B. C. & C. line, office Michigan n. Ohio, b. American.

Pease & Trowbridge, forwd. and com. mers. foot Lloyd.
Pease, William A. at 61 Main, h. Bowery n. North.
Pease, W. R. book-keeper, h. 99 Swan.
Peasland, Job. b. cor. Michigan and Carroll.
Peck, Chas E. Am. Exp. Co. h. 59 Ellicott.
Peck, Daniel, prop. Boston Hotel, cor. Chase and Ellicott.
Peck, G. W. clerk, b. Jefferson cor. Batavia.
Peck, H. boat builder, h. 5th ab. Pa.
Peck, H. pro'r Com'l Hotel, Ohio n. Main.
Peck, J. C. blacksmith, h. cor. Clinton and Mich.
Peck, Jesse, mason, h. cor. Jeff. and Batavia.
Peck, Wm. B. Am. Exp. Co. h. 150 Pearl.
Peck, Wm. G. cook, h. 34 William.
Peckham, John W. butcher, 15 Elk St. Market.
Peel, Geo. truckman, h. 27 Union.
Pegelo, John, bricklayer, h. Goodell alley n. Burton alley.
Peglo, Chs. bricklayer, h. Maple cor. Burton alley.
PEIRCE, LORING, undertaker, 153 Franklin. —See adv. p. 94.
Peiter, Philip, farmer, Barton n. Delaware.
Pell, Jno. farmer, Calvin bet. Burton and Amherst.
Peller, Geo. lab. h. Pine n. Cypress.
Peller, Jacob, teamster, b. J. F. Hofenis.
Pellman, Francis H. carp. h. 44 William.
Pelloran, P. b. Revere.
Peltzer, Wm. actor, h. 121 Oak.
Pembroke, Karrin. ship carp. h. 4th n. Virginia.
Pemsel, Casper, lab. h. Sycamore n. Walnut.
Pendergrass, Thos. lab. h. Erie basin n. Gen.
Pendergrast, Thos. ship carp. h. 9th.
Pendleton, N. firm Nibecker & P. h. cor. Erie and Lock.
Penfield, Danl. with T. V. N. Penfield, h. 38 W. Eagle.
Penfield, Henry F. h. Niagara n. Bidwell.
Penfield, J. H. book-keeper, firm M. S. Hawley & Co. b. cor. Main and Huron.
Penfield, T. V. N. printing and blank book manuf. 15 W. Seneca, h. 3o W. Eagle.
Penn, Henry L. clerk, 215 Main, h. 141 9th.
Pennels, Thos. farmer, h. Bat. beyond toll gate.
Pennels, Thos. Jr. farmer, b. Bat. beyond toll gate.
Pennen, Thomas, lab. 132 Folsom.
Penseyers, Philip, blacksmith, h. Syc. n. Mich.
Peoples, James A. machinist, b. 137 Elk.
Perger, F. clerk, h. Ellicott.
Perkins, Electa, Mrs. wid. h. Palmer ab. Va.
Perkins, L. P. attorney, 4 Hollister Buildings, h. 47 Chippewa.
Perkins, Thomas G. insurance agent, 4 Merchant's Exch. h. 82 Pearl.
Perkins, Wm. with Pratt & Co. h. 32 Goodell.
Permange, Michael, carp. h. High n. Ellicott.
Perolz, John, shoemaker, cor. Chicago and Miami.
Perrigo, Benj. moulder. h. Carroll n. Ala.
Perrin, Geo. ship carp. h. Fulton n. Hayward.
Perrine, Henry E. firm Morse & P. h. 89 Morgan.
Perrott, Geo. sea grass manuf. h. Ferry n. Jeff.
Perry, Israel B.* shoemaker, h. 165 Elk.

Perry, H. O. foreman, Shepard's iron works, h. Fulton n. Hamburgh.
Perry, Jas. dyeing establ't, 412 Main, h. same.
Perry, John. shoemaker, b. Genesee n. Oak.
Perry, Robert, saloon, cor. Com'l and Terrace, h. same.
Perry, Wm. H. sup. Great Western Dispatch, h. 8 E. Mohawk.
Persch, Henry C. grocer, Terrace cor. Church, h. same.
Persch, Jacob, shoemaker, h. 68 5th.
Person, Chas. whisky rectifier, 220 Elm, h. same.
Person, Henry, b. 220 Elm.
Pesch, Adam, lab. h. Mulberry n. Virginia.
Peseler, E. W. teacher, h. Pratt n. Sycamore.
Peter, Jacob, hair dresser, 232 Main, b. 3 Court.
Peter, J. F. firm P. & Ketchum. h. 39 E. Eagle.
Peter & Ketchum, dealers in cheese and dried fruit, 48 Main.
Petermann, Jacob, carp. h. 247 Oak.
Peters, August, wagon makcr. b. 51 Cherry.
Peters, Elizabeth, widow, h. 49 N. Division.
Peters, Fred. lab. h. Hydraulics n. city line.
Peters, Gottfried. tailor, h. 50 Cherry.
Peters, Henry, tinner, 237 Main, h. Potter n. arsenal.
Peters, John, lab. h. Maple n. High.
Peters, John, lab. h. 86 Cherry.
Peters, Peter, lab. h. 39 Cherry.
Peters, Samuel G. machinist, b. 264 S. Div.
Peters, Samuel, shoemaker, 156 Main, h. 264 S. Division.
Peterson, Charles, shoemaker, h. ov. 238 Main.
Peterson, Chas. mariner, h. Hickory n. Eagle.
Peterson, George, morocco dresser, b. Green n. Michigan.
Peterson, Henry, morocco dresser, b. Mrs. M. Peterson, Exch. n. Beak.
Peterson, John, wool dealer, N. Canal n. junc. Swan and Seneca.
Peterson, Matthias, grocer, h. 140 6th cor. Va.
Peterson, P. B. ins. agt. 44 Main, b. 29 Swan.
Petit, Ed. tailor. h. 209 Ellicott.
Petit, G. R. clerk, 212 Wash. h. 230 Franklin.
Petrie, John, upholsterer, with Sherman & Barnes, h. William n. Stanton.
Petrie, John, lab. h. William n. Stanton.
Petrie, M. fonndryman, Brayley & Pitts.
Petrie, Sherman, clerk. 436 Main.
Petrie, William. firm W. P. & Co. h. 85 Swan.
Petrie, William & Co. forwd. and com mers. 13 Central Wharf.
Petsch, Chas. F. clothing store, 46 E. Genesee, h. same.
Pettegrini, A. stationery, 47 Seneca.
Pettengill. J. T. moulder, h. La. n. Elk.
Pettibone, Jay, h. 31 E. Eagle.
Pettis, Joel, lab. h. Illinois n. Scott.
Pettis, W. H. b. Western.
Pettit, Sweet & Co. wholesale dealers in boots and shoes. 166 Main.
Pettit, Wm. B. firm P. Sweet & Co. h. 191 Del.
Petts, Jno. in ropewalk. b. H. Donahue.
Petty, Wm. carp. b. Exch. n. Chicago.
Petz, Conrad, lab. h. Lemon n. High.
Petzing. Jacob, baker, Genesee n. Jefferson.
Petzing, Peter, lab. h. Lutheran n. William.

Peugeot, George, h. 30 E. Huron.
Peugeot, Peter, h. 158 Ellicott.
Pfall, James, engineer, h. 7 Cypress
Pfalz, Francis, butcher, h. Genesee cor. Elm.
Pfann, Fred. blacksmith, Seneca n. Hydraulics, h. same.
Pfau, Gustavus, cooper, h. Tupper bel. Va.
Pfazler, M. shoem'r, h. Hamilton n. Thompson.
Pfeffen, John C. grocer, 275 Elm. h. same.
Pfeffer, Christian, ship carp. h. Mich. n. High.
Pfeffer, Ludwig, lab. h. Boston al. n. Burton al.
Pfeifer, Adam, lah. h. Jefferson n. William.
Pfeifer, Catherine. wid. h. Main cor. North.
Pfeifer, Chas. tailor, h. Sycamore n. Ash.
Pfeifer, Conrad, saloon, 4 Michigan. h. same.
Pfeifer, Geo. h. Jefferson cor. Perry.
Pfeifer, Henry, lab. h. William n. Jefferson.
Pfeifer, Louis, lab. h. Johnson n. Batavia.
Pfeiffer, Casper, shoemaker. Grey n. Genesee.
Pfeiffer, Geo. F. with F. J. Kraft, 29 E. Huron, h. 40 Goodell.
Pfeiffer, Henry, tanner, h. Grey n. Batavia.
Pfeiffer, Henry P. salesman, 243 Main, h. 229 Elm.
Pfeiffer, Jacob, tailor, h. 95 Pine.
Pfeiffer, John, carpenter, h. Milnor n. Batavia.
Pfeiffer, Jno. lab. h. Hickory n. Syc.
Pfeiffer, Lena, widow, h. Pratt n. William.
Pfeiffer, Louis, canal collector's off. h. 69 Syc.
Pfeiffer, Martin, lab. h. Goodell al. n. Tupper.
Pfeiffer, Phil. shoemaker, h. Clinton bel. Pratt.
Pfeiffer, Wm. wagoner, h. Michigan n High.
Pfeil, Adam, barber, 104 Exch. n. Nat. Hotel.
Pfeil, Henry, baker, b. Monroe n. William.
Pfeil, Jacob, cooper, b. Philip Stern.
Pfeil, John, baker, h. Monroe n. William.
Pfenning, Francis, tobac'nist, 61 Gen. h. same.
Pfifer, John, type founder. h. Hickory n. Bat.
Pfilter, lab. h. Monroe n. Peckham.
Pfister, And. lab. h. Milnor opp. Arsenal.
Pfister, Andrew, tailor, h. Maple n. Carlton.
Pfister, Geo. grocer, h. Maple n. Carlton.
Pfleger, John C. painter. b. Goodell n. Elm.
Pfleuger, John, painter, h. 98 Goodell.
Pfleuter, William, gardener, b. Jeff. n. Carlton.
Pflug, Jacob, tailor, h. Mich. n. High.
Pflug, Jacob, lab. h. Walnut n. Batavia.
Pflug, Michael, tailor, h. Maple n. High.
Pflum, Gustavus, cooper, h. 542 Michigan.
Pfohl, Jacob, teamster, h. cor. Clin'n and Oak.
Pfohl, Jacob H. flour merchant, firm P. & Co. 162 Batavia, h. same.
Pfohl, Louis, flour merchant, firm P. & Co. 162 Batavia, h. same.
Pfohmam, Jacob, brewer, h. Main n. Goodell.
Pfrang, Eliz. seamstress, h. Hickory n. Syc.
Pfrang, Juliana, widow, Hickory n. Sycamore.
Phelps, Calvin, h. 219 Niagara.
Phelps, Catharine, widow, boarding, 167 Seneca.
Phelps, C. B. dentist, h. 28 Chippewa.
Phelps, Geo. b. Revere House.
Phelps, J. D. builder, h. 30 Park.
Phelps, Orson, h. 467 Main.
Phersch, Mary, Mrs. h. r. 117 Oak.
Philip, Jacob, h. r. 249 Elm.
Philip, Rudolph, lab h. 408 S. Division.
Philips. Anton, carpenter, h. 64 E. Tupper.
Philips, Jacob, Sr. h. 249 Elm.

Philips, John, lab. h. 64 E. Tupper.
Phillbrook, Augustus P. blacksmith, h. Palmer n. Maryland.
Phillip, Rudolf, lab. h. S. Division n. R. R.
Phillip, S. & Co. clothiers, 94 and 192 Main.
Phillippi, Henry, carpenter, h. Abbott road n. Smith.
Phillippi, John, Fulton n. Market.
Phillippi, Wm. lab. h. Fox n. North.
Phillipps, Geo. grocer, Niag. n. Hamilton, h. same.
Phillips, A. baker, R. Ovens, b. 34 Seneca.
Phillips, Chas. shoemaker, b. Frank. Fisher.
Phillips, Chas. H., B. & E. R. R. b. 85 Seneca.
Phillips, Geo. fisherman, h. ac. creek.
Phillips, Henry, conductor, N. st. R. R. b. Ferry n. N. Washington.
Phillips, Henry H. clerk, Jewett & Root, b. 90 Clinton.
Phillips, Isaac, mariner, h. 53 Delaware.
Phillips, John, wagon maker, b. 38 Chicago.
Phillips, John, clerk, 120 Exch. b. same.
Phillips, J. S. painter. h. cor. Miss. and Perry.
Phillips, J. W. with Miles Jones.
Phillips, Oliver C. barber, h. Oak n. Virginia.
Phillips, Peter, cabinet maker, h. 90 Clinton.
Phillips, Philip, carp. Spruce n. Sycamore.
Phillips, S. * shoemaker, shop cor. Niagara and Amherst.
Phillips, Sarah, Mrs. saloon, 8 Terrace, h. same.
Phillips, Seneca. h. Ferry n. Adams.
Phillips, Stephen G. tallyman, b. 104 Fulton.
Phillips, Thos. foreman for I. Holloway & Co. h. Palmer ab. Maryland.
Phillips, Wm. cl'k, Adams & Co. b. 29 E. Swan.
Phillipson, Isaac, melodeon maker, h. Cottage n. Maryland.
Philpot, John N. com. mer. 26 Central Wharf, b. 180 E. Swan.
Philpot, J. N. b. 180 E. Swan.
Philpot, Robert S. mariner, h. 208 S. Div.
Philpot, Wm. R. clerk, b. 180 E. Swan.
Philpot, W. S. com. mer. 26 Central Wharf, h. 180 Swan.
Phofe, August, lab. h. Stanton n. Peckham.
Pickard, Frank, h. Clinton n. Bond.
Pickard, Frank, Jr. firm F. P. Jr. & Co. 22 and 29 Elk st. market, h. Clinton n. Bond.
Pickering, Chas. city clerk's office, h. Erie n. Franklin.
Pickering. Chs. E. clk. Buffalo City Bank, b. cor. Erie and Franklin.
Pickering, E. P. firm P. & Otto, h. 12 W. Swan.
Pickering & Otto, real estate agents, 37 Pearl.
Pickett, Jno. H. sail maker, b. J'sey n. Rogers.
Pickle. Mrs. widow, h. Hickory n. Swan.
Pidd, Jno. N. Y. & E. R. R. office cor. Exch. and Washington, b. cor. Exch. and Mich.
Pielman, Wm. lab. h. 536 Michigan.
Pierce, Andrew, clk. Pierce & Co. b. 80 Seneca.
Pierce, Augustus, moulder, b. 140 Elk.
Pierce. C. ship carp. h. N. Wash. n. Clinton av.
Pierce, Chas. L. firm P. & Co. h. 150 Elk.
Pierce, Chas. machinist, b. 6 Park.
Pierce. Chas. C. clerk, h. 191 7th.
PIERCE & CO. lumber dealers and shingle manuf. office and yard cor. Mich. and Scott.
—See adv. p. 84.

Pierce, Chas. S. agent Ladd, Webster & Co. h. 80 E. Seneca.
Pierce, Daniel, carp. cor. Hamburgh and Elk.
*Pierce, E. P. with J. Appleton, h. 159 9th.
Pierce, Francis F. h. 45 Cedar.
Pierce, Henry, lab. h. Bremen n. Vermont.
Pierce, J. shoemaker, 12 Court, h. same.
Pierce. Jacob G. with Sherman & Barnes, h. cor. Oak and E. Swan.
Pierce, J. B. Mrs. mantillas, cloaks, &c. 19 N. Division.
Pierce, J. B. clerk, with Hamlin & Mendsen, h. 19 N. Division.
Pierce, Jenny, widow, h. Main cor. North.
Pierce, Jerome, firm P. & Co. b. 80 Seneca.
Pierce, John, dep. sheriff, h. 150 S. Division.
Pierce, Thos. printer, with Sage & Sons, h. 112 W. Huron.
Pierce, Wm. C. Am. Exp. Co. b. 98 Folsom.
Pierce, Wm. P. scale manuf. J. Weeks, h. 380 Franklin.
Pierson, C. B. clerk, Pratt & Letchworth, b. 78 Franklin.
Pierson, Ed. cash. Farmers and Mechan. Bank, h. 173 Pearl. •
Pierson, Henry, barber, 25 Mohawk, h. same.
Pike, Wm. submarine diver, h 18 Illinois.
Pillard, Mrs. widow, h. 100 Elm.
Piller, Adam, lab. h. Batavia cor. Lutheran.
Pilliard, Fred. farmer, Del. n. town line road.
Pillure, Fred. drayman, h. 76 Sycamore.
Pinckner, William, gardener, b. ov. 7 Swan.
Pindorfer, John, h. 265 Elm.
Pindorfer, Paul, shoemaker, h. 238 Elm.
Pine, Pat. engineer, h. 17 Jackson.
Pine, Samuel, carpenter, b. 63 Clinton.
Pingre, Wilson, h. Batavia n. R. R. track.
Pinkney, Joseph, grainer, h. 102 Clinton.
Pinner, M. real estate agent, 236 Main, h. 139 Franklin.
Pinton, Gustavus, machinist, b. 67 Genesee.
Pipo, August, joiner, b. Monroe n. Batavia.
Pisto, John, lab. h. Hickory n. Genesee.
Pister, Nicholas, lab. h. Spring n. William.
Pitkin, J. F. with Hamlin & Mendsen.
Pitman, Ed. patt'n maker, b. 31 Elm.
Pitman, Geo. Mrs. nurse, h. 31 Elm.
Pittman, Henry,* shoemaker, 43 Seneca, h. 35 Carroll.
Pittman, N. moulder. b. Walnut bel. Sycamore.
Pittman, Peter, h. Walnut bel. Sycamore.
Pitts, Calvin W. machinist, foreman Brayley & Pitts, h. Georgia n. 6th.
Pitts, Jno. W. firm Brayley & P. b. American.
Pittsford, Henry, blacksmith, h. 312 Seneca.
Pitz, Adam, shoemaker, h. 218 Elm.
Pixley, Jas. G. machinist, h. 6 Carey.
Pixley, Philander, builder, h. 6 Carey.
Pixley, William, machinist. h. 52 Sycamore.
Place, John, drayman, h. 167 N. Division.
Plank, Geo. W. shoemaker. b. Globe Hotel.
Plantz, Elizabeth, wid. h. Spring n. Sycamore.
Plantz, Jacob, clerk, at 194 Main, h. Spring n. Sycamore.
Plase, S. b. American.
Plassar, Nicholas, carp. h. Clinton n. Spring.
Platt, A. B. wool and leather dealer. 4 Birkhead Buildings, h. 37 Ellicott.

PRATT & CO.

28, 30 AND 32 TERRACE ST.

PROPRIETORS OF THE

BUFFALO IRON & NAIL WORKS

IMPORTERS AND DEALERS IN

EVERY VARIETY OF

AMERICAN AND FOREIGN HARDWARE AND METALS,

MANUFACTURERS OF

BAR IRON, NAILS,

SPIKES, CUT TACKS, BRADS,

CLOUT, FINISHING AND SHOE NAILS.

Also, Commission Merchants for the sale of

PAILS AND TUBS, FIRE-PROOF SAFES

WATER LIME, PLATFORM SCALES, LEATHER BELTING, ETC.

Any size, shape, length or quality of Iron rolled to order and furnished to Manufacturers or Merchants on short notice.

SCRAP IRON WANTED.

For which the highest market price will be paid.

SAMUEL F. PRATT.   PASCAL P. PRATT.   EDWARD P. BEALS.

Platt, Clement, engineer, b. Mississippi n. Elk.
Platt, J. G. saw filer, Elk n. Ohio, h. 217 Wash.
Platt, L. B. firm L. B. P. & Co. h. 59 E. Eagle.
PLATT, L. B. & CO. oyster and fruit depot, 286 Main, h. 59 E. Eagle.—See adv. p. 50.
Playter, C. G. book-keeper, Pratt & Co. h. Niagara n. York.
Plembel, Jacob, tanner, h. 19 Bennett.
Pleuthner, Christiana J. wid. h. Mich. n. High.
Plimpton, Geo. A. book-keeper, 180 Main, b. 16 Eagle.
Plimpton, George D. book-keeper, 50 Main, b. 129 Pearl.
Plimpton, L. K. auction, com. and wool, 50 Main, h. 129 Pearl.
Ploeszel, Geo. lab. h. Boston alley n. Va.
Plogstead, John F. E. constable, b. 80 Bennett.
Pluemer, Rudolf, carp. h. 318 Ellicott.
Plug, John, engineer, h. Monroe n. Sycamore.
Plumeinstein, Edward, ship carp. 68 Del. place.
Plumley, Annie, h. 66 Court.
Plumley, Wm. lab. Dearborn n. Amherst.
Poacher, David, cooper, h. Eagle n. Jefferson.
Poetting, Henry, shoemaker, 20 S. Division, h. 65 Batavia.
Poetz, John, shoemaker, b. 583 Main.
Poh, Caroline, widow, washer. h. 122 Elm.
Poh, Catharine, widow, h. Walnut n. Bat.
Poh, Louis, stone cutter, h. r. 56 Bennett.
Poh, Louis, brass finisher, h. 91 Elm.
Pohl, Catharine, widow, h. Wm. n. Lutheran.
Pohlman, Chris. H. tanner, h. Grey n. Bat.
Police Justice office, Terrace n. Evans.
Police Station No. 1, Terrace n. Evans.
Police Station No. 2, Carroll n. Louisiana.
Police Station No. 3, Mohawk cor. Pearl.
Police Station No. 4, Sycamore n. Ash.
Pollard, Geo. lab. h. 14 Iron place, N. Wash.
Pollard, John, ship carp. h. 105 Fulton.
Pollen, E. last maker, b. 111 Carroll.
Polley, Amos, caulker, h. Ohio n. Elk.
Polley, Robt. machinist, b. Globe Hotel.
Pollock, John, moulder, b. 107 Fulton.
Pollock, Joseph, carp. h. Monroe n. Wm.
Pollock, Jos. watch maker, with T. Dickinson.
Pollock, Thomas, salesman, 162 Main, h. cor. Main and N. Division.
Pomainville, Frank, mason, h. 26 Chicago.
Pomainville, Frank, Jr. saloon, Franklin House h. Chicago n. Exchange.
Pomeroy, Emerson C. teacher, h. 138 Clinton.
Pomeroy, Robt. Mrs. h. Swan cor. Oak.
Pomeroy, Robt. clerk, b. Swan cor. Oak.
Pomeroy, S. T. nursery man, Ferry n. Del.
Pommerscheim, Geo. baker, 124 Seneca.
Pond, C. L. photographic artist, 198 Main, h. 20 Ellicott.
Pool, C. O. attorney, h. Franklin n. North.
Poole, Anna W. Miss, h. 41 W. Eagle.
Poole, Rushmore, with Homer & Co. h. 41 W. Eagle.
POOLEY & BUTTERFIELD, rope manuf. Forest avenue.—See adv. p. 53
Pooley, George P. firm P. & Butterfield, h. Bird avenue n. Dewitt.
Pooley, William, foreman, Jas. R. Evans & Co. h. 133 9th.
Pope, Bernhard, carp. h. 545 Michigan.

Pope, Chas. actor, h. 16 Delaware place.
Pope, Joseph R. actor, b. Chas. Pope.
Popcorn, Mrs. corn popper, h. 143 Elm.
Poppenberg, Albert, music teacher, h. Delaware n. Ferry.
Poppenberg, Gustavus, musician, h. 23 Cypress.
Poppenberg, Robt. musician, h. 12 Walnut.
Porcell, Edward, foreman, in stave yard, h. Bristol n. Spring.
Porn, Frederick. lab. h. High n. Maple.
Port, Fred. 162 Main, b. Vandalia n. Mackinaw.
Porter, A. D. tallyman, N. Y. C. R. R. freight office, b. Franklin House.
PORTER, SAMUEL. grocer, 360 Main, h. bet. Washington and High.—See adv. p. 41.
Porter, Stephen B. attorney, Erie Exch. b. 83 S. Division.
Porter, Walter, builder, 83 S. Division.
Porter, Wm. gardener, with Geo. Malcom, h. Main n. Ferry.
Porter, Wm. mariner, h. across creek.
Porter, Wm. J. printer, b. 200 Washington.
Porth, Henry, grocer, 543 Mich. h. 541 Mich.
Pos, Wm. lab. h. Spring n. Genesee.
Post, Henry, clerk, 174 Main, b. 62 Pine.
Post, John, painter, h. 62 Pine.
Post, John C. clerk, 4 E. Swan, b 62 Pine.
Post, Wm. farmer, Ontario cor. Tonawanda.
Postal. Annie, saloon, 52 Clinton.
Poth, Geo. H. h. 50 E. Genesee.
Potter, Amos K. clerk, 24 Main, b. r. 260 Sen.
Potts, Robt. carp. h. Perry n. Hamburgh.
Powell, David, sup. Buffalo Omnibus Co.
Powell, Edw'd, clerk, C. Wormwood, h. 91 9th.
Powell, Egbert H. clerk, N. Y. & E. R. R. h. Elk n. Louisiana.
Powell, John, stone mason, h. 91 9th.
Powell N. O. liquor dealer, 45 Seneca, h. same.
Powell, Wm. clerk, 180 Main. h. 83 Clinton.
Power, Pat. grocer, Sen. junc. Swan, h. same.
Powers, Daniel, mariner, h. across creek.
Powers, Jno. pork inspector, b. cor. Terrace and Genesee.
Powers, Jno. clerk, P. O. b. 80 Clinton.
Powers, Patrick, at Evans' elevator, h. Evans n. Water.
Pox, Jacob, lab. h. Elm n. Genesee.
Pralon, Fred. tailor, h. 418 S. Division.
Pralow, Jno. lab. h. Mulberry n. Carlton.
Pratt, Amos, lake capt. h. 10 Park place.
Pratt, Anson, com. merchant, 17 Central Wharf, h. 27 Johnson place.
Pratt, Byron, b. 14 Oak.
PRATT & CO. hardware, 28, 30 and 32 Terrace.—See adv. colored leaf opp. name.
Pratt, Francis, lab. h. Adams n. Sycamore.
Pratt. G. F. M. D. office 8 Swan, h. 155 E. Swan.
Pratt, H. Mrs. h. 75 E. Swan.
Pratt, James M. lake capt. h. 10 Tracy.
Pratt, John, carp. h. 261 Elm.
PRATT & LETCHWORTH, saddlery hardware, 34 Terrace.—See adv. colored leaf opp. name.
Pratt, Lucius, boat builder, Mich. cor. Green, h. 89 Swan.
Pratt, Martha, widow, h. 454 Michigan.
Pratt, P. P. firm P. & Co. h. 496 Main.
Pratt, Royal, boatman, h. Carroll n. Louisiana.

Pratt. S. F. firm P. & Co h. 83 E. Swan.
Pratt. Sophia, widow, h. 139 Swan.
Pratt, Thos. carp. b. G. W. Baskett.
Preas, Jno. with Jewett & Root, h. 37 Elm.
Preis, John,* boots and shoes, 349 Senaca, h. same.
Preisinger, John, lab. h. Mich. n. Carlton.
Prell, Simon, tailor, h. Johnson cor. High.
Premo, Louis, ship carp. h. Swan, at rail road crossing.
Prenatt, Elik, weighman, h. Ohio n. Chicago.
Prenett, Sylvester, engineer, h. Elk n. Van Rensselaer.
Presbrey, Carrie J. Miss, teacher, b. O. F. Presbrey.
PRESBREY, OTIS F. M. D. grape grower and vintry and city clerk's office, h. Prospect hill, vintry n. reservoir.—See adv. colored leaf opposite name.
Pressnen, Michael. lab. h. Perry n. Illinois.
Preston, Isaac H. ship carp. h. 226 E. Eagle.
Preston, John R. grocer, h. 194 Seneca.
Preuss, David, tanner, h. 545 Michigan.
Price, Charles, blacksmith, h. N. Wash. cor. Clinton avenue.
Price, Wm. policeman, h. Jeff. n. Swan.
Pride, Darius K. clerk, at Adams & Co. b. Seneca n. Chicago.
Pries, Henry, lab. h. Johnson n. Batavia.
Priest, Ann, widow, boarding house, Moore n. Miami.
Primm, Alexander, moulder, b. cor. Walnut and Batavia.
Primrose, Benj. type dresser, h. 29 Wm.
Prince, Geo. A. firm Geo. A. P. & Co. cor. 7th and Md. h. Niag. cor. Georgia.
PRINCE, GEO. A. & Co. melodeon manuf. 7th cor. Md.—See adv. opp. name.
Prince, John, melodeon maker, with Geo. A. Prince & Co. b. 11 Court.
Prince, Samuel N. with Geo. A. Prince & Co. b. 109 Niagara.
Prince, W. D. carp. h 155 Delaware.
Prine, H. last maker, h. 105 Carroll.
Prins, N. foundryman, at Brayley & Pitts.
Prior, George, milkman, h. 229 N. Division n. Hickory.
Prior, William S. joiner, h. Carroll n. Van Rensselaer.
Pritchard, Thos. joiner, h. Ohio n. Ind.
Probeck, Chs. lab. h. Cherry cor. Spruce.
Probeck, Conrad, mason, h. Jeff. n. Carlton.
Probeck, Henry, blacksmith, h. Brown n. Jefferson alley.
Prochnow, C. A. printer, h. 13 Walnut.
Proepster, John, lab. h. Watson n. Batavia.
Proessels, L. A. saloon, 4 Gen. h. 228 Main.
Proll, Annie M. widow. h. Johnson n. North.
Proll, S. tailor, with Altman & Co.
Prosch, Christoph, shoemaker, h. Locust n. Carroll.
Prosser, Erastus S. vice-pres't International Bank, h. Delaware above Summer.
Prothias & Heron, liquor dealers, 12 Main and 6 Central Wharf.
Prothias, John, firm P. & Heron, 12 Main.
Prouty, James, h. Elk cor. Louisiana.
Prouty, Wallace, lab. h. Ala. n. Elk.

Provoost, Benjamin A. clerk, Marine Bank, h. 114 Niagara.
Provoost, David, firm P. & Newkirk, h. Mich. below Swan.
Provoost, J. P. & Co. sail makers, chequered warehouse, Central Wharf.
Provoost, James P. firm J. P. P. & Co. h. 63 Seneca.
Provoost, J. P. Jr. firm J. P. P. & Co. h. 63 E. Seneca.
Provoost, John S. firm J. P. P. & Co. h. 63 Seneca.
Provoost Milton H. sail maker, cor. Prime and Lloyd, b. Western Hotel.
Provoost & Newkirk, sail loft, foot Lloyd.
Provoost, S. A. sail maker, Prime, h. 145 Niag.
Provoost, Samuel A. Jr. book-keeper, Marine Bank, b. 114 Niagara.
Provoost, Wm. K. firm J. P. P. & Co. h. 128 E. Eagle.
Provoost, Wm T. Lloyd cor. Prime, b. Western Hotel.
Pruchtl, John,* cooper, Batavia cor. Mattison, h. same.
Prumig, Chs. moulder, h. Spruce n. Syc.
Prushaw, Jas. machinist. h. Carolina cor. 5th.
Pryor, Jos. painter, h. Palmer ab. Carolina.
Pullen, Timothy, last maker, b. 111 Carroll.
Pulling, Geo. clerk. 288 Main, b. 13 Court.
Puls, Charles, printer, Commercial Advertiser, b. 98 Goodell.
Puls, Frederick, printer, Commercial Advertiser, b. 98 Goodell.
Puls, John, tailor, h. 98 Goodell.
Punsens, Jacob, porter, h. Spring n. Gen.
Purcel, Michael, Rev. h. Edward opp. Asylum.
Purcell, Henry, prop. New England Hotel, cor. Carroll and Michigan.
Purcell, Mich. lab. h. Folsom n. Kinney's alley.
Purdie, John, foundry, h. 55 N. Division.
Purtill, Jas. mariner, h. Jackson n. Genesee.
Purucker, David, cabinet maker, h. Maple n. High.
Pusse, Ludwig, wagon maker, h. Hickory n. Clinton.
Putnam, Caleb, porter, h. over 96 E. Seneca.
Putnam, George, with Hamlin & Mendsen, b. 10 Boston Block.
Putnam, H. W. boat-house and saloon, ft. Erie, h. 56 Pearl.
Putnam, Lucius, boatman, h. 112 Folsom.
Putnam, Willard A. book-keeper, h. Bonney's Hotel.
Pynshon, L. K. h. Carolina above Palmer.

Q.

Qofi, Adam,* blacksmith, Clinton n. Watson, h. same.
Quackenbush, E. C. boatman, h. Niagara n. Bouck avenue.
Quadlaender, John, peddler, h. Monroe n. Clinton.
Quadlaender, John. tanner, h. Wm. n. Walnut.
Qualey, Stephen, lab. h. Elk n. Michigan.
Qualmann, E. F. shoemaker, b. 15 Pearl.
Quarliegh, John, musician. h. Gen. n. 6th.
Queen City Ice Co. office Main cor. Seneca.

PRINCE & CO.'S

IMPROVED PATENT

MELODEONS

WARRANTED FOR FIVE YEARS.

Our Latest Improvement—Prince & Co.'s GRADUATED SWELL.

This is an entirely new idea ; and its want has been noticed by all acquainted with reed instruments. The old swell could never be made to operate gradually ; the instant the pedal was touched for opening it, the change would be instantaneous and abrupt.

Our New Swell is Constructed on Scientific Principles,

And we are satisfied, by our untiring study and experiment, that it is the only one by which the tone of reed instruments may be graduated from a mere whisper to the full power of the instrument, and vice versa. The volume of tone is also very much increased by this swell, and is now all that we could desire.

We have taken the necessary steps to secure a patent for our improvement, and shall not sell rights to other manufacturers.

This, in connection with our " DIVIDED SWELL " (which we patented in 1855), will be added to all the Melodeons which we manufacture in the future, and without extra charge. Persons unacquainted with the Melodeon and its history, will bear in mind that we are the pioneers and leading manufacturers, not only in the United States, but in the world.

We commenced the manufacture of Melodeons in the fall of the year 1847, and since that time have finished and sold

TWENTY-SEVEN THOUSAND.

These instruments are now in use mostly in the United States and Canada ; but also in Europe, Asia, Africa, South America, and the West Indies ; and from all these quarters we have the most flattering testimonials of the high estimation in which they are held.

At all Industrial Exhibitions they have invariably been awarded the

Highest Premium whenever exhibited in Competition with others.

All Melodeons of our manufacture, either sold by us or dealers in any part of the United States or Canadas, are warranted to be perfect in every respect, and should any repairs be necessary before the expiration of FIVE YEARS from date of sale, we hold ourselves ready and willing to make such repairs free of charge, provided the injury is not caused by accident or design.

GEO. A. PRINCE & CO.

See Advertisement on the other side.

Queen City Mills, Black Rock. pier.
Queen, Patrick, lab. h. Efner alley n. Ellicott.
Quermbach, John, shoemaker, 583 Main.
Quermbach. Jacob. tailor, h. Monroe between William and Peckham.
Quida, John, peddler, h. Cherry n. Jeff.
Quill, Margaret, wid. washer, h. Scott n. Ohio.
Quinlan, Chas. Abbott road. bel. R. R.
Quinlan, M. sailor. h. Fulton n. Alabama.
Quinlan, Thomas, lab. h. La. n. Ohio.
Quinlan, Thos. lab. h. across creek.
Quinn, Catharine, wid. h. across creek.
Quinn, Daniel, lab. h. Otto cor. Alabama.
Quinn, James, carp. h. N. Div. n. Grosvenor.
Quinn, John, sawyer. h. Ohio n. Wabash.
Quinn, Joseph, firm Q. & Forrester, h. 13 10th.
Quinn, Pat. sawyer, h. Ohio below South.
Quinn, Richard, hostler, Franklin House.
Quinn, Wm. lab. h. foot Church.
Quinton, John, lab. h. Blossom n. Amherst.
Quirk, Eliza, widow. h. 50 Sycamore.
Quirk. John, lab. h. Perry n. Mass.
Quirk, Leo, b. 50 Sycamore.
Quirk, Patrick, sawyer, h. across creek.

R.

Raach, Fred. book-binder, h. Maple n. Goodell.
Rabel, John, lab. h. Spruce n. Sycamore.
Rabel, P. J. tailor, 115 Walnut.
Rabas, Andreas, stone cutter, h. Cherry n. Va.
Rackel, Michael. lab. h. Sherman n. Genesee.
Radague, John, carp. h. 28 Scott.
Radagne, Joseph, caulker, h. 28 Scott.
Radcliffe. Stephen M. foreman, Jewett & Root, h. 101 Fulton.
Rader, Wm. clerk, Howard, Whitcomb & Co. b. 51 Exchange.
Rady, Thomas, lab. h. n. round house.
Rae, John, saloon, Elk n. Ohio.
Raeker, August, furniture ware-rooms, Batavia n. Elm, h. same.
Raering, Joseph, carp. h. Milnor n. Arsenal.
Raffle. Conrad. mason, h. 30 Ash.
Ragan, Chs. lab. h. Commercial n. Erie canal.
Ragan, Margaret, widow, Nicholas alley n. Seneca.
Ragan, Thomas, lab. h. Albany n. School.
Ragensburgen, Louis, cooper, Spruce n. Gen. h. 501 Michigan.
Rahm, Daniel C. Mrs. carpet weaver, h. Del. below Allen.
Rahm, George. lab. h. Gray n. Batavia.
Rahm, Geo. Jr. lab. h. Grey n. Batavia.
Raichel, Gottfrey, metal moulder, h. German alley n Genesee.
Raidart, Frank, printer. b. Jeff. n. Batavia.
Raidart, Peter, liquor dealer, h. Jeff. n. Bat.
Railroad House, S. W. Lyons, Ferry cor. Canal.
Rainer, Francis, musician. h. Mich. cor. Cherry.
Rainey, Hamilton, firm R. & Wheeler, 22 Prime, h. 69 E. Eagle.
Rainey & Wheeler, produce and commission merchants, 22 Central Wharf.
Rainforth. M. stone cutter. h. cor. 5th and Pa.
Raleigh, Edward, at Roberts, malt house, h. Delaware n. Ferry.
Ralnig, August, lab. h. Porter n. Van Renssel'r.

Ralph, Edmund S. clerk, S. O. Barnum, h. Ferry n. Main.
Ralph. R. L. builder, h. Huron bel. Morgan.
Ram, Victoria, widow, h. Burton n. Delaware.
Ramacciotte, Fran piano maker, h. 107 Carroll.
Ramage. Geo. tailor, h. 117 Seneca.
Ramage, G. A. b. 117 Seneca.
Ramers, John, teamster, Buffalo Agr. works, h. same.
Rammacher, Wm. at L Holloway's, h. Maple n. Carlton.
Ramsberger. Casper, lab. h. 231 Ellicott.
Ramsdell. Chas. shoe dealer, 214 Main, h. 42 Franklin.
Ramsdell, O. P. firm O. P. R. & Co. h. 84 Delaware.
Ramsdell. O. P. & Co. wholesale shoe dealers, 168 Main.
Ramsdell, Wm. sailor, h. Miami n. Louisiana.
Ramsey, Wm. captain, h. Fulton n. Alabama.
Ran, Michael, lab. h. 9th cor. Carolina.
Rand, Chas. M. sailmaker, firm Franklin & R. h. 201 Swan.
Rand & Felthousen, tinsmiths and coal oil dealers, 115 Main.
Rand, Rose, widow of Chas. h. 142 Eagle.
Randall, Adley, conductor, h. 89 Franklin.
Randall, Chs. clerk, with W. Johnson, b. cor. Main and Carlton.
Randall, Geo. H. at cor. Prime, h. Franklin cor. Tupper.
Randall, M. Union ticket office, 17 Exchange, h. cor. Morgan and Carey.
Randall. Nelson, coroner. over 9 E. Seneca, h. cor. Main and Carlton.
Randall, Volney, boot and shoe store, 78 Main, h. Main cor. Carlton.
Randel, Jessy, farmer, h. Delavan avenue n. Williamsville road.
Rankin. Archibald, stewart. on lake, h. 6 Wm.
Rankin, Francis, clerk, 319 Main, h. St. Paul n. Main.
Rankin, Francis, M. D. h. St. Paul n. Main.
Rankin, Hugh, sailor, h. cor. Perry and Hayward.
Rankin, M. M. com. merch. b. Bonney's.
Ranney, Orville W. salt dealer, 20 Central Wharf, h. 70 E. Swan.
Ranney, Philip, clerk, b. 70 Swan.
Ranschu, C. foundryman, Brayley & Pitts.
Ransom, Amasa R. hat store, 332 Main, h. 197 Swan.
Ransom, E. F. machinist, h. Fulton n. Ala.
Ransom, Giles F. engineer, lake, h. Fulton n. Alabama.
Ransom, John, book-keeper, John Weeks, b. 197 E. Swan.
Ransom, Rudolph, hatter, Tweedy & Smith, h. 197 Swan.
Rapold, Philip, watchman, h. Johnson n. Bat.
Rapp, Catharine, widow, h. Best n. Walden.
Rapp, Joseph, h. Shumway n. Peckham.
Rapp, Michael, lab. h. Washington cor. Burton alley.
Raquet, Louis, carp. h. Sycamore n. Hickory.
Rash. John, lab. h. Batavia n. Lutheran.
Rast, Lorenz,* butcher, h. Batavia cor. Adams.
Ratchen, John, lab. b. 87 Cherry.

Ratcliff, Stephen M. moulder, with Jewett & Root, b. 101 Fulton.
Ratcliffe, Geo. captain, h. Albany n. N. Adams.
Ratel, Jos. engineer, h. 12th n. Massachusetts.
Rath, Casper, milkman, h. Elm n. Burton alley.
Rath, John, ship carp. Moore n. Elk.
Rath, Joseph, shoemaker, h. Walnut n. Wm.
Rathbone, C. E. h. 256 Pearl.
Rathbone, R. W. flour insp. 16 Prime, h. 82 Morgan.
Rathbone, Samuel, h. 212 Franklin.
Rathbone, Samuel H. b. 256 Pearl.
Rathbun, Chas. H. firm Whitmore, R. & Co. h. 81 S. Division.
Rathbun, Chas. L. local ed Post, h. 215 Del.
Rathbun, Frank A. clerk, N. Y. & E. Bank, h. 24 Carroll.
Rathbun, Jos. A. att'y, 334 Main, h. 115 N. Div.
Rathbun, Thomas, office Whitmore, R. & Co. h. 24 Carroll.
Ratman, Edward, with Jewett & Root, h. 6 Maple.
Ratzel, Louis, butcher, h. cor. Sycamore and Walnut.
Rau, Elizabeth, widow, peddler, h. Spruce n. Sycamore.
Rau, John, tailor, h. over 388 Genesee.
Rau, John, cabinet maker, h. Wm. n. Walnut.
Rauert, Chas H. clerk, Chas. Best, h. Washington cor. Virginia.
Rauh, Joseph, peddler, h. Walnut n. Genesee.
Raubenstein, John G. saloon, cor. Lloyd and Canal. h. same.
Rauht, Philip, lab. h. 134 Spring.
Raum, Conrad, carp. h. Boston alley n. Va.
Raum, Erhut, tanner, h. Granger n. Chicago.
Rausch, Erhardt, lab. h. Lemon n. High.
Rausch, Geo. tailor, h. Mortimer n. Genesee.
Rausch, Jacob, grocer, h. Michigan cor. High.
Rausch, Leonard, carpenter, h. cor. Madison and Peckham.
Rauscher, Chas. moulder, h. 207 Elm.
Rauscher, Nicholas, lab. h. 207 Elm.
Rautenstrauch, Geo. cabinet maker, h. 159 Bat.
Ravels, Henry, saloon, cor. Oak and Batavia, h. same.
Rawley, Michael, lab. h. Exch n. Hamburgh.
Ray, A. M. widow, h. Virginia n. Carolina.
Ray, J. carpenter, b. N. Division n. Watson.
Ray, John, boarding, cor. Elk and Mississippi.
Ray, John, brick maker, h. Batavia beyond tollgate.
Ray, Thomas, machinist, b. 199 Exchange.
Ray, Thomas S. machinist, Buff. Steam Gauge Co. h. 286 Franklin.
Raymond, George, blacksmith, h. Dearborn n. Austin.
Raynolds, James, lab. h. 4th n. Georgia.
Raynor, Augustus, h. 273 Washington.
Raynor, C. A. book-keeper, Wm. H. Glenny, b. 305 Michigan.
Raze, Ansel S. h. 126 Swan.
Raze, Julina S. widow of Joel S. h. N. Canal n. R. R. crossing.
Reacher, Fred. F. sailor, h. Pratt n. Genesee.
Read, Elizabeth, widow, h. 38 E. Genesee.
Read, Elizabeth, Miss, b. 38 E. Genesee.
Read, J. J. P. h. 38 E. Genesee.

Read, Jas. carp. h. Pratt n. Eagle.
Read, Peter A. ship carpenter, b. 193 Exch.
Read, Wil'd S. foreman, M. Clor, h. 276 S- Div.
Read, Wm. foreman, O'Conner's ship-yard, h. Elk cor. Hayward.
Reader, Jane, Mrs. h. over 423 Main.
Ready, Martin, lab. h. Ohio n. Elk.
Ready, Thos. lab. b. Martin Ready.
Reaman, Francis H. grocer, cor. Clinton and Union. h. same.
Reaman, Geo. A. mason, h. 101 r. Clinton.
Reaman, John, lab. h. 103 Clinton.
Reardon, Daniel, lab. h. Mississippi n. Ohio.
Reardon, Hannah, widow, h. ac. creek.
Reardon, John, clerk, G. R. Wilson & Co. h. S. Sullivan.
Reardon, Mary, Mrs. boarding, h. 40 Oak.
Reber, Chas. tanner, h. Seneca n. junc. Swan.
Reber, Henry, lab. b. C. Schule.
Reber, Jacob, lab. h. Bennett n. Batavia.
Reber, John, milkman, h. Adams n. William.
Rebstock, Constantine, butcher, Niagara n. Hamilton.
Rebstock, Elias, book binder, h. 375 Wash.
Rebstock, Elizabeth, Mrs. dress maker, h. 375 Washington.
Rebstock, F. teamster, h. Dearborn n. Hamil'n.
Rechtenwald, Nicholas, Eagle Furnace, h. Pratt n. William.
Recktenwald, John, lab b. Milnor n. William.
Recktenwalt, Peter, flour dealer, cor. Bat. and Michigan, h. Milnor n. arsenal.
Recktewalt, Theresa, b. Milnor n. William.
Rector, W. D. mach'ist. N. Wash. n. Clint ave.
Redittberg, August, blacksmith, h. 255 Oak.
Redline, M. musician. h. Camp n. Sycamore.
Redlein, Geo. h. r. 160 Oak.
Redmond, Garrett, lab. Bidwell's ship yard, h. n. toll bridge.
Reeb, Adam, tailor, h. Genesee n. Michigan.
Reed, Ellen, Mrs. h. Pratt n. Eagle.
Reed, Gottfrey, shoemaker. b. L. Buehl.
Reed, Jas. carpenter, h. Main n. Bryant.
Reed, Margaret, widow, h. across creek.
Reed, Simeon R. gardener, h. 8 Chestnut.
Reed, Victoria, seamstress, h. 11 William.
Reed, Wm. carp. h. Hayward n. Fulton.
Reed, Wm. lab. b. Ohio n. R. R. track.
Reed, Wm. lab. h. Potter n. William.
Reebl, Wm. clerk, 220 Main, b. 571 Wash.
Reop, Christian, baker. b. r. 140 Genesee.
Rees, E. H. h. Washington ab. Carlton.
Reese. Geo. printer, 5 W. Seneca, h. 5 Boston Block.
Reese, Geo. W. printing office, 5 W. Seneca, h. 5 Boston Block.
Reese, Maria, teacher No 10, b. 5 Boston Bl'k.
Reeve, John, machinist, Carroll n. Ala.
Reeve, Wm. on lake, h. 8 Scott.
Reeves, Albert Z. printer, b. 25 Pearl.
Reeves, Chas. steamboat insp'r, h. 1 N. Pearl.
Reeves, Elizabeth, widow, h. 10th n. Md.
Reeves, Walter, sailor, h. Elk n. Louisiana.
Reffel, August, carp. h. Amherst n. Thomp.
Reffert, Fred. lab. h. Mich. n. Carlton.
Regan, Olney, lab. h. Elk n. Michigan.
Regelie, I. F. Chr. lab. h. 57 Cedar.
Regenauer, Catharine, wid. h. Pine n. Wm.

Regier, Henry, baker, h. r. 140 Genesee.
Regner, Xavier. tailor, h. Wm. n. Adams.
Rehbaum, Albert, blacksmith, h. Boston alley n. Tupper.
Rehbaum, Fred. blacksmith, h. Walnut n. Bat.
Rehbaum, Fred. lab. h. Walnut n. William.
Rehbaum, Julius, h. Walnut n. Batavia.
Rehberg. August, blacksmith, h. 255 Oak.
Rehm, Henry, butcher, 190 Niagara, h. same.
Rehm, Jacob, farmer. h. Utica cor. R. I.
Rehming, Mary, widow. h. Milnor n. Batavia.
Rehorn, Martin, shoemaker, Seneca n. junction Swan.
Rehorn, Peter, shoemaker, Exch. n. Van. Rensselaer.
Reibold, Chr.* shoemaker, Gen. n. Spring, h. same.
Reibold, Henry, lab. h. Genesee n. Mortimer.
Reice, Casper, lab. h. Ash n. Genesee.
Reicher, Constantine, lab. 5 Iron place, N.Wash.
Reichert, Andrew, shoemaker, h. Burton alley n. Elm.
Reichert, Barbara, widow, h. 8 Huron.
Reichert, Jacob, tailor. h. Boston alley n. Tup.
Reichert, Jno. butcher, h. Goodell cor. Elm.
Reichert, Geo. saloon, Ellicott n. Chip. h. same.
Reichert, Jacob, Batavia plank road n. Williamsville road.
Reichert, Jno. shoemaker, h. Locust n. Cherry.
Reichert, L. P. book-keeper, J. C. Jewett, 31 Main. b. 8 Huron.
Reichert, Wm. carp. h. East n. Parish.
Reichhold, Jno. lab. h. Johnson n. Genesee.
Reichle, Chs. engineer, h. 169 Clinton.
Reichle, Jno. painter, h. Clinton cor. Pratt.
Reichman, Fr. Joseph,* shoemaker, h. Syca. n. Ash.
Reichmann, R. shoemaker. h. 13 Sycamore.
Reid, Jno. book-keeper, 9 Water, b. Mansion.
Reid, Robt. shoemaker, Goodell all. n. Goodell.
Reid, Robt. Jr. with Turner Bros. b. Goodell alley n. Goodell.
Reid, Wm. book-keeper, D. Bell, f. 181 Terrace.
Reid, Wm. gardener, h. Niagara n. Georgia.
Reidel, Adam, lab. h. Genesee n. Johnson.
Reider, Christ. lab. h. Dearborn n. Austin.
Reidpath, Robert D. clerk, 1 E. Seneca, h. 297 Seneca.
Reidshau, Thos. miller, h. Parish n. Tona.
Reif. Anthony, saw maker, 222 Washington, h. Ellicott ab. Goodell.
Reif, Chs. carp. b. Delaware n. North.
Reif, Jos. h. 316 Ellicott.
Reifier, Jacob, carp. h. Spring n. Clinton.
Reigle, Jno. ship carp. h. Adams n. Peckham.
Reil, Jno.* butcher, Bat. n. Monroe, h. same.
Reil, Michael, lab. h. Mulberry n. High.
Reil, Franz, lab. h. Locust n. North.
Reilin. Henry. ship carp. h. 123 Genesee.
Reiling, Catharine, widow, h. 380 Genesee.
Reiley, F. lab. b. 160 Exchange.
Reilly, James, book-keeper, Republic office, h. York n. 12th.
Reilly, John G. cutter, 27 Main, h. Ontario.
Reilly, T. C. prop. R.'s Bazaar, 228 Main, h. 9 Niagara.
Reily, Jas. saloon, under Revere House.
Reily, Thos. lab. h. 67 Cedar.

Reily, Thos. policeman, h. 117 Cedar.
Reim, Adam, barber, h. 27 Exchange.
Reiman, Chs. lab. h. ov. 13 German alley.
Reiman, Chs. blacksmith, h. Bennett n. Wm.
Reiman, Jos. h. Ash n. Batavia.
Reiman, Philip, wagon maker,Wm. n. Hickory.
Reiman, S. carp. h. 2 Bennett.
Reimann, Gottfrey, lab. h. 13 German alley.
Reimann, Henry, shoemaker, h. 7 Water.
Reimann, Jacob, carp. h. Hickory n. Clinton.
Reimber, Chris. brewer, h. Wash. n. Virginia.
Reinauer, Bonifacius, carp. h. Madison n. Wm.
Reinecke, Fred. printer, Baker's Block, Genesee square, h. same.
Reinecke, Ottomar, printer, b. Fred. Reinecke.
Reinfaltner, E. h. Grape n. High.
Reinhagel, Geo. moulder, h. 207 S. Division.
Reinhard, Adam, piano maker, h. Mortimer n. William.
Reinhard, John R. picture frames and looking glasses, 403 Main, h. 114 Hickory.
Reinhard, Jno. lab. h. 112 Cedar.
Reinhardt, Berdiey, with H. Hitchler, cooper, h. 133 Spring.
Reinhardt, Christian, works Coml. Adv. b. Gen. cor. Mortimer.
Reinhardt, Daniel, tailor, h. Syca. n. Pratt.
Reinhardt, Fred. shoemaker, h. Walnut n. Va.
Reinhardt, Geo. J. saloon, 423 Main, h. same.
Reinhardt, Geo. A. grocer, Gen. cor. Morgan.
Reinhardt, Henry, stone cutter, h. Spruce n. Batavia.
Reinhardt, Henry, lab. h. Adams n. Sycamore.
Reinhardt, Jacob, lab. h. Best n. Main.
Reinhardt, Jacob, cap maker, 161 Main, h. 376 Genesee.
Reinhardt, Jno.* bakery, 156 Syc. h. same.
Reinhardt, Peter. cap maker, h. Carlton n. Jeff.
Reinhardt, Peter, policeman, 212 Genesee.
Reinhardt, P. J. brewer, h. 295 Genesee.
Reinhardt, Simon, tailor, h. Hickory n. Gen.
Reinhart, Chas. clothing store, 51 Genesee, h. same.
Reinheimer, Geo. stone cutter, Best n. Elm.
Reinig, C. widow, h. Genesee E. toll gate.
Reinig. Geo. ship carp. h. Wm. n. Jefferson.
Reining, Geo. h. Genesee n. toll gate.
Reining, John, shoemaker, 2 Commercial.
Reinlander. Jacob, basket maker, h. Lemon n. Virginia.
Reinlander, Peter, basket maker, h. Lemon n. Virginia.
Reinmund. Geo. lab. h. Shumway n. Batavia.
Reippel, Peter, carp. h. Walnut n. Batavia.
Reis, Andrew, carp. h. 562 Michigan.
Reis, Geo. brewer, b. L. Roth's brewery.
Reis, Henry, tailor, h. 105 Pine.
Reischel, Wm. cab maker, h. 202 Genesee.
Reiser, Caroline, widow, h. 10 Walnut.
Reiser, Charles, clerk, h. 10 Walnut.
Reiser, Joseph, shoemaker, h. 158 Genesee.
Reish, Thos. lab. h. Porter n. Bouck avenue.
Reiter, Frederick, lab. h. Watson n. Wm.
Reiter, Jacob, with J. & G. Fisher, 74 E. Gen.
Reiter, Roland, h. William n. Cedar.
Reith, Geo. brewer, b. Efner's brewery.
Reitz. Frederick, carp. b. 23 Ash.
Reitz, John, G. tailor, h. Hickory n. William.

Reitz, Peter. musician, h. Cypress n. Michigan.
Relf, Edward, saloon, 285 Main, h. same.
Relf, Geo. saloon, 198 Seneca, h. same.
Relf, Matilda, Mrs. 285 Main.
Relf, Perry. saloon, 285 Main. h. same.
Relph, Andrew, h. Main S. of toll gate.
Relph, Jesse,* brick maker, h. Genesee E. toll gate.
Remis, Michael, moulder, h. 46 Bennett.
Remlinger, Geo. peddler, b. Wm. cor. Pine.
Rendecker, Kate, seamstress, h. 128 Clinton.
Rendell, A. G. B. clerk, cor. Ellicott and Seneca, b. 303 E. Seneca.
Rendell, Elias D. R. manager, W. M. C. Ass. h. 303 E. Seneca.
Rendell, E. D. R. Jr. machinist, b. 303 E. Sen.
Rendla, John, rope maker, h. 124 Genesee.
Renker, Conrad, sawyer, b. Keane n. Genesee.
Renner, Leonhardt, lab. h. Peach n. High.
Renner, G. firm R. & Co. h. 128 Elm.
Renner, G. & Co. tailors, 281 Main.
Renning, Chas. tailor, h. Mich. n. Burton alley.
Renowden, Wm. clerk, b. 186 S. Division.
Rensler, David, blacksmith, h. 38 Bennett.
Renwick, Ralf. firm Carr & R. 354 Main, h. Mariner n. Virginia.
Renz, Matthias, merchant tailor, 172 Batavia, h. same.
Reoder, Antomy, grocer, Niagara n. School, h. same.
Resch, Henry, cooper, h. East n. R. R.
Reschlo, Jno. lab. h. N. Div. n. Grosvenor.
Resp, Philip, lab. h. Farmer n. East.
Retel, Caspar, M. D. h. 96 Pine.
Retel, John, turner. h. Adams n. Batavia.
Retel, John, M. D. Genesee n. Jeff. h. same.
Rettel, Mart. Pratt iron works. h. East n. Berry.
Retlang, Geo. lab. Carlton n. Seneca.
Retman, Adam. carpenter. h. 404 Michigan.
Rettig, M. lab. h. Sycamore n. Keane.
Reuling, Christian, shoemaker, h. 119 Genesee.
Reuling, Henry, carp. h. 140 Genesee.
Reus, Siegfried, h. Mortimer cor. Hickory.
Reuschling, Chris. h. Sycamore n. Keane.
Reuter, John, tailor, h. 28 Union.
Repeau, Henry, tanner. h. 2 Vine.¶
Repp, And. mason. h. Sycamore n. Spring.
Revie, Jno. lab. h. Genesee n. toll gate.
Rey, John, stone mason, h. Watson n. Batavia.
Reynolds, A. firm A. R. & Co. h. 223 Delaware.
Reynolds, A. & Co. groceries and drugs, 155 and 157 Main, and Wash. cor. Seneca.
Reynolds, Cha. miller, h. Dearbon n. Hamilton.
Reynolds, Cornelius, miller, h. 77 Church.
Reynolds, David S. constable, h. 318 S. Div.
Reynolds, Homer B. saloon, Chippewa opp. market, h. same.
Reynolds, H. H. electrician, 4 W. Swan, h. same.
Reynolds, Jno. mason, h. 7th n. Pennsylvania.
Reynolds, Lynus, dep. sheriff, h. 320 S. Div.
Reynolds, Sarah, wid. grocer, Staats cor. Court.
Rhall, James, cartman, h. cor. Va. and Court.
Rheinbold, Hennan, clerk, 432 Main, b. 96 Chippewa.
Rheinhardt, Philip, grocer, 72 W. Tupper.
Rhinhardt, Jacob, cap maker, Gen. n. Jeff.
Rhinbart, Fred. shoemaker. h. Maple n. Va.
Rhoads, Adam. lab. h. Jefferson n. William.

Rhobacker, Henry, lab. Exchange n. Michigan.
Rhode, Christian, lab. h. Ash n. Sycamore.
Ribbel & Cowan, merchant tailors, 257 Main.
Ribbel, Charles A. firm R. & Cowan, h. 83 W. Tupper.
Ribbel, Jacob, tailor, h. 49 Spruce.
Ribbell, Jacob, lab. h. Walnut n. William
Ribbling, B. b. Spruce n. Sycamore.
Rice, Alondrew, b. cor. Genesee and Walden.
Rice, Chas. gardener, h. Delaware n. Barker.
Rice, Chas. turner. b. 138 N. Division.
Rice, Chas. B. roofer. h. 154 9th.
Rice, Daniel S. carriage manufacturer. 296 Seneca, h. 138 N. Division.
Rice, Franklin H. blacksmith. b. 138 N. Div.
Rice, Geo. painter. h. 136 N. Division.
Rice, Harlow, tavern, Genesee n. Walden.
Rice, J. G. b. 29 Swan.
Rice, John, capt. h. 44 W. Tupper.
Rice, Victor M. h. 195 7th.
Rice, Wm. teacher, h. Washington n. High.
Rice W. G. carriage maker, b. 138 N. Division.
Rich, Andrew J. pres't Bank Attica, h. cor. Main and Tupper.
Rich, Ed. S. firm Manchester & R. h. North n. Delaware.
Rich, G. B. h. Main cor. Barker.
Rich, Geo. F. h. cor. Exchange and Wash.
Richard, Geo. cloth manuf. h. Niag. n. Amh'st.
Richard, Jno. tallyman N. Y. & E. R. R. h. Sycamore n. Michigan.
Richards, J. I. M. D. 148 Main. h. 4 Morgan.
Richards, Nancy A. Mrs. h. Oak n. High.
Richards, Nancy, Miss. teacher, b. Oak n. High.
Richards, Nettie A. Miss. teacher, b. Oak n. High.
Richardson, Dyre, carpenter, b. 502 Wash.
Richardson, E. K. capt. police No. 2, h. N. Canal n. R. R.
Richardson, E. engineer. b. Courier.
Richardson, G. at G. S. Hazard & Co. h. 14 7th.
Richardson, M. D. printer, h. 14 7th.
Richardson, Marshall, ship carp. h. 39 Del. pl.
Richardson, Robt. mariner, h. cor. Pa. and 7th.
Richardson, Rufus, painter, h. 502 Washington.
Richardson, S. B. furniture dealer, 5 Quay. h. Ferry n. Niagara.
Richardson, Wm. E. student, b. 14 7th.
Richardson, Wm. h. Bird ave. n. Washington.
Richardson, Wm. machinist, h 233 Seneca.
Richert, Geo. builder, h. 301 Ellicott.
Richey. Wm. clerk, Howard, Whitcomb & Co. h. 50 N. Division.
Richlieu, John, painter, h. Clinton n. Jeff.
Richmond, Chas. shoemaker, b. cor. Ohio and Indiana.
Richmond, Dean, office ft. Mich. b. American.
Richmond, Henry, b. American Hotel.
Richmond, J. M. com. merch. Ohio n. Mich. b. American.
Richmond, Lewis, shoemaker, b. cor. Ohio and Indiana.
Richmond, W. T. com. merch. h. North cor. Delaware.
Richtemann, Henry, carp. h. Johnson n. Bat.
Richter, Augustus, dress maker, h. Syc. n. Ash.
Richter, August, hatter. Sycamore cor. Ash.
Richterbaum, Francis, lab. h. Syc. n. Walnut.

Richterbolz, Conrad. cooper, h. 93 Cherry.
Richwald, David, clerk, 138 Main. b. 36 Exch.
Rick, John, watchman, h. 127 Pine.
Rick, Peter, carp. h. Niagara n. Austin.
Ricker, Martin, lab. h. Walnut n. Batavia.
Rickerd, Geo. H. Niagara st. R. R. h. E. Bennett n. Clinton.
Rickert, Fred. saloon, River n. bridge, h. same.
Rickert, Geo. saloon, 311 Ellicott.
Rickert, John, cooper, h. Amherst n. Tonaw'da.
Rickhard, Thos. sailor, b. N. Div. n. Jefferson.
Riddle, Henry S. engineer, h. 44 W. Huron.
Rider, John, lab. h. 32 Union.
Rider, John A. ship carp. h Elk n. R. R.
Riebercamb, John, baker, cor. Goodell and Mulberry, b. same.
Riebling, A. H. clerk, 211 Main, h. 320 Main.
Riebling, Burkhard. lab. h. Pratt n. Batavia.
Riebling, Conrad, tailor, b. 20 Pratt.
Riebling, J. B. clerk, 406 Main, h. 120 Pratt.
Rieblinger, Jos.* vinegar manuf. 320 E. Gen. h. same.
Riedel, John, carp. b. Adams n. Batavia.
Riedeman, Fred. lab. h. 15 Cypress.
Riedman, J. H. mason, b. 15 Cypress.
Riedl, John M. cooper, h. Locust n. North.
Riedy, John, grocer, Perry n Red Jacket.
Riedy, Pat. lab. b. Perry n. R. R. track.
Rieffenstahl & Bro. druggists, 396 Main.
Rieffenstahl, Julius, druggist, firm R. & Bro. h. 361 Michigan.
Riefler, John C.* shoemaker, 86 Eagle, h. 353 Michigan.
Riehl, Christ. lab. cor. Phillips and Military road.
Riehl, Frederick, grocer, cor. William and Lutheran, h. same.
Riehl, Geo. gardener, h. 571 Washington.
Riehl, John, peddler, h. Genesee n. Johnson.
Riehl, Philip, cooper, b. Genesee n. Johnson.
Rieman, F. H. Clinton House, cor. Watson and Clinton.
Rieman, Jacob, joiner, h. Hickory n. Clinton.
Rieman, Louis, wagon maker, h. Hickory n. Clinton.
Ries, John, shoemaker, h. 14 Bennett.
Ries, Jos. grocer, 398 Michigan, h. same.
Ries, Sarah, wid. h. 161 Batavia.
Riester, Catharine, widow, saloon, 585 Wash. cor. Burton alley, h. same.
Riester, Fernando J. glass stainer, b. Wash. cor. Burton alley.
Riesz, Frederick, h. 173 Batavia.
Riexinger, Thos. grocer, Elk n. Columbia.
Riger, John, lab. b. Maple n. Virginia.
Riggs, W. H. mess'ger, Am. Ex. Co. h. 11 6th.
Riggs, William, lab. h. 100 Fulton.
Ril, Mathias, lab. h. r. 186 Genesee.
Rilander, Joseph, lab. h. Raze n. Clinton.
Riley, Arabella, widow, h. Main n. Barker.
Riley, C. lab. h. across creek.
Riley, Ellen, wid. h. across creek.
Riley, James, blacksmith, h. Huron n. Ellicott.
Riley, John, hackman, Peddler's al. n. Seneca.
Riley, John C. tailor, Ontario n. Tonawanda.
Riley. John, sailor, h. Georgia n. 6th.
Riley, Mary, widow, h. Court n. Terrace.
Riley, Michael, saloon, 12 Canal.
16

Riley, Patrick, lab. h. 9th n. Carolina.
Riley, Pat. peddler, b. 104 Carroll.
Riley, Thos. grocer, h. 238 Seneca.
Riley, Thos. lab. h. Iron place, N. Washington.
Riley, Thos. b. 56 6th.
Rims, Geo. lab. h. Best n. Ellicott.
Rinck, B.* rope maker, Williamsville road n. Genesee.
Rindfusz, Henry, lab. h. Best n. Walden.
Ring. John. lab. h. Louisiana n. South.
Ring, Wm. M. D. h. 4 Boston Block, Niagara.
Ringer, A. veterinary surgeon, h. Ferry n. Jeff.
Ringer, Chas. mason. h. Ferry n. Jefferson.
Ringleben. Adam, cooper, h. Parish n. Thoms'n.
Rink, William, printer, h. Genesee n. Davis.
Rinker, Bernhardt, lab. h. Peckham n. Stanton.
Rinkert, Andrew, tanner, h. 338 Genesee.
Ripont, Fred. J. finisher. h. 531 Michigan.
Ripont, Jas. wood dealer, 81 Batavia, h. same.
Ripont, Peter, grocer, h. 81 Batavia.
Rippel, Jacob, grocer, 260 Genesee, h. same.
Ripstock, Stephen, cooper, Niagara n. Bird.
Ripthomer, H. b. Hickory cor. Clinton.
Risch, Casper, lab. h. Spring n. Sycamore.
Risch. Mary. wid. h. Spring n. Sycamore.
Rischar, John, lab. h. Elm n. Best.
Rister, Geo. lab. h. Fox n. Genesee.
Ritchie, H. B. railroad agent, h. 163 Franklin.
Ritchie, Martha. Miss, dressmaker, 45 Church.
Ritchie, Mary, Mrs. widow, h. 45 Church.
Riding, Jos. mason, h. Best cor. Ellicott.
Ritt, Gregory, firm R. & Hoffner, h. 131 Ellicott.
Ritt, M. L. firm Gardner, R. & Fox, b. 236 Ellicott.
Ritt, Nicholas, tailor, h. 216 Batavia.
Ritter, Charles, carp. h. Park ab. Allen.
Ritter, Felix, pattern maker. h. 107 Cedar.
Ritter, Frank, h. Eagle bel. Michigan.
Ritter, Fred. cabinet maker, h. 105 Cedar.
Ritter, Fred. lab. h. Watson n. William.
Ritter, Geo. tailor, h. Carlton n. Jefferson.
Ritter, Henry, painter, h. 145 Batavia.
Ritter, John, tinsmith, h. Union n. Clinton.
Ritter, Louis, tanner, h. Carroll n. Van Renss.
Ritter, Philip, Jr. boiler maker, b. Mary n. Ill.
Ritter, Wm. boiler maker. h. Mary n. Ill.
Rittmeier, Andrew, mason, h. Monroe n. Wm.
Rivers, Jos. peddler, b. 2 Centre.
Rivers, Martin. moulder. b. Miller's Block, Mich.
Rizer, Henry, lab. h. S. Div. bel. R. R. crossing.
Roach, Jas. joiner. h. Louisiana n. Perry.
Roach, Jas. lab. h. cor. Perry and Mississippi.
Roach, John, cartman, h. Virginia n. 6th.
Roach, Martin, lab. h. Michigan n. Ohio.
Roach, Michael, saloon, foot Erie, h. same.
Roach, Mrs. widow, h. 13th n. Connecticut.
Roach, Rich. cooper, b. Perry cor. Hamburgh.
Roan, Wm. mariner, h. 185 Terrace.
Roath, Ira, William n. Cedar.
Roauer, John, lab. h. Madison n. Batavia.
Robb, David, moulder, h. 10th n. Connecticut.
Robbins, Edwin C. attorney, with Geo. B. Hibbard, b. Mansion.
Robbins. E. H. Mrs. h. 132 6th.
Robbins. J. B. bowling saloon, 8 Commercial.
Robert. Christian, saddler, h. Goodell alley ab. Tupper.
Robert, Jos. lab. h. Oak n. Goodell.

Robert, Louisa, wid. h. 87 Watson n. Peckham.
Roberts, David, lab. h. Burwell place n Scott.
Roberts, Elijah, firm E. R. & Co. h. 9 Carroll.
ROBERTS, E. & CO. printer's warehouse, 49 E. Seneca.—*See adv. p. 70.*
Roberts, H. C. with R. C. Palmer & Co. h. 75 Hickory.
Roberts, Jas. sailor, h. Carolina n. 4th.
Roberts, J. saw maker, 222 Washington, h. 6th n. Pennsylvania.
Roberts, John B. painter, h. Elk n. Smith.
Roberts, J. D. malt house, Franklin cor. Allen, h. Allen cor. Delaware.
Roberts, Lewis, sailor, h. 10th n. Mass.
Roberts, Michael, grocer, Martin's Corners.
Roberts, S. A. clerk, Barrows & Co. h. Cottage n. Virginia.
Roberts, Thos. Elk st. market, h. Fulton cor. Chicago.
Roberts, Wm. C. firm E. R. & Co. b. 9 Carroll.
Robertson, A. farmer, h. Seneca n. toll bridge.
Robertson, G. W. hat store, 292 Main, h. 353 Franklin cor. Virginia.
Robertson, Jas. F. foreman B. E. I. W. h. Perry.
Robertson, Samuel, b. Revere.
Robertson, Wm. attorney, cor. Main and Lloyd, h. Abbott road.
Robertson, Wm. Jr. weighman, b. Seneca n. Chicago.
Robie, John E. editor Christian Advocate, Seneca cor. Pearl, h. Niagara n. Auburn.
Robin, F. S. firm Troutman & R. h. Clinton cor.. Jefferson.
Robin, Henry, shoemaker. h. Maple n. Carlton.
Robinet, Elizabeth, h. Parish n. East.
Robinson, A. firm R. & Co. h. Main cor. Riley.
Robinson, Amelia, b. J. Robinson.
Robinson, Chas. tel'gh operator, b. 35 E. Swan.
Robinson. Chas. fireman. b. Revere.
Robinson, Christ. blacksmith, b. Jno. Robinson.
Robinson, C. J. b. Western.
Robinson, Cynthia, Mrs. servant, 50 Sycamore.
Robinson, & Co. bankers, 182 Main.
Robinson. E. Miss, b. Batavia n. Walnut.
Robinson, Geo. lab. h. 447 Michigan.
Robinson, Jas. V. painter, h. Bat. n. Walnut.
Robinson, Jno lab. Iron place, N. Washington.
Robinson, Jno. Jr. blacksmith, b. with J. Robinson Sr.
Robinson, John, blacksmith, Ferry n. Main, h. same.
Robinson, Jos. ship carp. b. 4th n. Geo.
Robinson, Jos. blacksmith, h. Evans n. Canal.
Robinson Mary Ann, dressmaker, b. Batavia n. Walnut.
Robinson, M. L. supt. N. St. R. R. Co. h. 5th n. Hudson.
Robinson, Robt. blacksmith, b. Ferry n. Main.
Robinson, Sidney M. paper hanger, h. Batavia n. Walnut.
Robinson, Wm. h. 5th n. Carolina.
Robinson, Wm. M. D. office 2 Exchange up stairs, h. 53 Ellicott.
Robinson, Wm. M. D. office cor. Washington and Exchange, b. 53 Ellicott.
Robinson, Wm. blacksmith, LeCouteulx n. Canal, h. 227 Carroll.
Robinson, Wm. blacksmith, h. Butler n. Del.

Robinson, Wm. lab. h. Peugeot n. White's Cor. plank road.
Robinson, Wm. joiner, h. 202 S. Division.
Robinson, Wm. D. capt. marine inspector, Home Insurance Co. h. Terrace n. Church.
Robinson, Wm. F. saloon keeper, cor. Indiana and Ohio, h. same.
Robson, Arch. carp. b. cor. Watson and Howard.
Robson, J. O. gunmaker and jeweler, 111 Main, h. 121 S. Division.
Robson, Robt foreman gas works, h. 25 Jackson
Roby, Jas. lumber dealer and forwarder. h. 162 Pearl.
Roch, Dennis, sailor, h. 3 Scott.
Roch, Nicholas, saddler, h. 71 Genesee.
Roche, James. b. Oak n. High.
Roche, John, h. 2 W. Genesee.
Roche, John, cartman, h. 6th n. Virginia.
Roche, Owen, music dealer, h. 119 Franklin.
Rocheleau, Louis, engineer, h. Jeff. cor. Swan.
Rochester, Thos. F. M. D. 9 Court, h. same.
Rochte, Christ. lab. h. Ash n. Sycamore.
Rock, James, sailor, b. 5th n. Carolina.
Rockenbach, M. Mrs. wid. washer, h. 112 Pine.
Rocker, Louis, carp. h. Monroe n. Batavia.
Rockwell, Aug. artist, ov. 266 Main, h. 73 Eagle.
Rockwell. Fred. S. Am. Ex. office, h. Ga. n. 6th.
Rockwell, John M. firm G. B. Bull & Co. hardware merch'ts, 95 Main, h. 117 N. Division.
Rockwell, J. J. clerk, h. 311 Washington.
Rockwell, Richard W. tinsmith, b. 117 N. Div.
Rockwell, S. D. printer, firm R. & Baker, h. 16 E. Eagle.
Rode, Christian, lab. h. Ash n. Sycamore.
Rodenbach, John, book-binder, with J. M. Johnson, h. Pine n. William.
Rodenbach, Louis, baker, h. cor. William and Hickory.
Rodenberger, Fred. shoemaker, h. Ash n. Syc.
Rodger, Mary A. widow, h. 65 Ellicott.
Rodgers, Daniel, captain, b. 64 Court.
Rodgers, Edwin, clerk, with Hamlin & Mendsen, b. 44 Virginia.
Rodgers, John, cooper, h. Dearborn n. Austin.
Rodney, Chas. H. plumber, firm R. & Son, b. 10 Court.
Rodney, John, firm R. & Son. h. 110 9th.
Roe, John, ship carp. h. across creek.
Roe, Peter, ship carp. b. across creek.
Roeber, Frederika, widow, r. 536 Michigan.
Roeceloin, Geo. ash peddler, h. Lemon n. High.
Roeder, Chs. carp. h. Adams n. Peckham.
Roeder, Frank, lab. h. Adams n. Peckham.
Roeder. Jacob, clerk, 400 Main, b. cor. Clinton and Elm.
Roehner, Adam, shoemaker, h. 266 Elm.
Roehner, Frank, tailor, h. 50 Walnut.
Roehrer, John G. shoemaker, h. Main n. North.
Roelmer, Magdalena, widow, h. Pine n. Cypress.
Roemer, Elizabeth, widow, h. Watson n. Wm.
Roemer. Geo. b. 47 Genesee.
Roemhild, Geo. lab. h. Johnson n. Batavia.
Roesch, Geo. wagoner, Clinton n. Watson, b. same.
Roesch, John. lab. b. Michigan n. Carlton.
Roesch, Peter. lab. h. Lutheran n. Batavia.
Roeschman, Jos. rag peddler, h. Ellicott n. Dodge.

Roeser, Geo. brewer, 219 Oak.
Roesler, Wm. joiner, h. 12 Potter.
Roessel, Augustus, butcher, 10 Court st. market. h. 85 Batavia.
Roessel, Chs. peddler, h. 120 Pratt.
Roessel, Henry. carp. h. Williamsville road cor. Batavia plank road.
Roessel, Jacob, cigar maker, 12 E. Seneca, b. Seneca cor. Washington. ●
Roetling. Geo. blacksmith, h. Carlton n. Lemon.
Roettlingshoefer, John, baker, h. Genesee n. Adams.
Roffo, John, grocer, 5 Canal, h. same.
Rogentine, Henry, teamster, with I. D. White, h. Cherry n. Goodell.
Rogers, Alex. exp. mess. h. 75 Clinton.
Rogers & Bowen, lawyers, Erie cor. Pearl.
Rogers, Bradley D. prod. mer. b. 126 S. Div.
Rogers, Franklin, b. 39 N. Division.
Rogers, Fred. book-keeper, cor. Washington and Perry. h. 5 Carolina.
Rogers, H. W. firm R. & Bowen, h. Delaware cor. Tracy.
Rogers, Jane, widow, saloon, 2 Peacock.
Rogers, J. foreman, H M. Gaylord. b 73 Clinton.
Rogers, Laura Ann, widow of Edwin, h. 44 Virginia.
Rogers, Sherman S. att'y, 223 Main, h. 357 Franklin.
Rogers, Vincent, farmer, Main n. Buff. Plains.
Rogers, Wm. F., Col. N. Y. S. V. M. h. 39 N. Division.
Rogers, Wm. engineer, N. Y. C. R. R. b. Nat. Hotel.
Rohe, Peter J. h. 137 Eagle.
Rohe, Peter, h. Gen. cor. Williamsville road.
Rohr, John. tailor, Erie cor. Terrace, h. 38 Batavia n. Elm.
Rohrbacher, Gregory, h. 7 Cypress.
Rohrbacher, John F. shoemaker, b. 75 Ellicott.
Rohrback, John W. clerk. b. 99 Swan.
Rohman, Jno. butcher, b. cor. Elm and Clint'n.
Rohut, Wm. lab. h. 6 Michigan.
Rolandt, John, lab. h. North n. Michigan.
Rolf, August, cabinet maker, 112 Batavia.
Rolf, Edw'd, tailor, h. Hickory n. Batavia.
Roll, A. tailor, 27 Seneca, h. 38 Watson.
Rollant, Frank. teamster, h. Dodge n. Main.
Roller, B. grocer, h. 183 Batavia.
Roller, David, painter, h. Sherman n. Genesee.
Roller, Wm. boiler maker, h. Miami cor. Ala.
Rollin, Frank. baker, h. Hickory bet William and Clinton.
Rollins, Ellen, widow, h. Otto n. Hayward.
Rollins, Francis, lab. h. Niagara n. Amherst.
Rollins, Josiah A. melodeon maker, b. Mrs. M. Frost.
Rollo, Elizabeth, Mrs. h. Cherry cor. Goodell.
Roman, Jno. lab. h. 77 Genesee.
Romeis, Jno. h. Gray bet. Gen. and Batavia.
Romeis, —. tanner, with Schoellkopf & Breithaupt, h. Carroll n. Exchange.
Romer, Alex. carp. and join. h. r. 89 E. Sen.
Romer, Isaac J. builder, h. 208 Pearl.
Romer, John, carpenter, h. 9th n. Hampshire.
Romer, Matthias, shoemaker, b. R. Thorp.
Rommelmeyer, John, wood-sawyer, h. Fox n. Genesee.

Ronen, And. lab. h. 6 Michigan.
Roneyn, Matthew, ship carpenter, cor. Hamburgh and Fulton.
Rooney, W. P. clerk, b. 202 Swan.
Roop, Henry, prod. dealer, Prime cor. Dayton, h. 535 Main.
Roos, Geo. brewer, h. Roos alley n. Batavia.
Roos, Jacob, brewery, Hick. n. Bat. h. same.
Roos, Wm. brewer, Geo. Roos, b. same.
Roose, Henry, blacksmith, h. Bristol n. Spring.
Roosenberger, Jos. lab. h. Johnson n. North.
Root, Adrian R. provision and fish dealer, 64 Main, h. 47 W. Mohawk.
Root, B. A. sec'y Western Trans. Co. h. 129 Niagara.
Root, Chs. G. b. 44-Franklin.
Root, F. C. clerk. b. 129 Niagara.
Root, Francis, clerk, with John Root, 204 Sen.
Root, Francis H. firm Jewett & R. h. 309 Mich.
Root, Frank C., W. T. Co. b. 129 Niagara.
Root, John, grocer, 204 Seneca, b. Chicago cor. Carroll.
Root, J. S. with Jewett & Root, h. 47 Clinton.
Roperts, Chris. harness maker, h. Goodell al.
Rose, A. A. millwright, h. Clinton n. Walnut.
Rosa, Abraham, ship carp. h Hayward n. Ful'n.
Roscheoot, Bros. brewery, Spring cor. Cherry.
Roscheoot, Geo. brewer, firm R. Bros. h. Spring cor. Cherry.
Roscheoot, Jno. brewer, firm R. Bros. h. Spring cor. Cherry.
Rose, B. Mrs. widow, h. Niag. n. Amherst.
Rose, Edwin, contractor, h. 88 Franklin.
Rose, Frank. tailor, h. Grey n. Adams.
Rose, F. W. watch maker, h. Maple n. Goodell.
Rose, Harry, machinist. b. 12 Illinois.
Rose, Henry, baker, 124 E. Seneca, h. same.
Rose, Hugh, with Pratt & Co. b. 199 7th.
Rose, Jacob, mason, b. 298 Pearl.
Rose, John, grocer, h. Exch. n. Heacock.
Rose, John. miller, h. Spring n. Bristol.
Rose, Jos. with H. Gaylord, marble works, h. 298 Pearl.
Rose, Mary J. widow, cor. Exch. and Heacock.
Rose, M. W. cooper, h. Hayward n. Fulton.
Rose, Richard, shoemaker, h. 124 Elm.
Rose, Robt. N. Y. C. R. R. b. Globe.
Rose, Simon, clerk, 180 Main, h. 298 Pearl.
Rose, S. T. millwright, b. Western.
Rose, Thos. Mrs. milliner, 6 W. Eagle, h. same.
Rose, Thos. boat maker. h. 4th n. Genesee.
Rose, Thos. tallyman, h. 6 W. Eagle.
Rosa, T. S. saloon. 7 Revere Block, h. Com'l.
Rose, Wm. cooper, h. Grey n. Batavia.
Rose, Wm. R. R. b. Exchange n. Heacock.
Rosebach, Magdalena, widow, h. St. Paul n. Rosebach alley.
Rosee, H. wood worker, Brayley & Pitts.
Rosenau, D. clerk, 280 Main, h. same.
Rosenau, S. firm S. R. & Co. b. 52 N. Division.
Rosenau, S. & Co. wholesale millinery, 280 Main.
Rosenbauer, Augustus, goldsmith, b. 94 Cedar.
Rosenbauer, Geo. goldsmith, h. 407 Michigan.
Rosenberg, Herman, pastor, h. 13 Eagle.
Rosenberg, Jno. blacksmith, h. Lewis n. Amherst.
Rosenblatt, Anton F. carp. h. 157 Sycamore.

Rosenblatt, Catherine, widow, h. Grey n. Gen.
Rosencrantz, E. D. brass finisher, h. 82 Chip.
Rosencrantz, Ephraim, lamp maker, h. 82 Chip.
Rosendahl, Markus B. teacher, b. 21 Sycamore.
Rosener, Fred. cabinet maker, h 28 Ash.
Rosengren, N. J. tailor, h. 40 Cedar.
Rosenhahn, Gottfried, moulder, h. 407 Mich.
Rosenthal, A. B. butcher, 26 Commercial.
Rosenthal, Elias, cutter. 160 Main, h. 98 Main.
Rosert, Jno. farmer, h. Jefferson n. Best.
Rosner. Fred. shoemaker, h. 549 Michigan.
Rosner. Henry, tailor, h. Spruce n. Sycamore.
Ross, A. Mrs. h. 97 Seneca.
Ross, Andrew, engineer. h. 5th n. Court.
Ross. Benj. carpenter, S. L. R. R. shop, h. Alabama opp. Carroll.
Ross, Chas. G. printer, b. 97 Seneca.
Ross, D. firm R. & Stewart, h. Pollard n. E. Seneca.
Ross, David, book-keeper, 66 Lloyd, h. 179 S. Division.
Ross, Henry, fisherman, h. on turnpike n. toll-gate.
Ross, Henry, b. 35 Ellicott.
Ross. Hugh. blacksmith, b G. W. Baskett.
Ross, H. Schuyler, clerk, 289 Main, b. 97 Sen.
Ross, J. J. in Prince & Co's. factory, b. 6th n. Hudson.
Ross, Jeanette S. dressmaker, b. 129 Franklin.
Ross, Malcom, machinist, h. Carroll n. La.
Ross, Wm. hack driver, h. 137 Clinton.
Rosseel, Charles, firm G. R. Wilson & Co. h. 472 Main.
Rossel. Frank. peddler, h. Sherman n. Genesee.
Rosser, Susan, Mrs. h. 172 Oak.
Rossner, Fred. h. Adams n. Sycamore.
Rost, Michael, marble cutter, h. cor. Batavia and Elm.
Rost, Nicholas, farmer, on town line road bet. Main and Delaware.
Rotch. Frank, maltster, h. Elk n. Moore.
Roth, Anthony, tanner, b. 50 William.
Roth, Anthony, machinist, h. 54 Bennett.
Roth, Christ. grocer, h. Sycamore n. Pratt.
Roth, Chris. boiler maker, h. Gen. n. German.
Roth, Conrad, turner. h. Batavia n. Johnson.
Roth, Conrad, lab. h. Watson n. Peckham.
Roth, Frank. lab. h. Elk n. Chicago.
Roth, Fred. lab. h. 42 Cherry.
Roth, Fred. machinist, b. 34 Batavia.
Roth, Fred. shoemaker, b. 80 Cedar.
Roth, Geo. h. Hickory n. Sycamore.
Roth, Geo. blacksmith. b. Oak cor. Virginia.
Roth, Henry, shoemaker, h. 36 Cherry.
Roth, Henry, shoemaker, h. Mich. cor. Tupper.
Roth. Jno. A. Roth's Hall, 417 Mich. h. same.
Roth, Jno. G. grocer, Seneca n. Red Jacket Hotel.
Roth. John, boiler maker, Sycamore n. Pratt.
Roth, John, h. 16 Bennett.
Roth, John, carpenter, h. Walnut n. Sycamore.
Roth, Jno. Andrew, lab. h. Prime n. William.
Roth, Joseph, shoemaker, h. 119 Walnut.
Roth, Ludwig, h. Elm ab. Burton alley.
Roth, L. brewery, Main cor. North.
Roth, Martin, cap maker, h. 243 Oak.
Roth, Max, brewer, h. Sycamore cor. Walnut.
Roth, Michael, brewer, b. Max Roth.

Roth. Sebastian, shoemaker, Niagara cor. Virginia, h. same.
Roth, Wm. H. clerk Newman & Scovill.
Rothbart, John, cooper. h. 53 Maple bel. Va.
Rothenberger, Fred. shoemaker, h. Ash n. Syc.
Rothenbans, Geo. lab. h. Peckham cor. Watson.
Rothenhauser, Jacob, lab. b. 74 Genesee.
Rother, Augustus, wagon maker. h. 169 Elm.
Rother. Christian, saw filer. h. 169 Elm.
Rother, Gustavus, wagon maker, h. 169 Elm.
Rother, Jno. E. at Prince & Co.'s, h. 118 Clint'n.
Rothert, Fred. tailor, h. Michigan n. High.
Rothert, Wm. carpenter, h. Ketchum n. Carl'n.
Rothfuss, Gottfried. shoemaker, h. 9th ab. Ga.
Rottgurt, John, carpenter, b. 182 Batavia.
Rounds & Hall, gen. ins. agents, 7 Cent. Wharf and 2 Brown's Buildings cor. Sen. and Main.
Rounds. G. W. firm R. & Hall. 7 Cent. Wharf and 2 Brown's Buildings, h. 145 Franklin.
Rourke. Frank. lab. h. cor. La. and Fulton.
Row, Jno. brick maker, h. S. Division n. R. R. crossing.
Rowan, Martin M. Mrs. widow. clothier, 100 Main, h. same.
Rowan, Nathaniel J. apprentice with Julius Walker, b. 29 E. Swan.
Rowe & Co. dealers in oysters and liquors. 212 Washington.
Rowe, Geo. 12 Beak.
Rowe, Willis, firm R. & Co. h. 162 Seneca.
Rowley, C. C. b. Bonney's Hotel.
Rowley, J. F. paint dealer, 3 S. Division. h. Delavan ave. ab. Walden.
Rowley, Jas. cartman, h. Carolina bel. 5th.
Roy, Alex. blacksmith, h. Jeff. n. Peckham.
Royer, Jas. h. Ellicott n. Burton alley.
Royce, M. B. Mrs. h. 109 Seneca.
Royce, Jas. T. with Sherman & Barnes, b. 109 Seneca.
Royn, Thos. cooper, h. 244 Ellicott.
Rubel. Jacob, tailor, 183 Main, h. 280 Franklin.
Rubens, John. with W. H. Perry. b. 29 E. Swan.
Rubins. Chas. with Sternberg & Co. b. cor. Swan and Ellicott.
Rubins, Simeon, b. 107 S. Division.
Ruble, And. grocer, E. Eagle cor. Elm; h. same.
Ruble, John, clerk, cor. Eagle and Elm, b. 280 Franklin.
Rubrock, Frank. shoemaker, at 2 Exchange. h. 48 Bennett.
Rubrock. John, shoemaker, h. 48 Bennett.
Ruch, Michael, farmer, h. Ferry E. of Jeff.
Ruckdeskel, Henry, lab. h. Krettner n. Bat.
Ruckdeskel, John, lab. h. High cor. Smith's alley.
Ruckel. James H. blacksmith, b. 52 S. Div.
Ruckel, John H. book-keeper, Case & Co. 52 S. Division.
Rudd, Henry, waiter, h. 95 Oak.
Rude, Matta, patentee, b. 255 Washington.
Rudell, Wm. watchmaker, b. W. Genesee.
Ruden, Alex. B. printer, b. 15 Pearl.
Rudig. Conrad, hatter, 332 Main, h. Bristol n. Spring.
Rudof. Frank. carp. h. Tupper n. Virginia.
Rudolf, Frances, widow, h. Mich. n. High.
Rudolf. George, brick maker, h. S. Division n. R. R. crossing.

Rudolf, Henry, grocer, h. Spring n. Genesee.
Rudolf, Jacob, grocer, 434 Main, h 238 Pearl.
Rudolf, William, book-keeper, foot Washington, N. William.
Rudolph, Anna, Mrs. h. 230 Oak.
Rudolph, John, finisher, h. 179 Oak.
Rudolph, Joseph, tailor. h. 288 Elm.
Rudolph, Julia, cap maker, b. 230 Oak.
Rudy, John.* h. Amherst n. Thompson.
Ruediger, Charlotte. widow, b. B. Delitch.
Ruf, Jacob, h. Monroe n. Batavia.
Ruff, Ellis, blacksmith. h. Tonawanda n. Am't.
Ruff, John. coachman. at 170 Franklin.
Ruff, Michael. lab. h. Lewis n. Amherst.
Ruffier, Jos millwright, h. 97 Oak.
Rug, Peter, lab. h. Fox n. Genesee.
Rugenstein, Christoph. lab. h. Maple n. Carlton.
Ruger, A. machinist, b. 137 Elk.
Ruger, G. W. 230 Seneca.
RUGER, J. S. & CO. Queen City Iron Works, Chicago n. Ohio. h. Louisiana n. Elk.—See adv. pp. 58 and 59.
Ruger, J. W. Queen City Iron Works, Chicago below Elk, h. 230 Seneca.
Ruhl, Louis, baker. Swan n. junc. Seneca.
Ruhland, Andrew. lab. h. Adams n. Genesee.
Ruhland, John, artist. h. Batavia cor. Mich.
Ruhland, John, lab. h. Monroe n. Sycamore.
Ruhle, Henry. moulder, b. Wm. n. Cedar.
Ruhle, Wm. moulder, h. Wm. n. Cedar.
Ruhle, Wm. carp. h. Wm. n. Cedar.
Ruhlman, Geo. carp. h. Peckham n. Shumway.
Ruhlman, George saloon, Ohio n. Chicago, h. same.
Ruhlman, Lucas, grocer, Ohio n. swing bridge, h. same.
Ruhman, John, butcher, h. cor. Clinton and Elm.
Rulland, Michael, lab. h. Adams n. Batavia.
Rulofson, J. b. Revere House.
Rumrill, L. H. clerk, W. T. Co. h. 79 S. Div.
Rumsey, Aaron, firm A. R. & Co. h. Delaware cor. North.
RUMSEY, A. & CO. leather dealers, 2 and 4 Exchange.—See adv. p. 51.
Rumsey, Bronson C. firm A. R. & Co. h. Delaware cor. Tracy.
Rumsey, Dexter P. firm A. R. & Co. h. Delaware cor. Summer.
Rumsey, E. P. agent, G. W. R. R. h. 142 Swan.
Rumsey, Fayette, assessor, h. 171 Niagara.
Runcie. James, trunk manufacturer, 196 Main, h. 63 Clinton.
Runcie, S. Henry, 196 Main, b. 63 Clinton.
Runckel, John P. lab. h. Tupper below Oak.
Runckle, Geo. student, b. Tupper below Oak.
Rundell, Elizabeth, b. 19 Oak.
Runions, Wm. farmer, h. Bouck n. Preston.
Runk, Jacob, tailor, h. Spruce n. Genesee.
Runkel, Chattarina. widow, h. Spring n. Gen.
Runkel, Geo. H. tailor, h. Mich. ab. Goodell.
Runkel, Louis, moulder, h. Spring n. Gen.
Runner, F. cooper, East n. Hamilton.
Runnions, John, well digger, h. Best n. Main.
Rupner, Andrew, lab. h. German alley n. Gen.
Rupp, Francis V. shoemaker, h. Abbott plank road n. iron bridge.

Rupp. Fred. lab. h. Genesee n. Adams.
Rupp, George, clerk, Holbrook & Dee, b. 129 Clinton.
Rupp, George M. grocer, Clinton cor. Union, h. same.
Rupp, John, Delaware Street House. Delaware cor. Amherst.
Rupp, Mary, widow, seamstress, h. Walnut n. Sycamore.
Rupp, Peter, cooper, h. Thompson n. Hamilton.
Ruppel, Reinhardt, joiner. Mortimer n. Gen.
Ruppert, John, mason, h. Johnson n. Gen.
Rupprecht, Henry A. b. Batavia n. Pratt.
Ruprecht, Andrew, butcher, High n. Michigan, h. same.
Ruprecht, Geo. lab. h. Best n. Oak.
Ruprecht, John M. mason, h. Mich. n. High.
Ruprecht. M. Mrs. milliner. 91 Batavia.
Rusart, Charles, carp. h. Monroe n. Bat.
Rusch, Francisca, Mrs. h. r. 189 Ellicott.
Ruscher, Jacob, brewer, b. G. Bodamer.
Rusco, Lydia K. widow, h. 61 6th.
Ruscoe, Charles, mariner, h. 92 Cedar.
Rusert, Chas. carp. h. Monroe n. Peckham.
Russell, Charles H. b. 209 7th.
Russell, John E. stove mounter, h. 13th n. Clinton.
Russell, Josephine, h. 14 Batavia.
Russell, Kate, Miss, with Moore & White, b. Palmer n. Maryland.
Russell, Rudolph, h. Main n. Chapin.
Russell, Samuel, cattle dealer, h. Abbott n. Martin's Corners.
Russell, Thomas, lab. h. Miami n. Alabama.
Russell, Washington, farmer, h. Main n. Chapin.
Russell, W. C. firm Felthousen & R. h. 123 6th.
Rust, Catharine, widow, h. 258 Genesee.
Rutcak, John, shoemaker, h. Hickory n. Wm.
Ruthdruf, John, lab. b. Brown n. Jefferson.
Rutter, Thomas, alderman, h. Seneca n. 13th Ward House.
Ryan, Alex sailor, h. Exch. n. Hamburgh.
Ryan, Catharine, widow, variety store, Ohio n. Washington.
Ryan, Chs. machinist, b. 104 Exch.
Ryan, David. lab. h. S. Division below Emslie.
Ryan, Edward, lab. h. 5th n. Carolina.
Ryan, Edward, lab. h. Smith n. Elk.
Ryan, Elizabeth, widow, h. 10th cor. Md.
Ryan, James, ship carp. h. 12 Benk.
Ryan, James, truckman, b. Ala. n. Seneca.
Ryan, James, grocer, 57 Exch. h. same.
Ryan, James, lab. h. Niag. n. Farmer.
Ryan, James, lab. h. Elk n. Chicago.
Ryan, Jas. lab. h. Lock n. Terrace.
Ryan, Jas. carriage maker, h. 30 5th.
Ryan, Jas. tailor, h. 5 Commercial.
Ryan, Jas. W. carriage maker, b. 30 5th.
Ryan, John. clerk, h. 10th cor. Maryland.
Ryan, Jno. lab. h. Niag. n. Farmer.
Ryan, John, hatter, Terrace cor. Mechanic, h. same.
Ryan, Jno. grocer, Elk St. Market, h. 35 Lib'y.
Ryan, John, brewer. h. 30 6th.
Ryan, John, tinsmith, 237 Main, h. Folsom n. Kinney's alley.
Ryan, John, teamster. h. Carroll n. Michigan.
Ryan, John, lab. h. towpath n. round house.

Ryan, John, lab. h. Exchange n. Hamburgh.
Ryan, Lawrence, lab h. 5th n. York.
Ryan, Martin, ship carp. b. 107 Fulton.
Ryan, Mary, widow of John, h. 2 Scott.
Ryan, Mary, Mrs. h. 158 Georgia.
Ryan, Michael, sailor, h. 4th n Georgia.
Ryan, Michael, lab. h. Perry n. R. R. track.
Ryan, Michael, porter, 48 Main, b. 2 Scott.
Ryan, Morris, lab. h. 4th n. Genesee.
Ryan, Morris, grocer, Ohio cor. Wabash.
Ryan, Patrick, lab. h. Ohio n. South.
Ryan, Patrick, drayman, b. across creek opp.
Reed's Dock.
Ryan, Paul, cartman, h. 86 5th.
Ryan, Thos. carp. h. Perry n. R. R crossing.
Ryan, Thos. lab. h. Terrace n. Henry.
Ryan, Thos. C. waiter, Bonney's Hotel.
Ryan, Wm. ship carp. h. 4th n. Genesee.
Rye, Geo. stone cutter, h. Watson n. Batavia.
Ryghtman, David, saloon, 2 Canal.
Ryno, David, joiner, h. Cedar n. N. Division.

S.

Sabiskopskey, Ignatz, Rev. East n. Hamilton.
Suble, S. painter, h. Locust n. Cherry.
Sachs, Louis, tinsmith, h. 142 Batavia.
Sachs, Mary, widow, b. Brown n. Adams.
Sachsschuffer, Chs. tailor, b. 75 Cedar.
Sack, Catharine, widow, h. Batavia n Walnut.
Sackett, E. B. book-keeper, 11 Central Wharf,
b. 52 Swan.
Sackett, Grace A. Miss, teacher public school
No. 4, b. 201 Swan.
Sackett, John B. teacher public school No. 4, h.
218 Swan.
Sadler, Levi, peddler, 84 Carroll.
Saegel, Lorenz, lab. h. Peach n. High.
Saegelhaus, Christopher, carpenter, h. Cherry n.
Hickory.
Saeler, Edward, h. Seneca n. Red Jacket.
Saexhauer, Chris.* blacksmith, Gen. cor. Mich.
h. Tupper n. Michigan.
Safford, Elisha, staves and lumber, b. H. L.
Safford.
Safford, H. L.* stave manufactory, h. Niagara
n. Hamilton.
Safford, John A book-keeper, B. N. Y. & E. R.
R. b. 183 E. Seneca.
Safford, Jno. H. painter, h. Watson n. Howard.
Safford, J. F. mason, h. 183 Seneca.
Sage & Allison, architects, 7 Brown's Buildings,
joiners, Pearl n. Court.
Sage, Henry H. firm S. & Sons, h. 15 7th.
Sage, John, firm S. & Sons, h. 19 Court.
Sage, John B. firm S. & Sons, h. 19 Court.
Sage, R. C. firm S. & Allison, h. 170 Delaware.
SAGE & SONS, lithographers and engravers,
and map publishers, Arcade Buildings opp.
American Hotel.—See adv. p. 87.
Sage, Theo. B. grocer, 360 Main, b. 170 Del.
Sage & Tucker, druggists, 232 Main.
Sage, Wm. S. firm S. & Tucker, 232 Main, b. 19
Court.
Sahlen, Jacob, peddler, h. Watson n. William.
Sahlen, Wm. peddler, Grey n. Genesee.
Salender, Rudolph, tailor, h. Main n. Burton
alley.

Salisbury, Elias O. b. 38 W. Genesee.
Salisbury, Guy H. office 1 Niagara, 2nd story,
h. 110 W. Huron.
Salisbury, Lemuel C. printer, b. 110 Huron.
Salisbury, M. clerk, b. Delaware n. Allen.
Salisbury, Phebe, widow of H. A. h. 38 W.
Genesee.
Salisbury, W. J. builder. h. Delaware n. Allen.
Salles, Anna, washerwoman, h. 62 William.
Salles, Michael, saloon, Ellicott cor. Tupper, h.
same.
Salmon, S. J. clerk, supt's office B. & S. L. R.
R. b. 29 Swan.
Salmon, A. H. lab. h. Louisiana n. Perry.
Salow, Fred. shoemaker, h. Maple n. Virginia.
Saltar, Joseph, h. 189 Franklin.
Saltwell, Fred. stone cutter, b. Mich. n. North.
Salzer, Christ. lab. h. Mortimer n. Genesee.
Salzer, Christ. carp. h. 104 Pine.
Salzgeber, Louis, lab. h. 567 Washington.
Salzman, John, lab. h. Sherman n. Genesee.
Salzmann, Geo lab. h. Sherman n. Genesee.
Samco, Jno. in stave factory, h. Military road.
Sames, Wm. cigar maker, h. Kaene n. Gea.
Samo, Jas. R. M. D. 7 S. Division, h. 285 Oak.
Samo, Jos. 43 ' Main, b. 285 Oak.
Samo, Henry W. news depot, 432 Main, b. 285
Oak.
Samson & Hoffer, apothecaries, 364 Main.
Samson, Jas. grocer, Georgia cor. 5th.
Samson, Jos. 346 Main, h. Lutheran n. Wm.
Samson, Theo. machinist, h. Spring n Eagle.
Samuels, A. M. artist, b. 299 Michigan.
SAMUELS, NATHAN, daguerrean stock deal.
4 Weed's Block, h. 299 Mich —See adv. p.73.
Sanborn, Clark A. b. 62 E. Swan.
Sand, Katharine, wid. h. 238 Elm.
Sand, Paul, machinist, h. 238 Elm.
Sand, Valentine, carp. h. 253 Elm.
Sandam, Geo. saloon, 6 Revere Block, h. same.
Sandech, Andrew, basket maker, h. Fox n.
Genesee.
Sander, Adolph, clerk, cor. Ellicott and Clinton.
b. same.
Sander, Godfried, saddler. h. Hickory n. Bat.
Sander, Godfrey, cabinet maker, h. 170 Oak.
Sander, G. cab. maker, h. Spruce n. Batavia.
Sander, William A. butcher, h. 271 Elm.
Sanders, David, lab. b. W. A. Sutton.
Sanders, Harry B. ship carpenter, h. 109 9th.
Sanders, John W. carp. h. Parish n. East.
Sanders, John, cooper, h. East n. Austin.
Sanders, W. N. printer, b. Southern Hotel.
Sanders, Wm. painter, h. Fulton n. Hamburgh.
Sandon, John, carp. h. Louisiana n. Elk.
Sandrock, Geo. produce and com. 23 Central
Wharf, b. cor. Michigan and Eagle.
Sandrock, Geo. shoemaker, h. 9 E. Huron.
Sanerwein, Philip, brass finisher, 162 Main.
Sanford, Harroun & Co. R. R. printers, Courier
buildings, 178 Washington.
Sanford, Henry W. ship carp. h. Monroe n.
Howard.
Sanford, Isaac, clerk P. O. h. 82 Clinton.
Sanford, James W. book-keeper, Jas. Warren
& Co. b. 158 Pearl.
Sanford, Jos. H. firm S. Harroun & Co. h. 11
Union.

Sangster, Amos W. with H. Sangster, h. 247 Swan.
Sangster, Hugh, square lamp manuf. 41 Ohio, h. Alabama n. Elk.
Sangster, Jas. patentee, b. Hugh Sangster.
Sangster, Sophia, wid. h. 65 Batavia.
Sanwald, John, ash peddler, h. Locust n. High.
Sargeant, —, at Hatch's elevator, b. Genesee House.
Sargent, James. boatman. h. 99 Oak.
Sarsnett, Edward, b. 11 Wm. cor. Mark.
Sarsnett, Felander, sailor. h. 11 William.
Sauer, Charles. cooper, h. 94 Cedar.
Sauer, Christine, wid. h. Elm cor. Genesee.
Sauer, Frederick, carp. h. Hudson n. 10th.
Sauer, John, barber. Niagara n. Amherst.
Sauer, John, lab. 102 Cedar.
Sauer, Michael, shoemaker, h. Va. n. Garden.
Sauerteig, Robert, with Howell & Smith, b. 66 Bennett.
Sauerwein, Henry, saloon, 8 Court, h. same
Sauerwein, Philip, car fitter, h. Mark cor. Gay.
Sauken, Gustave. saloon. h. ov. 113 Genesee.
Saul, Nicholas, lab. h. 109 Cedar.
Saulter, Christian, tailor, b. 13 Main.
Saulter, Phil. truckman, b. Perry n. Hayward.
Saunders, Chs. piano maker, with A. & J. Keogh.
Saunders, Godfrey, harness maker, h. Batavia n. Hickory.
Saunders, John, piano maker, h. 213 N. Div.
Saunders, Riley, atty. b. Saunders' Exch. cor. Seneca and Chicago.
Saur. Jacob, locksmith, h. 164 Clinton.
Saurwine, at J. C. Harrison's, Reed's dock.
Sauter, Casper, brewer, h. 544 Michigan.
Sauter, Jacob, shoemaker, 8 W. Eagle, h. 20 Bennett
Sauter, John, lab. h. Sycamore n. Ash.
Sauter, Michael, lab. h. Walden n. Steele.
Savage, Thos. dairyman, h. Abbott road bel. R. R.
Savill, Wm. wagon maker, h. Abbott road n. Elk.
Sawin, Albert, atty. firm S. & Lockwood, h. 97 Niagara.
Sawin, Carlton T. with T. D. Dole, b. 20 Del.
Sawin, Chas. N. telegraph operator, B. N. Y. & E. R. R. b. Bloomer's.
Sawin, J. B. clerk, N. Y. & E. R. R. b. 20 Del.
Sawin, J. S. book-keeper, S. Sawin & Co. b. 20 Delaware.
Sawin & Lockwood, attys. 3 Hollister Block.
Sawin, Silas, firm S. S. & Co. h. 20 Del.
Sawin, S. & Co. builders, 8 W. Eagle.
Sawyer, Jas. D. prod. and com. mer. 11 Cent. Wharf, h. 49 Niagara.
Saxe, Chas. sailor. h. South n. Louisiana.
Sayles, Harvy. engineer, B. & S. L. R. R. h. Lee's Corner's, 13th Ward.
Sayles, P. M. atty. old post office buildings, b. 29 E. Swan.
Sayre, Chas. machinist, h. Seneca opp. Franklin House.
Scally, John, conductor, Niagara st. R. R. h. cor. R. L and 11th.
Scanlan, Ellen, milliner, b. Michigan bet. Swan and S. Division.

Scanlan, John. lab. h. Clinton n. Lockwood.
Scanlan, Martin. lab. h. Carroll cor. Hamburgh.
Scanlan, Michael, lab. h. across creek.
Scanlan, Michael, sailor, h. Kentucky n. South.
Scanlan, Pat. saloon, Joy cor. Water, h. same.
Scannell, Daniel, lab. h. Carroll cor. Heacock.
Scannell, Daniel, lab h. in Forest Lawn.
Scatcherd, James N. lumber dealer, Elk cor. Louisiana, h. 212 Seneca.
Schabio, Charlotte, midwife, h. Peckham n. Monroe.
Schabio, Peter, moulder, h. Peckham n. Adams.
Schabot, August, h. Hollister n. Spring.
Schabtack, Catharine, wid. h. Brown n. Jeff.
Schad, Geo. lab. h. Pratt n. William.
Schadler, John, shoemaker, 175 Wash. h. same.
Schaefer, Catharine, widow, 581 Washington.
Schaefer, Chas. shoemaker, h. Syc. n. Spring.
Schaefer, Christian,* vinegar manuf. 202 Oak.
Schaefer, Chris. grocery, Wm. cor. Walnut.
Schaefer, D. bl'ksmith, Bat. n. Watson, h. same.
Schaefer, F. brick maker, h. Seneca n. junc. Swan.
Schaefer, Francis, mason. h. Syc. n. Walnut.
Schaefer, G. A. clerk, White's Bank, h. 202 Oak.
Schaefer, Hen. mason. h. Monroe n. Peckham.
Schaefer, John C. vinegar manuf. h. 210 Gen.
Schaefer, John, dyer, h. Walnut n. Sycamore.
Schaefer, John, tailor, h. 210 Genesee.
Schaefer, John, grocer. h. Perry cor. Hayward.
Schaefer, Jno. lab. h. Cedar n. Batavia.
Schaefer, Lorenz, lab. h. Watson n. Batavia.
Schaefer, Mary, wid. h. Goodell n. Burton al'y.
Schaefer, Nicholas, grocer, Carroll cor. Heacock, h. same.
Schaefer, Philip, barber, 104 Exch. h. Mulberry n. Goodell.
Schaefer, Theodore, furnaceman, h. Burton alley n. Tupper.
Schaefer, Valentine. butch'r, h. Good'l n. Maple.
Schaefer, Valentine, joiner, h. Adams n. Bat.
Schaefer, Valentine,* butcher, Gen. n. Adams, h. same.
Schaeffer, Bartholomew, wagon maker, h. Hickory n. William.
Schaeffer, Frank,* tailor, 64 S. Div. h. same.
Schaeffer, Geo. cooper, h. Peckham n. Krettner.
Schaeffer, Jno. H. carp. h. Hinckley cor. Spring.
Schaeffer, Margaret, wid. grocer, 375 Genesee.
Schaefmann, Mich. lab. h. Mortimer n. Genesee.
Schaen, Chris. lab. h. Walnut n. Genesee.
Schaetzer, John, shoemaker, h. Monroe bel. Sycamore.
Schaf, Geo. lab. h. Mulberry n. High.
Schafer, Adam, baker, William n. Adam.
Schafer, Ann, widow, h. 284 Pearl.
Schafer, Caspar, lab. h. Adams cor. William.
Schafer, Catharine, wid. h. Shumway n. R. R. crossing.
Schafer. C. Mrs. widow, h. 256 Genesee.
Schafer, Chas. shoemaker, Main n. Eley Road.
Schafer, Jno. blacksmith, h. Watson n. Clinton.
Schaff. Jos. grocer, 32 Delaware place, h. same.
Schaffer, Adam, moulder, h. 86 Cherry.
Schaffer, Jacob, clerk, b. 423 Main.
Schafner, Henry, lab. h. Johnson n. Batavia.
Schall, Andrew, grocer, S. Div. cor. Jefferson.
Schall, Andrew, lab. h. Milnor n. Batavia.

Schall, Chas. painter, h. German al. n. Genesee.
Schall, Fred. carpenter, h. 322 Ellicott.
Schaller, Henry, lab. h. Batavia cor. Jefferson.
Schaller, John, carp. h. Hickory n. Batavia.
Schaller, Simon, gardener, h. Grey n. Genesee.
Scham, Jno. lab. h. ov. 18 Maple.
Schanama, B. tinsmith, h. 103 Genesee.
Schanbacher, Dan'l, shoemaker, h. 14th n. Vt.
Schanla, Finzanz,* shoemaker, Delaware n. Ferry, h. same.
Schannahan, B. lab. h. Mary bet. Ind. and Ill.
Schanne, Adrian, painter, h. 127 Walnut.
Schanne, Franciskay, wid. h. Hickory n. Bat.
Schanne, Jacob, painter, h. Walnut n. William.
Schanzlin, Jacob, brewer, Main cor. Del. ave.
Schanzlin, Jacob, Jr. brewer, h. J. Schanzlin.
Schap, H. wood worker, at Brayley & Pitts.
Schapter, Geo. joiner, h. 139 Oak.
Schapter, H. ship carpenter, h. 390 S. Division.
Schard, F. lab. h. Steele n. Walden.
Schard, J. A. lumber yard, h. 212 Seneca.
Scharf, John, butcher. h. Watson n. Peckham.
Scharf, John, clerk, 3 E. Seneca, b. 360 Swan.
Scharff, Chas. paper box manuf. 273 Main, b. same.
Scharpf, Christopher, butcher, 3 Seneca, b. 360 Swan.
Schattner, Joseph, moulder, h. 99 Pine.
Schau, Philip J. lab. h. 540 Michigan.
Schaub, Frank, milkman, h. Park ab. Virginia.
Schaub, Valentine. lab. h. Erie canal n. Md.
Schauf, Adam, paver, h. 134 Spring.
Schauf, Adam, lab. h. r. 134 Spring.
Schauf, Philip, lab. h. Mortimer n. Genesee.
Schauk, Peter, lab. h. 33 Walnut.
Schaulau, Christian, marble polisher, Cherry n. Jefferson.
Schaumloeffel, Jno. M. cooper, h. 542 Mich.
Schaumloeffel, Ludwig, tailor, h. Johnson n. Genesee.
Schaus, Peter, chair maker, b. 110 Hickory.
Schauten, Rich'd, barber, Genesee, h. 143 Bat.
Scheafer, Adam, grocer, Wm. cor. Adams.
Scheafer, Michael, lab. h. Clinton n. C. R. R.
Scheble, Jno. machinist, b. Wash. n. Goodell.
Schecker, Wolfgang. shoemaker, b. 75 Cedar.
Scheer, Cassimer, engineer, h.Dearborn n. R. R.
Scheer, F. book-binder, b. Amherst n. East.
Scheerer, Mich'l, tailor, h. S. Div. n Grosvenor.
Scheffel, Godfreid, h. 37 William.
Scheffel, Julius, policeman, h. 48 Sycamore.
Scheffel, Waltmeier, clerk, 211 Main b. 27 Wm.
Scheffer, Frank E. with U. S. Ex. h. 84 N. Div.
Scheffer, John H. clerk, L. B. Platt & Co. b. 84 N. Division.
Scheffler, Wm. butcher, h. Virginia cor. 11th.
Scheibler, Peter, brewer, b. 32 Genesee.
Scheid, Anna M. seamstress, b. Michael Sheid.
Scheid, Michael, lab. h. Pine n. William.
Scheidel, Jno. paper hanger, 147 Oak.
Scheidt, J. painter. L. W. Scheidt.
Scheidt, Lorenz W. lab. b. Monroe n. Peck'm.
Scheinmeister, August, h. r. 502 Washington.
Schell, Christian, switch tender, h. Monroe n. Peckham.
Schell, Dorothea, widow, h. 564 Washington.
Schell, John, blacksmith, h. Eagle n. Walnut.
Schell, Vincent, lab. h. Walnut n. Batavia.

Schelle, Chas. tailor, h. Pratt n. William.
Schelle, Fred. Rev. h. 163 Pearl.
Schelling, Fred. grocery, 8 Huron, h. same.
Schello, Peter, moulder, h. Ash n. Genesee.
Schemhorn, James. lab. h. 311 Seneca.
Schemm, B. lab. h. Hickory n. Sycamore.
Schenck, Jno. sawyer, b. 33 Walnut.
Schenk, Gottlieb, Mrs. h. Elm n. Burton alley.
Schenk, John, hostler. h. 10th n. Hampshire.
Schenk, Joseph, b. 66 Tupper.
Schenkel, John, marble cutter, b. Main n. Cold Spring.
Schenkelberger, Chas. machinist, h. Lutheran n. Batavia.
Schenkelberger, Jacob, saloon, Main cor. Mohawk. h. same.
Schenkelberger, Maria S. widow, h. Walnut n. Batavia.
Schenkelberger, Mary, Miss, seamstress, h. Walnut n. Batavia.
Schenkelberger, Regina, Miss, seamstress, b. Walnut n. Batavia.
Schep, Fred. lab b. Military road n. Amherst.
Scheper, Henry, ship carp. h. 390 S. Div.
Scherber, John. gilder, h. Michigan n. Carlton.
Scherber, Martin, finisher, h. Carlton n. Mich.
Schereitzer, Thos. cooper, h. Dearborn n. R. R.
Scherer, G. grocer, Vermont n. Rogers, h. same.
Scherer, John, lab. h. 306 Elm.
Scherer, Michael, moulder, h. Ash n. Syc.
Scherer, Nicholas. lab. h. Johnson n. Batavia.
Scherrer, Jos. tailor, h. 223 Elm.
Schermerhorn, B. clerk, 186 Main, b. 5 Franklin.
Schermerhorn, I. M. general freight agent, B. N. Y. & E. R. R. h. Wash. n. Carlton.
Schertel, Stephen, lab. h. Adams n. Sycamore.
Schett, Henry, lab. h. Spruce n. Genesee.
Schetter, John, brewer, with A. Ziegele.
Scheu's Brewery, Spring cor. Genesee.
Scheu, C. Mrs. widow, h. Amherst n. Thompson.
Scheu, Henry, baker, h. Ellicott n. Burton al.
Scheu, Henry, lab. h. 196 Elm.
Scheu, Jacob, brewer, Genesee cor. Spring, h. same.
Scheu, Martin, lab. h. Mulberry n. Goodell.
Scheu, Philip, Sr. brewer, h. High n. Main.
Scheu, P. J. h. Genesee cor. German alley.
Scheu, Solomon, h. 351 Genesee.
Scheu, Wm. grocer and feed store, Genesee n. Michigan, h. same.
Scheuauer, John, lab. h. Monroe n. Batavia.
Scheubeck, Peter, carp. h. Pine n. Cypress.
Scheubner, Chas. teamster, h. Gen. n. tollgate.
Scheubner, Nicholas, farmer, h. Jefferson cor. Brown.
Scheuer, Peter, lab. h. 8 Bennett.
Scheuerman, John, carp. h. Walnut n. Batavia.
Scheuerman, Jos. J. grocer, h. 259 Genesee.
Scheuerman, Joseph, carpenter, 411 Michigan, h. same.
Scheuk, Jacob, wagon maker, cor. Dearborn and Amherst.
Scheukelberger, Martin, clerk, P. O. h. Roos alley n. Batavia.
Scheurer, Jos. lab. h. Goodell alley n. Tupper.
Scheurmann, Joseph, grocer, 114 Pine.
Schible, Jos. basket maker, h. 54 Cedar.
Schick, Adam, shoemaker, h. Walnut n. Bat.

Schick. Adolf. with Pratt & Letchworth, b. cor. Hudson and 6th.
Schick. Anton, tailor, h. Goodell alley n. Goodell.
Schick, Jacob, carp. h. East n. Hamilton.
Schick, Jos. shoemaker, h. Tupper cor. Oak.
Schick, Peter, cooper, h. East n. Amherst.
Schick, Philip, tailor, h. 54 Bennett.
Schick, Wm. painter, h. Michigan n. North.
Schickedanz, Henry, tailor, h. 259 Elm.
Schickel, Bernhard, saloon, cor. Elm and Bat.
Schickel, B. saloon, b. Batavia n. Elm.
Schickendantz, Wm. 478 Michigan, h. same.
Schicker, Louis, beer peddler, h. Oak n. North.
Schiebel, Geo. lab. h. 266 Washington.
Schiebel, John, lab. b. 566 Washington.
Schieber, Barbara, widow, h. North n. Herman.
Schieder, Geo. carp. b. r. 443 Michigan.
Schieder, Mary, seamstress, b. 156 Batavia.
Schiedt, Lawrence,* cigar manuf. Genesee n. Hickory.
Schiefer, Chas. sailor, h. Spruce n. Genesee.
Schiefer, John, carp. h. Kaene n. Genesee.
Schiefer, Martin, butcher, h. Wm. cor. Hickory.
Schieffer, Swartz & Co. joiners, 42 Ash.
Schieffer, Fred. firm S. & Swartz, carp. 42 Ash.
Schieffer, Geo. saddler, h. Spruce n. Genesee.
Schieferle, John, carp. h. 60 Walnut.
Schieferle, Josepha, widow, h. 60 Walnut.
Schieferle, Stephen, carp. h. 60 Walnut.
Schiefferle, John, moulder, h. Spruce n. Bat.
Schiefferle, Mary, widow, b. Spruce n. Batavia.
Schieferstein, Geo.* confectionery, 258 Genesee, h. same.
Schiefler, John, baker, 52 Bennett, h. same.
Schiel, John, gardener, h. Maple cor. North.
Schiele, John,* sash and blind factory, cor. Oak and Clinton, h. Elm n. Carlton.
Schier, Peter, drover, h. 257 Genesee.
Schierman, Fred. baker, b. 34 E. Genesee.
Schierman, John, mason, h. Sycamore n. Pine.
Schiesel, Andrew, carp. h. 296 Elm.
Schiesel, Jas. lab. h. 296 Elm.
Schiffbauer, Chas. carp. h. Pratt n. Sycamore.
Schiffler, John, lock maker, h. Walnut n. Syc.
Schiffmacher, Nicholas, b. 118 Batavia.
Schifirstein, John, lab. h. Pratt n. William.
Schildknecht, Conrad, piano maker, h. Goodell n. Washington.
Schill, Chs. wagoner, h. Batavia n. Adams.
Schiller, Francis, brewer, b. J. Weppner.
Schiller. Geo. lab. h. Pratt n. William.
Schilling, John, blacksmith, b. Pine n. Batavia.
Schilling. Theo. h. Genesee n. tollgate.
Schillo, Emanuel, printer, b. Ash n. Sycamore.
Schillo, John, moulder, h. Pratt n. Sycamore.
Schillo, Nicholas, moulder, h. Walnut n. Wm.
Schillo, Peter, moulder, h. 10 Cypress.
Schillrothd, Geo. printer, Aurora office, h. 114 Cedar.
Schilp, John Chr. shoemaker, h. Mortimer n. Genesee.
Schimke, John, tailor, Erie, h. 260 Elm.
Schimpky, John, tailor, h. 260 Elm.
Schindler, Andrew, tailor, 2 Water, h. same.
Schindler, Bernhard, milkman, h. Herman cor. North.
Schindler, Chas. lab. h. Burton alley n. Mich.

Schinthal, Andrew, shoemaker, Batavia bet. Jefferson and Spring.
Schinthal, Jacob, machinist, b. Gen. n. Walnut.
Schinthal, Leopold, carp. h. Walnut n. Syc.
Schirber, John, lab. h. Genesee n. Jefferson.
Schirmann, Chas. mason, h Mortimer n. Gen.
Schirmer, Henry, organ builder, h. Locust ab. Cherry.
Schirra, Conrad. tailor, h. cor. Maiden and Fly.
Schittler, Frederlin, marble polisher, h. 13th n. Vermont.
Schizzel. Christopher. grocery, Mulberry n. Goodell, h. same.
Schlachter, Jacob, carpenter, h. Jefferson n. Peckham.
Schlachter, Louis, moulder. h. Walnut n. Bat.
Schladt, Christian, carp. b. 85 Cherry.
Schlag, Robert, firm Mohr & S. h. Ellicott n. Tupper.
Schlager, Fran. clerk. 72 Main, h. Pratt n. Wm.
Schlager, Louis, at 4 E. Sen. h. Pratt n. Clinton.
Schlageter. Isidore, tailor, h. 96 Pine.
Schlagter, B. h. 243 Elm.
Schlanger, John, tanner, h. Wm. cor. Jefferson.
Schlank. Robert, tailor, h. 227 Ellicott.
Schlatterrer, Stephen, grocer, b. Michigan n. Batavia.
Schlau, And. lab. h. 294 Oak.
Schleafer, John, butcher, h. Sycamore n. Ash.
Schlegel, C. firm S Bettinger & Co. h 399 Main.
Schlegel, Daniel, printer. b. Cherry cor. Locust.
Schlegel, Jno. lab. h. Lutheran n. William.
Schlegel, M. ash peddler, Mich. cor. Tupper.
Schlegel, Michael, tailor, h. 117 Pratt.
Schleher, John, lab. b. 39 Walnut.
Schleher, Peter, lab. h. 39 Walnut n. Sycamore.
Schleiger. Nicklaus, shoemaker, h. Batavia n. Hickory.
Schleininger, Francis, lab. h. 111 Pine.
Schleiweis, John, tailor, h. 90 Cherry.
Schleixbei, Conrad, brewer, b. A. Ziegele.
Schlemon, Fred. shoemaker, 23 Park place.
Schlenk, Michael, lab. with Howell & Smith, Davis n. Genesee.
Schlenker, Casper, harness maker, h. Jefferson cor. Peckham.
Schlenker, Erhardt, machinist. b. Wm. n. Jeff.
Schlenker, Ernhardt, shoemaker, b. 7 Comm'l.
Schlenker, Jacob, peddler, b. Adams n. Bat.
Schlenker, John, turner, h. Jeff. cor. William.
Schlenker, John M. lab. h. Adams n. Batavia.
Schlenker, Martin, lab. h. Adams n. Batavia.
Schlenter, Philip, baker, h. Miss. n. Perry.
Schley, Geo. cooper, h. Hamilton n. Thorp.
Schleyer, Michael, tailor, h. Herman n. Gen.
Schlingmeier, Geo. shoemaker. h. 171 Batavia.
Schlingmeier, Henry, shoemaker, 171 Batavia, h. same.
Schlink, Leonard, grocer, Main cor. Goodell.
Schlink, Michael, lab. h. Davis n. Genesee.
Schloeger, Conrad. brewer, h. 567 Main.
Schlorf, Fred. lab. h. 530 Michigan.
Schloss, Jacob, cigar maker, h. Pine n. Will'm.
Schlotter, Geo. lab. h. Lathrop n. Genesee.
Schlotzer, John, grocer, Clinton cor. Hickory.
Schlund, J. B. book-keeper, L. D. White, b. 34 W. Seneca.
Schmaering, C. wood worker, Brayley & Pitts.

Schmahl, C. wagon maker, cor. Gen. and Hickory, h. 5 Cherry.
Schmal, Chas. blacksmith, b. P. Schmal.
Schmal, Peter, blacksmith, 171 Gen. h. samo.
Schmall, L. saloon, h. 4th n. Carolina.
Schmall, William, b. C. Schmall.
Schmandt, Chs. painter, h. Cherry n. Spring.
Schmaus, John, milk peddler, h. Johnson n. Genesee.
Schmeink, Nicholas, Buff. Ag. Mach. Works, h. 91 Cedar.
Schmelzer, Christoph H./ tailor, h. 535 Mich.
Schmelzer, Fred. street inspector, h. 335 Mich.
Schmeltzer, Gottlieb, carpenter, h. 535 Mich.
Schmering, Clemens, carpenter, h. Ash n. Syc.
Schmering, J. H. grocer, William cor. Pearl.
Schmetter, Geo. lab. h. Pine n. Batavia.
Schmid, Daniel, trunk maker, 196 Main.
Schmid, John, carp. h. Mulberry n. Virginia
Schmidt, Adam, carp. h. Stanton n. Peckham.
Schmidt, Adam, lab. h. Michigan n. North.
Schmidt, Adam, cooper, h. Camp n. Genesee.
Schmidt, Andreas, tailor, h. 26 Walnut.
Schmidt, Anton, book store, 411 Main, h. same.
Schmidt, Anton, lab. h. Mich. n. High.
Schmidt, Anton, lab. h. Porter n. Hydraulics.
Schmidt, August, shoemaker, 147 Genesee, h. same.
Schmidt. August, cooper. h. Spring cor. Wm.
Schmidt, Barbara, wid. b. Syc. opp. Mortimer.
Schmidt, Casper, h. Shumway n. William.
Schmidt, Chas. trunk maker, 79 Sycamore.
Schmidt, Chas. lab. h. Elm cor. Virginia.
Schmidt, Christian, musician and piano maker, h. 412 Michigan.
Schmidt, Christian, tailor, h. 112 Batavia.
Schmidt, Christina, widow, h. 3 Cypress.
Schmidt, Christ. tanner, h. Lemon n. Carlton.
Schmidt, Conrad, lockmaker, h. William n. Cedar.
Schmidt, Elizabeth, widow, h. 274 Elm.
Schmidt, Ernst, locksmith b. Maple n. High.
Schmidt, Francis, saloon, Canal n. Erie, h. 70 William.
Schmidt, Francis J. teacher, b. Milnor n. Bat.
Schmidt, Franz, baker, h. Pine n. Baker.
Schmidt, Fred. tailor, h. Seneca bel. junc. Swan.
Schmidt, Fred. tinsmith, h. Clinton n. Cedar.
Schmidt. Fred. shoemaker, h. Walnut n. Bat.
Schmidt, Fred. teacher, b. Milnor n. Batavia.
Schmidt, Geo. bl'ksmith. h Watson n. Peckham.
Schmidt, Geo. baker, b. Batavia n. Pine.
Schmidt, Geo. tailor, b. 410 Michigan.
Schmidt, Geo. J. cooper, b. 3 Cypress.
Schmidt, Gottleib, painter, h. 460 Michigan.
Schmidt, Henry, tailor, over 263 Main, h. r. 138 E. Genesee.
Schmidt, Henry, shoemaker, Syc. n. Spring.
Schmidt, Henry, lab. h. Jefferson n. Peckham.
Schmidt, Jacob, cooper, h. 3 Cypress.
Schmidt, Jacob, tanner, h. 123 Pine.
Schmidt, Jacob, veterinary surgeon, b. 144 E. Genesee.
Schmidt, Jacob D. carp. h. Hollister n. Spring.
Schmidt, Joachim, tailor, h. Maple n. High.
Schmidt, Jno. butcher, 208 Oak, h. same.
Schmidt, Jno. porter, American. h. 117 Pine.
Schmidt, Jno. sailor, h. Connecticut n. 14th.

Schmidt, Jno. lab. h. Michigan n. Virginia.
Schmidt, Jno. moulder, h. Syc. n. Mortimer.
Schmidt, Jno. Ulrich, shoem'r, North n. Mich.
Schmidt, Jno. G. baker. 82 E. Gen. h. same.
Schmidt. Jno. lab. h. Gen. n. Jefferson.
Schmidt, Jno. L. grocer. Clinton n. Emslie.
Schmidt, Jno. P. woodsawyer, 47 Cedar.
Schmidt, Jno. lab. h. Locust n. North.
Schmidt, Jno. blacksmith, h. Hollister n. Spring.
Schmidt. John, lead works, h. cor. Michigan and Virginia.
Schmidt, John, mason. b. Adams n. Sycamore.
Schmidt, Jos. lab. h. Best cor. Ellicott.
Schmidt, Louis, upholsterer, with Hersee & Timmerman. h. 144 Genesee.
Schmidt, Ludwig,* shoemaker, Grey n. Batavia. h. same.
Schmidt, Margaret. widow, h. 144 E. Gen.
Schmidt, Mary, widow, h. 5 Cypress.
Schmidt, Mathias, carriage trimmer, h. Sycamore n. Spruce.
Schmidt, Matthias, tailor, h. 52 Goodell.
Schmidt, Matthias, teacher, h. Milnor n. Bat.
Schmidt, Max J. brewer, h. 525 Michigan.
Schmidt, Melchior, lab. h. 79 Spruce.
Schmidt, Michael, cabinet maker, 203 Main, h. Ellicott n. High.
Schmidt, Michael, upholsterer, h. 162 Bat.
Schmidt, Michael, peddler, h. Pratt n. Clinton.
Schmidt, Moritz, chair maker, h. Hickory n.Bat.
Schmidt, Nicholas, shoemaker, h. junc, Seneca and Exchange.
Schmidt, Peter, lab. h. Monroe n. Batavia.
Schmidt, Stephen, moulder, h. 111 Pine.
Schmidt, Stephen, lab. h. 117 Pine n. Batavia.
Schmidt, Wm. tailor. h. Lemon n. Carlton.
Schmidt, Wm. cooper, h. Kaene n. Sycamore.
Schmidtmeyer, Leonard, lab. h. Lemon n. High.
Schmied, Christ. cutler. h. Cedar n. Wm.
Schmied, Joseph, cabinet maker, h. Pine n. Cypress.
Schmiedel, L. grocer, Niagara n. Pennsylvania. h. same.
Schmieding, Chas. G. butter dealer, 29 Elk St. Market, h. Batavia n. Hickory.
Schmeiding, Chas. H. butter and cheese dealer, 33 Elk St. Market, h. Lutheran n. Batavia.
Schmieding, Ernst, butter dealer, b. Chas. G. Schmieding.
Schmiering, Bernhardt, last maker, h. William n. Bennett.
Schmiering, Joseph, lab. h. Pine cor. Cypress.
Schmill, Christopher, shoemaker, h. 134 Gen.
Schmitt, Adam, machinist, h. Adams n. Bat.
Schmitt, Anselm, saloon, 585 Main, h. same.
Schmitt, Bernhard, lab. h. Walnut n. Batavia.
Schmitt, C. grocer, cor. Wm. and Monroe.
Schmitt, Casper, cooper, Spring cor. Wm.
Schmitt, Catharine, widow, h. Batavia n. Williamsville road.
Schmitt, Chas. clerk, 364 Main, h. 153 Del.
Schmitt, Conrad, lab. h. Pratt n. Genesee.
Schmitt, F. farmer, b. Batavia n. Williamsville road.
Schmitt, Ferdinand, plasterer, h. Riley n. Jeff.
Schmitt, Fred. lab. h. Lutheran n. Wm.
Schmitt, Fred. blacksmith, h. Pratt n. Wm.
Schmitt, Frid. boiler maker, b. Spring n. Syc.

Schmitt, Geo. upholsterer, h. Pine n. Bat.
Schmitt, Geo. shoemaker, h. Camp n. Gen.
Schmitt, Geo. lab. h. Walden n. Ferry.
Schmitt, Jacob, mason, h. Adams n. Brown.
Schmitt, Jacob, lab. h. Madison n. Sycamore.
Schmitt, Jacob.* cooper, h. Kaene n. Gen.
Schmitt, Jno. G. blacksmith, h. Pine n. Cypress.
Schmitt, John, lab. h. Monroe bet. Batavia and Sycamore.
Schmitt, John, Sr. mason, h. Adams n. Brown.
Schmitt, John, lab. h. Adams n. Batavia.
Schmitt, John, paver. h. Kaene n. Genesee.
Schmitt, John, porter, 117 Pine.
Schmitt, Joseph, shoemaker, h. Burton alley n. Washington.
Schmitt, Jos. milkman. h. Hickory n. Bat.
Schmitt, Leonhard, lab.*h. Adams n. Syc.
Schmitt, Ludwig, shoemaker, 20 Main.
Schmitt, Margaret, midwife, h. Kaene n. Gen.
Schmitt, Mary, widow, h. Watson n. Bat.
Schmitt, Mathew, lab. h. Adams n Bat.
Schmitt, Michael, lab. h. Bundy alley n. Syc.
Schmitt, Michael, lab. h. Adams n. Wm.
Schmitt, Nicholas, cooper, Chippewa n. Main, h. same.
Schmitt, Peter, shoemaker, Gen. n. Jefferson.
Schmitt, Philip, lab. h. Batavia n. Johnson.
Schmitz, Adam, lab. h. Hickory bet. Sycamore and Genesee.
Schmitz, Jacob, grocer, Oak n. Burton alley, h. same.
Schmitz, John,* dyer, 2 Court, h. same.
Schmitz. John, huckster, h. Sycamore n. Jeff.
Schmitz, John A. lab. h. Hickory n. Sycamore.
Schmitz, John J. lab. h. Adams n. Peckham.
Schmitz, Peter J. dyer, h. 485 Wash.
Schmitz, Winand. lab. h. Boston alley below Goodell.
Schmoker, Jno. lab. h. 265 Exchange.
Schmuck, Albert, lab. h. Boston alley bel. Va.
Schmuck, Joseph, harness maker, Niagara n. Amherst, h. same.
Schmucker, John, lab. h. Hickory n. Bat.
Schmucker, Jos. carp. h. Locust n. North.
Schnabel, Jacob, lab. h. Pine n. Cypress.
Schnabel, Michael, lab. h. Davis bet. Sycamore and Genesee.
Schnabel, Paul. lab. h. Cypress n. Pine.
Schnabel, Peter, lab. h. Cypress n. Pine.
Schnaberger. B. brick maker, h. Fox. n. Gen.
Schnaeble, Michael, finisher, h. Davis n. Syc.
Schnapp, Conrad, cooper, h. 12 Cypress.
Schneicler, Wm. clothing store, 285 Genesee, h. same.
Schneider, Anthony. cooper, b. P. Debus.
Schneider, Chas. tanner, h. Spring n. Syca.
Schneider, Christian, blacksmith, h. 75 Gen.
Schneider, Francis, lab. h. Pratt n. Batavia.
Schneider, Frank. lab. h. Va. cor 11th.
Schneider, Fred. tailor, h. Mulberry n. Goodell
Schneider, Geo. h. 227 Ellicott.
Schneider, Jacob, cooper, h. Spring n. Gen.
Schneider, Jacob, tailor, b. Pratt n. Sycamore.
Schneider, James, tailor, cor. N. Div. and Main, up stairs, h. 225 Oak.
Schneider, Jas. wagoner. h. 268 Elm.
Schneider, John G. lab. h. 167 Batavia.
Schneider, John. lab. h. 42 Cherry.

Schneider, John, lab. h. Hickory n. Batavia.
Schneider, John. cooper, h. Grape n. Cherry.
Schneider, John, lab. h. 42 Cherry.
Schneider, John, carp. h. 201 Batavia.
Schneider, John, carp. h. 70 E. Tupper.
Schneider, Ludwig. saloon, Jeff. n. Sycamore.
Schneider, Ludwig, h. 191 Ellicott.
Schneider, Marcelle, blacksmith. h. 279 Oak.
Schneider, Michael, lab. h. 126 Pine n. Cypress.
Schneider, Michael, lab. h. Boston alley cor.Va.
Schneider, Philip, saloon. 427 Main.
Schneider, Philip, baker. 163 Batavia, h. same.
Schneider, Valentine, blacksmith, h. Pratt n. Genesee.
Schneider, —, lab. h. High n. Michigan.
Schneidewing. Christian, carp. 320 Ellicott.
Schnelee, Bernhard, cabinet ware rooms, Huron cor. Genesee. h. same.
Schnellbach, Jos. tailor, h. Lutheran n. Wm.
Schnellbach, Jacob, b. Jos. Schnellbach.
Schneller, Gotlieb, painter, h. Hickory n. Syc.
Schnellinger, George, butcher, h. Genesee cor. Herman.
Schnepp, Geo. lab. h. Mortimer n. Hinckley.
Schnickelberger. J. carp. h. Amherst n. Lewis.
Schnorr, Conrad, plasterer. h. Adams n. Brown.
Schnorr, Henry, gardener, h Ferry n. Dela.
Schnun, Michael, lab. h. 95 Cherry.
Schnur. John, moulder, h. 67 Tupper.
Schnur. Peter, lab. h. 63 E. Tupper.
Schoell, Henry, clerk, h. Milnor opp. arsenal.
Schoellkopf & Breithaupt, sheepskin factory, Carroll n. Van Rensselaer.
Schoellkopf & Co. North Buffalo Mills, office 10 Central Wharf.
Schoellkopf. J. F. flour and feed store, 388 Main, h. Franklin n. Allen.
Schoellkopf. J. F. firm J. F. S. & Co. h. Franklin n. Allen.
Schoeman, Jacob, tailor, h. 302 Elm.
Schoenblom, John, at Clark's distillery.
Schoenfeld, Frederick, lab. h. Best n. Oak.
Schoenfeld, Johanna, h. Wm. n. Milnor.
Schoenfelder, Robt. carp. h. Maple n. North.
Schoenl. And. lab. h. 228 Elm.
Schoenleber, Geo. lab. h. Pratt n. Batavia.
Schoenman, Jno. carp. b. Maple n. Goodell.
Schoenthal, W. Mrs. widow, b. ov. 239 Gen.
Schoenwald. Carrol. carp. h. Locust n. Va.
Schoepflin, J. machinist. h. Wm. n. Mortimer.
Schoepflin, Jacob, machinist, b. William n. Mortimer.
Schoey, Herman, mason, h. Seneca n. N. Y. & E. R. R. track.
Schoff, Jno. cigar maker. h. Tupper n. Oak.
Scholden, Theodore, peddler, h. Brayton n. R. I.
Schomers, Eberhard, lab. h. Lutheran n. Bat.
Schonhart, Andrew, baggageman. h. 93 Pine.
Schooman, Jno. Brayley & Pitts. h. 23 Maple.
Schoonover, James S. millwright, Fulton cor. Hamburgh.
Schop, Henry, gardener, h. Ferry n. Delaware.
Schork, Peter, lab. h. Walnut n. Batavia.
Schorner, Joseph, lab. h. Herman n. Genesee.
Schorp, Raimund, shoemaker, h. Hickory n. Genesee.
Schorr, Ernst, millinery, 48 E. Gen. h. Main n. Best.

Schossrin, Jno. shoemaker. h. Maple n. Cherry.
Schott, Geo. shoe store, 3 E. Gen. h. Carlton n. Oak.
Schott, Jacob, lab. on canal, h. Niagara cor. Hamilton.
Schott, John, peddler, h. Howard n. Jefferson.
Schottmuell, Jacob, grocer, Wm. cor. Pratt, h. same.
Schouten, Rich. barber. 404 Main, h. 141 Bat.
Schperch, Louis, lab. h. Locust n. Cherry.
Schradel, Lawrence, tanner, 246 Gen. h. over 250 Genesee.
Schrader, Chas. tailor, 445 Michigan.
Schrader, F. lab. h. Herman n. Genesee.
Schrader, J. L. clerk, Eve. Post, b. 445 Mich.
Schrader, Jno. M. St. R. R. h. Main n. North.
Schrader, Wm. carp. b. Mary Frost.
Schraer, Peter, lab. h. 303 Genesee.
Schrafft, A. shoemaker, Thompson n. Amherst.
Schragelman, Geo. lab. h. Spring n. Genesee.
Schram, Alois, tailor, h. Maple n. High.
Schram, Chas. machinist, h. Bennett n. Wm.
Schranck, Michael, grocer, cor. Perry and Elk St. Market.
Schravin, Henry, ship carp. h. 183 Eagle.
Schreck, F. L. school teacher, h. 155 Ellicott.
Schrefer, Geo. harness maker, h. Spruce n. Gen.
Schreiber, Adam. carp. h. Pratt ab. Batavia.
Schreiber, Andrew, lab. h. Watson n. Peckham.
Schreiber, David, lab. h. Adams n. Sycamore.
Schreiber, Joseph, cigar maker, b. cor. Pine and Clinton.
Schreiber, M. lab. h. Roos alley n. Wm.
Schreier, Geo. tailor, h. 10 Walnut.
Schreiner, Nicholas, foreman, E. B. Holmes & Co. h. Lutheran n. Wm.
Schremmel, Geo. lab. h. Lemon n. High.
Schremps, August, butcher, h. 137 Oak.
Schremps, Henry, lab. h. 208 Elm.
Schreyer, Geo. lab. h. Adams n. Brown.
Schriefer, John, mason, h. Adams n. Sycamore.
Schriver, Henry, boat knees maker, h. Spring n. Clinton.
Schriver, John, with J. Benson, 131 Main, h. 312 Ellicott.
Schroeck, Remkins, shoemaker, h. Adams n. Peckham.
Schroeder, Anthony, tanner, with Rumsey & Co. h. Pine n. William.
Schroeder, Herman, painter, h. 234 Elm.
Schroeder, John, carp. h. Walnut n. William.
Schroeder, John, lab. h. Best n. Michigan.
Schroeder, Peter, shoemaker. 412 Michigan.
Schroeder. Ulrich, lab. h. 258 Elm.
Schroeter, Christian, lab. h. Carlton n. Maple.
Schroeter, Fred. lab. h. Maple n. Virginia.
Schrott, Chas. grocer, 135 Bat. h. same.
Schrott, Christ. lab. h. r. Hamilton n. Dearborn.
Schrout, N. lab. h. 391 Swan.
Schrove, Chas. butcher, h. Pratt n. Clinton.
Schrum, A. A. with Hamlin & Mendsen, b. 160 Pearl.
Schryver, A. L. shoe dealer, 304 Main, h. 60 Chippewa.
Schryver, James B. 304 Main. b. 60 Chippewa.
Schu, B. farmer, h. Williamsville road n. Delavan avenue.
Schubach, Wm. carp. h. Stanton n. Lovejoy.

Schubbert, Geo. boiler maker. h. Syc. n. Pratt.
Schubek, James, grocer, Adams n. Sycamore, h. same.
Schubert, Franz, lab. h. Sherman n. Genesee.
Schubert, John, lab. h. Mortimer n. Genesee.
Schubert, Louis, carriage trimmer, h. Maple n. High.
Schuch, Mary, wid. b. Walnut n. William.
Schuckwa, Joseph, lab. h. Spring n. Hinckley.
Schuehle, Geo. lawyer, office ov. old post office building, h. 43 Clinton.
Schuele, Geo. lab. h. Pratt n. Clinton.
Schuele, Jacob, sash and blind maker, cor. Clinton and Oak. h. Elm n. Carlton.
Schueler, Peter. lab. b. 174 Genesee.
Schuerer, Andrew, shoemaker, b. 128 Batavia.
Schuerer, Anton, shoemaker, h. 128 Batavia.
Schuerer, Francis, shoemaker, b. 128 Batavia.
Schuerer, Joseph, shoemaker, b. 128 Batavia.
Schuerer, Wendel, shoemaker, b. 128 Batavia.
Schuettel, Martin, carp. h. Main n. Burton al.
Schuetz, Michael, lab. h. Best n. Oak.
Schuffner, Earnst, dealer in cigars, 360½ Main, h. same.
Schugans, Otto. musician, h. 162 Elm.
Schuh, Anton, shoemaker. b. 575 Washington.
Schuh, Matthias, R. R. h. 213 Elm.
Schuhman, Francis, grocer. 112 Hickory.
Schuhman, Joseph, shoemaker. b. Burton al. cor. Weaver.
Schuler, Christian, h. Brown n. Adams.
Schuler, G. printer, h. 6th cor. Hudson.
Schuler, John M. melodeon maker, h. Spruce n. Genesee.
Schuler, Jno. piano maker, b. 6th cor. Huron.
Schuler, Geo. paver, h. Lemon n. North.
Schuler, Jos. teamster, h. Monroe n. Brown.
Schulta, Herman, clerk. h. Spruce n. Sycamore.
Schultes, Maria, widow, h. Michigan n. Carlton.
Schultz, Daniel, farmer, b. 253 Genesee.
Schultz, F. wagon maker. h. Hickory n. Wm.
Schultz, Frederick, pump maker, 336 Genesee, b. same.
Schultz, Fred. h. 253 Genesee.   •
Schultz, Fred. wagon maker. b. 110 Exchange.
Schultz, Fred. tailor, 204 Main. h. 394 Mich.
Schultz, Fred. bootmaker. b. 546 Michigan.
Schultz, Fred. lab. h. 50 Bennett.
Schultz, Fred. cooper, b. Cherry n. Orange.
Schultz, Godfried, firm Anderson & Co. grocers, b. 400 Michigan.
Schultz, Harris, saloon, h. 138 N. Division.
Schultz, Henry, lab. h. Spring n. Genesee.
Schultz, Jacob, baker, b. John Foell.
Schultz, Jno. lab. h. 18 Maple.
Schultz, John, lab. h. Davis n. Genesee.
Schultz, John, lab. h. Spruce n. Batavia.
Schultz, John, lab. h. Ketchum alley n. Carlton.
Schultz, John P. tailor, 18 Main. h. same.
Schultz, Louis, coffee extract manuf. 252 E. Genesee, h. same.
Schultz, Ludwig, tailor, b. Johnson n. Gen.
Schultz, Peter, lumber dealer, h. Genesee cor. Pratt.
Schultz, Peter, Jr. lab. b. Genesee cor. Pratt.
Schuller, Conrad, grocer, Wm. cor. Walnut.
Schulz, Peter, plasterer, b. 456 Michigan.
Schulz, Philip, lab. h. 321 Ellicott.

Schum, Fran. shoemaker. 133 Main. h. 311 Oak.
Schum, John, tailor, h. Peach n. North.
Schumers, Hubert, carp. h. Goodell alley cor. Tupper.
Schnnborn, Jno. P. sailor, h. R. I. n. 11th.
Schunck, And. lab. h. Spring bet. Gen. and Syc.
Schunck, Christian, lab. h. Mulberry n. Good'l.
Schunck, Fred. lab. h. 259 Elm.
Schupp, George. carp. h. Carolina bet. Palmer and 9th.
Schury, William.* cabinet shop, 390 Seneca, h. same.
Schuster, Casper, farmer. h. Peck'm n. Adams.
Schuster, Christian, grocer, 387 Main. h. same.
Schuster, Fer. groc'r, Bat. cor. Johns'n, h. same.
Schuster, Geo. lab. h. High n. Michigan.
Schuster, Geo. lab. h. 73 Hickory.
Schuster, John, lab. h. Cherry n. Jefferson.
Schuster, Mich. shoemaker, h. Sycamore cor. Bundy's alley.
Schuster, William, paper hanger, h. 9 Scott.
Schusterbauer, Paul, mason, h. 251 Elm.
Schutrum, Catharine, widow, grocery, h. Bat. cor. Johnson.
Schutrum, Henry, peddler, h. 129 Sycamore.
Schutrum, Valentine, cigar maker, h. 129 Syc.
Schutz, John, carp. h Spruce n. Genesee.
Schutz, John, Jr. printer, h. 259 Oak.
Schutz, Joseph. moulder, h. William n. Walnut.
Schutz, Peter, printer, b. Spruce n. Genesee.
Schutz, Michael, engineer, h. Pine n. Batavia.
Schuyler, D. b H. Chandler, 163 Swan.
Schwab, Anton, bricklayer, h. Mulberry n High.
Schwab, John, lab. h. Main n. Burton alley.
Schwabl, Sebastian, grocer, 197 Bat. h. same.
Schwach, John. lab. h. 12th n. Vermont.
Schwalb, Jno. G. carp. h. Hickory n. Sycamore.
Schwan, Philip, mason, Elm cor. Virginia.
Schwaneknip, John, carp. h. Vary n. Spring.
Schwankin, John, chairmaker, Vary n. Spring.
Schwanz, Fred. porter, h. Pine n. Batavia.
Schwartz, Andrew, lab. h. Gen. n. Walden.
Schwartz, Chas. bakery, 365 E. Gen. h. same.
Schwartz, David, lab h. 539 Michigan.
Schwartz, Geo. saloon, 7 E. Genesee, h. same.
Schwartz, Henry, mason, h. Hickory n. Gen.
Schwartz, Jacob, carp. h. Walnut n. Wm.
Schwartz, Jacob, lab. h. Hollister n. Mortimer.
Schwartz, Jno. lab. h. Mulberry bel. Va.
Schwartz, John, mason, h. 137 Sycamore.
Schwartz, John, firm S. & Rebmann, h. Wash. cor. Chippewa.
Schwartz, John, lab. h. Bennett n. Batavia.
Schwartz, John, farmer, h. Main cor. Del. av.
Schwartz, John G. carp. h. Wash. n. Chippewa.
Schwartz, John W. ship. carp. h. 558 ½ ich.
Schwartz, Jos. saloon, Commercial n. Canal.
Schwartz, Mathias. lab. h. Batavia n. Lutheran.
Schwartz, Michael, teamster, h. Gen. cor. Camp.
Schwartz, Phelix. b. 40 Batavia.
SCHWARTZ & REBMANN, planing mill, &c. Elm ab. Batavia.—See adv. p. 85.
Schwartz, Wm. J. firm S. & Mache, h. 22 Wm.
Schwartz, Xavier, brewer, h. Grey n. Batavia.
Schwarzass, John, butcher, Brown n. Jefferson.
Schwarztt. Martin, shoemaker, h. Adams n. Peckham.
Schwaxzutt, Geo. butcher, h. Monroe n. Bat.

Schwegler, Jos. butcher, h. Ellicott n. Dodge.
Schweigel, Michael, lab. h. Canal n. Commer'l.
Schweigel, Peter, peddler, h. 218 Ellicott.
Schweiger, Martin,* tailor, h. Genesee n. Jeff'n.
Schweiger, Mary, wid. h. Adams n. Genesee.
Schweigert, Anthony, printer, b. Batavia cor. Milnor.
Schweigert, Frank, printer, b. Batavia cor. Milnor.
Schweigert, John, h. Batavia cor. Milnor.
Schweigert John, Jr. printer, b. Batavia cor. Milnor.
Schweighart, Jacob, grocer, Adams n. Sycam'e, h. same.
Schweinmeier, Anton. lab. h. 7 Cypress.
Schweis, Sebastian, turner, h. Goodell alley n. Tupper.
Schweitzer, Anton, carp. h. 522 Michigan.
Schweitzer, Jacob, lab. h. Hickory n. Sycamore.
Schweitzer, Jacob, lab. h. Mulberry n. Carlton.
Schweitzer, Max, mason, h. r. 372 Genesee.
Schwendeman, And. cutlery, Batavia n. Cedar.
Schwer, Paul. lab. b. 131 Genesee.
Schwetner, Geo. lab. h. Maple n. Goodell.
Schweyer, Henry, lab. h. Sycamore n. Keane.
Schweyer, Peter. lab. h. Genesee n. Kaene.
Schwinderman, Geo. h. Cottage n. Maryland.
Schwing, William. turner, h. Bat. cor. Bennett.
Schwinn, Jacob, wagon maker, h. Batavia n. Williamsville road.
Schwinn, Jno. C. shoemaker, h. Pine n. Bat.
Schwinn, Jno. W. umbrella maker, 377 Washington, h. same.
Schwinneman, Andrew, cutler, h. 165 Batavia.
Schwitzke, Chas. blacksmith, h. Wm. n. Adams.
Schwohn, Fred. clerk, h. Pine n. Batavia.
Schwowoda, Jno. carp. h. Monroe n. Batavia.
Scobell, Richard, book-keeper, L. S. R. R. ticket office, h. 97 9th.
SCOFIELD, AUGUST, fence maker, h. 113 Seneca.—See adv. p. 17.
Scofield, Wm. painter, h. Abbott road bel R. R.
Scolard, J. blacksmith. at Brayley & Pitts.
Scoonhurd, Andrew, baggageman, h. Pine n. William.
Scott, Ahira, apprentice, b. 61 Clinton.
Scott, David, saloon, 166 Exchange, h. same.
Scott, Edwin, ship carp. h. 61 Clinton.
Scott, Frank, ostler, 116 Pearl, h. Elm n. Gen.
Scott, Fred. carpenter, h. Main n. Utica.
Scott, F. B. sign painter, over 231 Main, res. at Lancaster.
SCOTT, GEO. W. grocer, 9 E. Seneca, h. 26 Carroll.—See adv. p. 40.
Scott, James, lab. h. 2 Centre.
Scott, James W. with Geo. A. Prince & Co. h. 6th n. Hudson.
Scott, J. W. piano finisher, 159 Washington, h. 277 Franklin.
Scott, J. Burt. saloon, St. James Hall, h. 338 Washington.
Scott, Levi, mariner, h. Louisiana n. South.
Scott, Mary, Miss, teacher No. 18, b. C. Barr, Main n. Perry.
Scott, Michael, h. Virginia n. 11th.
Scott, Pat. finisher, A. & J. Keogh, b. 140 N. Division.
Scott, Pat. waiter, Mansion, h. Lloyd n. bridge.

Scott, Robert, nailer, h. Niagara n. Forest ave.
Scott, Thos. J. ship carp. b. 69 W. Chippewa.
Scott, Wm. K. M. D. 39 W. Mohawk, h. same.
Scott, Wm. L. agt. N. Y. C. R. R. h. 96 Folsom.
Scott, W. M. b. National Hotel.
Scott, W. R. printer, Com. Adv. b. 200 Wash.
Scott. W. S. cashier, B. N. Y. & E. R. R. freight, h. Michigan n. Carlton.
Scovill, Erastus, firm Newman &S. h. 55 Del.
Scoville. J. firm J. & N. C. S. b. 131 S. Div.
SCOVILLE, J. & N. C. car wheel and chill tire foundry, La. opp. Lake Shore freight depot.—See adv. p. 61.
Scoville, M. at White's paint shop, b. 13 Court.
Scoville, Nathan A. boatman, h. Mass. n. 13th.
Scrafford, Chas. clerk, W. S. Abbott, b. cor. Hospital and 6th.
Scrafford. Mary, widow, h. Hospital n. 5th.
Scriven, W. M. lock-tender. ship lock.
Scroggs, G. A. sheriff.Erie co. b. Mansion.
Scurr, Henry, joiner, h. 38 Sycamore.
Seafisher. A. C. paper hanger, h. Marinor n. Virginia.
Seagar, Joseph, saloon, 3 Canal, h. same.
Seagler, Wm. paper hanger. h. 296 Franklin.
Seaman. Jas. cutter, 164 Main, h. 14 Ellicott.
Searl, Wm. A. rope maker, h. Forest ave. n. Washington.
Searle, Mary, Miss. private school, 85 Swan.
Sears, Chs. book-keeper. b. 203 Swan.
SEARS & CLARK, lumber dealers and builders, office and yard, River, Erie Basin.—See adv. p. 85.
Sears, Frank A. firm Langdon & S. h. 23 Niagara.
Sears, Selim, firm S. & Clark, h. Chip. bel. Del.
Sears, Thos. P. Buff. Mut. Ins. Co. h. 49 W. Tupper.
Seaver. Thos. traveling agt. Moffat's brewery, h. 7th n. Jersey.
Seba, James, b'acksmith. h. over 138 Main.
Seckel, Michael, lab. h. Pratt n. Batavia.
Seckinger, Andrew. harness maker, 31 E. Seneca, h. Michigan n. Goodell.
Seckler, Chas. butcher, b. Genesee cor. Elm.
Sedinger, Phelix, clerk, h. Dearborn n. Amh'st.
See, John L. Rev. pastor Dutch Reform church, h. 190 Franklin.
Seebach, G. A. cutter, 183 Main, h. Washington n. Chippewa.
Seeber, Conrad, grocer and turner, 174 Batavia, h. same.
Seeger, Geo. cigar maker, h. 396 Michigan.
Seeger, Fred. grocer, h. Batavia cor. Cedar.
Seekins, Wm. engineer, h. across creek.
Seelbach, Chs. printer, b. Cherry n. Orange.
Seeley, John, machinist. h. 326 Michigan.
Seeley, Jno. F. works Altman & Co. b. 326 Michigan.
Seely, Walter G. circulator, Com'l Adv. h. 106 S. Division.
Seeman, John, furnaceman, h. 71 E. Tupper.
Seemann, Charles, bricklayer, h. 321 Elm.
Seereiter, Jacob, E. A. Darling's, h. 132 Elm.
Seereiter, Mich. policeman, h. Wm. n. Bennett.
Sees, Jno. carp. h. Hickory n. Sycamore.
Seewald, Andrew, farmer, h. Gen. E. toll gate.
Segel, Wm. lab. h. 28 Bennett.

Sehnert, Adam, lab. h. Adams n. Sycamore.
Sehnert, Jno. A. lab. h. Adams n. Sycamore.
Seib. Henry, carp. h. Maple n. Virginia.
Seibald, Jno. S student at law, 158 Main, b. 101 Delaware.
Seibel, Conrad, lab. h. High cor. Ketchum al.
Seibel, Henry, lab. h. 33 Cherry.
Seibel, John F. grocer, 188 Niagara, h. same.
Seibert, Christian, wagoner, h. 514 Michigan.
Seibert, Francis. wagon maker, h. 48 Bennett.
Seiberts, Fritz, lab. h. 540 Michigan.
Seibert, John. shoemaker, h. Hickory n. Gen.
Seibert, Jno. C. moulder. h. Mads'n cor. How'd.
Seibort, J. barber, h. Michigan n. Cherry.
Seibert, John. moulder. h. Johnson n. Batavia.
Seibert, Jno. lab. h. Lathrop n. Genesee.
Seibert. Nicholas, lab. h. 104 Goodell.
Seibold, Conrad. lab. h. Adams n. Sycamore.
Seibold, Jacob, lab. b. 157 Cherry.
Seibold, Jacob, grocer, 176 Main, h. 1 Delaware.
Seibold, John, lab. h. r. 157 Cherry.
Seibold, Jno. S. b. 1 Delaware.
Seibold, Q. Adams, clerk, 176 Main, b. Court n. 4th.
Seibold, Wm. H. clerk, 176 Main, b. Church cor. Delaware.
Seidl, John, lab. h. Locust n. High.
Seidler, Geo. lab. h. Lemon n. North.
Seifang, Geo. sash and blind maker, h. S. Division n. Jefferson.
Seifert, Adam, lab. h. Sycamore n. Spring.
Seifert, And. butcher, b. Main cor. Burton alley.
Seifert, Andrew, mason, h. Fox n. Genesee.
Seifert, Casper. lab. h. Adams n. Sycamore.
Seifert, Elizabeth, midwife, Syc. n. Spring.
Seifert, Geo. cap maker, h. Oak bet. Huron and Genesee.
Seiffert, Fred. J. with J. C. Seiffert, b. 7 Wm.
Seiffert, Jno. beer peddler, b. Haefner's brew'y.
Seiffert, John C. cutlery and instrument manufacturer. 247 Washington, h. 7 William.
Seifreid, Catharine, widow, wash. h. 167 Bat.
Seigle, Anthony, moulder, h. 42 Maple.
Seiler, Michael, painter, h. 140 Oak.
Seiler, Ludwig. lab. h. r. Niagara n. Hamilton.
Seinor, M. printer, h. 82 Folsom.
Seinor, Thos. printer, b. 82 Folsom.
Seitman, Henry, lab. h. Austin n. East.
Seits, Jacob, peddler, h. Monroe n. Batavia.
Seitz, Chas. W. liquor dealer, h. Niagara cor. Amherst.
Seitz, E. cooper, Washington n. Scott.
Seitz, Henry, mason. h. 250 Genesee.
Seitz, John, lab. h. Goodell alley bel. Goodell.
Seitz, Jno. silver plater, b. 150 Genesee.
Seitz, Jno. cooper, h. East n. Amherst.
Seiz, Peter, lab. h. Goodell alley, bel. Goodell.
Sekler, Anthony, butcher, Genesee cor. Elm, h. same.
Selbach, Chas. shoemaker, h. Genesee bet. Jefferson and Adams.
Selbach, Fred. baker, h. Genesee n. Jefferson.
Selbert, Henry, lab. b. Hickory n. Sycamore.
Selden, Henry H. clerk, 220 Main, b. 287 Pearl.
Selegman, Louis, tailor, 18 Main. h. 18 Pratt.
Seles, Ann, washerwoman, h. 62 William.
Selhamer, Christopher, tinsmith, h. Adams n. Peckham.

Selkirk, Geo. sculptor, b. 173 Franklin.
Selkirk. J. H. architect, Swan n Main, h. 173 Franklin.
Sellar, Henry, engineer, h. Terrace.
Selle. A. Mrs. h. Hickory n. Genesee.
Selle, Theo. constable, h. High cor. Jefferson.
Selliox. John, machinist. h. 182 Oak.
Sellof. Chs. lab. h. Michigan n Carlton.
Sellstedt, Laurentius G. artist, 16 Granite Block, h. 39 W. Mohawk.
Selmser, Edward, prod. and com. merchant, h. 28 6th.
Selmser, E. P. firm Hayward & S. at 16 Cent. Wharf, h. 7th cor. Georgia.
Selves, John, brick maker, h. Bat. n. toll gate.
Selye, W. W. firm Clapp & Co. b. American.
Semar, Joseph, hostler, with H. Stern, Exch.
Semmelmann, F. lab. h. Watson n. Peckham.
Semor, A. P. cartman, h. Walnut n. Clinton.
Semple, Wm. H. agent, b. 255 Washington.
Sendker, Jas. shoemaker, h. 143 Oak.
Seneled, Frank. lab. h. Boston al. bel. Goodell.
Senf, Michael. miller, Amherst n. East.
Senfleet, Caroline, widow, washer, h. Pine n. Sycamore.
Sens, Peter, carp. h. Genesee n. Grey.
Senter, H. Mrs. h. Thompson n. Hamilton.
Serfes, Peter, lab. h. Gen. n. Batavia.
Sergeant, John F. sailor, h. 35 Court.
Sergent, Chs. W. mariner, h. Oak cor. Tupper.
Service, Wm. with Jas. Moffat, h. 55 Morgan.
Setten. F. farmer, h. r. 177 Cherry.
SEVERNS, OSCAR, tobacco dealer, 191 Main, h. 174 S. Div.—See adv. p. 74.
Seward. John, painter, h. 2 11th n. Carolina.
Seward. S. B. grocer, cor. Delaware and Tupper. h. 3 Tracy.
Sewell. John B. tailor, h. 173 Wash.
Sexauer. Christ. blacksmith, Gen. cor. Mich. h. 67 E. Tupper.
Sexton. Jason, h. 79 E. Swan.
Seyd, A. A. cigar maker, b. Bonney's Hotel.
Seyd, Emil, leather dealer, 121 Main, b. High cor. Ellicott.
Seyfrang, George, cabinet maker, h. 292 S. Div.
Seyfried, Jos. shoemaker, h. Ellicott n. High.
Seymour, C. L. freight agent. M. C. R. R. h. Morgan n. Chippewa.
Seymour, E. W. book-keeper, at International Bank, b. 52 Pearl.
Seymour, Edward, teamster, h. Carroll n. Ala.
Seymour, Erastus B. firm S. & Wells, h. Niag. Square.
Seymour, Henry S. b. 52 Pearl.
Seymour, Horatio, attorney, 190½ Main, h 24 Niagara
Seymour, Horatio, Jr. b. 24 Niagara.
Seymour, H. R. Mrs. widow, h. 52 Pearl.
Seymour. John A.* blacksmith, h. 422 Seneca.
Seymour, J. B. book-keeper, N. Y. & Erie Bank, b. E. B. Seymour.
Seymour & Wells, elevating and commission merchants, Ohio cor. Illinois.
Seymour, William H. melodeon maker, h. 9th n. Vermont.
Seymour, Wm. cartman, b. Eagle n. Pratt.
Shackelton, James, gardener, h. cor. Rogers and Utica.

Shader, E. H. sailor, b. 6 Commercial.
Shadrake, Ed manufacturer of yeast compound, 6 12th, b. 12 12th.
Shadrake, Francis, painter, 11 Swan, h. 13th n. North.
Shadrake, Fred. painter, S. W. cor. Washington and Swan, h. 12 12th.
Shaeffer, Nicholas, lab. b. Walnut n. Syc.
Shaffer, Henry, mason, h. Monroe n. Peckham.
Shaffer, Jacob, shoemaker. b. 4 Commercial.
Shaffer. Peter, caulker, h. Ohio n. toll bridge.
Shaffer, Peter,* shoemaker. 2 Mich. h. same.
Shaller, Michael. lab. b Ellicott n Goodrich.
Shaller, S. W. h. Ellicott n. Goodrich.
Shallerman, S. stove mounter, b. cor. Water and Maiden lane.
Shallow, Walter, lab. h. Ohio n. South.
Shamberger. Ann, widow, h. 135 Maple.
Shanahan, James, grocer, b. Canal n Ferry.
Shanahan, Jno. ferryman, h. 9th n. Hampshire.
Shang. Peter, blacksmith, b. 171 Genesee.
Shangle. John, grocer, Main n. Cold Spring.
Shank, Jacob, ship carp. h. 5th n. Virginia.
Shank. William D. agent, h. 91 Folsom.
Shanley, Richard, waiter at Bloomer's, h. 68 William.
Shannahan, D. on Niag. St. R. R. b. 7th n. R. I.
Shannahan, Michael, sailor, h. 29 Ohio.
Shannessy, M. grocer, 74 Carroll, h. same.
Shannessy, Patrick, lab. h. 15 Mechanic.
Shannon, M. engineer. b. across creek.
Shannon, Pat. lab. h. Clinton n. C. R. R.
Shanty, James, h. Cal. plank road n. city line.
Sharidon, John, U. S. recruiting service, 83 Main.
Sharp, Dewitt, lab. h. Miami n. Alabama.
Sharp, Mary, widow, Erie n. bridge.
Sharrer, Nicholas, lab. Johnson n. Bat.
Shattuck, Alvin, M. D. b. 45 S. Division.
SHATTUCK, CHARLES T. Justice of the Peace, over 144 Main.—See adv. p. 81.
Shattuck, Charles M. clerk, S. L. R. R. h. 152 Clinton.
Shaver, Jacob, Jr. clerk, h. 113 E. Eagle.
Shaver, James, book-keeper. h. 113 Eagle.
Shaver, Norman J. firm F. C. Hill & Co. h. cor. Virginia and Palmer.
Shaver, Peter, hostler, George Efner, b. Wm. n. Shumway.
Shaver, Wm. lab. b. Monroe n. Peckham.
Shavlin, Michael, grocer, 345 Seneca. h. same.
Shaw, Alex. engineer. h. 114 Folsom.
Shaw, C. A. h. 187 Delaware.
Shaw, Chas. W. tinsmith, Monroe n. Clinton.
Shaw, Edwin A. firm S. & Kibbe b. 64 Morgan.
Shaw. George W. coppersmith, Dudley Bros. h. Virginia n. 10th.
Shaw, John P. coppersmith. h. Eagle n. Jeff.
Shaw, John H. tinsmith, 198 Washington, h. 251 Swan.
Shaw & Kibbe, shook manufacturer, across creek.
Shaw, L. D. carp. h. 240 Carroll.
Shaw, Salmon, at Pratt & Co.'s, h. 233 Franklin.
Shaw. Winfield S. clerk, with R. L. Howard, h. 26 Delaware place.
Shay. Wm. mariner, h. across creek.
She, John, engineer, b. Chicago n. Elk.

Sheahan, Michael, carp. h. 65 5th.
Sheahan, John, joiner, b. Ga. bel. 5th.
Shean, Daniel, lab. h. Exch. cor. Hamburgh.
Shearer, Theodore, machinist, h. 399 S. Div.
Shearman, R. H. b. Mansion.
Sheehan, Jerry, lab. h. Exch. n. Heacock.
Sheehan, Michael, clerk, Revere House.
Sheehan, Owen, lab. h. La. n. Ohio.
Sheehan, P. lab. h. across creek.
Sheehan, Wm. lab. b. Ohio n. R. R. crossing.
Sheehan, Wm. prop'r. Dayton House, 5 Erie.
Shehan, Wm. lab. b. 9th n. York.
Sheehy, Jno. blacksmith, h. Mill n. Heacock.
Sheel, Jacob, lab. h. Porter n. Van. Rens'l.
Sheenan, Dennis, lab. h. cor. Perry and Ind.
Sheffelly, N. widow, h. Clinton n. Raze.
Sheffer, Louis, brakeman, N. Y. C. R. R. h. Hamburgh n. Carroll.
Sheffield, W. H. mariner, h. 12 Union.
Sheffler, Wm. h. Virginia n. Gardner.
SHELDON, ALEX. J. ink manuf. Wash. cor. M. and H. canal, h. 163 Pearl.—*See adv. p.* 79.
Sheldon, Geo. peddler, h. Maiden lane.
Sheldon, Jas. county judge, 190½ Main, h. 142 Franklin.
Sheldon, Mary E. Miss, select school, 155 Frank.
Sheldon, M. B. at Erie st. depot, b. Courter.
Sheldon, Philo, merchant. b. Brown's Hotel.
Sheldon, Wesley, shoemaker, b. National.
Sheldon, Wm. tailor. h. 40 Delaware.
Sheldon, —, b. National.
Shell, Hiram, blacksmith, Evans.
Shelly, Jno. lab. h. towpath n. round house.
Shelton, Silvia, widow, h. 155 Franklin.
Shelton. Wm. Rev. D. D. h. 62 Pearl.
Shepard, Chas. mill, sawyer, h. Blossom n. Amherst.
Shepard, Chas. E. att'y, 191 Main. b. Mansion.
SHEPARD IRON WORKS, Ohio, John D. Shepard agent.—*See adv. colored leaf opp. name.*
Shepard, John, D. at iron works, h. 14 Dela.
Shepard, Philo M. L. cashier N. Y. C. freight office. h. 28 E. Eagle.
SHEPARD, SIDNEY & CO. hardware dealers, 54 Main.—*See adv. p.* 60.
Shepard, Sidney, firm S. S. & Co. h. 58 Pearl.
Sheppard, Christian, shoemaker, h. 92 Cedar.
Sheppard & Cottier, piano forte and music emporium, 215 Main.
Sheppard, David, Mrs. widow, h. East n. Am.
Sheppard, Jas. D. firm S. & Cottier, h. Chip. n. Georgia.
Sheppard, John H. tallyman, N. Y. C. R. R. h. Monroe n. Clinton.
Sheppard, Thomas B. milk-dairy, h. Batavia n. city line.
Sheppard, Walter, prop. Eagle tav. cor. Parish and Niagara.
Sheppard, W. L. h. Palmer n. Carolina.
Sheppard, Wm. works C. R. R. b. 92 Cedar.
Sherber, John A. gilder, G. D. Teller, h. Mich. n. Carlton.
Sheridan, Jno. carp. h. Clinton n. C. R. R.
Sheridan, John, lab. h. 166 9th.
Sherlock, John, marble worker, h. 4th n. Va.
Sherman, A. P. Am. Exp. Co. h. 250 Seneca.
Sherman, Benj. F. butcher, h. 226 E. Seneca.

Sherman & Barnes, dry goods and carpet dealers, 205 Main.
Sherman, Chas. A. W. h. 308 Pearl.
Sherman, D. B. clerk, H. Wing & Co. b. 80 N. Division.
Sherman, Esther H. tailoress, h. 79 Chippewa.
Sherman, Geo. B. clerk, H. Wing & Co. h. 80 N. Division.
Sherman, H. C. foreman, Truscott's distillery. h 69 William.
Sherman, Henry, mason, h. 157 Elm.
Sherman, John, carp. h. 107 Folsom.
Sherman, Jos. distil'r, b. Tonawanda n. Austin.
Sherman, Margaret, widow, h. 109 Cedar.
Sherman, Michael, painter. b. 107 Cedar.
Sherman, Paul, R. R. inspector, b. 28 Oak.
Sherman, P. C. lum. and prod. deal. h. 28 Oak.
Sherman, R. D. firm S. & Barnes, h. North n. Delaware.
Sherman, R. J. at Sherman & Barnes', b. American.
Sherman, T. P. baggage master, h. 33 Elm.
Sherman, Wm. M. b. 28 Oak.
Sherman, Winslow, h. Forrest avenue.
Sherreff, John, harness maker, 2 Canal.
Sherrer, Dan. moulder, h. Forrest av. n. N.
Sherwood, Albert, firm A. S. & Co. h. 72 For.
Sherwood, A. & Co. prod. and com. 9 Central Wharf.
Sherwood, George, b. Western.
Sherwood, G. W. saloon, h. Koon's alley n. Blossom.
Sherwood, Griffin, b. 248 Pearl.
Sherwood, M. B. h. 452 Main.
Sherwood, M. B. Jr. h. 67 Chippewa.
Sherwood, Wm. C. h. Niag. cor. Carolina.
Shesler, John, brewery, h. cor. Clinton and Emslie.
Shethar, Geo. W. clerk, 61 Ohio, b. 48 Swan.
Shields, Michael, sailor, h. 6 Scott.
Shiels, Andrew, h. 63 Batavia.
Shiels, Chas. hostler, A. M. Clapp.
Shiels, Charles, book-keeper, Buffalo Savings Bank, h. 63 Batavia.
Shiels, Jas. Mrs. h. 454 Michigan.
Shiels, Jno. A. clerk, Pratt & Co. h. 63 Batavia.
Shifferens, Peter, carp. h. Eagle cor. Jefferson.
Shiffmacher, Balthasor, bricklayer, h. Spruce n. Sycamore.
Shilling, Jno. blacksmith, h. Pine n. Batavia.
Shiner, Rich. A. joiner, h. 13 7th.
Shipman, John, joiner. h. 240 Ellicott.
Shissler, Thos. Queen City Ice House, h. Revere.
Shlife, Wm. grocer, Clinton cor. Pratt, h. same.
Shmitt, Wm. shoemaker, b. F. Bechever.
Shoecraft, Albert, clerk, 318 Franklin, h. same.
Shoecraft, J. P. auctioneer, 5 W. Seneca, h. 13 Genesee.
Shoemaker, Catharine, wid. h. Roos alley n. Michigan.
Shoemaker, E. D. book-keeper, with S. Stewart & Co. b. R. G. Stewart.
Shoemaker, John, firm S. Stewart & Co. h. 117 Niag.
Shoemaker, Nicholas, printer, 358 Main, b. 82 Elm.
Shoemaker, V. 7 Com'l, h. Niagara ab. Virginia.

Shoemaker, Stewart & Co. distillers and produce dealers. 5 Central Wharf.
Shoepflen, Jacob, lab. h. William n. Monroe.
Shofer, John, blacksmith, h. Watson n. Clinton.
Sholtus, E. H. clerk. 211 Main, b. 61 Mohawk.
Shoop, Chas. pattern maker, h. 104 Clinton.
Shoop, Daniel, cabinet maker, h. 88 Cedar.
Shoop, Geo. tobacconist, 325 Main, b. 88 Cedar.
Shoop, John, machinist, b. 88 Cedar.
Shootss, Jas. moulder, h. Wm. n. Walnut.
Short, James, N. Y. C. R. R. depot, h. Ohio cor. Chicago.
Short, L. h. 358 Swan.
Short, Mike, lab. h. Seneca n. junc. Swan.
Short, Pat. emigrant agent, Wash. n. Scott, h. 151 E. Swan.
Short, Philip, lab. h. Vermont n. Rogers.
Shortel, Michael, key maker, with A. & J. Keogh, h. 33 Sycamore.
Shortell, Catherine, Mrs. wid. h. 33 Sycamore.
Shove, Lewis, Mrs. h. 115 W. Huron.
Shraft, A. F. saloon, La. n. Exch. h. same.
Shriver, Peter, engineer, h. Watson n. Clinton.
Shroeder, Wm. lab. h. Seneca n. R. R.
Shulter, Adam, cooper, h. Hamilton n. Thomp.
Shulter, Conrad, blacksmith, Dearborn n. Niag.
Shultz, Biron M. firm Dinwoodie & Shultz, b. cor. Swan and Ellicott.
Shultz, Ernst, lab. h. Adams n. Clinton.
Shultz, Frank, miller, h. Dearborn n. Amherst.
Shultz, R. blacksmith, N. Y. & E. R. R. h. Wm. n. Hickory.
Shumway, Horatio, atty. 12 Spaulding's Exch. h. 40 Franklin.
Shumway, J. B. policeman, h. 156 S. Divison.
SHURLY, C. J. jeweler, 151 Main, b. 13 Franklin.—See adv. p. 75.
Shurly, Edmund R. P. h. 225 7th.
Shurtleff, Charles A. with H. Utley, h. 129 Chippewa.
Shutrum, John, lab. h. Jeff. n. Clinton.
Shutt, Fred. tinsmith, b. 144 Carroll.
Shuttleworth & Co. exchange brokers, cor. Main and Seneca.
Shuttleworth, Henry J. firm S. & Co. h. 178 E. Swan.
Shuttleworth, Wm. painter, h. Spring between Clinton and William.
Shwanc, Anson, carp. h. r. Main n. Virginia.
Shwien, Philip, tailor, William n. Watson.
Siaal, John. lab. h. 214 Genesee.
Sibel, Conrad, lab. h. Watson n. Peckham.
Sibert, Christian, lab. h. S. Division n. railroad crossing.
Sibley, John C. attorney, Main cor. Niagara, h. 104 Delaware.
Sibley, John F. h. 37 Delaware.
Sibley, O. E. watches and jewelry, 186 Main, h. Morgan cor. Carey.
Sibley, R. J. h. Morgan cor. Carey.
Sicardi, Gomillo, barber, firm Scott & S. b. Washington n. Seneca.
Sichert, John, lab. h. Johnson n. North.
Sickens, Wm. lab. h. Palmer n. Maryland.
Sickinger, Andrew, saddler, h. 539 Michigan.
Sicks, Jacob, lab. h. Fox n. North.
Siddons, Robert, conductor, L. S. R. R. b. 137 Seneca.

Sidway, Franklin, b. Mrs. P. Sidway.
Sidway, James, b. Mrs. P. Sidway.
Sidway, Jno. J. grocer, Main cor. Huron.
Sidway, Jonathan, land office, Com'l cor. Terrace, b. Mrs. Wilbur, 408 Main.
Sidway, P. Mrs. widow, h. Hudson cor. 11th.
Siebeneller, Matthias, carp. h. 320 Elm.
Siebenpfeiffer, Charles, Rev. pastor, h. Amherst n. East.
Sieber, Louis, lab. h. Walnut below Sycamore.
Siebert, Friedricka, widow, h. 57 Cedar.
Siebert, Fred. b. 57 Cedar.
Siebert, John, lab. h. Batavia cor. Jefferson.
Siebold, Cornelius, lab. h. Elm ab. Gen.
Siebold, Erhard, painter, b. Elm above Gen.
Siebold, F. Mrs. h. Elm above Genesee.
Siebold, Henry, cabinet maker, h. Boston alley below Goodell.
Siebold, Jacob, lab. b. 157 Cherry.
Siebold, John, lab. h. r. 157 Cherry.
Siebold, Louis, wagoner, h. Burton alley n. Boston alley.
Siebold, Rosina, Mrs. hair worker, 130 E. Gen.
Siebrich, Geo.* tailor, 72 Michigan, h. same.
Siedal, William, brass finisher, h. Hickory n. Clinton.
Siefert, Henry, tanner, h. S. Division n. Jeff.
Sieffert, John C. cutlery and instrument manuf. 217 Wash. h. 7 William.
Sieffert, John F. with J. C. Sieffert, b. 7 Wm.
Siefried, Martin, lab. h. Hinckley cor. Spring.
Siegel, Adam, moulder, h. Walnut n. Gen.
Siegel, Andrew, lab. h. Spring n. Genesee.
Siegert, Michael, lab. h. Walnut n. Batavia.
Siegle, Gottleib, tailor, h. North n. Peach.
Siegle, John Wm. lab. h. Bat. n. Walnut.
Sieglebind, Henry, lab. h. Madison n. Bat.
Siegler, John, lab. h. Walnut n. Genesee.
Siegman, Geo. stone cutter, h. 92 Monroe.
Sies, Wm. farmer, h. Niag. n. city line.
Siess, John, baker, h. cor. Mich. and Burton al.
Sigel, John, painter, h. 18 Maple.
Sigwald, J. cutler, 57 Gen. h. same.
Sihrer, Jos. lab. h. Batavia cor. Ash.
Sikes, Edwin, chair maker, b. 154 E. Eagle.
Sikes, Edwin, chair maker, b. 313 Mich.
Sikes, S. D. chair factory, 300 Clinton, h. 154 E. Eagle.
Silas, Joseph, lab. h. Main n. toll gate.
Silber, Frank, tailor, Cherry n. Spring.
Silberberg, D. firm S. Bergman & Co. h. 366 Main.
Silberberg, S. clothier, 366 Main, h. same.
Silberhom, John, lab. h. Bundy alley n. Syc.
Silk, Wm. blacksmith, b. 5th cor. Md.
Sill, Harriet E. widow, h. Del. cor. Tupper.
Sill, W. H. printer, b. Southern Hotel.
Silner, Joseph, lab. h. Sherman N. of Gen.
SILSBY, M agent, Wheeler & Wilson, 207 Main.—See adv. p. 104.
Sime, William, surveyor, Franklin cor. Eagle, b. 126 Swan.
Simmerly, Albert, machinist, h. 111 Pine.
Simmonds, Daniel G. blacksmith, h. Carroll cor. Michigan.
Simmons, C. hackman, h. 5 Edward.
Simner, Henry, turner, b. ov. 522 Mich.
Simon, Catherine, widow, h. 73 Genesee.

17

Simon, F. grocer, 213 Genesee.
Simon. Henry, lab. h. Hinckley n. Spring.
Simon, Henry, bricklayer, h. North n. Oak.
Simon, Jacob, tanner, b. North cor. Oak.
Simon, John, carp. h. Gen. n. Johnson.
Simon. Mathias, moulder. h. 114 Cedar.
Simpson, George, tallyman, L. S. R. R. h. 216 S. Division.
Simpson, John, barber, h. Pine n. Clinton.
Simpson, John, auction and fancy store, 167 Main, h. same.
Simpson, John, brewer, b. St. Paul n. Main.
Simpson, Thos. capt. h. 228 S. Division.
Simpson, Wm. cook. h. Mortimer n. Syc.
Sims, Alex. stone cutter, h. Md. n. 10th.
Sims, E. captain, on lake, h. 7th n. Md.
Simson, Elisha, ship carp. h. Perry n. Ala.
Simson, Michael. lab. h. Sherman n. Gen.
Sinclair, A. A. printer, b. cor. Michigan and S. Division.
Sinclair, Wm. H. waiter, h. 77 Oak.
Sindele. Jos. shoemaker, h. Clinton n. Madison.
Singer, Frederick, farmer, h. Delaware avenue n. Williamsville road.
SINGER, I. M. & CO. 230 Main, H. D. Baldwin agent.—See adv. opp. name.
Sinsel, Wm. lab. h. Monroe n. Peckham.
Sinton, Ann. Mrs. b. Palmer n. Maryland.
Sippel, Adam, tailor, 408 Main, h. Oak n. Va.
Sippel, Conrad. tailor, 398 Main, h. same.
Sirret. Emile, importer and dealer in liquors, 317 Main, h. 382 Michigan.
Sirret, Eugene C. clerk, 317 Main, b. 382 Mich.
Sirret, Geo. E. carver, b. 382 Michigan.
Sirret, Lucian, clerk, P. O. b. 382 Michigan.
Sirrett, Belizer, clerk, H. Stilman. h. 114 Elm.
Sisson. Geo. B. machinist, h. 116 Carroll.
Sister Camiela, sup. Buff. sisters of charity hospital, cor. Pearl and Virginia.
Sister Kelly of sisters of charity, b. 12th cor. York.
Sister Mary Patrick of sisters of charity, b. 12th cor. York.
Sister Roasline Brown, principal foundling asylum.
Sister Rodrizgnaus of sisters of charity, b. 12th cor. York.
Sisters of the good sheppard, Best E. Jefferson.
Sister St. Augustin of sisters of charity, b. 12th cor. York.
Sister St. Mary of sisters of charity, b. 12th cor. York.
Sister St. Peter, sister superior of sisters charity, h. 12th cor. York.
Sisto, F. Rev. pater, St. Patrick's church, h. S. Division n. Emslie.
Sittel, Geo. carp. b. 482 Michigan.
Siver, Charlotte, widow, h. 224 Carroll.
Six, M. widow, seamstress, h. 51 Cherry.
Sizer, Henry S. clerk, U. S. Exp. b. Mrs. H. H. Sizer.
Sizer, H. H. Mrs. widow, h. cor. Niagara square and Delaware.
Sizer, Samuel, b. 235 7th n. Virginia.
Sizer, Thos. J. attorney, 7 Court, h. Main ab. Tupper.
Skaats, L. marble cutter, h. 8 Union.
Skelly, John, clerk, h. 11th n. Vermont.

Skelly, Peter, mason, h. 142 6th.
Skelton, Wm. J. clerk, h. 10th n. Maryland.
Skidmore, B. W. gro. E. Eagle, h. 20 E. Eagle.
Skillman, Theodore, h. Pine n. Clinton.
Skinner, Geo. tinner, h. 20 6th.
Skinner, John B. attorney, over cor. Court and Main, h. North opp. Bowery.
Skinner, Wm. lab. h. Ferry n. Jefferson.
Slade, Samuel, prin. school No. 8, b. 52 Swan.
Slade, Wm. H. clerk comp. office, b. 343 Wash.
Slaght, D. A. h. 82 S. Division.
Slagle, Peter, machinist, h. Palmer n. Md.
Slall, August, lab. Pratt n. William.
Slater, Edward, boarding, h. Mich. cor. Ohio.
Slatery, James. seaman, h. 5 Scott.
Slaughter, Louis, Mrs. widow, 75 Elm.
Slaven, Pat. lab. h. 13th n. Vermont.
Slavin, Wm. grocer. Illinois cor. Scott.
Slaytor. S. V. melodeon maker, h. 94 6th.
Sliger, Rudolf, mariner, h. Watson n. Wm.
Slinger, Jacob, brewer, h. Clinton n. Madison.
Sliter, Geo. boatman, h. Hayward n. Elk.
Sliter, Nicholas, hackman, h. 3 Centre.
Sloan, Alexander, grocer, 82 Main, h. 31 Oak.
Sloan. David, clerk, E. S. Bemis, b. 5 Green.
Sloan, Geo. clerk at 41 E. Seneca, b. 26 Ky.
Sloan, Hugh, grocer, 39 Exchange, h. same.
Sloan, James. h. Niagara n. Sloan.
Sloan, James, grocer, Washington cor. Perry.
Sloan, Jas. grocer. Main n. Ferry, h. same.
Sloan, Jas. carp. Kentucky n. Mackinaw.
Sloan, James, Jr. carp. b. Niagara n. Sloan.
Sloan, Peter, b. James Sloan.
Sloan, R. E. machinist, b. cor. Chicago and Exchange.
Sloan, Thos. grocer, 57 Exchange, h. same.
Sloan, Wm. grocer, 19 Exchange, h. same.
Sloan, Wm. W. Hydraulic brewery, Carroll n. Van Rensselaer, h. 7th n. Maryland.
Sloan, Wm. M. timber dealer, h. 62 Swan.
Sloat, John J. hatter, at 202 Main, h. 81 Elm.
Slocum, B. canal stable, h. 33 5th.
Slocum, Chas. H. hackman, h. 111 Walnut.
Slocum, Eliza, grocer, Franklin cor. Court.
Slocum, Giles, with J. B. Dubois, b. Bonney's.
Slocum, John, Wadsworth house, h. 53 Cedar.
Slocum, Michael, porter, Wadsworth house, h. 53 Cedar.
Slocum, Nicholas, porter, Wadsworth house, h. William n. Hickory.
Slocum, Quincy, h. 2 9th.
Slocum. Samuel N. agt. N. Y. C. R. R. h. 37 W. Mohawk.
Slocum, Seth, engineer, b. 92 Folsom.
Slocum, William, h. Amherst n. Jubilee bridge.
Sloop, Stephen, lab. h. Swan bel. Jefferson.
Sloss, Mary, Miss, b. 203 N. Division.
Sloter, Wm. carp. h. 81 Elm.
Slotzer, Louis, moulder, b. Philip Betz.
Slyter, A. with Altman & Co. h. 73 Chippewa.
Smacher, Jos. mason, h. Cherry n. Spruce.
Small, Daniel D. cigar dealer, 44 E. Swan, h. same.
Small, Francis, clerk, h. 83 Spruce.
Small, James, clerk, B. S. R. R. Co. b. Cold Spring.
Small, Jno. tailor, 43 Niagara.
Small, Mary, widow, h. Bundy alley n. Syc.

Smallbeck, Wm. lab. h. Pratt cor. Sycamore.
Smaltz, Jacob, lab. h. Ferry n. Jefferson.
Smart, Geo. engineer, h. 13th n. York.
Smead, H. D. printer, Com. Adv. b. Western.
Smead, S. E. clerk, h Clinton n. Michigan.
Smeltz, Vincent, carp. h. Austin n. East.
Smetg, John, moulder, h. E. Bennett opposite market.
Smid, Joseph, grocer, across creek.
Smink, Nicholas, varnisher, h. 91 Cedar.
Smit, Moses J. dealer in second hand clothing, 2 Commercial and 2 Pearl, h. 13 Carroll.
Smith, Adam, cooper, h Tonawanda n. East.
Smith, A. L. clerk, with F. S. Fitch, cor. Seneca and Michigan, h. same.
Smith, Albert, barber, h. 68 Bennett.
Smith, Albert, cigar maker. b. Elm n. Batavia.
Smith, Albert, sailor, 199 Oak.
Smith, Alfred H. firm Hiram S. & Co. h. 213 Pearl.
Smith, Anthony, lab. h. Amherst n. city line.
Smith, Barnard, tailor, h. 64 Delaware place.
Smith, B. F. conductor, N. Y. C. R. R. h. 172 E. Swan.
Smith & Bowen,* engravers on wood, 190½ Main.
Smith & Brother, hatters, 267 Main.
Smith, Caroline, widow, h. Perry n. Hayward.
Smith, Chas. at Brayley & Pitts. h. 333 Goodell.
Smith, Chas. sail maker, h. 11 William.
Smith, Chas. sailor, h. Fulton n. Chicago.
Smith, Chas. switchman, h. Hickory n. Wm.
Smith, Chas. D. barber, h. 56 Folsom.
Smith, Chas. E. farmer, h. 188 Genesee.
Smith, C. K. cooper, b. 6 Scott.
Smith, Cynthia B. widow, h. Allen n. Pearl.
Smith, D. C. book-keeper, b. 38 Oak.
Smith, Darius, boat builder, h. Wash. n. High.
Smith, David, lab. h. Ohio n. R. R. crossing.
Smith, Ed. brass founder, b. Folsom n. Chicago.
Smith, Edmond H. clerk, Heill & Co. b. Jas. D. Bishop.
Smith, Edward W. auctioneer, h. 205 Oak.
Smith, Edwin, firm Robinson & Co. h. 122 Franklin.
Smith, E. H. saddler, b. 229 Carroll.
Smith, Elias, cigar maker, 157 Main, b. 33 E. Genesee.
Smith, Eli B. milkman, h. Smith n. Exchange.
Smith, Elisha T. teller, Clinton Bank, h. Franklin n. Allen.
Smith, Eliza, widow, nurse, h. 322 Michigan.
Smith, Eliza, Miss. h. 156 Ellicott.
Smith, Eliza, Mrs. milliner, 52 Ellicott.
Smith, Elizabeth, widow, h. Monroe n. Wm.
Smith, Elliot, peddler, h. Clinton n. Walnut.
Smith, E. M. daguerrean, over 268 Main.
Smith, Ernst, tailor, h. Potter opp. arsenal.
Smith, Eugene W. shaving and bathing, 4 E. Seneca, h. 34 Clinton.
Smith, Ferdinand, plasterer, h. Riley n. Jeff.
Smith, Francis, blacksmith, b. Carolina n. 7th.
Smith, Francis, moulder, h. Hayward n. Emslie.
Smith, Francis, lab. h. Hamburgh n. Carroll.
Smith, Francis, toll-gate keeper, Genesee junction Best.
Smith, Frank, saloon. h. William.
Smith, Fred. steam plow manuf. b. 19 William.

Smith, Fred. lock maker. h. 418 Michigan.
Smith, Fred. lab. h. Lutheran n. William.
Smith, G. news-room, 302 Main, b. same.
Smith, Geo. conductor, N. Y. C. R. R. h. 88 S. Division.
Smith, Geo. Jr. b. cor. Seneca and Chicago.
Smith, Geo. lab. h. Peckham n. Stanton.
Smith, Geo. F. engraver, b. 57 Pine.
Smith, Geo. H. grocer. Terrace cor. Mechanic, h. same.
Smith, Geo. L. iron finisher, Brayley & Pitts.
Smith, George M. dentist, with Dr. Hayes, 247½ Main.
Smith, Geo W. moulder, h. 141 S. Division.
Smith, G. W. firm S. & Co. h. 38 Oak.
Smith, G. W. & Co. lumber dealers, cor. Clinton and Elm.
Smith, Greenman, h. 141 Seneca.
Smith, Greenman, harness maker, h. 35 Church.
Smith, Griffin. Rev. b. Tremont House.
Smith, H. book-keeper. Erie bel. slip, b. Revere.
Smith, Harry, firm S. & Brother, h. 21 7th.
Smith, Heman M. farmer, White's Corners pl'k road n. Martin's Corners.
Smith, Henry, app. with Fraser Bro. b. Michigan cor. Carlton.
Smith, Henry E. 127 Main, b. 199 Terrace.
Smith, Hiram, clerk, 29 Cent. Wharf, b. 74 6th.
Smith, Honorah L. widow. h. 5th n. Carolina.
Smith, Isaac H. farmer, h. White's Corners plank road n. Martin's Corners.
Smith, Isaiah, lab. b. 36 W. Seneca.
Smith, Jacob, joiner, Watson n. Clinton.
Smith, Jacob M. ship carp. h. Md. ab. Cottage.
Smith, James, h. 141 S. Division.
Smith, Jas. sailor, b. 22 Mississippi.
Smith, Jas. joiner, b. Fulton n. Hamburgh.
Smith, Jas. painter, 64 and 66 Lloyd, h. same.
Smith, James, lab. cor. Seneca and Ala.
Smith, James, grocer and baker, cor. Court and 5th, h. same.
Smith, Johanna, widow, h. 81 Elm.
Smith, James C. brick maker, h. Batavia E. of toll gate.
Smith, Jas. E. agt. U. S. Exp. Co. b. 29 E. Swan.
Smith, Jas. H. book-keeper, 91 Main, h. 71 Clinton.
Smith, Jas. I. teamster, h. Mechanic n. Canal.
Smith, James M. cashier, Clinton Bank, b. American.
Smith, Jas. P. mason, h. Mackinaw n. Hamb.
Smith, Jas. R. firm Mixer & S. b. 124 E. Eagle.
Smith, J. E. machinist, h. 2 Potter.
Smith, Jefferson, farmer, Main n. Buffalo Plains.
Smith, J. G. clerk, N. Y. C. R. R. freight office, Ohio, h. 169 N. Division.
Smith, Jno. farmer, military road n. Phillip.
Smith, Jno. brewer at P. Walsh, Clinton n. Cedar, h. same.
Smith, Jno. coppersmith, b. 108 Pratt.
Smith, Jno. h. Terrace n. Henry.
Smith, Jno. moulder, h. 119 Sycamore.
Smith, Jno. foreman, Niag. lead works, h. cor. Virginia and Michigan.
Smith, Jno. book-binder, h. 262 Carroll.
Smith, Jno. pocket book manuf. h. 35 Pine.
Smith, Jno. lab. h. Niagara n. Parish.
Smith, Jno. lab. h. towpath n. round-house.

Smith, Jno. prop. of the Shades, cor. Swan and Washington, h. 20 Oak.

Smith, Jno. lab. h. Mackinaw n. Alabama.

Smith, John A. machinist, h. Potter n. Batavia.

Smith, John A. grocer, Main n. poor house.

Smith, John B. at theatre, h. over 437 Main.

Smith, John C. tailor. h. and shop 219 Niag.

Smith, J. D. & Co. plumbers and gas fitters, 162 Main.

Smith, J. D. firm J. D. S. & Co. h. 240 7th.

Smith, John H. h. Abbott n. Martin's Corners.

Smith, John J. oyster and fruit dealer, 197 Main, h. 219 Niagara.

Smith, J. K. with Deihl & Parker, h. 45 N. Division.

Smith, John K. tailor, h. St. Paul bel. Main.

Smith, John M. ship carp. h. Jersey n. 11th.

Smith, Jno. M. canal forw'der, h. 124 E. Eagle.

Smith, John M. shoemaker, 7 Spaulding's Exchange, h. 74 Washington.

Smith, John N. shoemaker, 7 Com'l, h. 7 Canal.

Smith, John R. mariner, h. 30 Folsom.

Smith, John S. meat and epicurean market, 106 E. Seneca, h. same.

Smith, John S. furniture dealer, 58 Lloyd, b. Revere House.

Smith, John W. German teacher, h. South n. Amherst.

Smith, Joseph, boiler maker, h. 19 Illinois.

Smith, Joseph, painter, h. 12th n. Vermont.

Smith, Joseph, engineer, b. Folsom n. Chicago.

Smith, Joseph, butcher, h. Clinton n. Watson.

Smith, Joseph H. plow maker, 138 E. Seneca.

Smith, Jos. lab. h. Water.

Smith, Junius S. prod. com. mer. 28 Central Wharf, h. 158 E. Seneca.

Smith, L. J. mason, h. 53 E. Seneca.

Smith, Louis, waiter, American Hotel, h. Gen. n. Hickory.

SMITH, LUM, bill poster, b. 196 Chicago.—See adv. p. 70.

Smith, Lyman, farmer, h. Main n. Amherst.

Smith, Lyman, cabinet maker, 10 Canal.

SMITH, LYMAN R. atty. office old post office building. h. Main cor. North.—See adv. p. 82.

Smith, Matthias, clerk, b. 6 Commercial.

Smith, Michael, cabinet maker, h. Ellicott n. High.

Smith, Michael, h. 2 Bundy's alley.

Smith, Moritz, chair maker, h. Hickory n. Bat.

Smith, N. b. cor. Virginia and 11th.

Smith, Nathan, cattle dealer, h. Elk n. Red Jacket Hotel.

Smith, N. H. h. 13 Ellicott.

Smith, Nicholas, ship carp. h. Chicago n. Ex.

Smith, N. S. Rev. h. Delavan av. W. of Del.

Smith, O. B. firm Howell & S. h. 68 E. Seneca.

Smith, Otto, coppersmith, b. Michigan n. Gen.

Smith, Owen. lab. b. across creek.

Smith, P. Anthony, with Howard, Whitcomb, & Co. h. 67 William.

SMITH, PATRICK, gunsmith, 127 Main, h. 199 Terrace.—See adv. p. 53.

Smith, Peter, milkman, h. Hickory n. Clinton.

Smith, Philip A. h. 9 Genesee n. Pearl.

Smith, Robert, b. 141 S. Division.

Smith, R. W. at Bloomer's, b. same.

Smith, Samuel, firm Tweedy & S. h. 32 W. Tup.

Smith, Samuel, sailor, h. 6th ab. Hudson.

Smith, Samuel T. with Tweedy & S. b. 32 W. Tupper.

Smith, Sheldon T. clerk, b. 163 Franklin.

Smith, Sidney, actor, b. Wadsworth House.

Smith, Stephen, h. 239 E. Seneca.

Smith, Stephen,* blacksmith, Niag. cor. Mason.

Smith & Schermerhorn, produce deal's, 5 Scott.

Smith, Thomas, clerk, h. 486 Michigan.

Smith, Thos. cooper, h. Perry n. Louisiana.

Smith, Thos. h. 269 Main.

Smith, Thos. J. city sealer, h. Main n. Amherst.

Smith, Thos. Mrs. milliner, 267 Main.

Smith, Valentine, at Niagara Lead Works, h. Boston alley cor. Tupper.

Smith, Walker, butcher, h. Elk n. Smith.

Smith, Walter, brass finisher, h. 26 7th.

Smith, Willard, with Howell & Smith, b. 166 S. Division.

Smith, Wm. h. Allen bel. Main.

Smith, Wm. cooper, h. Mackinaw n. Tenn.

Smith, Wm. firm S. & Bro. b. 267 Main.

Smith, Wm. B. truckman, h. 5th n. Carolina.

Smith, Wm. C. ins. agent, 4 Brown's Buildings. h. 115 E. Eagle.

Smith, Wm. L. G. attorney, h. 173 Niagara.

Smith, William W. book-keeper, h. Hudson n. Palmer.

Smith, W. H. lumber dealer, firm G. W. S. & Co. h. 42 Oak.

Smith, W. H. grocer. Mich. cor. Eagle, h. same.

Smithmyer, Leonard, lab. h. Lemon n. High.

Smithson, James, h. 9 Terrace.

Smithwick, P. J. grain merchant, h. 178 9th.

Smuch, Francis, pump maker, Clinton n. Smith.

Snaith, Jno. clerk, 316 Main, b. 117 E. Seneca.

Sneider, A. lab. h. 123 William.

Sneider, Jos. carp. h. Wm. n. Cedar.

Sneidwin, Adam, cigar maker, b. J. Sneidwin.

Sneidwin, Geo. clerk, b. J. Sneidwin.

Sneidwin, John, blacksmith, Erie cor. Terrace. h. Ash n. Genesee.

Snell, Norman, Am. Exp. Co. h. Va. n. 9th.

Snell, Walter, canal barn, 6 Maiden lane, h. 56 6th.

Snell, W. S. gardener, h. Jersey n. 14th.

Snow, Augus. T. foreman, Wood, Hubbell & Co. h. 93 Niagara.

Snow, Frank M. firm Howard, Whitcomb & Co. h. 126 Franklin.

Snow, H. C. widow, nurse, h. Main cor. N. Div.

Snow, Jas. F. capt. on lake, h. 146 E. Eagle.

Snow, Olive, Mrs. dressmaker, h. 325 Ellicott.

Snow, Reuben G. dentist, 4 Church, h. same.

Snow, Wm. S. printer, h. 295 Ellicott.

Snowbank, Jno. painter, h. Pooley n. N. Wash.

Snyder, Christopher, blacksmith, 15 E. Eagle, h. Mich. cor. Sycamore.

Snyder, Franklin, porter, Hollister Bank, h 8 Bear.

Snyder, Geo. h. 200 Franklin.

Snyder, Henry, blacksmith, h. Mich. cor. Syc.

Snyder, J. at Brayley & Pitts.

Snyder, Jos. A. machinist, h. 58 Carolina.

Snyder, R. tailor. h. 36 Union.

Soder, Chas. W. grainer, h. Batavia n. Walnut.

Soens, Peter, cabinet maker, G. House, h. Gray n. Genesee.

Soergel, Jn. butcher. b. High cor. Ketchum all.
Soeter, Chas. h. Batavia n. Walnut.
Sohl, John, tailor, h. 18 Pratt.
Sohm, Otto, meat market, cor. Elm and Clinton, h. same.
Sohn, John. painter, h. Hickory n. Sycamore.
Solomon, Michael, turner, 257 Wash. h. 90 Hickory.
Soltvalt, Henry, stone cutter, h. Stanton n. Peckham.
Somerville, John, Mrs. h. 4th n. Georgia.
SOMERVILLE, SAMUEL, veterinary surgeon, office 8 Canal, h. 146 Swan.—*See adv.* p. 52.
Sommer, Conrad, barber, h. 5 Maiden lane.
Sommer, Fred. grocer, 387 Wash. h. same.
Sommer, Philip, barber, Bonney's Hotel, b. 5 Maiden lane.
Sondermon, Godfrey, gardener, h. Park n. North.
Sonner. Magdalene, wid. h. Elm cor. Virginia.
Sonnick, Peter, M. D. Ash cor. Gen. h. same.
Sonnick, Peter, lab. h. Batavia n. Hickory.
Sontag. Philip, saloon, River n. W. T. Co.
Sorg, Eliza, Miss. teacher No. 12, b. 27 Ellicott.
Sorg, John A. 207 Main. h. 177 Oak.
Sorg, William, carp. h. 2 Bennett.
Sorrel, John. nailer, h. Niagara n. Bird ave.
Soule, Andrew V. clerk, Moores & White, b. 30 W. Seneca.
Soule, Henry V. h. 30 W. Seneca.
Sour, Chas. butcher, William cor. Walnut.
Sour, Fred.* butcher, 58 6th, h. same.
Sour. Peter, carp. h. 10th ab. Jersey.
Souter, Isaac, engineer, b. 413 Swan.
Souter, Jos. engineer, h. Hayward n. Perry.
Southard, J. B. machinist, b. Saunder's Exch.
Southein, Philip, lab. h. 99 Batavia.
Southwick, Alfred P. engineer, h. 13th n. Conn.
Southwick, Henry, grocer. Mich. cor. Carroll.
Sovan, August, moulder. h. 382 Washington.
Sower, Jacob, locksmith, h. 164 Clinton.
Sowerby, Floaten, clerk, Thos. Clark, h. 12 Oak.
Spade, Lewis, tailor, 7 Canal, h. same.
Spang, Chris. cooper, h. Steele n. Waldron.
Sparks, Chas. joiner, 143 Pearl, h. 97 Pine.
Sparks, Reuben, Buffalo Agricultural Works, h. 87 N. Division.
Spaulding, E. G. pres. F. & M. Bank, 3 Spaulding's Exchange, h. Main cor. Goodell.
Spaulding, John T. clerk, canal col. office, h. 35 7th.
Spayth, G. h. 42 Delaware place.
Spayth, Henry, book-keeper. 288 Franklin.
Spearman, Simeon, clerk, J. T. Noye, h. 27 Niagara.
Speck, John, flour dealer. h. Wil'am n. Ben'ett.
Speck, Valentine. butcher, b. 422 Main.
Speidell, John, shoemaker, h. Amherst n. Lewis.
Speidell, Jos. blacksmith, h. Dearborn n. Hamilton.
Speiger, Chas. blacksmith, h. Sycamore cor. Bundy's alley.
Speiker, Chas. tinsmith, h. 146 Genesee.
Speiser, Mary, widow, h. Burton n. Wash.
Speisser, A. saloon, 5 Michigan.
Spell. Herman, tailor. h. 12 Cypress.
Spelman, Jane, wid. b. Clinton bel. R. R. cross'g.

Spence, J. carriage maker, b. National Hotel.
Spencer, Burrall, distiller, h. cor. Franklin and Huron.
Spencer, Edward S. h. Ferry ab. Delaware.
Spencer, Elihu A. clerk. 54 Main, h. 96 6th.
Spencer, Fanny. b. 36 E. Eagle.
Spencer, Jas. clerk, Erie cor. Canal, h. 62 S. Division.
Spencer, Jas. baker, h. 13 S. Division.
Spencer, Jane, widow. h. 237 Carroll.
Spencer, Jno. R. cash. 54 Main, b. 26 Carolina.
Spencer, O. C. carp. h. Mackinaw n. Hamb'gh.
Spencer, Warren P. Mer. College, Brown's Buildings, b. Courter House.
Spencer, W. H. tel. operator, L. S. R. R. h. Niagara n. Huron.
Spendellow, Henry, Cutter & Austin elevator, h. Ketchum n. Carlton.
Spendler, Chs. cabinet maker, h. Burton alley n. Ellicott.
Spengler, Gottlieb, shoemaker, h. 34 Union.
Spengler, Matthias,* baker, 179 Gen. h. same.
Sperling, John, lab. h. Walnut ab. Bat.
Sperri, Frank. shoemaker, b. 575 Main.
Spertzell, Justus, wholesale confectioner, 9 S. Division, h. same.
Sperwer, John. lab. h. High cor. Maple.
Speth, Gregory. stone cutter, h. 42 Del. place.
Speth, Vetal. shoemaker, h. Tupper bel. Va.
Spiegel, Marks, with Altman & Co. b. 152 Ellicott.
Spielman, Anton, lab. h. German al. n. Syc.
Spielman, Wendelin, lab. h. Mortimer n. Gen.
Spies, Henry,* baker, Gen. n. Kaene, h. same.
Spies, John, mason, h. Peach n. High.
Spies, John L. carpenter, h. Peach n. High.
Spies, Sophia, widow, h. Peach n. High.
Spiesz, Anton, cigar maker, h. Spring n. Syc.
Spiesz, Ehrhard, cooper, h. 22 Walnut.
Spiesz, John, prof. music, b. Huron cor. Main.
Spiesz, Jno. bar tender at Zeigele's saloon.
Spiez, Balthauser, cooper, b. Walnut n. Bat.
Spine, Mary, seamstress. b. Spring n. Batavia.
Spiner, Gottleib, lab. h. Spring n. Batavia.
Spiner, Jno. carp. b. Spring n. Batavia.
Spiner, Jno. tailor, b. 159 Main.
Spiner, Margaret, widow, h. Spring n. Batavia.
Spipinger, Matthew, lab. h. Gen. n. Jefferson.
Spire, Geo. firm Frank & Co. b. A. H. Frank.
Spitzmier, Mary, widow, h. Spring n. Batavia.
Spitzmiller, A. J. clk. 384 Main. h. 163 Ellicott.
Spoeri, Conrad, lab. h. Roos alley n. William.
Spohn, John. wagon maker, Wm. n. Walnut.
Spooner, Alden, Mrs. h. 33 Elm.
Spoth, Matthias, mason, b. Pratt n. Batavia.
Spraeger, Henry, lab. h. Sherman n. Batavia.
Sprague, A. B. exch. clerk, Manuf. & Traders' Bank, b. 57 N. Division.
Sprague, A. S. M. D. h. 57 N. Division.
Sprague, Chas. E. dis. clerk, Manuf. & Traders' Bank, b. 57 N. Division.
Sprague, E. C. firm S. & Fillmore, 222 Main, h. 65 Morgan cor. Carey.
Sprague & Fillmore, attorneys, 222 Main.
Sprague, H. S. clerk, Bank, b. 57 N. Division.
Sprague, Nelson, painter, b. 57 Washington.
Sprague, Noah P. deputy sheriff, h. Franklin cor. Niagara.

Sprenger, Henry, mason, h. 59 Maple.
Sprigg, Chs. P., M. St. R. R. h. N. William.
Sprigman, Louis, saloon, 4 Water, h. same.
Springer, O. F. boarding-house, 144 Carroll.
Springler, Jacob, saloon, 55 Exch. h. same.
Springweiler, Jacob, watchman, h. Pratt n. Wm.
Springweiler, Phillip, shoemaker, h. German alley n. Sycamore.
Sprissler, Frank, tanner, h. Mark cor. Gay.
Sprissler, Joseph, blacksmith, h. 16 Bennett.
Squibb, George, printer. h. 152 Clinton.
Squier, A. H. capt. h. Niagara n. Hudson.
Squier, F. B. agent Buff. Ag. M. Works, h. Delaware cor. Utica.
Squier, G. L. pres't Buff. Ag. M. Works, h. cor. Main and Edward.
Staadler, Christian, lab. h. Mortimer n. Gen.
Staats, Andrew. lab. h. 284 Genesee.
Staats, Jeremiah, cabinet maker, Staats cor. Mohawk, h. Genesee cor. Franklin.
Staats, P. widow, h. 117 Franklin.
Stabell Fred. rectifier, h. 11th n. R. I.
Stach, Lawrence, blacksmith, h. Green.
Stack, Jas. lab. N. Y. C. R. R. freight depot, h. Miami n. Louisiana.
Stack, Joseph, mason, Forest av. n. Main.
Stack, Morris, lab. h. ac. creek.
STACY, FRANCIS, tin and copper smith, 22 Com'l. h. same.—*See adv. p. 97.*
Stacy, Parmelia, dress maker, 10 E. Eagle.
Stadel, Lawrence, lab. h. Grey n. Genesee.
Stademan, Theo. piano maker, b. Syc. cor. Mich.
Stadler, Joseph, tailor, h. Adams n. Sycamore.
Staebler, Geo. with Geo. A. Prince & Co. h. 11th cor. Maryland.
Staedel, Wendelin, mason, h. 298 Elm.
Staehr, Geo. blacksmith, h. Kaene n. Gen.
Staendel, F. lab. h. Walnut n. Genesee.
Staffel, Philip, shoemaker, h. North cor. Mich.
Staffen, Francis, lab. P. O. h. 300 Elm.
Staffiger, Jacob, shoemaker. b. Walnut n. Bat.
Stafford, W. D. conductor, b. 85 Seneca.
Stafbenger, Philip, carp. h. Maple n. Va.
Stahl, Joseph, grocer, h. 115 Pine.
Stahl, Peter, paver. h. 119 Pine.
Stahl, Mathias, lab. 567 Washington.
Stahl, Michael, tanner, h. Mulberry n. High.
Stahleker, Fred. printer. b. 75 Batavia.
Stableker, Jacob, shoemaker, h. 75 Batavia.
Stalter, Anthony, shoemaker, h. Watson n. Peckham.
Stalter, John, mason, h. Watson n. Peckham.
Stambach, Frederick, farmer, h. Main n. Buffalo plains.
Stambach, H. E. clerk, 287 Main, b. 13 Frank'n.
Stambach, M. C. Mrs. h. 13 Franklin.
Stambach, P. C. firm W. P. & P. C. S. b. 13 Franklin.
Stambach, W. P. & P. C. clothing store, Main cor. Ohio.
Stamm. C. Mrs. h. Fulton cor. Chicago.
Stanbridge, Thos. weighman, b. Washington Hotel.
Stanfield, Chs. mariner, h. across creek.
Stanfield, F. scenic artist, H. Oak n. High.
Stansfield, F. J. Mrs. h. 2 9th.
Stanford, Harry, engineer, N. Y. C. R. R. h. 254 S. Division.

Stanford, Lawrence, carp. h. Ky. n. South.
Stangel, John, lab. h. Stanton n. Lovejoy.
Stanhope, L. Mrs. h. 19 Huron.
Stanler, Fred. h. iron bridge, Abbott road.
Stanley, Diana, wid. h. Clinton alley n. Wm.
Stanley, H. H. book-keeper, Erie County Savings Bank. b. Western.
Stanley, Thad. at Frontier mills, h. Ferry n. Adams.
Stanton, James, machinist, h. 6th n. Md.
Stanton, Pat.* blacksmith, h. 6th n. Md.
Stanton, Wm. h. Fulton n. Ohio basin slip.
Stannard, Frederick P. pattern maker, b. 29 Palmer.
Stannard, Gaylord, pattern maker, b. Fulton n. Hayward.
Stannard, Walter W. pattern maker, h. Fulton n. Hayward.
Staple, Benhard, carp. h. Spruce n. Syc.
Staple, Frank, h. cor. Rhode Island and 11th.
Staple, Frank. carp. h. Ash n. Sycamore.
Stapleton, John. lab. h. tow path bel. Gen.
Stapf, Jos. tanner, h. Mortimer n. Hinckley.
Star Brewery, St. Paul.
Starbaird, Caroline, widow, upholsterer, h. 26 Niagara.
Staring, Jno. h. 444 Washington.
Stark, August, lab. h. Maple n. Carlton.
Stark, Joseph, cabinet maker, h. 165 Oak.
Stark, Wm. H. on lake. h. 10th n. Jersey.
Stark, Wm. clerk, 251 Main, b. 26 Chippewa.
Starkey, —, with Hamlin & Mendsen, b. 29 Swan.
Starkweather. H. B. teller, Buffalo City Bank. b. 207 Franklin.
State. Pat. lab. h. Boston n. Cal. plank road.
Statterman, A. musician, b. over 17 Cherry.
Stattermann, Gotlieb, musician, h. Sycamore n. Michigan.
Stattermann, Theodore, piano maker. b. Sycamore n. Michigan.
Stattle, Christ. carp. h. Lewis n. Amherst.
Staub, Alois, lab. h. 143 Sycamore.
Staab, Jacob, lab. h. Sycamore n. Walnut.
Staub, Joseph, saloon, Washington cor. Seneca. h. 48 Sycamore.
Staubel, Christoph, grocer, cor. Cherry and Maple.
Staubele, Philip, watchman, 108 Elm.
Stauch, Diebold, grocer, h. 156 6th.
Stauch, Jacob, furnaceman, h. 85 Cherry.
Stauch, Jacob, Jr. moulder, b. 85 Cherry.
Stauch, Jno. finisher, 3 State. b. Fly cor. State.
Stauch, Phillip, police, h. 537 Michigan.
Stauch, Phillip, lab. h. r. 131 Genesee.
Staudacher, Bernhard, cooper, h. 8 Ash.
Stauman, Geo. lab. h. Madison n. Howard.
Stearn, Henry, saloon, 63 Exch. h. same.
Stearns, Eli, saloon, Bonney's Hotel, h. 120 Chippewa.
Stearns, Geo. tinsmith, h. 32 Union.
Stearns, G. C. book-keeper, A. Rumsey & Co. h. 76 E. Eagle.
Stearns, Nor'n, firm Elder & S. h. 78 E. Eagle.
Stearns, Samuel, Mrs. b. 78 E. Eagle.
Stechholz, Jno. cabinet maker, h. 71 Goodell.
Stechmeyer, Henry, lab. h. Steele n. Walden.
Steck, Jacob, b. 74 Genesee.

Steckhaus, Andrew, M. D. Bat. n. Adams, h. same.
Stedman, A. K. teamster, h. Hamburgh n. Fulton.
Steedman. Andrew, shoemaker, h. Tecumseh n. Hamburgh.
Steel. Jos. fruit dealer, h. 111 N. Division.
Steel, Wm. huckster, h. Ohio n. toll bridge.
Steele, Charles G. clerk, gas works, h. 37 Jackson.
Steele, John, starch factory, h. Dearborn n. Hamilton.
Steele, John, lab. h. 435 Main.
Steele, Oliver G. sec'y Gas Co. h. 194 Frank'n.
Steele. O G. Jr. clerk, American Express Co. b. 152 Pearl.
Steevert, Jno. lab. h. Adams n. Sycamore.
Steffan, Michael, leather dealer, 575 Main.
Steiacker, John, paver, h. Spring n. Syc.
Steichele, John C. hardware, 140 E. Genesee, h. same.
Steig, Bernhardt, lab. h. over 13 Cherry.
Steigel, Othea, widow, h. 210 S. Division.
Steger, Anthony, watchman, h. 58 Bennett,
Steiger, Balthauser, tanner, h. cor. Madison and Howard.
Steiger, Conrad, musician, h. Bat. n. Hickory.
Steiger, Peter, lab. Walnut n. Sycamore.
Steiger, Theobald, printer, h. Kaene n. Gen.
Steiboff, Henry W. lab. h. Spring cor. Hinckley.
Steiman, C. Mrs. widow, h. 146 Oak.
Stein, Chas. saloon, 93 Genesee, h. same.
Stein, Henry, baker. h. Mulberry cor. Cherry.
Stein, Jacob, h. Hickory cor. Batavia.
Stein, Jas. B. 240 Main, b. Swan n. Wash.
Stein, Wolf. peddler, h. 83 Elm.
Steinacker, Henry, shoemaker, Maple n. Cherry h same.
Steinbach, F. K. tailor, h. 552 Michigan.
Steinbach, Frank. tailor, h. 552 Michigan.
Steinebach, Peter, blacksmith, h. Milnor n. Bat.
Steiner, John, lab. h. cor. Maple and North.
Steiner, Nicholas, coach maker, b. cor. North and Maple.
Steinfeldt, Henry, brewer, h. Mulb. n. Carlton.
Steinforth, John, painter, h. Wm. n. Walnut.
Steingoetter, Andrew, grocer, Mich. cor. Pine.
Steininger, Florian, tailor, h. Hickory n. Syc.
Steinkircher, Casper, lab. h. Monroe n. Syc.
Steinkirchner, Geo. lab. h. Adams n. Batavia.
Steinla, Jos.* brush maker, 377 Gen. h. same.
Steinmann, Chas. teamster, h. Hickory n. Bat.
Steinmetz, Martin, mason, h. Fox n. Genesee.
Steinmiller, Francis, tailor, h. Spruce n. Bat.
Steinmiller, Adam, lab. h. Stanton n. Batavia.
Steinockle, Barbara, widow, h. 36 Delaware.
Steits, Valentine, tailor, h. Mich. ab. Goodell.
Stellwagen, Jas. firm J. S. & Kraetzer, h. 369 Main.
Stellwagen, John G. lab. h. Lutheran n. Bat.
STELLWAGEN, J. & KRAETZER, commission, 369 Main.—See adv. p. 37.
Stellwagen, Nichol. grocer, Cherry cor. Lemon.
Stelzle, Frank, lab. h. Walnut n. Batavia.
Stemmler, Daniel, shoemaker, Clinton cor. Watson.
Stench, Frederick. lab. h. 177 Genesee.
Stener, John, musician, h. 18 Maple.

Stengel, John, lab. h. Jefferson n. Best.
Stengel, John, saloon. 130 Sycamore.
Stengel, Jos. lab. b. 113 Hickory.
Stengelmeyer, S. lab. h. Michigan n. Genesee.
Stengle, Nicholas, lab. h. Locust n. Cherry.
Stenglein, Geo. mason, h. Monroe n. Sycamore.
Stephan, Chris. carpenter, h. Keane n. Gen.
Stephan, Francis, lab. h. 300 Elm.
Stephens, Francis J. saloon, b. Washington cor. Chippewa.
Stephan, Franciscus, carpenter, h. Pine n. Bat.
Stephens, Wm. tanner, h. Jefferson n. Batavia.
Stephens, Richard, lab. h. across creek.
Stephens, W. L. book-keeper, 57 Main, b. 93 N. Division.
Stephenson & Co. jewelers, 200 Main.
Stephenson, Fred. saloon, 297 Seneca. h. same.
Stephenson, Jos. teamster, h. r. 101 9th.
Stephenson, Thos. firm S. & Co. h. Del. n. Utica.
Sterling, Clara A. music teacher, b. 29 Swan.
Sterling, Clara, Miss. music teacher, b. 29 Swan.
Sterling, Geo. engineer, h. 44 6th.
Sterling, Thomas, clerk, h. 44 6th.
Sterman, Wm. lab. b. Richard Evans.
Stern, Philip, grocer, Wm. cor. Jeff. h. same.
Stern, Wendel, grocer, Genesee cor. Sherman.
Sterne, Jno. grocer. h. 402 Swan.
Sternberg, C. F. clerk, 8 Main, b. 100 S. Div.
Sternberg, Chester W. agent. N. Y. S. V. M. h. N. Pearl n. Virginia.
Sternberg, Ephraim, h. 148 Swan.
Sternberg, P. L. firm P. L. S. & Co. h. 100 S. Division.
STERNBERG, P. L. & CO. prod. and com. 4 Cent. Wharf, and 8 Main.—See adv. p. 36.
Sternitsky, Charles, cabinet maker, h. Ash n. Sycamore.
Sternitzky, Charles, miller, h. Walnut n. Syc.
Sterritt, John, carp. h. Niagara n. Sloan.
Stettenbenz, Anton, baker, 225 Ellicott. h. same.
Steuel, Chs. butcher, h. Maple n. North.
Steuernagel, Jno. shoemaker, Jefferson n. Syc.
Stevens, A. G. firm F. P. & A. G. S. dep'ty U. S. marshal, b. Del cor. Barker.
Stevens, Doct. bone setter. h. 223 Seneca.
Stevens Edward, att'y. 3 N. Div. b. 303 Wash.
Stevens, F. P. firm F. P. & A. G. S. h. Del. cor. Barker.
Stevens, F. P. & A. G. att'ys, 1 Weed's Block, Main cor. Swan.
Stevens, Henry. lab. h. East n. Farmer
Stevens, John H. brick layer, h. junc. Seneca n. Swan.
Stevens, Jno. breakman, h. cor. Ct. and 12th.
Stevens, Lawrence S. Rev. b. 224 S. Division.
Stevens, Lewis, clerk, N. Y. C. R. R. freight office, h. 144 Pearl.
Stevens, Milo, circulator Buff. Daily Courier, h. 298 Franklin.
STEVENS, PEABODY S liquor dealer. Main cor. Eagle, h. 154 Franklin.—See adv. p. 49.
Stevens, R. H. att'y, Harvey Block, Main cor. Swan, b. 28 Delaware.
Stevenson, Archibald J. sailor, h. r. 74 Chip'a.
Stevenson, E. A. Mrs. milliner, h. cor. Morgan and Eagle.
Stevenson, E. L. firm G. P. S. & Co. h. 297 Washington.

Stevenson, G. P. firm G. P. S. & Co. h. Washton cor. Lafayette.

Stevenson, G. P. & Co. livery stable, 303 Main.

Stevenson, Jas. L. agent G. P. S. & Co. h. 121 E. Eagle.

Stevenson, J. D. G. M. D. h. 237 7th.

Stevenson, Joel T. student, b. Wash. cor. Lafayette.

Stevenson, John S. sale stable, Wash. n. Mohawk, h. 39 Clinton.

Stevenson, W. H. confectioner, h. 178 Oak.

Stever, M. lab. h. Folsom n. Spring.

Steves, B. F. moulder, h. 92 Folsom.

Steves, Jane. widow, h. 92 Folsom.

Stewart, A. G. book-keeper, 89 Main, h. 62 W. Tupper.

Steward, Geo. H. carp. h. 146 Huron.

Steward, Jas. ship carp. h. Fulton n. Ala.

Stewart, Chs. clerk, b. 62 W. Tupper.

Stewart, Henry, car. insp. N. Y. C. R. R. h. 107 Clinton.

Stewart, Jas. lab. h. Lloyd bel. Canal.

Stewart, John W. clerk, post office, h. 138 S. Division.

Stewart, Margaret, widow, h. 7 Park place.

Stewart, Wm. propeller agent, b. National.

Stewart, W. W. asst. librarian, Young Men's Association, b. 138 S. Division.

Sticht, John, grocer, Niagara cor. Hamilton, h. same.

Sticker, Peter, lab. h. Blossom n. Jubilee bridge.

Stickney, Geo. clerk, b. 36 W. Seneca.

Stickney, Orrin, joiner, h. Niag. n. Brecken'ge.

Stickney, Orrin J. teamster, b. O. Stickney.

Stickney, Zillar, carp. h. Ferry n. Adams.

Stiefen, Jacob, lab. h. Blossom n. Amherst.

Stiegler, Robt. lab. h. Batavia n. Lutheran.

Stier, John, lab. h. 51 Delaware place.

Stiker, Chas. finisher, 3 State, h. Smith below Carroll.

Stiker, Chas. machinist, h. 229 E. Seneca.

Stiker, Valentine, finisher, h. 3 W. Bennett.

Stiker, Valentine, finisher, 9 Water, h. 25 Syc.

Stiles, Eliza, Mrs. h. 4 Hospital.

Still, Andella, dress maker, b. 63 6th.

Still, H. H. book-keeper, b. 29 Swan.

Stillinger, Geo. blacksmith, h. Stanton cor. Bat.

Stillman, Horace, hats and caps, 169 Main, h. 441 Main.

Stillson, Jerome B. local editor Com'l. Adv. b. 291 Ellicott.

Stilson, Jas. portrait painter, h. 291 Ellicott.

Stillwell, Myron, keeper Erie Co. poor house.

Stillwell, Reuben, teamster, L. B. Platt & Co. h. Perry cor. Alabama.

Stimers, Alvin C. engineer, h. 211 Swan.

Stimpson & Mathews, forwd. com mchts. 6. C. Wharf.

Stimpson, Wm. com. mer. 6 C. W'f, h. 129 Del.

Stines, Michael, painter, h. 5 Walnut.

Stinson, Ed. 36 Elk St. Market, h. 1 Pine.

Stinson, Rich. cooper, h. Perry n. Chicago.

Stislenger, And. blacksmith, h. Martin's Cor.

Stithers, Kate, grocery, 5th n. Carolina.

Stitts, H. H. book-keeper, b. 29 Swan.

St. John, Harry, with T. D. Dole, b. Western.

Stock, Fred. lab. h. Dearborn n. Farmer.

Stock, Geo. saloon, 135 Maple.

Stock, John, firm Ash & S. h. 557 E. Seneca.

Stock, Jno. grocer, Peckham cor. Krettner, h. same.

Stockbridge, Ira M. clerk. 5 Seneca, b. 40 Oak.

Stocker, Jno. C. lab. h. 547 Michigan.

Stocking, Jos. A. b. Delaware cor. Barker.

Stocking, Thos. R. over 270 Main, h. Delaware cor. Barker.

Stockley, T. B. carp. h. Chicago bel. Elk.

Stockmar, Constantine, tallyman, h. William n. Bennett.

Stockton, T. W. firm Brush & S. 190 Wash. h. 236 Pearl.

Stoddard, Geo. N. clerk, 308 Michigan.

Stoddard, Newton, carp. Blossom n. Batavia.

Stoeker, Frederick, joiner, h. Watson n. Clinton.

Stoesel, Jacob, carp. h. 314 Elm.

Stoezel, Joseph, tailor, h. Adams n. Sycamore.

Stohr, Maria, Mrs. midwife, h. Hamilton n. Thompson.

Stokes, John, printer, b. Washington.

Stoll, John, lab. h. 125 Pine.

Stoll, John, lab. h. Spruce n. Genesee.

Stollsteimar, Jacob, lab. h. Spring cor. Clinton.

Stollsteimer, Chas. grocer, h. Ohio n. Chicago.

Stolte, Ernst, lab. h. Spring n. Sycamore.

Stoltz, Sebastian, lab. h. 117 Oak.

Stone, Chas. farmer, Ontario n. railroad.

Stone, D. J. mechanic, h. 20 Palmer.

Stone, Geo. S. sailor, h. Virginia n. 5th.

Stone, John, salesman at Clark & Stone's, h. 78 Carroll.

Stone, John, b. Western.

Stone, Spencer, firm Adams & Co. h. 11 Ellicott.

Stonehouse, Conrad, lab. h. cor. Hamilton and Canal.

Stonehouse, Isabella, widow, h. r. 74 Chippewa.

Stonerock, John, carp. h. Hamilton n. East.

Stong, John, at Brayley & Pitts.

Storck, E. D. M. D. h. 161 Ellicott.

Storck, Mathias, saloon, Com'l. cor. Pearl.

Storck, Michael, policeman, h. 116 Sycamore.

Stork, John, peddler, h. Adams n. Brown.

Storms, Christian, brass finisher, 237 Main, h. Michigan n. William.

Storms, Jas. J. 54 Main, h. Palmer n. Carolina.

Storrs, W. R. agent, b. 44 Franklin.

Storum, William, steward, h. 58 Pine.

Story, Fred. C. clerk, Sherman & Barnes, Carolina cor. 6th.

Story, John W. book-keeper, 56 Main, h. 42 Pine.

Story, Joseph, staves and shook dealer, Marine Block, h. 303 Michigan.

Story, Thomas, with Jewett & Root.

Story, Wm. liquor dealer, b. Bloomer's.

Stotter, Nicholas, lab. h. Mich. n. Carlton.

Stoughton, Wm. engineer, h. 8 Bennett.

Stout, L. N. painter, b. 36 W. Seneca.

Stout, William, furniture dealer, 32 Quay, h. 51 Church.

Stover, Louis, with Manchester & Rich, h. cor. Michigan and Sycamore.

Stover, Theodore, liquor dealer, h. Sycamore cor. Michigan.

Stow, Wm. L., S. L. R. R. fr. off. b. 169 Swan.

Stowell, Mary H. M. D. over 1 Niag. h. same.

Strabel, Michael, tailor, h. Walnut n. Wm.

Strachan, Thomas, candle maker, h. Chicago n. Perry.
Strack, Gottfried, moulder, h. 12 Bennett.
Straebel, Catharine, widow, h. Cedar n. Wm.
Straessenger, Chris. Emigrant House, 124 Exch.
Straight, Chester L. dentist, over 280 Main.
Straight, L. C. clerk, Holbrook, Dee & Co. b. 37 W. Seneca.
Straight, M. B. dentist, 280 Main, h. 144 Pearl.
Strandgaard, Sidney, freight office, N. Y. C. R. R. h. 192 N. Division.
Strass, Chas. shoemaker, h. 1 Cedar.
Strass, Jos. E. clothing, &c. 5 Commercial.
Strassheimer, Conrad, stone mason, h. Kaene n. Genesee.
Strasser, F. blacksmith, h. cor. Peckham and Stanton.
Strasser, Frank. blacksmith, h. Peckham n. Lovejoy.
Strasser, Henry, grocer, cor. Fly and State.
Strasser, John, tanner. h. Ash n. Syc.
Strasser, Julia, Mrs. nurse, h. 241 Elm.
Strasser, Louis, grocer. 241 Elm, h. same.
Strasser, Mrs. widow, h. 86 Cherry.
Stratford, Alfred. carp. b. G. W. Baskett.
Straub, Anna, widow, washer, h. 8 Cypress.
Straub, George, gardener, h. Washington n. Virginia.
Straub, Henry, book-binder, h. cor. Virginia and Washington.
Straub, Jos. stone cutter, h. Johnson n. Gen.
Strausberg, F. lab. h. Boston alley n. Tupper.
Straus, John, cooper, h. East n. Farmer.
Strauss, Emanuel, clerk, 3 Commercial, h. cor. Potter and William.
Strauss, Mathias, barber, h. Mortimer n. Gen.
Strauss, Mathias, tanner, h. Exchange n. Van Rensselaer.
Straw, Anthony. lab. h. Main n. poor house.
Straw, Geo. finisher, b. North n. 14th.
Straw, John, lab. h. York n. 14th.
Streb, John, carp. h. 10th n. Hampshire.
Strebel, Thos. lab. h. Adams n. Batavia.
Streele, Joseph, dyer, 389½ Main.
Stregl, Michael, ash peddler, h. Grey n. Gen.
Stregle, John, lab. h. White's Corners plank road.
Stregle, Katharine, h. White's Corners plank road.
Streicher, B. cabinet maker, b. 32 Ash.
Streicher, Jno.* cabinet maker, r. 32 Ash.
Streicher, Julius, locksmith, h. Pine n. Wm.
Streifler, Jacob, lab. h. 34 Walnut.
Strele, Joseph, dyer, 58 Niagara, h. 142 Bat.
Streemer, E. mason, h. 186 N. Division.
Striber, Ed. prop. Genesee House, cor. Gen. and Main.
Striber, H. machinist, B. & E. R. R. h. Watson.
Stricker, Chs. 299 Main, h. Elm ab. Genesee.
Strickler, Alois, lab. h. r. 140 Genesee.
Striebach, Anson, mason, h. Genesee n. Jeff.
Striebach, Anton, mason, b. Pratt n. William.
Striebach, Simon, peddler, h. Johnson n. High.
Striegler, Chris. silver plater, h. 73 Bennett.
Striemacher, Fred. lab. h. 100 Cedar.
Strike, John, grocer, cor. N. Div. and Hickory.
Stringer, Geo. A. clerk, Rounds & Hall, b. 34 Morgan.

Stripf, Jos. gardener, h. 42 Delaware place.
Strobel. Jacob, Niag. lead works, h. Oak n. Genesee.
Strobel, Jacob, h. 153 Genesee.
Strobel, Geo. Niag. lead works, h. Edward n. Delaware.
Stroh. Chas. firm L. Wacker & Co. h. 563 Main.
Stroh, Jacob, coffin maker. h. 13 Sycamore.
Stroh, Lewis, lab. h. cor. Dearborn & Hamilt'n.
Strohacker, Peter, plumber, h. 163 Oak.
Strohauer, Henry, lab. h. Cottage n. Virginia.
Strohauer, Jacob, lab. h. Mulberry n. High.
Strohecker, C. Mrs. widow, h. 218 Genesee.
Strohecker, John, lab. b. 218 Genesee.
Strohm, Jacob, lab. h Clinton n. Jefferson.
Strohouer,Henry, lab. h. William n. Mortimer.
Strong, B. card engraver, with Geo. H. Strong. 246 Main, b. Western.
Strong, Geo. H. engraver, 246 Main, b. 287 Seneca.
Strong. John C. firm Strong Bros. 190½ Main, h. Niagara n. Jersey.
Strong, Morgan J. jeweler. h. 36 Morgan.
Strong, Samuel, h. Delaware cor. Chippewa.
Strong & Strong, attorneys, 190½ Main.
Strong, Wm. R. contractor, h. 130 Franklin.
Strootman, Herman, shoemaker and grocer, N. Division cor. Elm, b. same.
Strorr, Mark, belt maker, h. 223 N. Division.
Strub, Jos. stocking weaver, 83 Main.
Strube, Fred. Mrs. h. 342 Michigan.
Strube, Wm. piano maker, b. 342 Michigan.
Struebing, Chs. lab. h. Mulberry n. Carlton.
Strup, Theobold, stocking weaver, 435 Main, h. same.
Struve, A. P. clerk, h. 177 Oak.
Struve, Jno. tailor, h. Lutheran n. Batavia.
Stuart & Efner, mer. tailors, 204 Main.
Stuart, Wm. H. firm S. & Efner, h. 36 Morgan.
Stucki, Conrad, clerk. 286 Main, b. 6 Court.
Stubbl, Henry, shoemaker, 163 Clinton.
Stubbs, Jane, h. Elk opp. Moore.
Stuber, Peter, lab. Batavia n. Hickory.
Stucki, Eliz. widow, house cleaner, h. 118 Ced'r.
Stucki, John, Mrs. h. 6 Court.
Stuebinger, Louis, painter, h. Burton alley cor. Goodell alley.
Stuebo, Christy,carp. h. 411 Michigan.
Stuehler, John Nicholas, butcher, h. Walnut n. Sycamore.
Studer, Mary, wid. h. ov. 80 Sycamore.
Stuhlmiller, Henry, stone cutter, h. 13 Syc.
Stump, John, finisher. b. Walnut n. Batavia.
Stumpf, Andrew, shoemaker. h. 160 Clinton.
Stumpf, Geo. A. tailor, h. 129 Walnut.
Stumpf, John, grocer, Genesee bet. Elm and Oak, b. Hickory n. Cherry.
Stumpf, John, Jr. b. John Stumpf, Sr.
Stunrm & Gerlach, cabinet ware rooms, 132 E. Genesee.
Stunrm. John J. firm S. & Gerlach, b. 162 Elm.
Sturm. F. lab. h. Sycamore n. Ash.
Sturm, Geo. drover, h. Adams n. Batavia.
Sturm, Henry, mason. h. Spring n. Sycamore.
Sturman, Jas. waiter, Terrapin Lunch.
Sturman, S. W. brickmaker, h. 4th cor. Carolina.
Stuterly, Goblieb, lab. h. Madison n. Peckham.
Stutts, Rudolph. printer, h. Folsom bel. Spring.

Stutz, John, carp. h. Spring n. Clinton.
Stutz, Louis, teamster, Batavia n. Pratt.
Stutzman, Fred. teamster, h. Goodell cor. Goodell alley.
Stuzmann, Philip, engineer, h. 98 Tupper.
Stygall, James, barber, Lovejoy House, h. 14 Palmer.
Suckw, Sophia, wid. h. William n. Jefferson.
Sudderick, John, painter, h. 44 E. Eagle.
Sudderick, Margaret B. music and drawing teacher. h. 44 E. Eagle.
Sudrow, Wm.* wagoner, h. Batavia n. Adams.
Suentsel, Thos. tailor, h. Hickory n. Batavia.
Suesz, Geo. lab. h. Michigan n. North.
Sullivan, Catherine, wid. h. Wm. n. Walnut.
Sullivan, Cornelius, lab. h. Ohio n. Ohio basin.
Sullivan, Cornelius, lab. h. Conn. n. towpath.
Sullivan, Cornelius, baggageman, h. cor. Jackson and Genesee.
Sullivan, Daniel, lab. h. Genesee n. Canal.
Sullivan, Daniel, lab. b. cor. Scott and Market.
Sullivan, Daniel, ship carp. h. 4th n. Carolina.
Sullivan, Daniel, teamster, h. Niagara n. Breckenridge.
Sullivan, Daniel, lab. h. Ohio n. Mississippi.
Sullivan, Daniel, sailor, h. Fulton n. Hayward.
Sullivan, Dennis, lab. h. 34 N. Division.
Sullivan, Dennis, lab. h. Illinois n. Perry.
Sullivan, Dennis, lab. h. 3 Evans.
Sullivan, D. lab. h. across creek.
Sullivan, James, grocer, h. Chicago n. Elk.
Sullivan, John, lab. b. 38 Ohio.
Sullivan, Jeremiah, lab. h. La. n. Mackinaw.
Sullivan, Jerry, ship carp. b. 4th n. Carolina.
Sullivan, John, huckster, h. 12th n. Mass.
Sullivan, John, lab. h. Perry n. Illinois.
Sullivan, John, lab. h. Louisiana n. R. R.
Sullivan, Lawrence, lab. h. Miss. n. Perry.
Sullivan, L. lab. b. across creek.
Sullivan, Michael, lab. h. across creek.
Sullivan, Mrs. widow, h. Albany n. R. R.
Sullivan, Owen, lab. h. 17 Illinois.
Sullivan, Pat. lab. h. Columbia n. Ohio.
Sullivan, Timothy, b. 38 Ohio.
Sullivan, Wm. cooper, h. 225 Carroll.
Sully, Robt. carp. Mich. cor. Carroll.
Sully, Thomas, book-keeper, Brayley & Pitts, h. 106 W. Huron.
Sulzback, Fred. tailor, 23 Exch. h. Gray n. Bat.
Sumer, Philip, h. Maiden lane.
Summer, Jacob, cooper, h. Hamilton n. East.
Summer, John, cooper, h. Amherst n. Lewis.
Summer, John, lab. Amherst n. Lewis.
Sumner, Thos. boiler maker, b. 20 Perry.
Sumner, T. E. h. 37 7th.
SUOR, JOSEPH, turner, 11 Mechanic, h. Hopkins n. 5th.—*See adv. p. 67.*
Supple, John, lab. h. 8 Mechanic.
Sutcliff, John, carp. h. Tupper cor. Franklin.
Sutcliffe, John, machinist, 16 Water, h. 94 9th.
Sutcliffe, Wm. machinist, h. 95 Hospital.
Sutherland, Anson, millwright, J. T. Noye, h. 97 N. Division.
Sutherland, Oliver, fisherman, h. Elk n. La.
Sutler, John, lab. h. Mulberry n. Goodell.
Sutor, August, shoemaker, h. 524 Michigan.
Sutor, Augustus J. hair dresser, 232 Main, b. 524 Michigan.

Sutter, Anthony, lab. 4 Waldron cor. Ferry.
Sutter, Martin, lab. h. Steele n. Walden.
Sutter, Michael, lab. h. Walden n. Steele.
Sutton Brothers, steam engine builders, Le Couteulx cor. Canal.
Sutton, Francis, firm S. Bros. h. 220 Oak.
Sutton, Job C. cooper, h. 124 N. Division.
Sutton, Nicholas, firm S. Bros. h. 120 Seneca.
Sutton, Peter, firm S. Bros. h. 27 Huron.
Sutton, W. A. h. Main cor. Goodrich.
Sutton, Wm. h. 29 W. Seneca.
Swain, J. ship carp. h. 5th n. Pennsylvania.
Swain, John, M. D. h. Niagara n. Ferry.
Swan, Adin, firm S. & Thayer, h. 110 E. Eagle.
Swan, Augustus A. with Swan & Thayer, h. 129 E. Eagle.
Swan, Chris. lab. h. Shumway n. Peckham.
Swan, Geo. locksmith, h. 117 Pratt.
Swan, Russell, Pratt & Letchworth, h. 10 9th.
Swan, S. E. firm S. E. S. & Co. h. 123 E. Eagle.
Swan & Thayer, ford. and com. 25 C. Wharf.
Swan, W. cooper, h. cor. 7th and Hospital.
Swaney, Wm. cartman, h. 157 Elk.
Swankin, John, chair maker. h. Vary n. Spring.
Swanson, Henry, lab. h. W. cor. plank road n. city line.
Swanton, Stephen, gilder, 4 E. Swan, h. 155 Pearl.
Swanton, Wm. painter. b. 6th n. Maryland.
Swarcodt, Martin, shoemaker, h. 53 Adams.
Swarp, H. h. William cor. Cedar.
Swartz, A. S. contractor, h. 321 Michigan.
Swartz, Daniel, baker, 96 Elm.
Swartz, Dewitt C. clerk, Sherman & Barnes, h. 77 N. Division.
Swartz, Frank S. teamster, h. 30 Del. place.
Swartz, Frederick, firm Scheiffer & S. h. Mulberry n. Goodell.
Swartz, Henry P. pattern maker, h. Spruce n. Sycamore.
Swartz, Henry A. C. coppersmith. h. 558 Mich.
Swartz, Henry A. att'y, Erie Exchange.
Swartz, Jacob, pattern maker, h. 65 Spruce.
Swartz, Jacob C. ship joiner, b. Walnut n. Bat.
Swartz, John G. cigar maker, 207 Washington, h. Walnut n. Genesee.
Swartz, Joseph, ship joiner, h. 58 Walnut.
Swartz, Samuel, contractor, h. 77 N. Division.
Swartz, William, h. 22 William.
Swartzenburgh, Wm. H. policeman, h. 5th n. Hudson.
Sweegles, Wm. sailor, h. 77 Church.
Sweeney, Edward. blacksmith, h. 34 N. Div.
Sweeney, James, hostler, h. 175 Washington.
Sweeney, Jas. cashier, N. Y. & Erie Bank, h. John S. Ganson.
Sweeney, John, lab. h. Exchange n. Griffin.
Sweeney, Jno. lab. h. Ohio n. R. R. crossing.
Sweeney, Michael, lab. h. Mill n. Heacock.
Sweeney, Michael, lab. h. Bouck n. N. Wash.
Sweeney, Owen, lab. h. Arkansas n. Barton.
Sweeney, Peter, inventor, h. 157 Eagle.
Sweeney, Timothy, cutter, 9 Main, h. 5th n. Carolina.
Sweet, Albert. planing mill, h. 7 6th.
Sweet, Geo. H. land agent, h. 15 Elm.
Sweet, Geo. W. firm Pettit, S. & Co. b. Mrs. S. G. Walker, Franklin.

Sweet, G. J. M. D. b. 15 Elm.
Sweet, Joseph B. firm L. & J. B. S. h. Niagara n. Penn.
Sweet, Lorenzo, firm L. & J. B. S. h. Palmer n. Georgia.
Sweet, William C. firm Pettit, S. & Co. h. 50 Mohawk.
Sweet, Wm. boiler maker, b. Perry n. Ohio slip.
Swegler. Jos. at R. Bullymore's, h. cor. Dodge and Ellicott.
Sweigles, Eliz. Mrs. h. 28 Jackson.
Sweigles, Wm. boatman, h. Georgia cor. 5th.
Swicks, Thos. lock tender, h. East n. Parish.
Swidzert, John. lab. h. cor. Beak and Green.
Swigler, Chs. cook, h. 300 Seneca.
Sydow, Chas. A. lab. h. Walnut n. Sycamore.
Sydow, Chas. F. tailor, h. Walnut n. Sycamore.
Sydow, Rebecca, widow, seamstress, h. Walnut n. Sycamore.
Sykes, Chas. W. music teacher, h. 94 Niagara.
Sykes, Jno. lab. b. Revere.
Sylvester, Darius. moulder, h. 187 Eagle.
Sylvis, Dan. nailer, h. Forest avenue n. Niag.
Syms, S. W. barber, h. 135 N. Division.
Sypher, Chs. teamster, b. S. Hutter.
Syrher, John, cabinet maker, h. Seneca n. R. R.
Syrius, Jno. cooper, h. Ash bet. Syc. and Gen.

T.

Tabor, Frank, foreman, A. Rumsey & Co. h. 246 Carroll.
Taesey, Jno. lab. h. Jefferson n. Clinton.
Taff, Jno. M. spar maker, b. 102 N. Division.
Taff, Manuel C. pump and block-maker, Ohio n. Michigan, h. York cor. 14th.
Taff, Richard, spar maker, h. 102 N. Division.
Taggert, Archy, clerk, Robert Latta.
Taggert, Etta, teacher, b. 224 Swan.
Taggert, Jennie A. tailoress, b. 224 Swan.
Taggert, Wm. hair restorative, h. 224 Swan.
Taintor. Chas. lumber dealer, River, h. Delaware n. Barker.
Talbert, Louis, grocer, across creek.
Talbot, Eliza, widow, h. 97 Oak.
Talbot, Jno. ship broker, h. Dearborn n. An.h'st.
Talcott, Geo. W. sailor, h. Hayward n. Perry.
Talcott & Houghton, att'ys, 4 Arcade Building.
Talcott, John L. firm T. & Houghton, h. 173 Niagara.
Taller, Conrad, lab. h. 348 Genesee.
Tallman, Bocker, fisherman, h. Utica n. Mass.
Tallman, Jno. S. watchman. h. Madison n. Clin.
Talman, Wm. S. firm Mathews & T. b. Main cor. Huron.
Tanner, Alonzo, comptroller, h. 13 Johnson Place.
Tanner, H. boiler maker, b. 234 Carroll.
Tanner, Harvey, grocer, 234 Carroll, h. same.
Tanner, Henry, 236 Ellicott.
Tanner, Henry M. clerk, b. Main n. Ferry.
Tanner, Jos. pail maker, h. Thom'n n. Austin.
Tape, Christian, teamster, h. Grey n. Batavia.
Tappender, Henry, machinist, 377 Swan.
Tappender, Thos. blacksmith, 377 Swan.
Tate, Henry E. clerk, Howard, Whitcomb & Co. b. 32 N. Division.
Tate, Wm. shoemaker, h. E. Seneca.

Tate, Wm tailor, h. 32 N. Division.
Tattkomskey, Chs. painter, h. Bat. n. Pratt.
Tatu, Jos. mariner, h. Perry n. Ala.
Taufman, Christian, carpenter. h. 24 Bennett.
Taunt & Bristol, furniture dealers. 233 Main.
Taunt, Emery, firm T. & Bristol, h. 209 Pearl.
Tausch, Jno. lab. h. Ketchum alley n. High.
Tauscher, Jas. lab. h. Thompson n. Ham'l.
Taylor, Andrew, lab. h. Walnut n. Batavia.
Taylor, Anthony, farmer, h. 54 Swan.
Taylor. Augustus C. firm T. & Jewett, b. American.
Taylor, Benj. C. cook, h. 106 Walnut.
Taylor, Byron, brakeman. h. Wh's. Cor. pl'k r'd.
Taylor, D. carriage hardware, 2 E. Swan, h. 24 S. Division.
Taylor, Eliza, widow, saloon, 70 Washington.
Taylor, Ellen, widow, tailoress, h. ov. 4 Centre.
Taylor, Fred. W. clerk, J. Booth, h 42 Del.
Taylor, Henry D. clk. 2 E. Swan, b. 24 S. Div.
TAYLOR & JEWETT, ship chandlers. 4 and 5 Marine block, Ohio.—See adv. p. 43.
Taylor, Jno. ship carp. h. 296 Michigan.
Taylor. John J. clerk, h. 152 Seneca.
Taylor, Jno. fireman, N. Y. & E. R. R. b. 324 S. Division.
Taylor, Jno. clk. Murray, Cumming & Grant, b. 11 Oak.
Taylor, Louis, h. N. Wash. n. Forest avenue.
Taylor. Louisa, widow, h. 42 Delaware.
TAYLOR, MARTIN, book dealer, 299 Main. b. 76 Ellicott.—See adv. opp.
Taylor, Orson D. Jr. clk. 299 Main, b. 144 Pearl.
Taylor, Phil. boatman, h. Ferry n. Jefferson.
Taylor, P. A. clk. 325 Wash. b. Revere House.
Taylor, Robt. turner, h. Mackinaw n. Hamb'gh.
Taylor, R. M. farmer, h. Marilla n. Lee's Cors.
Taylor, Robt. S. machinist. b. R. Taylor.
Taylor, William, farmer, Main n. toll gate.
Taylor, Wm. nail maker, h. Perry n. Ala.
Taylor, Wm. upholsterer, h. 103 Clinton.
Taylor, Wm. chief engineer, fire department, h. 32 Oak.
Taylor, Wm. R. boot and shoe store, 236 Main, h. 304 Pearl.
Tayntor, E. farmer and contractor, h. Perry cor. Louisiana.
Tebas, Jno. with Wm. Bark, h. Cypress n. Pine.
Tebe, Henry, lab. h. Adams n. opp. Sycamore.
Tebes, Fred. lab. h. Grey n. Batavia.
Teckenmeyer, Julius, lab. h. 43 Hick'y ab. Bat.
Tedery. John, lab. h. Bennett opp. Market.
Tehard, Christian, cabinet maker, h. Cedar cor. William.
Teller, Geo. D. looking-glass and picture frame manuf. 170 Main, h. Hudson n. 9th.
Temmink, John, lab. h. Monroe n. Sycamore.
Templing. Louis, in iron works, h. Thompson cor. Austin.
Teppel, Jno. cabinet maker. h. Walnut n. Bat.
Terhaar, Chris. cabinet maker, h. cor. Cedar and William.
Terhaar, Jno. cabinet maker, 241 Main, h. 127 Pratt.
Terner, Henry, lab. h. Grey n. Tennessee.
Terro, William, lab. h. Ferry E. Walden.
Terry, Joseph, tinner, h. 136 Ellicott.
Tetter, —, furnaceman, h. Boston al. n. Tup'r.

Tetterling, Theodore, bricklayer, h. Burton alley n. Goodell.
Teuful, Geo. Jacob, shoemaker, h. Lutheran n. William.
Teuful, Jacob, shoemaker, b. with G. J. Teuful.
Teut, Ernst, butcher, b. William n. Hickory.
Thaler, Joseph, tailor, h. 163 Oak.
Thaler, Peter, machinist, h. Jefferson n. Bat.
Thayer, C. H. firm Swan & T. h. 131 E. Eagle.
Thayer, Edwin, att'y, 290 Main, h. 77 E. Eagle.
Thayer, E. S. h. 26 6th.
Thayer, G. H. b. 38 6th.
Thayer, Hiram P. custom house clk. h. 63 Oak.
Thayer, J. Houghton, ambrotype rooms, 274 Main, h. Jersey n. 11th.
Thayer, Joel, b. 38 6th.
Thayer, Nathan, h. 38 6th.
Thayer, Nathan W. foreman, Com. Adv. h. N. William n. Allen.
Thayer, William, shoemaker, b. cor. Seneca and Michigan.
Thaylor, John, clerk, 316 Main. h. 11 Oak.
Theiler, Anthony, lab. h. 147 Walnut.
Theisz, Peter, lab. h. Jeff. n. William.
Theobald, Abraham, blacksmith, h. 66 E. Tupper.
Theobald, Cassimer, clerk, Allen & Harvey, b. Clinton cor. Pine.
Theobald, Cassimer, firm T. & Krupp, 420 Mich.
THEOBALD, CHARLES, tinsmith, Main n. Huron, h. same.—See adv. p. 71.
Theobald, Geo. tailor, h. 106 Batavia.
Theobald, John, clerk, 352 Main, b. 420 Mich.
Theobald, Peter, lab. h. r. 3 Cherry.
Thiebold, W. H. carp. b. 369 Michigan.
Thesseen, Mathias, carp. h. Walnut n. Syc.
Thessen, Peter, blacksmith, b. 85 9th.
Theurer, Christian G. saloon, River bel. Erie.
Thielan, John, carp. h. Stanton n. Madison.
Thieringer, Martin, lab. h. 19 Sycamore.
Thies, Lewis, stone mason, h. 449 Michigan.
Thill, John, tailor, h. Hinckley n. Mortimer.
Thirston, W. H. student, Mercantile College, b. 128 Swan.
Thistlethwaite, Jeremiah, lumber dealer, office Genesee, h. 5 6th.
Thoma, Hortung, painter, 158 Bat. h. same.
Thoma, John B. painter, h. Hickory n. Wm.
Thomas, A. wood worker, at Brayley & Pitts.
Thomas, Alfred A. 192 Wash. b. 85 Niag.
Thomas, Alanson S. 157 Main, b. 35 N. Div.
Thomas, Calvin F. S. 192 Wash. h. 85 Niag.
Thomas, Catharine, widow, h. 536 Mich.
Thomas, Chas. L. tavern, Genesee cor. Jeff.
Thomas, Chs. boiler iron works, h. N. Wash.
Thomas, David, lab. h. Blossom n. Huron.
Thomas, E. A. commercial paper warehouse, 192 Washington.
Thomas, Ed. W. machinist, b. Carroll n. Ala.
Thomas, Edwin, produce and commission merchant, 10 C. Wharf, h. R. L bet. 6th and 7th.
Thomas, Edwin, Jr. liquor dealer, 199 Wash. b. Edwin Thomas.
Thomas, Enoch, clerk, h. 13 10th.
Thomas, Geo. boarding, h. 7 Scott.
Thomas, George H. salesman, 289 Main, h. 58 Ellicott.
Thomas, Hezekiah R. printer, h. 82 Folsom.

Thomas, Horace, dining saloon, 159 Main, h. 98 S. Division.
Thomas, Horace G. capt. N. Y. S. V. M. 21st Reg't, b. A. M. Clapp.
Thomas, Horace J. cashier, Hamlin & Mendsen, b. 98 S. Division.
Thomas, Isaac, machinist, h. Ohio n. Cherry.
Thomas, James L. farmer, h. Gen. n. Hickory.
Thomas, Jno. machinist, h. 5th cor. Carolina.
Thomas, John, carp. h. Oak n. Red Jacket.
Thomas, Jos. lab. h. Park n. Virginia.
Thomas, Jos. carp. h. 376 Michigan.
Thomas, M. fish dealer, across creek.
Thomas, Mrs.* milliner, 158 Batavia.
Thomas, Peter, musician, h. 3 Vine alley.
Thomas, Robert, marine inspector, h. Niagara n. Morgan.
Thomas, Robert, h. 213 Niagara.
Thomas, W. A. with H. Thomas, b. 157 Main.
Thomas, Wealthy, widow, h. 183 Ellicott.
Thomas, Wm. blacksmith, h. 447 Michigan.
Thommesser, Mathias, shoemaker, h. 4 Gen.
Thompson, A. Hull, h. Ferry n. Niagara.
Thompson, A. P. cashier, Buffalo City Bank, h. York cor. Niagara.
Thompson, Esther, widow, h. 116 Chippewa.
Thompson, E. P. firm T. & Co. h. cor. York and Niagara.
Thompson, Harry, h. Ferry n. Niagara.
Thompson, Harry, Jr. firm H. T. Jr. & Co. h. Ferry cor. Jefferson.
Thompson, Harry, Jr. & Co. grocers, Niagara n. Breckenridge.
Thompson, Henry, driver, b. Walnut n. Wm.
Thompson, Henry, b. J. Thompson.
Thompson, Henry, rope maker, h. Pooley place n. DeWitt.
THOMPSON, H. soap and candles, Chicago cor. Perry.—See adv. p. 77.
Thompson, H. lab. h. across creek.
Thompson, J. veterinary surgeon, h. Walnut between Clinton and William.
Thompson, James, waiter, b. 11 William.
Thompson, Jane, widow, h. 3 Hart Bl'k, Erie.
Thompson, Jane, widow, h 401 N. Division.
Thompson, John, sailor, h. Allen cor. College.
Thompson, John, sailor, h. across creek.
Thompson, John, engineer, h. 294 N. Division.
Thompson, Jno. sailor, h. Roos alley n. Wm.
Thompson, Jno. clerk, b. 279 Main.
Thompson, John W. on lake, h. 33 Blossom.
Thompson, Joseph, rope maker, h. 14th n. Vt.
Thompson, Margaret, h. across creek.
Thompson, Martin, butcher, h. 5 Gay.
Thompson, N. D. porter, h. 52 Pine.
Thompson, O. C. grocer, Niag. n. Breck'ge.
Thompson, O. F., L. S. R. R. b. Wadsworth House.
Thompson, Samuel, carp. b. 7 6th.
Thompson, Thos. fisherman, h. across creek, opposite Reed's dock.
Thompson, Thomas, shingle factory, h. Niag. n. Bird.
Thompson, Warren, carp. b. 50 Ohio.
Thompson, Wm. M. D. h. Delaware n. Ferry.
Thompson, Wm. with Hamlin & Mendsen.
Thompson, Wm. painter, h. 273 N. Division.
Thompson, Wm. lab. elevator, h. across creek.

Thompson, Wm. F. with Pratt & Letchworth, h. Palmer n. Hudson.
Thompson, Wm. J., Pratt & Co. b. 3 Franklin.
Thompson, Wm. P. with T. S. Hawks, b. 199½ E. Swan.
Thoms, Philip, distiller, h. Jeff. n. Peckham.
Thomson. James E. h. 188 Franklin.
Thorn, Martin, lab. h. Walnut n Batavia.
Thorn, Chas. surveyor, h. 171 Clinton.
Thorn, Fred. peddler, h. 297 Oak.
Thorn, Jacob, shoemaker, 7 Com'l. h. same.
Thorn, John, lab. 273 N. Division.
Thornton, Henry, h. Ferry cor. N. Wash.
Thornton, Thos. F. foreman, G. A. Prince & Co. h. 6th n. Pennsylvania.
Thornton, Thos. firm T. & Chester, b. Niagara n. Auburn.
Thorp, H. W. capt. on lake, b. Pa. n. Niagara.
Thorp, Martin, printer, Com. Adv. b. 125 Mich.
Thorp, N. B. prop. Tremont House cor. Seneca and Washington.
Thulman. Fred. gas works, h. 116 Clinton.
THURSTON, CHAS. J. glass stainer, 5 Terrace, h. 80 6th.—See adv. p. 73.
Thurston, Dwyer, b. 80 6th.
Thurston, Jno. M. carp. h. Seneca n. Van Rens.
Thurstone, Wm. h. 390 Franklin.
Tibbets, Chs. boatman, h. Mich. foot Fulton.
Tibbets, Geo. on Niagara St. R. R.
Tibbetts, Chas. at N. Y. & E. R. R. depot, h. 148 Clinton.
Tibbetts, Geo. painter, b. 9th ab. Hudson.
Tibbetts. Henry B. melodeon maker, h. 215 7th.
Tibbetts, Jno. teamster, b. Hudson ab. 12th.
Tibbits, Wm. at Prince & Co.'s h. 363 Frank'n.
Tice, Jno. painter, h. 12th n. R. I.
Tiede, Ernst, cooper, William cor. Spring.
Tiedt, John, wagon maker, Ellicott cor. Va. h. Jefferson cor. Utica.
Tiehrt, Christ. carp. h. William n. Cedar.
Tieschner, Geo. lab. h. Hickory n. Sycamore.
Tifft, Geo. H. firm G. W. T., Sons & Co. b. 178 Pearl.
TIFFT, G. W., SONS & CO. foundry and machine shop, Wash. cor. Ohio.—See adv. opp.
Tifft, Geo, W. firm G. W. T., Sons & Co. h. 173 Pearl.
Tifft, Jno. L. saloon, Lloyd cor. Canal, h. same.
Tifft, Jno. V. firm G. W. T., Sons & Co. b. 178 Pearl.
Tifft, Jos. N. firm G. W. T., Sons & Co. b. 180 Pearl.
Tifft, Wm. S. milkman, h. 126 S. Division.
Tigert. Jos. cabinet maker, h. 17 Spruce.
Tigh, Thos. grocer, b. Niagara n. Ferry.
Tilden, J. H. eclectic M. D. 28 S. Div. h. same.
TILDEN, THOS. B. builder, 11 Franklin, h. same.—See adv. p. 86.
Tillinghast, Dyre, att'y, clerk Sup'r Court, h. 297 Washington.
Tillinghast, Fred. A. wood yard, Swan below Ellicott, b. 255 Washington.
Tillinghast, H. D. firm T. & McMahon, h. 214 Niagara.
Tillinghast, H. P. clerk, b. 255 Washington.
Tillinghast & McMahon, attorneys, 58 Arcade Building.
Tillmann, Albert, shoemaker, b. Wash. Hotel.

Tilson, Mathew, h. 6 Iron place, N. Washington.
Timmerman, Benj. firm Hersee & T. h. Main n. High.
Timmerman, Christian, lab. h. Jeff. n. Peck'm.
Timmerman, Ed. cigar maker, h. Seneca n. R. R.
Timmerman Jos. grocer, 559 Seneca.
Timon, John, Rt Rev. h. Swan, cor. Terrace.
Timon, John, recruiting service, 83 Main.
Timon. Timothy, hostler, h. Green n. Canal.
Tiphaine, Victor, liquor and cigar dealer, 193 Main, h. 68 Mohawk.
Tiphaine, Victor L. h. 68 Mohawk.
Tipman, Jno. grocer, 33 Walnut, h. same.
Tippings, Geo. blacksmith, h. 111 Cedar.
Tischendorf, Gustav. pocket book maker, h. 33 Sycamore.
Titus, O. B. h. Franklin n. North.
Titus, Richard, waiter, h. 95 Oak.
Titus, Sarah A. Mrs. boarding house, 408 Main.
Titus, Thos. J. clerk, H. N. Smith, b. 408 Main.
Toban, Jno. lab. h. Chicago n. Ohio.
Tobias, & Reidpath, grocers, Sen. cor. Chicago.
Tobias, Wm. firm T. & Reidpath, b. 285 Swan.
Tobie, Edward, M. D. Main n. Amherst.
Todd. Jas. melodeon maker,.h. Palmer n. Va.
Todd, Mary, wid. of Jas. h. 88 E. Seneca.
Todd, Robert, sailor, h. 78 Perry.
Todd, Wm. at Fero & Barnard's, h. Gen. n. Morgan.
Todrig, Louise W. wid. Rev. F. T. T. h. 127 Franklin.
Token, Thos. soap maker, h. Chicago n. Perry.
TOLES, BENJ. dep. sheriff, h. 167 Franklin. See adv. p. 81.
Tolles, Geo. H. milkman, h. 75 Carroll.
Tolliver, John, boatman, h. Green n. Smith's boat yard.
Tomlinson, Thos. clk. B. & L. H. R. R. office, h. Georgia n. 5th.
Tompkins, Jno. engineer. h. 32 Scott.
Toney, James, sailor, h. Mill n. Heacock.
Tooker, M. Am. Express Co.
Toolan, Pat. sailor. b. 5th n. Georgia.
Toole, Pat. lab. b, Ohio n. Washington square.
TOOLEY, LEVI A. malt and drying house, n. foot Erie, h. Seneca cor. Franklin.—See adv. p. 74.
Toomey, Donald, lab. h. cor. Smith and Exch.
Topping, Jno. cash. U. S. Ex. Co. h. 191 Frank.
Topschal, Wm. cigar maker, h. Potter n. Gay.
Torrance, Geo. A. clerk, b. 29 E. Swan.
Torrance, —, clerk, Murray, Cumming & Grant, b. 29 E. Swan.
Torry, Abel R. clerk, 211 Main, h. 226 Pearl.
Torry, E. G. tanner, b. 14 Oak.
Torry, Geo. tailor, h. 125 S. Division.
Toshenbrager, John, lab. h. Porter n. Van Rensselaer.
Tospot, Timothy, boarding house, 11 William.
Tourat, Frederick, grocer, h. 382 Seneca.
Tout, John, sawyer, h. Perry n. R. R. track.
Tower, Henry, moulder, h. Conn. n. Rogers.
Tower, Paul, lab. h. Rogers cor. Conn.
Towle, James, carp. h. Rogers n. Summer.
Towne, Joseph H. D. D. h. Del. n. Summer.
Towns, Henry A. conductor, L. S. R. R. h. 420 Seneca.
Townsend, Alex. clerk, h. Oak n. High.

Townsend, Chas. cashier, Bank of Attica, h. 462 Main.

Townsend, Elizabeth, widow, h. 27 Palmer.

Townsend, Geo. W. clerk, Thos. Clark, b. 30 Morgan.

Townsend, Hosea W. 7 Court, h. 30 Morgan.

Townsend, Richard, stone hauler, h. Main n. Amherst.

Townsend, Richard A. book-keeper, 26 Cent. Wharf, h. 30 Morgan.

Townsend, Richard H. with J. Tupper, b. Palmer.

Townsend, Sarah A. teacher No. 32, b. 62 E. Eagle.

Toy, Charles, milk dealer, h. Batavia pl'k road. n. Williamsville road.

Toy, Thos. W. firm Hardiker & T. h. 209 Del.

Toy, Wm. cigar maker, h. 55 William.

Toynbee, Henry S. peddler, h. Pa. cor. 12th.

Tracy, Albert H. Mrs. h. Franklin cor. Court.

Tracy, Chas. E. ship joiner, h. Folsom n. Spring

Tracy, Frank W. b. Franklin cor. Court.

Tracy, Geo. caulker, h. Michigan foot Fulton.

Tracy, Jas. grocer, Niagara n. Breckenridge.

Tracy, Patrick, 13 Green.

Tracy, S. A. book-keeper, M. A. Campbell, b. Delaware cor. Church.

Trager. John, wagon maker, Kaene n. Syc.

Tragseil, Andrew, cook, h. r. St. Michael's Ch.

Trainor, H. J. peddler, b. 34 E. Seneca.

Tralles, F. W. piano maker, h. ov. 292 Genesee.

Trankle, F. silver plater, 201½ Wash. b. 1 Gay bel. Michigan.

Trankle, George L. peddler, h. Spring n. Gen.

Tranzer, Geo. lab. h. Boston alley cor. Burton alley.

Trapp, Gregory, lab. h. Walden n. Ferry.

Trask, Amos, machinist, h. Palmer n. Carolina.

Traufler. John, blacksmith, h. Walnut n. Bat.

Trautman, Elizabeth, Mrs. h. Locust n. High.

Trautman, Michael, lab. h. Locust n. High.

Trautman, Wm. stone polisher, N. Division cor. Hickory.

Trautmann, Frank. grocer, Clinton cor. Jeff.

Trautmann, Peter, lab. h. Shumway n. Lovejoy.

Trautwein, Chas. cigar maker, Gen. n. Spruce.

Trautwein, Louisa, wid. saloon, Gen. n. Spruce.

Travers, Caleb, h. North Canal n. Emslie.

Travers, Frank. drayman, h. Ind. n. Mary.

Traverse, Gilbert, capt. on lake, h. 78 Carroll.

Traynor. James, tailor, h. 6th n. Pennsylvania.

Trazer, Nicholas, lab. h. Raze n. Clinton.

Treat, Wm. M. D. office 7 S. Division, h. Michigan n. High.

Trebard, Martin, watchman, h. Peckham.

Trefts, J. moulder, h. 76 Morgan.

Tregilgus, Joseph, Buff. water works, h. Carolina bet. 10th and Palmer.

Tregillius, Jno. machinist, h. 7th n. Maryland.

Treinlay, Matthias, maltster, h. r. Ferry n. Main.

Trember, Geo. machinist, b. 164 Oak.

Trembly, Oliver, miller, h. Eagle Tavern.

Trenkle, Simeon, blacksmith, b. 227 Spring.

Treshler, John, cooper, 12 Cypress.

Trestel, Michael, piano finisher, b. cor. Cherry and Maple.

Tretbar, Charles F. book-keeper, Com'l. Adv. 161 Main, h. 87 Batavia.

Trettbar, C. F. book-keeper, h. 87 Batavia.

Treuebig, Joseph, cooper, Wm. cor. Spring.

Trible, John M. cooper, h. 73 Spruce.

Tricker, Wm. H. clerk, G. O. Vail & Co. b. 4 Boston Block.

Trier, Christian, saloon, 15 Long Wharf.

Trier, Geo. lab. b. Michigan n. Carlton.

Trier, Henry, clerk, 182 Washington, h. cor. Michigan and Carlton.

Trier, Louisa, widow, h. Michigan n. Carlton.

Tries, Chas. carpenter, h. Pratt n. Batavia.

Tries, Julius, cartman, h. Elm n. Genesee.

Trieschmann, Chas. b. 194 Washington.

Triller. Richard, carp. h. Sycamore n. Pine.

Trim, Wm. sailor, h. 24 Illinois.

Trimlett, Wm. C. printer, Com'l Adv. h. 5 Del. place.

Tripenzie, Ernest, joiner, b. 7 6th.

Tripp, Augustus F. firm S. Shepard & Co. h. 40 W. Eagle.

Tripp, Catherine, Mrs. saloon, cor. Elk and Liberty.

Tripp, Chas S. cutter, h. Butler n. Delaware.

Tripp, Job. gardener, Bat. cor. Wm'sville road.

Tripp, John P. milk dealer, h. Batavia cor. Williamsville road.

Tripp, Jos. P. painter, h. 286 S. Division.

Tripp, Samuel, merch. tailor, 326 Main, h. Butler n. Delaware.

Tripple, John, carp. h. Hickory n. Batavia.

Tritshler. Vincent, painter, Clinton cor. Pine.

Troedl, Casper, mason, h. Monroe n. Sycamore.

Troitl, Andrew. lab. h. Walnut ab. Batavia.

Trost, Chas. A. painter, h. 345 Swan.

Trost, John, lab. h. Monroe n. Sycamore.

Trostel, Fred. gunsmith, h. 369 Michigan.

Troue, Jno. wood peddler, b. Locust n. Cherry.

Trouge, Henry, cooper, h. Hamilton n. East.

Trout, Henry, machinist, h. 25 Clinton.

Trouten, John, rectifier, h. 5th n. Carolina.

Trowbner, Jno. lab. h. Shumway n. William.

Trowbridge, Charles, b. 298 Ellicott.

Trowbridge, E. B. painter, h. 298 Ellicott.

Trowbridge, Jas. fireman. b. 39 Seneca.

Trowbridge, Josia, h. 14 W. Swan cor. Pearl.

Trowbridge, J. S. city treas. h. 35 Pearl.

Trowbridge, L. B. firm Pease & T. h. 21 Johnson place.

Trowbridge, H. A. Miss. sales room 207 Main. b. 73 S. Division.

Trowbridge, Lewis, clerk, h. 14 W. Swan cor. Pearl.

True, Joseph, h. 48 Oak.

Truebig. Jos. cooper, h. Adams n. Batavia.

Truesdale, Gideon, blacksmith, h. Eagle n. Jeff.

Trude, Jerry. corker, h. Carroll n. Louisiana.

Truman, Otis E. book-keeper, b. 2 Tracy.

Truman, Thos. boiler inspector, 11 P. O. buildings, h. 2 Tracy.

Trumbell, Jas. cooper, h. Dearborn n. Farmer.

Trumer, Peter, moulder, h. Wm. n. Stanton.

Trunk, Lorenz, lab. h. 36 Walnut.

Truscott's Distillery, William cor. Pratt.

Truscott. Geo. distiller, h. 158 Delaware.

Tryon, Geo. H. receiver Great Western R. W. office, h. Chippewa cor. Morgan.

TRYON, M. H. tailor, 242 Main, h. Virginia n. Delaware.—*See adv. p. 83.*

TURNER BROTHERS,

MANUFACTURERS OF

Ginger Wine, Syrups, Cordials, Bitters, Native Wines, &c.

AT NEW YORK, BUFFALO, N. Y., AND SAN FRANCISCO, CAL.

ESTABLISHED IN THE YEAR 1844.

New York Manufactory, Washington, corner Franklin St.

Buffalo Manufactory, Niagara, near Carolina St.

San Francisco Manufactory, corner Broadway and Front Sts.

OUR GOODS ARE SOLD AT WHOLESALE BY THE PRINCIPAL

GROCERS, DRUGGISTS, LIQUOR AND WINE DEALERS

In all the principal Towns and Cities throughout North and South America, and in many parts of Europe and Asia ; also at retail, by dealers generally among all civilized nations.

PRICE CURRENT LIST FURNISHED ON APPLICATION, BY MAIL OR OTHERWISE.

POST OFFICE ADDRESS.—Turner Bros, New York; Turner Bros, Buffalo, N. Y; Turner Bros, San Francisco, Cal. All Communications should be addressed (to either of the above) to the place which is most convenient for transacting the business required. For particulars see Price List.

TURNER BROTHERS.

Tubesing, Chas. with E. Drew, over 136 Main, b. 159 Elm.
Tubesing, Elizabeth, Mrs. h. 257 Elm.
Tuck, H. Mrs. dressmaker. h. 9th n. York.
Tuck, Moses. painter, b. 9th ab. Jersey.
Tucker, Chauncey, att'y, 1 N. Y. & Erie Bank Building, h. North n. Delaware.
Tucker, David. b. Mansion.
Tucker, Evensa, sexton, h. 28 Cypress.
Tucker, Franklin, Mrs. h. 117 Oak.
Tucker, Henry C. att'y, 1 N. Y. & E. Bank Buildings, b. North n. Delaware.
Tucker, Jno. K. livery stable, Michigan n. Exchange. b. Wadsworth House.
Tucker, Mary, widow, h. 32 Green.
Tucker, Robt. grocer, 1 Oak, h. same.
Tucker, Thomas, shoemaker, 164 Seneca.
Tucker, Wm. cutter, h. 88 Mohawk.
Tucker. Wm. F. joiner, h. 169 Terrace.
Taerk. Jos. varnisher, h. 96 Goodell.
Tully, Chas. with Hamlin & Mendsen, h. Ill. n. Elk.
Tumblety, Owen, sailor, h. Fulton n. Chicago.
Tunison, T. C. grocer, Elk cor. Chicago, b. Elk cor. Michigan.
Tupper, John, cigar and tobacco dealer, 310 Washington, h. 140 S. Division.
Tupper, W. R. b. 140 S. Division.
Turnbull, John, lab. h. ac. creek.
Turner. Adam, engineer, h. Palmer n. Md.
TURNER BROTHERS, manufacture ginger wine, syrups, &c. 172, 174 and 176 Niagara. —See adv. opp.
Turner, Chas. J. machinist, h. Carroll n. Al.
Turner, Chester P. pump and block maker, h. 196 S. Division.
Turner, Chipman, h. Bidwell n. Niagara.
Turner, James, firm T. Bros. h. 170 Niagara.
Turner, Jas. G. Elk st. market, h. 297 Seneca.
Turner, O. Mrs. h. Bidwell n. Niagara.
Turner, Philip, h. cor. S. Division and Spring.
Turner, Thos. lab. h. Perry n. Hamburgh.
Turner, Thos. C. firm T. Bros. h. Va. n. 9th.
Turner, Wm. steward, h. 22 Pine.
Turner, Wm. pattern maker, b. 54 William.
Turner, Wm. B. printer, b. Bidwell n. Niagara.
Turpin, Pat. nail maker, b. Fulton n. Chicago.
Tuskar, Henry, lab. h. 197 Eagle.
Tuthill, Roswell P. boarding, h. 125 Michigan.
Tuton, Harvey, agent Wood, Hubbell & Co. b. 46 E. Swan.
Tuttle, David N. com. mer. h. 37 W. Eagle.
Tuttle, David W., N. Y. S. V. M. 21st Reg. b. 37 W. Eagle.
Tuttle, Elizabeth, teacher No. 20, b. East n. Amherst.
Tuttle, Geo. with L. B. Platt & Co. b. 59 E. Eagle.
Tuttle, Wm. h. East n. Amherst.
Tuttle, Wm. ass't sup't. L. H. R. R. b. Courter House.
Tweedy & Smith, hat, cap and fur store, 173 Main.
Tweedy, Wm. firm T. & Smith, h. 167 Del.
Tweedy, Wm. S. clerk, T. & Smith. b. 167 Del
Twichell, Abram, grocer, 406 Main, h. 199 Pearl.
Twichell, Collins, clk. A. Twichell, b. 199 Pearl.

Twichell, Samuel, Jr. h. Abbott road, 3½ miles from Main.
Tyler, Elihu, green house, h. N. Wm. n. North.
Tyler, Jos. cutter, 224 Main, b. Fr'nklin House.
Tyler, Jos. K. dep. sheriff, h. 102 E. Swan.
Tyler, J. H. law student, b. 102 Swan.
Tyler, Mary, E. Mrs. teacher No. 2, b. 32 Carolina.
Tyman, Peter, joiner, h. North cor. 11th.
Tyrrell, Wm. fireman, gas works, h. Ferry n. Walden.

U.

Ubelherr, Jacob, carpenter, h. 544 Michigan.
Ubeing. Anthony, boiler maker, h. 95 Pine.
Ubeing, John, painter, Batavia bel. Bennett.
Uebel, Charles, lab. h. 487 E. Genesee.
Uebler, Erhart, lab. h. Ketchum alley n. High.
Uebler, Matthias, butcher, h. Cedar n. Wm.
Uehlein, Martin, shoemaker, h. 133 Pine.
Uhlrig, Chs. baker, h. Goodell cor. Goodell al.
Uhly, Augustus,* tailor, 17 Pearl, h. same.
Uhrhan, Chas. painter, h. Locust n. Virginia.
Uhrlandt, Geo. F. clerk, Dinwoodie & Shultz, b. cor. Clinton and Pine.
Ulinger, Geo. lab. h. Jefferson n. Ferry.
Ullerich, Adam, lab. h. Goodell n. Maple.
Ullmer, Geo. carp. h. Spring n. Genesee.
Ullmer, Philip, carp. h. Sycamore cor. Spring.
Ullrich, Michael, tailor, b. 27 Main.
Ulmann, Geo. lab. h. Spring n. Genesee.
Ulmer, Fred. locksmith, h. 562 Michigan.
Ulmer, Margaret, widow, h. Spring n. Gen.
Ulmer, John, lab. h. Washington n. Exch.
Ulrich, Adam, lab. h. Goodell n. Michigan.
Ulrich, Gottlieb, printer, 358 Main, b. Ash n. Sycamore.
Ulrich, Henry, lab. h. Grey n. Batavia.
Ulrich, W. tailor, h. Ash n. Genesee.
Umbauhauer, Nicholas, tailor, Mulberry n. Va.
Umbehauer, Matthew, lab. h. Howard n. Madison.
Umbehauer, Wm. lab. h. 50 Bennett.
Umberhaun, Louis, cutter, with Altman & Co. h. 163 Elm.
Umlauf. Adam, mason, h. Carlton n. Mich.
Umlauf, Jno. J. mason, h. Michigan n. Carlton.
Unbauhauen, Henry, blacksmith, b. Howard n. Jefferson.
Unberhaun, Richard, tailor, h. Cedar n. Wm.
Underhill, Chas. B. foreman, 5 State, h. cor. 9th and Pennsylvania.
Underhill, Wm. G. miller, h. Ferry cor. Porter.
Unger, Chs. carp. h. Burton alley n. Wash.
Union Elevating Co. foot Erie.
Unterfinger, Simon, printer, Pratt n. Genesee.
Upham, C. Mrs. h. East n. Berry.
UPSON. JEFFERSON T. daguerreotype art't, 324 Main, h. 62 W. Huron.—See adv. p. 79.
Upton, John, lab. h. Exchange n. Hamburgh.
Urban, Geo. flour dealer, h. Doat n. Williamsville road.
Urban, Geo. firm U. & Co. 92 E. Gen. h. Doat.
Urban, Jacob, blacksmith, b. 145 Batavia.
Urban, Jacob, milk dairy, h. Walden n. Ferry.
Urban, Jacob, Sr. lab. Walden n. Best.
Urban, Louis, Mrs. widow, saloon, h. 570 Main.

Urff, John, shoemaker, h. Mortimer n. Gen.
Uschold, Andrew, lab. h. Mortimer n. Hinckley.
Uschold, Geo. lab. h. Mortimer n. Hinckley.
Uschold, Ulrich, moulder, h. Goodell n. Mich.
Usher, John, cap maker, cor. Folsom and Chicago.
Utley, Horace, piano forte manuf. etc. 38 Pearl, h. 74 Niagara.
Utz, Geo. lab. h. Maple n. Goodell.

V.

Vail, A. R. firm G. O. V. & Co. h. 207 Del.
Vail, Chauncey, 2nd gate keeper, Lake Shore road.
Vail, Geo. O. firm G. O. V. & Co. h. 4 Boston Block, Niagara.
VAIL, G. O. & CO. marble and slate dealers, Ohio cor. Chicago.—*See adv. p. 61.*
Vail, H. B. clerk, C. O. Leonard, b. 3 Illinois.
Vail, Isaac, Lake Shore R. R. b. National.
Valentine, Edward, carriage maker, 499 Main, h. 63 Delaware place.
Valentine, Edward, clerk, b. 138 Swan.
Valentine, Frank, plumber, with Levi L. Zook, h. Elm n. Sycamore.
Valentine, Fred. firm V. & O'Reilly, h. Park n. Virginia.
Valentine, Geo. mason, 5th n. Carolina.
Valentine, Jabez, mason, h. 10th 3d ab. Md.
Valentine, John, prod. dealer, h. 12th n. Vt.
Valentine, John, supt. Buff. agr'l mach. works, h. 138 Swan.
Valentine, Michael, lab. h. 11th n. Vermont.
VALENTINE & O'REILLY, lock manuf. 14 Court.—*See adv. p. 53.*
Valentine, Ursule, widow, h. 164 Elm.
Valentine, Wm. H. tinsmith, Levi L. Zook, h. 164 Elm.
Valentine, Wm. mason, h. Oak n. High.
Valiquette, Mitchell, boiler maker, h. Spring n. Clinton.
Vallat, Justus, engineer h. 296 Michigan.
Vallee, John, tinsmith, h. S. Division n. Jeff.
Valleer, Levi, harbor master, h. 54 Eagle.
Vallis, Thos. lab. h. Fulton n. Alabama.
Van Allen, J. D. Mrs. h. Wash. n. High.
Van Allen, Noah, law student, with F. P. & A. G. Stevens, b. Mrs. J. D. Van Allen.
Van Allen, P. J. farmer, Main opp. poor house.
Van Amburg, Henry, farmer, Ontario.
Vanater, Robt. engineer, h. 482 Michigan.
Vanatter, Chas. machinist, b. Walnut n. Gen.
Vanatter, Fred. fireman, b. Walnut n. Gen.
Van Benthusen, Jno. H. carp. h. 385 Swan.
Van Benthusen, John, clerk, 285 Main, b. 385 E. Swan.
Van Brunt, Wm. T. expressman, Kasson & Co. h. Exchange n. Alabama.
Van Bunsworth, J. b. 111 Carroll.
Van Buren, James, firm V. B. & Noble, com. merch. 29 C. Wharf, h. 62 W. Mohawk.
Van Camp, Matthew, filer, h. Dearborn n. R. R.
Vancamp, Gerhard, carp. b. 419 Michigan.
Vance, R. J. blacksmith, b. Commercial.
Van Cord, Lewis, foreman, at lead factory, h. 2 Cottage.
Van Demner, H. sawyer, La. n. Niagara.
Vandenberg, Anton, painter, h. 135 Pine.

Vandenberg, Moses, machinist, b. 3. Illinois.
Vanderblaz, Jno. ship carp. h. r. 206 Genesee.
Vanderbusch, Bernhard, lab. h. 137 Pine.
Vanderbush, Jno. lab. h. 264 Adams.
Vanderlin, Fred. tailor, h. 51 Genesee.
Vanderlip, Elias, Buffalo agricultural works, h. 257 Franklin.
Vanderlip, Harriet, widow, h. Bennett n. Wm.
Vanderlip, Henry L. book-keeper, b. N. Vanderlip.
Vanderlip, N. contractor, h. 9th n. Vt.
Vanderlip, Thomas, mason, b. 257 Franklin.
Vanderpoel, L. V. att'y, old P. O. building. b. Oak cor. Vine.
Vandervan, Henry, carp. h. 82 Batavia.
Vandervan, John, carp. h. Spruce n. Genesee.
Vandervief, Magdaline, Mrs. h. Elm n. Best.
Vanderwerf, Franz, lab. h. Porter n. Bouck.
Van Duzee, W. S. h. Main cor Riley.
Van Duzen, B. C. engraver, 158 Main, h. Reilly n. Utica.
Van Duzer, Fidelia, dress maker, 155 Swan.
Van Eps, Hiram, ov. 280 Main, h. same.
Vanevery, Samuel, engineer, h. Mackinaw n. Alabama.
Van. Greson H. ambrotypist, over 202 and 204 Main, h. same.
Vanherten, Martin, lab. h. ov. 441 Michigan.
Van Hoesen, E. H. shipping clerk, N. Y. C. R. R. freight office. h. 158 Clinton.
Vankampen, —, with Pierce & Co. b. Black Rock.
Van, Mary, widow, h. across creek.
Van Ornam, C. S. prod. dealer, Elk St. Market, h. E. Bennett n. Clinton.
Van Ornam, C. S. firm Van O. & Co. 4 Scott, h. Bennett opp. Clinton Market.
Van Santfleet, William, printer, Com'l. Adv. h. Pine n. Cypress.
Van Sicklen, Jas. cartman, h. 114 Elk.
VAN SLYCK, G. A. confectioner, 39 Seneca, h. same.—*See adv. p. 47.*
Van Slyck, A. Mrs. h. 7th n. R. I.
Van Slyke, Albert, clerk, b. 116 Franklin.
Van Slyke, Cornelius A. firm Van S. & Notter, h. Genesee cor. Franklin.
Van Slyke & Notter, boat builders, cor. Va. and Canal, foot Mechanic.
Van Valkenburg, Jas. policeman, h. 94 Carroll.
Van Valkenburgh, Nelson, hackman, h. 318 Michigan.
Van Velsor, B. Mrs. bakery, 296 Main, h. same.
Van Velsor, John, baker, 296 Main, h. 90 E. Eagle.
Van Vleck, Geo. H. book-keeper and oil agt. 5 River, b. 67 Clinton.
Van Vleck, Joseph, lumber dealer, 5 River, h. 67 Clinton.
Vanvranken, Jas. H. boatman, Elk n. Market.
Van Wie, A. joiner, h. Virginia cor. 4th.
Van, Wm. sailor, b. Mary Van.
Van, Wm. lab. h. across creek.
Van Woert, F. A. grocery and provision store. 75 Washington, h. same.
Van Woert, J. L. clerk, 190½ Main, h. 75 Wash.
Varley, Stephen, policeman, h. 391 Swan.
Varney, Eliza, toll-keeper, h. Bat. n. Williamsville road.

Varno, Chs. locksmith, h. 321 Elm.
Varoe, Wm. carp. h. Fulton cor. Hayward.
Vary, D. W. carp. and joiner shop, Clinton n. Spring, h. Vary alley n. Spring.
Vath, Joseph, carp. h. Burton alley n. Boston alley.
Vatter, Christian, moulder, h. 3 Cherry.
Vaughan, Dan. auctioneer, 6 Terrace, h. 145 9th.
Vaughan, Maurice, auction and com. 5 and 6 Quay, h. 22 Park place.
Vaughan, Otis, shoemaker. h. Vc. n. Niag.
Vaughn, Burlington R. machinist, h. Del. cor. Ferry.
Vaughn, Dennis, lab. h. Mill n. Hamburgh.
Vaughn, G. C. h. Del. cor. Ferry.
Vaughn, R. B. farmer, h. Del. cor. Ferry.
Vaugn, Anson, ship carp. h. 100 Carroll.
Vaux, J. P. cl'k Am. Exp. office, h. 156 Clint'n.
Vedder, E. B. attorney, 191 Main, h. Franklin n. North.
Vegiard, A. cutter, with Altman & Co. h. 184 E. Seneca.
Vegiard, Antina, tailor, 184 Seneca.
Veit, Lorenz, lab. h. Mulberry n. Virginia.
Venator, Robt. engineer, h. Walnut n. Gen.
Venderbush, Jno. brewer, h. Adams n. Syca.
Verigon, Augustus, machinist, h. 110 Elm.
Vermeher, August, carp. h. 319 Ellicott.
Vermilya, Wm. E. confectionery, etc. 137 Main, h. Palmer cor. Maryland.
Verplanck, Isaac A. judge Superior Court, office new Court House, h. North n. Del.
Versh, Adam, grocer, Syc. cor. Walnut, h. same.
Vester, Conrad, tailor, h. Syc. cor. Walnut.
Vestrup, John, mason, h. Jefferson n. Wm.
Vetter, Chas. tailor, h. Niagara n. Mass.
Vetter, Geo. joiner, h. Krettner n. Batavia.
Vetter, Matheas, lab. h. Hickory n. Batavia.
Vetter, Nicholas, tailor, h. Locust n. Carlton.
Vetter, Wm. tanner, h. 243 Elm.
Veyle, Chas. book-binder, b. Exch. n. Mich.
Viant, Wm. lab. h. Clinton n. Emslie.
Vickery, Edward, h. Exchange n. Heacock.
Vickery, Geo. H. clerk, Dock foot Evans, b. 50 Ellicott.
Vickery, Wm. R. h. 50 Ellicott.
Vief, Fred. mason, b. Walnut n. Batavia.
Vief, Fred. cigar maker, Canal cor. Evans, h. Walnut n. William.
Viele, Mrs. John B. h. 23 E. Tupper.
Vielwerth, Jacob, lab. h. Oak n. Best.
Viertel, John, lab. h. Cedar n. William.
Vignero, Joseph, farmer, h. Niagara n. Mass.
Vilas, B. D. printer, Com. Adv. b. 62 Eagle.
Vilhauer, Conrad, carp. h. Davis n. Genesee.
Vincent, Henry, lab. h. Ferry n. Main.
Vincent, Leatt, barber, over 263 Main.
Vine, Geo. butcher, Elk street Market, h. Vermont n. Hodge.
Vine, Jas. brick maker, h. Genesee E. tollgate.
Vine, Thos. Mrs. wid. h. Ferry n. Jefferson.
Vines, Caroline, wid. h. Batavia n. tollgate.
Vining, Geo. W. dep. city clerk, h. 46 Mohawk.
Vintlinger, John, blacksmith, h. Michigan n. Genesee.
Visscher, John R. clerk, b. 27 Ellicott.
Voas, Robert Wm. firm Voas & Ward, h. cor. Alabama and Carroll.

Voas & Ward, Buffalo City Bellows factory, Alabama cor. Carroll.
Voe, Geo. peddler. h. Ferry n. Delaware.
Voegtle, Geo.* bakery, h. Batavia n. Jefferson.
Voekele, Jacob, tailor, h. Seneca n. Hamburgh.
Voelk, John, sailor, b. Western Hotel.
Voelker, Peter,* butcher, Batavia cor. Monroe, h. same.
Vogel, Chas. shoemaker, h. 105 Genesee.
Vogel, Eliz. widow, h. Jefferson n. Carlton.
Vogel, Frank, saddler, h. Main n. Buff. Plains.
Vogel, John, tailor, h. North n. Elm.
Vogel, John, with Shephard & Co. h. 168 Clinton.
Vogel, John, cooper, h. 158 Sycamore.
Vogel, Jos. milkman, h. Watson n. Peckham.
Vogel, Peter, lab. h. 89 Cherry.
Vogel, Samuel,* saddler, Batavia n. Madison, h. same.
Vogel, Valentine, painter, 204 Genesee.
Vogelgesang, Abraham, tailor, h. 178 Gen.
Vogelsang, Casper, lab. h. Carlton n. Jeff.
Vogelsang, Frank, shoemaker, h. Carlton n. Jefferson.
Vogeslang, Henry, carp. h. Mich. n. North.
Voght, M. shoemaker, 139 S. Div. h. Milnor cor. Pine.
Voght, Mary, widow, h. 132 Sycamore.
Voght, John, tinsmith, 12 Walnut.
Voght, Peter, tinsmith, b. 132 Sycamore.
Vogt, Adam, lab. h. Delavan ave. n. Walden.
Vogt, Andrew, porter, Fire Marshal's, Franklin cor. Eagle, b. Utica n. Vermont.
Vogt, Andrew, h. Mulberry n. Virginia.
Vogt, Catharine, h. Milnor n. William.
Vogt, Casper, lab. h. 42 Cherry.
Vogt, Eliza, widow, seamstress, b. 132 Syc.
Vogt, Francis, clothing dealer, 11 Commercial, h. same.
Vogt, Geo. S. pastor, h. 192 Oak.
Vogt, Hubart, locksmith, h. Hickory n. Wm.
Vogt, John, lab. b. 290 Elm.
Vogt, Martin, shoemaker, h. Wm. n. Milnor.
Voigt, Charles R. cigar maker, h. 139 Batavia.
Voigt, Robert, locksmith, 15 E. Seneca, h. 70 Hickory.
Volckman, Alfred, h. 9th n. Pennsylvania.
Volger, Ed. variety store, 320 Main, h. same.
Volk, David, shoemaker, h. Mortimer n. Gen.
Volk, John, peddler, h. Herman n. Genesee.
Volk, John G. shoemaker, h. 90 Genesee.
Volk, Wm. gardener, h. Mulberry n. Carlton.
Volk, Wm. shoemaker, h. Spring n. Sycamore.
Volk, Wm. shoemaker, h. Mortimer n. Syc.
Volker,*Ferdinand A. boot maker, with G. Henning, h. 36 E. Maple.
Volker, Wm. M. D. 240 Genesee, h. same.
Volkeri, John,* blacksmith, Niagara n. Georgia, h. 85 9th.
Volland, Michael, cabinet maker, h. 10 Monroe n. Peckham.
Voller, Jos. lab. h. Genesee n. Herman.
Vollert, Geo. lab. h. Sherman n. Batavia.
Vollmer, Ann B. widow, 39 Batavia.
Vollmer, Fred. grocer, Elk n. Hayward.
Vollmer, Ignatz, tailor, h. Gen. n. Jeff'n.
Volmer, Jacob, lab. h. Genesee n. Spruce.
Volmer, Wm. H. b. 39 Batavia.

18

Vollmouth, Jacob, lab. h. Mich. foot Fulton.
Volrath, Jacob, peddler, h. 197 Cherry.
Voltz, Alois, gardener, h Ferry n. Jeff'n.
Voltz, Geo. grocer, 392 Main, h. same.
Voltz, John, clerk, 576 Main, b. same.
Voltz, Louis D. at county treasurer's office, h. 34 E. Tupper.
Voltz, Mathias, milk peddler, h. Elm n. High.
Volz, Christian, Rev. D. D. h. Hickory n. Wm.
Vomschedt, Wm. baker, 75 Gen. h. same.
Von'Rohr, Philip, student, Maple n. Virginia, h. same.
VonTable, Rudolf, machinist, cor. William and Cedar.
Vorce, D. G. Niagara St. R. R. h. over 423 Main.
Vordtriede, Julius, editor Buffalo Telegraph, h. 213 Oak n. Tupper.
Vorley, Peter, h. Swan cor. Hickory.
Vorse, Alden, sawyer, h. N. Wash. n. Niag.
Vorse, John P. cor. Georgia & 6th, b. 72 6th.
Vorst, John, flour dealer, 96 Batavia. h. same.
Vosburg, Cornelius, 16 Central Wharf, h. cor. Georgia and 7th.
Vosburgh, Mary, Miss b. cor. Niagara and Ferry.
Vosburgh, Mary J. wid. h. cor. Niagara and Ferry.
Vosburgh, P. M. atty. over old post office, h. 87 Niagara.
Vosburg, Theo. clerk, S. Pease, b. cor. Niag. and Perry.
Vosburgh, Wm. cor. Lloyd and Prime. b Western.
Voser, Robt. lab. h. Spruce n. Sycamore.
Vosinil, Marshall, farmer, town line road n. Main.
Voss, Chas. gilder, h. 96 Genesee.
Voss, John, printer, with J. M. Johnson, h. Maryland n. 6th.
Voss, P. D. lab. h. Pratt n. Sycamore.
Vosseller, Harriet A. teacher, 7 Illinois.
Vosseller, Hiram, b. 7 Illinois.
Vosseller, Nathan, Buff. stable, h. 7 Illinois.
Vosseller, Racila A. teacher School No. 3, b. 7 Illinois.
Vot, John, lab. h. Maple n. Carlton.
Vought, John H. firm A. Sherwood & Co. h. 456 Main.
Voutirlender, Anton, tailor, at 352 Main, b. 420 Michigan.
Vowinkle, John C. carp. h. Locust n. Carlton.
Vulcan Foundry, cor. Water and LeCouteulx.
Vunderlinden, E. tailor, h. 113 William.

W.

Wachtel, Henry, lab. h. Roos alley n. Wm.
Wackenheim, Michael, furnaceman, h. Mich. n. Carlton.
Wacker & Co. billiard table makers, 563 Main.
Wacker, Louis, firm W. & Co. h. 563 Main.
Wackermann, John M. glassware and crockery, cor. Genesee and Washington. h. same.
Wackerman, Mich. milkman, h. Best n. Main.
Wackler, Christian, machinist, h. 314 Elm.
Wacleman, Adam, huckster, h. Mortimer n. Genesee.

Wade, James, teamster, h. 54 Morgan.
Wade, Scuyler, h. 22 Niagara.
Wade, William, cartman, h. 6th n. Pa.
Wadsworth, Geo. firm W. & Williams, h. 45 W. Mohawk.
Wadsworth, Henry T. clerk, rolling mill, Black Rock, b. 45 W. Mohawk.
Wadsworth & Williams, city attys. over 219 Main.
Waegerer, Joseph, lab. h. Adams n. Batavia.
Wageman, A. fruit dealer, 8 E. Seneca, h. Oak n. Genesee.
Waggenblaz, Mrs. wid. h. 3 Cherry.
Wagner, Adam, h. 51 Delaware.
Wagner, Anna. Mrs. h. 197 Ellicott.
Wagner, Anton, peddler, h. ov. 177 Gen.
Wagner, Caspar, saloon, Seneca junc. Swan.
Wagner, Chas. grocer, Genesee cor. Jeff. h. same.
Wagner, Christian, lab. h. 64 Bennett.
Wagner, Christoph. shoemaker, 82 Main, h. 527 Michigan.
Wagner, Fred. blacksmith, h. Maple n. High.
Wagner, Fred. mill-stone builder, h. Maple n. Burton alley.
Wagner, Fred. wagon maker, h. Elm n. Gen.
Wagner, Geo. lab. h. Spring n. Sycamore.
Wagner, Geo. lab. h. Maiden lane.
Wagner, Geo. with Jewett & Root.
Wagner, Henry, lab. h. Shumway n. Wm.
Wagner, Henry, machinist, h. Pratt n. Bata.
Wagner, Jacob, lab. h. Stanton bet. Wm. and Peckham.
Wagner, Jacob,* baker, Mortimer n. Genesee, h. same.
Wagner, Jacob, peddler, h. r. 116 Cedar.
Wagner, Jacob, blacksmith, h. Clinton n. Wm.
Wagner, Jacob, carp. h. Maple n. Virginia.
Wagner, Jacob, tanner, h. Stanton n. Wm.
Wagner, Jas. lab. h. Mulberry n. High.
Wagner, John, lab. h. Bennett n. Batavia.
Wagner, John, moulder, h. Spruce n. Syca.
Wagner, John, lab. h. Pratt n. Clinton.
Wagner, John, lab. h. Watson n. Peckham.
Wagner, Joseph, lab. h. Gen. n. Carlton.
Wagner, Lewis, at Terrapin, h. ov. 140 Main.
Wagner, Martha L. widow, h. 95 Hospital.
Wagner, Matthew, clerk, 168 Main, h. 51 Tup.
Wagner, Michael, lab. h. 100 Hickory.
Wagner, Nicholas, ship carp. h. Milnor n. Wm.
Wagner, Nicholas, carp. b. Mortimer n. Gen.
Wagner, P. carp. h. 522 Michigan.
Wagner, P. A. shoe store, 7 Main, h. same.
Wagner, Peter, teamster, h. Mulberry bel. Va.
Wagner, Valentine, paver, h. Mortimer n. Gen.
Wagner, Valentine, Jr. awl maker, b. Mortimer n. Genesee.
Wagner, Wm. brewer, b. G. Roos.
Wagorneace, J. at Brayley & Pitts.
Wahl, Frank. with Jewett & Root, b. 208 Swan.
Wahl, Julius P. clerk, 294 Main, b. 208 Swan.
Wahl, Mathias, lab. h. Spruce n. Genesee.
Wahl. Peter, pattern maker. b. 208 Swan.
Wahle, Joseph, lab. 401 Michigan.
Wahlen. Mathias, lab. h. 79 Spruce.
Wait, Chas. H. firm Clapp, Matthews & Co. h. Summer n. Delaware.
Wait, Chs. ship carp. Van Slyke & Notters.

H. C. WALKER,

Inland Marine, Fire and Life

INSURANCE AGENT.

SECURITY INSURANCE CO.
OF NEW YORK.

Capital and Surplus, -- $640,000

Divides 75 per cent. of Profits among Customers.

FIRE, LAKE, RIVER and CANAL INSURANCE—CARGO and HULL

NORTH AMERICAN FIRE INSURANCE CO.
OF NEW YORK.

Capital and Surplus,--- $300,000

Divides 75 per cent. of Profits among Customers.

MANHATTAN FIRE INSURANCE CO.
OF NEW YORK.

Capital and Surplus,--$400,000

IRVING FIRE INSURANCE CO.
OF NEW YORK.

Cash Capital and Surplus,-- $250,000

PEOPLE'S FIRE INSURANCE CO.
OF NEW YORK.

Cash Capital,-- $150,000

NEW YORK LIFE INSURANCE CO.
OF NEW YORK.

Accumulated Capital,---$2,004,858

KNICKERBOCKER LIFE INSURANCE CO.
OF NEW YORK.

Accumulated Capital,--- $254,220

H. C. WALKER, Agent,
PRIME ST., CORNER HANOVER.

Wait, Hiram, saloon, Market n. Perry, h. same.
Waite, John H. printer, b. National.
Walbridge, C. E with Pratt & Co. b. Cottage n. Hudson.
Walbridge, G. B. with Pratt & Co. b. Cottage n. Hudson.
Walbridge, G. B. Mrs. wid. h. Cottage n. Hud.
Walder, J. H.* jeweler, 1 Genesee.
Waldob, Charles, moulder, h. 414 S. Division.
Waldow, Charles A. moulder, h. S. Div. cor. Grosvenor.
Waldrab, Andrew & Co. hatters, 9 E. Gen. h. Syc. cor. Oak.
Waldraff, John, shoemaker, Martin's Corners.
Waldren, E. G. h. 11 N. Division.
Waldron, C. A. justice, office 136 Main, h. 22 Carroll.
Waldron, Robert, saloon, 25 Exch. h. same.
Walemiller, Simon, finisher, h. Adams n. Syc.
Walker, A. steamboat inspector, office Gov't Building, h. 55 S. Division.
Walker, Alex. h. 6 Terrace.
Walker, A. R. on N. St. R. R.
Walker, Benj. lab. b. Peugeot n. White's Corner's plank road.
Walker, Chas. R. 255 Main, h. 159 Franklin.
Walker, Cynthia, h. ac. creek.
Walker, David, contr'tor. h. Mariner ab. Allen.
Walker, Ellmore H. Comm'l Reporter Express, b. 9th cor. Georgia.
Walker, Geo. book-keeper, 35 Seneca, h. 61 S. Division.
WALKER, H. C. ins. agent, Hanover cor. Prime, h. North n. Del.—See adv. opp.
Walker, Jas. lab. h. cor. 5th and Carolina.
Walker, Jas. shoemaker, 208 Seneca.
Walker, Jas. J. Am. Ex. Co. h. 108 Folsom.
Walker, Jas. heater, Forest ave. n. N. Wash.
Walker, Jesse, Mrs. h. Georgia cor. 9th.
Walker, Jno. tailor, b. 63 Exchange.
Walker, J. W. tinsmith, h. Wm. n. Walnut.
Walker, Joel L. att'y, 158 Main, h. cor. 9th and Virginia.
Walker, Julius,* jeweler, 185 Main, h. 4 E. Mohawk.
Walker, J. W. with E. P. Dorr, h. 34 7th.
Walker, Kingsbury, fisherman, b. ac. creek.
Walker, Martha, Mrs. dress maker. b. W. Gen.
Walker, Mary Ann, dress maker, b. W. Gen.
Walker, R. Eaton's planing mill.
Walker, Samuel N. tobacconist, 12 E. Seneca, h. 144 E. Swan.
Walker, Samuel B. machinist, S. Shepard, h. Fulton n. Alabama.
Walker, S. G. Mrs. h. 44 Delaware.
Walker, Stephen, carpenter, b. 173 Delaware.
Walker, Stephen, brakeman, b. Revere House.
Walker, W. B. G. clerk, 318 Main, b. 31 Elm.
Walker, Wm. H. firm O. P. Ramsdell & Co. h. 173 Delaware.
Walker, Wm. lab. h. ac. creek.
Walker, Wm. lab. h. Genesee n. canal.
Walker, Wm. machinist, h. 11th n. Hampshire.
Wall, David, foreman, Holloway & Co. b. Franklin n. Allen.
Wall, Frank. ship carp. h. Market opp. Elk st. market.
Wall, Hugh, hackman, b. 246 Pearl.

Wall, Jas. hack driver, h. 85 Carroll.
Wall, Thos. lab. h. S. Div. n. Emslie.
Wallace, E. J. with Jewett & Root, b. Huron cor. Ellicott.
Wallace, Pat. lab. h. cor. Exch. and Hamburgh.
Wallace, Robt. A. firm Harvey & W. h. 19 6th.
Wallace, Thos. machinist, h. 93 Hospital.
Wallace, Wm. engineer, Ft. E. R. W. Co. office, 1 Niagara.
Wallace, Wm. A. ship carp. h. 287 N. Div.
Wallace, Wm. H. telegraph operator, b. 96 9th.
Wallenhorst, Francis, engineer, h. Pratt n. Clin.
Wallenhorst, Geo. wagon maker, h. 36 Union.
Wallenmaier, John, baker, Niagara n. Hamilton, h. same.
Wallenwein, Adam, clerk, Mechanic cor. Terrace, h. same.
Wallet, Frank. farmer, h. Del. ave. E. Main.
Wallkamm, Jno. tailor. b. Wash. n. High.
Wallnholst, H. iron finisher, at Brayley & Pitts.
Wallon, Louis, Rev. h. Ash n. Sycamore.
Wallpole, Thos. ship joiner, h. 358 N. Div.
Walls, John, plasterer, h. Emily n. Delaware.
Walls, Geo. musician, h. 3 Vine alley.
Walpa, Jos tinsmith, h. Cherry cor. Spruce.
Walsh, James, clerk, 205 Main, h. 103 Ellicott.
Walsh, John, grocer, 151 Main, h. 97 9th.
Walsh, John, clerk, 207 Main, h. 103 Ellicott.
Walsh, Pat. firm Mills, W. & Co. h. 152 Elk.
Walsh, Peter, ship carp. h. 154 Elk.
Walsh, Richard, salesman, 207 Main, h. 103 Ellicott.
Walsh, R. Mrs. millinery, 261 Main, h. same.
Walsh, Thos. machinist, h. River n. Genesee.
Walsh, Wm. lab. h. towpath bel. Genesee.
Walshmet, Christoph, lab. h. Elm cor. Tupper.
Walter, Casper, lab. h. German alley n. Syc.
Walter, Catharine M. grocer, h. 67 Sycamore.
Walter, Chas. cooper, h. Mulberry bel. Va.
Walter, Chas. cigar maker, h. Jeff. n. Peckham.
Walter, Chs. ship carp. h. ov. 26 Cherry.
Walter, C. Mrs.* milliner, 148 Batavia, h. same.
Walter, Diebold, carpenter, h. Batavia cor. Ash.
Walter, F. C. shoemaker, h. 127 Pratt.
Walter, Franz, tailor, h. Locust n. High.
Walter, Geo. carpenter, h. 31 Maple.
Walter, Henry, mason, h. Krettner n. Batavia.
Walter, Henry, moulder, h. 525 Michigan.
Walter, Henry, jeweler, 411 Main, h. 46 E. Genesee.
Walter, John, brewer, h. Walnut n. Batavia.
Walter, John, lab. h. Jefferson n. Peckham.
Walter, John, Elk St. market, h. Carroll n. Heacock.
Walter, John, cooper, h. William cor. Spring.
Walter, John, butcher, h. cor. Swan and Jeff.
Walter, John, lab. h. S. Div. bel. Jefferson.
Walter, John R. book-keeper, with Schwartz & Rebmann. h. 67 Sycamore.
Walter, Matthew, painter, Cherry n. Jefferson.
Walter, Max, stone mason, h. Gulf n. Niagara.
Walter, Michael, turner, h. Carroll n. Heacock.
Walter, Peter, saw filer, h. 9 Cypress.
Walter, Richard, constable, h. 78 6th.
Walter, Thos. sailor, h. Spring n. Genesee.
Walter, Tobias, cabinet maker, h. 255 Elm.
Walter, Wm. I. shoemaker, 43 E. Seneca, h. 112 Pearl.

Walters, J. Wm. on lake, h. 240 E. Genesee.
Walther, Geo. shoemaker, Howard cor. Watson.
Waltz, Geo. lab. h. Clinton n. Madison.
Walz, Alois, baker, Burton n. Washington.
Walz, Cuspar, b. Mortimer n. Genesee.
Walz, Francis, carp. h. 35 Milnor.
Walz, Gebhard, peddler, b. 146 Genesee.
Walz, Geo. shoe store, 7 Commercial, h. Michigan n. Genesee.
Walz, Philip, policeman, Sycamore cor. Adams.
Wanamacher, Geo. lab. h. Elk n. Red Jacket Hotel.
Wandel, John, Mrs. meat store, cor. Elm and Sycamore.
Wandel, Jno. lab. h. Watson n. William.
Wander, Adam, mason, b. Adams n. Syc.
Wander, Daniel, clerk, P. J. Murphy, b. same.
Wander, Frederick, grocer, Batavia n. Spring, h. same.
Wander, Geo. tailor, h. Hinckley n. Mortimer.
Wander, Jos. mason, h. Hollister n. Spring.
Wander, Mary Ann, b. with Phillip Wander.
Wander, Paul, turner, h. 274 Elm.
Wander, Philip, carp. h. Pratt n. Batavia.
Wanger, Jacob, silver plater, h. cor. Ellicott and Chippewa.
Wanger, Jos. lab. h. Oak n. High.
Wangler, Geo. mason, h. Michigan n. Carlton.
Wanmaker, Conrad, shoemaker, Niagara cor. Staats, h. Oak cor. Sycamore.
Wannop, John, contractor, h. 38 Chippewa.
Wanter, Peter, tailor, h. Adams n. Sycamore.
Ward, Elizabeth, b. 99 Seneca.
Ward, Geo. H. clerk, h. 525 Washington.
Ward, Henry, bellows maker, h. Bristol n. Spring.
Ward, John, clerk, 16 Niagara, b. 69 6th.
Ward, Jno. lab. h. 13 Iron place, N. Wash.
Ward, Margaret, widow, h. Arkansas n. Adams.
Ward, Martin, lab. h. Exch. n. Hamburgh.
Ward, Robert, carriage painter, b. Genesee House.
Ward, Samuel B. agt. patent door fastener, B. & E. R. R. h. 295 Franklin.
Ward, Thos. sawyer, h. Perry n. Hamburgh.
Ward, Thos. sailor, h. 217 7th.
Ward, Wm. shoemaker, h. 99 Seneca.
Wardwell, Allen, book-keeper, Taylor & Jewett, h. 207 7th.
Wardwell, Geo. S. att'y, 180 Main, h. 207 7th.
Wardwell, Webster & Co. oil manuf. 157 Wash.
Wardwell, Wm. T. firm W. Webster & Co. h. 8 Boston Block, Niagara.
Warford, Lewis S. ship carp. h. Jackson n. Gen.
Warham, Jno. B. cabinet maker, 198 7th, h. cor. Virginia and 7th.
Warhouse, Elizabeth, widow, h. 165 Elm.
Warbus, Fred. W. shoemaker, h. 19 Eagle.
Warbus, Henry F. shoemaker, 2 Exchange, h. Milnor n. William.
Waring, Jane, Mrs. boarding house, 35 Swan.
Warke, Henry, tailor, h. Carlton n. Mulberry.
Warmwood, Geo. h. 72 Ellicott.
Warneke, Wm. blacksmith, h. Adams n. Gen.
Warner Brothers, clothiers, 43 and 45 Main.
Warner, Chas. wagon maker, Wm. Barker, h. Hickory n. Clinton.
Warner, Geo. W. at 29 C. Wharf, b. Western.

Warner, H. tailor, b. Wm. Schneider.
Warner, James N. painter, h. Main n. Allen.
Warner, Jesse, lab. h. Fulton n. Hamburgh.
Warner, Jno. firm W. Bros. h. Perry n. Beak.
Warner, Joseph, firm W. Bros. h. 45 Main.
Warner, Leobald, firm W. Bros. h. 45 Main.
Warner, Thomas N. painter, h. 10 Union.
Warner, Truman H. ship carp. Water bel. Joy, h. Perry n. Hayward.
Warr, Jas. iron works, h. cor. Bird and Niag.
WARREN & BROTHER, composition roofing, Main cor. Swan.—*See adv. opp.*
Warren, D. C. ticket agt. N. Y. & E. R. R. office, International Block, "Niagara Falls," h. 245 S. Division.
Warren, Eliza A. boarding house, 41 Church.
Warren, Evarts E. S. book-keeper, Pratt & Letchworth, b. 259 Franklin.
Warren, E. S. h. cor. Niagara and York.
Warren, Henry H. h. Bowery n. North.
Warren, Henry J. firm Kress & W. h. 9 Milnor.
Warren, J. D. firm R. Wheeler & Co. h. 373 Franklin.
Warren, Jno. firm W. & Bros. h. 382 Franklin.
Warren, J. Oscar, clerk, b. 382 Franklin.
Warren, Joseph, firm Joseph W. & Co. h. 259 Franklin.
Warren, Jos. & Co. prop. Buff. Daily Courier, 178 Washington.
Warriner, I. C. book-keeper, h. Franklin n. North.
Warren, M. clerk, city att'y office, b. 215 S. Div.
Warren, R. R. last maker, with H. Wing & Co. h. 374 Michigan.
Wartinger, M. sailor, h. 22 Maple.
Washburn, Alanson, receiver. N. Y. C. freight depot, h. 107 Delaware.
Washburn, S. F. healing physician, rooms and b. 29 Swan.
Washington, Francis, whitewasher, h. 91 Cedar.
Washington, Mary, widow, h. 106 Elm.
Wasinger, Michael, lab. h. Adams n. Sycamore.
Wasmer, Rudolph, last maker, Wing & Co. h. 14 Goodell.
Wasmuth, Geo. tanner, h. Walnut n. Batavia.
Wasser, Anthony, milkman, h. Pratt n. Wm.
Wasser, John, cooper, b. P. Stern.
Wasserberger, Nicholas, grocery, h. Mulberry bel. Virginia.
Wasmer, Samuel, shoemaker, h. 14 Goodell.
Wasson, A. U. S. Exp. Co. h. 155 Ellicott.
Wasson, Wm. h. Seneca W. of toll bridge.
Waterman, D. B. firm W. & Clark, h. 22 W. Eagle.
Waterman, D. W. carp. and joiner, 7th cor. Hospital, h. 266 Franklin.
Waterman, Gladin, joiner, h. 11th n. Virginia.
Waterman, P. Mrs. widow, h. 6 5th.
Waters, Albert E. clerk, St. Com'rs office, h. 116 S. Division.
Waters, Chas. Henry, clerk, b. 27 7th.
Waters, Chas. mechanic, with Pierce & Co. h. 47 Exchange.
Waters, George S. with R. O. Benton, h. 48 Morgan.
Waters, J. D. variety store, 385 Seneca.
Waters, John, tinsmith, h. alley bet. Franklin and Delaware.

Watson, John J. patentee. h. 327 Michigan.
Waters, Jno. U. S. recruiting service, 83 Main.
Waters, Levi J. street com'r, h. 116 S. Division.
Waters, Thomas, shingle maker, h. Howard n. Madison.
Waters, Wm. clerk. 42 Main, h. 218 Carroll.
Waters, Wm. S. with Bergman & Co. h. 218 Carroll.
Waterworth, Thos. on the lake, h. 51 Wm.
Watson, Geo. carver. with A. & J. Keogh.
Watson, G. V. clerk. b. 101 Swan.
Watson, Hannah. widow, h. Pine n. Eagle.
Watson, Isaac W. tinsmith, h. Elk n. La.
Watson, Josephine, widow, h. 275 Oak.
Watson, L. G. b. Western.
Watson, Samuel, machinist, b. 47 Exch.
Watson, S. L. com. merch. h. 9th n. Vermont.
Watson, S. V. R. land agent, office Ellicott cor. E. Swan, h. same.
Watson, Thos. ship carpenter, h. Clinton ave. n. N. Washington.
Wattinger, Jos. blacksmith, h. 98 Hickory.
Watts, Ann, widow of Wm. h. Perry n. Ala.
Watts, Geo. M. st R. R. h. Main n. Ferry.
Watts, Geo. H. whitewasher, h. 21 Ash.
Watts, Hen. capt. prop. Orontes. h. 158 S. Div.
Watts, John, ship carpenter, h. 68 Hickory.
Watts, John B. machinist, h. 68 Hickory.
Watts, Jno. tailor, h. 193 N. Division.
Watts, Jno. painter. b. Perry n. Hayward.
Watts, Joseph, h. 144 Ellicott.
Watts, Jos. Jr. brass finisher, b. 144 Ellicott.
Watts, Peter J. brass finisher, b. 144 Ellicott.
Watts, Robt. policeman, h. 210 N. Division.
Watts. Thos. farmer. h. 204 N. Division.
Waud & Abell. prod. and com. 24 Prime.
Waud, Richard H. book-keeper. h. 77 Clinton.
Waver, Orsamus. carp. h. 38 Chicago.
Wayland, John U. book-keeper, Buff. Savings Bank, h. 60 S. Division.
Weasheiser, S. tailor, b. Spruce n. Sycamore.
Weatejel. Charles, carpenter, h. Pratt bet. Wm. and Clinton.
Weaver, Nathan, M. D 243 Swan.
Weicherer, Jos. h. Adams n. Batavia.
Wechter, Lorenz, farmer, h. Delavan avenue n. Williamsville road.
Webb, Geo. J. printer, Com'l Adv. h. Vermont cor. 13th.
Webb, Isabella, teacher No. 18, b. Vt. cor. 13th.
Webb, Jas. printer, b. Vermont cor. 13th.
Webb, Jesse, ship carpenter, h. 47 Church.
Webb, Jos. keeper at penitentiary, h. 166 S. Div.
Webb, Martin, shoemaker, b. F. Hubel.
Webb, Peter J. saloon, Ohio n. Mississippi.
Webber, Adam, bl'ksmith. b. Hickory n. Eagle.
Webber, B. boot maker, 282 Swan.
Webber, Jno. tailor, h. William cor. Cedar.
Webber, Michael, wagon maker, h. 135 Clinton.
Webber, Sampson, shoemaker, h. Swan cor. Chicago.
Weber, Adam, policeman, h. Mortimer n. Syc.
Weber, Andrew, lab. h. Walnut n. Sycamore.
Weber, Annie M. widow, h. Williamsville road n. plank road.
Weber, Anton, tailor, h. Monroe n. Batavia.
Weber, Benedict.* boot and shoe manuf. 1 E. Swan, h. 282 E. Swan.

Weber, Chas.* brewer, Bat. n. Adams, h. same.
Weber, Chs.* cooper, Spring cor. William, h. same.
Weber, Ferdinand, shoemaker, 10 Terrace.
Weber, Fred. shoemaker, h. 402 Michigan.
Weber, Fred. lab. h. Farmer n. East.
Weber, Fred. J. blacksmith, h. 118 Oak.
Weber, Geo. grocer, Michigan cor. William.
Weber, Geo. D. lab. h. 222 Genesee.
Weber, Henry, cooper, h. Austin n. East.
Weber, Hermann, saddler, h. Main cor. Burton.
Weber, Jacob, carp. h. 232 Oak.
Weber, Jacob, saloon, Canal alley cor. 6th, h. same.
Weber, John, lab. h. 20 Maple.
Weber, John, lab. h. Carlton cor. Locust.
Weber, John, carp. h. Adams n. William.
Weber, John, lab. b. 78 Bennett.
Weber, John, saloon, Locust cor. Carlton, h. same.
Weber, Jno. Main st. brewery, Main n. Goodell, h. same.
Weber, Jno. lab. h. Sherman n. Genesee.
Weber, Jno. B. Lloyd cor. Prime, b. 281 Oak.
Weber, Jno. J. grocer, Tupper cor. Oak, h. same.
Weber, Jos. lab. h. Mulberry cor. Virginia.
Weber, Lorenz, cabinet maker, h. Spruce n. Sycamore.
Weber, Lorenz, on lake, h. 179 Oak.
Weber, Louis, h. 185 Oak
Weber, Martin, lab. h. 40 Cherry.
Weber, Matthias, h. Elm ab. Burton alley.
Weber, Michael, lab. h. Goodell n. Michigan.
Weber, Michael, tailor, h. r. 177 Genesee.
Weber, Nicholas, finisher, h. Mortimer n. Gen.
Weber, Nicholas, h. 223 Pearl.
Weber, Peter, basket maker, h. Genesee n. Va.
Weber, Peter, cap maker, h. 9 Sycamore.
Weber, Philip, brewer, b. 118 Batavia.
Weber, Philip, brass finisher, 237 Main, b. 34 E. Tupper.
Weber, Philip, paver, h. 242 Ellicott.
Weber, Philip J. gardener, h. 281 Oak.
Weber, Sarah. widow, washer, h. Bat. n. Pratt.
Webster, Alanson, contractor, h. 60 Ellicott.
WEBSTER, A. S. grocer, 33 Seneca, h. same. —See adv. p. 41.
Webster, Chas. H. clerk, Howard, Whitcomb & Co. b. 7 Union.
Webster, C. H. clerk, 318 Main, b. 65 S. Div.
WEBSTER & CO. grocers. 1 E. Seneca.—See adv. p. 41.
Webster, Daniel J. firm H. G. & D. J. Webster, b. 155 E. Seneca.
Webster, David, contractor, h. 7 Union.
WEBSTER, ELLIS, grocer, 7 Seneca, h. 12 Carroll.—See adv. p. 40.
Webster, Geo. B. Mrs. widow, h. Del. cor. Utica.
Webster, Geo. C. firm Wardwell, W. & Co. h. North n. Delaware.
Webster, Hiram, millwright, h. Seneca n. Van Rensselaer.
Webster, Hugh, firm W. & Co. h. 155 E. Sen.
Webster, Nelson, sailor, b. 34 N. Division.
Webster, Robert, grocer, cor. Perry and Mich. h. same.
Webster, Wm. joiner, h. Palmer n. Hudson.

Webster, W. C. music teacher, h. 223 Franklin.
Wechrung, Philip, finisher, h. 138 Elm.
Wechter, Jos. h. Tupper n. Ellicott.
Wechter, Lorenz. lab. Mulberry n. Goodell.
Weed, Alsop C. receiver, N. St. R. R. h. 12 W. Swan.
Weed, DeWitt C. & Co. hardware dealers, 222 Main.
Weed, DeWitt C. firm D. C. W. & Co. h. Connecticut cor. 7th.
Weed, Elias, prod. and com. mer. 17 C. Wharf, h. Delaware cor. Mohawk.
Weed, Hobart. clerk, D. C. Weed & Co. b. Swan cor. Franklin.
Weed, Walter, peddler, b. 91 Hospital.
Weeker, Maria, widow, washer, h. Milnor n. William.
Weeks, Jno. Buff. scale works, 81 Main, h. North cor. 13th.
Weeks, Jno. H. ship car'pter h. 375 Michigan.
Weertener, Erkard, bar tender, b. 53 Exch.
Wegand, August, shoe store, 397 Main, h. same.
Weglehner, Christ. lab. h. Lutheran n. Bat.
Weger, A. barber, h. William n. Hickory.
Weger, E. lab. h. William n. Hickory.
Weger, H. awl maker, h. William n. Hickory.
Weglin, Jno. U. baker, h. 169 Clinton.
Wegner, Adam, printer, b. 569 Washington.
Wegner, Martha, Mrs. h. 569 Washington.
Welch, Adam, silver plater, h. 318 Ellicott.
Weich, Gottlieb, tanner, h. Walnut n. Syc.
Weich, Joseph, lab. h. Mulberry n. Goodell.
Weick, Philip,* shoemaker, h. 130 E. Seneca.
Weick, Stephen, tailor, h. Fox n. Genesee.
Weid, Henry, gard'ner, h. Ketchum al. n. High.
Weid, John, tailor, h. 71 Goodell.
Weidenhaus, Christian, peddler, h. Pratt n. Bat.
Weidhaus, Henry, peddler, h. Pratt n. Bat.
Weidinger, Geo. lab. h. High n. Maple.
Weidinger, Geo. soap maker, h. Ketchum all. n. High.
Weidner, John G. pattern maker, h. 186 Oak.
Weidt, Joachim, lab. h. Spruce n. Sycamore.
Weidt, Joseph, at gas works, h. Spruce n. Bat.
Weiersheuser, Frank, tinsmith, h. 44 Bennett.
Weig, Geo. works Brayley & Pitts.
Weigand, Geo. maltster, b. John Weigand.
Weigand, Geo. machinist, h. Jefferson n. Wm.
Weigand, Jno. painter, h. Mulberry n. Good'll.
Weigand, John, lab. h. Johnson n. North.
Weigand, John, malthouse, h. Mich. n. Carlton.
Weigand, John, cigar maker, h. Pine cor. Bat.
Weigel, Michael, gardener, h. High n. Lemon.
Weigel, Theodore, wagon maker, h. Ferry n. Walden.
Weigel, Wolfgang, grocer, 150 Gen. h. same.
Weigeld, Balthaser, shoemaker, h. Walnut n. Sycamore.
Weigelmesser, Fred. hostler, 116 Pearl, h. Syc. n. Oak.
Weigle, Peter, policeman, h. 155 Oak.
Weil, Aaron, drover, h. Herman n. Genesee.
Weil, David, clerk, 153 Main, b. Revere House.
Weil, Geo. cigar maker, h. Herman n. Genesee.
Weil, Henry, drover, h. Herman n. Genesee.
Weil, Jacob, peddler, h. 18 Bennett.
Weil, Joseph, peddler, h. Pine n. Cypress.
Weil, Lazarus, peddler, h. Genesee n. Adams.

Weil, Simon, drover, h. Herman n. Genesee.
Welland, Chas. cooper, h. Louis n. Amherst.
Weiland, Gottfrey, firm Fischer & W. h. 233 Ellicott.
Weiler, Jacob, watch maker, h. 234 Batavia.
Weiler, John, with Bowen & Humason, h. Ex. n. Van Rensselaer.
Weiler, Ursula, widow, b. Goodell cor. Mich.
Weilfley, John, cooper, h. Mich. foot Fulton.
Weimar, John G. h. cor. Genesee and Walnut.
Weimar, Philip, baker, h. Locust n. Lemon.
Weimer, Mary C. wid. h. Spring n. William.
Weimer, Michael, lab. h. Walnut n. Batavia.
Weimert, Fred. grocer, Aurora plank road n. Whittmore's.
Wein, Geo. tailor, h. 168 Oak.
Weinbier, Michael, lab. h. Monroe n. Sycamore.
Weindle, John, cap maker, 144 Main, h. 420 Michigan.
Weiner, Peter, dept. keeper insane dept. Erie Co. poor-house.
Weingardner, Fred. H. coppersmith, h. 89 Ellicott.
Weinheimer, John, lab. h. William n. Jeff.
Weinshamer, P. lab. h. 34 Union.
Weinzierl, John, lab. h. Syc. n. Pratt.
Weippert, Jos. tailor, h. 84 Sycamore.
Weir, Geo. Jr. grocer, 107 N. Division.
Weir, Jas. grocer, Georgia n. 6th, h. same.
Weis, Chr. lab. h. 125 Pine.
Weis, Frederick,* shoemaker, Main n. Ferry, h. same.
Weisenburg, John, watchman, Niag. n. South.
Weisenheimer, Cath. b. Batavia n. Hickory.
Weisenheimer, Fred. sawyer, with S. D. Sikes, h. Batavia n. Hickory.
Weisenheimer, Henry, shoemaker, 4 Commercial, h. same.
Weisenzell, Nich. farmer, h. Delav. n. Krettner.
Weisheimer, Wm. cigar maker, h. 95 Goodell.
Weishuhn, P. H. W. h. r. 65 Batavia.
Weishuhn, Martin, sailor, h. Pratt n. Syc.
Weisner, Alex. book-keeper, h. 337 Seneca.
Weiss, Andreas, shoemaker, h. 75 Cedar.
Weiss, Ann M. grocer, 125 N. Div. h. same.
Weiss, Christ. cooper, Spring cor. William.
Weiss, Christ. lab. h. cor. Military road and Blossom.
Weiss, C. M. D. h. 19 Batavia.
Weiss, Conrad. lab. h. Spring n. Genesee.
Weiss, Fred, Jr. peddler, h. 20 Walnut.
Weiss, Fred. Sr. peddler, h. 18 Walnut.
Weiss, Jacob, vinegar fact. 62 Walnut, h. same.
Weiss, Jacob, miller, h. Porter n. Van Rens.
Weiss, John, saloon, 171 Genesee, h. same.
Weiss, Michael, lab. h. Monroe n. Sycamore.
Weiss, Michael, brewer, h. Walnut n. Bat.
Weiss, Nicholas, lab. h. Walnut n. Batavia.
Weiss, Peter, lab. h. 259 Elm.
Weissgerber, B. printer, h. Camp n. Gen.
Weissgerber, Leo. teamster, b. Jas. Doat.
Weissgerber, P. lab. h. Camp n. Genesee.
Weissgerber, Stephen, clerk, 222 Main, h. Camp n Genesee.
Weissleder, Rebecca, widow, h. 41 N. Div.
Weit, John, mason, h. Boston alley n. Virginia.
Weitermann, John, lab. h. 134 Spring.
Weitz, Henry, lab. h. Adams n. Batavia.

Weitz, Jacob, carp. Adams n. Batavia.
Welberry, Mary, widow, h. Fulton n. Hamb'h.
Welbert, D. lab. h. William n. Bennett.
Welch, Benj. Jr. commissary general, State of New York, b. American Hotel.
Welch, Bridget, saloon, 5th n. Carolina.
Welch, Catherine F. h. 102 Carroll.
Welch, Franklin, mechanic, Pierce & Co. h. N. Canal n. Emslie.
Welch, Geo. hackman, h. 80 E. Eagle.
Welch, Geo. boarding house. 120 Exchange.
Welch, Henry, grocer, h. over 88 E. Seneca.
Welch, Jacob, cooper, h. Walden n. Perry.
Welch, Jas. lab. h. Carroll n. Heacock.
Welch, Jas. carriage maker, h. 164 6th.
Welch, Jas. teamster, h. Carroll n. Chicago.
Welch, John, lab. h. Moore n. R. R.
Welch, John, contractor, h. 70 5th.
Welch, John, lab. h. Clinton n. Emslie.
Welch, John, peddler, h. 163 Elm.
Welch, Kate, widow, h. Elk below La.
Welch, Mary, widow, h. across creek.
Welch, Michael, lab. Van Rensselaer n. Porter.
Welch, Michael, h. Perry cor. Mississippi.
Welch, Michael, lab. h. 119 Batavia.
Welch & Millar, com. merch'ts and dealers in wool, hides and leather, 159 Washington.
Welch, Philip, lab h. Ohio n. Indiana.
Welch, R. C. h. Parish n. East.
Welch, Samuel M. firm Welch & Miller, h. 92 Niagara.
Welch, Thos. C. attorney, office cor. Seneca and Main, h. 118 Chippewa.
Welch, Timothy, cartman, h. Columbia n. Ohio.
Welch, Wm. huckster, h. 12th n. Vermont.
Welch, Wm. sailor, h. Johnson n. Batavia.
Welchly, Samuel, tanner, h. Am. n. Thomps'n.
Welchman, Henry, lab. h. Pratt n. Clinton.
Weldon, Walter, clerk, 293 Main, h. 62 E. Eagle.
Welhelm. C. with Hamlin & Mendsen, h. Swan cor. Oak.
Welker, Christ. lab. h. cor. East and Ton'wda.
Welker, John,* grocer, Ash cor. Sycamore, h. same.
Wellberry, Thos. blacksmith, h. Tennessee n. Mackinaw.
Weller, Adam, varnisher, h. Best n. Elm.
Weller, Alex. wagon maker, 15 E. Eagle, h. Mortimer n. Genesee.
Weller, Catharine, widow, h. Mortimer n. Gen.
Weller, Gottlieb, carriage maker, h. Mortimer n. Genesee.
Weller, Peter, blacksmith, h. 53 E. Tupper.
Weller, Peter, grocer, 238 Elm, h. same.
Wellmaier, William, cooper, h. Military road n. Amherst.
Wellman, Manley P. cooper, h. 49 Jackson.
Wellman Manley P. Jr. h. Court n. Hospital.
Wellman, Thos. bootmaker, h. 345 E. Seneca.
Wells, B. h. 296 Franklin.
Wells, Chandler J. h. 77 E. Swan.
Wells, C. C. commission merch't, &c., Coburn's elevator, h. 371 Franklin.
Wells' Elevator. n. foot Illinois.
Wells, Elijah, h. cor. Franklin and Chippewa.
Wells, Geo. saloon, Reed's dock, h. same.
Wells, Harry, with W. E. & Co. Hatch slip, h. 300 Michigan.

Wells, Israel, moulder, h. 5 Terrace.
Wells, M. A. widow, b. 18 Swan.
Wells, R. B. depot master, Erie street depot, h. 5th cor. Hudson.
Wells, Richard H. American Express Co. h. 172 Pearl.
Wells, William, firm Seymour & W. h. 304 Michigan.
Wells, Wm. D. engineer, h. 103 Fulton.
Wells, Wm. H. at Seymour & Mills' elevator, h. 304 Michigan.
Wells, W. H. Commercial office, h. cor. Church and Franklin.
Wellsteed, Arthur, foundry, b. Jno. Wellsteed.
Wellsteed, John, manuf. chapsega oil, h. R. I. cor. Utica.
Wellsteed, Thos. S. clerk, 334 Main, b. 2 Oak.
Welsh, John, lab. h. Wilkinson slip.
Welsh, Philip, brewer. h. Clinton n. Cedar.
Welt, Augustus, peddler, h. Wm. n. Shumway.
Welte, Chris. grocer, h. 286 Swan.
Welte, Franz, grocer, Genesee cor. Adams, h. same.
Welte, Jos. tinsmith, b. North n. Michigan.
Welter, Margaretha, widow, h. 3 Ash.
Welty, Michael, cor. Terrace & Evans, h. Sen. bel. Jefferson.
Welzel, Jno. N. grocer, Exch. n. Van Renssl'r.
Wendel, A. porter, h. 61 Tupper.
Wendel, Dan. W. steward, h. Elm n. High.
Wendel, Dan. W. Jr. b. Elm n. High.
Wendelbaus, Englebert, moulder, h. Cypress n. Pine.
Wendle, Jno. cap maker, h. 120 Michigan.
Wendling, Fred. clerk, 364 Main, h. 198 Elm.
Wendt & Speck, flour and feed store, Wm. n. Bennett.
Wendt, Wm. flour deal. h. Wm. n. Cedar.
Wendt, Wm. moulder, h. Wm. n. Cedar.
Wenner, Louis, shoemaker, h. Shumway n. Bat.
Wenraber, Jno. basket maker, b. 54 Cedar.
Wensing, H. grocer, William n. Cedar.
Wensing, Wm. b. William n. Cedar.
Wentz, Wm. gardener, h. Ferry n. Hamilton.
Wenz, James, M. D. h. 373 Michigan.
Wenzel, F. painter, h. 23 Walnut.
Wenzel, Wm. lab. h. Carroll n. Jefferson.
Wenzend, Geo. lab. h. 98 Goodell.
Weppner, Arnold I. butcher, 422 Main.
Weppner, August, butcher, h. 174 Genesee.
Weppner, Francis, firm F. W. & Co. 300 Mich. h. same.
Weppner, F. & Co. meat dealers, 300 Mich.
Weppner, Jacob,* brewer, h. Genesee n. Jeff.
Weppner, Jno. butcher, h. 174 Genesee.
Werdo, John, lab. h. Spruce n. Sycamore.
Wergus, Wm. piano maker, h. ov. 17 Syc.
Werich, Barbara, h. 279 Oak.
Werich, Henry, upholsterer, h. 277 Oak.
Werick. Jno. h. 316 Ellicott.
Werle, Anthony, tailor, 2 Com'l. h. Main ab. Chippewa.
Werle, Geo. A. grocer, Wash. cor. Burton alley.
Werle, Michael, gardener, h. Ferry cor. Jeff.
Werle, Mich. paver, h. Tupper n. Wash.
Wermatz, H. sexton, h. Genesee E. toll gate.
Werne, And. tailor, h. 439 Main.
Werner, Chas. lab. h. Gen. n. W'msville road.

Werner, Charles, wagon maker, h. Hickory n. Clinton.
Werner, Daniel, lab. h. Rogers n. Conn.
Werner, Jacob, tailor, h. Gen. n. Wm'ville road.
Werner, John, gardener, h. Pratt n. Syc.
Werner, Jno. lab. h. Cherry n. Lemon.
Werner, Jno. tailor, h. 551 Michigan.
Werner, Jno. butcher, b. 84 Batavia.
Werner, L. W.* daguerrean, 29 Mohawk, h. same.
Werner, Michael, shoemaker, h. Goodell cor. Washington.
Werner, Peter, lab. h. Watson n. Peckham.
Werner, Wm. lab. h. 87 Pine.
Wernicke, Gustavus, eng'r, Com'l Adv. office, b. cor. Mohawk and Main.
Werrich, Jos. painter, h. Genesee n. city line.
Wert, Adam, lab. h. Adams n. Batavia.
Wertsch, Chas. P. saloon, 155 Ellicott, h. same.
Wertz, Christ. cooper, h. Blossom n. Military road.
Wertz, Peter, lab. h. William n. Watson.
Wertz, Philip, blacksmith, b. Wm. n. Watson.
Werwatz, Albert, lab. b. Fox n. North.
Werwatz, Jacob, lab. h. Fox n. North.
Wesch, Fred. tailor, h. 132 Seneca.
Wescott, Cyrus A. joiner, h. Md. n. 7th.
Wesley, Alex. joiner, h. Monroe n. Eagle.
West, Geo. distiller, h. Hamilton n. Thompson.
West, John C. clerk, P. O. h. 73 S. Division.
West, Wm. W. butcher, Clinton market, Jeff n. bet. Carroll and Seneca.
Westcott, Martin, hackman, h. 246 Pearl.
Westerfelder, Ludwig, lab. h. White's Cor. pl'k road n. Lee's Corners.
Westerholst, H. iron finisher, Brayley & Pitts.
Westermeier, Peter, blacksmith, h. 165 Pine.
Western Elevating Co. 22 Cent. Wharf, across Buffalo creek.
Western Tran. Co. cor. River and Canal Slip.
Westfield, Joseph, sail maker, h. 84 5th.
Westfield, Wm. ship carp. b. Watson bet. Clinton and Howard.
Weston, Ed. W. with W. Johnson.
Weston, Elijah, vulcan foundry, Water cor. Le Couteulx, h. 115 S. Division.
Weston, H. J. with Bush & Howard, h. Niag. n. Forest avenue.
Weston, Judson, clerk, h. E. Bennett n. Clint.
Weston, W. H. clerk, L. H. R. R. b. 2 Oak.
Westphal, Chas. machinist, h. Wm. n. Krettner.
Westphal, Frederick, ash peddler, h. Goodell n. Michigan.
Westphal, Joachim H. teacher, h. Walnut n. William.
Weter, Henry, baker, b. 188 Elm.
Weter, John, lab. b. 188 Elm.
Weter, Joseph, grocer, 55 Genesee, h. same.
Weter, Peter, b. 55 Genesee.
Weter, Peter, ticket agt. h. cor. Wm. and Potter.
Weth, Margaret, wid. b. Spring cor. Hollister.
Wetter, Jacob, lab. h. Genesee n. Mortimer.
Wetts, Christ. cooper. h. Military road n. Am.
Wetzel, F. cooper, h. Mortimer n. William.
Wetzel, Geo. mason, h. r. 136 E. Genesee.
Wetzel, Henry, basket maker, h. Spring cor. Hollister.
Wetzel, Jacob, lab. h. Carlton n. Jefferson.

Wetzel, Valentine, basket maker, h. Spring cor. Hollister.
Wetzell, Frederick. cooper, h. Jeff. n. Peckh'm.
Wex, Lawrence, daguerrean artist, b. Eagle tavern.
Wex, Peter, peddler, h. 498 Michigan.
Weyant, Christian, shoemaker, h. Main n. Good.
Weyland, Chas. P. clerk, 347 Main, b. 73 Bat.
Weyland, Francis J. M. D. h. 73 Batavia.
Weyland, Francis, clerk, 145 Main. b. 73 Bat.
Whalen, E. engineer, h. Carolina ab. 5th.
Whalen, John, fisherman, h. lake shore.
Whalen, John, sail maker, b. 93 E. Seneca.
Whalen, Mich. lab. h. cor. Elk and Chicago.
Whalen, —, blacksmith, b. 199 Exchange.
Whalen, Pat. lab. h. Fulton n. Hayward.
Whalen, Wm. lab. h. Court n. 6th.
Whalon, Edward, teamster, h. 5th n. Va.
Whanon, Martin, lab. h. 53 Church.
Whaples, John W. machinist, h. 170 Seneca.
Wheaton, E. H. b. Western.
Wheeler, A. J. with Rainey & W. b. 53 E. Eagle.
Wheeler, E. D. Z. ass't rec. R. R. b. 51 E. Eagle.
Wheeler, G. L. agent N. S. Field, marble dealer, Del. n. Va. b. 362 Franklin.
Wheeler, Geo. S. cooper, h. Niagara n. Austin.
Wheeler, Geo. W. harness maker, b. 39 Oak.
Wheeler, Hannah, widow, h. 26 W. Genesee.
WHEELER, HEMMING & CO. Chromotypers, Com'l Adv. office.—See adv. p. 187.
Wheeler, Henry, coppersmith, S. Shepard & Co. h. 116 Palmer n. Virginia.
Wheeler, Isaac, soap and candle maker, 4 Batavia, h. Genesee n. Terrace.
Wheeler, Isaac G. soap dealer, h. 529 Wash.
Wheeler, J. H. H. receiver N. Y. C. and L. S. R. R. h. 51 E. Eagle.
Wheeler, Joel, firm Rainey & W. h. 53 E. Eagle.
Wheeler, John, shoemaker, h. St. Paul n. Main.
Wheeler, John B. hack driver, h. 101 Ellicott.
Wheeler, O. C. carriage maker, h. 99 9th.
WHEELER, R. & CO. publishers and proprietors Commercial Advertiser.—See adv. pp. 106, 107 and 110.
Wheeler, Rufus, firm R. W. & Co. h. 146 Pearl.
Wheeler, Sarah, widow of John, h. 93 Oak.
Wheeler, Solomon H. clerk, h. 172 N. Div.
WHEELER & WILSON'S SEWING MACHINES, 207 Main, M. Silsby, agent.—See adv. p. 104.
Wheeler, Wm. H. saloon, National Hotel.
Wheelock, John, stave dresser, b. National.
Whelan, Jas. auction and com. Quay n. Main, h. 90 E. Seneca.
Whinham, Robt. tailor, h. 16 Pine.
Whipple, Charlotte, Mrs. widow, 48 Morgan.
Whitaker, C. conductor N. St. R. R. b. Ferry n. Niagara.
Whitaker, Chaunc. H. mariner, h. Ferry cor. Adams.
Whitaker, Jac. M. D. 5 Kremlin Hall, b. Amer'n.
Whitaker, Harry, mariner, h. 209 7th.
Whitaker, W. D. Fly cor. Maid'n lane, h. same.
Whitcomb, Geo. h. 20 Carroll.
Whitcomb, Josh. M. firm Howard, W. & Co. h. 104 Delaware.
Whitcomb, Nathan, dentist, over 240 Main, h. 65 6th.

White, Adam, silver plater. h. 318 Ellicott.
White, Artemus, painter, 79 Main, b. cor. Geo. and 9th.
White, Betsey, widow. h. 202 Swan.
White, Chas. carp. h. Fulton bet. Hayward and Alabama.
White, Eliza, widow, b. Alexander McKaay.
White, E. R. at 205 Main, b. 29 Swan.
White, George C. President White's Bank, h. 51 E. Swan.
White, Gilbert, grocer, cor. Evans and Canal.
White, Henry, milliner. 358 Main, b same.
White, Henry, clerk, P. O. b. 100 Ellicott.
White, Henry, lab. h. Main n. Ferry.
White, Henry A. cabinet maker, with I. D. White, h. 34 W. Seneca.
White, Hiram C. seedsman and florist, 338 Main. h. 34 W. Tupper.
WHITE, H. G. painter and dealer in wall paper, 273 Main, h. 9th cor. Georgia.—See adv. p. 73.
White, H. T. clerk, 88 Main, b. 222 Niagara.
WHITE, ISAAC, cabinet manuf. 201 and 203 Main, h. 100 E. Swan.—See adv. p. 65.
White, I. J. firm L. & I. J. W. h. 13 Ellicott.
White, James P. M. D. h. and office 460 Main.
White, James, h. Niagara n. Ferry.
White, John, ship carp. h. Fulton n. Chicago.
White, John, h. Seneca n. Mineral.
White, John. engineer. h. 44 W. Huron.
White, J. P. b. 18 Delaware.
WHITE LEAD COMPANY, office 38 Lloyd. —See adv. p. 103.
White, Leonard, firm L. & I. J. W. h. 23 7th.
White, L. & I J. manufacturers of edge tools, Ohio cor. Indiana.
White, Mary A. widow, seamstress, h. 443 Michigan.
White, Mary, Mrs. h. 128 Clinton.
White, Michael, lab. h. across creek.
White, Michael, car maker, h. Pratt n. Wm.
White, Pat. grocer, 299 E. Seneca, b. same.
White, R. J. M. D. h. 386 Franklin.
White, R. J. cooper, b. cor. Niag. and Austin.
White, R. R. 11 C. Wharf, h. 55 W. Tupper.
White, S. Warner, Prime cor. Canal slip, b. N. Washington cor. Bird avenue.
White, Wm. baggageman, N. Y. C. R. R. h. Folsom n. Kinney's alley.
White, William C. firm Moores & W. b. 204 E. Swan.
White. Wm. W. printer, b. 446 Michigan.
White, W. C. merchant. h. 123 S. Division.
Whitehead, Lewis, h. 213 S. Div.
Whiteman, David, lab. h. Ind. n. Perry.
Whiteman, Wm. fisherman, h. Breckenridge n. Erie Canal.
Whiteman, Wm. lab. h. 14th, cor. Mass.
Whiteman, Z. b. 287 Michigan.
Whitfield, Jos. H. Jr. baggage master, b. 165 N. Division.
Whitford, John. carp. b. S. Div. bel. Cedar.
Whitford, Lot C. clerk, L. C. Woodruff, b. Gillespie cor. Eagle and Elm.
Whiting, A. bonnet dresser. b. 22 S. Div.
Whiting & Co. produce and com. 13 Central Wharf and 13 Prime.
Whiting, D. W. firm W. & Co. 2 N. Pearl.

Whiting, H. A. bonnet dresser, b. 22 S. Div.
Whiting, S. E. bonnet warerooms, 273 Main, h. 260 Pearl.
Whitmore, A. C. drover. h. Seneca n. Mineral.
Whitmore, H. carp. h. Folsom n. Chicago.
Whitmore. Peter, bl'ksmith, h. Pine n. Cypress.
WHITMORE, RATHBUN & CO. stone yard, Henry cor. Erie canal.—See adv. p. 69.
Whitney, B. T. M. D. dentist, 12 S. Div. h. same.
Whitney, Hezekiel. saw filer, Gen. cor. Chip.
Whitney, Mercy, widow, h. 14 E. Eagle.
Whitney, Milo A. attorney, over 156 Main, h. 18 N. Pearl.
Whitney, N. A. marble worker, h. 42 Court.
Whittaker, Thos. blacksmith, h. Perry bet. Ala. and Hayward.
Whittaker, Wm. ship carp. h. 5 Beak.
Whittet, Elizabeth, widow, h. 60 6th.
Whittet, Joseph, shipping master, 29 Central Wharf, b. 74 6th.
Whitty, Chs. watch maker, h. 104 Exchange.
Whitwell, Jno. lab. h. foot Church.
Wibert, Wm. h. 282 Pearl.
Wick, Adam, tinsmith, h. Bat. n. Madison.
Wick, John, mason, b. Best n. Oak.
Wick, Wm. lab. h. r. 99 Oak.
Widand, Gotlieb, tailor, b. Monroe n. Wm.
Wideman, John M. gunsmith, h. 228 Ellicott.
Wideman, Joseph, grocer. h. 400 Swan.
Widmer, Jacob, farmer, Elk n. Smith.
Wie, Mary, widow, h. 54 Goodell.
Wieckmann, Christian, prop. and ed'r Aurora, 67 Batavia, h. 69 Batavia.
Wiedemaur, Ludwig, gardener, h. 546 Mich.
Wieder, Wm. shoemaker, h. Kaene n. Syc.
Wiediger, Chas. carp. h. Pratt n. William.
Wiedrich, Michael, rec. of taxes, cor. Franklin and Eagle, h. 6 Walnut.
Wiegand. Augustus, barber, Main cor. Swan, h. William n. Walnut.
Wiegand, John, lab. h. Kaene n. Sycamore.
Wiegand, John, butcher. b. 126 Batavia.
Wiegand, Wm. carp. h. Pratt n. Sycamore.
Wiegele, Bartholomew, lab. h. Elm n. Burton alley.
Wiehardi, Louis, sailor, b. Water.
Wieland, Jacob, tanner, h. Clinton n. Jeff'n.
Wielandt, Chas. lab. h. Clinton cor. Watson.
Wieman, And. hatter, 382 Main, h. 41 Cherry.
Wiener, David, shoemaker, h. Bat. n. Ash.
Wierling, Herman,* blacksmith, Main n. Best, h. same.
Wieterkaeuer, Nicholas, mason, h. 491 Wash.
Wifenbach, Geo. paver, h. Spring n. Syc.
Wiggins, Dennis B. M. D. Niagara cor. Eagle, h. 107 Franklin.
Wigh, John, machinist. b. Cottage n. Md.
WIGHTMAN, GEO. D. wood engraver, 156½ Main. h. 10th n. Pa.—See adv. p. 89.
Wike, M. dry goods, 138 Seneca, h. same.
Wilber, Van Rensselaer, cabinet fin'r, h. 8 Va.
Wilbert, Jno. carp. h. Cherry n. Spruce.
Wilbor, Albert D. Rev. h. 289 Michigan.
Wilbur, E. S. Mrs. boarding house, 408 Main.
Wilbur, J. T. attorney, Exchange cor. Wash. h. 20 N. Pearl.
Wilbur. L. D. builder, h. 132 S. Division.
Wilcox, A. C. h. Wash. n. Carlton.

Wilcox, Chas. H. M. D. 22 W. Genesee, h. same.
Wilcox, B. h. Wash. n. Carlton.
Wilcox, Edmund, with D. S. Bennett & Co. h. 60 Pearl.
Wilcox, Geo. engineer, h. 24 Court.
Wilcox, Henry, carpenter, b. G. W. Baskett.
Wilcox, Herod J. finisher, h. 72 Pine.
Wilcox, Horace, com'l editor, Com'l Adv'r, b. 5 Carroll.
Wilcox, Jas. with D. S. Bennett & Co. h. 106 Huron.
Wilcox, J. S. box 3249 Post-office.
Wilcox, Lewis, machinist, h. 48 Oak.
Wilcox, Marian, widow, h. Carroll n. Ala.
Wilcox, Wm. b. 293 Michigan.
Wild, Conrad, blacksmith, h. Clinton n. Jeff.
Wild, John, gardener, High n. Lemon.
Wild, John, lab. h. Herman n. Genesee.
Wild, Jno. mason, h. 247 Elm.
Wilder, Alvin D. clerk, B. N. Y. & E. R. R. b. 380 Swan.
Wilder, F. machinist, b. 380 Swan.
Wilder, Geo. H. printer, Com. Adv. b. 5 Carroll.
Wilder, John, painter, h. 253 Elm.
Wilder, S. H. works at Brayley and Pitts.
Wilder, Wm. h. Riley bel. Main.
Wilds, H. N. butcher, h. cor. 9th and Mass.
Wilds, S. conductor, N. St. R. R. b. cor. 9th and Mass.
Wiley, Wm. harness maker. b. 126 Exchange.
Wilford, C. H. clerk, 211 Main, b. 27 William.
Wilford, Edward, att'y, h. 27 William.
Wilford, Edward, Jr. clerk, b. 27 William.
Wilgus, A. W. h. 75 S. Division.
Wilgus, F. A. shipper, b. 75 S. Division.
Wilgus, Lewis, h. Elk n. Smith.
WILGUS, NATHANIEL, paper-hanging depot, 231 Main, h. 66 W. Mohawk.—See adv. p. 73.
Wilhart, John, butcher, h. Monroe n. Batavia.
Wilhelm, Geo. lab. h. Monroe n. Sycamore.
Wilhelm, Jacob, mason, h. 166 Oak.
Wilhelm, Jno. shoemaker. b. 122 Walnut.
Wilhelm, Louis, grocer, Mich. cor. Goodell, h. same.
Wilhelm, Louis, with Hamlin & Mendsen, b. cor. Swan and Oak.
Wilhelm, Peter, carp. h. Hickory n. Sycamore.
Wilhelm, Samuel, carp. h. Hickory n. Syc.
Wilhem. Peter, shoemaker, h. 84 Sycamore.
Wilke, Nicholas, ship carp. Davis n. Genesee.
Wilker, Fred. shoemaker, b. East n. South.
Wilker, Fred. shoemaker. h. Niagara n. Austin.
Wilkes, W. A. h. Franklin ab. Allen.
Wilkeson, John, h. Niag. sqr. Court cor. Gen.
Wilkeson, Wm. h. Niag. sqr. Court cor. Gen.
Wilkeson, —, elevator, Ohio cor. Indiana.
Wilkie, M. firm Davis & W. Merchants' Exch. h. 221 Delaware.
Wilkins, Jos. E. farmer, h. Gen. n. city line.
Wilkins. John, farmer, h. Utica n. Mass.
WILKINS, RICHARD P. com. merch't, 13 Central Wharf, h. cor. Del. and Mohawk.—See adv. p. 36.
Wilkinson, Thos. exp. messenger, h. 253 Oak.
Wilkinson, Wm. builder, h. 118 W. Tupper.
Willard, Christopher, blacksmith, h. Monroe n. Batavia.

Willard & Curtiss, prod. and com. merchs. cor. Lloyd and Prime.
Willard, Levi, firm W. & Curtiss, b. Niagara square n. Court.
Willard, Nelson. h. Vermont cor. 7th.
Willard, Phineas S. mach'st, h. 195 Delaware.
Wille, Geo. fireman, h. 7 Maple.
Wille, Jno. watchman, h. 108 Goodell.
Willert, Conrad, lab. h. Johnson n. Batavia.
Willey, C. C. at Hamlin & Mendsen, b. Franklin House.
Willgaentz, Gottlieb, farmer, h. Gen. n. Williamsville road.
Willganz, Christian, cabinet maker, h. Carolina n. Palmer.
William, Andrew, blacksmith, h. N. Division n. Jefferson.
Williams, Aaron J. ship carp. h. 33 7th.
Williams, Adin W. section master, N. Y. C. R. R. h. 20 6th.
Williams, Alfred, carp. b. cor. Hudson and Palmer.
Williams, A. M. h. 177 S. Division.
Williams, Amos, h. 39 7th.
Williams, Andrew, painter, h. Hickory n. Bat.
Williams, A. G. firm W., Fargo & Co. h. 156 Franklin.
Williams, Avery, M. D. 57 E. Eagle.
Williams, Avery, clerk, 20 and 22 Pearl, h. 53 E. Eagle.
Williams, Benj. H. attorney, firm Wadsworth & W. b. 42 Goodell.
Williams, Chas. capt. h. Lutheran n. Batavia.
Williams, Chas. E. whitewasher, h. Elm n. Bat.
Williams, Chs. H. clerk, Newman & Scovill, b. cor. Barker and Main.
Williams, C. G. clerk, R. L. Williams, b. 92 E. Swan.
Williams, Daniel, constable, h. 34 Carroll.
Williams, Daniel, clerk, N. Y. & E. R. R. b. Brown's Hotel.
Williams, Daniel, tally clerk, B. C. & C. line, h. 92 Swan.
Williams, David R. M. D. h. East n. Parish.
Williams, Dudley D. h. 42 Goodell.
Williams, Edward, joiner, 9 Water, h. Palmer n. Hudson.
Williams, Edward P. cook, h. 7 William.
Williams, E. P. firm W., Fargo & Co. h. 21 Court n. Pearl.
Williams, E. W. carriage painter, b. 79 Chip.
Williams, Frank, civil engineer, h. 57 Del.
Williams, Fred. waiter, h. 7 William.
Williams, Geo. W. painter, h. 132 Folsom.
Williams, Geo. sailor, h. Hickory n. William.
Williams, Geo. S. h. Seneca cor Chicago.
Williams, Gibson T. president Clinton Bank, h. Main cor. High.
Williams, Henry, with N. Y. & E. R. R h. 9 William.
Williams, Henry, porter, b. 111 William.
Williams, H. J. ship carp. h. Bristol n. Spring.
Williams, Horace, b. 29 Swan.
Williams, H. S. glue manuf. h. Martin's Corners.
Williams, Jacob, clk. J. G. Deshler, b. 166 Oak.
Williams, James, D. D. h. 331 Michigan.
Williams, Jas. Pratt iron works, h. Forest n. Niagara.

Williams, James, lab. b. Hickory n. Seymour.
Williams, John, sailor, b. Perry n. Red Jacket.
Williams, John, lab. h. 6 Mechanic.
Williams, John, clerk, F. B. Myer, h. 33 Pine.
Williams, John, grocer, cor. Mich. and Scott, h. 4 Gay.
Williams, John, planer, b. Hickory n. Batavia.
Williams, John, lab. b. Smith Block, Exch.
Williams, John F. cor. Main and N. Division, b. Thomas.
Williams, John R. Mrs. wid. h. 57 Delaware.
Williams, John W. b. St. James.
Williams, Joseph R. clerk, Taylor & Jewett, h. 124 Tupper.
Williams, J. L. clerk. b. 92 E. Swan.
Williams, J. W. conductor N. Y. & E. R. R. b. St. James.
Williams, L. carp. h. Cold Spring.
Williams, Levi H. b. 70 6th.
Williams. Louis, ship carp. h. 145 Walnut.
Williams, M. D. agt. G. W. & L. O. Strs. Erie opp. depot, b. Revere House.
Williams, M. L. Mrs. wid. b. 79 Chippewa.
Williams, O. B. Am. Ex. Co. h. 204 Pearl.
Williams, O. V. engineer, b. Georgia n. 5th.
Williams. Orrin, carp. b. Cold Spring Cottage.
Williams, P. B. exp. messenger, h. 204 Pearl.
Williams, Ralph, sexton, h. 81 Clinton.
Williams, Richard, at Buff. Iron Works, h. N Washington n. Forest avenue.
Williams. Richard, prop. Erie Mills, office cor. Lloyd and Prime, h. 29 7th.
Williams, R. H. b. 94 Eagle.
Williams, R. L. com. mer. Marine Block, h. 152 Pearl.
Williams, Samuel, carp. h. Hickory n. Bat.
Williams, Samuel, Jr. painter, b. Hickory n. Batavia.
Williams, S. F. intelligence and house agency, 200 Washington, h. 94 E. Eagle.
Williams & Son, carriage factory, 499 Main, h. 34 W. Tupper.
Williams, Steadman, clerk, b. American.
Williams, Thos. carriage painter, h. 220 Ellicott.
Williams, V. R. exp. messenger, h. 32 Clinton.
Williams. Watkins, firm W. & Son, h. 34 W. Tupper
Williams, Watkins, moulder, Pooley place n. Bird ave.
Williams, Watkins M. coach painter, b. 79 Chippewa.
Williams, William, receiver Clinton Bank, b. American.
Williams, Wm. ticket agent, b. Revere House.
Williams, Wm. barber, h. 371 Michigan.
Williams, Wm. ship carpenter, h. 98 9th.
Williams, Wm. shoemaker, 55 Lloyd, h. 102 Fulton.
Williams, Wm. painter, h. Hickory n. Clinton.
Williams. Wm. shoemaker, 55 Lloyd, b. Catlin's coffee house.
Williams, Wm. lab. h. r. Hamilton n. Niagara.
Williams, Wm. H. firm W. & Son, b. Watkins Williams.
Williams Wm. I. carpenter and lumber dealer, 503 Main, h. 59 6th.
Williamson, M. carriage trimmer, h. Terrace n. Church.

Williban, Edwin, land agent, b. 44 Pearl.
Willis, Ann, Mrs. milliner, h. 122 Oak.
Willis, C. H. b. 122 Oak.
Willis, George, tailor, h. 122 Oak.
Willis, Michael, ship carp. h. 9th n. York.
Williston, R. Q. clerk, b. National.
Willox, Jno. dyer, h. Cherry n. Jefferson.
Willrich, And. Jr. cooper, Bat. cor. Walnut.
Wilmoth, Lorenzo, miller, h. East n. Hamilton.
Wilner, John, lab. h. Maple n. Goodell.
Wilson, Alfred, melodeon maker, h. 6th n. Hudson.
Wilson, Benj. engineer, h. 334 N. Div. n. Jeff.
Wilson, Caroline, Mrs. saloon, Lloyd bridge.
Wilson, Chas. A. clerk, b. 375 Michigan.
Wilson, Chas. B. clerk, b. 255 Washington.
Wilson & Co. Buff. City Mills, cor. Chicago and Miami.
Wilson, Dean, plumber. h. 329 Seneca.
Wilson, Edwin, engineer, h. 68 Ellicott.
Wilson, Geo. brick maker, h. Ferry n. Jeff.
WILSON, G. R. & Co. coal and iron dealers, junction Elk and Ohio.—See adv. p. 45.
Wilson, Guilford R. firm G. R. W. & Co. iron and coal merchants, h. Main cor. Tupper.
Wilson, Harvey L. 3 Niagara, b. 33 Ellicott.
Wilson, Isaac S. firm W. & Co. h. cor. Ferry and Niagara.
Wilson, Isaac, miller. b. cor. Ferry and Niag.
Wilson, James, machinist, b. Ala. n. Elk.
Wilson, James, carpenter. h. York cor. 10th.
Wilson, James, firm W. & Samuels, h. 195 E. Seneca.
Wilson, John, engineer, b. 334 N. Division.
Wilson. John, brick maker, h. Ferry opp. race course.
Wilson, Jno. nurse, B. G. Hospital.
Wilson, John, ship carpenter, Fulton n. Red Jacket.
Wilson, John, carpenter, h. 4 Hayward.
Wilson, John Q. A. harness maker, Canal n. Evans, h. 30 Carroll.
Wilson, John, hackman, b. Chippewa n. Del.
Wilson. Julia, Miss, at Sage & Sons, b. Julia A. Wilson.
Wilson, Julia A. widow, h. 375 Michigan.
WILSON, LEONARD, ins. agent, 3 Niagara, h. 33 Ellicott.—See adv. p. 95.
Wilson, Mary J. widow of James, h. 36 Union.
Wilson, Michael, carpenter, h. 13th n. Verm'nt.
Wilson, Richard, lab. h. 66 E. Seneca.
Wilson, Samuel, h. Breckenridge n. Niagara.
Wilson, Sarah, widow, h. r. 74 Chippewa.
Wilson, Wareham, book-keeper, Queen City Mills, b. Ferry cor. Niagara.
Wilson, Wm. ship carpenter, h. La. n. Elk.
Wilson, Wm. ship carp. h. Fulton n. Alabama.
Wilson, Wm. vegetable dealer, h. Lyman's al.
Wilson, Wm. lab. b. 334 N. Division.
Wilsey, Daniel, boatman, h. cor. Seneca and Hamburgh.
Wilter, Leonard, lab. h. Seneca n. Jefferson.
Wilting, Fred. grocer, Michigan cor. Cypress.
Wiltong, Aldolf. clerk, h. Batavia cor. Ash.
Wimmer, Adolph, lithographer, with Sage & Son, h. 125 N. Division.
Wimmer, Jos. teamster, h. Pine n. Batavia.
Winch, Byron, moulder, h. 130 S. Division.

Winchell, Jos. W. mariner, h. Carolina n. 7th.
Winchester, S. D. Mrs. matron Orphan Asylum. Virginia n. Delaware.
Wind, Henry, painter, h. William n. Jefferson.
Windisch, Geo. lab. h. Elm n. North.
Windisch, Geo. bricklayer, h. North n. Mich.
Windisch, Jacob, mason, h. Monroe n. Batavia.
Windisch, Margaret, wid. h. Elm n. North.
Wineford, Jacob, exp. messenger, h. 48 Gen.
Wing, C. J. firm H. Wing & Co. h. N. Div. cor. Oak.
WING, H. & CO. leather dealers, 6 and 8 Exchange.—See adv. p. 80.
Wing, Horace, firm H. W. & Co. h. 7 Carroll.
Wing, Horace, Jr. h. Delaware opp. Summer.
Wing, Wm. H. last maker, h. 359 Michigan.
Winkelses, Louis, Mrs. h. Dearborn n. Hamil'n.
Winkler, Franz X. grocer, Seneca cor. Emslie.
Winkler, John, tailor, h. Spring cor. Vary.
Winkler, John, lab. h. Jeff. n. Sycamore.
Winkler, John F. prof. Martin Luther College, Maple n. Virginia.
Winkler, John, lab. h. Mulberry n. Carlton.
Winkler, Louis, M. D. Batavia n. Pratt, h. same.
Winkler, Wolfgang, lab. h. Adams n. Batavia.
Winn, A. Curtis, conductor, h. 25 6th.
Winne, Chas. M. D. h. 287 Wash. office 13 E. Eagle cor. Washington.
Winne, Chas. K. M. D. 287 Wash. cor. Eagle, b. same.
Winship, Aaron N. real estate agt. cor. Wash. and Eagle, h. over 23 E. Huron.
Winship, A. J. clerk, 145 Main, b. Ellicott cor. Huron.
Winship, Jas. att'y. ov. 150 Main, h. 20 Park place.
Winslow, E. T. Mrs. h. 124 Franklin.
Winspear, Mary, Miss, teacher, b. 276 Ellicott.
Winter, Andrew, lab. h. Elm n. North.
Winter, Conrad, lab. h. Michigan n. High.
Winter, Dan'l. cabinet m'r, h. Sycamore n. Jeff.
Winter, Frank, grocer, h. Goodell cor. Oak.
Winter, Fred. blacksmith, h. Pratt n. Clinton.
Winter, George, tailor, h. Niagara cor. Parish.
Winter, George, farmer, h. Delavan ab. Williamsville road.
Winter, Jacob, carp. h. Mortimer n. Genesee.
Winter, John, lab. h. 98 Goodell.
Winter, John, mason, h. Oak n. Best.
Winter, John, with Jewett & Root, 92 Syc.
Winter, John M. clerk, with J. S. Newton, h. 153 9th.
Winter, Joseph, blacksmith, b. Oak n. North.
Winter, Leo, shoem'r, h. Batavia n. Krettner.
Winter, Nicholas, rag picker, h. Smith n. Exch.
Winter, Simon. carp. h. Krettner n. Batavia.
Winter, Wm. lab. h. Ontario n. Tonawanda.
Winterstein, Christian J. tailor, h. 162 Elm.
Wippert, Charles, clerk, h. Batavia n. Adams.
Wippert, C. W. foreman, 202 Main, b. Batavia cor. Adams.
Wippert, George, saloon, Batavia cor. Adams, h. same.
Wippert, Geo. Jr. carpet fitter, h. Batavia n. Adams.
Wippert, Wm. hatter, 202 Main, b. 6 Court.
Wircht, John, stone mason, h. Jefferson n. Sen.
Wirth, Adam, lab. h. Adams n. Batavia.

Wirth, Mary, widow, washer. h. Adams n. Bat.
Wirth, Mathias, potter, h. Watson n. Batavia.
Wirth, M. turner, b. Adams n. Batavia.
Wirth, Peter. brewer, b. Jefferson n. Genesee.
Wischerath, Wm. firm F. Weppner & Co. h. N. Division n. Michigan.
Wise, Wm. machinist, with T. Colligan.
Wisner, C. H. clerk, b. 65 S. Division
Wisner, Jno. with S. P. Wisner, h. cor. School and 9th.
Wisner, S. P. tobacco and cigar manuf. School n. 9th, h. Niagara n. Rhode Island.
Wissman, Gerhard H. tailor, Grey n. Batavia.
Wiswell, Daniel H. h. Palmer cor. Virginia.
Witer, A. lab. h. Herman n. Genesee.
Withers, Wm. shoemaker, h. 54 Palmer.
Witherspoon, O. Rev. pastor, St. John's church, h. 15 Oak.
Witholtz, Dorothy, widow, h. 48 Sycamore.
Witman, Jos. lab. h. Pratt n. Genesee.
Witmer, Joseph, lab. b. Elk n. Hayward.
Witrmee, Samuel, finisher, h. Exchange n. Van Rensselaer.
Witrum, Henry. lab. h. Batavia n. Hickory.
Witt, Louis,* hardware dealer, Genesee n. Pratt, h. same.
Wittenbenger, Jno. h. Main n. North.
Wittman, Ignatz, carp. h. Batavia cor. Grey.
Wittman, John, lab. h. Watson n. Batavia.
Wittman, John, lab. h. Maple n. High.
Wittman, John, lab. h. Mortimer n. Batavia.
Wittman, Nicholas, lab. h. S. Division cor. Grosvenor.
Wittne, Frank, lab. h. Ash n. Sycamore.
Wittung, F. lab. h. Mortimer n. Genesee.
Wittwer. Martin, lab. h. Maple n. Carlton.
Witzel, Andrew, lab. h. Johnson n. North.
Witzel, Ferdinand, lab. h. cor. Goodell and Mulberry.
Witzig, John A. shoemaker, h. 188 Seneca.
Woehnert, Geo. J. C. book-keeper, h. 37 Union.
Woehnert, John G. clerk, cor. Water and Norton, b. 347 Main.
Woeland, Jno. farmer, h. Walden n. Genesee.
Woerner, Lorenz, cabinet maker, h. Johnson n. Batavia.
Woesner, And. saddler, 250 Genesee, h. same.
Wofley, Gottleib, h. East n. Parish.
Wogan, Thos. h. 4th n. Carolina.
Wogan, Thos. Jr. moulder, b. 4th n. Carolina.
Wohlfeld, Wm. lab. h. Johnson n. Batavia.
Wolbert, Henry, hostler, b. 94 Swan.
Wold, Christian, painter, h. Best n. Main.
Woleben, Edward, real estate agt. h. 48 Pearl.
Wolefram, Fred. shoemaker, h. 6 W. Genesee.
Wolf, Chs. lab. h. 346 Michigan.
Wolf, Chs. W. com. merch. 2 Central Wharf.
Wolf, Chr.* barber, cor. Genesee and Hickory, h. same.
Wolf, Christian, blacksmith, h. 27 Hickory.
Wolf, Christian, shoemaker, h. 244 E. Genesee.
Wolf, Francis, lab. h. Clinton n. James.
Wolf, Frederick, cooper, h. Lewis n. Amherst.
Wolf, Frederick, capt. h. Hickory bet. William and Clinton.
Wolf, F. A. farmer, h. Williamsville road n. Ferry.
Wolf, Jacob, boatman, h. Tonawanda n. South.

Wolf, Jacob, grocer, Batavia cor. Pratt.
Wolf, Jacob, blacksmith, h. 12 Cypress.
Wolf, Jaco'), sailor, h. Bundy alley n. Syc.
Wolf, Jacob, lab. h. Forest avenue n. N. Wash.
Wolf, Jacob, engineer, h. Tonawanda n. East.
Wolf, John, grocer, Va. cor. 10th, h. same.
Wolf, John O. rectifier, 428 Main, h. same.
Wolf, John, tailor, h. Emslie cor. N. Canal.
Wolf, Margaret, widow, h. 211 Genesee.
Wolf, Martin, farmer, h. Cherry n. Spring.
Wolf, Michael, clerk, P. O. h. Court cor. Hosp'l.
Wolf, Michael, grocer, Hospital cor. Court, h. same.
Wolf, Michael, blacksmith, h. Best n. Ellicott.
Wolf, Philip. clerk, 400 Main, b. cor. Hickory and Genesee.
Wolf, Philip, shoemaker, h. 98 Hickory.
Wolf, Philip, lab. h. Vermont n. Hodge.
Wolf, Valentine. lab. h. Herman n. Gen.
Wolfenden, Edward, grocer, Ohio n. La.
Wolfer, Henry, teamster, h. Spring n. Gen.
Wolfer, Jacob, farmer, h. Delavan avenue n. Williamsville road.
Wolfert, Anna M. widow, h. 550 Michigan.
Wolfert. Anton, furnaceman, b. 550 Michigan.
Wolff, Chas. with T. D. Dole, b. 10 E. Huron.
Wolff, Christian, firm W. & Loegler, 362 Main, h. 10 E. Huron.
Wolff, Joseph, b. 113 Hickory.
Wolff, Joseph, turner, b. 98 Hickory.
Wolff & Loegler, saddlers and harness makers, 362 Main.
Wolffer, Lawrence, moulder, h. 40 Maple.
Wolfley, John, carp. h. Amherst n. Thompson.
Wolfshon, Jos. peddler, h. 163 Batavia.
Wollaber, Jacob, baggageman, N. Y. C. R. R. h. over 55 S. Division.
Wollenberg, Christian, shoemaker, h. Mulberry n. High.
Woller, Joseph, grocer, Michigan cor. Tupper, h. same.
Wolter. Henry G.* shoemaker, 8 W. Eagle, h. 126 Elm.
Woltge, William, book-keeper and cashier, at S. O. Barnum, 211 Main, h. 18 Ellicott.
Wolz, Geo. lab. h. Clinton n. Jefferson.
Wood, A. D. C. at Crocker's cattle yards Tifft's farm.
Wood, A. J. commission merchant 45 and 47 Ohio, h. Summer n. Delaware.
Wood, Asa D. contractor, 214 Main, h. 210 Pearl.
Wood, Byron. conductor, b. 185 E. Seneca.
Wood, F. P. pail and tub manufacturer, h. 82 W. Huron.
Wood, Franklin, caulker, b. 277 Exchange.
Wood, Geo. carp. and joiner, b. 35 Elm.
Wood, Henry, mariner, h. 32 Scott.
Wood. Henry, lab. h. Bennett n. Wm.
Wood. H. G. Rev. h. Bidwell n. Niagara.
WOOD. HUBBELL & CO. stove works, Scott n. Washington.—See adv. p. 45.
Wood, Jacob, sawyer, h. Maple n. Goodell.
Wood, Jas. cook, h. 20 Walnut.
Wood, Jonas, carp. h. Niag. n. Auburn.
Wood. J. D. steward, with T. D. Dole, b. 67 S. Division.
Wood, Martin, b. 111 Carroll.

Wood, Nathan,* shoemaker, h. Niag. n. Sloan.
Wood, Richard, farmer, h. Ferry n. Walden.
Wood, Sam. mariner, h. 79 6th.
Wood, Sarah, Mrs. widow, h. 26 W. Genesee.
Wood, Stephen, carp. b. Ferry n. Main.
Wood, Thos. cartman, b. Elk n. Ohio.
Wood, Warren, engineer water works, b. Niag. n. Auburn.
Wood, Wm. gardener, h. Northampton n. Main.
Wood, Wm. B. carp. h. 35 Elm.
Wood. Wm. Henry, book keeper, with Sutton & Bros. b. 35 Elm.
Wood. Willard W. with Thos. D. Dole, h. 57 S. Division.
Wood, W. J. porter, Bonney's Hotel.
Woodall, Thos. clerk, 271 Main, h. 63 Delaware place.
Woodall, Wm. gardener, h. 12th cor. Pa.
Woodard, Barnett, traveling agt. h. 3 Vine.
Woodburn, Jas. carpenter, h. 31 Scott.
Woodbury, Geo. melodeon manufactory, h. 327 Ellicott.
Woodbury. Hiram, tuner, G. A. Prince & Co. h. 327 Ellicott.
Woodcock, Wm. butcher, h. Elk n. Hayward.
Woodford, Emeline, Miss, dressmaker, b. Washington n. Carlton.
Woodhatch, Richard, cigar maker, 263 Main, b. 33 Genesee.
Woodruf, C. C. clerk, b. 53 E. Swan.
Woodruff. Jas. E. h. Delaware n. Allen.
Woodruff, J. M. agt. patent med. b. Bonney's.
WOODRUFF, L. C. paper warehouse, 24 and 26 Pearl, h 53 E. Swan.—See adv. p. 77.
Woodruff, Samuel, grocer, E. 394 Seneca.
Woodruff. Wm. b. Bonney's Hotel.
Woods, David, h. Virginia n. 4th.
Woods, John, blacksmith, b. cor. Main and Eley road.
Woods, Pat. lab. h. 43 Church.
Woods, Pat. lab. b. Wm. Flannigan.
Woods, Thos. D. lab. h. Exchange cor. Heacock.
Woodward, A. H. printer, h. 31 Palmer n. Va.
Woodward, D. M. grocer, Clinton cor. Union, h. 114 Clinton.
Woodward, O. B. ship carp. Water bel. Joy, h. Perry n. Hayward.
Woodward, Oscar B. ship carp. h. Perry n. Hayward.
Woodward, S. W. ship carp. h. Bowery n. Allen.
WOODWARD, WM. H. bonnet dealer, 287 and 289 Main and 19 Seneca, h. 58 Ellicott.—See adv. p. 87.
Woolbert, J. lab. h. William cor. Pine.
Wooster, Fred. at Howell's mill, h. Military road n. Amherst.
Wooster, Fred. teamster, h. Miami n. Chicago.
Worcester, Caroline, widow, h. 30 Chippewa.
Workman, Margaret, saloon, Canal n. State.
Wormwood, Chas. grocer, 6th cor. Carolina, h. 201 Terrace.
Wormwood, Eve, widow, h. 43 Cherry.
Worst, Chas.* jeweller, 53 Genesee, h. same.
Worst, Fred. jeweler, h. 172 Seneca.
Worster. Geo. cartman, h. 72 Washington.
Worster, Gottleib, miller, h. East n. Hamilton.
Worster, John, saloon, 72 Washington, h. same.
Worteuger, Joseph, h. Hickory n. Batavia.

Worth, Edward, sailor, h. Fulton n. Alabama.
Worth, Jno. sailor, cor. Vine and Elm.
Worthington, S. K. prod. com. merch. 16 Cent. Wharf, h. 418 Main.
Wortman, Samuel H. boot maker, 300 Michigan, h. same.
Wright, A. R. firm Kenyon & W. b. 262 Wash.
Wright, C. F. grocer. 6th cor. Geo. h. 72 6th.
Wright, C. L. foot Lloyd. h. 26 Delaware.
Wright, Chs. com. merch. 3 Central Wharf, b. Wadsworth.
Wright, Henry. machinist, h. 214 N. Division.
Wright, Jas. millinery, 265 Main, b. S. Division cor. Chestnut.
Wright, John, shoemaker, h. Fox n. Genesee.
Wright, Louisa L. widow, shirt maker, 64 N. Division.
Wright, Mary, widow, boarding house, 22 Chi.
Wright, Wm. H. joiner, h. Ala. n. Perry.
Wright, Wm. blacksmith, h. Fulton n. Ala.
Wright, W. B. private school, over 9 S. Division, b. N. Division cor. Washington.
Wright, W. H. machinist, h. Fulton n. Hayw'rd.
Wuertz, Katherine, Mrs b. 566 Washington.
Wuerz, Wm. machinist, h. 219 Oak.
Wuest, Fred. clothing, 162 Genesee, h. same.
Wuest, John, confect'r, 282 Main, h. 144 Elm.
Wuest, John A. tailor. h. 144 Elm.
Wuest, Jos. lab. h. Grey n. Genesee.
Wuest, Lewis, lab. b. Genesee cor. Elm.
Wuest, Oscar, student, M. L. College, Maple n. Virginia.
Wulliquez, Eugene, fireman, h. 99 Oak.
Wunch, Chas. carp. h. Jefferson n. Sycamore.
Wunsch, F. baker, h. 225 Ellicott.
Wunsch, Geo. baker, b. 34 E. Seneca.
Wurm, Fred. butcher, h. 518 Michigan.
Wursteisen, Philip, clerk, with French & Heusted, h. Seneca cor. Alabama.
Wurtzel, M. Rev. teacher, h. Ash bet. Gen. and Sycamore.
Wurtzel, Bernhard, tailor, h. Pine n. Batavia.
Wutz, John, lab. h. Johnson n. North.
Wyatt, Wm. ship. carp. h. Fulton n. Red Jack't.
Wybrantz, Geo. machinist, h. 12th n. R. L.
Wyckoff, C. C. M. D. h. 80 Pearl.
Wyman, Lawrence, shoemaker, b. 12 Com'l.
Wyman, James, marble cutter, b. 224 N. Div.
Wynhamer, Jas. G. liquor dealer, 1 Clinton, h. 309 Washington.
Wynhamer, Mary, Mrs. confectioner, 323 Main, h. 309 Washington.
Wynhamer, Phillis, Miss, clerk, 323 Main, b. same.

Y.

Yager, Chas. grocer, Goodell cor. Locust.
Yager, Henry, cooper, h. 15 Grey.
Yager, Henry, lab. h. Pratt n. Batavia.
Yager, Jno. potash maker, h. Monroe n. Syc.
Yager, Ottomer, ship carp. Eagle n. Pratt.
Yager, William, boiler maker, Le Couteulx n. Canal. h. Adams n. Batavia.
Yager, William, cooper, b. cor. Peckham and Monroe.
Yale, Herman, at Niag. lead works.
Yaraga, Anton, peddler, h. Cherry n. Spring.

Yaroux, Jacob, grocer, h. Hickory cor. Cherry.
Yates, John, lab. h. Puffer n. Walden.
Yaw, Ambrose P. firm A. P. Y. & Son, h. 474 Main.
Yaw, A. P. & Son, grocers, 44 Main.
Yaw, A. P. & Co. bankers, 44 Main.
Yaw, Geo. R. firm A. P. Y. & Son, b. 474 Main.
Yax, Darius, joiner, h. Georgia cor. 5th.
Yax, Jacob, Wash. Market, h. Oak cor. Tupper.
Yax, John, mason, h. 100 Batavia.
Yecht. Jacob, cook, h. 541 Michigan.
Yehle, Frank, butcher, h. 284 Pearl.
Yeldie, Jacob, carp. h. White's Cor. plank road n. iron bridge.
Yensen, Chas. lab. h. Cherry n. Spring.
Yeskee, Chs. h. 6 Water.
Yogo, Augustus, shoemaker, b. 6 Water.
York, Albert, clerk, Sherman & Barnes, b. 30 W. Seneca.
Youbanks, Wm. mariner, b. 10 William.
Young, Abraham, whitewasher, h. 79 Cedar.
Young, A. M. firm T. H. Mahama & Co. b. 92 W. Tupper.
Young, A. M. tailor, ov. 3 S. Div. h. 92 Tupper.
Young, Andrew, plumber, h. 64 N. Division.
Young, Barbara, b. M. Young.
Young, Benj. F. porter, h. 204 N. Division.
Young, Chs. boat carp. h. 9 Beak.
Young, Chas. clerk, h. 9 Beak.
Young, Chas. tuner, Prince & Co.'s. h. 92 9th.
Young, C. E. firm Y., Lockwood & Co. h. 48 Tupper.
Young, C. E. Mrs. dress maker, h. 9 Beak.
Young, Daniel, chair maker, with S. D. Sikes, h. Hickory n. Genesee.
Young, Eliza, milliner shop, 328 Main, h. same.
Young, Gertrude, pattern maker, ov. 344 Main, h. same.
Young, Hopkins, h. 344 Main.
Young, Jacob, book-binder, h. 211 Ellicott.
Young, Jacob, Jr. musician, b. Hickory n. Cherry.
Young, Jacob,* shoemaker, h. Hickory n. Cherry.
Young, Jas. shoemaker, over 123 Genesee.
Young, John, mason, b. 250 Franklin.
Young, John, miller, b. Eagle tavern.
Young, John, cooper, h. Jefferson n. Wm.
Young, Joseph, tailor, b. Jefferson n. Wm.
Young, Joseph, printer, h. 248 Franklin.
Young, Lockwood & Co. printers and stationers 159 Main.
Young, Martin, lab. h. Bat. opp. Milnor.
Young Men's Association Rooms, 304 Main.
Young Men's Christian Union Rooms, Arcade Buildings, 3d floor.
Young, Michael, peddler, b. 16 Spruce.
Young, Michael. shoemk'r, Hick'y n. Cherry.
Young, Peter, clerk, 330 Main, b. 250 Franklin.
Young, Peter, cooper, h. Dearborn n. Hamilt'n.
Young, Peter, turner, h. Hickory n. Cherry.
Young, Peter, tailor, h. 407 Michigan.
Young, Philip, moulder, b. Hickory n. Cherry.
Young, Theobald, cigar maker, 157 Main, h. 194 Elm.
Young, Thos. E. clerk, 251 Main. b. 62 Eagle.
Young, Valentine,* brush factory, 177 Bat.
Young, Wm. shoemaker, over 123 Genesee.

Young, Wm. baker, h. 74 5th.
Young, Wm. F. 169 Main, h. 122 Swan.
Young, W. M. law student, b. 305 Wash.
Young. Wm. C. civil engineer, h. 305 Wash.
Younglove, Abby, wid. Robert, h. 99 9th.
Younglove, Edward, b. Western.
Younglove, Elbridge G. artist, b. 99 9th.
Younglove, Robt. paper hanger, b. 99 9th.
Youngman, John, cooper, h. 12 Cypress.
Youngvert, Adam, saw filer, h. Clinton n. Smith.
Yox, John, mason, h. Jefferson n. Batavia.

Z.

Zabel, Wm. shoemaker, h. 202 Genesee.
Zabel, Dorothy, widow, h. 202 Genesee.
Zable, J. A. with Stevenson & Co. 200 Main.
Zacher, Chs. boiler maker. h. Goodell n. Maple.
Zacher, Chs. printer, b. 555 Michigan.
Zacher, John, blacksmith. b. 555 Michigan.
Zacher, Martin, lab. h. Hickory n. William.
Zahm, Geo. locksmith, 15 E. Seneca, b. 96 W. Tupper.
Zahm, Jno. clerk, 178 Main, h. 28 7th.
Zahm, Jos. blacksmith, h. over 16 Genesee.
Zahm, Joseph. Jr. clerk, h. 102 Pine.
Zahm, Michael, h. 26 7th.
Zahm, Peter, mason, h. 102 Pine.
Zahn, Jno. melodeon maker, h. Goodell alley below Goodell.
Zang, Nich. teamster, h. Mulberry ab. Goodell.
Zangele, Francis, bakery, 102 Syc. h. same.
Zanker, J. H. watchman, b. cor. Maiden lane and Water.
Zapp, Peter, lab. h. 294 Oak.
Zeamet, John, tailor. h. Mulberry n. Goodell.
Zeaus, Jacob, painter, h. Watson n. Peckham.
Zeb, Jacob J. bootmaker, 249 E. Seneca.
Zech, Michael, engineer. h. Adams n. Batavia.
Zeeb, John,* boot and shoemaker, 249 Seneca, h. same.
Zehnler, Alois, tailor, h. Best opp. Oak.
Zeigle, John, lab. h. 258 Franklin.
Zeiler, Geo. grocer, h. Goodell cor. Hickory.
Zeiliax, John, machinist, h. 182 Oak.
Zeis, John, tailor, h. Mulberry n. High.
Zeita, Mathias, lab. h. Mulberry n. North.
Zeitz, Andrew,* shoemaker, b. F. Zeitz.
Zeitz, Francis, bricklayer, h. Mulberry bel. Va.
Zeitz, Francis, shoemaker, 210 Genesee, h. same.
Zeitz, Theodore, machinist, h. r. 441 Mich.
Zekel, Fred. warehouseman, h. River.
Zell, Wm. wagon maker, h. Pratt n. Batavia.
Zeller, Barbara, wid. h. Locust n. High.
Zeller, Fred. clerk, 105 Main, h. 6 Court.
Zeller, Fred. brewer, with A. Ziegele.
Zeller, Fred. Mrs. wid. h. Goodell n. Maple.
Zeller, Louis, butcher, h. Maple n. High.
Zeller, Michael, lab. h. 592 Washington.
Zenker, Fred. August, cabinet maker, 112 Bat.
Zenner, Franz, lab. h. Herman n. Genesee.
Zent, Jos.* feed store, Main n. Best h. same.
Zentner, Mary, wid. h. 112 Cedar.
Zesch, Frank. printer, h. Elm ab. Batavia.
Zesch, Fred. tailor, h. 108 Elm.
Zickerman, John, lab. h. Ketchum all. n. High.

Ziegele, Albert, brewer, Main n. Virginia.
Ziegle, Anton, moulder, h. Mulberry n. Va.
Ziegle, John, lab. h. Mulberry n. Virginia.
Ziegler, Andrew, joiner, h. 51 Walnut.
Ziegler, Eucharius, mason, h. 106 Pine.
Ziegler, Valentine, shoemaker, h. 44 Bennett.
Ziele, Elizabeth, wid. h. Batavia cor. Ash.
Zieler, Geo. lab. h. Walnut n. William.
Zielonka, John, farmer, h. Genesee n. Williamsville road.
Ziemer. Adam, shoemaker, h. Kaene n. Syc.
Zier, John, grocer, Seneca n. Jefferson, h. same.
Zieres, Wolfgang, baker, b. Goodell cor. Good'l alley.
Zigler, Jacob. carp. h. Locust n. High.
Zillig, Geo. grocer, cor. Bennett and William.
Zimmer. Catherine, seamstress, b. Spring n. Hollister.
Zimmer, Fr. lab. h. Cherry n. Jefferson.
Zimmer, Jacob, lab. h. 179 Batavia.
Zimmer, Jacob, Jr. saloon, 69 Batavia, h. same.
Zimmer, Jacob, lab. h. 81 Spruce.
Zimmer, John, lab. h. Weaver alley n. Burton.
Zimmer, John, lab. h. Mich. n. Carlton.
Zimmer, Joseph, tailor, h. 147 Walnut.
Zimmer. Martin, policeman, h. Maple ab. Goodell.
Zimmer, Mary, wid. h. Spring n. Hollister.
Zimmer. Matthias, Jr. finisher, 241 Main, h. Spring n. Hollister.
Zimmer, Nicholas, lab. h. 75 Spruce.
Zimmer, P. cooper, h. Amherst n. Dearborn.
Zimmer, Flavian, lab. h. Watson n. Peck'm.
Zimmerman, Frederick, tanner, h. Lutheran n. William.
Zimmerman, Frederick, cabinet maker, h. 171 Clinton.
Zimmerman, Geo. grocer and lumber dealer, Pine n. Batavia.
Zimmerman, Geo. lab. h. Lutheran n. Wm.
Zimmerman, Geo. clerk, 383 Main, h. Sycamore n. Spring.
Zimmerman, Jacob, coach rep. h. 316 Elicott.
Zimmerman, Jacob, upholsterer, 205 Main, h. Pine n. William.
Zimmerman, John, carp. h. 115 Bennett.
Zimmerman, John P. lab. h. Lutheran n. Bat.
Zimmerman, John, book store, Pine n. Bat.
Zimmerman, John, carp. h. 316 Ellicott.
Zimmerman, Joseph A. lab. h. 14 Sycamore.
Zimmerman, Jos. gardener, h. 215 Elm.
Zimmerman, Joseph, boiler maker, Ohio n. Ohio Basin.
Zimmerman, Margaretta, widow, h. Elm cor. Tupper.
Zimmerman, Martin, lab. h. Pine n. William.
Zimmerman, Michael, butcher, h. 191 Ellicott.
Zimmerman, Peter, scale maker, h. Madison n. Batavia.
Zimmerman, Wm. Shepard's furnace, h. Bristol n. Spring.
Zimmerman, Wm. tinsmith, b. Lutheran n. Bat.
Zimmerman, Wm. lab. h. r. 24 Hickory.
Zimmermann, Geo. lab. h. Walden n. Ferry.
Zimmermann, Wm. piano maker, with A. & J. Keogh, h. 168 Oak.
Zimmermann, Wm. C. clerk, receiver's office, h. 283 Oak.

Zimper, Martin, lab. h. Walnut n. Eagle.
Zimpher, Elizabeth, widow, h. 100 Cedar.
Zimpher, Geo. lab. h. Pratt n. Sycamore.
Zimpher, Jacob, 99 Main, b. Adams cor. Peck'm.
Zimpher, Martin, carp. h. Mich. n. Carlton.
Zindl, Andrew, lab. h. Adams cor. Wm.
Zink, Bernhard, carp. h. Carlton n. Mich.
Zink, Geo. h. Niagara n. Hampshire.
Zink, Geo. W. clerk, 12 Cent. Wharf, h. Niag'.
ab. Massachusetts.
Zink, Geo. lab. b. Ferry n. Jefferson.
Zink, Henry, land office, h. 95 Ellicott.
Zinkel, Mathias, butcher, h. Gen. n. Herman.
Zinns, Fred. merchant tailor. h. 71 Batavia.
Zinns, Martin, tailor, h. 203 Ellicott.
Zinnuerly, Albert, machinist, h. 111 Pine.
Zintell, John W. carp. h. Adams cor. Brown.
Zinzin, Jno. tailor, h. Spring n. William.
Zinzin, Nicholas, paper peddler, b. Spring n.
William.
Zipp, Peter, grocer, h. 56 Pine.
Zipple, Casper, lab. h. 116 Cedar.
ZITTEL, FRED. lumber dealer, 335 Wash. h.
Wash. n. Carlton.—See adv. p. 86.
Zitter, Joseph, mason, h. Roos alley n. Wm.
Znick, Henry, with Pickering & Otto, b. 95
Ellicott.
Zober, Ludwig, shoemaker, h. 186 Oak.
Zoeller, Phil. blacksmith, h. Grey n. Batavia.
Zolitsch, Jno. wagoner, Main n. Best, h. same.

Zoll, John, clerk, P. O. h. 127 Pine.
Zoller, Jno. A. Ziegele's, h. Wash. n. Burton.
Zonne, Henry, tailor, h. 24 Union.
Zook, Anna, widow, h. 12 N. Division.
Zook, Daniel M. tinsmith, 5 Birkhead Building.
Commercial, h. 12 N. Division.
Zook, Jacob L. tinsmith, h. 11 Chestnut.
Zook, Jos. paper hanger, 272 Main, h. 12 N.
Division.
Zook, Levi L. weighman, Welch's Elevator, h.
Abbott plank road n. iron bridge.
Zook, Levi L. plumber and gas fitter, 5 Birk-
head Buildings, Com'l, h. Abbott road below
railroad.
Zook, Reuben, weigh master, Buff. Elevator, h.
12 N. Division.
Zorn, Michael, lab. h. Mulberry ab. Goodell.
Zuber, Jacob, 358 Main, b. Oak n. Genesee.
Zuber, Jno. printer, 358 Main, h. Pratt cor. Sye
Zuck, Joseph, peddler, h. Weaver's alley n. Va.
Zudick, Henry, engineer, h. 110 Clinton.
Zuehl, Jno. lab. h. 317 Elm.
Zuger, Cecilia, widow, h. Grey n. Genesee.
Zulauf, Andrew, lab. h. Sherman n. Genesee.
Zunk, Henry, cooper, h. 24 Hickory.
Zwicke, Jacob, grinder, h. Monroe n. Batavia.
Zwing, Jacob, moulder, h. Pratt n. Sycamore.
Zwing, Jno. lab. h. Krettner n. Batavia.
Zwirlein, Marcus, bird seller, h. Michigan ab.
Goodell.

BUFFALO BUSINESS DIRECTORY.

19

BUFFALO BUSINESS DIRECTORY.

Agricultural Warehouses.
See SEED STORES.

Kellogg & Bonnell, 178 Main.
Needham, George F. 247 Main.
Needham, Joseph P. 293 Main.
PRATT & CO. Terrace n. Pearl.

Agricultural Works.
Baker, Moses, Washington cor. Genesee.
Buffalo Agricultural Machine Works, Scott n. Washington.
Fischer & Weiland, 520 Main.
Howard, R. L. Chicago cor. Erie canal.
PITTS' AGRICULTURAL WORKS, Brayley & Pitts, proprietors, Carolina cor. 4th.
White, Hiram C. 338 Main.

Ambrotype Gallery.
See DAG. ARTISTS.

Bliss, H. L. over 293 Main.

Ambrotype Goods, &c.
Benton, R. O. over 204 Main.
SAMUELS, NATHAN, Weed's Block, Main cor. Swan.

American & U. S. Express Companies.
Seneca West of Main.

Apothecaries.
See DRUGGISTS.

Architects.
Balmarian, Buskel, 119 Batavia.
Otis, C. N. 5 Hollister Block.
Sage & Allison, 7 Brown's Buildings.
Selkirk, J. H. Swan n. Main.

Artists.
Andrews, A. over 216 Main.
Keller, H. H. 295 Main.
Keller, Wallace, 183 Terrace.
NIMBS, A. B. 303 Main.
Rockwell, Augustus, 266 Main.
Ruhland, John, Batavia cor. Michigan.
Samuels, A. M. 299 Michigan.
Sellstedt, Laurentius G. 16 Granite Block.
Stanfield, F. (scenic,) h. Oak n. High.
Upson, Jefferson T. 324 Main.

Artists' Materials.
Coleman, John H. 4 E. Swan.
DEUTHER, GEO. A. 12 Exchange.

Attorneys.
Allen, Wm. R. over 191 Main.
Allen, W. R. b. Bonney's.
Austin, Stephen G. 1 Granite Buildings.
Austin & Austin, Washington cor. Eagle.
Austin, Jonathan. Washington cor. Eagle.
Babcock & Moore, 330 Main.
Baker, Albert L. 1 Brown's Buildings.
Barker, Geo. P. 4 International Bank Build'gs.
Barton, Hiram, 6 Hollister Buildings, Main.
Bass, L. K. 18 Spaulding's Exchange.
Beckwith, Chas. 302 Main.
Bissell, Leavitt F. 3 Brown's Buildings.
Blanchard, Amos A. 9 Spaulding's Exchange.
Brodhead. W. W. 367 Washington.
Brown & Fisher, Fargo Buildings, over Clinton Bank.
Bryant, Reuben, 268 Main.
Bryant, Wm. C. 268 Main.
Bull, Absalom, Breckenridge n. Niagara.
Burrows, Roswell L. 1 Brown's Buildings.
Chapin, E. P. 7 Granite Block.
Chapin, Roswell, 148 Main.
Clark, Delevan F. 7 Arcade Buildings.
Clark, L. B. 13 Spaulding's Exchange.
Clarke, Chas. E. 2 Granite Block.
Cleveland, Grover, Erie cor. Pearl.
Clinton, DeWitt, 19 Arcade Buildings.
Coe, Spencer C. over 140 Main.
Colegrove, B. H. 6 Hollister Buildings.
Cook, Eli. cor. Main and S. Division.
Cook, Josiah, 136 Main.
Cornwell, Francis E. cor. Court and Main.

Cottle, O. O. 190½ Main.
Curtenius, J. L. 12 Spaulding's Exchange.
Cutler, W. H. over 223 Main.
Cutting, H. S. 227 Main.
Daniels, Chas. Erie Exchange.
Davis, Thad. C. 14 Spaulding's Exchange.
Davis, William, 3 Terrace.
Day, David F. 207 Washington.
Day, Hiram C. 164 Main.
Dorsheimer, William, 7 Court.
Douw, P. J. 146 Main.
Ewers, Tallmadge, 190½ Main.
Evans, Lewis M. 31 Ellicott.
Fairchilds, Joseph L. Co. clerk's office.
Fithian, Freeman J. 7 Court.
FORBUSH, E. B. Main cor. Swan.
Ford, Elijah, 216 Main.
Ford, James E. 216 Main.
Ganson, John, 18 Spaulding's Exchange.
Gardner, John T. 153 Main.
Germain, Rollin, 7 Court.
Gibbs, James S. 164 Main.
Goodrich, Guy H. 3 Weed's Buildings.
Gould, S. O. 19 Arcade Buildings.
Greene & Stevens, 3 North Division.
Greiser, J. P. 136 Main.
Gros, J. D. 152 Main.
Gurney, Wm. H. with Humphrey & Parsons.
Haddock, Lorenzo K. 8 Spaulding's Exchange.
Hamilton, Theodore B. 6 S. Division.
Hard, Samuel B. 20 Spaulding's Exchange.
Haven, Solomon G. 7 Court.
Hecox, William H. 261 Franklin.
Hibbard, George B. Seneca cor. Pearl.
Hodge, Lyman D. Spaulding's Exchange.
Hodge, P. A. 7 Seneca.
Hoffman, Phocian, 2 Exchange.
Hopkins & Halbert, 2 Exchange.
Howard, Austin A. ov. 279 Main.
Hoyt, James G. Court cor. Main.
Hubbell & Davis, 14 Spaulding's Exchange.
Hudson, John T. old Post Office Buildings.
Huetter, Charles, 4 Arcade Building.
Humphrey & Parsons, old Post Office Build'gs.
Johnson, G. W. 27 East Eagle.
Johnson, John, b. Delaware n. Allen.
Johnson, J. Girard, 3 Hollister Buildings.
Judson, J. S. A. b. 120 Pearl.
Kellogg, S. S. 152 Main.
Lanning & Miller, 6 Brown's Buildings.
Lapp, Christian, 98 Oak.
Larreau, L. D. 4 Arcade Buildings.
Le Clear, Ludovic, 3 Terrace.
Lewis, Loran L. 4 Arcade Buildings.
Macdonell, Allan, 5 Harvey Buildings.
Macomber, Chas. S. 152 Main.
Mann, W. W. 216 Main.
Marshall & Harvey, 330 Main.
MARVIN, LE GRAND & GEO. L. 156 Main.
Matterson, S. A. b. 116 6th.
McCumber & Le Clear, 3 Terrace.
McDonald, Hector, with Welch & Dundas.
McMahon, John E. 21 Spaulding's Exchange.
Merrill, Albert S. 148 Main.
Metz & Rathbun, 334 Main.
Mills, Josiah A. ov. 268 Main.
Murphy, John W. 174 Main.
Nicholas, Asher P. 3 Hollister Block.

Norris, John, ov. 146 Main.
Norton, C. D. 3 Weed's Block.
Noyes, George M. 11 Granite Block.
Palmer, Edward W. cor. Niagara and Virginia.
Parker, P. G. cor. Eagle and Main.
Perkins, Lyman P. 4 Hollister Buildings.
Pool, C. O. Franklin n. North.
Porter, Stephen B. Erie Exchange.
Rathbone, J. A. 334 Main.
Robbins, Edwin C. with Geo. B. Hibbard, Sen.
    cor. Pearl.
Robinson, William, Main cor. Lloyd.
Rogers & Bowen, Erie cor. Pearl.
Rogers, Sherman S. 223 Main.
Saunders, Riley, Saunders' Exchange.
Sawin & Lockwood, 3 Hollister Block.
Sayles, P. M. old Post Office Buildings.
Seymour, Horatio, 190½ Main.
Shepard, Charles E. 191 Main.
Shumway, Horatio, Spaulding's Exchange.
Sibley, John C. Main cor. Niagara.
Sizer, Thomas J. 7 Court.
Skinner, John B. ov. cor. Court and Main.
SMITH, LYMAN B. over old Post Office.
Sprague & Fillmore, 222 Main, Weed's Block.
Stevens, Edward, 3 N. Division.
Stevens, F. P. & A. G. 1 Weed's Block.
Stevens, R. H. Harvey Block.
Stevenson, J. D. G. 237 7th.
Strong & Strong, 190½ Main.
Swartz, Henry A. Erie Exchange.
Talcott & Houghton, 4 Arcade Buildings.
Tallmadge, Ewers, 190¼ Main.
Tanner, Alonzo, 268 Main.
Thayer, Edwin, 290 Main.
Tillinghast, Dyre, clerk sup'r. court.
Tillinghast & McMahon, 58 Arcade Buildings.
Tucker, Chauncey, 1 N. Y. & Erie Bank.
Tucker, Henry C. 1 N. Y. & Erie Bank.
Vanderpoel, I. V. old Post Office Buildings.
Vedder, E. B. 191 Main.
Vosburgh, P. M. old Post Office Buildings.
Wadsworth & Williams, ov. 219 Main.
Walker, Joel L. 158 Main.
Wardwell, George S. 180 Main.
Welch, Thomas C. cor. Seneca and Main.
Whitney, Milo A. ov. 156 Main.
Wilbur, J. T. Exchange cor. Washington.
Wilford, Edward, 27 William.
Winship, James, ov. 156 Main.

COPARTNERSHIPS OF ATTORNEYS.

Austin & Austin, Washington cor. Eagle.
    Austin, Benjamin H. Sen.
    Austin, Benjamin H. Jr.
Babcock & Moore, 330 Main.
    Babcock, George R.
    Moore, Mark B.
Brown & Fisher, Fargo Buildings.
    Brown, James C.
    Fisher, James H.
Greene & Stevens, 3 N. Division.
    Green, Wm. H.
    Stevens, Edward.
Hopkins & Halbert, 2 Exchange.
    Hopkins, Nelson K.
    Halbert, Norton A.

Humphrey & Parsons, old P. O. Buildings.
    Humphrey, James M.
    Parsons, Galusha.
Lanning & Miller, 6 Brown's Buildings.
    Lanning. Albert P.
    Miller, Wm. F.
Marshall & Harvey, 330 Main.
    Marshall, O. H.
    Harvey, Alex. W.
Marvin, Le Grand & Geo. L. 156 Main.
    Marvin, Le Grand.
    Marvin, Geo. L.
Metz & Rathbun, 334 Main.
    Metz, Christian, Jr.
    Rathbun, Jos. A.
Rogers & Bowen, Erie cor. Pearl.
    Rogers, Henry W.
    Bowen, Dennis.
Sawin & Lockwood, 3 Hollister Block.
    Swain, Albert.
    Lockwood, Stephen.
Sprague & Fillmore, 222 Main.
    Sprague, E. Carlton.
    Fillmore, Millard P.
Stevens, F. P. & A. G. 222 Main.
    Stevens, F. P.
    Stevens, A. G.
Talcott, & Houghton, 3 Arcade Buildings
    Talcott, John L.
    Houghton. Geo. W.
Tillinghast & McMahon.
    Tillinghast, Henry D.
    McMahon, John E.
Wadsworth & Williams, over 219 Main.
    Wadsworth. George.
    Williams, Benj. H.

Auction and Commission Merchants.

Bristol & Bierne, Arcade Buildings.
Irish, Charles G. Jr. 5 W. Seneca.
Locke, Wm. C. 5 Swan.
Shoecraft, J. P. 3 W. Seneca.
Simpson, John, 167 Main.
Plimpton, L. K. 50 Main.
Vaughan, Maurice, 5 and 6 Quay.
Whelan, James, Quay n. Main.

Awl Manufacturers.

PARR, GEORGE, cor. 5th and Court.

Awning Makers.

Lerquemain, John E. Walnut cor. Clinton.

Axe Makers.

White, L. & I. J. 32 Ohio.

Bakers.

Barth, Philip, 5 Canal.
Beck, Fred. Pratt n. Sycamore.
Beyer, Ernst, 238 Genesee.
CLARKE, WILLIAM H. Main cor. Huron and
    junc. Elk and Ohio.
Colston, John, 426 Main.
Cook, Fred. Seneca bel. R. R. track.

Dietrich, Charles. Jefferson n. Clinton.
Esslinger, Charles, Batavia n. Hickory.
Faber, Theibold, Genesee n. Pratt.
Fischer, Gottlieb, Genesee cor. Johnson.
Foel, Christian. 140 Genesee.
Foel, John, Ellicott ab. Chippewa.
Hauf, Jacob, 110 Sycamore.
Hellriegel, Wm. 356 Genesee.
Hesse, Charles, 175 Elm.
Ihrig, Christian, 374 Genesee.
Johe, Jacob, Batavia n. Spring.
Kamm, Baptist, Hickory n. Batavia.
Knower, Timothy, under Western.
Koch, Jacob, 116 Seneca.
Koehler, Frank, 138 Batavia.
Lochte, Henry, 180 Genesee.
Math, John M. Walnut n. Batavia.
Mathews, Conrad. Genesee n. Spruce.
McGlinn, Jas. Niagara cor. Pennsylvania.
MUGRIDGE, GEORGE, Ohio n. Main.
Ovens, Robt. 34 E. Seneca.
Riebercamb, John. cor. Goodell and Mulberry.
Reinhardt, John, 156 Sycamore.
Rose, Henry, 124 Seneca.
Schneider, Philip, 163 Batavia.
Schwartz, Charles, 365 Genesee.
Spencer, John E., S. Division cor. Washington.
Spengler, Matthaus, 179 Genesee.
Spies, Henry, Genesee n. Kaene.
Voegle, George, Batavia n. Jefferson.
Wagner, Jacob, Mortimer n. Genesee.
Zangele, Francis, 102 Sycamore.

Bandbox Makers.
See BOX MAKERS.

Bankers and Brokers.

Chard, Wm. A. 11 Exchange.
Church, Alvah, Washington cor. Exchange.
Graham, James, Wadsworth House.
Hills, Horace, 247 Main.
Hubbard, Geo. L. Spaulding's Exchange.
Jackson, J. 5 Exchange.
Lee, Edward L. Exchange cor. Main.
MANCHESTER & RICH, Main cor. Seneca.
Robinson & Co. 182 Main.
Shuttleworth & Co. cor. Main and Seneca.
Yaw, A. P. & Son, 44 Main.

Barbers and Hair Dressers.

Armstrong. Geo. 11 William.
Banleon, Charles, 86 Batavia.
Bartel, John C. Erie n. Canal.
Barthauer, Charles F. American.
Baum, Herman, Pearl cor. Terrace.
Cook, Edward, 9 Exchange.
Davidson, John, 23 Seneca.
Eatons, Richard, Mansion House.
Ester, David, Elk street Market.
Krause, W. J. Commercial Hotel.
Moxley, Henry, 188 Main.
Peter, Jacob, 232 Main.
Pfeil, Adam, 104 Exchange.
Schauten, Richard, 404 Main.
Smith, Eugene W. 4 E. Seneca.
Suter, A. J. 232 Main.

294   COMMERCIAL ADVERTISER DIRECTORY.

Schaefer, Philip, 104 Exchange.
Sommer, Philip, Bonney's Hotel.
Stygall, James. Lovejoy House.
Wolf, Chas. cor. Genesee and Hickory.
Wright, Mary, 22 Chicago.

Basket Makers.

Braxmeir, Thomas, Jefferson n. Peckham.
Naun, Cornelius, 220 Ellicott.
Wetzel, Henry, Spring cor. Hollister.
Wetzel, Valentine, Spring cor. Hollister.

Bathing Apparatus.

JOHN C. JEWETT, 259 Main.

Bell Hangers.

BANGASSER & BROTHERS, 15 Seneca.
Taylor, Dennis, 2 E. Swan.
VALENTINE & O'REILLY, 14 Court.

Bell Ringer in Tower.

Broch, John, 35 Sycamore.

Bellows Makers.

Beaman, Wm. F. William n. Jefferson.
Voss & Ward, Buffalo City Bellows Factory,
    Alabama n. Carroll.
Ward, Henry, Bristol n. Spring.

Bells.

Dudley, James, 93 Main.
Good, Adam, Ohio n. Washington.

Belting.

Newman, W. H. H. 42 Main.
PRATT & CO. Terrace.

Bill Posters.

SMITH, LUM, 196 Chicago.

Billiard Rooms.

Darling, E. A. 306 Main.
Fox, W. H. 208 Washington.

Billiard Table Makers.

Staats, Jeremiah, Staats n. Niagara.
Wacker & Co. 563 Main.

Bird Cage Maker.

JEWETT, JOHN C. 259 Main.

Bird Stuffer.

Lawson, Richard, Washington n. Perry.

Blacking and Ink Makers.

BUFFALO BLACKING & INK CO. Wash.
    cor. Erie canal.

Blacksmiths.

Bamberg, Chris. Batavia cor. Roos alley.
Barth, Jacob, Batavia n. Pratt.
Bauer, Michael, Goodell n. Elm.
Beck, Michael, Elk n. Michigan.
Becker, Christian, Peckham n. Watson.
Beyers, Wm. Main n. Puffer.
Boier, Ralph, Washington cor. Virginia.
Boltzki, Jacob, Seneca n. old city line.
Brauman, Peter, 499 Main.
Brennan, P. & Co. Genesee n. Pearl.
Casey, John, Clinton n. Walnut.
Coak, Joseph, Washington cor. Greene.
Demster, Robert, 5 Mississippi.
Duff, A. M. cor. Terrace and Henry.
Duggan, Daniel, Elk n. Louisiana.
Endel, Chas. Genesee n. Walden.
French, Harlow, 374 Washington.
Holzhausen, August, Genesee cor. Oak.
Hook, Thomas, Terrace cor. Henry.
Huff, Valentine, Genesee n. Walden.
Kerber, Joseph, Genesee cor. Adams.
McCormick, Frank. 115 Pearl.
Nisbet, Samuel, Ohio n. Michigan.
Pailey, Benjamin, Terrace.
Robinson, Wm. LeCouteulx n. Canal.
Schaefer, D. Batavia n. Watson.
Seymour, John A. 422 Seneca.
Silk, Wm. 49 Church.
Sneidwin, John, Erie cor. Terrace.
Stanton, Pat. 6th n. Maryland.
Volkert, John, Niagara n. Georgia.
Wierling, Herman, Main n. Best.

Blank Book Makers.

BREED, BUTLER & CO. 288 Main.
Collins, T. F. 156½ Main.
JOHNSON, J. M. over 161 Main.
Jones. William, 196 Washington.
Leavitt, James S. 70 Lloyd.
Penfield, T. V. N. 15 W. Seneca.
TAYLOR, MARTIN, 299 Main.
Young, Lockwood & Co. 165 Main.

Bleachers.

Boutelle, L. 21 Eagle.
Crossland, J. Ford, E. Seneca bel. Post Office.
Woodward, W. H. 287 & 289 Main or 19 Seneca.

Block and Pump Makers.
See PUMP MAKERS.

Boarding Houses.

Barber. Mary, Mrs. 255 Washington.
Barnard, Geo. A. 62 Eagle.
Beiser, L. Ph. A. Washington cor. Huron.
Billings, Harriett, 27 Ellicott.
Brownell, Minerva, 105 Carroll.
Clemons, Ann, Miss, 436 Main cor. Chippewa.
Coy, Emeline, 381 Michigan.
Cutler, Clara, Mrs. 509 Washington.
Dean, James, 20 Washington.
Frost, Mary, Palmer n. Maryland.
Frost, N. Mrs. 137 E. Seneca.
Hawkins, L. Mrs. 36 W. Seneca.

Hill, Marcus, 83 Seneca.
Howe, Joseph H. 27 Ohio.
Lewis, Samuel, Mrs. 52 E. Swan.
Luigart, Mathias, 32 E. Genesee.
Lyon, H. E. Mrs. 29 Swan.
Monroe, Melissa, 7 6th.
Moore, J. O. Mrs. 62 Swan.
Munson, M. T. 60 S. Division.
Nash, Thomas, 20 Exchange.
Newell, Bridget, 189 Exchange.
Noble, Mary, 74 Chippewa.
Nolan, Michael, 111 Carroll.
Noxon, Eliza, 44 Pearl.
Phelps, Catharine, 167 Seneca.
Reardon, Mary, Mrs. 40 Oak.
Saexhauer, Chris. Genesee cor. Michigan.
Springer, O. F. 114 Carroll.
Stephens, Susan, 24 Chicago.
Titus, S. A. Miss, 408 Main.
Tospot, Timothy, 11 William.
Tuthill, R. P. 125 Michigan.
Waring, Jane, Mrs. 35 Swan.
Warren, Eliza A. 41 Church.
Wilbur, E. S. Mrs. 408 Main.

Boat and Ship Builders.

Beck, Charles C. foot of Joy.
Brown, James, across Buffalo creek.
Haukins & Johns, across Buffalo creek.
Hingston, J. T. foot of Hudson.
MASON & BIDWELL, opp. foot Chicago.
McGilvray, Duncan, 125 6th.
Newton & Van Slyke, Green n. Michigan.
Pratt, Lucius H. cor. Green and Michigan.
Van Slyke & Notter, Virginia cor. Canal.
Woodward, O. B. junction Joy and Water.

Boiler Makers.

DAVENPORT & NELSON, Le Couteulx
 cor. Canal.
SHEPARD IRON WORKS, Ohio n. Bridge.

Bonnet Warerooms.

Hollerith, Geo. 272 Main.
Whiting, S. E. 273 Main.
Woodward, Wm. H. 287 and 289 Main.

Book Binders.

Chichester, James L. 182 Washington.
Collins, T. F. 156½ Main.
JOHNSON, J. M. 161 Main.
Jones, William, 196 Washington.
Leavitt, J. S. 70 Lloyd.
Penfield, T. V. N. 15 Seneca.
TAYLOR, MARTIN, 299 Main.
Young, Lockwood & Co. 159 Main.

Book Sellers.

Baer, Conrad, 410 Main.
Bessir, J. W. 27 Genesee.
Black, Robert, 17½ East Seneca.
BREED, BUTLER & CO. 188 Main.
Butler, Theodore, 159 Main.
Haefner, Francis, 222 Ellicott.
Hager, Robert, 364½ Main.

Hawks, T. S. 10 East Seneca.
HILL, J. F. & CO. 201 Main.
Hog, Joseph, Sr. Batavia near arsenal.
OTIS. H. H. 226 Main.
Schmidt, Anton, 411 Main.
TAYLOR, MARTIN, 299 Main.
Zimmerman, John, Pine n. Batavia.

Boot Makers.

See SHOEMAKERS.

Chamot, C. P. 217 Washington.
Denicombe, John, 7 Genesee.
Dennis, Robert, 96 Barker's Block.
Guild, E. T. 52 Exchange.
Henning, G. 20 South Division.

Boot and Shoe Dealers.

Abbott, Walter S. 240 Main.
Brown, John C. 43 East Seneca.
Buehl, Louis A. 372 Main.
Clor, Michael, 133 Main.
Diebold, George, 12 Commercial.
Draper & Rathbun, 253 Main.
Ferkel, Martin, 394 Main.
Field, Thomas C. 196 Main.
Forbush, Brown & Co. 91 Main.
Forsyth, Robert, 51 Seneca.
Guild, E. T. 52 Exchange.
Kreiner, G. & Co. 106 Exchange.
Lander, James, 156 Main.
Mabie, M. T. 278 and 410 Main.
Manhard, Frank. cor. Exchange and Chicago.
Matteson, Harry H. 256 Main.
McWilliams & Sons, 310 Main.
Moores & White, 218 Main.
Paige, Timothy, 238 Main.
Petit, Sweet & Co. 166 Main.
Ramsdell, Charles, 214 Main.
Ramsdell, O. P. & Co. 168 Main.
Randall, Volney, 78 Main.
Schott, Geo. 3 Genesee.
Schryver, A. L. 304 Main.
Taylor, William R. 236 Main.
Wagner, P. A. 7 Main.
Wegand, August, 397 Main.

Botanic Medicines.

Hill, M. W. 245 Main.
Wiggins, Dennis, Niagara near Pearl.

Bottlers.

HOWELL & SMITH, 36 E. Seneca.
KNIGHT, J. 324 and 330 Main.

Box Makers, (fancy.)

Day, Norris, Niagara cor. Maryland.
Drescher, Casper I. 117 Pine.
Gackle, Jno. 273 Main.
Gegla, Jno. Jr. Genesee n. Spruce.
Scharff, Chas. 273 Main.

Brass Founders.

BROWN & McCUTCHEON, junction Elk
 and Ohio.

Colligon, F. cor. Washington and Perry.
Dudley, J. D. & Co. 3 and 5 State.
GOOD, ADAM, 21 Ohio.

Brewers.

Albrecht, Frederick, Genesee cor. Jefferson.
Beck & Baumgarten, 209 Oak.
Bodamer, Gottlob, Genesee n. toll gate.
Boyle, Hugh, St. Paul n. Main.
Frederich, Henry, Spruce n. Cherry.
Gerber, Charles Main n. Virginia.
Gibbons, Charles, W. St. Paul n. Main.
Haas, Davis, Spring cor. Cherry.
Haberstro, Joseph L. High n. Main.
Haefner, Aloys, Michigan cor. High.
Heiser, Godfrey, 149 Seneca.
Hiemenz, Nicholas, 118 Batavia.
Kaltenbach, Xavier P. Lutheran n. Batavia.
Loerch, F. 200 Genesee.
Moffat, James, Mohawk cor. Morgan.
Nefzer, Fred. Goodell cor. Goodell alley.
Roos, Jacob, Hickory n. Batavia.
Scheu, Jacob, Genesee cor. Spring.
Scheu, Philip, Sr. High n. Main.
Weber, Charles, Batavia n. Adams.
Weppner, Jacob, Genesee n. Jefferson.
Ziegel, Albert, Main n. Burton alley.

Brick Makers.

Balcom, P. A. Cold Spring.
Brush, Milton, Clinton n. railroad crossing.
Brush, Nathaniel, Clinton n. railroad crossing.
Brush, William C., N. Canal n. Swan.
Hornbuckle, Richard, Batavia n. toll gate.
Kirkhover, Lewis, 420 Seneca.
Relph, Jesse, Genesee E. toll gate.

Britannia Ware.

Hill, F. C. 269 Main.
JEWETT, J. C. 259 Main.
Laudenbacher, Frederick, Pearl cor. Seneca.
PRATT & CO. 28, 30 and 32 Terrace.

Broom Makers.

Chrysler, George, 36 Green.

Brush Makers.

Chrysler, George, 36 Green.
Eberlein, Christian, Mortimer n. Sycamore.
Young, Valentine, 177 Batavia.
Steinla, Joseph, 377 Genesee.

Buffalo Steam Gauge Co.

Cor. Washington and Perry.

Builders.

See CARPENTERS AND JOINERS.

Allison, George M. 143 Pearl.
Ambrose, John, h. Main n. Steele.
Barnes, Bradford, 296 Michigan.
Chapin, Cooley S. Elm n. Clinton.
Cook, Lyman, Oak n. Clinton.

Gould, L. D. 36 Carroll.
HARRADEN, JAMES, 3 Elm.
Hefford, Thomas, 19 Oak.
Hodge & Baldwin, Niagara cor. Carolina.
Jones, Nathaniel, 74 N. Division.
Knapp, Stephen L. 253 Seneca.
Lock, Charles H. 185 Delaware.
Lord, F. A. Eaton's planing mill.
Morgan, Amos, 35 and 27 Elm.
Pixley, Philander, 6 Carey.
Phelps, J. D. 30 Park.
Porter, Walter, 83 S. Division.
Ralph, R. L. Huron below Morgan.
Salisbury, W. J. Delaware n. Allen.
Sawin, S. & Co. 8 W. Eagle.
Sears & Clark, River, Erie Basin.
TILDEN, THOMAS B. 11 Franklin.
Warren, Truman H. Water below Joy.
Waterman, Darius W. 7th cor. Hospital.
Wilbur, L. D. 132 S. Division.
Wilkinson, Wm. h. 118 Tupper.

Building Movers.

Chamberlain, John, Perry n. Chicago.
Chamberlain, Jno. 109 S. Division.
Denio, John R. Eagle n. Hickory.
Hemstreet, B. F. 14 Mohawk.
Lauber, Geo. Elm n. Burton alley.

Butchers.

ALBERGER, JOB, Terrace cor. Franklin.
Baetenger, Elizabeth, 286 Genesee.
Barnes, J. L. 199 E. Seneca.
Barnes, J. & Son, 3 E. Seneca.
Behringer & Klaes, 14 Niagara.
Beierlein, John S. Washington Market.
Bennett, Jas. P. 17 Elk Street Market.
BULLYMORE, RICHARD, Michigan n. Elk
  Street Market.
BULLYMORE, THOMAS, 326 Main.
Farthing, Geo. 12 Elk Street Market.
Farthing J. & J. 291 Main.
Farthing, Thomas, 1 Elk Street Market.
Feizel, Charles. Genesee cor. Spruce.
Fisher, Henry, Genesee cor. Hickory.
Goembel, Paul, 63 W. Chippewa.
Hacker, Martin, 342 Main.
Herrman, Jos. Vermont n. 13th.
Hitzel, Jacob, 237 Genesee.
Hock, John, 115 Batavia.
Hoffer, Fred. 374 Main.
Klein, J. P. 61 Exchange.
Kuebler, John, Genesee cor. Grey.
Lamb, Henry, 1 Birkhead Buildings.
Lees, John, 23 Elk Street Market.
Rast, Lorenz, Batavia cor. Adams.
Rehm, Henry, 190 Niagara.
Reil, Jno. Batavia n. Monroe.
Roessel, Augustus, 10 Court St. Market.
Schaefer, Valentine, Genesee n. Adams.
Schmidt, John, 208 Oak.
Sour, Fred. 58 6th.
Voelker, John, Batavia cor. Monroe.
Wandel, John Mrs. cor. Elm and Sycamore.
Weppner, Arnold L. 422 Michigan.
Weppner, August, 174 Genesee.

Weppner. F. & Co. 300 Michigan.
West, William W. Clinton market.

Butter and Egg Dealers.

See GROCERS.
See PROVISION DEALERS.

Cabinet Makers.

See FURNITURE DEALERS.

Barrett, Stephen John, r. N. Y. and E. Bank.
Bell, Robt. W. 161 Washington.
Galligan, William, 34 and 36 Ellicott.
Hersee & Timmerman. 307 and 309 Main.
Hersee, Harry, 241 Main.
Knettle, Christopher, 161 Batavia.
Krieger, M. 218 Genesee.
Luhmann, C. F. 98 E. Genesee.
Meyer, John. 241 Main.
Schury, William, 390 Seneca.
Sikes, S. D. 300 Clinton.
Staats, Jeremiah, Staats cor. Mohawk.
Streicher, John, 32 Ash.
Stunrm & Gerlac, 132 E. Genesee.
Taunt & Bristol, 233 Main.
WHITE, ISAAC D. 201 and 203 Main.

Candle Makers.

See SOAP AND CANDLE MAKERS.

Car and Car-Wheel Makers.

Buff. Car-Wheel Works, Louisiana cor. canal.
SCOVILLE, J. & N. C. Louisiana opp. Lake Shore Freight Depot.

Carpenters and Joiners.

See BUILDERS.

Innemann, Fred. Delaware n. North.
Schieffer & Swartz, 42, Ash.
Sparks, Charles, 143 Pearl.
Waterman, D. W. 7th cor. Hospital.
Waterman, G. 11th n. Virginia.

Carpet Dealers.

Hamlin & Mendsen, 206, 208 and 212 Main.
SHERMAN & BARNES, 205 Main.

Carpet Weavers.

Apel, Louis W. 516 Michigan.
Beer, Anne, 79 Sycamore.
Mathaes, Gottleib C. 222 Genesee.
Nitzhcke, Henry, 142 Elm.
Nitzhcke, J. G. 146 Elm.
Rahm, Daniel C. Delaware bel. Allen.

Carriage and Wagon Manufacturers.

Behrens, Andrew, Virginia cor. Ellicott.
Bowen, Daniel, Seneca bel. Chicago.
CHAMBERLAIN & CO. Niag. cor. Mohawk.
Chamberlain, H. S. cor. Pearl and Mohawk.
Colley, David D. Washington n. S. Division.
Godwin D. C. 15 East Eagle.

Harvey & Wallace, Lock n. Courter House.
Hewson & Miller, 48 Exchange.
Knight, T. M. 214 Elm.
Niebecker & Pendleton, Washington ab. Gen.
Rapelyea, John. 79 Elm.
Rice, Daniel S. 296 Seneca.
Williams & Son, 499 Main.

Carriage Hardware.

PRATT & LETCHWORTH, Terrace.
Taylor, D. 2 East Swan.

Carriage Spring Manufacturer.

Mills A. & Son, 20 and 22 Elm.

Carvers.

DREW. EDWARD, 136 Main.
Howell, James R. 439 Main.

Chair Manufacturers.

Galligan, William, 34 and 36 Ellicott. ·
Hersee & Timmerman, 307 Main.
Sikes, S. D. 300 Clinton.
WHITE, ISAAC D. 201 Main.

Cheese Merchants.

ANDERSON, A. S. & CO. 56 Main and 27 and 29 Hanover.
BEARD & HAYWARD, Wash. cor. Green.
BOGARDUS, S. ov. 29 Main.
Damon, Hiram, 25 Main.
HEAD. JOSEPH A. 60 Main.
Moore, George A. 68 Main.
Peter & Ketchum, 48 Main.

Chemists.

See DRUGGISTS.

Chromotype Printers.

WHEELER, HEMMING & CO. 161 Main.

Cider and Vinegar Makers.

See VINEGAR FACTORIES.

Cigar Dealers.

See TOBACCONISTS.

ADAMS, JAMES & CO. 207 Washington.
Barrows, E. G. & Co. 213 and 215 Washington.
DIEHL & PARKER, 263 Main.
Diehl, Henry, 322 Main.
Doerffel, Hermann, 54 E. Genesee.
Geyer, F. C. W. 342 Main.
Hayen, Jacob F. Terrace.
Lloyd, Alfred A. 263 Main.
Neu, George, Batavia cor. Ash.
Schiedt, Lawrence, Genesee n. Hickory.
SEVERN, OSCAR, 191 Main.
Tiphaine, V. L. 193 Main.
Tupper, John. 310 Washington.
Walker, Samuel N. 12 E. Seneca.

Cistern Builders.

Debas, Andrew, Batavia cor. Walnut.
Dennis, James H. 265 Swan.

Cistern Pumps.

Hill, F. C. 269 Main.

Civil Engineers.

See SURVEYORS.

Cloth Manufacturers.

Newman, Peter, Spring cor. Batavia.
Richard, Geo. Niagara n. Amherst.

Clothes Cleaners.

Harris, Peyton, 379 Michigan.
Johnson, Charles, Pearl cor. Terrace.

Clothiers.

See TAILORS AND DRAPERS.

Abrahams, Abraham, 98 Main.
Alexander, I. 138 Main.
Alexander, J. 160 Main.
Altman, A. & Co. 140 Main.
Altman & Co. wholesale, 40 Pearl.
Burman, Jacob, 116 and 148 Main.
Bennett, Samuel, 126 and 128 Main, and 1 and 2 Terrace.
Bergman, S. & Co. 142 and 198 Main.
Black & Alexander, 10 Com'l, 98 and 160 Main.
Boasberg, N. second-hand, 5 Commercial.
Bogert & Dolittle, 164 Main.
Boland & Son, 104 Main.
Broch, Henry, 157 Main.
Clark & Storms, 308 Main.
Claus, Daniel, 123 Genesee.
Friedenburgh, Julius, 124 Main.
Greenshield & Laux, Commercial cor. Canal.
Hart, Henry, 171 Main.
Heinminghoffen, Charles P. 15 E. Genesee.
Hermann, John, 2 W. Genesee.
Hyman, B. & Son, 120 and 154 Main.
Hoefeller, S. & Bros. 140 Main.
Horvitz, T. 99 Main.
Lazarus, Ephraim, 38 Main.
Levi, Emanuel, Gothic Hall and 184 Main.
Lichtenstein, Edward, 13 Main.
Mohr & Schlag, 382 Main.
Newman, Emanuel, Ohio cor. Columbia.
Nickles, Reinhard, 94 Genesee.
Petsch, Chas. F. 46 E. Genesee.
Philips, S. & Co. 94 and 192 Main.
Reinhart, Charles, 51 Genesee.
Schneider, William, 285 Genesee.
Silberg, S. 366 Main.
Stambach, W. P. & P. C. Main cor. Ohio.
Straas, J. E. 5 Commercial.
Vogt, Francis, 11 Commercial.
Warner, Brothers, 43 and 45 Main.
Worle, Anthony, 1 Commercial.
Wuest, Fred. 162 Genesee.

Coal Dealers.

BULL, CADWALLADER, River, opp. Erie Basin.
Daken, Geo. foot Genesee.
DE FOREST & COYE, foot Genesee and Erie Basin.
EVANS, CHARLES W. foot Erie.
FARNHAM & HODGE, Erie cor. River.
Joy, Walter, Main cor. Seneca.
MADDEN, EDWARD, Erie and Ship Canal.
PARKER, JASON & CO. Norton and Ship Canal.
WILSON, G. R. & CO. junction Elk and Ohio.

Coffee Ext. Manufacturers.

Gese, Julius & J. G. 68 William.
Shultz, Louis, 252 E. Genesee.

Coffee and Spice Dealers.

Benson & Co. Arcade Buildings.
CHASE, JAMES H. 271 Main.
Ferris, P. J. Hanover cor. Canal.

Coffin Makers.

See UNDERTAKERS.

FARWELL, E. & H. D. Niagara cor. Pearl.
Kraft, Francis J. 29 E. Huron.
Meacham, George, Carey bel. Morgan.
Nothnagel & Pfeifer, Ash n. Batavia.

Commercial Colleges.

Bryant & Stratton, Brown's Building.
HICKS, D. CLINTON, over 194 Main.

Commission Merchants.

See PRODUCE MERCHANTS.

See FORWARDERS.

Abell, William H. 24 Central Wharf.
Allen, J. W. foot Main.
Annin, J. V. W. 9 Central Wharf.
Anthony, Jacob C. 2 Central Wharf.
Arnett, Henry M. 7 Central Wharf.
Beckwith, Brothers, 1 Central Wharf.
BENTLY, J. R. & CO. 17 Central Wharf.
Bettis, Heron H. 26 Central Wharf.
Bigelow, Wm. H. 15 Central Wharf.
Bissell, Sheldon & Co. 7 Central Wharf.
Blackman & Gilbert. 13 Central Wharf.
BOYD, ROBERT D. 10 Central Wharf.
Boynton, T. C. over 9 Central Wharf.
Boughton & Jackson, cor. Michigan and Scott.
Brownell, Isaac W. 10 Central Wharf.
Buell, J. S. cor. Lloyd and Prime.
Clark, Cyrus. 5 Central Wharf.
COBB & CO. 20 and 21 Central Wharf.
COBB, WM. H. & CO. 12 and 14 Canal.
Coit, G. C. & Son, 70 Main.
CUTTER & AUSTIN, Norton and Ship canal.
Cutter & Nims, 6 Central Wharf.
Darragh. John, 14 Central Wharf.
DAW, HENRY & SON, 26 Central Wharf.

Deshler, John G. 14 and 15 Central Wharf.
Dought, John, 4 Central Wharf.
Durfee, Philo, 2 Central Wharf.
Eames, M. R. 20 Central Wharf.
Ellis, A. D. 9 Central Wharf.
Enos. L. & Co. 22 Central Wharf.
Evans, Edwin T. cor. Water and Ship Canal.
Evans, J. C. cor. Water and Ship Canal.
Fish & Avery, 18 Central Wharf.
FLEEHARTY, J. 27 Central Wharf.
Foster, W. C. & Co. 20 Central Wharf.
Gibson, W. L. 28 Central Wharf.
Greenvault & Co. 73 Main.
Griffin, A. L. 23 Central Wharf.
Griffin & McDonald, 17 Central Wharf.
Guthrie, S. S. 11 Central Wharf.
HAWLEY, M. S. & Co. 18 Central Wharf.
Hayward & Selmser, 16 Central Wharf.
Hazard, Geo, S. & Co. 25 Central Wharf.
HEAD, JOSEPH A. 60 Main.
Heimlich, P. J. Jr. 12 Central Wharf.
Hopkins & Co. 8 Central Wharf.
HORTON, A. W. 10 Central Wharf.
Howard, W. S. 9 Central Wharf.
Howcutt, John, 15 Commercial Wharf.
Howe, Otis B. 13 Prime.
Johnson, Wallace, 89 Main.
Jones, Isaac A. 10 Central Wharf.
Judson & Avery, 24 Central Wharf.
King, Rufus S. 12 Central Wharf.
LITTLE & ARNOLD, foot Commercial.
Lockwood & Kinne, 11 Central Wharf.
Mann, Charles J. 15 Central Wharf.
Mann, W. B. & Co. 17 Central Wharf.
McNaughton, John, 58 Main.
Millikin, C. A. 68 Lloyd.
Moore, J. A. Central Wharf.
Morgan, H. G. Central Wharf.
Morse, Nelson & Co. 28 Central Wharf.
Morton & Foot, 7 Central Wharf.
Munderback, J. S. Central Wharf.
Niles & Co. 5 Central Wharf and 10 Main.
Noble, R. P. 23 Central Wharf.
ORR, ALEX. B. 58 Main.
PARKER, JASON. 23 Central Wharf.
Parsons, Silas, 17 Prime.
Patterson, F. W. 13 Central Wharf.
Philpot, John N. 26 Central Wharf.
Philpot, William S. 26 Central Wharf.
Pratt, Anson, 17 Central Wharf.
Rainey & Wheeler, 22 Central Wharf.
Rankin, M. M. b. Bonney's Hotel.
Richmond, J. M. Ohio n. Michigan.
Richmond, W. T. North cor. Delaware.
Sandrock, George, 23 Central Wharf.
Sawyer, James D. 11 Central Wharf.
Seymour & Wells, foot Illinois.
Sherwood, A. & Co. 9 Central Wharf.
Smith, J. S. 28 Central Wharf.
Steelwagen, J. & Kraetzer, 369 Main.
STERNBERG, P. L. & CO. 4 Central Wharf.
Stimpson & Mathews, 6 Central Wharf.
Swan, S. E. & Co. 25 Central Wharf.
Swan & Thayer, 25 Central Wharf.
Taintor, Charles, River.
Thomas, Edwin, 10 Central Wharf.
Tuttle, David N. Central Wharf.
VanBuren, James, 23 Central Wharf.

Vandenburgh, H. P. & Co. Marine Block.
Watson, S. L. h. 9th n. Vermont.
Waud & Abell, 24 Central Wharf.
Weed, Elias, 17 Central Wharf.
Welch & Millar, 159 Washington.
Wells, C. C. Coburn's elevator.
Whitting & Co. 13 Central Wharf.
Wilkins, Richard P. 13 Central Wharf.
Willard & Curtiss, Lloyd cor. Prime.
Williams, R. L. Marine Block.
Wolf, Chas. W. 2 Central Wharf.
Wood, A. J. 45 and 47 Ohio.
Worthington, S. K. 16 Central Wharf.
Wright, Chas. 3 Central Wharf.

Compass Manufacturers.

Andrews & Son, 221 Main.

Composition Roofing.

WARREN & BROTHERS, Main cor. Swan.

Confectioners.

BENSON. JOHN, 131 Main.
Bierman, Henry, 350 Main.
Bouyon, Paul, 298 Main.
Loebrich, George, 127 Genesee.
McARTHUR, J. J. 297 Main.
Mesnard, John, 75 Genesee.
Schiefersttein, Geo. 258 Genesee.
Spertzell, Justus, 9 South Division.
VanSlyck, G. A. 39 East Seneca.
Vermilya, Wm. E. 137 Main.
Wuest, John, 282 Main.
Wynhamer, Mary, Mrs. 323 Main.

Contractors.

Barton, Theodore D. 532 Main.
Beckwith, L. W. 20 Goodell.
Bristol, Henry, 214 Main.
Brown, Warren, Thompson n. Hamburgh.
Butler, Ormond, Jr. 4 Park Place.
Deiler, Geo. Hamilton n. Dearborn.
Douglas, W. H. 214 Main.
Dunn, V. R. Niagara cor. Virginia.
HOWELLS, JAMES, junction Church and Genesee.
Olson, G. Wadsworth n. North.
Rose, Edwin, 88 Franklin.
Swartz, A. S. 321 Michigan.
Swartz, Samuel, 77 North Division.
Tayntor, E. Perry cor. Louisiana.
Vanderless, N. 9th n. Vermont.
Walker, David, Mariner ab. Allen.
Wannop, John, 38 Chippewa.
Webster, A. 60 Ellicott.
Webster, David, 7 Union.
Welch, John, 70 5th.
Wood, A. D. 214 Main.

Coopers.

Ade, John M. h. Genesee n. Sherman.
Argus, Anthony. Amherst n. Military road.
Bennett, Eligh, Mortimer n. William.
Binder, Marzoff, Tonawanda n. Hamilton.

Clark, David N. Burwell Place.
Debus, Andrew, Batavia cor. Walnut.
Ditmar, Frederick, German alley n. Sycamore.
Ebling, John, Lewis n. Amherst.
Friedman, John, Amherst n East.
Frieschlag, Jacob & Bro. Clinton n. Jefferson.
Hitschler, Henry, Spring above Genesee.
Hoefle, John, William cor. Spring.
Jensen, Thomas, Washington cor. Perry.
Jungman, John, Pratt n. Sycamore.
Miller, Jacob, East n. South.
Pruchtl, John, Batavia cor. Mattison.
Weber, Chs. Spring cor. William.

Coppersmiths.
See TINSMITHS.

Britton, Nicholas. Commercial cor. Pearl.
Brown & McCutcheon, 3 Elk junction Ohio.
Dudley Brothers, 57 Main.
HART, BA L & HAR , 237 Main.
HILL, F. CL& CO. 269 Main.
Schmitt, Jacob, Kaene n. Genesee.
Shaw, John H. 198 Washington.
SHEPARD, S. & CO. 54 Main.

Crockery and Glass Dealers.
GLENNY, WM. H. 162 Main.
Gram, F. & Co. 344 Main.
HOMER & CO. 175 Main.
Newman, Geo. F. 344 Main.
Wackerman, John M. 415 Main.

Cutlers.
Seiffert, John C. 217 Washington.

Daguerreotype Artists.
Benton, Russell O. 204 Main.
Beyer, Mart, 538 Michigan.
Brent, Henry, Genesee n Spruce.
Buell, Chas. W. 214 Main.
Butler, Anna, 293 Main.
Clark, Geo. W. Mrs. 348 Main.
Evans, O. B. Main cor. Erie.
Feckes, Benj. F. 324 Main.
KNIGHT, W. M. 2 Arcade Buildings.
Koegel, Chas. 34 E. Genesee.
Macdonell, D. 232 Main.
Macdonell, R. 275 Main.
Miller, John. 505 Michigan.
NIMBS, A. H. 303 Main.
Pond, C. L. 198 Main.
Smith, E. M. over 268 Main.
Thayer, J. Houghton, 274 Main.
UPSON, JEFFERSON T. 324 Main.
Werner, L. W. 29 Mohawk.

Daguerreotype Stock.
SAMUELS, NATHAN, 4 Weed's Block.

Decorative Painters.
See PAINTERS.

Dentists.
Brown, Benoni S. 301 Washington.
Giffing, Isaac H. 203 Main.
Harvey, Leon F. 5 S. Division cor. Wash.
Hayes, George E. 247½ Main.
Lewis, John, Sr. over 278 Main.
Oliver, F. 2 Erie.
Oliver, William G. 11 Niagara.
Phelps, C. B. 28 Chippewa.
Reynolds, H. H. 4 W. Swan.
Snow, Reuben G. 4 Church.
Straight, C. L. over 280 Main.
Whitcomb, Nathan, over 240 Main.
Whitney, B. T. 12 S. Division.

Derricks.
Bishop, James D. Palmer n. Virginia.
Campbell, John A. 258 Seneca.

Distillers.
See RECTIFIERS.

Ayers, W. J. 8 Hanover.
Boyle, Hugh, St. Paul n. Main.
CLARK, THOMAS, Washington cor. Perry.
Emerick, Louis, 44 E. Genesee.
GILLET, HENRY T. 18, 20, 22 Lloyd.
Miller, H. B. Spring n. Batavia.
Shoemaker, Stewart & Co. 5 Central Wharf.
Truscott's Distillery, William cor. Pratt.
Wolf, John O. 428 Main.

Dress Makers.
Alton, Mary, over 12 Niagara.
Baumeister, Margaret, Hickory n. Sycamore.
Bliss, Madam, 295 Main.
Chandler, Elizabeth, Mariner n. Virginia.
Dimery, Maria, 117 Pearl.
Drew, Mary E. 40 N. Division.
Duell, Fanny, 47 Clinton.
Earle, Helen, over 12 Niagara.
Estes, C. M. 131 Chippewa.
Gibson, I. Miss, 63 Chippewa.
Hammond, Mary, 346 Main.
Hebron, Mary, 187 S. Division.
Hersee, Jane, Washington cor. Chippewa.
Hill, Matilda, Jefferson n. Howard.
Humberstone, Elizabeth, 1 Church.
Kendrick, Jane, 47 Delaware.
Knodel, M. widow, 480 Michigan.
Martin, Amelia, 217 Oak.
McKernon, Margaret, 31 Clinton.
Rebstock, Elizabeth, 375 Washington.
Richter, Augustus, Sycamore n. Ash.
Ritchie, Martha, 45 Church.
Robinson, Mary Ann, Batavia n. Walnut.
Ross, Jeanette S. 129 Franklin.
Stacy, Parmelia, 10 E. Eagle.
Tuck, H. Mrs. 9th n. York.
Vanduzee, Fidelia, 155 Swan.
Young, C. E. 9 Beak.

Dry Goods—Wholesale.
BETTINGER & CO. 399 Main.
Holbrook, Dee & Co. 220 Main.

HOWARD, WHITCOMB & CO. 207 Main.
Hamlin & Mendsen, 206, 208 and 212 Main.
Murray, Cumming & Grant, 316 Main.
Sherman & Barnes, 205 Main.

Dry Goods.

See FANCY GOODS.

Bettinger & Co. 399 Main.
Beyer, Jacob, 113 Genesee.
Beyer, Philip, 430 Main.
Chase & Bird, Niagara cor. Amherst.
Cone, H. 194 Main.
Dahlman, L. & Co. 274 Main.
Dihl, Frank, Clinton n. Walnut.
Fitch, F. S. cor. Seneca and Michigan.
Georger, F. A. & Co. 400 Main.
Greenburg. Harris, 400 Seneca.
Haberstro, Joseph, 401 Main.
Hamlin & Mendsen, 206, 208 and 212 Main.
Hausle & Son, 146 E. Genesee.
Holbrook, Dee & Co. 220 Main.
HOWARD, WHITCOMB & CO. 207 Main
and 216 Washington.
Loewi & Geirshofer, 306 Main.
Lorenz, Philip G. 31 E. Genesee.
Murray, Cumming & Grant, 316 Main.
Murray & Grant, 288 Main.
Pardridge, C. W. & E. 318 Main.
Rosenau & Co. 280 Main.
Sherman & Barnes, 205 Main.
Titus, O. B. 285 Main.
Wike, M. 138 Seneca.

Druggists.

Champlin, O. H. P. Arcade Buildings.
Coleman, John H. 4 E. Swan.
Davis, Epenetas H. 10 Terrace.
DIEHL, JOHN P. 402 Main.
FRANCIS, JULIUS E. 268 Main.
Gibbons, John J. 195 Main.
HOLLISTER & LAVERACK, 202 Wash.
Holman, Edward D. 145 Main.
Jenner, R. 438 Main.
King, Wm. Jr. 249 Main.
Mathews, A. I. 255 Main.
Peabody, Wm. II. 251 and 432 Main.
Reynolds, A. & Co. 155 and 157 Main, and
Washington cor. Seneca.
Rieffenstahl & Bro. 396 Main.
Sage & Tucker, 232 Main.
Samson, Hoffer, 364 Main.
Wiggins, D. B. Niagara n. Pearl.

Dyers.

Brokenbourg, S. 193 E. Genesee.
CHESTER, LUCAS, 18 Batavia.
CLAUDE, LOUIS & CO. 306 Michigan.
Hertel, Ferdinand, Sycamore n. Michigan.
Hertel, Fred. 6 Court.
Idrick, Conrad, 144 Batavia.
Perry, James, 412 Main.
Schmitz, John, 2 Court.
Strele, Joseph, 389½ Main.
Strele, Joseph, 58 Niagara.

Eating Houses.

Bloomer House, 1 W. Eagle.
Boggis, Wm. Pearl cor. Eagle.
Broezel, John, under old Post Office.
Catlin, Ira, 25 Commercial.
Cotter, Thomas, under Spaulding's Exchange.
Fowler, George L. Terrapin Lunch, Main cor.
Terrace.
Red Jacket, Main cor. Seneca.
Thomas, H. 159 Main.
Wheeler, Wm. H. Wadsworth House.

Edge Tool Makers.

Lang, Michael, Batavia cor. Ash.
White, L. & I. J. Ohio cor. Indiana.

Electrotyper.

Lyman, N. Seneca n. Pearl.

Elevators.

	Storage Capacity.	Elevation per Hour.
Seymour & Wells	150,000	3,000
Wells	80,000	3,500
Union	100,000	4,000
Wilkeson	200,000	4,000
Sternberg	200,000	4,000
Coburn Square	250,000	4,000
Empire	250,000	4,000
Erie Basin	200,000	4,000
Buffalo	100,000	2,000
Corn Dock	300,000	6,000
Dart	175,000	3,000
Evans	200,000	2,500
Hatch	200,000	4,500
Grain Dock	100,000	2,500
Main street	200,000	4,000
Sterling	100,000	3,500
Central	400,000	6,000
Total	3,205,000	64,50)

Engine Manufacturers.

BELL'S STEAM ENGINE WORKS, Norton
cor. Water.
BUFFALO EAGLE IRON WORKS, Missis-
sippi cor. Perry.
Buffalo Steam Engine Works, foot Washington.
COLLIGON, F. Washington cor. Perry.
Dunbar & Howell, Eagle Iron Works.
GOOD, ADAM, 21 Ohio.
SHEPARD IRON WORKS, Moore cor. Ohio.

Engravers, Copper and Stone.

DREW, EDWARD, 136 Main.
MOONEY, L. 200 Main.
SAGE & SONS, 209 Main.
Strong, George H. 246 Main.

Engravers on Wood.

DREW, EDWARD, 136 Main.
MITCHELL, WILLIAM J. 136 Main.
Smith & Bowen, 190½ Main.

Vanduzee & Barton. 161 Main.
WIGHTMAN, GEORGE D. 156½ Main.

Engravers, (Relief-Line.)

JEWETT & HEMMING, 161 Main.

Exchange and Stock Brokers.

See BANKERS.

Express Companies.

'AMERICAN, 9, 11 and 13 W. Seneca.
UNITED STATES, 15 W. Seneca.

Fancy Goods Dealers.

See VARIETY STORES.

Barnum, S. O. 211 Main.
Comstock & Co. 230 Main.
HOFFMAN, JULIUS, 294 Main.
Volger, E. F. 320 Main.

Fence Makers—Iron, &c.

Dennis, Dan. 265 E. Swan.
EDDY & BINGHAM, Clinton Iron Works,
  Jackson cor. Church.
JONES, GEORGE. Terrace cor. Henry.
SCOFIELD, AUGUST, at J. R. Evans & Co's.

File Manufacturer.

COLLINSON, SAMUEL, Hospital bel. Court.
Jetter, Jacob, 118 E. Genesee.

Fireworks Manufacturers.

See PYROTECHNISTS.

MORRIS, J. S. & SON, Niag. School and 10th·

Fish-rod Manufacturer.

Mitchell, James, 155 Delaware.

Fish Dealers.

Higgins, D. C. & Co. Lloyd n. Canal.
Hoag, Darius, Michigan n. Bridge.
Johnson & Bros. Lloyd n. Erie canal.
Mesmer, Michael, 277 Main.
Neff, A. Lloyd n. Canal.
Root, Adrian R. 64 Main.

Flour Dealers.

See PRODUCE MERCHANTS.

See COMMISSION MERCHANTS.

See FLOUR AND FEED DEALERS.

See GRAIN MERCHANTS.

Abernethy, Andrew, Elk n. Louisiana.
Brown, Alexander, 289 Seneca.
CANDEE, GILBERT, Michigan cor. Carroll.
COBB & CO. 20 and 21 Central Wharf.
COBB, WM. H. & CO. 12 and 14 Canal.
DAW, HENRY & SON, 26 Central Wharf.

Heimlich, P. J. Jr. 12 Central Wharf.
Heywood, R. H. 81 Seneca.
Hollister, James, Central Wharf.
Houck, Philip, 91 Genesee.
Pfohl & Co. 162 Batavia.

Flour and Feed Dealers.

See FLOUR DEALERS.

Abernethy, Andrew, Elk n. Louisiana.
Brown, Alexander, 289 Seneca.
CANDE, GILBERT, Michigan cor. Carroll.
COBB, WM. H. & CO. cor. Terrace and Evans.
Cutter & Bailey, 201 Washington.
Dickey & Marsh, 212 Washington.
Diebold, A. Canal ab. Maiden lane.
Diebold, Sebastian, 133 Batavia.
Fischer, J. & G. 74 E. Genesee.
French & Hustead, 204 Washington.
Hamlick, Philip, 191 N. Division.
Hannivan & Albro, 36 E. Seneca.
Harvey & Allen, 206 Washington.
Hasteed. E. S. 41 Seneca.
Houck, Philip, 91 Genesee.
Pfohl, Jacob H. 162 Batavia.
Pfohl, Louis, 162 Batavia.
Recktenwalt, Peter, cor. Batavia and Wash.
Scheu, Wm. Genesee n. Michigan.
Schoelkopf, J. F. 388 Main.
Vorst, John, 96 Batavia.
Wendt & Speck, William n. Bennett.
Zent, Joseph, Main n. Batavia.

Flour Inspector.

Brainard, Richard, 17 Central Wharf.
Rathbone, R. W. 16 Prime.

Flour Mills.

Buffalo City Flour Mills, Chicago n. Miami.
Clinton Mills, Black Rock Pier.
CUTTER & AUSTIN, Elevator, Norton cor.
  Ship Canal.
Erie Mills, Black Rock.
EVANS, CHARLES W. ship canal cor. Water.
Frontier Mills, Upper Black Rock.
Globe Mills, Thornton & Chester. ft. Amherst.
HOLMES, E. & B. Michigan n. R. R. Depot.
North Buffalo Mills, P. Bauer & Schoelkopf.
  W. Canal n. Amherst.
Queen City Mills, Upper Black Rock.
Wadsworth Mills, Benjamin Campbell, 61 Ohio.

Flour Mill Manufacturers.

ALLEN, Z. G. agent, Miami n. Chicago.
Exelby, R. Miami.
HENRY, S. H. Water cor. Le Couteulx.
NOYE, JOHN T. Washington cor. Canal.

Forwarders.

See COMMISSION MERCHANTS.

See PRODUCE MERCHANTS.

Bissell, Sheldon & Co. 7 Central Wharf.
Fish, S. H. & Co. 18 Central Wharf.

Foster & Co. 20 Central Wharf.
Griffin, A. L. 23 Central Wharf.
Jones, Isaac A. 10 Central Wharf.
Judson & Avery, 24 Central Wharf.
LITTLE & ARNOLD, foot Commercial.
Morse & Nelson, 28 Central Wharf.
MORTON, FOOTE & CO. 7 Central Wharf.
Niles, H. & Co. Marine Block.
Petrie, William & Co. 13 Central Wharf.
Pease & Trowbridge, foot Lloyd.
STERNBERG, P. L. & CO. 4 Central Wharf.
Stimpson & Mathews, 6 Central Wharf.
Swan & Thayer, 25 Central Wharf.
Van Buren & Noble 23 Central Wharf.
Western Transportation Company, Erie Basin.
Wood, A. J. 45 and 47 Ohio.

Foundries, (Brass.)

BANGASSER & BROTHER, 15 E. Seneca.
GOOD, ADAM, 21 Ohio.
TIFFT, GEORGE W. SONS & CO. cor. Washington and Ohio.

Foundries, (Iron.)

BULL, GEORGE B. & CO. Swan cor. Jeff.
DUNBAR & HOWELL, Eagle Iron Works, Mississippi.
HUBBARD, CHAS. J. Carroll cor. Chicago.
TIFFT, GEORGE W. SONS & CO. cor. Washington and Ohio.

Fresco Painters.

BURNS, GEORGE L. 204 Washington.
Stanfield, F. h. Oak n. High.
THURSTON, CHARLES J. 5 Terrace.
WHITE, H. G. 273 Main.

Fruit Dealers.
See OYSTER DEALERS.

Beamer, S. 94 E. Seneca.
Blakely, J. & W. 31 Main.
DODGE, A. L. 17 Main.
Libby. James, 182 Washington.
PLATT, L. B. & CO. 286 Main.
Rowe & Co. 212 Washington.
Smith, John J. 197 Main,
Wageman, A. 8 E. Seneca.

Fur Dealers.
See HATTERS.

Furnaces—Hot Air.

HARDIKER & TOY, cor. Niagara and Pearl.
HART, BALL & HART, 257 Main.
Hill, F. C. 269 Main.
JEWETT, JOHN C. 259 Main.

Furnace Builders.
Kneeland, E. G. 36 Clinton.

Furniture Dealers.
Galligan, William, 34 and 36 Ellicott.

Hersee, Harry, 241 Main.
Hersee & Timmerman, 307 and 309 Main.
Mesner, Peter, 243 Main.
Raeker, August, Batavia n. Elm.
Richardson, S. B. 5 Quay.
Smith, John S. 58 Lloyd.
Stout, William, 32 Quay.
Taunt & Bristol, 233 Main.
Whalen, James, 3 Quay.
WHITE, ISAAC D. 201 and 203 Main.

Gardeners.

Bayliss, Charles, Delaware bel. Bryant.
Henking, Ernst, at Prospect Hill.

Gas Light Co.
Buffalo Gas Light Co. Genesee cor. Jackson.

Gas Fitters.
See PLUMBERS.

Carr, W. A. 354 Main.
Day, Geo. 9 W. Eagle.
HART, BALL & HART, 237 Main.
Hill, F. C. 269 Main.
Irr & Irlbacher, 1, 2 and 3 Mohawk.
Zook, Levi S. 5 Birkhead Buildings, Com'l.

Gents' Furnishing Goods.
MILLINGTON, E. H. 314 Main.

Gilders.
See FRAME MAKERS.

Howell, J. R. 439 Main.
Howell, William, 439 Main.
Teller, George D. 170 Main.

Glass Stainers.

BURNS, GEORGE L. 204 Washington.
Myers, William H. over 79 Main.
THURSTON, CHARLES J. 5 Terrace.
WHITE, H. G. 273 Main.

Glaziers.
See PAINTERS.

Glove Maker.
Leonard, Norman, 27 E. Seneca.

Glue Manufacturers.
Evans, Richard, Abbott Road n. Iron Bridge.
Williams, Richard, Martin's Corners.

Gold Beaters and Workers.
Dennis & Cottier, Washington cor. Exchange.

Gold Pen Manufacturers.
Brown, Samuel, 185 Main.
Carpenter, Geo. W. 159 Main.
FELTON, JOHN, 159 Main.

Goldsmith.

Boader. Joseph, 403 Main.

Grain Merchants.

See COMMISSION MERCHANTS.

See PRODUCE MERCHANTS.

See FLOUR DEALERS.

BENTLEY, J. R. & CO. 17 Central Wharf.
Blackmar & Gilbert, 13 Central Wharf.
BOYD, R. D. & CO. 13 Central Wharf.
Brownell, Isaac W. 10 Central Wharf.
COBB & CO. 20 and 21 Central Wharf.
COBB, WM. H. & Co. 12 and 14 Canal.
CUTTER & AUSTIN, Norton and ship canal.
Cutter & Nimbs, 8 Central Wharf.
DAW. HENRY & SON, 26 Central Wharf.
DESHLER, J. G. 14 and 15 Central Wharf.
EVANS, CHARLES W. Norton cor. Water.
Hawley, M. S. & Co. 18 Central Wharf.
Hazard, G. S. & Co. 25 Central Wharf.
King, R S. 12 Central Wharf.
Mann, W. B. & Co. 17 Central Wharf.
Selmser & Hayward, 16 Central Wharf.
Smithwick, P. J. 178 9th.
STERNBERG, P. L. & CO. 4 Central Wharf.
Worthington, S. K. 16 Central Wharf.

Grape Culturists and Domestic Wine.

PRESBREY, OTIS F. M. D. 214 Niagara, City Clerk's office.
Williams, Horace, Abbott Road ab. Martin's Corners.

Grape Grower and Vintry.

PRESBREY, OTIS F. Prospect Hill n. Res.

Green Grocers.

Baylis, Charles, 5 Scott.
Keel, Charles A. Bullymore Block.
PLATT, L. B. & CO. 286 Main.

Groceries and Provisions.

Adams, Jno. n. cor. Exchange and Wash.
Adams, Hiram & Co. 37 E Seneca.
Adams, J. F. n. Whitmore's tavern.
Adoff, L. P. Genesee cor. Oak.
Allinger, Francis, Niagara n. Austin.
Aiple, Daniel, 435 Seneca.
Albert, Charles, Milnor cor. William.
Albrecht. Jacob, S. Division cor. Pine.
Allen, John P. Chicago n. Exchange.
Argus, George, Niagara cor. Hamilton.
Argus, George, Niagara n. Amherst.
Armbraster, Joseph, Genesee cor. Canal.
Anderson, A. S. & Co. 56 Main.
Antony, James, 3 Water.
Baker, Louis, Batavia n. Hickory.
Balmer. George J. cor. Erie and Lock.
Banks, Levi A. 16 Niagara.
Barber, Daniel, 396 Seneca.
Barnard, Ira, Jr. 182 E. Swan.
Barnum, George G. 74 Main.
BEARD & HAYWARD, Wash. cor. Green.

Becker, John, Genesee n. Jefferson.
Becker, John P. 356 Michigan.
Becker, Lorenz, 72 Bennett.
Becker. Philip & Co. 384 Main.
Bell, Brampton, 22 E. Eagle.
Benzing, Gott N. Clinton cor. Madison.
Benzinger, Christian. Clinton cor. Jefferson.
Berlin, Louis, 560 Seneca.
Beyer, Philip & Co. 482 Main.
Billeb, Ernst, Batavia cor. Grey.]
Bilz, Joseph, Genesee cor. Elm.
Blackmond, Edwin F. Ferry cor. Adams.
Blum, Peter, 12 Huron.
Blumenburg, William, 154 Batavia.
Boas, Samuel, 234 Main.
Borst, John, 159 Elk.
Boyle, Ellen, S. Division n. Jefferson.
Brady, Daniel, Palmer n. Maryland.
Braids, Robert, cor. 14th and Vermont.
Braun. Paul. Genesee cor. Pratt.
Brechte, John, Niagara n. Massachusetts.
Brown, Daniel, Old Packet Dock.
Brown, Robert, Michigan bet. Elk and Ohio.
Brunner, Frank, Walnut n. Batavia.
Buck, Thomas, 257 Swan.
Buettler, Matthias, 117 Batavia.
Bulger, James, 11 Reed's Dock.
Burckhard, Christian, Vermont cor. 12th.
Burdgers, James, Terrace n. Mechanic.
Byrne, James, 30 Ohio.
Caburet, P. F. Huron cor. Ellicott.
Callanan. Cornelius. 32 Terrace.
CALLENDER. SAMUEL N. 229 Main.
Carey. Richard J. Abbott n. N. Y. C. R. R.
Carmichael, Robert. Carolina cor. Palmer.
Cole, Alexander, 163 Seneca.
Corroll, Michael, 5th n. Carolina.
Cowan, Chas. 96 Main.
Chapman, J. Y. 29 Central Wharf.
Chase & Bird, North Buffalo.
Chavel, Peter, Washington cor. Tupper.
Churchill & Parker, 336 Main.
Clemens, Jacob, Seneca n. 13th Ward House.
Clifford, James, Hudson n. Niagara.
Comstock, Martin. 21 Main.
Cowing, H. O. Niagara cor. Bird avenue.
Currier. Joseph. 163 Main.
Dahl, Henry, Genesee cor. Johnston.
Davis, A. I. Chippewa cor. Franklin.
Davis, John, Elk bel. Alabama.
Dean, A. M. 266 S. Division.
Debus, Andrew, Batavia cor. Walnut.
Debus, Philip, Peckham cor. Monroe.
Denny, Jacob, Hospital cor. Court.
Diebold, B. Canal cor. Maiden lane.
Diebold, Joseph, Batavia cor. Adams.
Dier. Christ. Canal n. Erie.
Dinwoodie & Co. 30 Clinton.
Dinwoodie & Shultz, S. Division cor. Michigan.
DOBBINS, SAMUEL, Swan cor. Michigan.
Gollwitzer, Michael, Michigan cor. Sycamore.
Good, Adam J. 277 Genesee.
Goodwin, Patrick, Elk opp. Moore.
Gottman, Henry, 295 Genesee.
Graf, G. Batavia n. Hickory.
Graf. Philip, Oak cor. Tupper.
Grass, A. Wm. cor. Hickory.
Griffin, John, Hudson cor. 7th.

DODGE. A. L. 17 Main.
Dolan, James. Niagara cor. Breckenridge.
Dolan, Patrick, 122 Exchange.
Doll, Sebastian, Canal cor. Evans.
Doran, E. W. Niagara n. Pennsylvania.
Dorst, Frederick, Niagara cor. Huron.
Dorst, Jacob, 367 Main.
Dorst, Philip, Main cor. Allen.
Duggan, Patrick M. 169 E. Seneca.
Dunlop, Robert. Jr. 10th ab. Carolina.
Dunne, Mary, Mrs. cor. Eagle and Cedar.
Dwyer, Mary, cor. 4th and Georgia.
Eckels, Stephen, opp. Guard Lock.
Edwards, John, Louisiana n. Tennessee.
Eley, Samuel, Main cor. Eley Road.
Elsheimer, George, Genesee cor. Johnson.
Emerling, Philip. Batavia cor. Monroe.
Endres, George, 80 E. Genesee.
Ernst, Henry, Eagle cor. Pratt.
Ewig, Peter, Goodell n. Michigan.
Faber, Jacob, Abbott Road bel. Smith.
Fallis, Janet, Chippewa cor. Franklin.
Faver, Peter, Huron cor. Ellicott.
Feith, Nicholas, Sycamore n. Spruce.
Fenstermacher, William, 475 E. Seneca.
Fero & Barnard, Canal n. Evans.
Festus, Peter, 247 Seneca.
Fink, John, 199 Batavia.
Finley, James, Carolina cor. 9th.
Fisher, Francis, Elm cor. Tupper.
Fix, George, 555 E. Seneca.
Flach, Julius E. Sycamore cor. Oak.
Flach, Richard, Ellicott cor. Clinton.
Fogerty, James, Clinton n. Montgomery.
Fogerty, John, Perry n. Hayward.
Forsyth, Thomas, Main n. Cold Spring.
Fougeron, Joseph, Niagara cor. Mohawk.
FUCHS BROTHERS, 390 Main.
Gaetz, Michael, Sr. Canal cor. Evans.
Gage, George, 5 E. Seneca.
Garrigan. Matthew, cor. 6th and Pennsylvania.
Gastel, Jas. cor. Goodell and Mulberry.
Geary, W. & Co. 59 Main.
Geier, John, 109 Pine.
Gerhardt, John P. Elk cor. Alabama.
Germany, Philip, Batavia cor. Bennett.
Gerst, Jacob, Niagara n. Amherst.
Gilbert, A. D. 100 Chippewa.
Gill, Patrick, Ohio cor. Michigan.
Goetz, Joseph, Genesee cor. Spruce.
Gross, George, Hickory n. Sycamore.
Gruner, Valentine, Chicago cor. Ohio.
Gygli, Fred, Clinton cor. Walnut.
Haderer, John, Genesee cor. Fox.
Hagelin, Adolph, William n. Pine.
Hahring, John, Batavia cor. Emslie.
Haines, Nathan, 145 S. Division.
Haller, Fred. Eagle cor. Hickory.
Haller, Martin, Walnut, n. Batavia.
Hanson, John, Jackson cor. Wilkeson.
Hanter, George E. 2 Birkhead Buildings.
HARRIES, EDWARD, 180 Main.
Harris, Chas. D. 27 Commercial.
Hartman, Chas. F. Goodell cor. Elm.
Hasack, Conrad, 226 Batavia.
Hauenstein, George. High cor. Michigan.
Heidelbach, George. Clinton n. Cedar.
Heiszler, Jacob, Main n. Ferry.

Hellriegel, Henry, 576 Main.
Hellriegel, Philip, Mrs. Genesee cor. Elm.
Henner, Joseph, 5 Sycamore.
Hennessee, Thomas, Louisiana cor. Exchange.
Henry, Nicholas, Spruce cor. Genesee.
Herbold, Fred. 142 E. Genesee.
Herman, Joseph, Clinton cor. Pine.
Herr, Francis J. Best n. Oak.
Hibsch, Michael, Eagle cor. Union.
Himelsbach, Joseph, 11th cor. Virginia.
Hinderkirch, Alois, 569 Main.
Hoffmier, Louis, Niagara cor. Massachusetts.
Holfelner, Mathias, Batavia cor. Pine.
Hollendreher, John, Batavia n. Jefferson.
Hollerith, Matthias, 405 Main.
HOLLISTER & LAVERACK, 202 Washin'n.
Holman, E. D. 145 Main.
Hotchkiss, Fred. A. Maryland cor. Palmer.
Howley, Edward, 331 E. Seneca.
Huff, Oliver W. 7th cor. Carolina.
Hughes, Wm. 274 Seneca.
Ingalls, David S. 346 Main.
Jaeger, George, 145 Batavia.
James, Nelson, 409 Seneca.
JOHNSTON, A. M. 52 Main.
Judson, Libeus. 113 Seneca.
Kappel, Valentine, Genesee cor. Hickory.
Keena, Peter, Perry cor. Illinois.
Kennedy, James, 343 Seneca.
Kersten, C. Mulberry n. Virginia.
Kiersch, Emanuel, cor. Seneca and Michigan.
Kirch, Jno. Niagara n. Austin.
Kirch, Peter, Niagara n. Hamilton.
Kirsch, Peter, 119 Seneca.
Klein, Jacob, Clinton cor. Spring.
Klotz, William, Niagara n. South.
Knauper, Michael, Goodell cor. Mulberry.
Koenig, Chris. 331 Genesee.
Kohlbrenner, Jacob, Maple cor. Goodell.
Kohlgrubber, Fred. H. 155 Batavia.
Krathwol, John, 448 Washington.
Kress, Valentine, Amherst cor. Lewis.
Krupp, George, 147 Batavia.
Kruse, Henry C. 23 Canal.
Kuempel, Louis, Pratt n. Batavia.
Kull, Fred. cor. Lloyd and Prime.
Lachner, George, 577 Main.
Laing A. & Co. 71 Main.
Laing, Jacob, 51 Main.
Lamey, Margaret, Perry cor. Mississippi.
Lapp, Jacob, Mart Block, Ohio.
Latta, Robert, Niagara n. Mohawk.
Lattau, Michael, 7 Canal.
Lavin, Mary, 407 Seneca.
Lawless, Thomas, Elk opp. Moore.
Leader, John J. cor. Perry and Illinois.
Leech, John W. Alabama opp. Carroll.
Lenk, George, Mulberry cor. Carlton.
Leonard, C. O. Ohio cor. Illinois.
Leonard, Patrick B. Genesee n. Bridge.
Lichtnam, John, 407 Main.
Liebel, John, 94 Goodell.
Liebler, John J. 70 William.
Lincoln, Barney, cor. N. Division and Michig'n.
Loosen, Frederick, Batavia cor. Spruce.
Love, David, Perry cor. Washington.
Love. A. B. 191 Niagara.
Mabis, John, Niagara n. Parish.

20

Mahoney, Dennis, 318 E. Genesee.
Mantz, Jacob, Genesee cor. Spring.
Martin, Dominick, Pennsylvania cor. 5th.
Martin. Jacob, cor. Batavia and Hickory.
MATHEWS & TALLMAN, 334 Main.
McCarty, John, 260 Seneca.
McDonald, James, 99 Exchange.
McDonell, Martin, 55 Main.
Meister, William, Tonawanda n. Niagara.
Messing, William, Jr. 189 E. Genesee.
Meyer, J. W. A. Batavia cor. Walnut.
Miller, Bernhert, 505 Michigan.
Miller & Greiner, 28 and 30 Main.
Miller, Rosina, 467 Michigan.
Millring, William, 104 Tupper.
Milliken, C. A. 68 Lloyd.
Mischo. John, Batavia cor. Pine.
Moessinger, George, 120 Genesee.
Moon, Merrill A. 11 Seneca.
Mooney, Robt. Elk n. Marvin.
Moore. U. D. Morgan n. Mowhawk.
Morrow, Hugh, 129 Chippewa.
Morse, Alanson, 27 Central Wharf.
Mugler, Philip, 380 Seneca.
Mugridge, James. cor. Louisiana and Carroll.
Mugridge, Joseph, 92 Seneca.
Muldon, Gerald, N. Division cor. Cedar.
Munshauer, Geo. Elm cor. Sycamore.
Munzert, Nich. Batavia n. Monroe.
Murphy, T. J. Franklin cor. Tupper.
Nagel, Lorenz, Cherry n. Lemon.
Nash, Jas. cor. Genesee and Terrace.
Neeb, Henry, Michigan n. High.
NEWMAN & SCOVILL, foot Lloyd.
Noeller, Geo. Genesee n. Sherman.
O'Brian, John, 27 Commercial.
O'Brien, Catharine, 56 5th.
O'Grady, Thos. cor. Exchange and Heacock.
O'Harra, John, 37 N. Division.
O'Neil, Wm. 44 Ohio.
O'Shea, Daniel, 6th cor. Virginia.
Ottenot, Nicholas, 425 Main.
Parish, Wm. H. Elk cor. Louisiana.
Persch, Henry C. Terrace cor. Church.
Peterson, Mathias, 6th cor. Virginia.
Pfeffen, John C. 275 Elm.
PORTER, SAMUEL, 360 Main.
Porth, Henry, 543 Michigan.
Power, Patrick, Seneca junc. Swan.
Preston, John R. 194 Seneca.
Reaman, Francis H. Clinton cor. Union.
Reinhardt, Geo. A. Genesee cor. Morgan.
Reinhardt, Phillip, 72 West Tupper.
Reynolds, A. & Co. 155 and 157 Main.
Reynolds, Sarah, Court cor. Staats.
Riehl, Fred. William cor. Lutheran.
Rice, Joseph, 398 Michigan.
Riley. Thos. 238 Seneca.
Ripont, Jas. 81 Batavia.
Rippel, Jacob, 260 East Genesee.
Riedy, John, Perry n. Red Jacket.
Roffo, John, 5 Canal.
Root, John. 204 Seneca.
Roberts, Michael, Martin's Corners
Roth, Christ. Sycamore n. Pratt.
Ruhlman, Lucas, Ohio n. Swing Bridge.
Ruble, A. E. Eagle cor. Elm.
Rudolf, Jacob, Main cor. Chippewa.

Rupp, Geo. M. Clinton cor. Union.
Ryan, Jas. 57 Exchange.
Ryan, John, Elk St. Market.
Sage. Theodore B. 360 Main.
Samson, Jas. Georgia cor. 5th.
Schaefer, Chris. William cor. Walnut.
Schaefer, John, Perry cor. Hayward.
Schaefer, Nicholas, Carroll cor. Heacock.
Schaeffer, Margaret, 375 Genesee.
Schaff, Joseph, 32 Delaware place.
Schall, Andrew, South Division cor. Jefferson.
Schelling, Fred. 8 Huron.
Scheu, Wm. Genesee n. Michigan.
Scheuerman, Jos. L. 259 Genesee.
Scheurmann, Jos. 114 Pine.
Schizzel, Christopher, Mulberry n. Goodell.
Schlatterer, Stephen, Michigan n. Batavia.
Schlink, Leonard, Main cor. Goodell.
Schlotzer, John, Clinton cor. Hickory.
Schmiedel, L. Niagara n. Pennsylvania.
Schmitz, Jacob, Oak n. Burton alley.
Schranck, Michael, Perry cor. Elk.
Schuman, Francis, 112 Hickory.
Schuster, Chris. 387 Main.
Schuster, Fer. Batavia cor. Johnson.
Schwabl, Sebastian, 197 Batavia.
Schweighart, Jacob, Adams n. Sycamore.
SCOTT, GEORGE W. 9 East Seneca.
Seeber, Conrad, 174 Batavia.
Seibel, John F. 188 Niagara.
Seibold, Jacob, 176 Main.
Seward, S. B. cor. Delaware and Tupper.
Shannessy, Pat. 74 Carroll.
Shevelin, Michael, 345 E. Seneca.
Sidway, John J. cor. Main and Huron.
Simon, F. 213 Genesee.
Skidmore, B. W. 21 E. Eagle cor. Ellicott.
Sloan, Alex. 82 Main.
Sloan, Hugh, 39 Exchange.
Sloan, Jas. Washington cor. Perry.
Sloan, Jas. Main n. Ferry.
Sloan, Thos. 57 Exchange.
Sloan, Wm. 19 Exchange.
Slocum. Eliza, Franklin cor. Court.
Smith, Geo. H. Terrace cor. Mechanic.
Smith, Wm. H. Michigan cor. Eagle.
Sommer, Fred. 387 Washington.
Southwick, Henry, Michigan cor. Carroll.
Stahl, Jos. 115 Pine.
Staubel, Christoph, cor. Cherry and Maple.
Stauch, Diebold, 156 6th.
Stern, Philip, William cor. Jefferson.
Stern, Wendel, Genesee cor. Sherman.
Sterne, John. 402 Swan.
Steingotter, Andrew, Michigan cor Pine.
Stellwagen, Nichol, Cherry cor. Lemon.
Sticht, John, Niagara cor. Hamilton.
Stithers, Kate, 5th n. Carolina.
Strasser, Henry, cor. Fly and State.
Strasser, Louis, 241 Elm.
Strike, John, cor. N. Division and Hickory.
Stumpf, John, Genesee bet. Elm and Oak.
Tanner. Harvey, 234 Carroll.
TAYLOR & JEWETT, 4 and 5 Marine Block.
Thompson, Harry, Jr. & Co. Niag. n. Bredige.
Thompson, O. C. Niag. n. Breckenridge.
Timmerman, Jos. 359 Seneca.
Tipman, Jno. 33 Walnut.

Tobias & Reidpath, Seneca cor. Chicago.
Tourat, Fred. 382 Seneca.
Tracy, James, Niagara n. Breckenridge.
Trautmann, Frank, Clinton cor. Jefferson.
Tucker, Robt. 1 Oak.
Tunison. T. C. Elk cor. Chicago.
Twichell, Abram, 406 Main.
Van Ornam, P. C. & Co. Scott n. Michigan.
Van Woert, F. A. 75 Washington.
Versh, Adam, cor. Sycamore and Walnut.
Vollmer, Fred. Elk n. Hayward.
Voltz, Geo. 392 Main.
Wagner, Charles, Genesee cor. Jefferson.
Walsh, John, 151 Main.
Wander, Frederick, Batavia n., Spring.
Weber, George, Michigan cor. William.
Weber, John J. Tupper cor. Oak.
WEBSTER, A. S. 33 E. Seneca.
WEBSTER & CO. 1 E. Seneca.
WEBSTER, ELLIS, 7 E. Seneca.
Webster, Robert, cor. Perry and Michigan.
Weigel, Wolfgang, 150 Genesee.
Weimar, John G. Genesee n. Pratt.
Weir, George, Jr. 107 N. Division.
Weir, James, Georgia n. 6th.
Weiss, Ann M. 125 N. Division.
Welker, John, Ash cor. Sycamore.
Weller, Peter, 238 Elm.
Welte, Franz, Genesee cor. Adams.
Welzel, John W. Exch. cor. Van Rensselaer.
Wensing, H. William n. Cedar.
Weter, Joseph, 55 Genesee.
White, Gilbert, cor. Evans and Canal.
White, Patrick, 299 E. Seneca.
Wilhelm, Louis, Michigan cor. Goodell.
Williams, John, cor. Michigan and Scott.
Wilting, Fred Michigan cor. Cypress.
Winkler, Franz X. Seneca cor. Emslie.
Winter, Frank. Goodell cor. Oak.
Wolf, Jacob, Batavia cor. Pratt.
Wolf, John, Virginia n. 10th.
Wolf, Michael, Hospital cor. Court.
Wolfenden, Edward, Ohio n. Louisiana.
Woller, Joseph, Michigan cor. Tupper.
Woodruff, Samuel, 394 Seneca.
Woodward, D. M. Clinton cor. Union.
Wormwood, Charles, 6th cor. Carolina.
Wright, C. F. 6th cor. Georgia.
Yager, Charles, Goodell cor. Locust.
Yarous, Jacob, Hickory cor. Cherry.
Yaw, A. P. & Son, 44 Main.
Zeiler, George, Goodell cor. Hickory.
Zillig, George, Bennett cor. William.
Zimmerman, George, Pine n. Batavia.

Grocers—Wholesale.

Adams, Hiram & Co. 37 East Seneca.
Anderson, Alexander S. 56 Main.
BEARD & HAYWARD, Wash. cor. Green.
DODGE, A. L. 17 Main.
HARRIES, EDWARD, 108 Main.
HOLLISTER & LAVERACK, 202 Wash.
JOHNSTON, A. M. 52 Main.
Johnson & Steward, Market n. Perry.
Laing. A. & Co. 71 Main.
LAING, JACOB, 51 Main.
MATHEWS & TALLMAN, 334 Main.

Miller & Greiner, 26 and 28 Main.
Milliken, C. A. 68 Lloyd.
NEWMAN & SCOVILL, Lloyd cor. Prime.
Reynolds, A. & Co. 155 Main.
TAYLOR & JEWETT, Marine Block.
Yaw, A. P. & Son, 44 Main.

Gunsmiths.

Robson, James O. 111 Main.
SMITH, PATRICK, 127 Main.

Hair Braiders.

Grauss, J. J. 328 Main.
MAJOT, A. 273 Main.

Hardware and Cutlery.

Corning, E. & Co. 30 and 32 Pearl.
Hadley & Husted, 119 and 217 Pearl.
HAUCK & KIEFER, 393 Main.
Hausle & Son, 146 E. Genesee.
Heimlich, C. 348 Main.
JEWETT, JNO. C. 259 Main.
KELLOGG & BONNELL, 178 Main.
Kress & Warren, 383 Main.
Krueger, John F. W. 23 E. Genesee.
Newbould, Frederick W. 23 Main.
PRATT & CO. 28, 30 and 32 Terrace.
PRATT & LETCHWORTH, 34 Terrace.
SHEPARD. SIDNEY & CO. 54 Main.
Steichele, John C. 140 E. Genesee.
Weed, Dewitt C. 222 Main.
Witt, Louis, Genesee n. Pratt.

Harness, Saddle and Trunk Makers.

See SADDLERS AND HARNESS MAKERS.

Carpenter, John H. 285 Main.
Cook & Lytle, 10 Exchange.
Cooper, N. 29 E. Seneca.
Echardt, John, 148 Seneca.
Kolb, Charles A. 355 Main.
Kolb, George M & Co. 117 Main.
Lane, John, Evans n. Canal.
Woll & Loegler, 362 Main.

Hats, Caps and Furs.

Ambs, Gervas, 17 E. Genesee.
Bassett, Gustavus, 161 Main.
Comstock, M. L. 202 Main.
Datt, August, 73 Genesee.
Eichier, Gottlieb, Genesee n. Sherman.
Emig, John, 385 Main.
Georger, Charles, 388 Main.
Georger, Frank, 382 Main.
Henkel, H. 125 Main.
Hinman, G. W. 144 Main.
Mackenzie, C. 151 Main.
McCool, James, 80 Main.
Ransom, A. R. 332 Main.
Robertson, G. W. 292 Main.
Ryan, John, Terrace cor. Mechanic.
Smith & Brother, 267 Main.
Stillman, H. 169 Main.

Tweedy & Smith, 173 Main.
Waldrab, Andrew & Co. 9 E. Genesee.
Wippert, Wm. 202 Main.

Hay Dealers.

Baker, Moses, Genesee cor. Washington.
Holzworth, C. Market cor. Fulton.

Hides, Tanners' Oil, &c.

See LEATHER.

Horse Bucket Manufactory.

Holley, Allen, Bristol n. Spring.

Horse Collars.

Frazer, D. & Brother, 28 Terrace.

Horse Dealers.

Fowler, Seymour. h. Seneca n. Red Jacket H'l
Friday, George, Kaene n. Genesee.

Hotels.

American Hotel, Main ab. Eagle.
Bloomer. T. T. 1 W. Eagle.
BONNEY'S HOTEL, Washington cor. Carroll.
Boston Hotel. Clinton cor. Ellicott.
BROWN'S HOTEL, Seneca cor. Michigan.
City Hotel. Exchange cor. Michigan.
Cold Spring House, Main, Cold Spring.
Commercial Hotel, Main cor. Ohio.
COURTER HOUSE, Erie cor. Terrace.
Elk Street House, Michigan cor. Elk.
FRANKLIN HOUSE, Seneca cor. Ellicott.
GLOBE HOTEL, 37 Exchange.
London Hotel, Niagara n. Auburn.
Mansion House. Main cor. Exchange.
Metropolitan Hotel, opp. Niagara Falls depot.
National Hotel, Exchange opp. N. Y. C. R. R.
  depot.
New England, Michigan cor. Carroll.
Railroad House, Ferry cor. the Canal.
Red Jacket. Seneca, 2½ m. from Main.
REVERE HOUSE, opp. Niag. F. R. R. depot.
Saunders' Exchange, Seneca cor. Chicago.
St. James Hotel, Main cor Eagle.
SOUTHERN HOTEL, Michigan cor. Seneca.
Thirteenth Ward House, Seneca n. Dole.
Tremont House, cor. Washington and Seneca.
United States Hotel, Terrrace cor. Pearl.
Wadsworth House, Michigan cor. Exchange.
WASHINGTON HOTEL, 15 Commercial.
Waverley House, Erie cor. Canal.
WESTERN HOTEL, Terrace cor. Pearl.

House Furnishing Goods.

Hadley & Husted, 217 Main.
JEWETT, JOHN C. 259 Main.

Ice Dealers.

Queen City Ice Co., Clark & Waterman, Main
  cor. Seneca.
Niagara Ice Company, 190½ Main.

Importers of Wines and Liquors.

Barrows, E. G. & Co. 213 & 215 Washington.
DAMAINVILLE. A. 165 Main.
FUCHS, BROTHERS, 390 Main.
KNIGHT, J. 324 Main.
Sirrit, Emile, 317 Main.
Tiphaine, V. L. 193 Main.
Weisser, Henry, 347 Main.

Ink Manufacturer.

Sheldon. Alexander J. Washington cor. Main
  and Hamburgh Canal.

Inspectors.

See FLOUR INSPECTORS.

JONES, MILES, Prime cor. Dayton.
LANGDON & SEARS, 22 and 24 Hanover.
Long. Lucius, 10 Central Wharf.
Newell, V. C. & Bro. Dayton n. Prime.
Roop, Henry, 4, 6 and 7 Dayton.
Truman, Thomas, 11 Post Office Buildings.

Insurance Agents.

Barker, A. 3 Brown's Buildings.
Brown & Johnson, Yaw's Buildings.
Chambers, Hiram, 179 Main.
Davis & Wilkie, Merchant's Exchange.
DOBBINS, D. P. 4 Thompson Block.
DORR, E. P. cor. Prime & Lloyd.
Fish & Armstrong, 44 Main.
GARDNER, RHITT & FOX, 5 Central
  Wharf and 10 Main.
Hubbard, George L. 5 Spaulding's Exchange.
Loersch, J. P. cor. Sycamore and Oak.
Kolhofer, John, 32 E. Tupper.
Krettner, Jacob, 281 Main.
Niles & Brewster, 5 Central Wharf and 10 Main.
Palmer, Monteath & Co. 21 Central Wharf.
Perkins, Thomas G. Merchant's Exchange.
Peterson. P. B. 44 Main.
Rounds & Hall, 7 Central Wharf and 2 Brown's
  Buildings.
Smith. William C. 4 Brown's Buildings.
WALKER, H. C. Hanover cor. Prime.
WILSON, LEONARD, 3 North Division.

Intelligence Office.

Williams, S. F. 200 Washington.

Iron Merchants.

Bull, Cadwallader, Ohio cor. Chicago.
Corning, Erastus & Co. Pearl cor. Seneca.
PRATT & CO. 28, 30 and 32 Terrace.
Weed, DeWitt C. Main cor. Seneca.
WILSON, G. R. & CO. junc. Elk and Ohio.

Iron Railing Works.

EDDY & BINGHAM, Church cor. Jackson.
JONES, GEORGE, Terrace cor. Henry.

Iron Smelting Works.

Palmer & Wadsworth, Buffalo creek n. Lake
  Shore Railroad track.

Thompson & Co. Buffalo creek n. Lake Shore Railroad track.

Iron Works.

BELL'S FOUNDRY, Norton.
Buffalo Iron Works, Niagara n. Scajaquada Creek.
BULL, G. B. & CO. Swan cor. Jefferson.
Dunbar & Howell, Eagle Iron Works, Mississippi cor. Perry.
EDDY & BINGHAM, Jackson cor. Church.
HUBBARD, C. J. Globe Foundry, Carroll n. Chicago.
JONES, GEORGE, Terrace cor. Henry.
RUGER, J. S. & CO. Chicago n. Ohio.
SCOVILLE, S. & N. C. Louisiana opp. Lake Shore Freight Depot.
SHEPARD IRON WORKS, Ohio cor. Miami.
TIFFT, GEORGE W. SONS & CO. Washington cor. Ohio.

Ivory Turners.

Solomon, M. 257 Washington.

Japanned Ware.

Dudley Brothers, 57 Main.
JEWETT, JOHN C. 259 Main.
Laudenbacher, Fred. cor. Pearl and Seneca.
PRATT & CO. 28, 30 and 32 Terrace.
SHEPARD, SIDNEY & CO. 54 Main.

Jewelers.

Appleton, Jas. Jr. 196 Main.
Castle. Dan. 135 Main.
DICKINSON, THOMAS, 370 Main.
Goodrich, Erastus H. Bonney's Hotel.
Hotchkiss, Hiram, 210 Main.
Hotchkiss, J. W. 189 Main.
Hovey, D. A. 266 Main.
JUENGLING, HENRY F. 3 Niagara.
Keyes, Lewis, 8. E. Seneca.
KING, B. H. over 202 Main.
Oelrich, Frederick, 295 Main.
Robson, J. O. 111 Main.
SHURLY, C. J. 151 Main.
Sibley, O. E. 186 Main.
Stephenson & Co. 200 Main.
Walder, J. H. 1 Genesee.
Walker, Julius, 185 Main.
Walter, Henry, 411 Main.
Worst, Chas. 52 Genesee.

Jewelry and Silver Ware.

See JEWELERS.

Jewelers (Working.)

KING, B. H. over 202 Main.

Keg Manufacturers.

See COOPERS.

McClure & McCreary, Eaton's Planing Mill.

Ladies' Hair Dressers.

MAJOT, ACHILLES, over 73 Main.

Lamp and Lantern Manufacturers.

Cleveland, L. cor. Washington and Perry.
Sangster, Hugh, 41 Ohio.
STACY, F. 22 Commercial.

Land Agents.

See REAL ESTATE AGENTS.

Beardsley, Josiah, 190½ Main.
Garrett, C. 190½ Main.
Goodrich, Guy H. 3 Weed's Buildings.
Griffin, Harmon, over 427 Main.
Hastings, C. J. Main cor. Seneca.
Janes, Nelson, 2 Hollister Block.
Kelly, Daniel, Breckenridge n. N. Wash.
Lyon & Co. Brown's Buildings.
Maynard, R. H. 67 Seneca.
Meech, Asa B. Main cor. Swan.
Paul & Mooney, 11 Arcade Buildings.
Pickering & Otto, 37 Pearl.
Sidway, Jonathan, Commercial cor. Terrace.
Sweet, George H. h. 15 Elm.
Watson, S. V. R. cor. Swan and Ellicott.
Williban, Edwin, 44 Pearl.
Zink, Henry, 95 Ellicott.

Lampblack Manufacturers.

WARREN BROTHERS, Main cor. Swan.

Lard Oil and Candles.

PEASE, F. S. 61 Main.
WARDWELL, WEBSTER & CO. 157 Wash.

Last Makers.

WING, H. & CO. 6 and 8 Exchange.

Lawyers.

See ATTORNEYS.

Leather Dealers.

Behm, Gottfried, 224 Genesee.
Bowen & Humason, 109 Main.
Bull, J. B. & Co. 21 and 23 Lloyd.
Bush. John & Co. 29 E. Seneca.
BUSH & HOWARD, 91 Main.
CASE, NEHEMIAH, Washington cor. Exch.
Chretien, John, 3 E. Genesee.
Curtis & Demings, 72 Main.
Dascomb, John, hide dealer, 207 N. Division.
Eckhardt, Geo. 246 Genesee.
Hunter, John B. 2 Birkhead Buildings.
HUTCHINSON, J. M. 40 and 42 Lloyd.
Laub & Brothers, 11 E. Genesee.
Niederlander, Chretien & Co. 253 Main.
Platt, A. B. 4 Birkhead Buildings.
RUMSEY. A. & CO. 2 and 4 Exchange.
Schoellkopf, J. F. & Co. 103 and 105 Main.
Seyd, Emil & Co. 124 Main.

Welch & Millar, 159 Washington.
WING, H. & CO. 6 and 8 Exchange.

Lightning Rods.

BANGASSER & BROTHERS, 15 Seneca.

Lithographers.

Mooney, L. 200 Main.
SAGE & SONS, 209 Main.

Liquor Stores.

See GROCERS AND IMPORTERS OF LIQUORS.

Abel, Chas. L. Ohio, Com'l Hotel Block.
Ayres, W. J. 6 and 8 Hanover.
Barr, Robert, 212 Washington.
Barrows, E. G. & Co. 213 and 215 Washington.
Becker, John C. 372 Michigan.
Best, Charles A. 180 Washington.
Blakely, J. & W. 31 Main.
BOAS, S. 234 Main.
Bosse, Charles, Seneca junction Swan.
DAMAINVILLE, A. 163 Main.
DIEHL & PARKER, 263 Main.
Fero, John R. Terrace n. Evans.
FITCH, F. S. Seneca cor. Michigan.
FUCHS, BROS. 390 Main.
GILLETT, HENRY T. 18, 20 and 22 Lloyd.
Grimard, Gustavus, 356 Main.
Kamper, Charles, 112 Exchange.
Kerr & Laing, 83 Main.
KNIGHT, J. 324 Main.
Laing, A. & Co. 71 Main.
Laing, Jacob, 51 Main.
Loveridge, Edward D. 176 Washington.
Metscher, George, Ellicott ab. Chippewa.
Murray & Brothers, 7 Terrace.
Powell, W. O. 45 Seneca.
Prothias & Heron, 12 Main and 6 Cent. Wharf.
Seitz, C. W. Niagara n. Amherst.
Sirrit, Emile, 317 Main.
STEVENS, PEABODY S. Main cor. Eagle.
Tiphaine, V. L. 193 Main.
Weisser, Henry, 347 Main.
Wynhammer, James G. 1 Clinton.

Livery Stables.

Burton, Lauren, 30 Pearl.
Callahan, Richard, 264 Washington.
CHEESEMAN & DODGE, 116 Pearl.
DICKEY & BOWEN, Southern Hotel.
Efner, George B. 8 Ellicott.
Harris, D. P. Miller & Co. Terrace cor. Lock.
Harris, Joseph, Ferry n. Washington.
Lord, Casper R. 123 Ellicott.
Mace, James C. boarding, 217 Washington.
Metzger, George, 326 Washington.
MOUNT, FORMAN, Terrace bel. U. S. Hotel.
Stevenson, George P. & Co. 303 Main.
Stevenson, John S. Genesee n. Main.
Tucker, J. K. Michigan n. Exchange.

Locksmiths.

BANGASSER & BROS. 15 E. Seneca.

FLACH, D. & BRO. 17 Mohawk.
Taylor, D. 2 Swan.
VALENTINE & O'REILLY, 14 Court.

Looking Glasses and Frames.

Coleman, J. H. 6 E. Swan.
DEUTHER, GEORGE, 12 Exchange.
Hog, Joseph, Batavia n. arsenal.
Reinhard, John R. 403 Main.
Teller, George D. 170 Main.

Lumber Dealers.

Booth, John, Ohio n. Ohio Basin.
Brown, Sylvester, 71 E. Seneca.
Bugbee, Oliver, Dock cor. Long Wharf.
Campbell, M. A. Ohio n. toll bridge.
Churchyard, Joseph, Clinton cor. Adams.
Colie, S. D. Mich. bet. Seneca and Exchange.
Craig, F. S. Michigan n. Elk.
DART & BROTHERS, planing mill, Ohio Basin cor. Mackinaw.
Drecher & Co. Batavia cor. Elm.
Duthie, James, Niagara cor. Georgia.
EATON PLANING MILL. Court cor. Hosp'l.
EVANS, JOHN R. & CO. Mechanic n. Ter.
Fischer, J. & G. 74 E. Genesee.
Frink, H. A. & Co. 22 Central Wharf.
Hawkins, Wm. River n. Erie Basin.
Hill, H. F. Revere Block.
Hodge & Baldwin, Niagara cor. Carolina.
HOLMES, E. & B. n. N. Y. C. R. R. depot.
Hotchkiss, Wheeler, 4th cor. Hospital and 7th cor. Carolina.
Hotchkiss, T. W. River n. Erie Basin.
Hoyt, Bradley, Bird ave. n. N. Washington.
Hoyt, Gabriel, cor. Genesee and River.
Leaton, John, 6th n. Fort Porter.
Mixer & Smith, Mart Block. Ohio.
Monneir, George F. 110 Elm.
NEWTON, ISAAC S. Church bel. Terrace.
Noyes, J. S. 5 River.
PARK, PAUL, Genesee cor. 4th.
PIERCE & CO. Michigan cor. Scott.
Scatcherd, James N. Elk cor. Louisiana.
Schults, Peter, Genesee cor. Pratt.
SEARS & CLARK, River, Erie Basin.
Sherman, P. C. h. 28 Oak.
Smith, G. W. & Co. Clinton cor. Elm.
Taintor, Charles, River.
Thistlethwaite, J. foot Genesee.
Van Vleck, J. 5 River.
ZITTLE, FREDERICK, 335 Washington.

Machinists and Machinery Dealers.

Bailey, Geo. 9 and 10 Water.
Barton, P. F. at Vulcan Foundry.
BELL, DAVID, Norton n. Water.
BROWN & McCUTCHEON, Elk junc. Ohio.
COLLIGON, F. Perry cor. Washington.
Frank & Co. n. Eaton's Planing Mill.
GOOD, ADAM, 15 Ohio.
MONNIN, CHARLES, 9 Water.
Reegar, J. S. & Co. Chicago n. Ohio.
SHEPARD IRON WORKS, Ohio.
Weeks, John, 81 Main.

Maltsters.

Blackmar & Gilbert, Main cor. Ferry.
Malcom, George. Main cor. Ferry.
Meidenbauer, John, Michigan n. High.
Roberts, J. D. Allen cor. Franklin.
TOOLEY, LEVI A. n. foot Erie.
Weigand, John, Michigan n. Carlton.

Mantilla Makers.

Hill, Mary, Jefferson n. Howard.
Pierce, J. B. Mrs. 19 N. Division.

Marble Dealers and Workers.

CRAWFORD. JOHN. 84 and 86 Niagara.
GAYLORD, H. M. Erie cor. Terrace.
Gregory, V. R. & Co. Washington n. S. Div.
Hayford, Riley, with G. O. Vail & Co.
Kunz & Gross, Main n. Chippewa.
VAIL. GEO. O. & Co. Ohio cor. Chicago.
Wheeler, G. S. Delaware n. Allen.

Marine Inspectors.

Anderson, Andrew. Captain, 9th n. Pennsyv'a.
Berryman, John, 205 E. Swan.

Match Makers.

Heimlich, Christian, 234 E. Genesee.
Jung, Michael, 228 Oak.

Meat Markets.

See BUTCHERS.

Melodeon Dealers.

Blodgett & Bradford, 209 Main.
Sheppard & Cottier, 215 Main.

Melodeon Manufactory.

PRINCE, GEO. A. & Co. Maryland cor. 7th.—
See adv. opp. p. 236.

Merchant Tailors.

See TAILORS AND DRAPERS.

Mercantile Colleges.

Bryant & Stratton, Brown's Buildings.
HICKS, D. CLINTON over 194 Main.

Midwives.

See NURSES.

Milkmen.

Anot, Peter, Walden n. Ferry.
Bailey, Jas. B. Batavia cor. Williamsville Road.
Balcom, A. W. Batavia n. toll-gate.
Benzinger, John, Jefferson n. Clinton.
Betzmeyer, Andrew, Walden N. of Best.
Bibus, Michael, 204 Elm.

Bosche, John, Best n. Main.
Christ, Henry. Hickory n. Batavia.
Chur, Chris. Gen. n. Williamsville Road.
Curtis, W. B. Batavia n. Williamsville Road.
Doll, Fred. Genesee n. Williamsville Road.
Diemker, David, Grey n. Genesee.
Dieping Geo. N. Division n. Hickory.
Finkler, John, 321 Elm n. Virginia.
Franklin, Jas. Walden n. Batavia.
Gass, Peter, Ferry E. of Walden.
Geyer, Geo. Genesee n. Williamsville Road.
Green, Starr, 91 S. Division.
Hale, Wm. C. 203 S. Division.
Hall, Jacob, Maryland above Cottage.
Hall, Jas. W. Main n. Ferry.
Hay, M. W. 28 Carroll.
Harkness, Stephen. Exchange n. Heacock.
Heitzman, Conrad, Genesee n. Jefferson.
Hoffheins, Geo. F. Genesee n. toll-gate.
Hoffman. Michael, William cor. Roos Alley.
Hook, Henry, r. 338 Genesee.
Jones, Michael. William n. Spring.
Keaner, John, Cherry n. Jefferson.
Kraemer, Andrew, German Alley n. Genesee.
Mertz, Jacob, Williamsville Road n. Perry.
Mullett, John, Niagara n. Clinton.
Murphy, John, 251 Seneca.
Prior, Geo. 229 N. Division.
Tifft, Wm. S. 126 S. Division.
Tripp, John P. Batavia cor. Williamsville Road.
Toy, Chas. Batavia n. Williamsville Road.
Urban, Jacob, Walden n. Ferry.
Wackerman, Michael, Best n. Main.

Milliners.

ANGELS, SALLY, 284 Main.
Bates, C. Mrs. 275 Main.
Batt, Anton, 125 Genesee.
Brennen, Martin, 302½ Main.
Clarke, E. A. Mrs. 283 Main.
Crossland, J. F. Mrs. 32 E. Seneca.
Dodd, Martha J. 8 S. Division.
King, Samuel, 5 S. Division.
Schorr, Ernst, 48 E. Genesee.
Walter, Catharine, 148 Batavia.
Wright, James, 265 Main.
Young, Eliza, 328 Main.

Millinery Goods.

ANGELS, SALLY, 284 Main.
Beckman, Peter, 386 Main.
Lee. E. H. Miss, 279 Main.
Rielly's Bazaar, 288 Main.
Rosenau, S. & Co. 280 Main.
Wright, James, 265 Main.
WOODWARD, W. H. 287 and 289 Main.

Mill Furnishings.

ALLEN, Z. G. Miami n. Shepard Iron Works.
Henry, S. H. Vulcan Foundry, Water.
NOYE, JOHN T. Washington cor. Scott.

Millstones.

ALLEN, Z. G. agent, Miami n. Shepard Iron Works.

Henry, S. H. Vulcan Foundry, Water.
NOYE, JOHN T. Washington cor. Scott.

Millwrights.

ALLEN, Z. G. agent, Miami n. Shepard Iron Works.
Cogswell, M. C. at Eagle Iron Works.
Exelby, R. Miami.
Henry. S. H. Vulcan Foundry, Water.
NOYE, JOHN T. Washington cor. Scott.

Mittens and Gloves.

Leonard, Norman, 27 E. Seneca.

Mowing Machines.

Buffalo Agricultural Machine Works, Scott cor. Washington.
Howard, R. L. Chicago n. Hamburgh canal.
Miller, Bennett & Co. Water cor. Le Couteulx.

Musicians.

Berger, Moritz, Spruce n. Genesee.
Braudt, Wm. Spruce n. Genesee.
Beler, Frank, 30 Goodell.
Berch, John, Bundy's alley n. Sycamore.
Boerner, Fred. cor. Washington and Genesee.
Boller, Christian, 70 Tupper.
Bomberg, Jno. A. Spring n. Genesee.
Cournea, James, 197 Washington.
Cramer, Peter, Jr. 94 Batavia.
Delano, James, 19 Johnson Place.
Delvecchio, Chs. H. 17 E. Eagle.
Duga, Charles, 10 Maple.
Haycraft, J. 44 Pearl.
Poppenberg, Albert, Delaware ab. Ferry.
Poppenberg, Gustavus, 22 Cypress.
Schmidt, Christian, 412 Michigan.
Vining, Geo. W. 46 Mohawk.

Musical Instruments.

Blodgett & Bradford, 209 Main.
Sheppard & Cottier, 215 Main.

Music Stores.

Blodgett & Bradford, 209 Main.
Sheppard & Cottier, 215 Main.

Music Teachers.

Adam, Karl, D. G. Pearl ab. Virginia.
Bagnell, Elizabeth, Miss, College n. Virginia.
Baker, Everett L. 427 Main.
Bamberg. John A. Hickory n. Sycamore.
Banken, Wm. W. Cedar cor. Clinton.
Bushart, Wm. 161 Batavia.
Crowther, Rodney, Mrs. 46 6th.
Denton, Robert, Jr. 5 9th.
Dossert, John, St. Paul cor. Ellicott.
Grimmer, Charles, 411 Main.
Krausskoph, William, 36 Goodell.
Poppenberg. Albert. Delaware n. Ferry.
Raze, A. S. 126 Swan.
Spiesz, John, Huron cor. Main.
Sterling, Clara A. 29 Swan.

Sterling, Clara, Miss, 29 Swan.
Sykes, Charles W. 94 Niagara.
Vining, George W. 46 Mohawk.
Webster, W. C. 223 Franklin.

Nailers.

Niesence, Michael, Gen. cor. Spruce.

Newspapers.

See Page 25.

News and Periodical Depots.

Beadle, Irwin P. Mrs. 227 Main.
Bergtold, Chas. A. 147 Main.
Black, Robert, 17 E. Seneca.
Conry, T. J. 17½ Seneca.
Corbin, Peter, N. Y. & E. depot.
Dyer. Margaret, Wadsworth House Block.
Felton, B. F. 205 Washington.
Hawks, T. S. 10 E. Seneca.
HILL, J. F. & Co. 201 Main.
McFarlane, Mary, Wadsworth House.
McWhorter, John, N. Y. C. R. R.
Samo, Henry W. 432 Main.
Smith, G. 301 Main.

Notaries Public.

See Page 16.

Nurserymen.

Buffalo Nursery, D. S. Manley, Utica bet. Delaware and Roger.
Hollander Nursery, White's Corners plank road n. Martin's Corners.
Nieuwer, Wm. Hopkins road n. Abbott plank road.
Pomeroy, S. T. Ferry n. Delaware.

Nurses and Midwives.

Amstuts, Catherine, midwife, h. Hickory n. Syc.
Ashley, Dorothy, nurse, 75 Delaware.
Austin, Anna, Mrs. nurse, Hamburgh n. Sen.
Baldwin, Eliza, 436 Michigan.
Berry, Elizabeth, 271 S. Division.
Bersch, Johanna, 82 Sycamore.
Bettis, Sallie, 48 Morgan.
Butler, Hope, (colored,) city nurse, 92 Lloyd, up stairs.
Cook, Mrs. B. 4 Vine.
Crandall, Lodema, Mrs. Huron cor. Ellicott.
Dory, B. Mrs. Vermont n. 11th.
Dunker, Maria, Locust n. High.
Fairchild, Maria, 75 Delaware.
Fenerstein, P. Mrs. h. 150 Clinton.
Gibson, Ellen, 68 William.
Graham. Eliza, Buff. Orphan Asylum.
Jann, Barbara, Sherman n. Genesee.
Jones, Isabella, Staats cor. Niagara.
Jones, S. Mrs. Wm. n. Spring.
Kester, Ann, 435 Main.
Lang, Susanna. 500 Michigan.
Lindenberg, Marie E. 201 Genesee.
Mehen, Mary, Connecticut n. 12th.
Miller, Mary P. 213 N. Division.

Nagel, Caroline, 77 Hickory.
Ohnesorge, Anna, 12 Potter.
Schabio, Charlotte, Peckham n. Monroe.
Schmitt, Margaret, Kaene n. Genesee.
Seifert, Elizabeth, Sycamore n. Spring.
Sloss, Maria, 222 Clinton.
Smith, Eliza, 322 Michigan.
Stohr, Maria, Hamilton n. Thompson.

Oil Dealers and Manufacturers.

Atwater & Hawes, cor. Maryland and 3d.
PEASE, F. S. 61 Main.
Wardwell, Webster & Co. 157 Washington.
Wellsteed, John, (capsega) R. I. cor. Utica.
WARREN & BROTHER, Main cor. Swan.

Opticians.

ANDREWS & SON, 221 Main.

Organ Builder.

HOUSE, GERRITT, Clinton opp. new Court House.

Organ Melodeons.

PRINCE, GEORGE A. & CO. 7th cor. Maryland.—See adv. opp. p. 236.

Organists.

Baker, Everett, L. 427 Main.
Baum, Charles F. cor. Cherry and Michigan.
Blodgett, J. R. 209 Main.
Denton, Robert, Jr. 5 9th.
Dossert, John, 79 Ellicott.
Krauskopf, Wm. 36 Goodell.
Poppenberg, Albert, Delaware above Ferry.
Sykes, Charles W. 94 Niagara.

Oyster and Fruit Dealers.

Blakely, J. & W. 31 Main.
Granniss & Co. 315 Main
PLATT, L. B. & CO. 286 Main.
Rowe & Co. 212 Washington.
Smith, John J. 197 Main.

Pail and Tub Factories.

Wood, Francis, agent Niagara Co. 82 Huron.

Painters, Sign and House.

Bean, J. & W. M. 174 Main.
Buchanan, Henry, 15 E. Mohawk.
Burns, George L. 204 Washington.
Churchill, W. Sumner, 157 Main.
Dalton & Kingston, 247 Main.
Gerlach, Jacob, 233 Genesee.
Ingalls & Lamphier, 107 Main.
Kieffer, Klein, Genesee n. Sycamore.
Klein, Charles, 43 Spruce.
Melancon & Courtney, Terrace cor. Pearl.
Monforte, Joseph C. 157 Main.
Rowley, J. F. 3 S. Division.
Scott, F. B. over 231 Main.
Shadrake, Edward. 11 Swan.
WHITE, H. G. 273 Main.

Paintings, Dealers in.

Coleman's Gallery, over 4 E. Swan.
Teller, George D. 170 Main.

Paints and Oils.

See DRUGGISTS.

Coleman, John H. 4 E. Swan.
Reynolds & Co. 157 Main.
Bickel, John G. Ellicott cor. Genesee.
Rowley, J. F. 3 S. Division.

Paper Hangers.

BIRGE & CO. 174 Main.
Elder & Stearns, 270 Main.
Hamlin & Mendsen, 212 Main.
WHITE, H. G. 273 Main.
WILGUS, N. 231 Main.

Paper Hangings.

BIRGE, & CO. 174 Main.
Elder & Stearns, 270 Main.
WHITE, H. G. 273 Main.
WILGUS, NATHANIEL, 231 Main.

Paper Wharehouses.

Brush & Stockton, 190 Washington.
Ingersoll, M. 196 Washington.
JEWETT, E. R. & CO. 161 Main.
Nelson, E. 177 Washington.
WOODRUFF, L. C. 24 and 26 Pearl.
Young, Lockwood & Co. 165 Main.

Parasol Dealers.

See UMBRELLAS.

Pattern Makers.

Gage, William, 3 Scott.
Stannard, Walter W. for Jewett & Root.
Young, Gertrude, ov. 344 Main.

Pattern Emporiums.

Bliss, Madam, 295 Main.
Henking, E. Mrs. 370 Main.

Pavers.

Frederick, John, Mortimer cor. Hollister.

Hornung, Charles, Genesee cor. Elm.
HOLLOWAY, ISAAC, Michigan n. C. R. R. Depot.
HOWELLS, JAMES. Genesee cor. Church.
WHITMORE, RATHBUN & CO. opp. Niagara Falls Depot.

Philosophical Instruments.

ANDREWS & SON, 221 Main.

Physicians.

Adam, Augustus, 29 Pearl.
Amos & Sons, 48 E. Genesee.

Barnes, Josiah, 6 Exchange.
Bartlett, F. W. 70 Pearl.
Bates, L. W. at Buffalo Gen. Hospital.
Beers, Alfred H. 6 S. Division.
Berry, Elizabeth W. 271 S. Division.
Bissell, E. L. cor. Main and Mohawk.
Blanchard, Henry C. Main cor. Eagle.
Boardman, John, 4 W. Eagle.
Bristol, Moses, h. Delaware cor. Ferry.
Brown, J. N. 79 Franklin.
Brownell, E. C. Elk n. Hayward.
Burwell, Bryant, 120 Franklin.
Burwell, George N. 66 Pearl.
Cary, Walter, 68 Delaware.
Clark, Joseph W. 283 Main.
Comstock, Albert L. Albany cor. Jefferson.
Congar, H. M. 137 Pearl.
Cronyn, John, 76 Pearl.
Damainville, L. ov. 163 Main.
Dayton, C. L. Niagara cor. Amherst.
Dayton, L. P. Niagara cor. Amherst.
Dellenbaugh, Charles C. 358 Main.
Dellenbaugh, Frederick, 87 Batavia.
Dellenbaugh, S. & Son, 358 Main.
Devening, Daniel, 361 Michigan.
Dodge, Lewis, homœop. 56 Pearl.
Eastman, Sandford, 24 W. Genesee.
Edmunds, James J. Michigan foot Fulton.
Felgenmacher, J. A. 140 Batavia.
Firmenich, Joseph, 302 Main.
Flagg, Samuel D. Jr. 294 Main.
Fullam, John W. Niagara cor. Breckenridge.
Furlonge, Joseph, Dudley Hall.
Garvin, H. D. 1 Hart Block, Erie.
Gay, Charles C. F. Main cor. Mohawk.
Gese, Louis, 421 Michigan.
Goldberger, J. S. 79 Oak.
Goldberger, I. S. 239 Ellicott.
Gould, William, 125 Pearl.
Gray, E. P. 6 W. Swan.
Gregg, R. R. 237 Washington.
Griswold, A. S. oculist, 23 Church.
Grumholzer, I. J. 136 Genesee.
Hadley, George, Main n. Utica.
Hadley, James, Main n. Utica.
Harvey, Chas. W. S. Division cor. Washington.
Harvey, Leon F. 5 S. Division.
Hauenstein, John, 357 Washington.
Hayer, F. F. Erie Co. Poor House.
Hill, J. D. 2 W. Eagle.
Hill, M. W. botanic physician, 245 Main.
Hinkley, A. S. homœop. 51 Ellicott.
Hoyt, Onson C. 498 Washington.
Hughes, J. H. Michigan cor. Carroll.
Hunt, S. B., N. Pearl ab. Virginia.
Hutchins, C. B. 238 Main.
Hutchinson, Elisha, 43 7th.
Kenyon & Wright, 262 Washington.
King, J. E. ov. 8 E. Seneca.
Kughler, G. D. 126 Pearl.
Leake, W. J. 18 Mart Block.
Learned, Samuel, S. 22 Division.
Lewis, Geo. W. homœop. 131 Pearl.
Lockwood, N. S. ov. 266 Main.
Lockwood, Thomas, Adams Block, Wash.
Lockwood, T. 21 Niagara.
Loeper, J. C. Goodell n. Michigan.
Loerch, Philip, 198 Genesee.

Loomis, H. N. 79 Franklin.
Lothrop, Joshua R. Washington cor. Seneca.
Lothrop, Thomas, Niagara n. Clinton.
Mackay, Edward, 123 Pearl.
Mayer, Martin, 85 Franklin.
McCray, G. W. Commercial cor. Water.
Mead, Chas. 159 Elk.
Miller, A. C. 42 William.
Miner, Julius F. 15 Ellicott.
Mixer, S. F. 74 E. Swan.
Nichell, Henry, 58 Sycamore.
Pratt, G. F. 8 W. Swan.
Rankin, Francis, St. Paul n. Main.
Retel, Caspar, 96 Pine.
Retel, John, Genesee n. Jefferson.
Richards, J. I. 148 Main.
Ring, William, 4 Boston Block.
Robinson, Wm. 2 Exchange, up stairs.
Rochester, Thos. F. 9 Court.
Samo, James B. 7 S. Division.
Scott, William K. 39 W. Mohawk.
Sonnick, Peter, Ash cor. Genesee.
Sprague, A. S. 57 N. Division.
Steckhaus, Andrew, Batavia n. Adams.
Stevens, J. F. 593 Seneca.
Stevenson, J. D. G. 237 7th.
Storck, E. 161 Ellicott.
Stowell, Mary H. 26 Niagara.
Sweet, George J. 15 Elm.
Thompson, William, Delaware n. Ferry.
Tilden, J. H. eclectic, 28 S. Division.
Tobie, Edward, Main n. Amherst.
Treat, William, 7 S. Division.
Trowbridge, Josiah, 14 W. Swan.
Volker, Wm. 240 Genesee.
Weiss, C. h. 19 Batavia.
Wenz, James, 373 Michigan.
Weyland, Francis J. h. 73 Batavia.
White, James P. 460 Main.
White, R. J. 386 Franklin.
Whitney, B. T. 12 S. Division.
Whittaker, Jacob, 5 Kremlin Hall.
Wiggins, Dennis B. botanic, Niagara n. Eagle.
Wilcox, Chas. H. 22 W. Genesee.
Williams, Avery, 57 E. Eagle.
Williams, D. R. East n. Parish.
Winkler, Louis, Batavia n. Pratt.
Winne, Charles, 287 Washington.
Winne, Chas. K. Washington cor. Eagle.
Wyckoff, C. C. 80 Pearl.

Piano Forte Dealers.

Blodgett & Bradford, 209 Main.
Devine, Francis F. cor. Niagara and Maryland.
KEOGH, A. & J. 257, 259 and 261 Washing'n.
Sheppard & Cottier, 215 Main.
Utley, Horace, 38 Pearl.

Piano Forte Hardware.

Utley, Horace, 38 Pearl.

Piano Forte Makers.

KEOGH, A. & J. 257, 259 and 261 Washing'n.
Kurtzeman, Heinze, Staats cor. Mohawk.

Piano Forte Tuners.

Denton, R. 5 9th.
Devine, Francis F. Niagara cor. Maryland.
Parks, James S. 209 Main.
Woodbury, Hiram, G. Prince & Co.

Picture Frame Dealers.

Brodie, Archibald, Niagara n. Eagle.
Coleman, Wm. ov. 4 Swan.
DEUTHER, GEORGE A. 12 Exchange.
Hog, Joseph, Batavia n. arsenal.
Reinhard, John R. 403 Main.
Teller, George D. 170 Main.

Plane Makers.

Axe, George. 233 E. Seneca.
Bingham, Robert, cor. Howard and Adams.
WHITE, L. & L. J. 32 Ohio.

Planing Mills.

DART PLANING MILL, Ohio Basin cor.
  Mackinaw.
EATON'S PLANING MILL, Court cor.
  Hospital.
EVANS, JOHN R. & Co. Mechanic n. Terrace.
HOLMES, E. & B. Michigan n. Central R. R.
PIERCE & CO. Michigan cor. Scott.
SWARTZ & REBMANN, Elm ab. Batavia.
Sweet, Albert, 7 6th.

Planing Mill Makers.

HOLMES, E. & B. Michigan n. C. R R. Depot.

Plow Manufacturers.

Baker, Moses, cor. Genesee and Washington.
Smith, Frederick, 19 William.
Smith, Joseph H. 138 E. Seneca.

Plumbers.

See GAS FITTERS.

Carr, Wm. 354 Main.
HARDIKER & TOY, 325 Main.
HART, BALL & HART, 237 Main.
HILL, F. C. 269 Main.
Irr & Irlbacher, 1, 2 and 3 Mohawk.
Smith, J. D. & Co. 162 Main.
ZOOK, LEVI L. 5 Birkhead Buildings, Com'l

Pocket-Book Maker.

FELTON, JOHN, 159 Main.

Pomologist.

Hodge, Benjamin, Main cor. Utica.

Pork Dealers and Inspectors.

JONES, MILES, Prime cor. Dayton.
LANGDON & SEARS, 22 and 24 Hanover.
Newell, V. C. & Brother, 3 Dayton.
Roop, Henry, 4, 6 and 7 Dayton.

Porter and Cider Vaults.

LONDON DOCK VAULTS, 330 Main.
HOWELL & SMITH, 36 Seneca.
Wynhamer, J. G. 1 Clinton.

Portrait Painters.

NIMBS, A. B. 303 Main.
Rockwell, Augustus, 266 Main.

Potters.

Braun, Charles W. 327 Seneca.

Printers—Newspapers, Book, and Job.

Bailey, Geo. machinery and printing, 9 & 10
  Water.
BENDER, PHILIP H. 358 Main.
BRUNCK, HELD & CO. 194 Washington.
BRYAN, GEORGE J. 182 and 184 Wash.
Clapp, A. M. & Co. 158 Main.
Clapp, Matthews & Waite, 158 Main.
Faxon, James, 157 Main.
HAGAN, MICHAEL, 111 Main.
Penfield, T. V. N. 15 W. Seneca.
Reese, Geo. W. 5 W. Seneca.
Rockwell & Baker, 196 Washington.
WHEELER, R. & CO. 161 Main.
WARREN, JOSEPH & CO. 178 Washington.
Wieckman, Christian, 67 Batavia.
Young, Lockwood & Co. 159 Main.

Printers' Joiners.

GERARD, A. H. Mechanic n. Terrace.
ROBERTS, E. & Co. 49 E. Seneca.

Printing Ink, Etc.

Fellows, Jeremiah C. 227 Main.

Produce Merchants.

See COMMISSION MERCHANTS.

See GRAIN MERCHANTS.

Barker, Dudson B. Elk street Market.
Betz, Ferdinand. Clinton Market.
Boyd, R. D. 13 Central Wharf.
COBB & CO. 20 & 21 Central Wharf.
Connelly, James, Elk street Market.
Fish & Avery, 18 Central Wharf.
FLEEHARTY, J. 27 Central Wharf.
Gelring, Geo. J. 32 Elk st. Market.
Gemmel, Mathias, Clinton Market.
Gould, Phares, 18 Central Wharf.
Griffin, A. L. 23 Central Wharf.
Griffin & McDonald, 17 Central Wharf.
Guthrie, S. S. 11 Central Wharf.
Hanegan, Mary, 35 & 37 Elk street Market.
Hawley, M. S. & Co. 18 and 19 Central Wharf.
Hayward & Selmser, 16 Central Wharf.
Hazard, George S. 25 Central Wharf.
HEAD, J. A. 60 Main.
Heimlich, P. J. Jr. 12 Central Wharf.
HORTON, A. W. 10 Central Wharf.
Howe, Otis B. 13 Prime.
Johnson, J. B. & Co. Bullymore Block.

Johnson, Wallace & Co. Market n. Perry.
Johnson, Wallace,, 89 Main.
Judson & Avery, 24 Central Wharf.
Mann, Charles J. 14 Central Wharf.
PARKER, JASON, 23 Central Wharf.
Patterson, F. W. 13 Central Wharf.
Raney & Wheeler, 22 Central Wharf.
Rogers, Bradley D. 126 S. Division.
Roop, Henry, Prime cor. Dayton.
Root, A. R. 64 Main.
Sawyer, James D. 11 Central Wharf.
Sherman, P. C. 28 Oak.
Sherwood, A. C. & Co. 9 Central Wharf.
Smith, Junius S. 28 Central Wharf.
Smith & Schermerhorn, 5 Scott.
STERNBERG, P. L. & CO. 4 Central Wharf.
Worthington, S. K. 16 Central Wharf.

Provision Dealers.

ALBERGER, JOB, Terrace. cor. Franklin.
BULLYMORE, RICHARD, Michigan and
   Elk street Market.
BULLYMORE, THOMAS, 326 Main.
Barnes, J. & Son, 3 Seneca.
JONES, MILES, Prime cor. Dayton.
LANGDON & SEARS, 22 and 24 Hanover.
McPherson, John, Elk street Market.
Meyer, Charles, 22 Washington Market.
Nowell, V. C. & Bro. Dayton n. Prime.
Roop, Henry, 4, 6 and 7 Dayton.
Van Wort, F. A. 75 Washington.
Weppner, Francis, 300 Michigan.

Publishers.

BENDER. PHILIP, 358 Main.
BREED, BUTLER & CO. 188 Main.
BRUNCK & HELD, 194 Washington.
Bryan, Geo. J. Washington n. Gothic Hall.
Butler, Theodore, 159 Main.
Clapp, A. M. & Co. 158 Main.
Faxon, James, 157 Main.
Hagan, Michael, 111 Main.
Hog, Joseph, Batavia n. Arsenal.
Johnson, Fry & Co. 190½ Main.
WARREN, J. & CO. 193 Washington.
WHEELER, R. & CO. 161 Main.

Pump and Block Makers.

Beyer, Louis, Michigan cor. Cherry.
Howard, Daniel, Evans cor. Water.
Klein & Dobinson, Evans cor. Water.
Taff, Manuel C. Ohio n. Michigan.
Taff, Richard, Ohio n. Michigan.

Pump Tubing and Curbs.

HOLMES, E. & R. Michigan n. C. R. R. Depot.
PRATT & CO. 28, 30 and 32 Terrace.

Pyrotechnists.

MORRIS, J. S. & SON, Niagara bel. Water
   Works.

Railroad Printing, Etc.

Bailey, Geo. 9 Water.
Sanford, Harroun & Co. Courier Buildings.

Real Estate Agents and Dealers.

See LAND AGENTS.

Beardsley, Josiah, 190½ Main.
Goodrich, Guy H. Weed's Block.
Hastings, Chauncey J. 3 Brown's Buildings.
Lyon & Co. Brown's Buildings, Seneca.
Maynard, R. H. 69 Seneca.
Meach, Asa B. Swan cor. Main.
Pickering & Otto, 37 Pearl.
Pinner, M. 236 Main.
WILSON, LEONARD, 3 Niagara.
Winship, Aaron N. cor. Washington and Eagle.
Woleben, Edward, 48 Pearl.

Rectifiers and Distillers.

See DISTILLERS.

Clark, Thomas, cor. Washington and Perry.
GILLET, H. T. 18, 20 and 22 Lloyd.
Green, James, Niagara n. Pennsylvania.
Person, Charles, 220 Elm.
Trouten, John, h. 5th n. Carolina.
Wolf, John O. 428 Main.

Refrigerators.

JEWETT, JOHN C. 259 Main.

Regalia Makers.

Day, Lester, 82 Niagara.
Drew, W. H. Exchange cor. Washington.

Rope Makers.

Donoghue, Hugh, Vermont n. Brayton.
Kimmet, Francis, 29 Carolina.
POOLEY & BUTTERFIELD, N. Washington
   n. Bird.
Rinck, B. Williamsville road n. Genesee.

Rubber Goods.

Newman, W. H. H. 46 Main.

Saddle and Harness Makers.

See HARNESS MAKERS.

Ach & Stock, 557 Seneca.
Carpenter, John H. 285 Main.
Cook & Lytle, 10 Exchange.
Cooper, N. 29 E. Seneca.
Georger, Lewis, junc. Ohio and Elk.
Kolb, Charles A. 355 Main.
Kolb, George M. & Co. 117 Main.
Vogel, Samuel. Batavia n. Madison.
Wolf & Loegler, 362 Main.

Saddlery, Coach and Trunk Hardware.

PRATT & LETCHWORTH, 34 Terrace.
Taylor, D. 2 E. Swan.

Sail Makers.

FRANKLIN & RAND, Marine Block.
Proovost, Jas. P. & Co. Chequered Warehouse, Central Wharf.
Provost & Newkirk, n. foot Lloyd.

Salt Dealers.

Morse, C. H. 22 Central Wharf.
Ranney, Orville W. 20 Central Wharf.

Sand Dealers.

Myers, Edward H. cor. Erie and Peacock.

Sash and Blind Makers.

Altenburg, John E. Swan n. N. Y. C. R. R.
Boynton, Theodore N. 48 Clinton.
Evans, J. R. & Co. Mechanic.
HOLMES, E. & B. Michigan n. Central R. R. Depot.
HUSTED, E. & G. 142 Seneca.
Schiele, John, cor. Oak and Clinton.
Schuehle, Jacob, Clinton cor. Oak.

Sausage Makers.

ALBERGER, JOB, Terrace cor. Franklin.
BULLYMORE, RICHARD, Michigan n. Scott.
BULLYMORE, THOMAS, 326 Main.

Saw File Makers.

COLLINSON, SAM. Hospital bel. Court.

Saw Filers and Setters.

Newman, Frederick, Mohawk cor. Main.
Rother, Christian, 169 Elm.
Walter, Peter, 9 Cypress.

Saw Manufacturer.

Roberts, John, 222 Washington.

Saw Mills, Panel.

HOLMES, E. & B Michigan n. Central R. R. Depot.

Scale and Safe Dealers

Brown, H. C. Arcade Buildings.
Dudley, J. G. 93 Main.
PRATT & CO. 28, 30 and 32 Terrace.
Weeks, John, 81 Main.

Schools, (Private.)

Ernst, John F. cor. Mohawk and Pearl.
Meissner, Ernst G. 136 E. Genesee.
Nardin, E. Miss, 27 and 29 S. Division.
Shelton, Mary E. Miss, 175 Franklin.
Wright, W. B. over 9 S. Division.

Schools.

For PUBLIC SCHOOLS see p. 20.

School Furniture Makers.

Chase, W. & Son, 198 7th.

Scroll Sawyers.

HOLMES, E. & B. Michigan n. Central R. R. Depot.

Sea Grass.

Hastings, Wm. Dearborn n. Amherst.

Seamstresses.

Archer, Mary, 112 Batavia.
Blackmann, Mary, widow, 81 Sycamore.
Blattner, Mary, Miss, 118 Batavia.
Borck, Catherine, 50 Bennett.
Brames, Elizabeth, Miss, Pratt n. William.
Combs, S. M. Mrs. cor. Wash. and Genesee.
Crowley, Catherine, 32 Main.
Deller, Margaret. Pratt n. William.
Denzinger, Barbara, 156 Batavia.
Denzinger, Maria, widow, 156 Batavia.
Dillsworth, Sarah J. 188 Genesee.
Dorer, Catherine, r. 449 Michigan.
Dorr, Margaret, 112 Batavia.
Emerick, Christiene, 102 Pine.
Fair, Catharine, 16 Pratt.

Seedsmen.

See NURSERYMEN.

Needham, George F. 247 Main.
Needham, Joseph P. 293 Main.
White, Hiram C. 338 Main.

Sewer Builder.

Webster, A. 60 Ellicott.

Sewing Machines.

BALDWIN, HENRY D. agent, 230 Main.
CLARK, EDWIN, 272 Main, Kremlin Block.
Irwin, Comstock & Co. 221 Main.
SINGER, I. M. & CO. 230 Main.
WHEELER & WILSON, 207 Main.

Sheepskin Dealers.

See WOOL DEALERS.

Schoellkoff & Breithaupt, Carroll n. Van Rensselaer.

Shingle Manufacturers.

PIERCE & CO. Michigan cor. Scott.
Thompson, Thomas, North Buffalo.

Ship Brokers.

Billings & Dickinson, 29 Central Wharf.
Dill, Reuben, 2 Ohio.

Ship Carpenters.

See BOAT AND SHIP BUILDERS.

Ship Chandlers.

Bemis, Philo S. 6 and 7 Ohio.
Mack, Wm. J. 22, 23 and 24 Long Wharf.
MORSE & PERRINE, cor. Lloyd and Erie Canal.
NEWMAN & SCOVILL, Lloyd cor. Prime.
TAYLOR & JEWETT, 4 and 5 Marine Block.

Ship Smiths.

Donaldson & Brothers, Indiana cor. Ohio.
Kinnear, Sylvester, 14 Water.
Shepard, Andrew J. Ohio ab. Michigan.

Shirt and Collar Makers.

Gorton & Matteson, 208 Main, up stairs.
Wynhammer, M. Mrs. 309 Washington.

Shoemakers and Dealers.

Albert, John, 9 Commercial.
Argus, Henry, 242 Main.
Becherer, F. Seneca n. junc. Swan.
Becker, Ferdinand, Seneca junc. Swan.
Bedmaier, Frank, cor. Niagara and Amherst.
Birnbach, Joseph, Michigan n. S. Division.
CHAMOT. C. P. 207 Washington.
Costello, Thomas, 112 Pearl.
Denicombe, John, 7 Genesee.
Dillon, Jas. Elk n. Louisiana.
Doyle, Jno. Hayward cor. Fulton.
Eberhardt, B. cor. Ohio and Indiana.
Elseasser, Wm. cor. Kaene and Genesee.
Fellner, Godfred. 10th n. Hampshire.
Furey, Wm. 103 Eagle.
Graser, John, 139 Batavia.
Griesert, Wm. 300 Seneca.
Handrich. John, 10th n. Maryland.
Hellriegel, Henry, 8 Commercial.
Henning, G. 20 S. Division.
Herrman, J. H. Michigan n. Batavia.
Hess, Frank, 182 S. Division.
Hess, George, 14 Main.
Huebel, Ferdinand, Niagara cor. Morgan.
Jacobi. Herman, 6 Water.
Judevine, H. 316 Michigan.
Kennedy. John, Georgia bel. 5th.
Kreber, Adam, 195 Genesee.
Kreiger, Benjamin, 341 Genesee.
Landefiele, C. Clinton above Hickory.
Langfed, Jno. Genesee cor. Camp.
Lauscbach, Wm. Commercial Hotel.
Lehman, Nicholas, 7 Swan.
Linnenkohl, Wm. 75 Ellicott.
Lohouse, F. W. 3 Clinton.
Lung, Anton, Mortimer n. Sycamore.
Maiers, Stephen, 125 Pine.
Mayer, Peter, 23 Genesee.
Michael, J. Vermont n. 13th.
Murphy, James, 88 E. Seneca.
Nucken, Hubert, 12 Commercial.
O'Rourk, James, Ohio n. Mississippi.
O'Rourk, Pat. 25 Ohio.
Perry, Israel B. 165 Elk.
Phillips, S. cor. Niagara and Amherst.
Pittman, Henry, 43 Seneca.

Preis, Jno. 349 Seneca.
Reibold, Chr. Genesee n. Spring.
Richman, Fr. Sycamore n. Ash.
Riefler, John C. 86 Eagle.
Roth, Sebastian, Niagara cor. Virginia.
Shaffer, Peter, 2 Michigan.
Schanla, Finzanz, Delaware n. Ferry.
Schlingmeier, Henry, 171 Batavia.
Schmidt, August, 147 Genesee.
Schmidt, Ludwig. Grey n. Batavia.
Schuer, Anton, 128 Batavia.
Thorn. Jacob, 7 Commercial.
Vaughan, Otis, Virginia n. Niagara.
Voght, M. 139 S. Division.
Wagner, Christoph, 82 Main.
Wagner, P. A. 7 Main.
Walz, Geo. 7 Commercial.
Warhus, Henry F. 2 Exchange.
Weber, B. 1 E. Swan.
Weber, Ferdinand, 10 Terrace.
Weick, Philip, 130 E. Seneca.
Weis, Fred. Main n. Ferry.
Williams, Wm. 55 Lloyd.
Wolter, Henry G. 8 West Eagle.
Wood, Nathan, Niagara n. Sloan.
Young, Jacob, Hickory n. Cherry.
Zebb, John, 249 Seneca.
Zeitz, Andrew, 210 Genesee.

Shook Manufacturers.

See STAVE DEALERS.

Hale, H. H. Marine Block.
Shaw & Kibbe, across creek.

Silver Platers.

BANGASSER & BROTHER, 15 E. Seneca.
Trankle, F. 201½ Washington.
VALENTINE & O'REILLY, 14 Court.

Silver Smith.

Dubois, Philo, 11 E. Swan.

Slate Dealers.

HAYFORD, RILEY, Washington Dock. foot Chicago.
VAIL, GEO. O. & CO. Ohio cor. Chicago.

Soap and Candle Makers.

Achtziger, John, h. Clinton n. C. R. R.
Atkinson. Ed. J. Burwell Place.
Bryson, Wm. Hudson n. 5th.
DANTZER & CO. cor. Exchange and Chic.
Gilbert, John, Delaware n. Barker.
Gowans & Beard, Chicago cor. Perry.
Lutz, Wm. Batavia n. Spring.
THOMPSON, H. Chicago cor. Perry.
Wheeler, Isaac, 4 Batavia.

Soda and Sarsaparilla Makers.

Gibbons & Hager, 57 Exchange.
TURNER, BROTHERS, Niagara n. Virginia.

Spar Maker.

Taff, Richard, Ohio n. Michigan.

Spice Factories.

See COFFEE AND SPICE.

Spring Bed Manufacturers.

Bame, Samuel S. 45 Chippewa.
Galligan, Wm. 34 Ellicott.

Stair Builder.

Briggs & Martin, cor. Terrace and Mechanic.

Staple and Fancy Dry Goods.

See DRY GOODS.

Starch Manufacturer.

Steele, John, Dearborn n. Hamilton.

Stationers.

BREED, BUTLER & Co. 188 Main.
Butler, Theodore, 159 Main.
FELTON, JOHN, 159 Main.
JEWETT, E. R. & Co. 161 Main.
Leavitt, James S. 70 Lloyd.
Leech, J. H. cor. Main and Exchange 3d story
TAYLOR, MARTIN, 299 Main.
Young, Lockwood & Co. 159 Main.

Stave Dealers.

Clarke, E. H. 2 Main.
Dutton, E. H. 2 Main.
Fink, John, stave cutter, East n. Hamilton.
Frink, H. A. & Co. 22 Central Wharf.
Hale, Henry H. Marine Block, Ohio.
Harbeck, H. A. 1 Central Wharf.
Parmelee, S. 2 Main.
PIERCE & CO. Michigan cor. Scott.
Safford, Elisha, b. H. L. Safford.
Safford, H. L. h. Niagara n. Hamilton.
Story, Jos. Marine Block.

Steam Engine Manufacturers.

BELL, DAVID, Norton.
GOOD, ADAM, 21 Ohio.
SHEPARD IRON WORKS, Ohio opposite N. Y. C. R. R. foot depot.
TIFFT, GEORGE W., SONS & CO. Washington cor. Ohio.

Steam Saw-Mills.

DART & BROTHERS, Ohio Basin.
Eaton, S. Hospital cor. Court.
HOLMES, E. & B. Mich. n. C. R. R. depot.
PIERCE & CO. office Michigan cor. Scott.
SWARTZ & REBMANN, Elm above Batavia.

Stencil Plate Cutters.

DREW, E. 136 Main, up stairs.

Stereotypers.

Felton, Charles E. 7 E. Seneca.
WHEELER, R. & Co. 161 Main.

Stocking Weaver.

Strup, Theobold, 435 Main.

Stone Dealers.

Harron, Robt. Erie opp. Courter House.
HOLLOWAY, ISAAC, corner Michigan and Hamburgh canal.
HOWELLS, JAMES, junc. Carlton and Gen.
WHITMORE, RATHBUN & CO., Henry cor. Erie canal.

Storage and Forwarding.

See FORWARDERS.

Stove Dealers.

See COPPER AND TINSMITHS.

BULL, GEORGE B. & CO. Main cor. Quay.
CANDEE, F. C. 354 Main.
Hadley & Husted, 119 and 217 Main.
HILL, F. C. 269 Main.
JEWETT, JOHN C. 259 Main.
JEWETT & ROOT. Mississippi.
Shaw, John H. 198 Main.
Wood, Hubbell & Co. Scott n. Washington.

Surgical Instruments.

KING, WM. Jr. 249 Main.
Mathews, A. I. 255 Main.
Peabody, W. N. 251 Main.

Surveying Instrument Maker.

ANDREWS & SON, 221 Main.

Surveyors.

Charles, Stephen D. Prosser Buildings.
Colburn, Ransom II. 14 Spaulding's Exchange.
Cox, Gustavus, Main cor. Huron.
Emslie, Peter, City Buildings.
Keeler, J. W. 2 Prosser Block.
Lovejoy, Henry, Swan cor. Michigan.
Peacock, William W. 268 Main.
Rehn, Fred. Prosser's Buildings, Pearl corner Seneca.
Sime, William, Franklin cor. Eagle.
Williams, Frank, 57 Delaware.

Syrup Makers.

GIBBONS & HAGER, 57 Exchange.
TURNER BROTHERS, Niagara ab. Carolina.

Tailoresses.

Creamer, John, Mrs. 19 Park place.
Daly, Catharine, Perry n. Louisiana.
Hale, Lovina, 103 Clinton.

Tailors and Drapers.

See CLOTHIERS.

Aarons, Aaron, 21 Exchange.
Arey, Chas. Abbott n. iron bridge.
Baer, George, 31½ Genesee.
Bogart & Doolittle, 164 Main.
Boland & Son, 104 Main.
Bomel, F. F. 278 Main.
Bruce, Harlow, ov. 140 Main.
Clark & Storms, 308 Main.
COOLEY, W. S. 7 Seneca.
Corr, W. 198 Main. ●
Diebold, Andrew, 11 Commercial.
Dodsworth, Wm. cor. Main and Lloyd.
DUBOIS, J. B. 149 Main.
Fallon, James, 224 Main.
Flucht, Philip, Ash n. Sycamore.
Hart, Henry, 171 Main.
Hettrichs, Peter, 108 Exchange.
Hey, John, 15 Sycamore.
Jones, H. P. Main opp. American.
KENNETT, THOMAS, 183 Main.
Kreiger, A. 255 Genesee.
Marcus, Julius, 157 Main.
McMurray, Thomas, Main cor. Eagle.
Metzger, Jacob, 34 Main.
Nicklis, William, 27 Main.
Renner, G. & Co. 281 Main.
Renz, Matthias, 172 Batavia.
Ribbel & Cowan, 257 Main.
Rohr, John, Eric cor. Terrace.
Schaeffer, Frank. 64 S. Division.
Schmidt, Henry, ov. 263 Main.
Schweiger, Martin, Genesee n. Jefferson.
Siebrich, George, 72 Michigan.
Sippel, Adam, 408 Main.
Sippel, Conrad, 398 Main.
Stuart & Efner, 204 Main.
Sweet, L. 230 Main.
Theobald & Krupp, 352 Main.
Tripp, Samuel, 326 Main.
TRYON, M. H. 242 Main.
Uhey, Augustus, 17 Pearl.
Warner Brothers, 43 and 45 Main.
Werle, Anthony, 2 Commercial. ●
Young, A. M. ov. 3 S. Division.

Tanners.

See LEATHER DEALERS.

Palmer & Gardner, Seneca n. Hydraulics.

Teacher, (French.)

Malhoubie, Charles, Delaware ab. Virginia. ·

Teachers, (Penmanship.)

Bryant & Stratton, Brown's Buildings.
HICKS, D. CLINTON, ov. 194 Main.

Tile Manufacturer.

Mattrice, Frederick M. 10th ab. Jersey.

Tin and Coppersmiths.

Adler, Max, Court n. 6th.
BRITTON, NICHOLAS, Com'l. cor. Pearl.
BROWN & McCUTCHEON, junction Elk and
 Ohio.
Candee, F. C. 72 Main.
CASE & CO. Ohio cor. Washington.
Ditmar, Geo. Genesee n. Hickory.
Duborn, A. M. 22 Commercial.
Dudley Brothers, 57 Main.
Felthousen & Russell, 113 Main.
HART. BALL & HART, 237 Main.
HAUCK, A. & KIEFER, 395 Main.
Herd, B. 235 Genesee.
Hersch. Adolph, 344 Genesee.
HILL, F. C. 269 Main.
JEWETT, JOHN C. 259 Main.
Loebig, Michael, Genesee n. Hickory.
Naurt, Julius, Michigan cor. N. Division.
Shaw, John H. 198 Washington.
STACY, FRANCIS, 22 Commercial.
THEOBOLD, CHARLES, Main n. Huron.
Zook, Daniel M. 5 Birkhead Building.

Tobacconists.

See CIGAR DEALERS.

ADAMS, JAMES & CO. 207 Washington.
Diehl, Henry, 322 Main.
Haehn, Otto F. 40 East Seneca.
Hayen, Jacob F. 5 Terrace.
SEVERNS, OSCAR, 191 Main.
Walker, Samuel N. 12 East Seneca.

Toys, Importers of.

Barnum, S. O. 211 Main.
Christoph, Eugene, 150 Main.
Flersheim's 275 Main.
HOFFMAN, JULIUS, 294 Main.
Volger, Edward, 320 Main.

Trunk Makers.

Karn, Adam, Jr. h. Maple cor. Carlton.
Kihlberg, John, 219 Main.
Kolb & Co. 117 Main.
Leonard. N. 27 E. Seneca.
Runcie, Jas. 169 Main.

Turners.

Brown, Jno. 160 Elm.
Hoenes, Henry, Madison cor. Batavia.
Mutter, Fuetell, 123 Walnut.
Solomon, M. 257 Washington.
SUOR, JOSEPH, Mechanic n. Terrace.

Type Founder.

Lyman, N. 18 W. Seneca.

Umbrella and Parasol Makers.

Flammer, Mathew, Adams n. Batavia.
Hesse, E. 103 Genesee.

Malony, Jas. Scott cor. Mississippi.
MILLINGTON, ED. H. 314 Main.

Umbrella Maker.

Schivum, Jno. W. 377 Washington.

Undertakers.

See COFFIN MAKERS.

Atkins, Robt. F. 100 Pearl.
FARWELL, E. & H. D. 13 and 15 Niagara.
Gombert, Wm. Batavia cor. Pine.
Kraft, Francis J. 29 E. Huron.
PIERCE, LORING, 153 Franklin.
Rodney & Atkins, 16 Court.

Upholsterers.

See PAPER HANGERS.

Albright, Michael. 203 Main.
Armstrong. Charles, 3 Birkhead Buildings, Commercial.
BARTLETT, GEO. cor. Clinton and Hickory.
Elder & Stearns, 270 Main.

Variety Stores.

Barnum, S. O. 211 Main.
Christoph, Eugene, 150 Main.
Deery, Thomas, 408 Main.
DeYoung, J. J. 147 Main.
Flersheim's, 275 Main.
HOFFMAN, JULIUS, 294 Main.
JEWETT, JOHN C. 259 Main.
Ryan. Catharine, Ohio n. Washington.
Schmidt, Jacob, 144 Genesee.
Volger, Ed. 320 Main.
Waters, J. D. 385 Seneca.

Veterinary Surgeons.

SOMERVILLE, SAMUEL, 8 Canal.
Thompson, J. Walnut n. Clinton.

Vinegar Factories.

Abel, Louis, h. 70 Delaware place.
Gentsch, Bernard, Batavia n. Walnut.
HOWELL & SMITH, 36 E. Seneca.
Klipfel, Chas. 331 Seneca.
Korzelius, Jno. Batavia cor. Pine.
Menning. C. R. Batavia n. Walnut.
Rieblinger, Jos. 320 E. Genesee.
Schaefer, C. 202 Oak.

Vise Maker.

Hickman, Arthur, Illinois n. Ohio.

Wagon Makers.

Barker, Wm. 98 Seneca.
Bowell, Daniel, 209 Seneca.
Brack. Jacob, Genesee n. Walden.
Buffum, H. A. Seneca n. Whittmore's tavern.

CHAMBERLAIN & CO. Niag. cor. Mohawk.
Graft, Jno. G. Genesee cor. Michigan.
Heller, Christ. Monroe n. Batavia.
Heller, Jno. 562 Seneca.
Hunsinger, Michael, Niagara n. Hamilton.
Lang, A. cor. Chicago and Perry.
Ledebor, Henry, Adams n. Sycamore.
Rice, D. S. 296 Seneca.
Roesch, Geo. Clinton n. Watson.
Sudrow, Wm. Batavia n. Adams.

Washblueing Manufacturer.

Asmuss. John. 177 Genesee.

Washboard Manufacturers.

HOLMES, E. & B. Michigan n. C. R. R. depot.

Watches and Watchmakers.

Bosson, Jas. 78 Exchange.
CASTLE, DAN. B. 135 Main.
Church, Ralph, Swan cor. Washington.
Denze, Mathew, 200 Genesee.
DICKINSON, THOMAS, 370 Main.
Getrost, John, 501 Michigan.
Goodrich, E. H. 183 Washington.
Hotchkiss, Hiram, 210 Main.
Hotchkiss, J. W. 197 Main.
LOEBRECK, CHARLES, 382 Main.
SHURLY, C. J. 151 Main.
Sibley, O. E. 186 Main.
Stephenson & Co. 200 Main.
Walker, Julius, 185 Main.

Water Coolers and Filters.

JEWETT, JOHN C. 259 Main.

Water Lime.

Newman & Bros. cor. Ship canal and Water.

Water Works Company.

Buffalo Water Works Company, Erie n. Pearl.

Wax Flowers.

Husser, Wm. Mrs. 60 6th.

Well Diggers.

Runions, John, Best n. High.

Whip Makers.

Leonard, Norman, 27 Seneca.
Monroe, William C. 359 Main.

White Lead Factories.

Buffalo White Lead Works, 6th cor. Georgia.
NIAG. WHITE LEAD CO. office 38 Lloyd.

21

Wig Makers, etc.

Graus, S. J. J. 328 Main.
MAJOT. ACHILLES, over 273 Main.

Willow and Wooden Ware.

Barnum. S. O. 211 Main.
Christoph, Eugene, 150 Main.

Willow Wagon Maker.

Avery. George, 384 Swan.

Wine Dealers.

Barrows, E. G. & Co. 213 and 215 Washington.
Champlin. O. H. P. Arcade Buildings.
DAMAINVILLE, A. 163 Main.
GIBBONS & HAGAR, 57 Exchange.
KNIGHT, J. 324 and 330 Main.
Murray & Brother, 7 Terrace.
PRESBREY, O. F.—*See adr. opp. p. 238.*
Tiphaine, V. L. 193 Main.
TURNER BROS. (Fruit Wines.) Niag. n. Va.

Wire Works.

Buffalo Wire Works, 115 Main.

Wood Dealers.

Coatsworth, Thomas, Erie cor. Erie canal.
Daniel, John M. Michigan cor. canal.
Hulbert, Edwin, Green rear N. Y. C. Depot.
KELDERHOUSE, JOHN, foot Church.

Wool and Pelt Dealers.

Bush, John & Co. 29 Seneca.
Coit, G. C. & Son. 70 Main.
Peterson, John, Swan junc. Seneca.
Platt, A. B. 4 Birkhead Buildings.
Welch & Millar, 155 Washington.

Yeast Maker, (Patent.)

Ehlers. Louis, Watson n. William.

THE OLD CITY
Dyeing Establishment

NO. 18 BATAVIA STREET, BUFFALO.

Near the Bell Tower.

Respectfully solicits the Patronage of the Citizens, promising that no effort on his part shall be wanting to give satisfaction.

GOODS RECEIVED AND DELIVERED BY EXPRESS.

GENTLEMEN'S AND LADIES' GARMENTS

Cleaned and Re-Dyed in the best manner.

LACE CURTAINS

Bleached and made to look like new.

CRAPE SHAWLS,

Cleansed or Dyed any Shade.

CARPETS CLEANED

At very moderate rates.

SILK DRESSES DYED AND FINISHED.

Rugs, Mats and Table Covers, Damask Curtains

CLEANSED OR RE-DYED.

KID GLOVES Cleansed by a New Process to Vie with New.

All kinds of Machinery for ▮▮▮▮▮▮▮▮▮▮▮ Work,

▮▮▮▮▮▮▮▮HESTER.

Lightning Source UK Ltd.
Milton Keynes UK
UKHW012226110219
337137UK00006B/1249/P